Lecture Notes in Artificial Intelligence   12431

Subseries of Lecture Notes in Computer Science

Series Editors

Randy Goebel
  University of Alberta, Edmonton, Canada
Yuzuru Tanaka
  Hokkaido University, Sapporo, Japan
Wolfgang Wahlster
  DFKI and Saarland University, Saarbrücken, Germany

Founding Editor

Jörg Siekmann
  DFKI and Saarland University, Saarbrücken, Germany

Xiaodan Zhu · Min Zhang ·
Yu Hong · Ruifang He (Eds.)

Natural Language Processing and Chinese Computing

9th CCF International Conference, NLPCC 2020
Zhengzhou, China, October 14–18, 2020
Proceedings, Part II

Springer

Editors
Xiaodan Zhu
ECE & Ingenuity Labs Research Institute
Queen's University
Kingston, ON, Canada

Yu Hong
School of Computer Science
and Technology
Soochow University
Suzhou, China

Min Zhang
Department of Computer Science
and Technology
Tsinghua University
Beijing, China

Ruifang He
College of Intelligence and Computing
Tianjin University
Tianjin, China

ISSN 0302-9743 ISSN 1611-3349 (electronic)
Lecture Notes in Artificial Intelligence
ISBN 978-3-030-60456-1 ISBN 978-3-030-60457-8 (eBook)
https://doi.org/10.1007/978-3-030-60457-8

LNCS Sublibrary: SL7 – Artificial Intelligence

This Springer imprint is published by the registered company Springer Nature Switzerland AG
The registered company address is: Gewerbestrasse 11, 6330 Cham, Switzerland

Preface

Welcome to 9th CCF International Conference on Natural Language Processing and Chinese Computing (NLPCC 2020). Following the success of previous conferences held in Beijing (2012), Chongqing (2013), Shenzhen (2014), Nanchang (2015), Kunming (2016), Dalian (2017), Hohhot (2018), and Dunhuang (2019), this year's NLPCC was held at Zhengzhou, which is located in the central part of China. As a leading international conference on natural language processing (NLP) and Chinese computing (CC), organized by the CCF-NLP (Technical Committee of Natural Language Processing, China Computer Federation, formerly known as Technical Committee of Chinese Information, China Computer Federation), NLPCC 2020 serves as an important forum for researchers and practitioners from academia, industry, and government to share their ideas, research results and experiences, and promote their research and technical innovations in the various fields.

The fields of NLP and CC have boomed in recent years, and the growing number of submissions to NLPCC is testament to this trend. After unfortunately needing to reject 25 submissions that did not meet the submission guidelines, we received a total of 404 valid submissions to the entire conference, inclusive of the main conference, student workshop, evaluation workshop, and the special explainable AI (XAI) workshop. Of the 377 valid submissions to the main conference, 315 were written in English and 62 were written in Chinese. Following NLPCC's tradition, we welcomed submissions in nine topical areas for the main conference: Conversational Bot/QA; Fundamentals of NLP; Knowledge Base, Graphs and Semantic Web; Machine Learning for NLP; Machine Translation and Multilinguality; NLP Applications; Social Media and Network; Text Mining; Trending Topics (Explainability, Ethics, Privacy, Multimodal NLP, etc.)

Acceptance decisions were made by multiple virtual scientific Program Committee (PC) meetings due to the COVID-19 pandemic, attended by the general, PC, and area chairs. After our deliberations for the main conference, 83 submissions were accepted as oral papers (with 70 papers in English and 13 papers in Chinese) and 30 as poster papers. 9 papers were nominated by the area chairs for the Best Paper Award in both the English and Chinese tracks. An independent Best Paper Award Committee was formed to select the best paper from the shortlist. The proceedings included only the accepted English papers; the Chinese papers appear in the journal *ACTA Scientiarum Naturalium Universitatis Pekinensis*. In addition to the main proceedings, 2 papers were accepted for the student workshop, 8 papers were accepted for the evaluation workshop, and 4 papers were accepted to the special Explainable AI (XAI) workshop.

We were honored to have four internationally renowned keynote speakers – Claire Cardie (Cornell University, USA, and ACL Fellow), Ido Dagan (Bar-Ilan University, Israel, and ACL Fellow), Edward Grefenstette (Facebook AI Research, UK), and Danqi Chen (Princeton University, USA) – share their expert opinions on recent developments in NLP via their wonderful lectures.

The organization of NLPCC 2020 is due to the help of a great many people:

- We are grateful for guidance and advice provided by general co-chairs Mark Steedman and Xuanjing Huang, and Organization Committee co-chairs Hongying Zan, Xiaojun Wan, and Zhumin Chen. We especially thank Xiaojun Wan, as the central committee member who as acted as a central adviser to both of us as PC chairs, in making sure all of the decisions were made on schedule.
- We would like to thank the student workshop co-chairs Jin-Ge Yao and Xin Zhao, evaluation co-chairs Shoushan Li and Yunbo Cao, XAI workshop co-chairs Feiyu Xu, Dongyan Zhao, Jun Zhu, and Yangzhou Du, as well as techical workshop co-chairs Xiaodong He and Feiyu Xu.
- We are indebted to the 18 area chairs and the 251 primary reviewers, for both the English and Chinese tracks. This year, in the special COVID-19 period, they operated under severe load, and completed their high-quality reviews. We could not have met the various deadlines during the review process without their hard work.
- We thank tutorial co-chairs Xipeng Qiu and Rui Xia for assembling a comprehensive tutorial program covering a wide range of cutting-edge topics in NLP.
- We thank sponsorship co-chairs Dongyan Zhao and Derek Wong for securing sponsorship for the conference.
- Yu Hong and Ruifang He for ensuring every little detail in the publication process was properly taken care of. Those who have done this form of service work know how excruciating it can be. On behalf of us and all of the authors, we thank them for their work, as they truly deserve a big applause.
- Above all, we thank everybody who chose to submit their work to NLPCC 2020. Without your support, we could not have put together a strong conference program.

Stay safe and healthy, and we hope you enjoyed NLPCC 2020.

August 2020

Xiaodan Zhu
Min Zhang

Organization

NLPCC 2020 is organized by China Computer Federation, and hosted by Zhengzhou University and the National State Key Lab of Digital Publishing Technology.

Organization Committee

General Chairs

Mark Steedman   The University of Edinburgh, UK
Xuanjing Huang   Fudan University, China

Program Committee Chairs

Xiaodan Zhu   Queen's University, Canada
Min Zhang   Tsinghua University, China

Student Workshop Chairs

Jin-Ge Yao   Microsoft Research Asia, China
Xin Zhao   Renmin University of China, China

Evaluation Chairs

Shoushan Li   Soochow University, China
Yunbo Cao   Tencent, China

Technical Workshop Chairs

Xiaodong He   JD.com, China
Feiyu Xu   SAP, Germany

Tutorial Chairs

Xipeng Qiu   Fudan University, China
Rui Xia   Nanjing University of Science and Technology, China

Publication Chairs

Yu Hong   Soochow University, China
Ruifang He   Tianjin University, China

Journal Coordinator

Yunfang Wu   Peking University, China

Conference Handbook Chair

Yuxiang Jia   Zhengzhou University, China

Sponsorship Chairs

Dongyan Zhao   Peking University, China
Derek Wong   University of Macau, Macau

Publicity Co-chairs

Wei Lu   Singapore University of Technology and Design,
                                Singapore
Haofen Wang   Tongji University, China

Organization Committee Chairs

Hongying Zan   Zhengzhou University, China
Xiaojun Wan   Peking University, China
Zhumin Chen   Shandong University, China

Area Chairs

Conversational Bot/QA
Yu Su   The Ohio State University, USA
Quan Liu   iFlytek, China

Fundamentals of NLP
Lili Mou   University of Alberta, Canada
Jiajun Zhang   Institute of Automation, Chinese Academy of Sciences,
                                China

Knowledge Graph and Semantic Web
Xiang Ren   University of Southern California, USA
Min Liu   Harbin Institute of Technology, China

Machine Learning for NLP
Mo Yu   IBM T.J Watson Research Center, USA
Jiwei Li   Shannon.AI, China

Machine Translation and Multilinguality
Jiatao Gu   Facebook AI, USA
Jinsong Su   Xiamen University, China

NLP Applications
Wei Gao   Singapore Management University, Singapore
Xiangnan He   University of Science and Technology of China, China

Text Mining
Wei Lu   Singapore University of Technology and Design,
                                Singapore
Qi Zhang   Fudan University, China

Social Network
Xiangliang Zhang   King Abdullah University of Science and Technology,
                                Saudi Arabia
Huaping Zhang   Beijing Institute of Technology, China

Trending Topics

Caiming Xiong   Salesforce, USA
Zhiyuan Liu   Tsinghua University, China

Treasurer

Yajing Zhang   Soochow University, China
Xueying Zhang   Peking University, China

Webmaster

Hui Liu   Peking University, China

Program Committee

Wasi Ahmad   University of California, Los Angeles, USA
Xiang Ao   Institute of Computing Technology, Chinese Academy
                          of Sciences, China
Lei Bi   Beijing Normal University, Zhuhai, China
Fei Cai   National University of Defense Technology, China
Pengshan Cai   University of Massachusetts Amherst, USA
Hengyi Cai   Institute of Computing Technology, Chinese Academy
                          of Sciences, China
Deng Cai   The Chinese University of Hong Kong, Hong Kong,
                          China
Yi Cai   South China University of Technology, China
Yixin Cao   National University of Singapore, Singapore
Yixuan Cao   Institute of Computing Technology, Chinese Academy
                          of Sciences, China
Ziqiang Cao   Microsoft STCA, China
Hailong Cao   Harbin Institute of Technology, China
Kai Cao   New York University, USA
Ching-Yun Chang   Amazon.com, UK
Hongshen Chen   JD.com, China
Muhao Chen   University of Southern California and University
                          of Pennsylvania, USA
Yidong Chen   Xiamen University, China
Chengyao Chen   Wisers AI Lab, Canada
Jian Chen   Beijing Normal University, Zhuhai, China
Yubo Chen   Institute of Automation, Chinese Academy of Sciences,
                          China
Lei Chen   Beijing Normal University, Zhuhai, China
Wenliang Chen   Soochow University, China

Kehai Chen   National Institute of Information and Communications
                          Technology, Japan
Boxing Chen   Alibaba, China
Qingcai Chen   Harbin Institute of Technology, China
Bo Chen   iscas.ac.cn, China
Gong Cheng   Nanjing University, China
Chenhui Chu   Kyoto University, Japan
Yiming Cui   Harbin Institute of Technology, China
Mao Cunli   Kunming University of Science and Technology, China
Xinyu Dai   National Key Laboratory for Novel Software
                          Technology, Nanjing University, China
Xiang Deng   The Ohio State University, USA
Xiao Ding   Harbin Institute of Technology, China
Li Dong   Microsoft Research Asia, China
Zi-Yi Dou   Carnegie Mellon University, USA
Qianlong Du   National Laboratory of Pattern Recognition, Institute of
                          Automation, Chinese Academy of Sciences, China
Junwen Duan   Harbin Institute of Technology, China
Nan Duan   Microsoft Research Asia, China
Miao Fan   Baidu Research, China
Yufei Feng   Queen's University, Canada
Yang Feng   Institute of Computing Technology, Chinese Academy
                          of Sciences, China
Shi Feng   Northeastern University, China
Guohong Fu   Soochow University, China
Wei Gao   Singapore Management University, Singapore
Yeyun Gong   Microsoft Research Asia, China
Yu Gu   The Ohio State University, USA
Jiatao Gu   Facebook AI Research, USA
Zhijiang Guo   Singapore University of Technology and Design,
                          Singapore
Han Guo   University of North Carolina at Chapel Hill, USA
Xu Han   Tsinghua University, China
Qinghong Han   Peking University, China
Tianyong Hao   South China Normal University, China
Jie Hao   Florida State University, USA
Lei Hou   Tsinghua University, China
Linmei Hu   Beijing University of Posts and Telecommunications,
                          China
Wei Hu   Nanjing University, China
Lifu Huang   University of Illinois at Urbana-Champaign, USA
Xuanjing Huang   Fudan University, China
Jing Huang   JD.com, USA
Minlie Huang   Tsinghua University, China
Guimin Huang   Guilin University of Electronic Technology, China
Chenyang Huang   University of Alberta, Canada

Jiangping Huang	Chongqing University of Posts and Telecommunications, China
Yuxiang Jia	Zhengzhou University, China
Ping Jian	Beijing Institute of Technology, China
Wenbin Jiang	Baidu Research, China
Tianwen Jiang	Harbin Institute of Technology, China
Shengyi Jiang	Guangdong University of Foreign Studies, China
Zhanming Jie	ByteDance, Singapore
Peng Jin	Leshan Normal University, China
Wan Jing	Associate Professor, China
Chunyu Kit	City University of Hong Kong, Hong Kong, China
Fang Kong	Soochow University, China
Xiang Kong	Language Technologies Institute, Carnegie Mellon University, USA
Lun-Wei Ku	Academia Sinica, Taiwan, China
Kenneth Kwok	Principal Scientist, Singapore
Oi Yee Kwong	The Chinese University of Hong Kong, Hong Kong, China
Yanyan Lan	Institute of Computing Technology, Chinese Academy of Sciences, China
Man Lan	East China Normal University, China
Hady Lauw	Singapore Management University, Singapore
Wenqiang Lei	National University of Singapore, Singapore
Yves Lepage	Waseda University, Japan
Maoxi Li	Jiangxi Normal University, China
Chenliang Li	Wuhan University, China
Jian Li	The Chinese University of Hong Kong, Hong Kong, China
Peifeng Li	Soochow University, China
Hao Li	ByteDance, Singapore
Ru Li	Shanxi University, China
Fei Li	University of Massachusetts Lowell, USA
Binyang Li	University of International Relations, China
Junhui Li	Soochow University, China
Bin Li	Nanjing Normal University, China
Zhixu Li	Soochow University, China
Zuchao Li	Shanghai Jiao Tong University, China
Xiujun Li	Microsoft Research Redmond, USA
Xiang Li	Xiaomi AI Lab, China
Lishuang Li	Dalian University of Technology, China
Yachao Li	Soochow University, China
Jiaqi Li	Harbin Institute of Technology, China
Hao Li	Rensselaer Polytechnic Institute, USA
Yuan-Fang Li	Monash University, Australia
Albert Liang	Google, USA
Lizi Liao	National University of Singapore, Singapore

Lei Sha	University of Oxford, UK
Haoyue Shi	Toyota Technological Institute at Chicago, USA
Xiaodong Shi	Xiamen University, China
Kaisong Song	Alibaba Group, China
Yiping Song	Peking University, China
Ruihua Song	Microsoft Xiaoice, China
Chengjie Sun	Harbin Institute of Technology, China
Jingyuan Sun	Institute of Automation, Chinese Academy of Sciences, China
Lichao Sun	University of Illinois at Chicago, USA
Xiaobing Sun	Singapore University of Technology and Design, Singapore
Xu Tan	Microsoft Research Asia, China
Yiqi Tang	The Ohio State University, USA
Zhiyang Teng	Westlake University, China
Zhiliang Tian	Hong Kong University of Science and Technology, Hong Kong, China
Jin Ting	Hainan University, China
Ming Tu	ByteDance, USA
Zhaopeng Tu	Tencent, China
Masao Utiyama	NICT, Japan
Xiaojun Wan	Peking University, China
Huaiyu Wan	Beijing Jiaotong University, China
Mingxuan Wang	ByteDance, China
Bo Wang	Tianjin University, China
Tianlu Wang	University of Virginia, USA
Shaonan Wang	National Laboratory of Pattern Recognition, Institute of Automation, Chinese Academy of Sciences, China
Bailin Wang	The University of Edinburgh, UK
Di Wang	Woobo, USA
Zhen Wang	The Ohio State University, USA
Xuancong Wang	MOH Office for Healthcare Transformation, Singapore
Rui Wang	NICT, Japan
Zhichun Wang	Beijing Normal University, China
Zhigang Wang	Tsinghua University, China
Longyue Wang	Tencent, China
Dingquan Wang	Google, USA
Xun Wang	University of Massachusetts Amherst, USA
Zekun Wang	Harbin Institute of Technology, China
Chuan-Ju Wang	Academia Sinica, Taiwan
Zhongyu Wei	Fudan University, China
Zhuoyu Wei	Microsoft Research Asia, China
Gang Wu	Northeastern University, China
Changxing Wu	East China Jiaotong University, China
Yu Wu	Microsoft Research Asia, China
Chien-Sheng Wu	Salesforce, USA

Xiaoqing Zheng	Fudan University, China
Zihao Zheng	Harbin Institution of Technology, China
Junsheng Zhou	Nanjing Normal University, China
Guangyou Zhou	Central China Normal University, China
Hao Zhou	ByteDance, China
Ganbin Zhou	Tencent, China
Guodong Zhou	Soochow University, China
Luowei Zhou	Microsoft, USA
Muhua Zhu	Tencent, China
Haichao Zhu	Harbin Institute of Technology, China
Yanyan Zou	Singapore University of Technology and Design, Singapore
Jinsong Su	Xiamen University, China
Congying Xia	University of Illinois at Chicago, USA
Cheng Yang	Beijing University of Posts and Telecommunications, China
Qiang Yang	KAUST, Saudi Arabia
Mo Yu	IBM Research, USA
Jianguo Zhang	University of Illinois at Chicago, USA
Huaping Zhang	Beijing Institute of Technology, China
Yunbo Cao	Tencent, China
Junyi Li	China Academy of Electronics and Information Technology, China
Min Yang	Chinese Academy of Sciences, China
Xuefeng Yang	ZhuiYi Technology, China
Sreya Dey	SAP, India
Yangzhou Du	Lenovo, China
Shipra Jain	Uttar Pradesh Technical University, India
Yao Meng	Lenovo, China
Wenli Ouyang	Lenovo, China

Organizers

Organized by

China Computer Federation

Hosted by

Zhengzhou University

State Key Lab of Digital Publishing Technology

In cooperation with:

Lecture Notes in Computer Science

Springer

ACTA Scientiarum Naturalium Universitatis Pekinensis

Sponsoring Institutions

Primary Sponsors

Zoneyet

Zoneyet 中业

Diamond Sponsors

JD Cloud & AI

AISpeech

Alibaba

Platinum Sponsors

Microsoft

Baidu

Huawei

Lenovo

China Mobile

PingAn

中国平安人寿保险

Golden Sponsors

Niutrans

Tencent AI Lab

Xiaomi

Gridsum

Silver Sponsors

Leyan

Speech Ocean

Contents – Part II

Explainable AI Workshop

Student Workshop

Evaluation Workshop

Contents – Part I

Oral - Conversational Bot/QA

Fundamentals of NLP

Knowledge Base, Graphs and Semantic Web

Machine Learning for NLP

Machine Translation and Multilinguality

NLP Applications

Social Media and Network

Text Mining

Trending Topics (Explainability, Ethics, Privacy, Multimodal NLP)

DCA: Diversified Co-attention Towards Informative Live Video Commenting

Zhihan Zhang[1]([✉]), Zhiyi Yin[1], Shuhuai Ren[2], Xinhang Li[3], and Shicheng Li[1]

[1] School of Electronic Engineering and Computer Science, Peking University,
Beijing, China
{zhangzhihan,yinzhiyi,lisc99}@pku.edu.cn
[2] School of Software Engineering, Huazhong University of Science and Technology,
Wuhan, China
renshuhuai007@gmail.com
[3] College of Software, Beijing University of Aeronautics and Astronautics,
Beijing, China
hestiaskylee@gmail.com

Abstract. We focus on the task of Automatic Live Video Commenting (ALVC), which aims to generate real-time video comments with both video frames and other viewers' comments as inputs. A major challenge in this task is how to properly leverage the rich and diverse information carried by video and text. In this paper, we aim to collect diversified information from video and text for informative comment generation. To achieve this, we propose a Diversified Co-Attention (DCA) model for this task. Our model builds bidirectional interactions between video frames and surrounding comments from multiple perspectives via metric learning, to collect a *diversified* and *informative* context for comment generation. We also propose an effective parameter orthogonalization technique to avoid excessive overlap of information learned from different perspectives. Results show that our approach outperforms existing methods in the ALVC task, achieving new state-of-the-art results.

1 Introduction

Live video commenting, also known as Danmaku commenting, is an emerging interaction mode among online video websites [2]. This technique allows viewers to write real-time comments while watching videos, in order to express opinions about the video or to interact with other viewers. Based on the features above, the **A**utomatic **L**ive **V**ideo **C**ommenting (ALVC) task aims to generate live comments for videos, while considering both the video and the surrounding comments made by other viewers. Figure 1 presents an example for this task. Automatically generating real-time comments brings more fun into video watching and reduces the difficulty of understanding video contents for human viewers. Besides, it also engages people's attention and increases the popularity of the video.

© Springer Nature Switzerland AG 2020
X. Zhu et al. (Eds.): NLPCC 2020, LNAI 12431, pp. 3–15, 2020.
https://doi.org/10.1007/978-3-030-60457-8_1

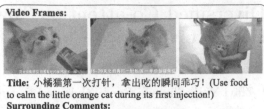

Fig. 1. An example of the ALVC task. The inputs are video frames and surrounding comments. The ground-truth comment (written by human) is the desired output. Compared to previous SOTA, our model generates comment with richer information from both video frames (*the orange cat*) and surrounding comments (*it is eating*).

Despite its usefulness described above, the ALVC task has not been widely explored. Ma et al. [15] is the first to propose this task, which is the only endeavor so far. They employ separate attention on the video and surrounding comments to obtain their representations. Such approach does not integrate visual and textual information and may lead to a limited information diversity. In fact, the surrounding comments are written based on the video, while they also highlight important features of the video frames. Thus, we aim to collect *diversified* information from video and text by building interactions between these two modalities.

As an effective method in multi-modal scenarios, co-attention has been applied in multiple tasks [11,14,19,30]. Based on previous works, we propose a novel **D**iversified **C**o-**A**ttention (DCA) model to better capture the complex dependency between video frames and surrounding comments. By learning different distance metrics to characterize the dependency between two information sources, the proposed DCA can build bidirectional interactions between video frames and surrounding comments from multiple perspectives, so as to produce *diversified* co-dependent representations. Going a step further, we propose a simple yet effective parameter orthogonalization technique to avoid excessive overlap (*information redundancy*) of information extracted from different perspectives. Experiment results suggest that our DCA model outperforms the previous approaches as well as the traditional co-attention, reaching state-of-the-art results in the ALVC task. Further analysis supports the effectiveness of the proposed components, as well as the information diversity in the DCA model.

2 Diversified Co-Attention Model

Given video frames $v = (v_1, \cdots, v_n)$ and surrounding comments $x = (x_1, \cdots, x_m)^1$, the ALVC task aims at generating a reasonable and fluent comment y. Figure 2 presents the sketch of our DCA model.

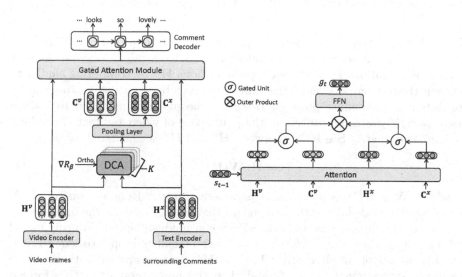

Fig. 2. An overview of the proposed DCA model (left) and the details of gated attention module (right).

2.1 Video Encoder and Text Encoder

The video encoder and text encoder aim to obtain representations of video frames and surrounding comments, respectively. The encoders are implemented as GRU networks. The hidden representations of each video frame v_i and each word x_i is computed as:

$$h_i^v = \mathrm{GRU}\big(h_{i-1}^v, f(v_i)\big), \quad h_i^x = \mathrm{GRU}\big(h_{i-1}^x, e(x_i)\big) \tag{1}$$

where $f(\cdot)$ refers to a convolutional neural network (CNN) used to transform raw images into dense vectors, and $e(x_i)$ is the word embedding of x_i. The visual and textual representation matrices are denoted as $\mathbf{H}^v = \{h_1^v, \cdots, h_n^v\} \in \mathbb{R}^{n \times d}$ and $\mathbf{H}^{\perp} = \{h_1^x, \cdots, h_m^x\} \in \mathbb{R}^{m \times d}$, respectively. Here we assume that h_i^v and h_i^x share the same dimension. Otherwise, a linear transformation can be introduced to ensure that their dimensions are the same.

---

[1] We concatenate all surrounding comments into a single sequence x.

2.2   Diversified Co-Attention

To effectively capture the dependency between video frames and surrounding comments, we propose a **D**iversified **C**o-**A**ttention (DCA) mechanism, which builds bidirectional interactions between two sources of information from different perspectives via metric learning [9]. We first elaborate on our DCA from *single perspective* and then extend it to *multiple perspectives*.

Single Perspective. The single-perspective DCA is adapted from original co-attention [14], but introduces techniques of metric learning. We first connect video representations $\mathbf{H}^v$ and text representations $\mathbf{H}^x$ by computing similarity between them. Conventionally, the similarity score between two vectors can be calculated as their inner product. However, the model is expected to learn a **task-specific distance metric** in the joint space of video and text. Therefore, the similarity matrix $\mathbf{S} \in \mathbb{R}^{n \times m}$ between $\mathbf{H}^v$ and $\mathbf{H}^x$ is calculated as:

$$\mathbf{S} = \mathbf{H}^v \mathbf{W} (\mathbf{H}^x)^{\mathrm{T}} \tag{2}$$

where $\mathbf{W} \in \mathbb{R}^{d \times d}$ is a learnable parameter matrix. Here we constraint $\mathbf{W}$ as a *positive semidefinite matrix* to ensure that Eq. (2) satisfies the basic definition [26] of the distance metric. Since $\mathbf{W}$ is continuously updated during model training, the *positive semidefinite* constraint is difficult to keep satisfied. To remedy this, we adopt an alternative: $\mathbf{H}^v$ and $\mathbf{H}^x$ are first applied with the same linear transformation $\mathbf{L} \in \mathbb{R}^{d \times d}$, and then the inner product of transformed matrices is computed as their similarity score:

$$\mathbf{S} = (\mathbf{H}^v \mathbf{L})(\mathbf{H}^x \mathbf{L})^{\mathrm{T}} = \mathbf{H}^v \mathbf{L} \mathbf{L}^{\mathrm{T}} (\mathbf{H}^x)^{\mathrm{T}} \tag{3}$$

where $\mathbf{L}\mathbf{L}^{\mathrm{T}}$ can be regarded as an approximation of $\mathbf{W}$ in Eq. (2). Since $\mathbf{L}\mathbf{L}^{\mathrm{T}}$ is *symmetric positive definite*, it is naturally a *positive semidefinite matrix*. Each element $\mathbf{S}_{ij}$ denotes the similarity score between v_i and x_j. $\mathbf{S}$ is normalized row-wise to produce vision-to-text attention weights $\mathbf{A}^x$, and column-wise to produce text-to-vision attention weights $\mathbf{A}^v$. The final representations are computed as the product of attention weights and original features:

$$\mathbf{A}^x = \mathrm{softmax}(\mathbf{S}), \quad \mathbf{A}^v = \mathrm{softmax}(\mathbf{S}^{\mathrm{T}}) \tag{4}$$
$$\mathbf{C}^x = \mathbf{A}^x \mathbf{H}^x, \quad \mathbf{C}^v = \mathbf{A}^v \mathbf{H}^v \tag{5}$$

where $\mathbf{C}^v \in \mathbb{R}^{m \times d}$ and $\mathbf{C}^x \in \mathbb{R}^{n \times d}$ denote the co-dependent representations of vision and text. Since $\mathbf{H}^v$ and $\mathbf{H}^x$ guide each other's attention, these two sources of information can mutually boost for better representations.

Multiple Perspectives. As distance metrics between vectors can be defined in various forms, learning a single distance metric $\mathbf{L}$ does not suffice to comprehensively measure the similarity between two kinds of representations. On the contrary, we hope to provide an informative context for the comment decoder from *diversified* perspectives. To address this contradiction, we introduce a multi-perspective setting in the DCA.

We ask the DCA to learn **multiple distance metrics** to capture the dependencies between video and text from different perspectives. To achieve this, DCA learns K different parameter matrices $\{\mathbf{L}_1, \cdots, \mathbf{L}_K\}$ in Eq. (3), where K is a hyper-parameter denoting the number of perspectives. Intuitively, each $\mathbf{L}_i$ represents a learnable distance metric. Given two sets of representations $\mathbf{H}^x$ and $\mathbf{H}^v$, each $\mathbf{L}_i$ yields a similarity matrix $\mathbf{S}_i$ as well as co-dependent representations $\mathbf{C}_i^x$ and $\mathbf{C}_i^v$ from its unique perspective. DCA is then able to build bi-directional interactions between two information sources from multiple perspectives. Finally, a mean-pooling layer is used to integrate the representations from different perspectives:

$$\mathbf{C}^x = \frac{1}{K}\sum_{k=1}^{K}\mathbf{C}_k^x, \quad \mathbf{C}^v = \frac{1}{K}\sum_{k=1}^{K}\mathbf{C}_k^v \qquad (6)$$

2.3 Parameter Orthogonalization

One potential problem of the above multi-perspective setting is *information redundancy*, meaning that the information extracted from different perspectives may overlap excessively. Specifically, the parameter matrices $\{\mathbf{L}_k\}_{k=1}^{K}$ may tend to be highly similar after many rounds of training. According to [13], to alleviate this problem, $\{\mathbf{L}_k\}_{k=1}^{K}$ should be as orthogonal as possible. We first try to add a regularization term R_β into the loss function as an orthonormality constraint [3]:

$$R_\beta = \frac{\beta}{4}\sum_{i=1}^{K}\sum_{j=1}^{K}\left(\text{tr}\left(\mathbf{L}_i\mathbf{L}_j^{\mathrm{T}}\right) - \mathbb{I}(i=j)\right)^2 \qquad (7)$$

where $\text{tr}(\cdot)$ is the trace of the matrix and β is a hyper-parameter. However, we empirically find that the simple introduction of regularization term may cause the collapse of model training. Thus, we propose an approximate alternative: after back propagation updates all parameters at each learning step, we adopt a post-processing method equivalent to the aforementioned orthonormality constraint by updating $\{\mathbf{L}_k\}_{k=1}^{K}$ with the gradient of regularization term R_β:

$$\nabla_{\mathbf{L}_i}R_\beta = \beta\left(\sum_{k=1}^{K}\text{tr}\left(\mathbf{L}_i\mathbf{L}_k^{\mathrm{T}}\right)\mathbf{L}_k - \mathbf{L}_i\right) \qquad (8)$$

$$\mathbf{L}_i \xleftarrow{update} (1+\beta)\mathbf{L}_i - \beta\sum_{k=1}^{K}\text{tr}(\mathbf{L}_i\mathbf{L}_k^{\mathrm{T}})\mathbf{L}_k \qquad (9)$$

The orthonormality constraint ensures that $\{\mathbf{L}_k\}_{k=1}^{K}$ are nearly orthogonal, suggesting that the information carried by these matrices rarely overlaps [13]. By reducing *information redundancy* in the multi-perspective setting, the orthogonalization technique ensures the *diversity* of information collected by DCA.

2.4   Gated Attention Module

In order to integrate the co-dependent representations from the DCA and original representations from the encoders, a Gated Attention Module (GAM) is designed following the DCA. Given the hidden state s_{t-1} of the decoder at timestep $t-1$, we first apply attention mechanism on the co-dependent and original representations respectively, using s_{t-1} as query:

$$\widehat{c}^x = \mathcal{A}(s_{t-1}, \mathbf{C}^x), \quad \widehat{h}^x = \mathcal{A}(s_{t-1}, \mathbf{H}^x) \tag{10}$$

where $\mathcal{A}$ is the attention mechanism [1]. Then, $\widehat{c}^x$ and $\widehat{h}^x$ are passed through a gated unit to generate comprehensive textual representations:

$$w^x = \sigma(\mathbf{U}_c^x \widehat{c}^x + \mathbf{U}_h^x \widehat{h}^x + b_x), \quad r^x = w^x \odot \widehat{c}^x + (1 - w^x) \odot \widehat{h}^x \tag{11}$$

where $\mathbf{U}_c^x$, $\mathbf{U}_h^x$ and b_x are learnable parameters, σ denotes the sigmoid function and $\odot$ denotes element-wise multiplication. r^x is the balanced textual representation of $\widehat{c}^x$ and $\widehat{h}^x$. Symmetrically, we obtain the balanced visual representation r^v through Eq. (10)–Eq. (11) based on $\mathbf{C}^v$ and $\mathbf{H}^v$.

In the ALVC task, the contribution of video information and textual information towards the desired comment may not be equivalent. Therefore, we calculate the final context vector $g_t \in \mathbb{R}^d$ as:

$$g_t = \mathcal{FFN}\big(r^x \otimes (\alpha \odot r^v)\big) \tag{12}$$

where α is a learnable vector. $\otimes$ denotes the outer product and $\mathcal{FFN}$ denotes a feed-forward neural network. The outer product is a more informative way to represent the relationship between vectors than the inner product, which we use to collect an informative context for generation.

2.5   Decoder

Given the context vector g_t obtained by the GAM, the decoder aims to generate a comment $y = (y_1, \cdots, y_l)$ via another GRU network. The hidden state s_t at timestep t is computed as:

$$s_t = \mathrm{GRU}\big(s_{t-1}, [e(y_{t-1}); g_t]\big) \tag{13}$$

where y_{t-1} is the word generated at time-step $t-1$, and semicolon denotes vector concatenation. The decoder then samples a word y_t from the output probability distribution:

$$y_t \sim \mathrm{softmax}(\mathbf{O}s_t) \tag{14}$$

where $\mathbf{O}$ denotes an output linear layer. The model is trained by maximizing the log-likelihood of the ground-truth comment.

In order to test the universality of the proposed components, we also implement our model based on Transformer [22]. Specifically, the text encoder, video encoder and comment decoder are implemented as Transformer blocks. Since this extension is not the focus of this paper, we will not explain it in more detail. Readers can refer to [22] for detailed descriptions of the Transformer architecture.

3   Experiments

3.1   Data and Settings

We conduct experiments on the Live Comment Dataset[2] [15]. The dataset is collected from the popular Chinese video streaming website Bilibili[3]. It contains 895,929 instances in total, which belong to 2,361 videos. In experiments, we adopt 34-layer Resnet [5] pretrained on ImageNet to process the raw video frames in Eq. (1). We set the number of perspectives to $K = 3$ in Eq. (6) and β in Eq. (9) is set to 0.01. We adopt the Adam [8] optimization method with initial learning rate $3e - 4$, and train the model for 50 epochs with dropout rate 0.1.

3.2   Baselines

The baseline models in our experiments include the previous approaches in the ALVC task as well as the traditional co-attention model. For each listed Seq2Seq-based models, we implement another Transformer-based version by replacing the encoder and decoder to Transformer blocks.

- **S2S-Video** [24] uses a CNN to encode the video frames and a RNN decoder to generate the comment. This model only takes the video frames as input.
- **S2S-Text** [1] is the traditional Seq2Seq model with attention mechanism. This model only takes the surrounding comments as input.
- **S2S-Concat** [23] adopts two encoders to encode the video frames and the surrounding comments, respectively. Outputs from two encoders are concatenated and fed into the decoder.
- **S2S-SepAttn** [15] employs separate attention on video and text representations. The attention contexts are concatenated and fed into the decoder.
- **S2S-CoAttn** is a variant of our model, which replaces the DCA module using traditional co-attention [14].

Accordingly, the Transformer versions are named as **Trans-Video**, **Trans-Text**, **Trans-Concat**, **Trans-SepAttn** and **Trans-CoAttn**.

3.3   Evaluation Metrics

Automatic Evaluation. Due to the *diversity* of video commenting, we cannot collect all possible comments for reference-based comparison like BLEU. As a complement, rank-based metrics are applied in evaluating diversified generation tasks such as dialogue systems [4, 25, 33]. Given a set of candidate comments, the model is asked to sort the candidates in descending order of likelihood scores. Since the model generates the sentence with the highest likelihood score, it is reasonable to discriminate a good model based on its ability to rank the ground-truth comment on the top. Following previous work [15], the 100 candidate comments are collected as follows:

---

[2] https://github.com/lancopku/livebot.
[3] https://www.bilibili.com.

◇ **Ground-truth:** The human-written comment in the original video.

◇ **Plausible:** 30 most similar comments to the video title in the training set. Plausibility is computed as the cosine similarity between the comment and the video title based on TF-IDF values.

◇ **Popular:** 20 most frequently appeared comments in the training set, most of which are meaningless short sentences like "Hahaha" or "Great".

◇ **Random:** Comments that are randomly picked from the training set to make the candidate set up to 100 sentences.

We report evaluation results on the following metrics: **Recall@k** (the percentage that the ground-truth appears in the top k of the ranked candidates), **MR** (the mean rank of the ground-truth), and **MRR** (the mean reciprocal rank of the ground-truth).

Table 1. Results of automatic evaluation. **R@k** is short for **Recall@k**. Lower **MR** score means better performance, while other metrics are the opposite.

Seq2Seq	R@1	R@5	R@10	MRR	MR	Transformer	R@1	R@5	R@10	MRR	MR
S2S-Video	4.7	19.9	36.5	14.5	21.6	Trans-Video	5.3	20.7	38.2	15.1	20.9
S2S-Text	9.1	28.1	44.3	20.1	19.8	Trans-Text	10.5	30.2	46.1	21.8	18.5
S2S-Concat	12.9	33.8	50.3	24.5	17.1	Trans-Concat	14.2	36.8	51.5	25.7	17.2
S2S-SepAttn	17.3	38.0	56.1	27.1	16.1	Trans-SepAttn	18.0	38.1	55.8	27.5	16.0
S2S-CoAttn	21.9	42.4	56.6	32.6	15.5	Trans-CoAttn	23.1	42.8	56.8	33.4	15.6
DCA (S2S)	**25.8**	**44.2**	**58.4**	**35.3**	**15.1**	**DCA (Trans)**	**27.2**	**47.6**	**62.0**	**37.7**	**13.9**

Table 2. Results of human evaluation. We average the scores given by 5 annotators. Scores in bold indicate significant improvement (⩾0.5).

Models	Fluency	Relevance	Informativeness	Overall
S2S-Concat	2.7	2.4	2.6	2.6
S2S-SepAttn	3.1	2.8	2.5	3.1
S2S-CoAttn	3.5	3.2	2.7	3.3
DCA (S2S)	3.7	3.5	**3.4**	3.6
Trans-Concat	3.0	2.5	2.5	2.7
Trans-SepAttn	3.2	2.7	2.8	3.3
Trans-CoAttn	3.6	3.3	3.3	3.5
DCA (Trans)	3.7	3.6	**3.8**	3.7

Human Evaluation. In human evaluation, we randomly pick 200 instances from the test set. We ask five human annotators to score the generated comments from different models on a scale of 1 to 5 (higher is better). The annotators are required to evaluate these comments from the following aspects: **Fluency** (whether the sentence is grammatically correct), **Relevance** (whether the comment is relevant to the video and surrounding comments), **Informativeness** (whether the comment carries rich and meaningful information) and **Overall** (the annotator's general recommendation).

3.4 Experiment Results

According to the results of **automatic evaluation** (Table 1), our DCA model assigns higher ranks to ground-truth comments. These results prove that DCA has stronger ability in discriminating highly relevant comments from irrelevant ones. Since the generation process is also retrieving the best sentence among all possible word sequences, it can be inferred that DCA performs better at generating high-quality sentences.

Additionally, our DCA model receives more favor from human judges in **human evaluation** (Table 2). This proves that DCA generates comments that are more consistent with human writing habits. We also discover that the margin between DCA and baselines in *Informativeness* is larger than the other perspectives. Assisted by the proposed components to obtain diversified information from video and text, sentences generated by DCA are more informative than the other models.

The experiments show consistent results in Seq2Seq models and Transformer models. Hence, the proposed DCA modules are believed to have good **universality**, which can adapt to different model architectures.

3.5 Ablation Study

In order to better understand the efficacy of the proposed methods, we further conduct an ablation study on different settings of our model, with results presented in Table 3.

As the results suggest, there is a significant drop in the model's performance while replacing the DCA module with traditional co-attention. Compared to traditional co-attention, DCA has advantages in its multi-perspective setting, *i.e.*, learning multiple distance metrics in the joint space of video and text. DCA builds interactions between two information sources from multiple perspectives, hence extracting richer information than traditional co-attention.

Table 3. Experiment results of the ablation study. **Ortho.** represents parameter orthogonalization. "**-DCA**" means using traditional co-attention to replace DCA.

Models	Seq2Seq Architecture					Transformer Architecture				
	R@1	R@5	R@10	MRR	MR	R@1	R@5	R@10	MRR	MR
Full Model	25.8	44.2	58.4	35.3	15.1	27.2	47.6	62.0	37.7	13.9
-GAM	24.1	43.8	57.5	35.0	15.4	26.2	47.5	60.4	37.3	15.1
-Ortho.	22.7	43.2	57.2	33.4	15.8	24.7	45.8	59.5	35.6	14.9
-DCA	21.9	42.4	56.6	32.6	15.5	23.1	42.8	56.8	33.4	15.6

Besides, results show that the parameter orthogonalization technique and the GAM module are also critical to our model's performance. By alleviating the *information redundancy* issue in DCA's multi-perspective setting, the orthogonalization technique ensures the *diversity* of information collected by DCA. GAM uses gated units to integrate information from co-dependent and original representations, as well as to balance the importance of video and text. Such approach helps GAM collect an informative context for comment generation.

3.6   Visualization of DCA

To illustrate the contribution of parameter orthogonalization to the information diversity of our model, we visualize the similarity matrices $\{\mathbf{S}_k\}_{k=1}^K$ in DCA. In the vanilla DCA (shown in Fig. 3(a)), each $\mathbf{S}_i$ is generated by a distance metric $\mathbf{L}_i$ through Eq. (3). However, the similarity matrices are highly similar to each other. This shows that the information extracted from K perspectives suffers from the *information redundancy* problem, which is consistent with our hypothesis in Sect. 2.3. After introducing the parameter orthogonalization (shown in Fig. 3(b)), apparent differences can be seen among these similarity matrices. This further explains the performance decline after removing the orthogonalization technique in Table 3. The parameter orthogonalization ensures the discrepancy between distance metrics $\{\mathbf{L}_k\}_{k=1}^K$, helps DCA generate *diversified* representations, thus alleviates information redundancy and improves information diversity.

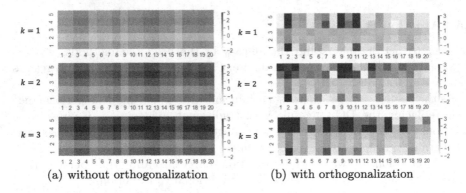

(a) without orthogonalization   (b) with orthogonalization

Fig. 3. Visualization of similarity matrices in DCA with or without parameter orthogonalization. Here we set $K = 3$. Horizontal axis: 20 words in a surrounding comment. Vertical axis: 5 surrounding video frames. Deeper color denotes higher relevance.

4   Related Work

Automatic Article Commenting. One similar task to our work is automatic article commenting. Qin et al. [18] is the first to introduce this task and constructs a Chinese news dataset. Ma et al. [16] proposes a retrieval-based commenting framework on unpaired data via unsupervised learning. Yang et al. [29] leverages visual information for comment generation on graphic news. Zeng et al. [32] uses a gated memory module to generate personalized comment on social media. Li et al. [10] models the news article as a topic interaction graph and proposes a graph-to-sequence model. Compared to article commenting, the ALVC task aims to model the interactions between text and video, and video is a more dynamic and complex source of information. The co-dependent relationship between a video and its comments makes this task a larger challenge for AI models.

Video Captioning. Another similar task to ALVC is video captioning. Venu-gopalan et al. [23] applies a unified deep neural network with CNN and LSTM layers. Shen et al. [20] proposes a sequence generation model with weakly supervised information for dense video captioning. Xiong et al. [27] produces descriptive paragraphs for videos via a recurrent network by assembling temporally localized descriptions. Li et al. [12] uses a residual attention-based LSTM to reduce information loss in generation. Xu et al. [28] jointly performs event detection and video description via a hierarchical network. Compared to video description, the ALVC task requires not only a full understanding of video frames, but also interaction with other human viewers. This requires effective modeling of the intrinsic dependency between visual and textual information.

Co-Attention. Our model is also inspired by the previous work of co-attention. Lu et al. [14] introduces a hierarchical co-attention model in visual QA. Nguyen et al. [17] proposes a dense co-attention network with a fully symmetric architecture. Tay et al. [21] applies a co-attentive multi-pointer network to model user-item relationships. Hsu et al. [6] adds co-attention module into CNNs to perform unsupervised object co-segmentation. Yu et al. [31] applies a deep modular co-attention network in combination of self-attention and guided-attention. Li et al. [11] uses positional self-attention and co-attention to replace RNNs in video question answering. Compared to previous co-attention methods, DCA considers the issue of obtaining co-dependent representations as distance metric learning. Equipped with the parameter orthogonalization technique, DCA is able to obtain rich information from multiple perspectives.

5   Conclusion

This work presents a diversified co-attention model for automatic live video commenting to capture the complex dependency between video frames and surrounding comments. By introducing bidirectional interactions between the video and text from multiple perspectives (different distance metrics), two information sources can mutually boost for better representations. Besides, we propose an effective parameter orthogonalization technique to avoid excessive overlap of information extracted from different perspectives. Experiments show that our approach can substantially outperform existing methods and generate comments with more novel and valuable information.

References

1. Bahdanau, D., Cho, K., Bengio, Y.: Neural machine translation by jointly learning to align and translate. In: ICLR 2015 (2015)
2. Chen, Y., Gao, Q., Rau, P.L.P.: Watching a movie alone yet together: understanding reasons for watching Danmaku videos. Int. J. Hum. Comput. Interact. **33**(9), 731–743 (2017)
3. Cissé, M., Bojanowski, P., Grave, E., Dauphin, Y.N., Usunier, N.: Parseval networks: improving robustness to adversarial examples. In: ICML 2017 (2017)
4. Das, A., et al.: Visual dialog. In: CVPR 2017 (2017)
5. He, K., Zhang, X., Ren, S., Sun, J.: Deep residual learning for image recognition. In: CVPR 2016 (2016)
6. Hsu, K., Lin, Y., Chuang, Y.: Co-attention CNNs for unsupervised object co-segmentation. In: IJCAI 2018 (2018)
7. Jiang, T., et al.: CTGA: graph-based biomedical literature search. In: BIBM 2019 (2019)
8. Kingma, D.P., Ba, J.: Adam: a method for stochastic optimization. In: ICLR 2015 (2015)
9. Kulis, B.: Metric learning: a survey. Found. Trends Mach. Learn. **5**(4), 287–364 (2013)
10. Li, W., Xu, J., He, Y., Yan, S., Wu, Y., Sun, X.: Coherent comments generation for Chinese articles with a graph-to-sequence model. In: ACL 2019 (2019)
11. Li, X., et al.: Beyond RNNs: positional self-attention with co-attention for video question answering. In: AAAI 2019 (2019)
12. Li, X., Zhou, Z., Chen, L., Gao, L.: Residual attention-based LSTM for video captioning. World Wide Web **22**(2), 621–636 (2018). https://doi.org/10.1007/s11280-018-0531-z
13. Lin, Z., et al.: A structured self-attentive sentence embedding. In: ICLR 2017 (2017)
14. Lu, J., Yang, J., Batra, D., Parikh, D.: Hierarchical question-image co-attention for visual question answering. In: NeurIPS 2016 (2016)
15. Ma, S., Cui, L., Dai, D., Wei, F., Sun, X.: LiveBot: generating live video comments based on visual and textual contexts. In: AAAI 2019 (2019)
16. Ma, S., Cui, L., Wei, F., Sun, X.: Unsupervised machine commenting with neural variational topic model. ArXiv preprint arXiv:1809.04960 (2018)
17. Nguyen, D., Okatani, T.: Improved fusion of visual and language representations by dense symmetric co-attention for visual question answering. In: CVPR 2018 (2018)
18. Qin, L., et al.: Automatic article commenting: the task and dataset. In: ACL 2018 (2018)
19. Seo, M.J., Kembhavi, A., Farhadi, A., Hajishirzi, H.: Bidirectional attention flow for machine comprehension. In: ICLR 2017 (2017)
20. Shen, Z., et al.: Weakly supervised dense video captioning. In: CVPR 2017 (2017)
21. Tay, Y., Luu, A.T., Hui, S.C.: Multi-pointer co-attention networks for recommendation. In: KDD 2018 (2018)
22. Vaswani, A., et al.: Attention is all you need. In: NeurIPS 2017 (2017)
23. Venugopalan, S., Rohrbach, M., Donahue, J., Mooney, R.J., Darrell, T., Saenko, K.: Sequence to sequence - video to text. In: ICCV 2015 (2015)
24. Vinyals, O., Toshev, A., Bengio, S., Erhan, D.: Show and tell: a neural image caption generator. In: CVPR 2015 (2015)

25. Wu, W., et al.: Proactive human-machine conversation with explicit conversation goal. In: ACL 2019 (2019)
26. Xing, E.P., Ng, A.Y., Jordan, M.I., Russell, S.J.: Distance metric learning with application to clustering with side-information. In: NeurIPS 2002 (2002)
27. Xiong, Y., Dai, B., Lin, D.: Move forward and tell: a progressive generator of video descriptions. In: ECCV 2018 (2018)
28. Xu, H., Li, B., Ramanishka, V., Sigal, L., Saenko, K.: Joint event detection and description in continuous video streams. In: WACV 2019 (2019)
29. Yang, P., Zhang, Z., Luo, F., Li, L., Huang, C., Sun, X.: Cross-modal commentator: automatic machine commenting based on cross-modal information. In: ACL 2019 (2019)
30. Yu, A.W., et al.: QANet: combining local convolution with global self-attention for reading comprehension. In: ICLR 2018 (2018)
31. Yu, Z., Yu, J., Cui, Y., Tao, D., Tian, Q.: Deep modular co-attention networks for visual question answering. In: CVPR 2019 (2019)
32. Zeng, W., Abuduweili, A., Li, L., Yang, P.: Automatic generation of personalized comment based on user profile. In: ACL 2019 (2019)
33. Zhou, H., Zheng, C., Huang, K., Huang, M., Zhu, X.: KdConv: a Chinese multi-domain dialogue dataset towards multi-turn knowledge-driven conversation. In: ACL 2020 (2020)

The Sentencing-Element-Aware Model for Explainable Term-of-Penalty Prediction

Hongye Tan$^{(\boxtimes)}$, Bowen Zhang, Hu Zhang$^{(\boxtimes)}$, and Ru Li

School of Computer and Information Technology, Shanxi University, Taiyuan, China
{tanhongye,zhanghu}@sxu.edu.cn

Abstract. Automatic term-of-penalty prediction is a key subtask of intelligent legal judgment (ILJ). Recent ILJ systems are based on deep learning methods, in which explainability is a pressing concern. In this paper, our goal is to build a term-of-penalty prediction system with good judicial explainability and high accuracy following the legal principles. We propose a sentencing-element-aware neural model to realize this. We introduce sentencing elements to link the case facts with legal laws, which makes the prediction meet the legal objectivity principle and ensure the accuracy. Meanwhile, in order to explain why the term-of-penalties are given, we output sentencing element-level explanations, and utilize sentencing elements to select the most similar cases as case-level explanations, which reflects the equity principle. Experiments on the datasets (CAIL2018) show that our model not only achieves equal or better accuracy than the baselines, but also provide useful explanations to help users to understand how the system works.

Keywords: Term-of-penalty prediction · Explainable · Sentencing elements

1 Introduction

Automatic term-of-penalty prediction is an important subtask of intelligent legal judgment. A few recent works have utilized deep learning methods to make legal judgment [1, 11–14]. However, deep neural networks lack explainability, which is a pressing concern.

For legal judgment, the most important principle is *"taking the law as criterion and the fact as ground"*, which is the principle of objectivity. That requires the case facts used for term-of-penalty prediction must be consistent with the laws. For example, in the process of sentencing decision for a traffic accident case, the relevant legal articles take some crucial elements as important factors for deciding the penalties, such as *"whether caused serious injury or death to victims"*, *"whether hit-and-ran"* and so on. And the case description contains the key information of *"died on the spot"* and *"drove and left the scene"*. So the appropriate term-of-penalties can be given based on whether the key facts are in accordance with the relevant sentencing elements.

Besides that, another important principle for legal judgement is *"similar cases should be with similar judgements"*, which is the principle of justice and equity.

Based on the above analysis, we think that: besides high accuracy, good term-of-penalty prediction systems should follow the two principles, and clearly explain to

X. Zhu et al. (Eds.): NLPCC 2020, LNAI 12431, pp. 16–27, 2020.
https://doi.org/10.1007/978-3-030-60457-8_2

users how they achieved that. We propose a sentencing element-aware neural model for term-of-penalty prediction with good explainability and high accuracy. The model uses sentencing elements to link the case facts with the legal articles, making sure the prediction is in line with the objectivity principle and ensure the accuracy. Specifically, sentencing elements are firstly summarized from the legal articles. Then, the model recognizes the sentencing elements in the case, and utilizes the attention mechanism to obtain the sentencing element-aware representation of case facts to predict term-of-penalties. Meanwhile the model utilizes the sentencing elements to provide two types of explanations. (1) the key facts coinciding with the sentencing elements, telling users why the penalties are given; (2) the sentencing element similar cases, explaining to users that there exist similar cases with the similar penalties.

Experiments on the CAIL2018 dataset (provided by 2018 Competition of AI and Law challenge in China) [2] show that: our sentencing element-aware model not only achieves equal or better accuracy than the baselines, but also provides useful explanations. The main contributions of this paper are summarized as follows:

- We propose a sentencing element-based neural model to predict term-of-penalties, taking both accuracy and judicial explanations into consideration.
- We introduce sentencing elements to the model, capturing key factors in the case facts and the legal articles.
- We fully utilize sentencing elements to provide two kinds of explanations: the sentencing element-level explanations and the case-level explanations.

2 Related Works

Researchers have tried to combine AI with law for decades. Early researchers implemented the rule-based expert systems to assist in predicting judicial acts [3, 4]. With the development of machine learning technologies, text categorization methods and manually-designed features have been utilized for judicial prediction [5–10]. Recently, deep neutral networks have begun to be used to make legal judgments [11–14].

But only a few works concentrated on term-of-penalty measurement [3, 5–7, 14, 21]. Some earlier works focus on sentencing for certain kinds of cases [5–7]. Recent works focus on sentencing for all kinds of cases due to the availability of big legal data. For example, Zhong et al. utilized topological learning and the CNN model to predict legal laws, charges and term-of-penalties simultaneously under a joint framework [14]. Chen et al. proposed the Deep Gating Network (DGN) for charge-specific feature selection and aggregation to improve term-of-penalty prediction [21].

Few previous ILJ works provide explicit explanations. Zhong et al. [1] proposed a method based on principle of Element Trial, iteratively questioning and answering to provide interpretable results. Their questions and answers serve as the element-level explanations for charge prediction. Our work is like their ideas on Elemental Trial, but besides the sentencing element-level explanations, we provide case-level ones.

Our model is to some degree inspired by the work of Hu et al. [12], but is different from theirs in the following aspects: (1) We focus on term-of-penalty prediction, while their goal is to improve the prediction of few-shot and confusing charges. (2) Our sentencing elements are relevant to term-of-penalty and mainly about the degree of harm caused by criminal acts, while their attributes are for confusing charge prediction. (3) Besides using sentencing elements to ensure the accuracy of term-of-penalty prediction, we take them as the sentencing element-level explanations and further utilize them to select the similar cases as case-level explanations.

3 Methodology

We formulate the task of term-of-penalty prediction as a classification problem: given the case fact description $x = \{t_1, t_2, \ldots, t_m\}$ and the set of term-of-penalty $Y = \{y_1, y_2, \ldots, y_l\}$, the learned model predicts the term-of-penalty y ($y \in Y$) as $y^* = \arg\max P(y|x)$.

3.1 Sentencing Elements

In order to capture the key legal factors for term-of-penalty prediction, we induce seven sentencing-element groups from Chinese Criminal Law and the Supreme People's Court's Guidance Opinions on Sentencing for Common Crimes.

- Means of crimes. This group of sentencing-element describes the way adopted by the offender in the act of committing a crime, which includes whether the offender carry a lethal weapon, or disguised as an army-man or a policeman, etc.
- Degree of injury to victims. This relates to the extent of the victim's injury caused by the offender. Specifically, the injury can be minor, serious or to be death.
- Characters of victims. This sentencing-element group focuses on whether the victims are some special people, such as infants, the young under 14 and the elder.
- Amount of properties. The properties involved in a crime may be money, drugs, goods, and materials etc., and the amounts can be large, huge, particularly huge or not large.
- Characters of properties. These sentencing elements focus on whether the properties are for military use, or for fighting disasters or relieving disaster victims.
- Locations of crimes. These elements are whether the crime is committed in the victim's house, or on public transports, or in some public financial institution etc.
- Other situations. These sentencing elements relate to some behaviors, resulting in a heavier (or lighter) punishment, such as the offender's surrendering to the police, or returning stolen goods, or committing crimes repeatedly etc.

In this paper, we consider 29 sentencing elements for 31 common crimes including traffic accident crime, intentional injury crime, theft crime, robbery crime and so on. The sentencing elements can be binary-valued (0 or 1) or multi-valued, indicating different degrees of harm. For example, the value of the sentencing element of "the amount of money involved in the case" can be not large (0), large (1), huge (2), and particularly huge (3).

We use the following methods to annotate sentencing elements for training corpus.

Binary-valued sentencing element annotation. We analyze the case descriptions and summarize the rules, which are triggered by some keywords. To ensure the rules' accuracy, we keep 61 keywords without ambiguity. We manually annotate 100 samples for evaluation, and the precision is almost 100% and the recall is about 95%.

Multi-valued sentencing element annotation. From the relevant legal articles and the provided penalties, we can infer the values of these sentencing elements. For example, for a case of the crime of theft, the legal articles' description is: "*If the theft amount is large, the offender will be sentenced to fixed-term imprisonment of not more than three years...*". We analyze the CAIL2018 dataset and find that one case generally involves one multi-valued sentencing element, indicating that there is almost no conflict among the sentencing elements.

3.2 Our Model

We propose a neural model using sentencing elements to predict penalties. As shown in Fig. 1, it consists of the following parts: case encoding, sentencing element-aware attention, sentencing element prediction, term-of-penalty prediction, explanations.

(1) Case Encoding. This layer takes the word2vec representation of each token in the input $x = \{t_1, \ldots, t_m\}$ as inputs and maps it into the corresponding vector representation. In order to consider the contexts, we employ BERT [15] and LSTM [16], both of which have achieved outstanding results for many tasks. Through BERT and LSTM, we get the representation $d \in \mathbb{R}^{m \times s}$, including the contextual information and history. Here s is the dimension of LSTM hidden layer.

(2) Sentencing Element-aware Attention. In order to capture the information relevant to sentencing, we propose a sentencing element-aware mechanism. The mechanism takes the hidden state sequence $d = \{d_1, \ldots, d_m\}$ (d_i is the i-th time step hidden state representation) as input and calculates the attention weights $a = \{a_1, \ldots, a_k\}$ of all sentencing elements; and then gets the sentencing element-aware representation $\bar{r}$. The calculations are as follows:

$$a_{i,j} = \frac{exp(tanh(W^a d_j)^T v_i)}{\sum_t exp(tanh(W^a d_t)^T v_i)}, \quad \forall i \in [1, k], \quad \forall j \in [1, m] \tag{1}$$

$$\bar{r}_i = \sum_t a_{i,j} d_t \tag{2}$$

$$\bar{r} = \frac{\sum_i \bar{r}_i}{k} \tag{3}$$

where the context vector v_i is used to calculate the attention weight for i-th sentencing element, the time step $t \in [1, m]$ and W^a is a weight matrix that all sentencing elements share.

(3) Sentencing Element Prediction. Based on the sentencing element-aware representation, the layer calculates the probability distribution z_i on the i-th sentencing element value, and obtains the sentencing element prediction results $p = [p_1, \ldots, p_k]$. The calculations are as Eq. (4) and (5), where the weight matrix W_i^p and b_i^p are weight matrix and bias vectors of the i-th sentencing element.

$$z_i = softmax(W_i^p \bar{r}_i + b_i^p), \tag{4}$$

$$p_i = argmax(z_i), \tag{5}$$

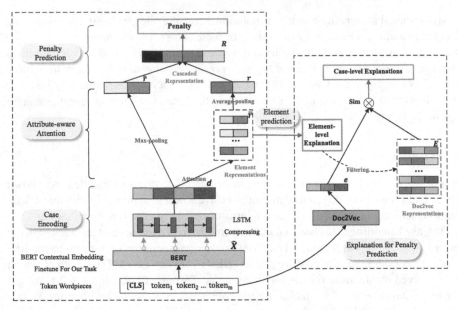

Fig. 1. Architecture of our model.

(4) **Term-of-penalty Prediction.** This layer concatenates the sentencing element-aware representation r and the sentencing element-free representation $\tilde{r} = [\tilde{r}_1, \cdots, \tilde{r}_s]$, and get the representation R. Then, the layer utilizes the softmax function to predict the term-of-penalty distribution y and outputs the term-of-penalty $\tilde{z} = argmax(y)$.

(5) **Training.** The training tasks include penalty prediction and sentencing element prediction. We use the common cross-entropy loss as the objective functions for the two training tasks, as shown in Eq. (6) and (7). The final loss function is Eq. (8):

$$L_{penalty} = -\sum_{i=1}^{l} y_i \cdot \log(\hat{y}_i) \tag{6}$$

$$L_{attr} = -\sum_{i=1}^{k} \sum_{j=1}^{4} z_{ij} \cdot \log(\hat{z}_{ij}) \tag{7}$$

$$L = L_{sen} + L_{attr} \tag{8}$$

where y_i is the ground-truth term-of-penalty label, $\hat{y}_i$ is the predicted term-of-penalty probability and l is the number of penalties, z_{ij} is the ground-truth sentencing element label, $\hat{z}_{ij}$ is the predicted sentencing element probability, k is the number of sentencing elements. And the maximum number of the value for a multi-valued sentencing element is four, so we set $j \in [1, 4]$.

(6) **Explanations.** In this part, we output the sentencing elements predicted by the model as the sentencing element-level explanations. Besides, we take similar cases as case-level explanations to tell users that there exist similar cases with the similar penalties, which is consistent with the equality and fairness principle of *"similar cases should*

be with similar judgements" in the judicial field. Here, we obtain the document representation *e* by utilizing Doc2vec [18], which is an unsupervised algorithm to obtain the vector representation of a document. And we use E to denote the collection representation for all cases. Then, our model chooses the cases with the same sentencing elements from the dataset by calculating the *cosin* similarity between the target case vector *e* and the selected case vector e_i. Finally, the top-k (k is set to 3) similar cases are output as the case-level explanations.

4 Experiments

4.1 Datasets and Baselines

Our experimental dataset is from the dataset of 2018 Competition of AI and Law challenge in China (CAIL2018), which contains about 1,700,000 cases and each case consists of fact descriptions and judgment results in Chinese. Since the Supreme People's Court of China has issued sentencing guidelines for common crimes, we focus on term-of-penalty prediction for these 31 common crimes. From the CAIL2018 dataset, we extract 1,229,225 cases for common crimes. And the sizes of the training set, the invalidation set and the test set are 990,881, 127,942 and 110,402 respectively.

We compare our model with the following models for text classification:

TFIDF-SVM [18]: SVM is a strong classifier in many classification tasks. Here, the model uses the TFIDF weights as term features for text classification.

CNN [19]: Convolutional neural networks (CNNs) are effective neutral network models, which uses hierarchical architectures and can extract the most informative features. CNNs have achieved state-of-the-art results on many NLP tasks.

Multi-Filter CNN [20]: A variant of CNNs, using filters of different sizes to form multi-window convolution neural network for text coding and classification.

LSTM [16]: LSTM is another kind of effective neutral network model. Here we use a multi-layer LSTM model for text coding and classification.

BERT [15]: Bert is a model proposed by Google, which adopts Transformer and self-attention mechanisms to learn contextual relations between words in a text, and has achieved outstanding results for a lot of NLP tasks. We design two variants of BERT model. One is BERT-FN, the BERT with full connection layer. The other is BERT-LSTM, the BERT with LSTM.

4.2 Experimental Details

We adopt the Adam as the optimizer because it makes the learning rate self-adapted during the training and leads to faster convergence. Then we set the initial learning rate to 10^{-3} and we adopt the two-layer LSTM. Meanwhile, we utilize dropout to alleviate over-fitting and set it to 0.8. We set the hidden state size to 768 and the maximum document length to 350. In addition, we set the batch size to 90 and epochs to 50.

4.3 Evaluation Metrics

We adopt the official evaluation metric (the score based on deviation) in CAIL2018. The metric is computed as Eq. (9), (10) and (11), where v is the deviation, l_p is the predicted label and l_a is the ground-truth label, $score_i$ is the score of the current predicted label, and $Score$ means the system score. If the ground truth is death penalty or life imprisonment, the score will be 1.0 and $l_p = 2$ or $l_p = -1$.

$$v = \left| \log(l_p + 1) - \log(l_a + 1) \right| \tag{9}$$

$$score_i = \begin{cases} 1, & 0 < v \le 0 \cdot 2 \\ 0 \cdot 8, & 0 \cdot 2 < v \le 0 \cdot 4 \\ 0 \cdot 6, & 0 \cdot 4 < v \le 0 \cdot 6 \\ 0 \cdot 4, & 0 \cdot 6 < v \le 0 \cdot 8 \\ 0 \cdot 2, & 0 \cdot 8 < v \le 1 \\ 0, & v > 1 \end{cases} \tag{10}$$

$$Score = \frac{\sum_{i=1}^{N} score_i}{N} * 100 \tag{11}$$

In ablation experiments, we employ accuracy (Acc.), macro-precision (MP), macro-recall (MR) and macro-F1 as our evaluation metrics.

4.4 Category Merging

The cases in CAIL2018 involve three types of term-of-penalties: life imprisonment, death penalty and fixed-term imprisonment. Among them, fixed-term imprisonment is measured in month with the range from 0 to 300 months and has 236 different penalties in total. But most of the penalties (about 80%) are in the scope of 0–18 months, meaning that the data distribution is imbalanced. To address the problem, we merge the fine-grained penalty categories according to the CAIL2018 evaluation metric.

From the Formula (11), it can be seen that: the smaller the deviation, the higher the score is. And the full score is obtained when the deviation v is within 0.2. We think that for the sentencing term-of-penalty interval $[l_m, l_n]$, if the interval median l_p satisfies $\left| \log(l_p + 1) - \log(l_m + 1) \right| \le 0.2$ and $\left| \log(l_p + 1) - \log(l_n + 1) \right| \le 0.2$, i.e. $\log(l_n + 1) - \log(l_m + 1) \le 0.4$, then the deviation v is small. In the dataset, the minimum and maximum terms of imprisonment are 0 month and 300 months respectively, and $\log 300 \approx 8$. So according to $(8/0.4 = 20)$, we can divide the whole interval [0,300] into 20 small intervals. One small interval corresponds to one term-of-penalty category, and the corresponding median is the label of the term of term-of-penalty. In this way the fine-grained categories are mapped into the coarse-grained ones. Specifically, because few cases have the penalties more than 180 months, we can regard these penalties as one category. Therefore, we finally map the categories of terms of imprisonment into 20 labels (including "death penalty" and "life imprisonment"). The number of the categories is much less than it used to be.

4.5   Results and Analysis

Comparison with Baselines. The prediction results are shown in Table 1, where CAIL-A, CAIL-E and CAIL-D respectively represent the dataset without category merging, the one with category merging using the equal interval, and the one with category merging based on the evaluation metric of CAIL2018.

From Table 1, we can see that our model consistently performs better than all baselines, showing that sentencing elements can help to capture crucial information for term-of-penalty prediction. And all methods on the datasets with category merging (CM) outperform those on the dataset without CM. Moreover, the methods on the dataset with CM based on the evaluation metric perform best, showing that the strategy alleviate the data imbalance problem and improve the performance.

We can also see that all the deep learning methods outperform TFIDF-SVM, showing that deep learning models can get more semantic information from the inputs. In the deep learning models, Multi-Filter CNN outperforms CNN and LSTM because it uses many filtering windows with different sizes and obtains more information with different granularities, such as words, phrases, and short terms. And LSTM is better than CNN, indicating that LSTM can solve the long-distance dependence of sequences and is more suitable for handing long textual descriptions. BERT-LSTM outperforms all the other models because it realizes the dynamic vector representations and grasps the contextual semantic information better.

Table 2 lists the performance of our model for the metrics of Acc., MP, MR and macro-F1. It can be found that compared with the two variants of BERT model, our model gets better performance for the metrics of Acc. and MP and macro-F1. To the best of our knowledge, few published researches focus on term-of-penalty prediction except Zhong et al. [14] and Chen et al. [21]. From their papers, we get that the performances of Zhong et al. [14] are Acc (38.3), MP (36.1), MR (33.1) and macro-F1 (32.1), and the performance of Chen et al. [21] is 75.74 for the metric of the score based on deviation. However, since the Supreme People's Court's Guidance Opinions on Sentencing for Common Crimes only involves 31 common crimes, we define the sentencing elements for these common crimes. Thus, we cannot compare our results with theirs. But their datasets and ours are all from CAIL2018, so our experimental results have reference values to some degree. And we can see that our system's performance is equivalent to theirs.

Ablation Analysis. In the experiments, the input sequence includes the corresponding charge of the case besides the factual description, because conviction needs to be carried out before sentencing in the process of a criminal judgement. We design ablation tests to investigate the effectiveness of the charge information and sentencing elements. As shown in Table 3, the performance drops after the sentencing elements and the charges are both removed. And the performance decreases more after the sentencing elements are removed, showing that the sentencing elements contribute more to the model than the charges.

Out of our expectations, the value of the metric of MP drops after the charges are removed. We analyze the outputs and find that the accuracy of death penalty is very low. The reason is that the definition of death penalty in Chinese Criminal Law is: "death

Table 1. Comparison with baselines.

Datasets	CAIL-A	CAIL-E	CAIL-D
Metric	Score based on deviation		
TFIDF-SVM	54.33	56.10	60.51
CNN	59.01	64.20	72.54
Multi-Filter CNN	60.15	65.97	73.68
LSTM	59.23	67.99	74.58
BERT-LSTM	63.70	69.85	77.62
Our model	**65.00**	**71.72**	**79.81**

Table 2. Comparison with BERT models.

Metrics	Acc.	MP	MR	Macro-F1
BERT-FN	42.1	42.0	28.3	29.6
BERT-LSTM	43.7	**44.6**	29.1	31.3
Our model	**46.7**	44.3	**32.0**	**34.3**

Table 3. Ablation study for our model.

Metrics	Acc.	MP	MR	Macro-F1
Our model	**46.7**	44.3	**32.0**	**34.3**
– Charges	45.8	**46.1**	30.5	32.4
– Sentencing elements	42.0	43.2	29.7	31.8
– Charges & - sentencing elements	43.3	44.8	28.9	31.5

penalty only applies to criminals who commit extremely serious crimes", which is very abstract and too difficult to compute.

4.6 Explainability Study

Our model fully utilizes sentencing elements to provide explanations. In the case shown in Table 4, the sentencing elements identified by the model are "the crime caused the victim's death" and "the offender hit-and-ran", which are the key factors for term-of-penalty prediction in a traffic accident crime. From the sentencing elements, users can know why the model gives the penalties.

Table 5 shows the top 3 cases selected with sentencing-element filtering (SEF) and without SEF, which are used as case-level explanations for the case in Table 4. We can

Table 4. Examples of sentencing element-level explanations.

Case description	At 19:40 on March 27, 2014, the defendant Yuan, ..., He knocked down the pedestrian Wang, causing Wang to die on the spot. Yuan drove and left the scene and was caught by the police later
Term	42 months
Sentencing element-level explanations	**The crime caused the victim's death; the offender hit-and-ran**

see that the cases selected with SEF are more similar with the case in Table 5, and the penalties are less deviated than those selected without SEF.

Table 5. Examples of case-level explanations.

No.	Case selected with SEF	Case selected without SEF
1	**Case description:** At about 15:20 on October 3, 2015, ... And Li **died** despite rescue. After the accident, Zhao abandoned his car and **fled the scene**. **Term:** 42 months.	**Case description:** At about 19:30 on February 28, 2015, ... The defendant Zhao abandoned his car and escaped. Liu died on the same day despite of rescue. **Term:** 42 months.
2	**Case description:** At about 21:00 on October 11, 2013, ... The accident results in Zhao's **death**. After the accident, Zhao **drove away**. **Term:** 42 months.	**Case description:** At about 17:40 on November 8, 2012, ... The accident caused Ji to be injured and died on that day despite of recue in the hospital. **Term:** 8 months.
3	**Case description:** At about 17:50 on December 16, 2015, ... The accident resulted in Zhao's **death** and ,... . After the accident, Sun abandoned his car and **fled.** **Term:** 36 months.	**Case description:** At about 18:40 on May 5, 2015,... . The accident resulted in Zhao's injury and Zhao died after rescue, which was a major traffic accident. **Term:** 12 months.

We random select 600 cases and carry on the statistical analysis for their similar cases obtained with SEF and without SEF. Table 6 shows the results, where exact match means the similar cases with the same term-of-penalty, and approximate match means the deviation of the term-of-penalty of the similar case is less than 15%. We can see that quality of case selected with SEF has significantly improved.

Table 6. Exact and approximate matching statistics of similar case selection.

Method	Exact match	Approximate match
Without SEF	53.3%	57.2%
With SEF	**60.5%**	**65.6%**

5 Conclusions

In this paper, we propose a neural model of automatic term-of-penalty prediction and take both accuracy and explanations into consideration. The model gets the better or equal accuracy by introducing sentencing elements to capture the key factors relevant to sentencing, and the model provides two kinds of explanations: sentencing element-level explanations and case-level explanations. In future, we will utilize more sentencing elements to understand more concrete details of the cases and we will analyze the bias in the dataset to further improve the accuracy of term-of-penalty prediction. Besides, we will explore more ways such as legal articles to provide legal-article-level explanations.

Acknowledgments. This work was supported by the National Social Science Fund of China (No. 18BYY074).

References

1. Zhong, H., Wang, Y., Tu, C., et al.: Iteratively questioning and answering for interpretable legal judgment prediction. In: Proceeding of AAAI (2020)
2. Xiao, C., Zhong, H., Guo, Z., et al.: CAIL2018: a large-scale legal dataset for judgment prediction (2018)
3. Shapira, M.: Computerized decision technology in social service. Int. J. Sociol. Soc. Policy **10**, 138–164 (1990)
4. Hassett, P.: Can expert system technology contribute to improved bail conditions. Int. J. Law Inf. Technol. **1**, 144–188 (1993)
5. Lin, W., Kuo, T.T., Chang, T.J.: Exploiting machine learning models for Chinese legal documents labeling, case classification, and sentencing prediction. In: Proceedings of ROCLING, p. 140 (2012)
6. Schild, U.: Criminal sentencing and intelligent decision support. AI Law **6**, 151–202 (1998)
7. Chen, C.T.H.: A decision support system for sex-crime sentencing. Inf. Manag. **20**(4), 449–482 (2013)
8. Aletras, N., Tsarapatsanis, D., Preotiuc-Pietro, D., Lampos, V.: Predicting judicial decisions of the european court of human rights: a natural language processing perspective. PeerJ Comput. Sci. **2**, e93 (2016)
9. Sulea, O.M., Zampieri, M., Vela, M., Van Genabith, J.: Exploring the use of text classification in the legal domain. In: Proceedings of ASAIL Workshop (2017)
10. Katz, D.M., Bommarito II, M.J., Blackman, J.: Predicting the behavior of the supreme court of the United States: a general approach. PLoS ONE **12**(4), e0174698 (2017)
11. Luo, B., Feng, Y., Xu, J., Zhang, X., Zhao, D.: Learning to predict charges for criminal cases with legal basis. In: Proceedings of EMNLP (2017)

12. Hu, Z., Li, X., Tu, C., Liu, Z., Sun, M.: Few-shot charge prediction with discriminative legal sentencing elements. In: Proceedings of COLING (2018)
13. Ye, H., Jiang, X., Luo, Z., et al.: Interpretable charge predictions for criminal cases: learning to generate court views from fact descriptions. In: Proceedings of NAACL (2018)
14. Zhong, H., Guo, Z., Tu, C., et al.: Legal judgment prediction via topological learning. In: Proceedings of EMNLP (2018)
15. Devlin, J., Chang, MW., Lee, K., et al.: BERT: pre-training of deep bidirectional transformers for language understanding (2018)
16. Tang, D., Qin, B., Feng, X., et al.: Effective LSTMs for target-dependent sentiment classification. Comput. Sci. (2015)
17. Le, Q., Mikolov, T.: Distributed representations of sentences and documents. In: International Conference on Machine Learning, pp. 1188–1196 (2014)
18. Suykens, J.A.K., Vandewalle, J.: Least squares support vector machine classifiers. Neural Process. Lett. 9(3), 293–300 (1999)
19. Johnson, R., Zhang, T.: Effective use of word order for text categorization with convolutional neural networks. Eprint Arxiv (2014)
20. Kim, Y.: Convolutional neural networks for sentence classification. In: Proceedings of EMNLP (2014)
21. Chen, H., Cai, D., Dai, W., et al.: Charge-based prison term prediction with deep gating network. In: Proceedings of EMNLP-IJCNLP (2019)

Referring Expression Generation
via Visual Dialogue

Lingxuan Li[(✉)], Yihong Zhao, Zhaorui Zhang, Tianrui Niu,
Fangxiang Feng, and Xiaojie Wang

School of Artificial Intelligence, Beijing University of Posts and Telecommunications,
Beijing, China
{lingxuanli,zhaoyihong,zhangzhaorui,niwtr,fxfeng,xjwang}@bupt.edu.cn

Abstract. Referring Expression Generation (REG) is to generate
unambiguous descriptions for the referred object in contexts such as
images. While people often use installment dialoguing methods to extend
the original basic noun phrases to form final references to objects. Most
existing REG models generate Referring Expressions (REs) in a "one-
shot" way, which cannot benefit from the interaction process. In this
paper, we propose to model REG basing on dialogues. To achieve it, we
first introduce a RE-oriented visual dialogue (VD) task ReferWhat?!,
then build two large-scale datasets RefCOCOVD and RefCOCO+VD
for this task by making use of the existing RE datasets RefCOCO and
RefCOCO+ respectively. We finally propose a VD-based REG model.
Experimental results show that our model outperforms all the existing
"one-shot" REG models. Our ablation studies also show that modeling REG as a dialogue agent can utilize the information in responses
from dialogues to achieve better performance which is not available in
the "one-shot" models. The source code and datasets will be seen in
https://github.com/llxuan/ReferWhat soon.

Keywords: Referring expression generation · Visual dialogue

1 Introduction

Generating a referring expression (RE) for unambiguously referring to an object
in the visual world is an important challenge problem for Artificial Intelligence.
Referring Expression Generation (REG) and its dual task Referring Expression
Understanding (REU), which is to find the object being referred to in a context,
bridge the symbolic language and the physical world.

The research on REG can be traced back to the work of Winograd [27].
Early works largely focus on structured object descriptions for synthetical and
simplified visual scenes [3]. The first end-to-end REG model of real and complicated visual scenes is proposed by Mao et al. [19], their work enables enormous
progress of the REG research on complex scenes. Recently, Yu et al. [29] and
Tanaka et al. [24] modeled the REG problem under a speaker-listener framework

© Springer Nature Switzerland AG 2020
X. Zhu et al. (Eds.): NLPCC 2020, LNAI 12431, pp. 28–40, 2020.
https://doi.org/10.1007/978-3-030-60457-8_3

	(a)	**REG in a "One-shot" Way:** RE: Black pencil on the notebook.

	(b)	**REG in a Dialoguing Way:** A: Give me a pencil, please. B: What color is it? A: Black. B: On the table or the notebook? A: The one on the notebook. B: Here you are.

Fig. 1. Two ways for REG: in a "one-shot" way and in a dialoguing way.

and jointly trained the REG and REU modules by reinforcement learning (RL). The resultant model [24] has achieved the state-of-art (SOTA) performance.

Existing REG models mainly generate a complete RE in a "one-shot" way, e.g. in Fig. 1(a), the RE is generated as a whole. Although "one-shot" is a way for people to generate REs, Clark and Wilkes-Gibbs [2] found that people often use episodic, installment, and other collaborative dialoguing methods to extend the original basic noun phrase to form final references to objects. In Fig. 1(b), A and B collaboratively generate RE *"Black pencil on the notebook"* implicitly. The responses from B contain some extra information that can give guidance for A, the RE Generator (**REGer**), to generate a new and distinguish description in the next turn. Such information is unavailable in "one-shot" REGer.

We, therefore, propose to model REG basing on dialogues. We believe that a dialogue-based REG model can perform better by making more use of extra information coming from the collaboration between interlocutors. The contributions of this paper can be summarized as follows:

1. We propose to model REG basing on the dialoguing method. To achieve it, we first introduce a RE-oriented VD game ReferWhat?!, and then build two large-scale RE-oriented VD datasets for RE, namely RefCOCOVD and RefCOCO+VD, basing on the existing RE databases.
2. We propose a VD-based REG model that utilizes the feedbacks of REUer to build REs through dialogues. Experimental results show that our VD-based REG model outperforms all the existing "one-shot" REG models.

2   Related Work

2.1   Referring Expression Generation

The study of REG was initiated by Winograd [27]. Krahmer and van Deemter [13] gave a perfect survey on the early works which largely focused on structured object descriptions or simple visual scenes. With the availability of large-scale databases on RE, works on RE move to referring the real objects in complex scenes. The first deep model for REG is a CNN-LSTM framework [19]. Based on this model, some researches made improvements on the extraction of image features [14,28], some researches added attribute features for the objects [16], and others studied the effects of different sampling methods in the decoding stage of REG [31]. They all promoted the study of REG.

However, all models above generate RE in a "one-shot" way, including the following models that involve implicit single-round dialoguing. Luo and Shakhnarovich embedded the REU model into the REG model through collaborative learning [17]. Yu et al. used RL to jointly train REG and REU models [29]. The existing strongest model [24] is based on [29] and adds the attention mechanism module.

Our work is partly inspired by previous works on the installment generation of RE. Fang et al. [7] demonstrated that collaborative models (episodic and installment model) significantly outperform non-collaborative models on an artificial scene. Zarrieß and Schlangen [30] also showed the effectiveness of installment models on a real scene. However, they are essentially modeled in pipelines.

Differing from all the existing works, we put the REG in an explicit multi-round dialogue between REGer and REUer. Through dialogue, our model can gradually add new distinctive descriptions to the referential object.

2.2 Referring Expression Datasets

The early RE datasets are mostly small-scale and involve synthetic or simplified visual scenes [13]. RefCLEF [9] is the first large-scale RE dataset of real visual scenes, collected on ImageCLEF [20] through the ReferIt game. Later, RefCOCO and RefCOCO+ [28] were collected by the same game interface, but based on MSCOCO [15]. Another dataset, RefCOCOg [19], is also collected on MSCOCO, but in a non-interactive way. Recently, Tanaka et al. [24] collected the RefGTA dataset on the GTA V game scene in a way similar to [19].

All RE datasets in previous works lie in the form of pairs (object, RE). In this paper, we extend the form into triples (object, dialogue, RE), where each dialogue shows a process of extending a basic noun to form the final references of the target object by collaborative interactions.

2.3 Visual Dialogue

Recently many VD tasks [4,12] have been proposed. Among them, the most relevant task to ReferWhat?! is GuessWhat?! [5], in fact, our ReferWhat?! is an extension to GuessWhat?! in three aspects:

Goal. As a goal-driven dialogue task, GuessWhat?! was proposed to solve the inaccurate evaluation of dialogue generation. But The goal of ReferWhat?! is to explore the generation and comprehension of RE under an interactive dialogue.

Behavior. The dialogues in GuessWhat?! is promoted by Questioner, Oracle can only passively answer questions. However, the dialogues in ReferWhat?! can be jointly advanced by both REGer and REUer.

Evaluation. GuessWhat?! only evaluates the success rate of dialogue, while ReferWhat?! also evaluates the quality of RE generated from a dialogue.

3 ReferWhat?! Game and Data

ReferWhat?! is a RE-oriented VD game for REGer and REUer. Firstly, REGer is supposed to propose an object in an image and to give an initial description of the object. If REUer cannot unambiguously distinguish the referential object from others according to the initial description, he/she can either report this situation to REGer or ask a question for more information. In the former case, REGer should append new information about the referential object, while in the latter case, REGer needs to answer the question. These two players interact in this way and thus forming a dialogue. Once REUer locates the object unambiguously according to the dialogue history, the game ends successfully, consequently, the dialogue includes a RE of the referential object.

3.1 Data Building

Firstly, the RE will be analyzed and divided into several syntactical blocks. For each RE, its headword is identified by Stanford Dependency Parser [18], and its syntactical tree is parsed by Berkeley Neural Parser [11]. Then, based on the headword and syntactical tree, a RE is segmented into several blocks according to some rules. Each block either contains the headword (called "Type 1" block, only one) or modifies the headword (called "Type 2" block, maybe several).

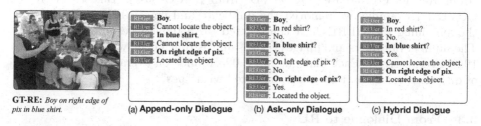

Fig. 2. Examples of the three types of dialogues generated during the construction of RE-oriented VD datasets. The referential object is indicated by a red box. (Color figure online)

Secondly, **append-only dialogues** are built based on these analyzed blocks. In an append-only dialogue, REUer only responds whether he/she can locate the target object, and REGer keeps on appending new information until REUer locates the target object successfully. Only when all blocks in the analyzed RE are mentioned in dialogue, can REUer locate the target object. Figure 2(a) gives an example. REGer is supposed to say the "Type 1" block of RE firstly. If there remains "Type 2" blocks, then REUer will keep on replying "*cannot locate object*" till REGer uses up all "Type 2" blocks. Each block in analyzed RE only can be said by REGer once, and the choice of a block in each turn is random. In this way, a RE is transformed into a dialogue between REGer and REUer. For a RE with more than one "Type 2" blocks, several different dialogues can be built when the "Type 2" blocks are appended in different orders.

Table 1. Statistics of the two RE-oriented VD datasets.

Dataset	#dialogues	#REs	#targets	#images	avg (#round)	yes%
RefCOCOVD	767,550	155,881	50,000	19,994	3.023	46.15%
RefCOCO+VD	530,383	152,773	49,856	19,992	2.595	47.39%

Then, **ask-only dialogues** are built by transforming from the append-only dialogues. In an ask-only dialogue, REUer keeps on asking questions and receiving answers from REGer until it can locate the target object, as shown in Fig. 2(b). Negative sampling on the attributes of objects and the relations between objects is used to make questions raised by REUer with different answers.

Lastly, **hybrid dialogues** are generated by combining append-only dialogues with its corresponding ask-only dialogues. As shown in Fig. 2(c), once REUer cannot locate the target object, he/she can randomly choose to ask a question or report *"cannot locate the object"* in every round.

3.2 Data Statistics

Table 1 demonstrates the statistics of our RE-oriented VD datasets RefCOCOVD (from RefCOCO) and RefCOCO+VD (from RefCOCO+). Take the RefCO-COVD for example, we removed the duplicate and empty REs in RefCOCO, the remaining 155,881 REs have constructed 767,550 dialogues in RefCOCOVD. The number of targets and images is the same as RefCOCO, which is 50,000 and 19,994 respectively. Each dialogue has 3.023 rounds on average. About 46.15% of questions raised by REUer are answered with *"yes"*.

3.3 From Dialogue to RE

All the dialogues above end with REUer saying *"located the object"*, therefore each dialogue contains a RE for the target object, as Fig. 2(a–c) show. To extract a RE from dialogue, we first filter the utterances containing blocks of analyzed RE, then merge them into one sentence.

For example, in an append-only dialogue, only the REGer's utterances cover key information of RE. Similar to [30], we extract REs from REGer's utterances G by the following two steps. Firstly, removing the duplicate words in G. As the same words can be mentioned in different REGer turns in dialogue, although the utterances are different. The words redundant offer no new information thus should be removed. Secondly, generating all possible permutations of REGer's utterances. Since a dialogue can be formed by the blocks of an RE in different orders. For each permutation, concatenating them as one candidate RE. In most cases, all of them are good REs.

4   VD-Based REG Model

This section illustrates a VD-based REG model, which includes four modules as shown in the left part of Fig. 3. A REUer simulator is designed for the RL stage.

4.1   REGer Model

Visual Encoder. Given an image I, the bounding boxes of the referential object r and a set of other objects $O = \{o_1, \ldots, o_M\}$, the visual and spatial features of them are calculated following Mao et al. [19]. All of them are fed into a CNN to get the feature representations $f_I, f_r, f_{o_1}, \ldots, f_{o_M}$. Then, the spatial feature of r is $l_r = \left[\frac{x_{tl}}{W}, \frac{y_{tl}}{H}, \frac{x_{br}}{W}, \frac{y_{br}}{H}, \frac{w \cdot h}{W \cdot H} \right]$, where (x_{tl}, y_{tl}), (x_{br}, y_{br}) are the coordinates of its bounding box, W, H are the width and height of I, and w, h are the width and height of r, respectively. The context feature of r is $v_r = W_r[f_I, f_r, l_r] + b_r$.

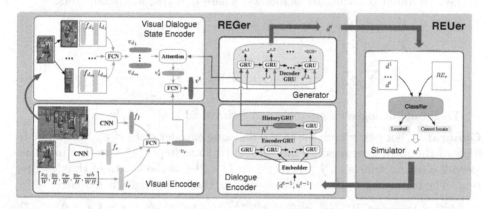

Fig. 3. The framework of our VD based REG model. The referential object is notated by the red bounding box, the other objects are notated by the blue box. (Color figure online)

Dialogue Encoder. A hierarchical GRU is used to encode the dialogue. The EncoderGRU in the lower level is to encode a pair of turn from the REGer and REUer. The upper level encoder is HistoryGRU, which encodes the dialogue history by making use of the pairs embedding.

Let $\left[d^i, u^i \right]$ be the dialogue pairs between REGer and REUer in the i-th dialogue round, L be the length of it. Then for t-th round:

$$p^t = [d_e^{t-1}, u_e^{t-1}] = \text{Embedder}\left([d^{t-1}, u^{t-1}] \right), \qquad\qquad t > 0 \quad (1)$$

$$h_e^{t,j} = \text{ReLU}\left(\text{EncoderGRU}\left(p^{t,j}, h_e^{t,j-1} \right) \right), \quad t > 0, L \geq j > 0 \quad (2)$$

$$h^t = \text{ReLU}\left(\text{HistoryGRU}\left(h_e^{t,L}, h^{t-1} \right) \right), \qquad\qquad t > 0 \quad (3)$$

Visual Dialogue State Encoder. To make REUer locate the target object successfully, the information provided by REGer should be both new and distinguishable, which means it should not be mentioned before and should be helpful to distinguish the target object from other objects. To achieve these, we first introduce the difference operations to capture distinguishable information and then design an inverse-attention mechanism to capture new information.

The visual and spatial difference feature between r and o_k are computed following [28]: $\delta f_{d_k} = \frac{f_r - f_{o_k}}{\|f_r - f_{o_k}\|}$, $\delta l_{d_k} = \left[\frac{[\Delta x_{tl}]_k^r}{w_r}, \frac{[\Delta y_{tl}]_k^r}{h_r}, \frac{[\Delta x_{br}]_k^r}{w_r}, \frac{[\Delta y_{br}]_k^r}{h_r}, \frac{w_{o_k} h_{o_k}}{w_r h_r} \right]$, where $[\Delta x]_k^r = x_r - x_{o_k}$, and $o_k, k \in \{1, 2, \ldots, m\}$ is one of the other objects belonging to the same category as the referent. The final difference feature between r and o_k is: $v_{d_k} = W_d [\delta f_{d_k}, \delta l_{d_k}] + b_d$.

An inverse-attention mechanism is used to assign different weight α on these distinguishable features $v_d = [v_{d_1}, \ldots, v_{d_m}]^T$, according to the current dialogue history embedding. We expect the model put more attention on the distinguishable information that have not appeared in history. The fused difference feature at the t-th round is calculated as follows, where μ, W_a, b_a are parameters.

$$s^t = \mu^T \cdot \tanh \left(W_a \left[v_d, h^t \right] + b_a \right) \tag{4}$$

$$\tilde{s}^t = -1 \times s^t \tag{5}$$

$$v_d^t = \sum_{i=1}^m \alpha_i^t v_{d_i} = \sum_{i=1}^m \mathrm{softmax}(\tilde{s}^t) v_{d_i} = \sum_{i=1}^m \frac{e^{\tilde{s}_k^t}}{\sum_{j=1}^m e^{\tilde{s}_j^t}} v_{d_i} \tag{6}$$

The visual dialogue encoder state at t-th round is $v^t = W_v [v_r, v_d^t] + b_v$.

Generator. For t-th round, the visual dialogue encoder state v^t and the embedding of the word generated at the $(j-1)$-th time step $x^{t,j-1}$ are fed into the DecoderGRU at time step j, where $j \in [1, L]$ and L is the length of the description. The history encoding h^t replaces $x^{t,0}$ as the beginning of a sentence.

$$h_w^{t,j} = \mathrm{DecoderGRU} \left([v^t, x^{t,j-1}], h_w^{t,j-1} \right), \qquad j > 1, t > 0 \tag{7}$$

$$x^{t,j} = \mathrm{Embedder} \left(\arg\max \left(\mathrm{softmax} \left(W_w h_w^{t,j} + b_w \right) \right) \right) \tag{8}$$

4.2 Training

Supervised Learning (SL). The negative log-likelihood loss function shown in Eq. (9) is employed for training, where N is the number of training data, T is the maximum round of dialogues, θ is the parameters of the model.

$$L_1(\theta) = -\sum_{n=1}^N \sum_{t=1}^T \log p \left(d_n^t | r_n, D_n^{t-1}, \theta \right) \tag{9}$$

The max-margin maximum mutual information (MMI) training [29] is also used to maximize the distances between the positive pair (D_n, r_n) and two negative pairs $(D_n, \hat{r_n})$, $\left(\hat{D}_n, r_n \right)$, where $\hat{r_n}$ and $\hat{D}_n$ are randomly chosen from the other referents in dataset. This encourages the model to refer the referential object more accurately. Formally:

$$L_2(\theta) = \sum_{n=1}^{N} \sum_{t=1}^{T} \max(0, m_1 - \log p(d_n^t | r_n, D_n^{t-1}, \theta) + \log p(d_n^t | \hat{r_n}, D_n^{t-1}, \theta)) \quad (10)$$

$$L_3(\theta) = \sum_{n=1}^{N} \sum_{t=1}^{T} \max(0, m_2 - \log p(d_n^t | r_n, D_n^{t-1}, \theta) + \log p(d_n^t | r_n, \hat{D}_n^{t-1}, \theta)) \quad (11)$$

where m_1, m_2 are predefined margins. The final goal in SL is to find the θ that minimizes total loss, i.e. $\theta = \arg\min\left(L_1(\theta) + \lambda_2 L_2(\theta) + \lambda_3 L_3(\theta)\right)$.

Reinforcement Learning (RL). Following Yu et al. [29] and Tanaka et al. [24], we adopt the REINFORCE [26] in the RL stage. The goal is to find the policy $\pi_\theta(as)$ that maximizes the expectation reward $J(\theta) = E_{\pi_\theta}[R_{\pi_\theta}(as)]$, where $R_{\pi_\theta}(as)$ is the cumulated reward function, $a_n^{t,j}$ means the action of choosing word $w_n^{t,j}$ as the j-th word of t-th round for the n-th sample, and the state $s_n^{t,j} = \left(r_n, I_n, O_n, D_n^{t-1}, (w_n^{t,1}, \ldots, w_n^{t,j-1})\right)$. According to [26], we have:

$$\nabla_\theta J = E_{\pi_\theta}\left[(R_{\pi_\theta}(a,s) - b)\nabla_\theta \log \pi_\theta(a,s)\right] \quad (12)$$

$$R_{\pi_\theta}(as) = \sum_{n=1}^{N} \sum_{t=1}^{T} \sum_{j=1}^{L} \gamma_n^{t-1} r\left(a_n^{t,j}, s_n^{t,j}\right) \quad (13)$$

Same as [23], we use a 2-layer FCN as our baseline function b to reduce the variance of gradient estimation. Following [21], we integrate the CIDEr [25] score between the ground-truth RE RE_{gt} and the RE converted from the generated dialogue RE_{conv} into the reward function to improve the quality of generation.

$$r\left(a_n^t, s_n^t\right) = \begin{cases} \max(\text{CIDEr}(RE_{gt}, RE_{conv}), 0), & \text{if successful} \\ \min(\text{CIDEr}(RE_{gt}, RE_{conv}) - 1, -0.1), & \text{otherwise} \end{cases} \quad (14)$$

4.3 REUer Simulator

We designed a rule-based simulator which only depends on the ground-truth REs to interact with the REGer model in RL. Let $RE_{gt} = \{re_1, \ldots, re_k\}$ be the representation of k different ground-truth REs of the same referent, and G be the words in REGer's utterances. We first use the NLTK toolbox to exclude stopping words in re_i then build entity set c_i basing on the remaining words. If $\exists i \in \{1, \ldots, k\}, G \supset e_i$, then the simulator considers G equals to RE_{gt}, and it will output *"located the object"*, otherwise it will output *"cannot locate the object"*. A synonym dictionary is also built to improve the accuracy.

5 Experiments

5.1 Experimental Settings

We choose all the existing "one-shot" REG models trained by MMI loss and evaluated without re-ranking as our baseline models. We use two types of CNNs pre-trained on ImageNet [6], namely VGG16 [22] and ResNet152 [8], to train our VD-based REG model on the append-only dialogues in RefCOCOVD and RefCOCO+VD. All above models are evaluated on the test sets of RefCOCO and RefCOCO+ under the scores of Meteor [1] and CIDEr [25] of REs. For ablation studies, we use ResNet152 to encode visual features.

5.2 Parameter Settings

The sizes of GRU's hidden state, word embedding, and the visual feature are all set to 1024. The maximum number of dialogue round and sentence length is 3 and 8, respectively. In the training period, we choose Adam [10] as our optimizer. All hyper-parameters are kept the same between SL and RL except the learning rate, which is initialized to 1×10^{-4} and decays 3% every epoch in SL, while it is fixed at 1×10^{-6} in RL. While testing, the beam search method is used to select the sampled expression, and the beam size is 3.

Table 2. Referring expression generation results on RefCOCO and RefCOCO+.

Model		CNN	RefCOCO				RefCOCO+			
			TestA		TestB		TestA		TestB	
			Meteor	CIDEr	Meteor	CIDEr	Meteor	CIDEr	Meteor	CIDEr
SL	MMI [19]	VGG16	0.175	–	0.228	–	0.136	–	0.133	–
	Visdif [28]	VGG16	0.185	–	0.247	–	0.142	–	0.135	–
	CG [17]	VGG16	0.197	–	0.243	–	0.146	–	0.135	–
	Attr [16]	VGG19	0.222	–	0.258	–	0.155	–	0.155	–
	BOC [14]	VGG16	0.184	–	0.249	–	0.153	–	0.14	–
	DS [31]	VGG19	–	0.658	–	1.112	–	0.400	–	0.527
	SLR [29]	VGG16	0.268	0.704	0.327	1.303	0.208	0.496	0.201	0.697
	Ours	VGG16	**0.305**	**0.791**	**0.345**	**1.398**	**0.216**	**0.533**	**0.209**	**0.768**
	EU [24]	ResNet152	0.301	0.866	0.341	1.389	**0.243**	**0.672**	0.222	0.831
	Ours	ResNet152	**0.320**	0.865	**0.360**	**1.460**	0.237	0.615	**0.230**	**0.835**
RL	SLR [29]	VGG16	0.268	0.697	0.329	1.323	0.204	0.494	0.202	0.709
	Ours	VGG16	**0.312**	**0.840**	**0.350**	**1.412**	**0.231**	**0.569**	**0.233**	**0.822**
	EU [24]	ResNet152	0.310	0.859	0.342	1.375	0.241	0.663	0.225	0.812
	Ours	ResNet152	**0.326**	**0.914**	**0.366**	**1.473**	**0.258**	**0.684**	**0.247**	**0.895**

5.3 Experiment Results

Table 2 shows the results of our model and other existing models on RefCOCO and RefCOCO+. From Table 2, we can see that, for models trained by SL, our model significantly outperforms all other existing models on the majority of test sets. For models trained by RL, our model also outperforms all existing models on all metrics on both datasets.

Figure 4 gives some examples generated by our model, which is trained by RL and uses ResNet152 as the encoder of the image. It can be seen that the REG process conducted in a dialoguing way is clearer than the REG process conducted in a "one-shot" way. We can easily understand how the referential information of the target object is appended step-by-step in a dialogue, while in the "one-shot" way, the generation process is unexplainable, almost a black box.

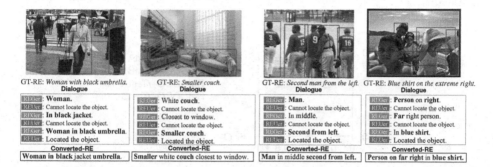

Fig. 4. Examples generated by our VD-based REG model. The target object is notated by a red box, and candidate objects are bounded with blue boxes. (Color figure online)

Table 3. Ablation study results on modules of our VD-based REG model.

Model		RefCOCO				RefCOCO+			
		TestA		TestB		TestA		TestB	
		Meteor	CIDEr	Meteor	CIDEr	Meteor	CIDEr	Meteor	CIDEr
SL	Full	0.320	0.865	0.360	1.460	0.237	0.615	0.230	0.835
	w/o Attention	0.313	0.857	0.359	1.478	0.234	0.603	0.229	0.834
RL	Full	0.326	0.914	0.366	1.473	0.258	0.684	0.247	0.895
	w/o Attention	0.319	0.899	0.361	1.471	0.250	0.663	0.248	0.904

5.4   Ablation Studies

Model Analysis. From Table 3, we can find that the attention mechanism does improve the performance, no matter on SL or RL. Comparing Table 3 with Table 2, it can be seen that our VD-based REG model still outperforms the strongest existing model, even without attention mechanism. This result indicates that the effectiveness of improvement mainly comes from the dialoguing framework itself.

Collaboration Analysis. In this experiment, we damage the collaboration gradually by lowering the correct rate of responses from REU. We replace each original response in training data with a wrong response with a probability of

α. The $\alpha \in [0,1]$, the higher α means the more original responses are replaced with wrong responses, thus the collaboration is damaged more.

Figure 5 illustrates the experimental results of the models trained under different levels of collaboration on SL. As we can see, with the increase of α, the performances in all datasets decrease. This result shows that the collaboration between REGer and REUer is important to REG. Our VD-based REG model can grasp the information behind collaboration to promote the performances significantly.

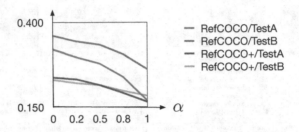

Fig. 5. Meteor scores of models trained with REUer of different error rates on SL.

6   Conclusion and Future Work

In this paper, we set the RE problem in the frame of VD by proposing a RE-oriented dialogue task ReferWhat?!, where REGer and REUer generate and understand REs cooperatively in an interactive dialogue. The installment and interactive ways on REG and REU are similar to that in human-human referential conversation. We develop two large-scale datasets RefCOCOVD and RefCOCO+VD for ReferWhat?! based on existing RE datasets. A dialogue-based REGer model is also proposed. The model is the first step to a full VD-based REG model with the capability of answering questions raised by REUer. The quantitative experiments show our model outperforms previous "one-shot" models by increasingly making use of new information during a dialogue.

References

1. Banerjee, S., Lavie, A.: METEOR: an automatic metric for MT evaluation with improved correlation with human judgments. In: Proceedings of the ACL Workshop on Intrinsic and Extrinsic Evaluation Measures for Machine Translation and/or Summarization, pp. 65–72. Association for Computational Linguistics, Ann Arbor (2005). https://www.aclweb.org/anthology/W05-0909
2. Clark, H.H., Wilkes-Gibbs, D.: Referring as a collaborative process. Cognition **22**(1), 1–39 (1986)
3. Dale, R., Reiter, E.: Computational interpretations of the Gricean maxims in the generation of referring expressions. Cogn. Sci. **19**(2), 233–263 (1995)

4. Das, A., et al.: Visual dialog. In: Proceedings of the IEEE Conference on Computer Vision and Pattern Recognition, pp. 326–335 (2017)
5. De Vries, H., Strub, F., Chandar, S., Pietquin, O., Larochelle, H., Courville, A.: GuessWhat?! Visual object discovery through multi-modal dialogue. In: Proceedings of the IEEE Conference on Computer Vision and Pattern Recognition, pp. 5503–5512 (2017)
6. Deng, J., Dong, W., Socher, R., Li, L., Li, K., Fei-Fei, L.: ImageNet: a large-scale hierarchical image database. In: 2009 IEEE Conference on Computer Vision and Pattern Recognition, pp. 248–255 (2009)
7. Fang, R., Doering, M., Chai, J.Y.: Collaborative models for referring expression generation in situated dialogue. In: Twenty-Eighth AAAI Conference on Artificial Intelligence (2014)
8. He, K., Zhang, X., Ren, S., Sun, J.: Deep residual learning for image recognition. CoRR abs/1512.03385 (2015)
9. Kazemzadeh, S., Ordonez, V., Matten, M., Berg, T.: ReferItGame: referring to objects in photographs of natural scenes. In: Proceedings of the 2014 Conference on Empirical Methods in Natural Language Processing, pp. 787–798 (2014)
10. Kingma, D.P., Ba, J.: Adam: a method for stochastic optimization (2014)
11. Kitaev, N., Klein, D.: Constituency parsing with a self-attentive encoder. In: Proceedings of the 56th Annual Meeting of the Association for Computational Linguistics (Volume 1: Long Papers), pp. 2676–2686. Association for Computational Linguistics, Melbourne (2018)
12. Kottur, S., Moura, J.M.F., Parikh, D., Batra, D., Rohrbach, M.: CLEVR-Dialog: a diagnostic dataset for multi-round reasoning in visual dialog. In: NAACL-HLT (1), pp. 582–595 (2019). https://aclweb.org/anthology/papers/N/N19/N19-1058/
13. Krahmer, E., van Deemter, K.: Computational generation of referring expressions: a survey. Comput. Linguist. 38(1), 173–218 (2012)
14. Li, X., Jiang, S.: Bundled object context for referring expressions. IEEE Trans. Multimedia 20(10), 2749–2760 (2018)
15. Lin, T.-Y., et al.: Microsoft COCO: common objects in context. In: Fleet, D., Pajdla, T., Schiele, B., Tuytelaars, T. (eds.) ECCV 2014. LNCS, vol. 8693, pp. 740–755. Springer, Cham (2014). https://doi.org/10.1007/978-3-319-10602-1_48
16. Liu, J., Wang, L., Yang, M.H.: Referring expression generation and comprehension via attributes. In: Proceedings of the IEEE International Conference on Computer Vision, pp. 4856–4864 (2017)
17. Luo, R., Shakhnarovich, G.: Comprehension-guided referring expressions. In: Proceedings of the IEEE Conference on Computer Vision and Pattern Recognition, pp. 7102–7111 (2017)
18. Manning, C., Surdeanu, M., Bauer, J., Finkel, J., Bethard, S., McClosky, D.: The Stanford CoreNLP natural language processing toolkit. In: Proceedings of 52nd Annual Meeting of the Association for Computational Linguistics: System Demonstrations, pp. 55–60 (2014)
19. Mao, J., Huang, J., Toshev, A., Camburu, O., Yuille, A.L., Murphy, K.: Generation and comprehension of unambiguous object descriptions. In: Proceedings of the IEEE Conference on Computer Vision and Pattern Recognition, pp. 11–20 (2016)
20. Müller, H., Clough, P., Deselaers, T., Caputo, B.: ImageCLEF: Experimental Evaluation in Visual Information Retrieval, vol. 32. Springer, Heidelberg (2010). https://doi.org/10.1007/978-3-642-15181-1
21. Rennie, S.J., Marcheret, E., Mroueh, Y., Ross, J., Goel, V.: Self-critical sequence training for image captioning. CoRR abs/1612.00563 (2016)

22. Simonyan, K., Zisserman, A.: Very deep convolutional networks for large-scale image recognition. In: International Conference on Learning Representations (2015)
23. Strub, F., De Vries, H., Mary, J., Piot, B., Courville, A., Pietquin, O.: End-to-end optimization of goal-driven and visually grounded dialogue systems. In: IJCAI (2017)
24. Tanaka, M., Itamochi, T., Narioka, K., Sato, I., Ushiku, Y., Harada, T.: Towards human-friendly referring expression generation. CoRR abs/1811.12104 (2018)
25. Vedantam, R., Lawrence Zitnick, C., Parikh, D.: CIDEr: consensus-based image description evaluation. In: Proceedings of the IEEE Conference on Computer Vision and Pattern Recognition, pp. 4566–4575 (2015)
26. Williams, R.J.: Simple statistical gradient-following algorithms for connectionist reinforcement learning. Mach. Learn. **8**(3–4), 229–256 (1992)
27. Winograd, T.: Understanding natural language. Cogn. Psychol. **3**(1), 1–191 (1972)
28. Yu, L., Poirson, P., Yang, S., Berg, A.C., Berg, T.L.: Modeling context in referring expressions. In: Leibe, B., Matas, J., Sebe, N., Welling, M. (eds.) ECCV 2016. LNCS, vol. 9906, pp. 69–85. Springer, Cham (2016). https://doi.org/10.1007/978-3-319-46475-6_5
29. Yu, L., Tan, H., Bansal, M., Berg, T.L.: A joint speaker-listener-reinforcer model for referring expressions. In: Proceedings of the IEEE Conference on Computer Vision and Pattern Recognition (2017)
30. Zarrieß, S., Schlangen, D.: Easy things first: installments improve referring expression generation for objects in photographs. In: Proceedings of the 54th Annual Meeting of the Association for Computational Linguistics (Volume 1: Long Papers), pp. 610–620. Association for Computational Linguistics, Berlin (2016). https://www.aclweb.org/anthology/P16-1058
31. Zarrieß, S., Schlangen, D.: Decoding strategies for neural referring expression generation. In: Proceedings of the 11th International Conference on Natural Language Generation, pp. 503–512. Association for Computational Linguistics, Tilburg University, The Netherlands (2018)

Hierarchical Multimodal Transformer with Localness and Speaker Aware Attention for Emotion Recognition in Conversations

Xiao Jin[1], Jianfei Yu[1], Zixiang Ding[1], Rui Xia[1(✉)], Xiangsheng Zhou[2], and Yaofeng Tu[2]

[1] Nanjing University of Science and Technology, Nanjing, China
{xjin,jfyu,dingzixiang,rxia}@njust.edu.cn
[2] ZTE Corporation, Shenzhen, China
{zhou.xiangsheng,tu.yaofeng}@zte.com.cn

Abstract. Emotion Recognition in Conversations (ERC) aims to predict the emotion of each utterance in a given conversation. Existing approaches for the ERC task mainly suffer from two drawbacks: (1) failing to pay enough attention to the emotional impact of the local context; (2) ignoring the effect of the emotional inertia of speakers. To tackle these limitations, we first propose a Hierarchical Multimodal Transformer as our base model, followed by carefully designing a localness-aware attention mechanism and a speaker-aware attention mechanism to respectively capture the impact of the local context and the emotional inertia. Extensive evaluations on a benchmark dataset demonstrate the superiority of our proposed model over existing multimodal methods for ERC.

Keywords: Multimodal emotion recognition · Hierarchical multimodal transformer · Local context modeling · Emotional inertia

1 Introduction

Emotion is interlinked in different cultures and is an important part of daily life. Due to its importance, emotion detection has been a hot topic in NLP in the past decade, where much work has been done for emotion detection in sentences or documents. With the rapid growth of online conversational data (especially multimodal conversations) in recent years, emotion recognition in conversations (ERC) has attracted enormous attention, primarily due to its potential applications in many downstream tasks such as user behavior modeling, dialogue generation, etc. Given a conversation with multiple utterances[1], the goal of the ERC task is to predict the emotions expressed in each utterance.

As an important subtask in sentiment analysis, ERC has been extensively studied in the literature. Existing approaches to ERC can be generally classified into three categories. One line of work focuses on textual conversations by

---

[1] Utterance is typically defined as a unit of speech bounded by breathes or pause [10].

© Springer Nature Switzerland AG 2020
X. Zhu et al. (Eds.): NLPCC 2020, LNAI 12431, pp. 41–53, 2020.
https://doi.org/10.1007/978-3-030-60457-8_4

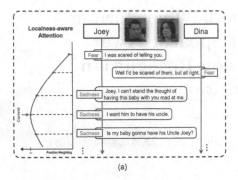 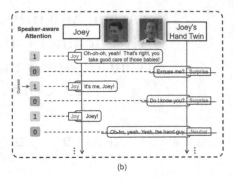

(a)   (b)

Fig. 1. (a) An example for illustrating the localness-aware attention; (b) An example for illustrating the speaker-aware attention. The numbers in the figure represent attention weights.

designing effective solutions to model the context of each utterance [19]. Another line of work aims to simulate human behavior to predict emotions by considering textual, acoustic, and visual information together [11,13]. Moreover, the last line of work primarily focuses on text and audio, with the goal of leveraging the acoustic features to improve the performance of textual emotion recognition [12,18]. In this work, we aim to extend the last line of work by proposing an effective multimodal architecture to integrate textual and audio information.

While previous studies have shown the success of integrating textual and acoustic features for ERC, most of them still have the following shortcomings: (1) They simply consider the emotional impact of the whole conversation or historical utterances (i.e., global context) over the current utterance, but ignore the fact that the surrounding utterances (i.e., local context) may have a higher emotional impact than the other long-distance utterances; (2) Although several previous studies incorporate the speaker information into their models, most of them use separate sequences to distinguish different speakers (e.g., self and others) [7,9], which will disentangle the correlated emotions between different speakers and largely increase the model complexity.

To address the above two limitations, we propose a new ERC model based on Transformer [14], named Hierarchical Multimodal Transformer with Localness and Speaker Aware Attention (HMT-LSA). Specifically, we first propose a Hierarchical Multimodal Transformer (HMT) as our base model, where two lower-level Transformers are employed to respectively obtain the textual and audio representations for each utterance, and two mid-level Transformers are stacked on top to capture the intra-modal dynamics within audio utterances and textual utterances respectively, followed by a higher-level Transformer to capture the inter-modal interactions between textual utterances and audio utterances. Based on HMT, to address the first limitation mentioned above, we propose a localness-aware attention mechanism, which learns to dynamically assign weights to each utterance based on their relative position to the current utterance (see Fig. 1a). Moreover, to tackle the second limitation, we further design a speaker-aware attention mechanism, which essentially employs self or inter-personal masks to model the speaker's emotional inertia (see Fig. 1b). Finally, the localness and speaker aware attention are integrated into HMT for emotion predictions of each utterance.

Experiment results on a benchmark dataset (MELD) show the following: (1) Our HMT-LSA model can consistently outperform a number of unimodal and multimodal approaches for ERC, including the state-to-the-art multimodal approach; (2) Further analysis demonstrates the usefulness of our proposed localness-aware and speaker-aware attention mechanism.

2   Related Work

Methods for ERC. One line of work focused on the influence of context on the current conversation content. Early work chose recurrent neural networks to model all contextual information in sequence, assisting the prediction of conversational emotions through contextual information [11]. Recent work has selected historical context to retrieve more relevant information [8,19]. Another line of work also centered on the speaker information. Sequence-based modeling methods usually split a dialogue into multiple sequences according to speaker masks, but these methods were slightly complicated in model design [7,9]. Meanwhile, some studies proposed to add speaker nodes or edge relation type definition based on the graph convolutional networks (GCN) to achieve context-sensitive and speaker-sensitive dependence modeling [6,18].

Methods for Localness-Aware Attention. Yang et al. [16] first proposed the localness modeling which enhanced the Transformer's ability to capture relevant local context. Until now, it has been widely used in many fields such as machine translation [15], speech synthesis. In this work, we follow this line of work. But different from these previous studies, we propose a Hierarchical Multimodal Transformer framework composed of the reformed Transformer LSA-Transformer to better focus on speaker-related local context information.

3   Methodology

3.1   Overall Architecture

Task Formulation. Given a dialogue d and its associated audio as input, the goal of ERC is to classify each utterance in d into one of the pre-defined emotion types based on the contextual information in a dialogue. Let $d = \{u_1, u_2, \ldots, u_n\}$ denote a dialogue of multiple utterances, and $y = \{y_1, y_2, \ldots, y_n\}$ be the corresponding labels, where $y_i \in \mathcal{Y}$ and $\mathcal{Y}$ is pre-defined emotion labels [4].

In this work, we propose a Hierarchical Multimodal Transformer with Localness and Speaker Aware Attention (HMT-LSA) framework to model such a "word-utterance-dialogue" hierarchical structure. The overall architecture of HMT-LSA is shown in Fig. 2, which mainly contains two layers (Sect. 3.3). The lower layer is a unimodal encoder, which contains the word-level utterance reader and the dialogue-level encoder. The utterance reader consisting of multiple

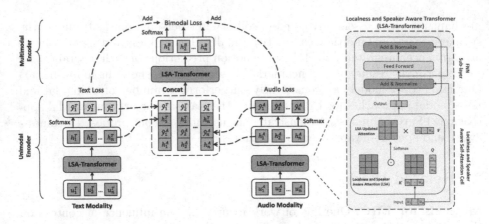

Fig. 2. The framework of our HMT-LSA model.

Transformers aims to encode word-level features into an utterance representation. Then a unimodal dialogue-level LSA-Transformer (Sect. 3.4) enhances the above utterance representation by combining the position (Sect. 3.5) and speaker (Sect. 3.6) information. The upper multimodal encoder layer takes the concatenation of LSA enhanced utterance representations and corresponding labels as input to obtain the fused multimodal utterance representations. Next, we also utilize an LSA-Transformer to add local context information to them. Moreover, we introduce an auxiliary task (Sect. 3.7) at the dotted arrows in Fig. 2 to capture the inter-modality and the intra-modality dynamics, and finally feed to a softmax layer for emotion classification.

3.2 Unimodal Feature Extraction

Textual Features. To compare fairly with the current state-to-the-art model ConGCN [18], the pre-trained word embeddings extracted from the 300-dimensional GloVe vectors are adopted to represent all words in an utterance $\{\mathbf{w}_1^i, \mathbf{w}_2^i, \ldots, \mathbf{w}_k^i\}$, where $\mathbf{w}_k^i$ represents the word embedding of the k-th word in the i-th utterance. After feeding into the utterance reader layer (mentioned in Sect. 3.3), each utterance is remapped into utterance-level textual representation $\mathbf{u}_i^T \in \mathbb{R}^{d_t}$ of dimensions d_t.

Acoustic Features. We first format each utterance-video as a 16-bit PCM WAV file and use P2FA [17] to obtain the aligned word-level audio timestamps. To extract the audio features, we feed the word-level audio features into the open-sourced software OpenSMILE [5]. Here we choose the INTERSPEECH 2009 Emotion Challenge (IS09) feature set to obtain 384-dimensional word-level audio features. To be consistent with the length of the textual features, we generate a random vector with the same dimension as the audio features for each punctuation and insert it into the audio features according to its original position. Similar to textual feature extraction, the generated word-level audio features also passes through the utterance reader layer to obtain the final utterance-level representation $\mathbf{u}_i^A \in \mathbb{R}^{d_a}$ of dimensions d_a.

3.3 Hierarchical Multimodal Transformer

We first propose a Hierarchical Multimodal Transformer framework to model such a "word-utterance-dialogue" structure, which contains the following layers:

- **Utterance Reader.** Utterance reader is a word-level encoder consisting of multiple Transformers [14]. Each utterance corresponds to a Transformer module, which accumulates the context information for the words in this utterance. Next, though a word-level attention mechanism [1], we obtain the utterance representation by the weighted sum of all words encoded with the above-mentioned Transformers.
- **Unimodal Encoder.** For text modality, a dialogue-level standard Transformer is used to accumulate the emotional impact of the whole conversation on the current utterance. This approach enhances the ability of the output utterance representation $\tilde{\mathbf{h}}_i^T$ to capture context information and emotional dynamics. Similarily we use another Transformer to capture the intramodality dynamics within the audio features and then we can obtain the acoustic utterance representations $\tilde{\mathbf{h}}_i^A$.
- **Multimodal Encoder.** After obtaining the unimodal utterance representations, we directly concatenate these features to generate multimodal features $\tilde{\mathbf{u}}_i^B$ for each utterance. Then followed by another Transformer to capture inter-modality interactions between the audio and textual features, through this operation we obtain the final multimodal representation $\tilde{\mathbf{h}}_i^B$.

3.4 Localness and Speaker Aware Attention

Standard Transformer's attention takes the following form [14]:

$$\mathrm{ATT}(\mathbf{Q}, \mathbf{K}) = \mathbf{weight} \cdot \mathbf{V}, \qquad \mathbf{weight} = \mathrm{softmax}(\frac{\mathbf{Q}\mathbf{K}^{\mathbf{T}}}{\sqrt{D}}), \qquad (1)$$

where $\{\mathbf{Q}, \mathbf{K}, \mathbf{V}\} \in \mathbb{R}^{I*D}$ is query, key, value respectively, D is the dimension of the layer states, and I is the dimension of the input matrix.

As shown in Fig. 3, when predicting the emotion of u_4, we find that the speaker's recently stated utterance u_2 has the greatest correlation with its emotions. At this time, if we only consider the nearest u_3 and u_5, it may lead to the final emotional misjudgment. Therefore, it is very important to filter out the relevant local context information on emotion judgment. However, the standard Transformer cannot better solve the problem of giving each token different weights based on its importance in a sequence. To address this problem, we propose a localness and speaker aware attention **LSA**, which is placed to mask the logit similarity **weight** in Eq. 1, namely:

$$\mathbf{LSA} = \mathbf{LA} \odot \mathbf{SA}, \qquad (2)$$

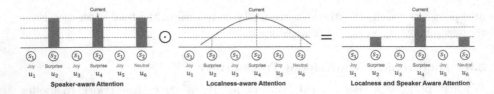

Fig. 3. Describe the process of calculating localness and speaker aware attention by using speaker and localness context information. In this example, s_1 and s_2 respectively represent Joey and Joey's Hand Twin in Fig. 1b. $\odot$ indicates the element-wise product operation.

$$\mathrm{ATT}(\mathbf{Q}, \mathbf{K}) = (\mathbf{weight} \odot \mathbf{LSA})\mathbf{V}, \tag{3}$$

where $\{\mathbf{LA}, \mathbf{SA}\} \in \mathbb{R}^{I*I}$ are speaker-aware attention and localness-aware attention respectively and the **weight** denotes the self-attention score. The **SA** module is used to describe the speaker's emotional inertia during the conversation and the **LA** module is to filter local context information. Here, we do element-wise product operation on above **LA** and **SA** to produce the localness and speaker aware attention **LSA**, which combines both local context and speaker information. In this way, the emotion of the current utteracnce is less affected by the long-distance utteracnces of the same speaker. Finally we add the logit similarity **weight** with **LSA** to modify the distribution of attention weights to obtain the Localness and Speaker Aware Transformer (LSA-Transformer).

3.5   Localness-Aware Attention

Fixed-Window. A simple idea is given a fixed window FW. Our model only pays attention to the influence of utterances in this window range on the current utterance. According to the relative positions of u_i and u_j, the attention **LA** obtained by this method is defined as:

$$\mathrm{LA}_{i,j} = \begin{cases} 1, & \text{if } |j - i| \leq f; \\ 0, & \text{otherwise}, \end{cases} \tag{4}$$

where $\mathbf{LA} \in \mathbb{R}^{I*I}$ represents the localness-aware attention, f denotes the size of the fixed window, which is set to 5 throughout the whole training and testing process.

Position Weighting. Based on the observation of the corpus, we find that the emotion of current utterance is more affected by the utterances close to it. But the fixed-window method treats utterances in the window equally. To solve this problem, we calculate the relative position weighting of u_i and u_j:

$$\mathrm{PW}_{i,j} = \begin{cases} \mathrm{MAX} - C(j - i)^2, & \text{if } i, j \leq n; \\ 0, & \text{otherwise}, \end{cases} \tag{5}$$

where n is the actual length of the dialogue, and both MAX and C are hyper-parameters. Here, we set MAX and C to 5 and 1.5 respectively. Finally, the **PW** obtained above is then subjected to sigmoid function and regularization to obtain the localness-aware attention:

$$\mathbf{LA} = \text{sigmoid}(\mathbf{PW}). \tag{6}$$

3.6 Speaker-Aware Attention

In Fig. 1b, Joey and Joey's Hand Twin habitually maintain their initial emotions, which are difficult to be quickly influenced by others. This phenomenon is called emotional inertia. In this paper, we design self-personal masks that focus on the utterances of the current speaker to model the emotional impact of this interlocutor's emotional flow on the current utterance. Specifically, in Fig. 1b, "1" indicates that the attention weight given to all utterances of the current speaker, and the remaining utterances mask "0" which means the influence of these utterances is not considered. Here, the calculation of **SA** as follows:

$$\mathbf{SA}_{i,j} = \begin{cases} 1, & \text{if } s_i = s_j; \\ 0, & \text{otherwise,} \end{cases} \tag{7}$$

where s_i and s_j is the speaker of u_i and u_j.

3.7 Emotion Prediction with Auxiliary Tasks

After the unimodal dialogue-level encoder, we obtain the LSA enhanced utterance textual representations $\mathbf{h}_i^T$ and stacking an extra softmax function to yield the textual modal label distribution $\hat{\mathbf{y}}_i^T$. Next, we minimize the cross-entropy loss between ground truth distribution of textual modality $\mathbf{y}_i^T$ and the prediction distribution $\hat{\mathbf{y}}_i^T$ eventually produced $loss_T$. Similarly, the LSA enhanced utterance representation of audio modality $\mathbf{h}_i^A$ performs the same operation as above to get the prediction distribution $\hat{\mathbf{y}}_i^A$ and corresponding losses $loss_A$.

Unlike the Hierarchical Multimodal Transformer, the i-th multimodal utterance representation is encoded as the concatenation of $\mathbf{h}_i^T$, $\mathbf{h}_i^A$, $\hat{\mathbf{y}}_i^T$, and $\hat{\mathbf{y}}_i^A$. Then, we feed it into the multimodal encoder (mentioned in Sect. 3.3) to calculate the final prediction distributions $\hat{\mathbf{y}}_i^B$ and the corresponding losses $loss_B$. The final loss is the weighted sum of $loss_T$, $loss_A$, and $loss_B$:

$$loss = \xi_T loss_T + \xi_A loss_A + \xi_B loss_B. \tag{8}$$

4 Experiments

4.1 Experimental Settings

Datasets. The publicly available multi-party conversational dataset MELD [12] is an enhanced version of the EmotionLines dataset [2] for the multimodal scenario. After removing a few outliers of EmotionLines, MELD eventually contains more than 300 speakers, 1400 dialogues, and 13000 utterances. Each utterance combined with multimodal information to select the most appropriate emotion label from *anger, disgust, sadness, joy, neutral, surprise*, and *fear*.

Hyperparameters. For all comparison experiments, the maximum numbers of words in each utterance and utterances in each dialogue are set to be 50 and 33, respectively. The network is trained based on the Adam optimizer with a mini-batch size 2 and a learning rate 1e−5. Besides, one layer of standard Transformer and LSA-Transformer are used in unimodal encoder, while only two layers of LSA-Transformer are used in multimodal encoder, and their hidden size and attention heads are 768 and 12 respectively.

Table 1. Performance of our HMT-LSA model and the other baseline systems on the MELD with uni-modality. *Indicates no results reported in original paper.

Audio Modality								
Models	Anger	Disgust	Fear	Joy	Neutral	Sadness	Surprise	W-avg.
BC-LSTM	21.90	0.00	0.00	0.00	66.10	0.00	16.00	36.40
ICON	31.50	0.00	0.00	8.60	66.90	0.00	0.00	37.70
DialogueRNN	32.10	**5.10**	0.00	11.20	53.00	8.30	15.60	34.00
ConGCN	**34.10**	3.00	**4.70**	15.50	64.10	**19.30**	25.40	42.20
HMT (Audio)	8.98	0.00	0.00	42.14	75.85	0.00	28.01	47.19
HMT-LSA(FW+self)	25.10	0.00	0.00	**42.59**	75.76	0.00	30.54	49.62
HMT-LSA(PW+self)	26.06	0.00	0.00	41.88	**75.86**	0.32	**31.28**	**49.79**
Text Modality								
BC-LSTM	38.90	0.00	0.00	45.80	77.00	0.00	47.30	54.30
ICON	30.10	0.00	0.00	48.50	76.20	18.90	46.30	54.60
DialogueRNN	41.50	0.00	5.40	47.60	73.70	23.40	44.90	55.10
ConGCN	43.20	8.80	6.50	52.40	74.90	22.60	49.80	57.40
BERT-BASE	39.69	16.96	4.61	50.17	73.51	23.48	49.45	56.07
DialogueGCN	*	*	*	*	*	*	*	58.10
AGHMN	39.40	14.00	**11.50**	52.40	76.40	**27.00**	49.70	58.10
KET	*	*	*	*	*	*	*	58.18
HMT (Text)	38.32	15.79	0.00	50.23	76.98	25.53	50.22	56.38
HMT-LSA(FW+self)	42.95	26.97	3.85	**55.16**	77.04	20.69	50.93	59.16
HMT-LSA(PW+self)	**43.53**	**27.30**	2.50	54.75	**77.19**	23.04	**51.46**	**59.47**

Table 2. Performance of our HMT-LSA model and the other baseline systems on the MELD with multi-modality.

Models	Anger	Disgust	Fear	Joy	Neutral	Sadness	Surprise	W-avg.
BC-LSTM	44.50	0.00	0.00	49.70	76.40	15.60	48.40	56.80
ICON	44.80	0.00	0.00	50.20	73.60	23.20	50.00	56.30
DialogueRNN	45.60	0.00	0.00	53.20	73.20	24.80	51.90	57.00
ConGCN	46.80	10.60	**8.70**	53.10	76.70	**28.50**	50.30	59.40
BERT-BASE	40.48	0.00	3.85	43.47	74.11	23.64	42.09	54.20
HMT	42.20	22.45	3.77	51.06	76.47	21.88	46.83	57.69
HMT-LSA(FW+self)	**47.02**	22.45	3.77	**56.03**	**77.55**	21.68	52.34	60.19
HMT-LSA(PW+self)	46.03	**23.57**	4.63	55.02	77.27	25.91	**52.95**	**60.21**

4.2 Compared Systems

We compare our model with the following several baseline systems for ERC task: (1) **BC-LSTM** [11] only encodes the context by Bi-LSTM to obtain content-sensitive utterance representation; (2) **ICON** [7] models a contextual summary that incorporates speaker emotional influences into global memories by using a RNN-based network; (3) **DialogueRNN** [9] selects three GRU to model the emotional state of different speaker dependencies; (4) **ConGCN** [18] chooses GCN to address context propagation and speaker dependency modeling issues present in the RNN-based approaches; (5) **BERT-BASE** [3] a multi-layer bidirectional Transformer encoder. Here, we only replace the textual encoder in the HMT-LSA with BERT. Due to the limitation of our GPU memory, we only experiment on the base version of BERT; (6) **DialogueGCN** [6] employs GCN to leverage self and inter-speaker dependency in textual conversations; (7) **AGHMN** [8] builds the memory bank for capturing historical context and proposes an Attention GRU for memory summarize; (8) **KET** [19] presents a Transformer combined with contextual utterances and external commonsense knowledge; (9) **Hierarchical Multimodal Transformer, namely HMT** replaces all LSA-Transformer with the standard Transformer and removes the auxiliary tasks in HMT-LSA; (10) **HMT-LSA(FW+self)** uses fixed-window for LA module in HMT-LSA; (11) **HMT-LSA(PW+self)** uses position weighting for LA module in HMT-LSA.

4.3 Main Results

HMT vs HMT-LSA. From Table 1 and Table 2, we can observe that our HMT-LSA model outperforms HMT with a significant margin for both unimodal and multimodal approaches. This shows the effectiveness of our localness-aware attention, speaker-aware attention, and the auxiliary tasks.

Comparison with Baselines. First, comparing all the unimodal approaches, we find that the audio modal HMT-LSA network variant has the most improvement, which is about 7.5% higher than the state-of-the-art model ConGCN.

Table 3. Ablation study for components of HMT-LSA.

Table 4. The effects of different speaker masks.

Table 5. The effects of window size.

Methods	F_1
HMT-LSA(PW+self)	**60.21**
w/o LA Module	59.11
Replacing LA with GD	59.04
w/o SA Module	59.50
w/o AT Module	59.26

SA Module	F_1
Self	**60.21**
Other	59.78
Dual	59.92

Window Size	F_1
3	59.71
5	**60.19**
7	60.07
9	59.66

We consider that it may be because the speech is segmented and the random vector is inserted into the audio feature matrix according to the punctuation position, so that the audio modal is integrated into the pause information. This strategy improves the classification effect of most kinds of majority emotions significantly, but is not very sensitive to the minority emotion characteristics. Besides, our method surpasses the current state-of-the-art model KET in text modality, indicating that it is very necessary to consider speaker information for modeling the emotion dynamics.

Second, comparing all the multimodal approaches with their corresponding unimodal experimental results, all multimodal experimental results are significantly improved. This means that the added audio information is very useful for the correct classification of emotions. Besides, compared with ConGCN, our model shows better performance in each emotion category and the final overall classification results, especially Disgust increased by 12.97%. This result shows that compared with using all the context information directly, it is possible to filter out the relevant context content and reduce the noise caused by irrelevant conversation content. This agrees with our first motivation.

Comparison of Different Network Variants. Both variants of the HMT-LSA framework show excellent results in multimodal emotion detection. Since HMT-LSA(PW+self) is slightly better than HMT-LSA(FW+self) of different modalities, which implies that we need to consider the position of different utterances and give different weights on this task.

4.4   Ablation Study

To investigate the effectiveness of each component in the HMT-LSA framework, we separately remove the speaker-aware attention (SA) module, the auxiliary task (AT) module, and the localness-aware attention (LA) module.

As shown in the Table 3 report, we find that all the above-mentioned modules provides help for emotion detection. It is obvious that LA module is a very important component in our model. Without it, our results decline by 1.1%, which shows that choosing context information within the appropriate range will reduce the negative impact of irrelevant dialogue content. Besides, we replace the LA module with the Gaussian distribution (GD) proposed by

[16], and find that the experimental result dropped by 1.17%. Then we find that the AT module makes important contributions to the final results, which shows that unimodal prediction labels and loss supervision help to enforce the intra-modality and inter-modality features sensitive to emotions. This agrees with our second motivation. Discarding the SA module will also drop the performance, which indicates that one's emotions are often affected by themselves or others.

Analysis of Different Speaker Masks. One's emotions are often influenced by others, so we propose inter-personal masks to simulate this phenomenon that caters to others' emotions. Through the observation of Table 4, we find that using self-personal masks (self) get the best experimental results, indicating that emotional inertia often exists in daily conversation. Moreover, the effect of only considering the other person (other) is slightly lower than that of considering the emotional impact of both (dual). Here, "self" and "other" denote self and inter-personal masks, while "dual" simultaneously considers self and inter-personal masks.

Analysis of the Effects of Window Size. Table 5 illustrates the experimental performance using different window sizes for HMT-LSA(FW+self). We observe that as the window increases, the experimental results gradually deteriorate. This phenomenon shows the importance of local context modeling.

Table 6. Comparison results of the HMT-LSA(PW+self) model and its variants.

Role	Utterances	Truth	Audio	Text	HMT	HMT-LSA
Phoebe	Can I tell you a little secret?	Neutral	Neutral	Neutral	Neutral	Neutral
Rachel	Yeah!	Joy	Joy	**Neutral**	Joy	Joy
Phoebe	I want to keep one	Neutral	Neutral	Neutral	Neutral	Neutral
Rachel	Ohh, I'm gonna be on the news!	Joy	Joy	Joy	**Sadness**	Joy

4.5 Case Study

Table 6 shows Phoebe reveals the secret that she wants to leave one of her upcoming children, and Rachel is always in a state of euphoria as a listener. Here, HMT-LSA can correctly predict the emotion of the last utterance is "Joy", while HMT makes the opposite prediction. This is because the SA module makes HMT-LSA pay attention to the emotional inertia. Besides, it is difficult to determine the emotion of utterance only based on the text "Yeah!". But the remaining methods that contain audio modality can predict correctly, which indicates the importance of incorporating multimodal information.

5   Conclusion

In this paper, we studies the task of multimodal ERC, and propose a Hierarchical Multimodal Transformer with Localness and Speaker Aware Attention (HMT-LSA), that can effectively capture the impact of the local context and the emotional inertia over emotion predictions of the current utterance. Experimental results show the effectiveness of our HMT-LSA model, in comparison with several state-of-the-art methods on MELD.

Acknowledgments. We would like to thank three anonymous reviewers for their valuable comments. This work was supported by the Natural Science Foundation of China (No. 61672288). Xiao Jin and Jianfei Yu contributed equally to this paper.

References

1. Bahdanau, D., Cho, K., Bengio, Y.: Neural machine translation by jointly learning to align and translate. arXiv preprint arXiv:1409.0473 (2014)
2. Chen, S.Y., Hsu, C.C., Kuo, C.C., Ku, L.W., et al.: Emotionlines: an emotion corpus of multi-party conversations. arXiv preprint arXiv:1802.08379 (2018)
3. Devlin, J., Chang, M.W., Lee, K., Toutanova, K.: Bert: pre-training of deep bidirectional transformers for language understanding. arXiv preprint arXiv:1810.04805 (2018)
4. Ekman, P.: An argument for basic emotions. Cogn. Emotion **6**(3–4), 169–200 (1992)
5. Eyben, F., Wöllmer, M., Schuller, B.: Opensmile: the munich versatile and fast open-source audio feature extractor. In: Proceedings of the 18th ACM International Conference on Multimedia, pp. 1459–1462 (2010)
6. Ghosal, D., Majumder, N., Poria, S., Chhaya, N., Gelbukh, A.: Dialoguegcn: a graph convolutional neural network for emotion recognition in conversation. arXiv preprint arXiv:1908.11540 (2019)
7. Hazarika, D., Poria, S., Mihalcea, R., Cambria, E., Zimmermann, R.: ICON: interactive conversational memory network for multimodal emotion detection. In: Proceedings of the 2018 Conference on Empirical Methods in Natural Language Processing, pp. 2594–2604 (2018)
8. Jiao, W., Lyu, M.R., King, I.: Real-time emotion recognition via attention gated hierarchical memory network. arXiv preprint arXiv:1911.09075 (2019)
9. Majumder, N., Poria, S., Hazarika, D., Mihalcea, R., Gelbukh, A., Cambria, E.: Dialoguernn: an attentive rnn for emotion detection in conversations. Proc. AAAI Conf. Artif. Intell. **33**, 6818–6825 (2019)
10. Olson, D.: From utterance to text: the bias of language in speech and writing. Harvard Educ. Rev. **47**(3), 257–281 (1977)
11. Poria, S., Cambria, E., Hazarika, D., Majumder, N., Zadeh, A., Morency, L.P.: Context-dependent sentiment analysis in user-generated videos. In: Proceedings of the 55th Annual Meeting of the Association for Computational Linguistics (volume 1: Long papers), pp. 873–883 (2017)
12. Poria, S., Hazarika, D., Majumder, N., Naik, G., Cambria, E., Mihalcea, R.: Meld: a multimodal multi-party dataset for emotion recognition in conversations. arXiv preprint arXiv:1810.02508 (2018)

13. Tsai, Y.H.H., Bai, S., Liang, P.P., Kolter, J.Z., Morency, L.P., Salakhutdinov, R.: Multimodal transformer for unaligned multimodal language sequences. arXiv preprint arXiv:1906.00295 (2019)
14. Vaswani, A., et al.: Attention is all you need. In: Advances in Neural Information Processing Systems, pp. 5998–6008 (2017)
15. Yang, B., Li, J., Wong, D.F., Chao, L.S., Wang, X., Tu, Z.: Context-aware self-attention networks. Proc. AAAI Conf. Artif. Intell. **33**, 387–394 (2019)
16. Yang, B., Tu, Z., Wong, D.F., Meng, F., Chao, L.S., Zhang, T.: Modeling localness for self-attention networks. arXiv preprint arXiv:1810.10182 (2018)
17. Yuan, J., Liberman, M.: Speaker identification on the scotus corpus. J. Acoustical Soc. Am. **123**(5), 3878 (2008)
18. Zhang, D., Wu, L., Sun, C., Li, S., Zhu, Q., Zhou, G.: Modeling both context-and speaker-sensitive dependence for emotion detection in multi-speaker conversations. In: See Proceedings of the Twenty-Eighth International Joint Conference on Artificial Intelligence, pp. 10–16. IJCAI (2019)
19. Zhong, P., Wang, D., Miao, C.: Knowledge-enriched transformer for emotion detection in textual conversations. arXiv preprint arXiv:1909.10681 (2019)

Poster

Generating Emotional Social Chatbot Responses with a Consistent Speaking Style

Jun Zhang[1], Yan Yang[1(✉)], Chengcai Chen[2], Liang He[1], and Zhou Yu[3]

[1] School of Computer Science and Technology, East China Normal University,
Shanghai, China
`51194506048@stu.ecnu.edu.cn`, `{yanyang,lhe}@cs.ecnu.edu.cn`
[2] Xiaoi Research, Shanghai, China
`arlenecc@xiaoi.com`
[3] University of California, Davis, USA
`joyu@ucdavis.edu`

Abstract. Emotional conversation plays a vital role in creating more human-like conversations. Although previous works on emotional conversation generation have achieved promising results, the issue of the speaking style inconsistency still exists. In this paper, we propose a Style-Aware Emotional Dialogue System (SEDS) to enhance speaking style consistency through detecting user's emotions and modeling speaking styles in emotional response generation. Specifically, SEDS uses an emotion encoder to perceive the user's emotion from multimodal inputs, and tracks speaking styles through jointly optimizing a generator that is augmented with a personalized lexicon to capture explicit word-level speaking style features. Additionally, we propose an auxiliary task, a speaking style classification task, to guide SEDS to learn the implicit form of speaking style during the training process. We construct a multimodal dialogue dataset and make the alignment and annotation to verify the effectiveness of the model. Experimental results show that our SEDS achieves a significant improvement over other strong baseline models in terms of perplexity, emotion accuracy and style consistency.

Keywords: Emotional conversation · Speaking style · Multimodal

1 Introduction

For chatbots, having the ability to express emotion is very important to deliver more human-like conversations. Addressing the emotion factor in dialogue systems can enhance user satisfaction [9] and contribute to a more positive perception of the interaction [19]. Recently, the sequence-to-sequence (Seq2Seq) based models have achieved significant success in building conversational agents [8,13–15,18,19]. Such a framework was also utilized to improve the ability of the model to express a desired emotion by Zhou et al. [19] and Song et al. [13]. However, people with different personalities express their emotions in different ways.

© Springer Nature Switzerland AG 2020
X. Zhu et al. (Eds.): NLPCC 2020, LNAI 12431, pp. 57–68, 2020.
https://doi.org/10.1007/978-3-030-60457-8_5

Table 1. Examples of different speaking styles with explicit and implicit expressions

Raj	We really suck at paintball	Explicit
Sheldon	That was **absolutely humiliating**	Explicit
Leonard	Some battles you win, some battles you lose	Implicit

Table 1 shows an example scene in *The Big Bang Theory*, where *Sheldon* uses specific words to express negative feelings, such as "absolutely" and "humiliating". While *Leonard* prefers to use third person quotes to express sadness that does not involve emotion words. Since existing models learn from large-scale and complex datasets, the generated responses always contain inconsistent speaking styles. There are few works on the issue of inconsistent speaing style. Li et al. [8] incorporated a speaker vector into Seq2Seq model to tackle the problem of response consistency. Qian et al. [10] and Zhang et al. [18] proposed to endow a chatbot with an explicit profile. Therefore, there is still a lot of room to improve the consistency of speaking style.

In this paper, we propose a Style-Aware Emotional Dialogue System (SEDS) to generate responses for a desired emotion with a consistent speaking style based on the multimodal inputs, including text and audio. SEDS is equipped with three novel components, an emotion encoder, a personalized lexicon and a speaking style classifier. Since multimodal information (such as intonation, pause) can help the model recognize the emotion in the sentence and understand the meaning of a sentence [3], we propose the emotion encoder to capture user's emotion features from multimodal inputs. Then the model can generate more coherent responses instead of vague responses, such as "I don't know". Additionally, as shown in Table 1, We have observed that language styles can be expressed in both explicit and implicit ways. On the one hand, using the words with strong speaking style is an explicit way. The personalized lexicon is proposed to extract word-level information to model the explicit way. On the other hand, using neutral words to assemble sentences is an implicit way. We create an auxiliary task, a speaking style classification task, along with the generation task to learn the implicit form of speaking styles. We construct a MultimodalBigBang dataset that has both text and audio information of the popular American TV series, *The Big Bang Theory*, and train SEDS on it. Experimental results show that SEDS largely enhances the expression of emotions and the consistency of speaking styles.

2   Method

Figure 1 shows an overview of our model. The encoder contains a text encoder and an emotion encoder. The text encoder takes the previous user utterance as input and produces its semantic representation, and the emotion encoder integrates text and audio information to encode the user's emotion. The decoder has an emotion attention mechanism to utilize emotion information from text and audio, and a personalized lexicon-based attention mechanism that encourages higher usage of words with strong speaking styles. Additionally, an internal

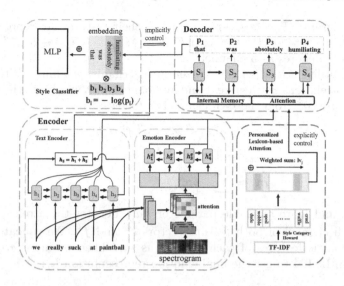

Fig. 1. The architecture of the Style-Aware Emotional Dialogue System (SEDS)

memory is used to model emotions. In the training process, we construct an auxiliary task, a speaking style classification, to guide SEDS to learn the implicit expression style.

2.1 Encoder

Text Encoder. We use a bidirectional gated recurrent unit (GRU) [2,4] to convert an utterance $X = [x_1, x_2, \cdots, x_M]$ into hidden states $H = [h_1, h_2, \cdots, h_M]$. The hidden representation h_i is computed as follows:

$$\overrightarrow{h_i} = GRU_{forward}(Emb(x_i), \overrightarrow{h_{i-1}}) \tag{1}$$

$$\overleftarrow{h_i} = GRU_{backward}(Emb(x_i), \overleftarrow{h_{i+1}}) \tag{2}$$

$$h_i = [\overrightarrow{h_i}; \overleftarrow{h_i}] \tag{3}$$

where $i = 1, 2, \cdots, M$, and $Emb(x)$ denotes the word embedding of x.

Emotion Encoder. We use the emotion encoder to extract the emotion representation based on the multimodal inputs, since audio information (such as speech intonation and pause) contains rich emotion information. Previous studies have proved that the convolutional neural network (CNN) and the long short term memory (LSTM) [6] can capture emotional information well, and significantly improve the emotion recognition accuracy [3,11]. We also use two types of neural networks in the emotion encoder. First, the emotion encoder uses different convolutional neural networks (CNNs) to encode multimodal inputs. Specifically, for each input utterance text $X = [x_1, x_2, \cdots, x_M]$ and audio spectrogram $SP = [sp_1, sp_2, \cdots, sp_T]$, their features are represented by $E^k = [e_1^k, e_2^k, \cdots, e_{d_m}^k] \in R^{d_w \times d_m}$ and $F^k = [f_1^k, f_2^k, \cdots, f_{d_t}^k] \in R^{d_s \times d_t}$, respectively, where k denotes k-th channel.

Then we utilize a multi-channel attention mechanism to improve the ability to capture correlations between text and audio. Formally, we obtain the weighted acoustic feature m_t^k from the k-th channel as follows:

$$c_{i,t}^k = tanh(v^T e_i^k + u^T f_t^k + b) \tag{4}$$

$$a_{i,t}^k = \text{softmax}\,(c_{i,t}^k) \tag{5}$$

$$m_t^k = \sum\nolimits_{i=1}^{d_m} a_{i,t}^k \cdot f_t^k \tag{6}$$

where v, u, and b are trainable parameters. $a_{i,t}^k$ denotes the attention weight between k-th channel of both feature vectors e_i^k and f_t^k. We concatenate the weighted acoustic features of each channel as m_t. Then we input m_t into an additional Bi-LSTM to get the final emotion representation h_t^e:

$$\overrightarrow{h_t^e} = LSTM_{forward}(m_t, \overrightarrow{h_{t-1}^e}) \tag{7}$$

$$\overleftarrow{h_t^e} = LSTM_{backward}(m_t, \overleftarrow{h_{t+1}^e}) \tag{8}$$

$$h_t^e = [\overrightarrow{h_t^e}; \overleftarrow{h_t^e}] \tag{9}$$

where $t = 1, 2, \ldots, d_t$. $\overrightarrow{h_t^e}$ and $\overleftarrow{h_t^e}$ are the t-th hidden states of the forward and backward LSTMs, respectively. Before training SEDS, we pre-train the emotion encoder on an emotion classification task.

2.2   Decoder

Our decoder extends a vanilla GRU with additional mechanisms to generate a response $Y = [y_1, y_2, \cdots, y_N]$ with a desired emotion and speaking style. The decoder's hidden state s_j at time step j, is given by:

$$s_j = GRU([I_j; v_e; v_s; mv_j; lv_j; M_{r,j}^I], s_{j-1}) \tag{10}$$

where I_j is the concatenation of context vector c_j and word embedding $Emb(y_{j-1})$. v_e and v_s are the embeddings of a given emotion category and style category, respectively. mv_j is a weighted emotion representation. lv_j is a style vector. $M_{r,j}^I$ is the information read from an emotion state.

To enhance the generation of emotion words, we choose a word to generate from either the emotion or the generic vocabulary.

$$\alpha_j = \text{sigmoid}\,(v_u^\top s_j) \tag{11}$$

$$P_g\,(y_j = w_g) = \text{softmax}\,(W_g^o s_j) \tag{12}$$

$$P_e\,(y_j = w_e) = \text{softmax}\,(W_e^o s_j) \tag{13}$$

$$y_j \sim o_j = P\,(y_j) = \begin{bmatrix} (1 - \alpha_j)\,P_g\,(y_j = w_g) \\ \alpha_j P_e\,(y_j = w_e) \end{bmatrix} \tag{14}$$

where $\mathbf{v_u}$, $\mathbf{W_g^o}$ and $\mathbf{W_e^o}$ are trainable parameters. $\alpha_j \in [0,1]$ is the probability of generating an emotion word. P_e and P_g are the probability distributions of generating emotion word w^e or generic word w^g, respectively.

Emotion Attention. We use attention mechanism to obtain the weighted emotion representation $\boldsymbol{mv}_j$ based on the hidden state $\boldsymbol{s}_{j-1}$ and the emotion representation $\boldsymbol{h}_t^e$. We compute $\boldsymbol{mv}_j$ as follows:

$$c_{j,t} = tanh(\boldsymbol{\alpha}_e^T \boldsymbol{s}_{j-1} + \boldsymbol{\beta}_e^T \boldsymbol{h}_t^e) \tag{15}$$

$$a_{j,t} = \text{softmax}\,(c_{j,t}) \tag{16}$$

$$Attn(\boldsymbol{s}_{j-1}, \boldsymbol{h}_t^e, \boldsymbol{\alpha}_e^T, \boldsymbol{\beta}_e^T) = \sum\nolimits_{t=1}^{d_t} a_{j,t} \cdot \boldsymbol{h}_t^e \tag{17}$$

$$\boldsymbol{mv}_j = Attn(\boldsymbol{s}_{j-1}, \boldsymbol{h}_t^e, \boldsymbol{\alpha}_e^T, \boldsymbol{\beta}_e^T) \tag{18}$$

where $\boldsymbol{\alpha}_e$ and $\boldsymbol{\beta}_e$ are trainable parameters.

Personalized Lexicon. The words a person often uses reflect his speaking style. We use a personalized lexicon-based attention mechanism to explicitly enhance the probabilities of the words with strong speaking styles during decoding process. A style vector $\boldsymbol{lv}_j$ is computed as the weighted sum of the word embeddings in a personalized lexicon by the attention mechanism. At each step j, the style vector $\boldsymbol{lv}_j$ is computed as follows:

$$\boldsymbol{lv}_j = Attn(\boldsymbol{s}_{j-1}, Emb(w_k^z), \boldsymbol{\alpha}_p^T, \boldsymbol{\beta}_p^T) \tag{19}$$

where $\boldsymbol{\alpha}_p$ and $\boldsymbol{\beta}_p$ are trainable parameters and w_k^z is the k-th word in the personalized lexicon belonging to the given style category z. In this way, the decoder will assign higher probabilities to words associated with a specific speaking style.

To construct the personalized lexicon for each speaking style, we group different speakers' utterances into separate word sets. Then we use tf-idf to select the top 1,000 words for each style as its personalized lexicon.

Internal Memory. Studies from psychology showed that emotional responses are relatively short lived and involve the dynamic emotion states [1]. Following Zhou et al. [19], we simulate a dynamic internal emotion state during generating emotional sentences. In the internal memory module, we dynamically update the emotion state $\boldsymbol{M}_e^I$ and read information $\boldsymbol{M}_{r,j}^I$ from $\boldsymbol{M}_e^I$ through a write gate $\boldsymbol{g}^w$ and a read gate $\boldsymbol{g}^r$, respectively:

$$g_j^r = \text{sigmoid}\,\left(\mathbf{W_g^r}\,[Emb\,(y_{j-1})\,;\boldsymbol{s}_{j\,1}\,;c_j]\right) \tag{20}$$

$$g_j^w = \text{sigmoid}\,\left(\mathbf{W_g^w}\,\boldsymbol{s}_j\right) \tag{21}$$

$$\boldsymbol{M}_{e,j+1}^I = \boldsymbol{g}_j^w \otimes \boldsymbol{M}_{e,j}^I \tag{22}$$

$$\boldsymbol{M}_{r,j}^I = \boldsymbol{g}_j^r \otimes \boldsymbol{M}_{e,j}^I \tag{23}$$

The emotion state gradually decays during the decoding process. It should decay to zero after the emotion is fully expressed.

Loss Function. The loss function of the decoder consists of three terms as follows:

$$L_{MCE} = -\sum\nolimits_{j=1}^{N} p_j \log(o_j) \tag{24}$$

$$L_{WCLA} = -\sum\nolimits_{j=1}^{N} q_j \log(\alpha_j) \tag{25}$$

$$L_{REG} = \|M_{e,N}^I\| \tag{26}$$

$$L_{decoder} = L_{MCE} + L_{WCLA} + L_{REG} \tag{27}$$

where L_{MCE} is the cross-entropy between predicted word distribution o_j and ground-truth distribution p_j. The others are regularization terms. L_{WCLA} constrains the selection of an emotion or a generic word, and $q_j \in [0, 1]$ is the true choice of an emotion word or a generic word in Y. L_{REG} is used to ensure that the emotion state decreases to zero.

2.3 Style Classifier

A speaking style can also be presented without using any personalized words, *i.e.* in an implicit way. Inspired by Song et al. [13], we propose a sentence-level style classifier as an auxiliary classification task to guide the model to learn the implicit way of expression. Formally, we first obtain the response $Y = [y_1, y_2, \cdots, y_N]$ and the generated probabilities of words $P = [p_1, p_2, \cdots, p_N]$. Then we use them as the style classifier's inputs to obtain sentence feature $Sf(Y)$. Finally, we compute style probability distribution $Q(S|Y)$ as follows:

$$Sf(Y) = \sum\nolimits_{j=1}^{N} -\log(p_j) \cdot Emb(y_j) \tag{28}$$

$$Q(S|Y) = \text{softmax}\,(W \cdot Sf(Y)) \tag{29}$$

where $W \in R^{K \times d}$ is a weight matrix, K denotes the number of style categories, and d is the dimension of word embedding. The classification loss is defined as:

$$L_{CLA} = -P(z)log(Q(S|Y)) \tag{30}$$

where $P(z)$ is a one-hot vector of the desired style category z. Instead of averaging over the word embedding $Emb(y_j)$, we use entropy $-log(p_j)$ for the weighted sum. This is because we find the entropy has a much stronger correlation with speaking style than the former method. Our interpretation is that the words with a high probability of generation have little correlation with the speaking style, and using the entropy $-log(p_j)$ can obtain the speaking style information. The introduction of the style classifier can help to generate responses in the implicit way and enhance the speaking style consistency.

2.4 Training Objective

The overall training objective is the weighted sum of the decoder loss and the style classification loss as follow:

$$L = L_{decoder} + \lambda L_{CLA} \tag{31}$$

Table 2. Emotion-labeled MultimodalBigBang dataset statistics

Training	Total	35693	
	Utterances	Neutral	5,208
		Happiness	18,271
		Sadness	8,405
		Anger	2,419
		Disgust	1,390
Validation		2,000	
Test		2,000	

where λ denotes a hyperparameter that balances the importance of the decoder loss and classifier loss. The first term ensures that SEDS can generate the response with a desired emotion. The second term guarantees that the response reflects the given speaking style.

3   MultimodalBigBang Dataset

Since there is no audio and text aligned dialogue dataset, we construct a new dialogue dataset with speaking style labels, namely, MultimodalBigBang. We crawl the subtitles of an American television comedy, *The Big Bang Theory*, and manually align subtitles with audio. We choose the six main characters as six distinctive speaking styles, including *Sheldon* (11,741), *Leonard* (9,809), *Penny* (7,702), *Howard* (5,942), *Raj* (4,697) and *Amy* (3,478).

As Zhou et al. [19], we use the outputs of an emotion classifier fine-tuned on the processed CMU-MOSEI [17] dataset as the emotion labels. We choose the BERT classifier to annotate MultimodalBigBang, due to its superior performance, as shown in Table 3a. The statistics of the emotion-labeled Multimodal-BigBang are shown in Table 2. Since the size of the MultimodalBigBang dataset is relatively small, we first train a standard Seq2Seq model on the Twitter dataset for 20 epochs and then apply the pre-trained model to the MultimodalBigBang dataset until the perplexity on the develop set converges.

4   Experiments

We conduct both automatic and human evaluation to measure the quality of the responses generated by different models. We evaluate response generation quality on three aspects: *Content*, *Emotion*, and *Speaking Style*.

4.1   Data Preprocessing

We downsample the raw audio signals from 44,100 Hz to 8,000 Hz. Then we apply the Short Time Fourier Transform (STFT) to convert audio signals into

Table 3. (a) Emotion classification accuracy (E-acc) on the processed CMU-MOSEI dataset and style classification accuracy (S-acc) on MultimodalBigBang. (b) Response generation results with automatic evaluation metrics. S-Con stands for style consistency

(a)

Method	E-Acc	S-Acc
LSTM	63.05	56.20
Bi-LSTM	64.01	57.30
BERT	64.73	61.70

(b)

Method	Perplexity	E-Acc	S-Con
Seq2Seq	56.37	19.60	18.04
Seq-sv	55.42	20.00	23.40
ECM	54.68	67.10	20.35
SEDS w/o SCla	54.18	68.05	25.95
SEDS w/o Ee	54.47	69.11	28.45
SEDS w/o Pla	53.94	67.74	24.70
SEDS	**53.57**	**70.30**	**30.80**

spectrograms. We use Hamming window during the STFT process and set the length of each segment to 800. Finally, the spectrograms are converted to log-scale with a fixed size of 200×400.

4.2 Training Details

We implement our SEDS[1] in Tensorflow. A 2-layer GRU structure with 512 hidden cells in each layer is used for the text encoder and decoder. We use a 1-layer bidirectional LSTM with the size of the hidden state set to 128 in the emotion encoder. The size of vocabulary is set to 42,000. The word embedding size is set to 300. The emotion embedding size and style embedding size are set to 100 and 300, respectively. The size of personalized lexicon for every speaking style is limited to 1,000. We adopt the beam search in the decoder to generate diverse responses. The beam size is set to 5. We use Adam [7] algorithm with the mini-batch method for optimization. We set the mini-batch size and learning rate to 64 and 1e-4, respectively. We run the two stages of training for approximately three days on a Tesla P100 GPU card.

4.3 Baseline Models

We consider several models for comparison with SEDS: (1) **Seq2Seq**: We implement the Seq2Seq model as described in Vinyals and Le [15] with the attention mechanism; (2) **Seq-sv**: We implement the Seq2Seq model with a speaker vector as described in Li et al. [8]; (3) **ECM**: We use the same model proposed in Zhou et al. [19]. Because the code of EmoDS model [13] has not yet been made available, it is not included among the baseline models.

To understand the effects of the three new components introduced in SEDS, we conduct ablation studies as follows: (3) SEDS w/o SCla: SEDS without the

---

[1] https://github.com/562225807/SEDS.

Table 4. Human evaluation results on response content (Cont.) and emotion (Emot.)

Model	Overall		Neutral		Happiness		Sadness		Anger		Disgust	
	Cont.	Emot.	Cont.	Emot.	Cont.	Emot.	Cont.	Emot.	Cont.	Emot.	Cont.	Emot.
Seq2Seq	1.89	0.32	1.84	0.32	1.97	0.55	1.96	0.40	1.83	0.16	1.85	0.17
ECM	2.09	0.56	2.14	0.51	2.07	0.69	2.15	0.60	**2.08**	0.56	**2.04**	0.43
SEDS	**2.10**	**0.66**	**2.17**	**0.60**	**2.12**	**0.70**	**2.19**	**0.73**	2.06	**0.66**	1.96	**0.61**

Table 5. Human evaluation results on recognizing speaking style

Model	Overall	Sheldon	Leonard	Penny	Howard	Raj	Amy
Seq2Seq	0.23	0.15	0.19	0.29	0.26	0.27	0.23
ECM	0.27	0.32	0.31	0.31	0.24	0.24	0.19
SEDS	**0.40**	**0.50**	**0.37**	**0.36**	**0.46**	**0.34**	**0.38**

style classifier; (4) SEDS w/o Ee: SEDS without the emotion encoder; (5) SEDS w/o Pla: SEDS without the personalized lexicon-based attention mechanism.

5 Results

5.1 Automatic Evaluation Metrics

We use perplexity, emotion accuracy and style consistency to evaluate the quality of generated responses [19]. We train two additional classifiers to predict emotion and speaking style, then we use them to evaluate response's emotion and speaking style consistency. Both classifiers are fine-tuned BERT classifiers.

5.2 Automatic Evaluation Results

Table 3b shows the automatic evaluation results. SEDS outperforms all the other methods in all three evaluation metrics. SEDS achieves significant improvements on both emotion accuracy and style consistency. It indicates that enhancing the consistency of speaking styles in emotional conversation helps the model generate responses more consistent with the emotion labels. This is because that our model can better distinguish and learn the different expression styles of speaking under the same emotion. The ablation studies show that all three new components improve the consistency of speaking style in responses. The personalized lexicon has the most significant improvement compared with other components, because words with strong speaking style widely exist in sentences and are the most explicit feature of the speaking style. As we can see, without the emotion encoder, the perplexity of the model increases the most. It indicates that multimodal information can help model generate more fluent and coherent responses.

5.3   Human Evaluation Setting

To better verify the quality of the generated responses, we evaluate the model by human evaluation using three metrics: content accuracy, emotion accuracy and speaking style accuracy. We randomly sample 500 utterances from the test set. The samples are divided into five sets of 100 utterances, with each set corresponding to a specific emotion. We also randomly sample 600 utterances for speaking style evaluation, 100 utterances for every speaking style. Given an utterance, the model generates a new utterance with a given emotion and speaking style.

We then present the generated responses to three human annotators. They assess the responses in terms of content, emotion and speaking style. We ask annotators to provide a binary similarity score between the generated and the ground-truth response in terms of emotion accuracy and speaking style consistency. Annotators also evaluate each response in terms of content quality on a three-point Likert scale. Here content quality is defined as the fluency and meaningfulness of the response. To measure inter-rater consistency among three annotators, their final results are calculated with the Fleiss's kappa [5]. The Fleiss's kappa for emotion, content and style consistency are 0.56,0.43,0.59, respectively.

5.4   Human Evaluation Results

Table 4 presents the human evaluation results on content and emotion accuracy. SEDS obtains much higher scores than the other models in most cases with an overall emotion score of 0.66. And SEDS performs poorly on anger and disgust due to the relatively small size of training data in these categories. Note that there is a large gap between the performances of Seq2Seq and SEDS on emotion score because Seq2Seq can not express the specified emotion.

The results on speaking style are shown in Table 5. Compared with other methods, SEDS achieves the best performance, indicating that it generates more consistent responses. Note that the utterances of Sheldon generated by SEDS are much better than other benchmarks, which indicates that SEDS performs better in the response generation with obvious speaking style.

6   Error Analysis

To intuitively show the emotional expression with a consistent speaking style in the generated responses, we provide some examples in Table 6. SEDS can generate more personalized responses in both explicit and implicit ways. For example, "scientist" is a characteristic word for *Sheldon*. He often uses a direct tone to express interest in scientific inventions because he is a neurotic scientist. *Penny* perfers to use strong emotional words to express disgust, like "ridiculous". As in Table 6, although SEDS generates responses with more consistent speaking styles, it still has several problems. For example, there are high probabilities of generating people's names, such as "Sheldon". Our interpretation is that some speakers frequently mention other people's names during conversations, which leads to some of the names were selected into personalized lexicon during the automatic lexicon building process.

Table 6. Sample responses generated by Seq2Seq, ECM and SEDS when given the conditioned emotion and style categories. We bold all the personalized words.

Utterance	Model	Condition	Response
How cool would that be if we could make one of those a reality?	Seq2Seq	Sheldon Happiness	I don't know
	ECM		Well, it's not you
	SEDS		I'm a **scientist**. I'm the wise
People love training monkey	Seq2Seq	Howard Disgust	Oh, do that
	ECM		Oh, my god
	SEDS		Sheldon, god, **ridiculous**
I obviously don't make my point with those people	Seq2Seq	Penny Sadness	Well, what are you doing here?
	ECM		I'm sorry, I don't know. I'm not even sure
	SEDS		I'm sorry, I'm not going to go away
That lab monkey told me he loves me in sign language	Seq2Seq	Sheldon Happiness	Well done
	ECM		Well, it's okay
	SEDS		Well, I think we're going to need parties

7   Related Work

Recently Seq2Seq [14] model greatly improved the quality of responses in conversation systems. Zhou et al. [19] addressed the problem of emotional expression in chatbots and proposed the Emotional Chat Machine (ECM), which was equipped with three mechanisms, emotion embedding, internal memory and external memory. Song et al. [13] proposed an emotional dialogue system (EmoDS) to model emotion in both explicit and implicit ways. Li et al. [8] proposed a speaker model and speaker-address model to tackle the problem of response consistency.

Prevouis works showed that multimodel information is important for enhancing the model's performance on several tasks. Choi et al. [3] and Xu et al. [16] indicated that emotion recognition benefited from the use of speech-textual information. Shi and Yu [12] suggested that incorporating user sentiment features extracted from multimodal information into the model can shorten the dialogue length and improve the task success rate.

8   Conclusions

We propose the Style-Aware Emotional Dialogue System (SEDS) with three novel components, namely, an emotion encoder, a personalized lexicon, and a style classifier. We construct a new multimodal dataset to verify the effect of SEDS. Experimental results show that SEDS can better deliver an emotional conversation with a consistent speaking style than other baseline models.

In the future, we will consider how to boost the coherence and speaking style consistency of responses based on pre-trained language models, since the pre-trained model shows great power in the natural language processing domain. This is a meaningful and significant challenge that makes a chatbot more personalized.

References

1. Alam, F., Danieli, M., Riccardi, G.: Annotating and modeling empathy in spoken conversations. Comput. Speech Lang. **50**, 40–61 (2018)
2. Cho, K., et al.: Learning phrase representations using RNN encoder-decoder for statistical machine translation. In: EMNLP, pp. 1724–1734 (2014)
3. Choi, W.Y., Song, K.Y., Lee, C.W.: Convolutional attention networks for multimodal emotion recognition from speech and text data. In: Proceedings of the first Grand Challenge and Workshop on Human Multimodal Language (Challenge-HML), pp. 28–34 (2018)
4. Chung, J., Gulcehre, C., Cho, K., Bengio, Y.: Empirical evaluation of gated recurrent neural networks on sequence modeling. In: NIPS 2014 Workshop on Deep Learning, December 2014
5. Fleiss, J.L., Cohen, J.: The equivalence of weighted kappa and the intraclass correlation coefficient as measures of reliability. Educ. Psychol. Measure. **33**(3), 613–619 (1973)
6. Hochreiter, S., Schmidhuber, J.: Long short-term memory. Neural Comput. **9**(8), 1735–1780 (1997)
7. Kingma, D.P., Ba, J.: Adam: a method for stochastic optimization. arXiv preprint arXiv:1412.6980 (2014)
8. Li, J., Galley, M., Brockett, C., Spithourakis, G., Gao, J., Dolan, B.: A persona-based neural conversation model. In: ACL, pp. 994–1003 (2016)
9. Prendinger, H., Mori, J., Ishizuka, M.: Using human physiology to evaluate subtle expressivity of a virtual quizmaster in a mathematical game. Int. J. Hum. Comput. Stud. **62**(2), 231–245 (2005)
10. Qian, Q., Huang, M., Zhao, H., Xu, J., Zhu, X.: Assigning personality/profile to a chatting machine for coherent conversation generation. In: IJCAI, pp. 4279–4285 (2018)
11. Satt, A., Rozenberg, S., Hoory, R.: Efficient emotion recognition from speech using deep learning on spectrograms. In: INTERSPEECH, pp. 1089–1093 (2017)
12. Shi, W., Yu, Z.: Sentiment adaptive end-to-end dialog systems. In: ACL, pp. 1509–1519 (2018)
13. Song, Z., Zheng, X., Liu, L., Xu, M., Huang, X.J.: Generating responses with a specific emotion in dialog. In: ACL, pp. 3685–3695 (2019)
14. Sutskever, I., Vinyals, O., Le, Q.: Sequence to sequence learning with neural networks. Advances in NIPS (2014)
15. Vinyals, O., Le, Q.: A neural conversational model. arXiv preprint arXiv:1506.05869 (2015)
16. Xu, H., Zhang, H., Han, K., Wang, Y., Peng, Y., Li, X.: Learning alignment for multimodal emotion recognition from speech. Proc. Interspeech, pp. 3569–3573 (2019)
17. Zadeh, A.B., Liang, P.P., Poria, S., Cambria, E., Morency, L.P.: Multimodal language analysis in the wild: CMU-MOSEI dataset and interpretable dynamic fusion graph. In: ACL, pp. 2236–2246 (2018)
18. Zhang, S., Dinan, E., Urbanek, J., Szlam, A., Kiela, D., Weston, J.: Personalizing dialogue agents: i have a dog, do you have pets too. In: ACL, pp. 2204–2213 (2018)
19. Zhou, H., Huang, M., Zhang, T., Zhu, X., Liu, B.: Emotional chatting machine: emotional conversation generation with internal and external memory. In: AAAI (2018)

An Interactive Two-Pass Decoding Network for Joint Intent Detection and Slot Filling

Huailiang Peng[1,2,3], Mengjun Shen[1,2], Lei Jiang[1,2(✉)], Qiong Dai[1,2], and Jianlong Tan[1,2]

[1] Institute of Information Engineering, Chinese Academy of Sciences, Beijing, China
{penghuailiang,shenmengjun,jianglei,daiqiong,tanjianlong}@iie.ac.cn
[2] School of Cyber Security, University of Chinese Academy of Sciences, Beijing, China
[3] Institute of Computing Technology, Chinese Academy of Sciences, Beijing, China

Abstract. Intent detection and slot filling are two closely related tasks for building a spoken language understanding (SLU) system. The joint methods for the two tasks focus on modeling the semantic correlations between the intent and slots and applying the information of one task to guide the other task, which helps them to promote each other. However, most existing joint approaches only unidirectionally utilize the intent information to guide slot filling while ignoring the fact that the slot information is beneficial to intent detection. To address this issue, in this paper, we propose an Interactive Two-pass Decoding Network (ITD-Net) for joint intent detection and slot filling, which explicitly establishes the token-level interactions between the intent and slots through performing an interactive two-pass decoding process. In ITD-Net, the task-specific information obtained by the first-pass decoder for one task is directly fed into the second-pass decoder for the other task, which can take full advantage of the explicit intent and slot information to achieve bidirectional guidance between the two tasks. Experiments on the ATIS and SNIPS datasets demonstrate the effectiveness and superiority of our ITD-Net.

Keywords: Spoken language understanding · Intent detection · Slot filling · Interactive two-pass decoding

1 Introduction

Spoken language understanding (SLU) [17] plays a vital role in task-oriented dialog systems. It generally contains intent detection task and slot filling task which aim to identify the intent of the user and extract semantic constituents (i.e., slots) from the natural language utterance, respectively. Generally, the entire utterance corresponds to one intent label, and each token (i.e., word) in the utterance corresponds to a slot label. For example, as shown in Table 1, the intent of the utterance "Play the song Little Robin Redbreast" is *PlayMusic*,

© Springer Nature Switzerland AG 2020
X. Zhu et al. (Eds.): NLPCC 2020, LNAI 12431, pp. 69–81, 2020.
https://doi.org/10.1007/978-3-030-60457-8_6

Table 1. An example with annotations of slots in IOB (In-Out-Begin) format and intent sampled from the SNIPS [3] dataset.

Utterance	Play	The	Song	Little	Robin	Redbreast
Slots	O	O	B-music_item	B-track	I-track	I-track
Intent	PlayMusic					

and there are a *music_item* slot with value "song" and a *track* slot with value "Little Robin Redbreast". Formally, given an utterance $X = (x_1, \cdots, x_T)$ with T tokens, intent detection aims to decide the intent label y^I of the utterance, and slot filling aims at mapping the utterance to its corresponding slot label sequence $Y^S = (y_1^S, \cdots, y_T^S)$.

Methods for the two tasks can be divided into pipeline approaches and joint methods. Traditional pipeline approaches implement the two tasks separately. Intent detection is usually treated as an utterance-level classification problem [15, 16]. Slot filling is generally formulated as a sequence labeling problem [13, 21]. Although pipeline methods can handle each task flexibly with separate models, they generally suffer from error propagation [6, 23]. Moreover, the intent and slots are highly correlative, and the two tasks are not independent [14, 23]. Hence, many joint methods are proposed to handle the two tasks simultaneously with a unified model. Early joint methods [11, 12, 23] just implicitly model the relationships between the intent and slots by utilizing a united loss function and shared representations of the utterance. More recent approaches [5, 6, 10, 14] try to explicitly model such relationships and apply the information of one task to guide the other task via the gate mechanism or the Stack-Propagation framework for improving the performance of the latter task. Though achieving promising performances, most of existing joint methods only unidirectionally apply the intent information to guide slot filling while ignoring the fact that the slot information is useful to intent detection.

To address the above issue, we propose an Interactive Two-pass Decoding Network (ITD-Net) for joint intent detection and slot filling, which explicitly establishes the token-level interactions between the intent and slots by performing an interactive two-pass decoding process. Through directly feeding the task-specific information obtained by the first-pass decoder for one task to the second-pass decoder for the other task at each token, ITD-Net can effectively utilize explicit intent information to guide slot filling and apply explicit slot information to instruct intent detection, thus achieving bidirectional guidance between the two tasks. Concretely, in the first decoding stage, the first-pass intent decoder and the first-pass slot decoder capture task-specific features from the vector representations of the input utterance, and generate first-pass intent output distributions and first-pass slot output distributions, respectively. These first-pass outputs are treated as explicit intent and slot information, which are further fed into the second-pass decoders to provide guidance. In the second decoding stage, the second-pass intent decoder performs token-level intent label decoding with the guidance provided by the slot information, and the intent of the whole utterance is determined by majority voting from the intent predictions of each token in the utterance. The second-pass slot decoder works similarly with the guidance of the intent information and generates the final slot label sequence. The experimental results on the ATIS [7,18] and SNIPS [3] datasets show the effectiveness and superiority of the proposed ITD-Net.

To summarize, the contributions of this work are as follows:

- We propose an Interactive Two-pass Decoding Network (ITD-Net) for SLU, which explicitly builds the interactions between the intent and slots and achieves bidirectional guidance between intent detection and slot filling, thus improving the performance of both tasks.
- We devise an interactive two-pass decoding process in the ITD-Net. Through directly feeding the task-specific information obtained by the first-pass decoder for one task to the second-pass decoder for the other task, the explicit intent and slot information can be effectively utilized to guide the prediction of the slots and intent.

2   Related Work

Considering the strong correlations between the intent detection task and slot filling task, joint models for the two tasks are proposed in recent years [11,12,23]. Zhang et al. [23] proposed a joint model based on recurrent neural networks (RNNs). To make the best of the explicit alignment information in slot filling and additional supporting information provided by the context vector [1], Liu et al. [11] devised an attention-based encoder-decoder model with aligned inputs and an attention-based bidirectional RNN model. However, these early joint methods just implicitly model the relationships between the intent and slots through applying a united loss function and shared utterance representations, which cannot take full advantage of the intent and slot information.

Accordingly, some more recent joint approaches [6,10] explicitly model such relationships through the gate mechanism and apply the intent information to guide slot filling. Goo et al. [6] designed a slot-gated model that introduces a slot gate to model slot-intent relationships for improving the performance of slot filling. Li et al. [10] proposed a self-attentive model with the intent-augmented gate mechanism, which utilizes the intent embedding as the gate for labeling slot. However, Qin et al. [14] argued that it is risky to simply rely on the gate function to summarize or memorize the intent information, and the interpretability of how the intent information guides the slot filling procedure is weak. Hence, they proposed a Stack Propagation framework with token-level intent detection for SLU, in which the output of intent detection is directly utilized as the input of slot filling to better instruct the slot prediction process. Compared with [14], our ITD-Net also employs the predicted slot information to enhance intent detection, thus achieving bilateral guidance between the two tasks.

To fully exploit the cross-impact between the two tasks, Wang et al. [20] devised a Bi-model that contains two inter-connected bidirectional long short term memory (Bi-LSTM) networks [8], one is for intent detection, and the other is for slot filling. To establish the bidirectional interrelated connections for the two tasks, E *et al.* [5] introduced an SF-ID network. To harness the hierarchical relationships among words, slots and intents in the utterance, Zhang *et al.* [22] proposed a capsule-based model, which utilizes a dynamic routing-by-agreement schema to accomplish joint modeling for the two tasks. To address the poor generalization ability of traditional natural language understanding (NLU) models, Chen *et al.* [2] designed a joint model based on the Bidirectional Encoder Representation from Transformer (BERT) [4].

3 Approach

In this section, we will describe our Interactive Two-pass Decoding Network (ITD-Net). Inspired by [14], ITD-Net performs token-level intent detection, which can provide token-level intent information for slot filling, thus alleviating the error propagation caused by incorrect utterance-level intent predictions. Formally, token-level intent detection is treated as a sequence labeling problem that maps the input utterance $X = (x_1, \cdots, x_T)$ to a sequence of intent labels $(o_1^I, \cdots, o_T^I)$.

As illustrated in Fig. 1, ITD-Net consists of a self-attentive encoder and an interactive two-pass decoder. The interactive two-pass decoder contains two first-pass decoders $(\mathcal{D}_1^I, \mathcal{D}_1^S)$ and two second-pass decoders $(\mathcal{D}_2^I, \mathcal{D}_2^S)$. Each of them is implemented by a separate unidirectional LSTM. Briefly speaking, the encoder firstly generates the context-aware vector representations of the input utterance. Then an interactive two-pass decoding process is executed, and the intent label and the slot label of each token in the utterance are obtained. Finally, the intent of the utterance is determined by majority voting from the intent predictions of each token. In the following, all the W with different superscripts are the model parameters to be learned, and all the bias terms are omitted for readability.

3.1 Self-Attentive Encoder

The self-attentive encoder aims at making use of the contextual information and temporal features to obtain the sequence representations of the utterance. It is composed of an embedding layer, a self-attention layer and a Bi-LSTM layer.

Embedding Layer. Considering that the character-level information (e.g., morphemes, capitalization and prefix) is beneficial to identify slot labels [10], we utilize a 1D convolution layer followed by an average pooling layer to generate the character-level embedding of a token. The embedding of each token is acquired by concatenating its word-level and character-level embedding. The obtained embeddings of all tokens in the utterance are represented as $E = (e_1, \cdots, e_T) \in \mathbb{R}^{T \times d_e}$, where d_e is the dimension of the token embedding.

Self-attention Layer. We apply the self-attention mechanism to capture the contextual information for each token in the utterance. Following [19], we first

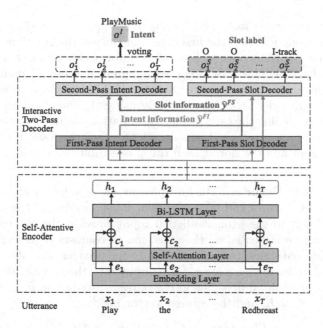

Fig. 1. Framework of the proposed Interactive Two-pass Decoding Network (ITD-Net) for joint intent detection and slot filling.

map the embeddings E to queries Q and keys K of dimension d_k and values V of dimension d_v by utilizing different linear projections. Then the output of the self-attention layer (i.e., the context-aware representations for the utterance) $C = (c_1, \cdots, c_T) \in \mathbb{R}^{T \times d_v}$ is computed as the weighted sum of the values:

$$C = \mathrm{softmax}(\frac{QK^\top}{\sqrt{d_k}})V. \tag{1}$$

Bi-LSTM Layer. To exploit the temporal features of the utterance, we further utilize the Bi-LSTM [8] to encode the utterance. Concretely, the embeddings E and the context-aware representations C of the utterance are concatenated as the input of the Bi-LSTM layer. And the Bi-LSTM reads the input forwardly and backwardly to produce the encoder hidden states $H = (h_1, \cdots, h_T) \in \mathbb{R}^{T \times d_h}$:

$$h_t = [\overrightarrow{h}_t, \overleftarrow{h}_t]; \ \overrightarrow{h}_t = \overrightarrow{\mathrm{LSTM}}(\overrightarrow{h}_{t-1}, [e_t, c_t]); \ \overleftarrow{h}_t = \overleftarrow{\mathrm{LSTM}}(\overleftarrow{h}_{t+1}, [e_t, c_t]), \tag{2}$$

where d_h is the dimension of the hidden vector.

3.2 Interactive Two-Pass Decoder

The interactive two-pass decoder divides the decoding process into two stages. In the first decoding stage, the first-pass intent decoder $\mathcal{D}_1^I$ and the first-pass slot decoder $\mathcal{D}_1^S$ perform token-level intent prediction and slot label prediction, respectively. They extract task-specific features and produce the first-pass intent output distributions $\widehat{\boldsymbol{y}}^{FI}$ and the first-pass slot output distributions $\widehat{\boldsymbol{y}}^{FS}$ separately, which can be treated as explicit intent information and slot information. In the second decoding phase, the second-pass intent decoder $\mathcal{D}_2^I$ performs information augmented decoding with the guidance of the slot information $\widehat{\boldsymbol{y}}^{FS}$. The second-pass slot decoder $\mathcal{D}_2^S$ works similarly using the intent information $\widehat{\boldsymbol{y}}^{FI}$. Through directly feeding the task-specific information obtained by the first-pass decoder for one task to the second-pass decoder for the other task, the interaction between the intent and the slot at each token is established explicitly.

First-Pass Intent Decoder. The first-pass intent decoder $\mathcal{D}_1^I$ aims to capture token-level intent features and perform intent label decoding. At each decoding step t, in addition to the explicit aligned input provided by the encoder, the dynamic context vector based on the attention mechanism [1] is introduced for providing additional supporting information to the decoder [11]. Mathematically speaking, the decoder hidden state $\boldsymbol{s}_t^{FI}$ is computed by the previous decoder state $\boldsymbol{s}_{t-1}^{FI}$, the previous emitted first-pass intent output distribution $\widehat{\boldsymbol{y}}_{t-1}^{FI}$, the aligned encoder hidden state $\boldsymbol{h}_t$ and the context vector $\boldsymbol{cv}_t^{FI}$:

$$\boldsymbol{s}_t^{FI} = \mathrm{LSTM}(\boldsymbol{s}_{t-1}^{FI}, [\widehat{\boldsymbol{y}}_{t-1}^{FI}, \boldsymbol{h}_t, \boldsymbol{cv}_t^{FI}]), \tag{3}$$

where $\boldsymbol{cv}_t^{FI} = \sum_{i=1}^T \alpha_{ti}^{FI} \boldsymbol{h}_i$. The attention weight $\alpha_{ti}^{FI} \propto \exp(g(\boldsymbol{s}_{t-1}^{FI}, \boldsymbol{h}_i))$, where g is a feedforward neural network [1]. $[\widehat{\boldsymbol{y}}_{t-1}^{FI}, \boldsymbol{h}_t, \boldsymbol{cv}_t^{FI}]$ is the concatenation of the three vectors, serving as current input to the LSTM network.

Then the first-pass intent output distribution $\widehat{\boldsymbol{y}}_t^{FI}$ of the t-th token in the utterance is computed as follows:

$$\widehat{\boldsymbol{y}}_t^{FI} = \mathrm{softmax}(\boldsymbol{W}^{FI} \boldsymbol{s}_t^{FI}), \tag{4}$$

where $\widehat{\boldsymbol{y}}_t^{FI} \in \mathbb{R}^{n_I}$ and n_I is the number of intent labels.

Finally, the first-pass intent output distributions $\widehat{\boldsymbol{y}}^{FI} = (\widehat{\boldsymbol{y}}_1^{FI}, \cdots, \widehat{\boldsymbol{y}}_T^{FI})$ is obtained, which can be regarded as explicit intent information. It is leveraged to constrain the slots into a specific intent in the second-pass slot decoder $\mathcal{D}_2^S$.

First-Pass Slot Decoder. The first-pass slot decoder $\mathcal{D}_1^S$ extracts the features specific to slot filling task from the vector representations $\boldsymbol{H}$ of the utterance and executes slot label decoding. At each decoding step t, based on the aligned input $\boldsymbol{h}_t$ and the context vector $\boldsymbol{cv}_t^{FS}$, the decoder state $\boldsymbol{s}_t^{FS}$ and the first-pass slot output distribution $\widehat{\boldsymbol{y}}_t^{FS}$ of the t-th token is calculated as:

$$\begin{aligned} \boldsymbol{s}_t^{FS} &= \mathrm{LSTM}(\boldsymbol{s}_{t-1}^{FS}, [\widehat{\boldsymbol{y}}_{t-1}^{FS}, \boldsymbol{h}_t, \boldsymbol{cv}_t^{FS}]), \\ \widehat{\boldsymbol{y}}_t^{FS} &= \mathrm{softmax}(\boldsymbol{W}^{FS} \boldsymbol{s}_t^{FS}), \end{aligned} \tag{5}$$

where $\boldsymbol{cv}_t^{FS} = \sum_{i=1}^T \alpha_{ti}^{FS} \boldsymbol{h}_i$ and $\alpha_{ti}^{FS} \propto \exp(g(\boldsymbol{s}_{t-1}^{FS}, \boldsymbol{h}_i))$. The ouput $\widehat{\boldsymbol{y}}_t^{FS} \in \mathbb{R}^{n_S}$ and n_S is the number of slot labels. Slot label dependencies are naturally modeled by feeding the previous output $\widehat{\boldsymbol{y}}_{t-1}^{FS}$ to the current decoding step.

The generated first-pass slot output distributions $\widehat{\boldsymbol{y}}^{FS} = (\widehat{\boldsymbol{y}}_1^{FS}, \cdots, \widehat{\boldsymbol{y}}_T^{FS})$ is treated as explicit slot information, which is further utilized in the second-pass intent decoder $\mathcal{D}_2^I$ to provide guidance.

Second-Pass Intent Decoder. The second-pass intent decoder $\mathcal{D}_2^I$ aims at making use of the slot information to improve intent detection. At each decoding step t, it directly leverages the explicit slot information $\widehat{\boldsymbol{y}}_t^{FS}$ to provoke the token-level intent associated with a particular slot. Concretely, the decoder state $\boldsymbol{s}_t^{AI}$ at time t is updated as:

$$s_t^{AI} = \mathrm{LSTM}(s_{t-1}^{AI}, [\widehat{\boldsymbol{y}}_{t-1}^{AI}, \boldsymbol{h}_t, \boldsymbol{cv}_t^{AI}, \widehat{\boldsymbol{y}}_t^{FS}]), \tag{6}$$

where the context vector $\boldsymbol{cv}_t^{AI} = \sum_{i=1}^T \alpha_{ti}^{AI} \boldsymbol{h}_i$. The weight α_{ti}^{AI} is computed based on the previous decoder state $\boldsymbol{s}_{t-1}^{AI}$ and the encoder hidden state $\boldsymbol{h}_i$.

Afterward, the decoder state $\boldsymbol{s}_t^{AI}$ is used for predicting the token-level intent label o_t^I of the t-th token in the utterance:

$$\widehat{\boldsymbol{y}}_t^{AI} = \mathrm{softmax}(\boldsymbol{W}^{AI} \boldsymbol{s}_t^{AI}); \ o_t^I = \mathrm{argmax}(\widehat{\boldsymbol{y}}_t^{AI}), \tag{7}$$

where $\widehat{\boldsymbol{y}}_t^{AI} \in \mathbb{R}^{n_I}$ is the intent label distribution of the t-th token.

Lastly, the predicted intent o^I of the entire utterance is obtained by majority voting from the token-level intent predictions $(o_1^I, \cdots, o_T^I)$ of all tokens:

$$o^I = \mathrm{argmax} \sum_{t=1}^T \sum_{i=1}^{n_I} v_i \mathbb{1}[o_t^I = i], \tag{8}$$

where $v_i \in \mathbb{R}^{n_I}$ denotes a 0–1 vector of which the i-th unit is one and the others are zero. $\mathbb{1}[\cdot]$ is the indicator function.

Second-Pass Slot Decoder. The second-pass slot decoder $\mathcal{D}_2^S$ aims to take advantage of the intent information to enhance slot filling. At each decoding step t, with the guidance and constraint provided by the first-pass intent output distribution $\widehat{\boldsymbol{y}}_t^{FI}$, the decoder state $\boldsymbol{s}_t^{AS}$ is computed as follows:

$$s_t^{AS} = \mathrm{LSTM}(s_{t-1}^{AS}, [\widehat{\boldsymbol{y}}_{t-1}^{AS}, \boldsymbol{h}_t, \boldsymbol{cv}_t^{AS}, \widehat{\boldsymbol{y}}_t^{FI}]), \tag{9}$$

where the context vector $\boldsymbol{cv}_t^{AS} = \sum_{i=1}^T \alpha_{ti}^{AS} \boldsymbol{h}_i$, and $\alpha_{ti}^{AS} \propto \exp(g(\boldsymbol{s}_{t-1}^{AS}, \boldsymbol{h}_i))$.

Then the decoder state $\boldsymbol{s}_t^{AS}$ is utilized to predict the final slot label o_t^S of the t-th token in the utterance:

$$\widehat{\boldsymbol{y}}_t^{AS} = \mathrm{softmax}(\boldsymbol{W}^{AS} \boldsymbol{s}_t^{AS}); \ o_t^S = \mathrm{argmax}(\widehat{\boldsymbol{y}}_t^{AS}), \tag{10}$$

where $\widehat{\boldsymbol{y}}_t^{AS} \in \mathbb{R}^{n_S}$ is the slot label distribution of the t-th token.

3.3   Joint Optimization

The joint loss function $\mathcal{L}$ of the token-level intent detection and slot filling is defined as the sum of the cross-entropy losses from both tasks:

$$\mathcal{L} = \mathcal{L}^I + \mathcal{L}^S; \; \mathcal{L}^I = -\sum_{t=1}^{T}\sum_{i=1}^{n_I} y_{t,i}^I \log(\widehat{\boldsymbol{y}}_t^{AI}); \; \mathcal{L}^S = -\sum_{t=1}^{T}\sum_{j=1}^{n_S} y_{t,j}^S \log(\widehat{\boldsymbol{y}}_t^{AS}), \quad (11)$$

where $\mathcal{L}^I$ and $\mathcal{L}^S$ denote the individual cross-entropy loss of intent detection and slot filling, respectively. $y_{t,i}^I$ and $y_{t,j}^S$ are the gold intent label and gold slot label separately. During training, we set the actual intent label y^I of the utterance as the gold intent label of each token in the utterance.

4   Experiments

4.1   Datasets and Metrics

To evaluate the efficiency of ITD-Net, we conduct experiments on two datasets, ATIS [7,18] and SNIPS [3]. The Airline Travel Information Systems (ATIS) is a single-domain dataset that consists of audio recordings of people making flight reservations. The SNIPS is a multi-domain dataset which refers to the custom-intent-engines collected by Snips personal voice assistant.[1] We follow the same format and division as [6] for both datasets. For ATIS, the training, development and test sets contain 4,478, 500 and 893 utterances, respectively. There are 21 intent types and 120 slot labels in the training set. For SNIPS, the above three sets include 13,084, 700 and 700 utterances separately. There are 7 intent types and 72 slot labels in the training set.

Three evaluation metrics are used to measure model performance [6]. Concretely, the accuracy is used for intent detection. The F1-score is adopted for slot filling. Furthermore, the sentence-level semantic frame accuracy (sentence accuracy) is utilized to indicate the overall performance of the two tasks. It refers to the proportion of the utterances whose intent label and all slot labels are both correctly predicted in the whole evaluation corpus.

4.2   Implementation Details

For the embedding layer, the dimension of the word-level embedding is set to 128 and 256 for the ATIS and SNIPS dataset, respectively. For the character-level embedding, each character in a token is first converted to a 12-dimensional vector. In the 1D convolution layer, the convolution filter sizes are set to {2, 3}, and the number of filters corresponding to each filter size is set to 64 and 128 for the ATIS and SNIPS dataset, respectively. Consequently, the dimension d_e of the token embedding is 256 for ATIS and 512 for SNIPS. Following [14],

---

[1] https://github.com/snipsco/nlu-benchmark/tree/master/2017-06-custom-intent-engines.

for the self-attention layer, the dimension d_v of the values V is set to 128. For the Bi-LSTM layer, the hidden size d_h is set to 256. For each unidirectional LSTM that is utilized as the decoder, the hidden size is set to 64. The batch size is 16 for training and evaluation. Adam [9] is utilized for model optimization with the learning rate of 1e-3. The dropout is applied to reduce over-fitting, and the dropout rate is set to 0.4. We choose the model that achieves the best performance on the development set and then evaluate it on the test set.

4.3   Ablation Study

We conduct ablation experiments to validate the effectiveness of various components in our ITD-Net. Specifically, we first investigate the effect of the interactive two-pass decoder. Then we explore the effect of the self-attention mechanism adopted in the self-attentive encoder.

Effect of Interactive Two-Pass Decoder. To verify whether the second-pass decoder for one task can make the most of the explicit information of the other task (i.e., the first-pass output distributions generated in the first decoding stage) to improve the model performance, we perform the following ablations:

- **Without Second-Pass Intent Decoder**: the second-pass intent decoder $\mathcal{D}_2^I$ is removed, and the output $\widehat{y}^{FI}$ of the first-pass intent decoder is adopted for predicting the token-level intent label sequence $(o_1^I, \cdots, o_T^I)$.
- **Without Second-Pass Slot Decoder**: the second-pass slot decoder $\mathcal{D}_2^S$ is ablated, and the output $\widehat{y}^{FS}$ of the first-pass slot decoder is used for final slot label prediction.
- **Without Both Second-Pass Decoders**: both second-pass decoders ($\mathcal{D}_2^I$ and $\mathcal{D}_2^S$) are removed, which means we only conduct one-pass decoding. $\widehat{y}^{FI}$ and $\widehat{y}^{FS}$ are utilized to predict the intent and slots, respectively.

The result of the ablation experiments is shown in Table 2. From the table, we can observe that without the second-pass intent decoder or the second-pass slot decoder, the model performance on both datasets decreases. Moreover, when removing both second-pass decoders, the performance drops a lot. Concretely, in the ATIS dataset, we see 0.71%, 0.90% and 2.69% drop on the slot F1-score, intent accuracy and sentence accuracy, respectively. In the SNIPS dataset, we observe 1.22%, 1.14% and 3.14% drop on the above three metrics. This indicates that the intent information is helpful for slot filling and the slot information is also beneficial to intent detection. More importantly, in the interactive two-pass decoder, the second-pass decoders can make the best of task-specific information offered by the first-pass decoders to boost the performance of both tasks.

Effect of Self-attention Mechanism. To study the benefits of the self-attention mechanism we used in the ITD-Net, we remove the self-attention layer from the self-attentive encoder, and the token embeddings generated by the

Table 2. Ablation experiments of the proposed ITD-Net on ATIS and SNIPS datasets.

Model	ATIS			SNIPS		
	Slot (F1)	Intent (Acc)	Sentence (Acc)	Slot (F1)	Intent (Acc)	Sentence (Acc)
ITD-Net (full)	**96.23**	**97.54**	**88.24**	**95.20**	**98.57**	**88.43**
W/o second-pass intent decoder	96.04	96.98	87.23	94.70	98.00	87.14
W/o second-pass slot decoder	95.94	96.86	87.23	94.93	98.57	88.00
W/o both second-pass decoders	95.52	96.64	85.55	93.98	97.43	85.29
W/o self-attention	95.83	96.98	87.46	94.76	98.00	87.86

Table 3. Intent detection and slot filling results on ATIS and SNIPS datasets.

Model	ATIS			SNIPS		
	Slot (F1)	Intent (Acc)	Sentence (Acc)	Slot (F1)	Intent (Acc)	Sentence (Acc)
Attention BiRNN [11]	94.20	91.10	78.90	87.80	96.70	74.10
Slot-Gated (Full Atten.) [6]	94.80	93.60	82.20	88.80	97.00	75.50
Slot-Gated (Intent Atten.) [6]	95.20	94.10	82.60	88.30	96.80	74.60
Self-Attentive Model [10]	95.10	96.80	82.20	90.00	97.50	81.00
Bi-model [20]	95.50	96.40	85.70	93.50	97.20	83.80
SF-ID Network ID-First (without CRF) [5]	95.58	96.58	86.00	90.46	97.00	78.37
SF-ID Network ID-First (with CRF) [5]	95.80	97.09	86.90	92.23	97.29	80.43
Stack-Propagation Model [14]	95.90	96.90	86.50	94.20	98.00	86.90
ITD-Net (ours)	**96.23**	**97.54**	**88.24**	**95.20**	**98.57**	**88.43**

embedding layer is directly utilized as the input of the Bi-LSTM layer. From Table 2, we can see that without the self-attention layer, the model performance on all evaluation metrics of both datasets decreases. Concretely, in the ATIS dataset, we observe 0.40%, 0.56% and 0.78% drop on the slot F1-score, intent accuracy and sentence accuracy, respectively. In the SNIPS dataset, the afore-mentioned three metrics drop 0.44%, 0.57% and 0.57% separately. We believe the reason is that the self-attention mechanism can capture the contextual infor-mation for each token, which is useful to the prediction of the token-level intent and slot.

4.4   Comparison with State-of-the-Arts

We compare ITD-Net with existing baselines for joint intent detection and slot filling. The results are presented in Table 3.[2] Among the baselines, [5,6,10] lever-age the gate mechanism to model the slot-intent relationships, [14] utilizes the predicted intent information to guide slot filling. We can see that the ITD-Net outperforms all baselines. Compared with the state-of-the-art *Stack-Propagation*

---

[2] For the *SF-ID Network*, we adopt the results of the model using the ID-First mode from [5]. For all other baselines, we obtain the results from [14].

Model [14], in the ATIS dataset, the ITD-Net achieves 0.33% improvement on slot F1-score, 0.64% improvement on intent accuracy and 1.74% improvement on sentence accuracy. In the SNIPS dataset, the ITD-Net achieves 1.00%, 0.57% and 1.53% improvements on the above three evaluation metrics, respectively. This result verifies the superiority of our ITD-Net.

Compared with *Stack-Propagation Model.* that only unidirectionally exploits the predicted intent information to guide slot filling, such improvements further indicate that the slot information is beneficial to intent detection. By directly utilizing the explicit slot information (i.e., the first-pass slot output distributions obtained in the first decoding stage) as the extra input of the second-pass intent decoder to provide guidance, our ITD-Net improves the intent accuracy and further improves the other two evaluation metrics through joint learning.

Besides, the ITD-Net significantly outperforms the SF-ID Network [5]. Compared with *SF-ID Network ID-First (with CRF)*, in the ATIS dataset, the ITD-Net gains 0.43%, 0.45% and 1.34% improvement in terms of slot F1-score, intent accuracy and sentence accuracy, respectively. In the SNIPS dataset, the ITD-Net achieves 2.97%, 1.28% and 8.00% improvements on the three metrics mentioned above, respectively. This implies that directly utilizing the explicit output label distribution of one task to guide the other task is more effective than using the gate mechanism to implicitly establish the interactions between the two tasks. The noticeable improvement on intent accuracy in the SNIPS dataset further indicates that the token-level intent prediction can improve the performance of intent detection as it can reduce the predicted variance [14].

5 Conclusion

In this paper, we propose an Interactive Two-pass Decoding Network (ITD-Net) for joint intent detection and slot filling. The ITD-Net explicitly models the token-level interactions between the intent and slots and implements bilateral guidance between the two tasks by carrying out an interactive two-pass decoding process. Experiments on the ATIS and SNIPS datasets show the superiority of our ITD-Net. In the future, we plan to incorporate powerful pre-trained language models such as BERT to further boost the model performance.

Acknowledgments. This paper is supported by National Key Research and Development Program of China under Grant No.2017YFB0803003 and National Science Foundation for Young Scientists of China (Grant No.61702507).

References

1. Bahdanau, D., Cho, K., Bengio, Y.: Neural machine translation by jointly learning to align and translate. In: Proceedings of the 3rd International Conference on Learning Representations (ICLR) (2015)
2. Chen, Q., Zhuo, Z., Wang, W.: Bert for joint intent classification and slot filling. arXiv preprint arXiv:1902.10909 (2019)

3. Coucke, A., et al.: Snips voice platform: an embedded spoken language understanding system for private-by-design voice interfaces. arXiv preprint arXiv:1805.10190 (2018)
4. Devlin, J., Chang, M.W., Lee, K., Toutanova, K.: Bert: pre-training of deep bidirectional transformers for language understanding. In: Proceedings of the 17th Annual Conference of the North American Chapter of the Association for Computational Linguistics: Human Language Technologies (NAACL) (2019)
5. E, H., Niu, P., Chen, Z., Song, M.: A novel bi-directional interrelated model for joint intent detection and slot filling. In: Proceedings of the 57th Annual Meeting of the Association for Computational Linguistics (ACL), pp. 5467–5471 (2019)
6. Goo, C.W., et al.: Slot-gated modeling for joint slot filling and intent prediction. In: Proceedings of the 16th Annual Conference of the North American Chapter of the Association for Computational Linguistics: Human Language Technologies, pp. 753–757 (2018)
7. Hemphill, C.T., Godfrey, J.J., Doddington, G.R.: The atis spoken language systems pilot corpus. In: Speech and Natural Language: Proceedings of a Workshop Held at Hidden Valley, Pennsylvania (1990)
8. Hochreiter, S., Schmidhuber, J.: Long short-term memory. Neural Comput. 9(8), 1735–1780 (1997)
9. Kingma, D.P., Ba, J.: Adam: a method for stochastic optimization. In: Proceedings of the 3rd International Conference on Learning Representations (ICLR) (2015)
10. Li, C., Li, L., Qi, J.: A self-attentive model with gate mechanism for spoken language understanding. In: Proceedings of the 2018 Conference on Empirical Methods in Natural Language Processing (EMNLP), pp. 3824–3833 (2018)
11. Liu, B., Lane, I.: Attention-based recurrent neural network models for joint intent detection and slot filling. In: Proceedings of the 17th Annual Conference of the International Speech Communication Association (INTERSPEECH) (2016)
12. Liu, B., Lane, I.: Joint online spoken language understanding and language modeling with recurrent neural networks. In: Proceedings of the 17th Annual SIGdial Meeting on Discourse and Dialogue (SIGDIAL) (2016)
13. Mesnil, G., et al.: Using recurrent neural networks for slot filling in spoken language understanding. IEEE/ACM Trans. Audio Speech Lang. Process. 23(3), 530–539 (2015)
14. Qin, L., Che, W., Li, Y., Wen, H., Liu, T.: A stack-propagation framework with token-level intent detection for spoken language understanding. In: Proceedings of the 2019 Conference on Empirical Methods in Natural Language Processing (2019)
15. Ravuri, S., Stolcke, A.: Recurrent neural network and lstm models for lexical utterance classification. In: Proceedings of the 16th Annual Conference of the International Speech Communication Association (INTERSPEECH) (2015)
16. Sarikaya, R., Hinton, G.E., Ramabhadran, B.: Deep belief nets for natural language call-routing. In: Proceedings of the 2011 IEEE International Conference on Acoustics, Speech, and Signal Processing (ICASSP), pp. 5680–5683 (2011)
17. Tur, G., De Mori, R.: Spoken Language Understanding: Systems for Extractingsemantic Information from Speech. John Wiley & Sons, Hoboken (2011)
18. Tur, G., Hakkani-Tür, D., Heck, L.: What is left to be understood in atis. In: Proceedings of the 2010 IEEE Spoken Language Technology Workshop (SLT), pp. 19–24 (2010)
19. Vaswani, A., et al.: Attention is all you need. In: Proceedings of the Advances in Neural Information Processing Systems (NIPS), pp. 5998–6008 (2017)

20. Wang, Y., Shen, Y., Jin, H.: A bi-model based rnn semantic frame parsing model for intent detection and slot filling. In: Proceedings of the 16th Annual Conference of the North American Chapter of the Association for Computational Linguistics: Human Language Technologies (NAACL) (2018)
21. Yao, K., Peng, B., Zweig, G., Yu, D., Li, X., Gao, F.: Recurrent conditional random field for language understanding. In: Proceedings of the 2014 IEEE International Conference on Acoustics, Speech and Signal Processing, pp. 4077–4081 (2014)
22. Zhang, C., Li, Y., Du, N., Fan, W., Yu, P.S.: Joint slot filling and intent detection via capsule neural networks. In: Proceedings of the 57th Annual Meeting of the Association for Computational Linguistics (ACL) (2019)
23. Zhang, X., Wang, H.: A joint model of intent determination and slot filling for spoken language understanding. In: Proceedings of the 25th International Joint Conference on Artificial Intelligence (IJCAI), vol. 16, pp. 2993–2999 (2016)

RuKBC-QA: A Framework for Question Answering over Incomplete KBs Enhanced with Rules Injection

Qilin Sun[1,2](✉) and Weizhuo Li[3]

[1] Academy of Mathematics and Systems Science and Key Lab-MADIS, Chinese Academy of Sciences, Beijing 100190, China
`sunqilin@amss.ac.cn`
[2] School of the Mathematical Sciences, University of Chinese Academy of Sciences, Beijing 100049, China
[3] School of Modern Posts and Institute of Modern Posts, Nanjing University of Posts and Telecommunications, Nanjing 210003, China
`liweizhuo@amss.ac.cn`

Abstract. The incompleteness of the knowledge base (KB) is one of the key issues when answering natural language questions over an incomplete knowledge base (KB-QA). To alleviate this problem, a framework, RuKBC-QA, is proposed to integrate methods of rule-based knowledge base completion (KBC) into general QA systems. Three main components are included in our framework, namely, a rule miner that mines logic rules from the KB, a rule selector that selects meaningful rules for QA, and a QA model that aggregates information from the original knowledge base and the selected rules. Experiments on WEBQUESTIONS dataset indicate that the proposed framework can effectively alleviate issues caused by incompleteness and obtains a significant improvement in terms of micro average Fl score by 2.4% to 4.5% under different incompleteness settings.

Keywords: Question answering · Incomplete knowledge base · Knowledge base completion

1 Introduction

Open-domain question answering (QA) over knowledge base (KB), also known as KB-based question answering (KB-QA), is a hot topic and has attracted massive attention recently. Most state-of-the-art approaches based on the assumption that evidence required to answer questions has existed in the KB completely. However, it is insufficient to cover full evidence required by open-domain questions due to inevitable incompleteness and restricted schema of the KB [1]. As illustrated in Fig. 1, it's easy to answer the question "What is the name of Justin Bieber's brother?" by utilizing evidence that Justin Bieber has a sibling relation with Jaxon Bieber. However, the question would turn to be non-trivial if

© Springer Nature Switzerland AG 2020
X. Zhu et al. (Eds.): NLPCC 2020, LNAI 12431, pp. 82–94, 2020.
https://doi.org/10.1007/978-3-030-60457-8_7

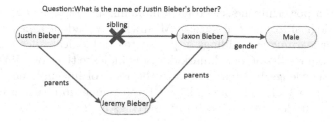

Fig. 1. An example for answering the question "What is the name of Justin Bieber's brother?".

the link between Justin Bieber and Jaxon Bieber is missing. Some researchers utilize textual evidence to alleviate this issue [1,2]. Nevertheless, textual evidence is not always accessible.

Knowledge base completion (KBC) aims to infer missing facts using existing information in the knowledge base. Various techniques have been devised for this task, such as rule-based approaches [3,4] and embedding-based approaches [5,6]. The effectiveness of KBC motivates us to explore its potential for enhancing the performances of QA over incomplete KBs by inferring missing evidence. In this paper, rule-based approach is adopted for two reasons. On the one hand, results in the work [7] show that rules with high confidences can cover a significant fraction of the test cases. On the other hand, confidences of rules are powerful priors about the quality of inferred facts.

A naive option is to take state-of-the-art KBC methods to infer missing facts firstly, then execute the process of QA as usual. Figure 1 shows how a rule-base KBC system would work for the question mentioned above in this naive option. Specifically, a logical rule like "people who have the same parent are siblings" could infer the missing sibling relation between Justin Bieber and Jaxon Bieber. Although straightforward, it is still a nontrivial task to exploit facts inferred by KBC. Because both rule-based and embedding-based approaches for KBC tasks usually infer missing facts that are very likely (but not necessarily) hold, e.g., "The spouses very likely have the same nationalities." The major challenge for utilizing works of KBC to enhance QA is how to reduce noises introduced during inferring missing facts.

To address this challenge, we propose a framework to integrate methods of **rule-based** knowledge base completion into general **question answering** systems, called RuKBC-QA. Firstly, we utilize a rule miner to extract massive logic rules from the KB automatically. Then, we design a rule selector to select meaningful rules for QA. This rule selector is conducted by estimating scores of rules and logical forms of questions alternately. Finally, we inject selected rules into a general QA system through aggregating information from the original KB and selected rules. The contributions of our study are summarized as follows.

– We propose a novel paradigm of QA over an incomplete KB that integrates methods of rule-based KBC into general QA systems. To the best of our knowledge, this is the first work that focuses on the impact of KBC to QA over an incomplete KB.

- We design a powerful rule selector via modeling interactions between logical rules and logical forms of questions. Meanwhile, we adopt a new mechanism tailored for learning embeddings of predicates and logical rules jointly.
- Experimental results on benchmark datasets indicate that logical rules mined from the knowledge base can alleviate the issue of incompleteness, and the proposed framework yields a significant improvement in terms of micro average F1 score under various incomplete settings by 2.4% to 4.5%.

2   Related Work

Our work is related to two research topics, the first one is question answering over knowledge base (KB-QA), the other one is knowledge base completion (KBC).

The mainstream methods for KB-QA fall into two major categories: semantic parsing and information retrieval. Semantic parsing based approaches [8,9] learn parsers which parse questions into its logical forms and then query knowledge base to obtain answers from KB. Information retrieval based approaches [10–12] collect a set of candidate answers and then select the final answers by analyzing the low-dimensional representations for questions and candidate answers. Nevertheless, most methods focus on the case where the KB is sufficient to cover the full evidence required for QA. Recently, several works [1,2,13] utilize textual evidence to improve QA over incomplete KBs. Although fusing evidence from multi-sources is effective, textual evidence is not always accessible. Adversely, we aim to boost the performance of QA over incomplete KBs through exploiting methods in KBC, namely, structure information in the KB.

KBC refers to the task of automatically predicting missing facts based on existing ones in the KB. Various techniques have been devised for this task, which can be roughly divided into two groups: rule-based and embedding-based. Rule-based approaches first learn logical rules and then infer missing facts by instantiating rules against existing facts. Methods of this kind focus on rule learning from KBs, which include First-Order Inductive Learner (FOIL) [3,14], differentiable learning [4], etc. The second group learns low-dimensional vector representations for entities and predicates in KBs [5,6]. The representations are leveraged to infer missing facts via mathematical operation of vectors. While successful in addressing different issues, methods in KBC introduce noise inevitably. Therefore, we design a metric to measure gains of rules for the QA task and select rules using question answer pairs to reduce the noise introduced.

3   Background

This paper focuses on the knowledge bases $\mathcal{K}$ that is a collection of triples (e_1, p, e_2), where $e_1, e_2 \in \mathcal{E}$ are the entities (e.g., Justin Bieber) and $p \in \mathcal{P}$ is a binary predicate (e.g., sibling). For compatibility with symbols of logical rules, we denote (e_1, p, e_2) as $p(e_1, e_2)$. We employ Freebase [15] to illustrate the proposed framework.

We consider *Horn rules* in this paper. A Horn rule R is an expression of the form $\mathbf{B} \Rightarrow p(x,y)$, where $p(x,y)$ is the head or conclusion of the rule, and $\mathbf{B}$ is a sequence of atoms $p_1(x_1,y_1),\dots,p_m(x_m,y_m)$ called the body, e.g., $parents(x,z), parents(y,z) \Rightarrow sibling(x,y)$. An *instantiation* of R means that all variables in R have been substituted by concrete entities in $\mathcal{E}$. A *prediction* of R is the instantiated head if all the instantiated atoms in the body exists in KB. For instance, if relations $parents$(Justin Bieber, Jeremy Bieber) and $parents$(Jaxon Bieber, Jeremy Bieber) hold, $sibling$(Justin Bieber, Jaxon Bieber) is a prediction of the rule mentioned above. We denote predictions of R w.r.t. $\mathcal{K}$ as $Pr(R, \mathcal{K})$, and the predictions of a set of rules $\mathcal{R}$ w.r.t. $\mathcal{K}$ as $\mathcal{K}_{\mathcal{R}}^{+} = \cup_{R \in \mathcal{R}} Pr(R, \mathcal{K})$. Then, the complemented knowledge base can be expressed by $\mathcal{K}_{\mathcal{R}} = \mathcal{K}_{\mathcal{R}}^{+} \cup \mathcal{K}$. Note that a rule miner usually associates each rule R with a confidence level $\lambda_R \in [0,1]$ since mined rules may not be consistent with all the facts in $\mathcal{K}$. Rules with higher confidence levels are more likely to hold. For convenience, we further group rules by their heads and donate all rules whose head predicate is p as $\mathcal{R}_p = \{R | R \in \mathcal{R}, \text{The head of } R \text{ is } p\}$. Rules that can infer the fact $p(e_1, e_2)$ are denoted by $I(p, e_1, e_2)$. Therefore, each inferred fact in $\mathcal{K}_{\mathcal{R}}^{+}$ corresponds to a set of rules.

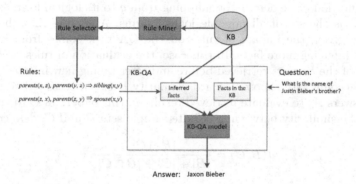

Fig. 2. A overview of proposed framework for question answering over an incomplete knowledge.

4   Framework

This work is aimed to improve the performance of KB-QA systems by inferring missing facts using rules mined from the knowledge base $\mathcal{K}$. We focus on KB-QA systems which is trained through a set of question-answers pairs $D = \{(q, A_q)\}$, where q and A_q are the question and corresponding answers, respectively. As illustrated in Fig. 2, our approach consists of three key components:

1. *Rule miner* mines a set of logic rules $\mathcal{R}$ from the available triplets in $\mathcal{K}$ automatically, e.g., $parents(z, x), parents(z, y) \Rightarrow spouse(x, y)$. We employ AMIE+, a successful rule miner, because AMIE+ calculates partial

completeness assumption (PCA) based confidence level. The PCA based confidence level is not only a powerful priori about the quality of the rule, but also more suitable than the standard one in a web-extracted KB (e.g., Freebase) designed under an open-world assumption.

2. *Rule selector* evaluates each rule in $\mathcal{R}$ and select rules which are considered helpful for QA. We utilize the selected rules $\mathcal{R}_s$ to infer missing facts in knowledge base.

3. *KB-QA model* takes a neural language question q, the origin knowledge base $\mathcal{K}$ and inferred facts as input, and then outputs answers.

4.1   Rule Selector

The core of rule selection is evaluating the impact of rules on the QA task. The facts inferred by selected rules need to be not only less noisy but also related to QA task. In KB-QA, a question is usually assumed to be associated with an unknown logical form. This logical form can be translated to a query on the knowledge base, and the retrieved results identify with answers to the question. In this part, we firstly discuss interactions between rules and logical forms, then present an iterative algorithm to evaluate rules.

For a question q, we denote the mapping from q to its logical form as $L(q) \in \mathcal{L}$, where $\mathcal{L}$ is the set of all possible logical forms. Assuming that the golden mapping is given, the impact of rules on the QA task comes from enriching answers by inferring more facts. In this case, the evaluation of rules becomes an evaluation of the answers retrieved before and after taking new inferred facts by rules into account. We choose Jaccard similarity between retrieved results and correct answers A_q to evaluate retrieved results in this paper. Jaccard similarity measures the similarity between two finite sample sets B and C, defined as

$$J(B, C) = \frac{|B \cap C|}{|B| + |C| - |B \cap C|} \tag{1}$$

For a logical form $l \in \mathcal{L}$, let the answers retrieved before and after the injection of a single rule R are $Q(l, \mathcal{K})$ and $Q(l, \mathcal{K}, R)$ respectively. We compute the gain of R as:

$$\mathrm{gain}(R|L(q), q) = J(Q(L(q), KB, R), A_q) - J(Q(L(q), KB), A_q) \tag{2}$$

In the above equation, we get the gain of R under the conditions of $L(q)$ and q, because the rule R only works during retrieving the KB if $L(q)$ is known. We define the score of R as the average conditional scores on all questions in training data D, namely:

$$\mathrm{gain}(R) = \frac{1}{|D|} \sum_{q \in D} \mathrm{gain}(R|L(q), q) \tag{3}$$

However, the mapping from question q to its logical form is unknown even in train data. Researchers calculate the confidence whether a logical form is correct for question q by evaluating retrieved results as mentioned above. Namely, for a logical form $l \in \mathcal{L}$,

$$\text{conf}(l|q, \mathcal{K}) = J(Q(l, \mathcal{K}), \; A_q) \tag{4}$$

Although it's simple over a complete knowledge base, calculating confidences over an incomplete knowledge base is not an easy task. The missing facts would lead to incorrect estimates of the logical form. For example, the right logical form for question q may get a zero score due to missing facts. Rules can alleviate this problem by inferring some missing facts. If facts inferred by rules are accurate, the confidence of l becomes

$$\text{conf}(l|q, \mathcal{K}, \mathcal{R}) = J(Q(l, \mathcal{K}_\mathcal{R}), \; A_q) \tag{5}$$

In the case of inaccurate rules, we exploit the confidence levels of rules to estimate $\text{conf}(l|q, KB, \mathcal{R})$. We first assign a truth value to the fact $p(e_1, e_2) \in \mathcal{K}_\mathcal{R}$ as:

$$\pi(p, e_1, e_2) = \begin{cases} 1 & \text{if } p(e_1, \; e_2) \in \mathcal{K} \\ max(\{\lambda_R | R \text{ can infer the fact } p(e_1, \; e_2)) & otherwise \end{cases} \tag{6}$$

Then we utilize t-norm based fuzzy logics [16] to model the truth value of retrieved answer for l. Namely, the truth value of a retrieved answer is estimated as a composition of the truth values of its constituent triples. In this work, we only consider triples in the logical form are connected by logical conjunction, which is computed as $\pi(a \wedge b) = \pi(a) \bullet \pi(b)$. It is enough to cover most of the correct logical forms in popular QA benchmarks, like WebQuestions [17] and ComplexQuestions [18]. So each retrieved answer is assigned a score $\pi(a|l, \mathcal{K}_\mathcal{R})$. Then we estimate $\text{conf}(l|q, \mathcal{K}, \mathcal{R})$ as:

$$\text{conf}(l|q, \mathcal{K}, \mathcal{R}) = \frac{\displaystyle\sum_{a \in Q(l, \mathcal{K}_\mathcal{R}) \cap A_q} \pi(a|l, \mathcal{K}_\mathcal{R})}{|A_q| + \displaystyle\sum_{a \in Q(l, \mathcal{K}_\mathcal{R})} \pi(a|l, \mathcal{K}_\mathcal{R}) - \displaystyle\sum_{a \in Q(l, \mathcal{K}_\mathcal{R}) \cap A_q} \pi(a|l, \mathcal{K}_\mathcal{R})} \tag{7}$$

By substituting J with its definition in Eq. 1, we know that Eq. 5 is a specialization of Eq. 7 when confidences of all rules equal to 1. In Eq. 3, we assume $L(q)$ is given. We modify this equation to Eq. 8 for handling uncertainty of $L(q)$.

$$\text{gain}(R) = \frac{1}{|D|} \sum_{q \in D} \sum_{l \in \mathcal{L}} \text{conf}(l|q, \mathcal{K}, \mathcal{R}) * \text{gain}(R|l, q) \tag{8}$$

We select rules with gain greater than 0, namely, $\mathcal{R}_s = \{R|R \in \mathcal{R} \text{ and gain}(R) > 0\}$.

Because both the selected rules and logical forms for questions are hidden, we iteratively calculate $\text{conf}(l|q, \mathcal{K}, \mathcal{R})$ and $\text{gain}(R)$ using Eqs. 7 and 8. Namely, we assume that $\text{gain}(R)$ is known when we calculate $\text{conf}(l|q, \mathcal{K}, \mathcal{R})$ and vice versa. Algorithm 1 summarizes the iterative estimation of logical forms and mined rules.

Algorithm 1: Rule Selector

Require: knowledge base $\mathcal{K}$, mined rules $\mathcal{R}$, possible logical forms $\mathcal{L}$, labeled
   question and answer pairs $D = (q, A_q)$
Ensure: selected rules $\mathcal{R}_s$
 1: $\mathcal{R}_s^0 \leftarrow \mathcal{R}, i \leftarrow 0$
 2: **repeat**
 3:   $i \leftarrow i + 1, \mathcal{R}_s^i \leftarrow \emptyset$
 4:   **for** each question $q \in D$ **do**
 5:     **for** each logic form $l \in \mathcal{L}$ **do**
 6:       compute conf$(l|q, \mathcal{K}, \mathcal{R})$ using equation 7
 7:     **end for**
 8:   **end for**
 9:   **for** each rule $R \in \mathcal{R}$ **do**
10:     compute gain(R) using equation 8
11:     add R to $\mathcal{R}_s^i$ if gain$(R) > 0$
12:   **end for**
13: **until** $\mathcal{R}_s^i = \mathcal{R}_s^{i-1}$

4.2   Inject Rules into KB-QA Model

Our proposed framework is universal and can be integrated into many existing
KB-QA Systems. We illustrate step by step below on how to inject selected rules
into information extraction based models for the KB-QA task. The information
extraction based QA models first retrieve candidate answers for questions, then
project questions and candidate answers into a unified low-dimensional space
and finally measure their matching scores by calculating similarities between
their low-dimensional representations. There are two key points in information
extraction based models: (i) How to represent the question? (ii) How to represent
entities in the knowledge base? Figure 3 shows the architecture we adopt to learn
representations of questions and answers.

Candidate Generation. For each question q, we use the entity linking tool
S-MART [19] to identify named entities in the question. The tool can generate a
score for each named entity. We use the one with the highest score as the topic
entity of question, denoted as e. After getting the topic entity, we collect all the
entities connected to it directly or connected with paths of length 2 when the
middle existential variable can be grounded to a compound value type (CVT)
node (CVT node is not a real-world entity, which is used to collect multiple
fields of an event.). These entities constitute the candidate set for the question
q, denoted as C_q.

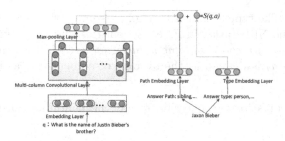

Fig. 3. The architecture used to learn representations of questions and answers.

Representations of Questions. We employ the multi-column convolutional neural networks (MCCNNs) [11] to learn fixed-length representations for questions. As shown in Fig. 3, we use two separate convolutions to learn different aspects of questions, one for paths from the candidate answer to the topic entity and the other one for types of the candidate answer. We ignored the context information used in [11] because we found that the context information had little effect in our experiments and make the learned model vary large. For question $q = w_1, \ldots, w_n$, we first look up a word embedding matrix $E_w \in \mathbb{R}^{d \times v_w}$ to transform every word into a vector, where d is the dimension of the embeddings and v_w denotes the vocabulary size of natural language words. Then, the embeddings are fed into two separate convolutional layers, each followed by a max-pooling layer that extracts the most salient local features to form a fixed-length vector. We denote the two fixed-length vector as $f_1(q), f_2(q)$, respectively.

Answer Representation. Corresponds to the representations of questions, we directly learn two embedding vectors for each candidate answer $a \in C_q$:

1. *Answer Path.* We assign an embedding matrix $E_p^k \in \mathbb{R}^{d_k \times v_p}$ for predicates in the knowledge base and an embedding matrix $E_R^k \in \mathbb{R}^{d_k \times |\mathcal{R}_s|}$ for selected rules, where d_k is the dimension of embeddings and v_p is the number of predicates. In the previous work [10,11], answer path representation is the average of embeddings assigned to predicates between the candidate answer a and the topic entity e in q. Additionally, if the fact $p(e_1, e_2)$ is missing but connected by selected rules in $\mathcal{R}_s$, we utilize the average embeddings of rules that can infer $p(e_1, e_2)$, namely, rules in $I(p, e_1, e_2)$ (defined in Sect. 3). Through learning different embeddings for predicates and rules, the model can distinguish between predicates and rules and identify meaningful rules. Formally, the embedding of fact $p(e_1, e_2)$ is represented as:

$$f_p = \begin{cases} E_p^k & \text{if } p(e_1, \ e_2) \in \mathcal{K} \\ ave_{R \in I(p,e_1,e_2)} E_R^k & \text{if } p(e_1, \ e_2) \in \mathcal{K_R} - \mathcal{K} \end{cases}$$

Then, the answer path embedding $g_1(a)$ is defined as the average of embeddings assigned to facts between the candidate answer a and the topic entity e in q.

2. *Answer Type.* The type of an entity, e.g., person, carries very useful information for various NLP tasks. In Freebase, entities and their types are associated using predicate *common.topic.notable_types*. As in [11], the answer type embedding $g_2(a)$ is defined as the average of embeddings assigned to types of a.

The matching scores for the question q and the candidate answer a is computed as:

$$S(q, a) = f_1(q) \cdot g_1(a) + f_2(q) \cdot g_2(a)$$

Training. By identifying correct answers in the candidate set, we divide the candidate set into two parts, namely, correct answer set P_q and incorrect answer set N_q. During training, we randomly sample k incorrect answers $a' \in N_q$ as negative instances for each correct answer $a \in P_q$. The loss function for pairs (q, a) and (q, a') is given as:

$$loss(q, a, a') = max\{0, \lambda - S(q, a) + S(q, a')\}, \text{ where } \lambda > 0$$

Inference. In the inference stage, we calculate score $S(q, a)$ for every candidate answer a in C_q. Then we compute the highest scores S_q^{max}. We use an auxiliary threshold to determine whether a candidate should be adopted. The final answer set is calculate as:

$$\hat{A}_q = \{a | S_q^{max} - S(q, a) < \tau) \text{ and } a \in C_q\}, \text{ and } S_q^{max} = max_{a \in C_q} S(q, a)$$

where τ is a threshold that is estimated on the development data.

5   Experiments

5.1   Setup

Dataset and Experimental Settings. We evaluate our system on the WebQuestions dataset [17], which contains 3,778 question-answer pairs for training and 2,032 for testing. These questions are crawled via Google Suggest API, and their answers are obtained from Freebase. We split the training instances into the training set and the development set by 80%/20%. To make Freebase fit in memory, we only keep the triples where one of the entities appears in either the WebQuestions training/development set or in ClueWeb extractions [20], which is similar to the preprocessing in [10,11].

To evaluate the robustness of our QA systems across different degrees of KB completeness, we follow the settings of [1], where facts in the KB is downsampled to various degrees. Specifically, we downsample facts to 10%, 30%, and 50% of the original to simulate KB with different degrees of completeness. For each setting, we treat these downsampled facts as the input of AMIE+ [3] to extract logical rules. To make the extraction more efficient, we only consider rules with less than 3 atoms in the body. We find that inverse equivalence rules dominate the task of knowledge base completion, which is verified similar cases in [7]. However, inferring missing facts using these trivial rules may overestimate the performance of our framework in real-world scenarios. Therefore, we remove inverse equivalence rules in our experiments.

We initialize the word embeddings with Stanford's publicly available 50-dimensional Glove vectors [21]. The development set is used for tuning the hyperparameters in our model and early stopping of training. The window size of MCCNNs is 5. The dimension of each column of convolutional layers and the dimension of answer embeddings are set to 64. The margin parameter λ in loss function is set to 0.5.

Evaluation Metric and Baselines. We re-implement the original MCCNN method from [11] as the baseline. To provide an in-depth analysis of the function of rules, we consider the following variations of the original MCCNN:

- **MCCNN.** This is the original MCCNNs only utilizes downsampled facts.
- **MCCNN-LM.** To clarify that the inferred facts are useful for QA over incomplete KB, rules with a high confidence level are used to infer missing facts. In this case, **MCCNN** use additional facts inferred by rules only at inference time, namely, merging inferred facts in the inference stage (late merge).
- **MCCNN-EM.** In addition to **MCCNN-LM**, the inferred facts are used at both training and inference time (early merge) to verify whether the early merging of inferred facts is helpful or not.
- **RuKBC-QA.** This is our proposed framework that employs the proposed rule selector to select rules automatically and jointly learn embeddings of predicates in the KB and mined rules.

Rules in **MCCNN-LM** and **MCCNN-EM** are filtered by a confidence threshold tuned on the development set. We adopt the micro average F1 score as our evaluation metric.

5.2   Results and Discussion

Main Results. We show the micro average F1 scores under different incomplete settings in Table 1. Overall, **MCCNN-EM** and **MCCNN-LM** perform better than the original **MCCNN**. And our proposed **RuKBC-QA** obtains a considerable improvement in terms of micro average F1 score by 2.4% to 4.5% when the KB is incomplete, which outperforms all the baselines with a significant gap. The results indicate that merging additional facts inferred by rules is valuable when the KB is incomplete. Early fusion of those additional facts performs better than late fusion. The proposed **RuKBC-QA** equipped with a well-designed rule selector and joint embeddings of predicates and logical rules further boost the performances. It is worth mentioning that the rules are selected automatically in

Table 1. Comparisons with baseline models under various incompleteness settings.

Methods	10% KB	30% KB	50% KB	100% KB
	F1	F1	F1	F1
MCCNN	7.0	19.7	28.0	**41.9**
MCCNN-LM	8.2	21.5	29.4	41.9*
MCCNN-EM	8.8	22.6	30.0	41.9*
RuKBC-QA	**9.4**	**23.7**	**32.5**	41.6
RuKBC-QA w/o joint learning	**9.4**	23.1	31.8	41.0

*As the tuned threshold for confidence level is 1, the model reduce to the original MCCNN.

our model, while **MCCNN-EM** and **MCCNN-LM** need to tune the thresholds on the development set. We also observe that our model benefits most when the completeness of the KB is moderate. This is because more rules are mined as the KB completeness increases, and the negative impact of noises introduced by rules increases at the same time. Under the full setup, **RuKBC-QA** drops the performance slightly due to noise introduced by selected rules.

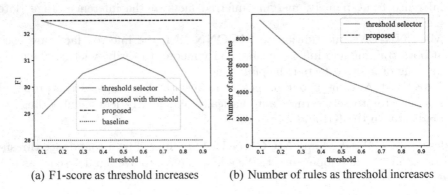

(a) F1-score as threshold increases   (b) Number of rules as threshold increases

Fig. 4. The comparison of our proposed selector with a threshold-based one in various thresholds.

Impact of Rule Selector. In this part, we illustrate our selector is superior to the one utilizing a threshold to filter mined rules in both performance and time consumption. We conduct experiments under the setting 50% sampling rate, and substitute our selector by the threshold-based with various confidence thresholds.

As shown in Fig. 4(a), the proposed rule selector outperforms the threshold-based selector under all threshold configurations. The performance of the threshold-based selector is sensitive to the choice of threshold. A higher threshold will reduce the number of mined rules, while a lower one might introduce incredible rules. Both of them can not obtain the ideal performance for KB-QA. We further combine our proposed selector with the threshold-based one to check whether our proposed selector can benefit from an elaborate threshold. We apply the proposed selector on rules filtered by a confidence threshold without changing other components in our framework. The result is tagged with "proposed with threshold" in Fig. 4(a). We discover that the performance will decrease as the threshold increases, which indicates that the proposed selector can effectively filter several noise rules. Besides, the sharp deterioration when the threshold is higher than 0.7 shows that models benefit the most from high-quality rules.

The time consuming of rule-based inference varies dramatically with specific questions and implementations of rule reasoners. However, the inference time is proportional to the number of selected rules which does not depend on the specific question and the reasoner implementation. Therefore, we compare the time consumption by counting the number of selected rules. As shown in Fig. 4(b), our proposed selector only needs far fewer rules than the threshold-based one.

Impact of Joint Learning. To study the effect of joint learning embeddings of predicates and logical rules, we perform experiments by substituting embeddings of a rule with embeddings of its head (see the last row in Table 1). As shown in Table 1, joint learning embeddings of predicates and logical rules lead to better performance.

6   Conclusion and Future Work

This paper investigates question answering over an incomplete knowledge base. A novel framework is proposed to integrate methods of rule-based knowledge base completion into general QA systems which enables the question answering system to utilize missing facts inferred by mined rules. Meanwhile, a powerful rule selector is introduced to reduce noisy facts inferred by rules, and a mechanism for leveraging information from origin knowledge base and rules. Our experiments reveal two main conclusions. (i) Rule-based knowledge base completion can boost the performance of question answering over incomplete KB by inferring missing facts. (ii) The framework further improves the performance with a significant gap under various incomplete settings.

Future work will focus on extending the system to cover both rule-based methods and embedding-based methods in knowledge base completion. Furthermore, integrating text evidence into our framework will also be considered.

Acknowledgement. This work is supported by National Key Research and Development Program of China under grant 2016YFB1000902; And NSFC Project No. 61472412 and No. 61621003.

References

1. Sun, H., Dhingra, B., Zaheer, M., Mazaitis, K., Salakhutdinov, R., Cohen, W.W.: Open domain question answering using early fusion of knowledge bases and text. In: EMNLP, pp. 4231–4242 (2018)
2. Xiong, W., Yu, M., Chang, S., Guo, X., Wang, W.Y.: Improving question answering over incomplete KBs with knowledge-aware reader. In: ACL, pp. 4258–4264 (2019)
3. Galarraga, L., Teflioudi, C., Hose, K., Suchanek, F.M.: Fast rule mining in onto-logical knowledge bases with AMIE+. VLDB J. **24**(6), 707–730 (2015)
4. Omran, P.G., Wang, K., Wang, Z.: Scalable rule learning via learning representation. In: IJCAI, pp. 2149–2155 (2018)
5. Bordes, A., Usunier, N., Garcia-Duran, A., Weston, J., Yakhnenko, O.: Translating embeddings for modeling multi-relational data. In: NIPS, pp. 2787–2795 (2013)
6. Schlichtkrull, M., Kipf, T.N., Bloem, P., van den Berg, R., Titov, I., Welling, M.: Modeling relational data with graph convolutional networks. In: Gangemi, A., et al. (eds.) ESWC 2018. LNCS, vol. 10843, pp. 593–607. Springer, Cham (2018). https://doi.org/10.1007/978-3-319-93417-4_38
7. Meilicke, C., Fink, M., Wang, Y., Ruffinelli, D., Gemulla, R., Stuckenschmidt, H.: Fine-grained evaluation of rule- and embedding-based systems for knowledge graph completion. In: Vrandečić, D., et al. (eds.) ISWC 2018. LNCS, vol. 11136, pp. 3–20. Springer, Cham (2018). https://doi.org/10.1007/978-3-030-00671-6_1
8. Yih, W., Chang, M.-W., He, X., Gao, J.: Semantic parsing via staged query graph generation: question answering with knowledge base. In: ACL, pp. 1321–1331 (2015)
9. Cheng, J., Reddy, S., Saraswat, V.A., Lapata, M.: Learning an executable neural semantic parser. Comput. Linguist. **45**(1), 59–94 (2019)
10. Bordes, A., Chopra, S., Weston, J.: Question answering with subgraph embeddings. In: EMNLP, pp. 615–620 (2014)
11. Dong, L., Wei, F., Zhou, M., Xu, K.: Question answering over freebase with multi-column convolutional neural networks. In: ACL, pp. 260–269 (2015)
12. Jain, S.: Question answering over knowledge base using factual memory networks. In: NAACL, pp. 109–115 (2016)
13. Das, R., Zaheer, M., Reddy, S., McCallum, A.: Question answering on knowledge bases and text using universal schema and memory networks. In: ACL, pp. 358–365 (2017)
14. Schoenmackers, S., Etzioni, O., Weld, D.S., Davis, J.: Learning first-order horn clauses from web text. In: EMNLP, pp. 1088–1098 (2010)
15. Bollacker, K.D., Evans, C., Paritosh, P., Sturge, T., Taylor, J.: Freebase: a collab-oratively created graph database for structuring human knowledge. In: SIGMOD, pp. 1247–1250 (2008)
16. Hájek, P.: Metamathematics of Fuzzy Logic, vol. 4. Springer, Dordrecht (2013)
17. Berant, J., Chou, A., Frostig, R., Liang, P.: Semantic parsing on freebase from question-answer pairs. In: EMNLP, pp. 1533–1544 (2013)
18. Bao, J.-W., Duan, N., Yan, Z., Zhou, M., Zhao, T.: Constraint-based question answering with knowledge graph. In: COLING, pp. 2503–2514 (2016)
19. Yang, Y., Chang, M.W.: S-MART: novel tree-based structured learning algorithms applied to tweet entity linking. In: Proceedings of ACL, pp. 504–513 (2015)
20. Lin, T., Etzioni, O., et al.: Entity linking at web scale. In: AKBC-WEKEX, pp. 84–88 (2012)
21. Pennington, J., Socher, R., Manning, C.D.: GloVe: global vectors for word repre-sentation. In: EMNLP, pp. 1532–1543 (2014)

Syntax-Guided Sequence to Sequence Modeling for Discourse Segmentation

Longyin Zhang[1,2], Fang Kong[1,2(✉)], and Guodong Zhou[1,2]

[1] Institute of Artificial Intelligence, Soochow University, Suzhou, China
`lyzhang9@stu.suda.edu.cn`, {`kongfang,gdzhou`}`@suda.edu.cn`
[2] School of Computer Science and Technology, Soochow University, Suzhou, China

Abstract. Previous studies on RST-style discourse segmentation have achieved impressive results. However, recent neural works either require a complex joint training process or heavily rely on powerful pre-trained word vectors. Under this condition, a simpler but more robust segmentation method is needed. In this work, we take a deeper look into intra-sentence dependencies to investigate if the syntax information is totally useless, or to what extent it can help improve the discourse segmentation performance. To achieve this, we propose a sequence-to-sequence model along with a GCN based encoder to well utilize intra-sentence dependencies and a multi-head biaffine attention based decoder to predict EDU boundaries. Experimental results on two benchmark corpora show that the syntax information we use is significantly useful and the resulting model is competitive when compared with the state-of-the-art.

Keywords: EDU segmentation · GCN model · Syntax information

1 Introduction

As a representative linguistic theory about discourse structure, Rhetorical Structure Theory (RST) [14] segments each sentence into a sequence of elementary discourse units (EDUs), as shown in Fig. 1. Under this theory, both the English RST Discourse Treebank (RST-DT) [2] and the Chinese Discourse Treebank (CDTB) [12] are annotated. The past decade has witnessed the progress in RST parsing [13,18,24]. Since EDUs are bottom-level units in RST-style discourse trees, discourse segmentation (i.e., EDU segmentation), which aims at determining EDU boundaries, is crucial to the overall performance.

Early works on EDU segmentation mainly focus on feature-based methods [9,20] which are time consuming and labor-intensive. Recently, neural models are proposed to better capture lexical semantics with distributed representations. Among them, Wang et al. [23] propose an end-to-end segmenter based on the LSTM-CRF framework. Li et al. [11] propose to use the pointer network to solve the problem of sparse boundary tags. Most recently, Lin et al. [13] employ the same model as Li et al. [11] and improve the segmentation performance through the joint learning with sentence-level discourse parsing. However,

© Springer Nature Switzerland AG 2020
X. Zhu et al. (Eds.): NLPCC 2020, LNAI 12431, pp. 95–107, 2020.
https://doi.org/10.1007/978-3-030-60457-8_8

the aforementioned works are mainly concerned with lexical semantics and rely on powerful pre-trained word vectors. In this work, we aim at investigating to what extent the intra-sentence syntax information can help improve discourse segmentation. In the literature, Braud et al. [1] first demonstrate that shallow syntax features are not that effective in EDU segmentation. However, statistics show that a great percentage of EDU boundaries are directly related to the dependents of root units in structure. With this in mind, we take a deeper look into intra-sentence dependencies to figure out the effect of syntax information in EDU segmentation. Besides, there exit segmentation works on English, Spanish, German and so on, but studies on Chinese are much less. With the release of CDTB corpus, more and more works [8,21,24] have been proposed on Chinese parsing, which calls for a generic segmentation model for different languages.

In this work, we seek further improvements on EDU segmentation to help reduce error propagation in RST-style discourse parsing [17]. Inspired by [11], we propose a sequence-to-sequence model to first encode the input text for N-gram and syntactic information and then decode the sequence to obtain EDU boundaries. In particular, we integrate a GCN model into the sentence encoder to better leverage dependency structures for sentence encoding and equip the decoder with a deep multi-head biaffine attention for EDU boundary determination. To obtain a generic segmentation model for different languages, we conduct several experiments on both RST-DT and CDTB corpora to examine the effect of our proposed approach. Experimental results show that the syntax information we use is useful and the resulting model is competitive when compared with the state-of-the-art (SOTA) works in EDU segmentation.

[Mr. Gonzalez said]$_{EDU}$ [several senators told him]$_{EDU}$ [that they "could get some road blocks out of the way]$_{EDU}$ [if there could be some understanding on Garn's insistence on Wall."]$_{EDU}$

[一九六零年，年仅五岁的马友友首次公开演出，]$_{EDU}$ [一鸣惊人，]$_{EDU}$ [自此跻身音乐大师之列。]$_{EDU}$

Fig. 1. Examples of EDU segmentation in both English and Chinese.

2 EDU Segmentation Model

The proposed segmentation model mainly consists of two stages: (i) the syntax-guided sentence encoding and (ii) the biaffine attention based EDU boundary decoding. Among them, the sentence encoding stage aims at equipping the word unit representation with lexical, contextual, and dependency structure information. While the biaffine attention based decoder is utilized to control the EDU boundary determination process. For clarity, we use a sample sentence with $n = 6$ words in Fig. 2 to illustrate the proposed model architecture.

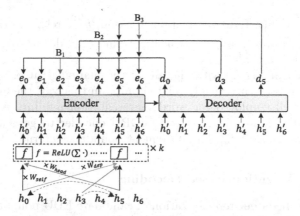

Fig. 2. The encoder-decoder architecture of the proposed syntax-guided EDU segmentation model. The partial dependency structure is shown with dash lines at the bottom, where the *head* and *dep* indicate that the edge is directed along or opposite the dependency arc, and the *self* denotes that the edge is a self-loop one.

2.1 Syntax-Guided Sentence Encoding

Formally, given an input sentence, we get its distributed representation $U = [u_1, \ldots, u_n]$ by concatenating the word embeddings and POS tag embeddings. Since the input text is sequential in format, we simply employ L layers of bidirectional GRUs to generate context-aware word representation as

$$[h_1, \ldots, h_n] = \mathbf{BiGRU}^{(L)}(U, \theta) \tag{1}$$

Our ultimate goal in this part is to fuse explicit syntax information into sentence representation. This is done by employing intra-sentence dependency structures to refine the obtained context-aware word vectors. Theoretically, a fake root is usually added in dependency structures and only one word is the dependent of the root which we refer to as *root-dep*. For the convenience of computation, we manually add a zero vector, h_0, at the start of the input sequence in Fig. 2 to serve as the root unit. To clearly illustrate the architecture of the encoder, we build partial dependency structures between h_0, h_3 and h_5 for example, as shown in Fig. 2.

Formally, given a unit g, the edge set $E(g)$ contains all the units connected to g including the unit g itself. Inspired by [16], we employ a mapping table $M(g, g')$, where $g' \in E(g)$, to determine whether the edge $\langle g, g' \rangle$ is directed (a) along, (b) opposite, or (c) is a self-loop one (e.g.., the edge $\langle h_5, h_0 \rangle$ is directed along the dependency arc). After k layers of GCNs, the final representation of the given unit g is formulated as

$$h_g^{'(k)} = f\Big(\sum_{g' \in E(g)} W_{M(g,g')}^{(k-1)} h_{g'}^{'(k-1)} + b^{(k-1)} \Big) \tag{2}$$

where $f(\cdot)$ denotes the ReLU activation function, $h_g^{'(0)}$ refers to the previously obtained context-aware word vector in Eq. 1, and $h_g^{'(k)}$ denotes the refined representation of the unit g.

As illustrated in Fig. 2, with the aid of the mapping table, information is shared between those syntactically related units. In this way, the explicit syntax information is well employed for word representation refining. After that, we take the refined vectors as input to a BiGRU encoder to generate candidate EDU boundaries, $[e_0, \ldots, e_n]$, for subsequent boundary determination.

2.2 Biaffine Attention Based Decoding

After achieving the latent representation of candidate EDU boundaries, we take the previously refined word vectors, $[h'_0, \ldots, h'_n]$, as input to our uni-directional GRU decoder and obtaining

$$\tilde{d} = \overrightarrow{e}_n \oplus \overleftarrow{e}_n \tag{3}$$

$$d_t = \mathbf{GRU}(h'_t, \theta) \tag{4}$$

where $\tilde{d}$ denotes the concatenation of last hidden states in both directions of the previous encoder which also serves as the initial state of the decoder, h'_t and d_t refer to the input and output of the decoder at the t-th time step.

During the pointing phase, we compute the attention [5] scores between the decoder output d_t and the encoder outputs corresponding to the candidate EDU boundaries (i.e., $e_m = \{e_i | t \leq i \leq n\}$). Since the deep biaffine attention mechanism can strip away irrelevant information before attention computation, we apply two multi-layer perceptrons before the biaffine classifier. And the attention score is computed as

$$e'_m = \mathbf{MLP}^{(\mathrm{enc})}(e_m) \tag{5}$$

$$d'_t = \mathbf{MLP}^{(\mathrm{dec})}(d_t) \tag{6}$$

$$A_t = e'_m \mathbf{U} d'_t + e'_m \mathbf{u} \tag{7}$$

where N is the number of candidate boundaries, $e'_m \in \mathbb{R}^{N \times D_1}$, $d'_t \in \mathbb{R}^{D_2}$ are outputs of the two MLPs, $\mathbf{U} \in \mathbb{R}^{D_1 \times D_2}$, $\mathbf{u} \in \mathbb{R}^{D_1}$ are model parameters, and $A_t \in \mathbb{R}^{N \times 1}$ denotes the attention weights assigned to candidate boundaries.

Here, the pointing phase is basically completed. However, due to the utilization of GCN based hierarchical encoder, the representation of input sequences usually consists of varied information (lexical, syntactic and contextual information) while the original attention mechanism only focuses on a specific component of the representation. Inspired by Chen et al. [4], we tackle this problem by extending the pointing phase to a multi-head way as

$$\mathbf{A}_t = \sum_{k=1}^{K} (e'_m \mathbf{U}^{(k)} d'_t + e'_m \mathbf{u}^{(k)}) / K \tag{8}$$

where $\mathbf{U}^{(k)} \in \mathbb{R}^{D_1 \times D_2}$ and $\mathbf{u}^{(k)} \in \mathbb{R}^{D_1}$ are model parameters of the k-th biaffine attention module, $\boldsymbol{A}_t \in \mathbb{R}^{N \times 1}$ is the averaged weights assigned to the N candidate units. In this way, the final averaged attention weight is a integrated result with different aspects taken into consideration.

At this point, the overall structure of the segmentation model permits continuous EDU boundary detection. For the example in Fig. 2, given the decoder outputs d_0, d_3 and d_5, the boundaries e_2, e_4 and e_6 are picked out in turn.

2.3   Model Training with Similarity Penalization

To optimize our supervised discriminative segmentation model, we employ the negative log-likelihood loss (NLL Loss) in this work to maximize the probability of selecting the correct EDU boundary at each decoding step.

In particular, we aim at reducing the redundancy of the multi-head attention and encouraging the diversity between those attention vectors mentioned in Sect. 2.2. To achieve this, we add an additional penalization term to the loss function to maximize the cosine distance between each two attention vectors. And the general loss objective at the t-th decoding step is detailed as

$$\mathcal{L}(\Theta) = \mu \sum_{k=1}^{K} \sum_{l=k+1}^{K} \cos(\boldsymbol{A}_t^{(k)}, \boldsymbol{A}_t^{(l)}) - \log(\hat{p}_{i,t}) + \frac{\lambda}{2} \|\Theta\|^2 \qquad (9)$$

where Θ denotes the set of model parameters, μ is a balancing parameter, λ is the l_2 regularization parameter, and $\hat{p}_{i,t}$ estimates the conditional probability of selecting the correct EDU boundary i at the t-th decoding step.

3   Experimentation

3.1   Data and Metrics

RST-DT. The RST-DT corpus annotates 385 articles from the Wall Street Journal. It is divided into a training set of 347 articles (6846 sentences) and a test set of 38 articles (870 sentences). Following previous studies, we use the 10% data of the shuffled training set as the development corpus.

CDTB. Motivated by the Penn Discourse Treebank and the Rhetorical Structure Theory, Li et al. [12] propose the Connective-driven Dependency Tree (CDT) scheme and manually annotate a Chinese Discourse Treebank (CDTB) with 500 Xinhua newswire documents. For supervised learning, the corpus is divided into a training set of 425 documents (4058 sentences), a test set of 50 documents (487 sentences) and a development set of 25 documents (200 sentences).

To avoid the overestimate of segmentation performance, following previous works [11,13], we evaluate the proposed segmenter with respect to sentence-internal EDU boundaries. We measure the **Precision**, **Recall** and **F₁**-score for segmentation performance. For fair comparison, all scores we report in this paper are micro-averaged ones.

3.2 Experimental Settings

We employed the 300D word embeddings provided by GloVe [19] and the People's Daily News for RST-DT and CDTB respectively, and did not fine-tune the pre-trained vectors during training. For preprocessing, we used the Stanford CoreNLP toolkit [15] and the pyltp toolkit for English and Chinese respectively to obtain POS tags and intra-sentence dependency structures.

We optimized the following hyper-parameters during training: for both corpora, the learning rate is 0.001, the dropout rate is 0.2, the hidden size of GRUs is set by 200, and the layer numbers of GRUs and GCNs in the sentence encoder are set by 3 and 1 respectively. The hidden size of MLPs in the deep biaffine attention is set to 64 and 256 for RST-DT and CDTB respectively. We use the Adam optimizer with an l_2 (10^{-5}) regularization term to minimize the loss objective. For both corpora, we train the segmentation model iteratively on the training set by 15 rounds and the batch size is set by 20. The segmentation system is implemented with PyTorch framework and the codes will be published at https://github.com/NLP-Discourse-SoochowU/EDU_Segmentation.

3.3 Overall Experimental Results

In this paper, we compare with previous SOTA works on two benchmark corpora, i.e., the English RST-DT corpus and the Chinese CDTB corpus. For RST-DT, we compare with four strong baseline systems using the same evaluation metric. Among them, Lample et al. [10] propose an LSTM-CRF model for sequence labeling. Wang et al. [23] propose an end-to-end segmenter using a self-attention based LSTM-CRF model. Li et al. [11] propose a sequence-to-sequence segmentation model using the pointer network. Most recently, Lin et al. [13] employ the same model as Li et al. [11] and further improve the performance by joint learning with sentence-level discourse parsing.

Nevertheless, existing works mainly focus on the popular RST-DT corpus, while for the under-developed Chinese CDTB corpus, there are few relevant publications. Under this condition, we duplicate the segmentation model of Lample et al. [10] and Li et al. [11] in this work to serve as strong baseline systems. The overall results are detailed in Table 1. From the overall experimental results we can find that,

- Comparing the two different experimental settings (i.e., with and without intra-sentence dependencies), the utilization of dependency structures can significantly improve the segmentation performance on both corpora. And this suggests the effectiveness of our approach of utilizing explicit syntax information to discourse segmentation.
- Moreover, to clarify the effectiveness of the syntax information, we compare with other works depending on context-aware semantics without using those powerful pre-trained word vectors. The results show that our proposed method achieves the best performance without using any hand-crafted features.

Table 1. Comparison with previous works on both RST-DT and CDTB corpora. Superscript * indicates the model is superior to Li et al. [11] with a *p-value* ≤ 0.05 and † denotes the duplicated systems.

	Method	P	R	F_1
EN	Lample et al. [10]	89.1	87.8	88.5
	Wang et al. [23]	87.9	84.5	86.2
	Li et al. [11]	91.6	92.8	92.2
	Lin et al. [13]	90.6	92.3	91.4
	Ours (without dep)	92.7	90.9	91.8
	Ours (with dep)	**92.8***	**92.9***	**92.9***
CH	Lample et al. [10] †	90.9	92.1	91.2
	Li et al. [11] †	92.0	92.1	92.1
	Ours (without dep)	90.7	91.1	90.9
	Ours (with dep)	**93.3***	**93.0***	**93.2***

Table 2. Comparison with the SOTA work using contextualized word vectors.

Method	P	R	F_1
Lin et al. [13]	94.1	96.6	95.3
Ours	94.1	95.9	95.1

Recent years have witnessed the effectiveness of contextualized word representation in many NLP tasks, and the SOTA EDU segmenter also employs ELMo to boost the segmentation performance. For reference, we follow the principle of "control variates" to compare with the model of Lin et al. [13] without using their "Joint Training" method, as shown in Table 2. As expected, the results show that our model achieves results similar to theirs.

3.4 Effect of Model Depth

In practice it has been observed that increasing the scale of deep learning, with respect to the model depth (or model parameters), the number of training instances, or both, can drastically improve ultimate classification performance. Therefore, we perform several additional experiments to test the effect of our model w.r.t. the depth of our hierarchical sentence encoder.

To better illustrate this, we give two sets of comparisons with respect to the layer number of GRUs (shown in Table 3) and GCNs (shown in Table 4) respectively. The results in Table 3 indicate that multi-layer GRUs in the sentence encoder is effective in both corpora and the segmentation model achieves the best performance when the layer number equals to 3. Accordingly, Table 4 reports the segmentation performance with respect to the layer number of GCNs. Comparing the first two rows, the GCN model we use can significantly improve

Table 3. Performance comparison with respect to the layer number of GRU.

Layer number	RST-DT	CDTB
1	90.6	91.3
2	92.0	91.8
3	**92.9**	**93.2**
4	91.4	**93.2**
5	91.6	92.7

Table 4. Performance comparison with respect to the layer number of GCN.

Layer number	RST-DT	CDTB
0	91.3	90.9
1	**92.9**	**93.2**
2	92.2	92.1
3	91.8	93.1

the performance of EDU segmentation in both corpora, and this improvement is especially evident in the Chinese corpus. Furthermore, comparisons between the second row and the last two rows show that integrating multi-layer GCNs into the sentence encoder does not show any further improvements in the experiments. On the whole, the overall results above indicate that a multi-layer GRU encoder along with GCNs can well capture intra-sentence dependencies and thus strengthen the sentence representation learning for EDU segmentation.

3.5   Effect of Multi-head Biaffine Attention

To illustrate the effectiveness of the multi-head biaffine attention mechanism, we give another group of comparison with respect to the number of attention heads, as shown in Table 5. The experimental results show that our proposed segmentation model achieves great performance in both corpora when the head number equals to two. Comparing the first row with the last two rows, an interesting phenomenon is revealed that the performances of our model on P, R, and F_1 are more stable when a multi-head attention is leveraged. This means that with the multi-head pointing phase, the proposed model no longer blindly pursues the improvement of F_1 score but develops a balanced development of recall and precision. On the whole, the experimental results indicate that the multi-head attention we use is useful for EDU segmentation in both corpora.

Table 5. Performance comparison with respect to the number of the multi-head biaffine attention heads.

Head number	RST-DT			CDTB		
	P	R	F_1	P	R	F_1
1	91.8	92.7	92.2	92.7	91.9	92.3
2	**92.8**	**92.9**	**92.9**	**93.3**	**93.0**	**93.2**
3	92.5	92.4	92.4	92.5	92.7	92.6

4 Case Study

To qualitatively illustrate the robustness of our model, we give two visualization examples of EDU segmentation, as shown in Fig. 3. From the example, the sentence "When they did, his commanders didn't have the initiative to do more than block a couple of roads." in Fig. 3(a) is segmented into three EDUs step by step and the boundaries colored in red are assigned with significant weights. Although the word "more" is also assigned with relatively high boundary weights (i.e., 7.6 and 1.1), the proposed model can still avoid mistaking it for an EDU boundary. Furthermore, we randomly select a Chinese segmentation example in Fig. 3(b) for comparison. From the examples, both English and Chinese EDU boundaries are assigned with extremely high weights. Differently, punctuations like "," are more probable to be EDU boundaries in Chinese, and this language phenomenon can be easily found in the CDTB corpus.

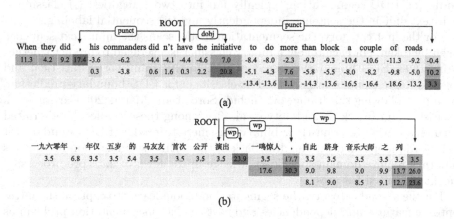

Fig. 3. Visualization of EDU segmentation for examples in both English and Chinese. EDU boundaries in both examples are colored in red. Following Tesnière [22], the dependency arcs we provide point from heads to dependents. (Color figure online)

To study the correlation between the EDU segmentation process and the syntactic information we use, we give another analysis about the randomly selected

Table 6. The proportion of EDU boundaries syntactically related to *root-dep* units.

	RST-DT	CDTB
Proportion	60.7%	37.9%

examples in Fig. 3. In dependency structure, a fake root is usually added and only one word is the dependent of the root, which we refer to as the *root-dep* unit (e.g.., the word "have" in Fig. 3(a)). Intuitively, we draw partial dependency structure between EDU boundaries and *root-dep* units for the two examples respectively. And the partial dependency structures in both examples reveal an interesting language phenomenon that those words identifying EDU boundaries are direct dependents of *root-dep* units. Scrupulously, we further display the proportion of EDU boundaries related to *root-dep* units in Table 6, and the results show that this language phenomenon is common in both corpora. Under the conduction of explicit dependency structures, those text units serving as dependents of *root-dep* units are well equipped with "hints" for EDU boundary determination. Hence, we have reason to believe that the refining method we use is stable and useful for RST-style discourse segmentation for languages like English and Chinese.

5   Related Work

Conventionally, given a sentence, the segmentation model identifies EDU boundaries and segments input sentences into EDU sequences. In general, previous studies on EDU segmentation typically fall into two categories: (i) classifying each text unit in the sentence independently and (ii) sequential labeling.

For the first category, the segmentation model scans the input text sequence token by token. For each token, a binary classifier is leveraged to predict whether to insert an EDU boundary after it or not. In this framework, statistical and Logistic Regression models are used as classifiers for EDU boundary prediction. Examples following this framework include Sorcuit and Marcu [20], Carlson et al. [3], Fisher and Roark [7] and Joty et al. [9]. Among these studies, hand-crafted features are used to train their binary classifiers to predict EDU boundary for each word independently. The drawback of these EDU segmentation methods is that they require domain-specific knowledge in the form of data pre-processing and hand-crafted features.

For the second category, the segmentation model learns to capture the intra-sentence features and dependencies and cast the EDU segmentation problem as a sequence labeling task. Following this framework, Feng and Hirst [6] propose a CRF based discourse segmentation model with some hand-crafted features. In last few years, recurrent neural networks with CRF output layer achieved SOTA performance in many sequence labeling tasks [10,23]. However, EDU segmentation suffers from the problem of tags sparsity which has limited the performance of CRF models. Recently, sequence-to-sequence neural models [11] are employed to alleviate this problem. Lin et al. [13] employ the same model as Li et al. [11]

and further improve the segmentation performance with contextualized word representation and the joint learning strategy.

In the literature, varied studies [6,20] have demonstrated the usefulness of syntax information in EDU segmentation. However, the recent study [1] proves that hand-crafted syntax features are less useful than expected. In this case, we take a deeper look into intra-sentence dependencies to investigate if the syntax information is totally useless, or to what extent it can help improve the segmentation performance. Moreover, the methods mentioned above are all implemented in the English discourse corpus, but in other languages like Chinese, there are few related works on. In this work, our segmentation model falls into the second category, where a sequence-to-sequence model with a deep multi-head biaffine attention is leveraged for EDU segmentation. In particular, we employ a GCN model in the work to better utilize intra-sentence dependencies. It is worth mentioning that, we perform experiments on both RST-DT and CDTB corpus to obtain a generic model for different languages.

6 Conclusion

In this paper, we propose a sequence-to-sequence model along with a deep multi-head biaffine attention for RST-style discourse segmentation. In particular, we use a GCN model to well leverage dependency structures for word unit representation enhancing. Experimental results on two benchmark corpora show that our approach of utilizing syntax information is effective and our final syntax-guided segmentation model is competitive when compare with the state-of-the-art. We will extend EDU segmentation to discourse parsing in our future work.

Acknowledgments. The authors would like to thank the anonymous reviewers for the helpful comments. We also thank Xin Tan for her helpful discussions. This work is supported by Artificial Intelligence Emergency Project 61751206 under the National Natural Science Foundation of China, Project 61876118 under the National Natural Science Foundation of China and the Priority Academic Program Development of Jiangsu Higher Education Institutions.

References

1. Braud, C., Lacroix, O., Søgaard, A.: Does syntax help discourse segmentation? not so much. In: Proceedings of EMNLP2017, pp. 2432–2442. Association for Computational Linguistics, Copenhagen, Denmark (2017)
2. Carlson, L., Marcu, D.: Discourse tagging reference manual. ISI Technical report ISI-TR-545 54, 56 (2001)
3. Carlson, L., Marcu, D., Okurovsky, M.E.: Building a discourse-tagged corpus in the framework of rhetorical structure theory. In: van Kuppevelt, J., Smith, R.W. (eds.) Current and New Directions in Discourse and Dialogue. Text, Speech and Language Technology, vol. 22, pp. 85–112. Springer, Dordrecht (2003). https://doi.org/10.1007/978-94-010-0019-2_5

4. Chen, Q., Ling, Z.H., Zhu, X.: Enhancing sentence embedding with generalized pooling. In: Proceedings of the 27th COLING, pp. 1815–1826. Association for Computational Linguistics, Santa Fe, New Mexico, USA (2018)
5. Dozat, T., Manning, C.D.: Deep biaffine attention for neural dependency parsing. In: Proceedings of ICLR 2017 (2017)
6. Feng, V.W., Hirst, G.: Two-pass discourse segmentation with pairing and global features. arXiv preprint arXiv:1407.8215 (2014)
7. Fisher, S., Roark, B.: The utility of parse-derived features for automatic discourse segmentation. In: Proceedings of the 45th ACL, pp. 488–495. Association for Computational Linguistics, Prague, Czech Republic (2007)
8. Jia, Y., Feng, Y., Ye, Y., Lv, C., Shi, C., Zhao, D.: Improved discourse parsing with two-step neural transition-based model. ACM Trans. Asian Low-Resour. Lang. Inf. Process. (TALLIP) **17**(2), Article no. 11 (2018)
9. Joty, S., Carenini, G., Ng, R.T.: CODRA: a novel discriminative framework for rhetorical analysis. Am. J. Comput. Linguist. **41**(3), 385–435 (2015)
10. Lample, G., Ballesteros, M., Subramanian, S., Kawakami, K., Dyer, C.: Neural architectures for named entity recognition. In: Proceedings of the 2016 Conference of the NAACL: Human Language Technologies, pp. 260–270. Association for Computational Linguistics, San Diego, California (2016)
11. Li, J., Sun, A., Joty, S.: SegBot: a generic neural text segmentation model with pointer network. In: Lang, J. (ed.) Proceedings of the 27th IJCAI, pp. 4166–4172. International Joint Conferences on Artificial Intelligence (2018)
12. Li, Y., Feng, W., Sun, J., Kong, F., Zhou, G.: Building Chinese discourse corpus with connective-driven dependency tree structure. In: Proceedings of EMNLP2014, pp. 2105–2114. Association for Computational Linguistics, Doha, Qatar (2014)
13. Lin, X., Joty, S., Jwalapuram, P., Bari, M.S.: A unified linear-time framework for sentence-level discourse parsing. In: Proceedings of the 57th ACL, pp. 4190–4200. Association for Computational Linguistics, Florence, Italy (2019)
14. Mann, W.C., Thompson, S.A.: Rhetorical structure theory: toward a functional theory of text organization. Text-Interdisc. J. Study Discourse **8**(3), 243–281 (1988)
15. Manning, C., Surdeanu, M., Bauer, J., Finkel, J., Bethard, S., McClosky, D.: The Stanford CoreNLP natural language processing toolkit. In: Proceedings of 52nd ACL: System Demonstrations, pp. 55–60. Association for Computational Linguistics, Baltimore, Maryland (2014)
16. Marcheggiani, D., Titov, I.: Encoding sentences with graph convolutional networks for semantic role labeling. In: Proceedings of EMNLP2017, pp. 1506–1515. Association for Computational Linguistics, Copenhagen, Denmark (2017)
17. Marcu, D.: The Theory and Practice of Discourse Parsing and Summarization. MIT Press, Cambridge (2000)
18. Morey, M., Muller, P., Asher, N.: How much progress have we made on RST discourse parsing? A replication study of recent results on the RST-DT. In: Proceedings of EMNLP2017, pp. 1319–1324. Association for Computational Linguistics, Copenhagen, Denmark (2017)
19. Pennington, J., Socher, R., Manning, C.: Glove: global vectors for word representation. In: Proceedings of EMNLP2014, pp. 1532–1543. Association for Computational Linguistics, Doha, Qatar (2014)
20. Soricut, R., Marcu, D.: Sentence level discourse parsing using syntactic and lexical information. In: Proceedings of the 2003 Human Language Technology Conference of NAACL, pp. 228–235 (2003)
21. Sun, C., Kong, F.: A transition-based framework for Chinese discourse structure parsing. J. Chin. Inf. Process. **32**(12), 26–34 (2018)

22. Tesnière, L.: Eléments de syntaxe structurale. Klincksieck (1959)
23. Wang, Y., Li, S., Yang, J.: Toward fast and accurate neural discourse segmentation. In: Proceedings of EMNLP2018, pp. 962–967. Association for Computational Linguistics, Brussels, Belgium (2018)
24. Zhang, L., Xing, Y., Kong, F., Li, P., Zhou, G.: A top-down neural architecture towards text-level parsing of discourse rhetorical structure. In: Proceedings of the 58th ACL, pp. 6386–6395. Association for Computational Linguistics, Online (2020)

Macro Discourse Relation Recognition via Discourse Argument Pair Graph

Zhenhua Sun, Feng Jiang, Peifeng Li, and Qiaoming Zhu[✉]

School of Computer Science and Technology, Soochow University, Suzhou, China
{zhsun7016,fjiang}@stu.suda.edu.cn, {pfli,qmzhu}@suda.edu.cn

Abstract. Most previous studies used various sequence learning models to represent discourse arguments, which not only limit the model to perceive global information, but also make it difficult to deal with long-distance dependencies when the discourse arguments are paragraph-level or document-level. To address the above issues, we propose a GCN-based neural network model on discourse argument pair graph to transform discourse relation recognition into a node classification task. Specifically, we first convert discourse arguments of all samples into a heterogeneous text graph that integrates word-related global information and argument-related keyword information. Then, we use a graph learning method to encode argument semantics and recognize the relationship between arguments. The experimental results on the Chinese MCDTB corpus show that our proposed model can effectively recognize the discourse relations and outperforms the SOTA model.

Keywords: Macro discourse relation · Discourse argument pair graph · Graph convolutional network

1 Introduction

In recent years, the focus of many natural language processing (NLP) applications shifts from the clause-level or sentence-level shallow semantic analysis (e.g., traditional lexical, syntactic analysis, and semantic role labeling) to discourse analysis that requires deep semantic understanding. Compared with sentence-level, discourse analysis as a larger granularity of text analysis has gradually become a NLP research hotpot.

Discourse analysis is to analyze the internal structure of natural texts and recognize the semantic relationship between discourse arguments [1]. According to the granularity of discourse arguments, discourse analysis can be divided into two levels: micro-level and macro-level. The micro-level discourse analysis focuses on sentences and sentence groups, while the macro-level focuses on paragraphs and chapters. Discourse analysis studies texts from both structural and semantic perspectives, and can be widely used in various NLP applications, including question answering [2], automatic summarization [3], sentiment analysis [4], and information extraction [5].

Generally, discourse analysis consists of three sub-tasks, namely structure construction, nuclearity identification, and relation recognition. The task of relation recognition

X. Zhu et al. (Eds.): NLPCC 2020, LNAI 12431, pp. 108–119, 2020.
https://doi.org/10.1007/978-3-030-60457-8_9

is to determine how two adjacent discourse arguments are connected semantically. In principle, the discourse connectives between discourse arguments play a decisive role in relation recognition. According to whether there is a connective between discourse arguments, discourse relations are divided into explicit and implicit. For explicit relation recognition, due to the presence of connectives, simple rule-based methods can achieve satisfactory performance. For implicit relation recognition, the lack of connectives poses a huge challenge to this task. Thus, it is important to grasp the semantics expressed by discourse arguments to identify discourse relations better.

In Chinese, there are few connectives that indicate semantic relations between macro-level discourse arguments (paragraphs). Therefore, Chinese macro discourse relations can be regarded as implicit relations [6]. In this paper, we focus on recognizing macro discourse relations in Chinese. As shown in Fig. 1, an example from the Macro Chinese Discourse Treebank [7] illustrates the macro discourse relations.

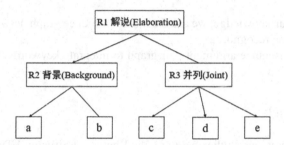

Fig. 1. The macro discourse tree of chtb_0019 in MCDTB.

According to the text of chtb_0019 (see Appendix), the overall topic is "the construction of Ningbo Free Trade Zone has achieved fruitful results". Paragraph *a* is the subject paragraph due to it is consistent with the overall topic. Paragraph *b* tells the basic situation of Ningbo Free Trade Zone and forms the background of the incident mentioned in paragraph *a*. The three paragraphs *c*, *d*, and *e* describe the detailed process of the incident described in paragraph *a* from the aspects of import and export trade, implementation of policies, and enterprise operating mechanisms. Therefore, these three paragraphs constitute a *Joint* relation internally, and an *Elaboration* relation with paragraphs *a* and *b* externally. In Fig. 1, leaf nodes (*a–e*) are elementary discourse arguments (EDUs), and internal nodes are discourse arguments (DUs), representing the discourse relation between two children.

Compared with micro-level, macro-level discourse arguments (that contain one or more paragraphs) are longer and have various internal expression forms. These characteristics pose a huge challenge to the semantic modeling of macro discourse arguments. Whether it is a semantic representation method based on word vectors or a sequence learning method such as LSTM, CNN, etc., it will be powerless when dealing with long texts such as macro discourse arguments. In addition, Chinese is a paratactic language, and recognizing Chinese discourse relations relies more on the deep semantics of discourse arguments, especially the topical coherence. In most cases, only using discourse arguments themselves cannot provide enough semantic information for Chinese discourse relation recognition. Furthermore, we need the global semantic clues of the topic behind discourse arguments [8].

Compared with the traditional model and sequence learning model, the graph-based neural network method can directly process complex structural data and retain global information to better learn long-distance dependence. Yao et al. [17] applied a graph-based learning method to text classification, which achieved better performance. They treated a single text as a document node and learned the representation of the node through document-word edge. However, this method can't be directly transferred into discourse relation recognition that is a pairwise task. Therefore, we expand this method and build a discourse argument pair graph to learn the difference and connection between discourse arguments, which are not reflected in the original method. Experimental results show that our method can effectively identify the discourse relations. The main contributions are summarized as following:

- To the best of our knowledge, we are the first to introduce graph networks to Chinese discourse relation recognition.
- We propose a discourse argument pair graph to integrate keywords information and global information.

2 Related Work

In English, most previous studies based on the Rhetorical Structural Theory Discourse Treebank (RST-DT) [9] and the Penn Discourse Treebank (PDTB) [10]. RST-DT [9] annotates 385 documents from the Wall Street Journal using the RST tree scheme and contains more than 20 types of rhetorical relations. PDTB [10] is another discourse corpus with 2312 annotated documents from the Wall Street Journal and contains many types of relations. Two corpora do not explicitly distinguish between micro-level and macro-level discourse relation. On the RST-DT, Li et al. [12] proposed attention-based hierarchical neural networks to encode arguments for discourse parsing. On the PDTB, Bai and Zhao [13] proposed a deep enhanced representation to represent arguments at the character, sub-word, word and sentence levels for relation recognition.

In Chinese, most previous studies based on the Chinese Discourse Treebank (CDTB) [11] and the Macro Chinese Discourse Treebank (MCDTB) [7]. CDTB [11] annotates 500 documents and 17 discourse relations, which is a micro-level corpus. MCDTB [7] is only available macro Chinese discourse corpus using RST-style including the structure, nuclearity, and relation, which currently annotates 720 news documents and contains 3 categories that further clustered into 15 sub-relations. On the micro-level, Xu et al. [8] applied a topic model to learn topic-level representation of arguments for relation recognition. On the macro level, Zhou et al. [6] proposed a traditional macro discourse relation recognition model, which combines macro semantic representation based on word vectors and structural features of discourse arguments to fill the gap in macro discourse research. With the popularity of deep learning, Jiang et al. [14] proposed a neural network model based on the gating mechanism for identifying macro discourse relationships. The model first encodes the discourse arguments through LSTM and attention mechanism, and then uses topic gating and structure gating to filter the arguments semantic representation to recognize relations.

3   GCN-Based Neural Network on Discourse Argument Pair Graph

In this paper, we focus on recognizing discourse relation between macro discourse arguments in Chinese. Macro discourse arguments have complex long-range dependencies, and recognizing their relations relies more on the deep semantics of discourse arguments, especially on global information such as topical coherence. To solve the problems suffered from long-distance dependence and lack of global information, we propose a GCN-based Neural Network model on Discourse Argument pair Graph (DAGGNN) and the overall architecture of the model is shown in Fig. 2.

Firstly, we calculate TF-IDF of the argument-word pair and point-by-point mutual information (PMI) of the word-word pair in the corpus. Then we construct the discourse argument pair graph to learn the semantic representation of the arguments and fuse the global information. This graph contains the aforementioned two kinds of information: the keyword information (TF-IDF) and the global information (PMI). The keyword information TF-IDF serves as a priori attention information, allowing the model to place emphasis on words that are important to arguments. The global information PMI derives from the global words co-occurrence that represents the semantic link between words, enabling the model to learn topic coherence between arguments. In addition, we apply the graph convolutional network [15] on the established graph to learn the semantic representation of arguments with global information. Finally, a multi-layer perceptron is introduced to learn the semantic matching between arguments and complete the discourse relation recognition.

3.1   Discourse Argument Pair Graph

First, we give the task definition of discourse relation recognition. Based on the number of arguments, the discourse relations can be divided into binary relations and multiple relations. Following previous work [6, 14], we convert multiple relations into binary relations. Finally, the task of discourse relation recognition turns into the task of classification of discourse argument pair. That is, given the discourse arguments *arg1* and *arg2*, this task is to recognize the relation between them. In this section, we will introduce the details of building the discourse argument pair graph, including node representation, edge link, and graph construction.

Node Representation. A discourse argument is a sequence of words $arg = \{w_1, w_2, \ldots, w_m\}$. In the discourse argument pair graph that we construct, there are three kinds of nodes, namely the *arg1* node, *arg2* node and *w* word node. The argument node *arg1* and *arg2* respectively represents two arguments in a sample holding a specific relation. The word node *w* refers to a word that appears in the corpus. We decompose each sample that is a form of (*arg1*, *arg2*, *relation*) into two argument nodes *arg1* and *arg2* in the graph, because we found that treating each sample as a document node is not a suitable choice in the preliminary experiments, which cannot fully reflect the semantic difference and connection between *arg1* and *arg2*. Thus, our graph consists of argument nodes of all samples and all word nodes, and it is built on the entire corpus.

We use the *word2vec* [16] to pre-train word embedding on a large-scale Chinese corpus to initialize the representation of nodes. Compared with one-hot encoding in Yao et al. [17], word embedding method not only alleviates the cold start problem, but also brings more accurate word semantics. Extensive experiments have proved that pre-trained word embedding is beneficial to many NLP tasks [19, 20]. For each word w_i, we represent it as a vector e_i. We also represent each argument arg_i as a vector e_arg_i by averaging the vectors of words it contains.

Edge Link. As mentioned above, there are word nodes and argument nodes in the graph. Therefore, we need to establish three kinds of edges among these nodes: word-word edge, arg-word edge and self-loop edge.

Word-Word Edge. We construct "word-word" edges based on the global word co-occurrence in a corpus. The global word co-occurrence can be explicitly used in arguments representation learning. Specifically, we use PMI metric to measure the global word co-occurrence on all arguments with a fixed-size sliding window. Formally, given the word pair $\langle i, j \rangle$, the PMI is calculated as follows:

$$PMI(i, j) = \log \frac{p(i, j)}{p(i) * p(j)} \tag{1}$$

$$p(i, j) = \frac{\#W(i, j)}{\#W} \tag{2}$$

$$p(i) = \frac{\#W(i)}{\#W} \tag{3}$$

where $\#W$ is the total number of sliding windows in all arguments, and $\#W(i)$ is the number of sliding windows that contain the word i in all arguments. $\#W(i, j)$ is the number of sliding windows containing the word pairs $\langle i, j \rangle$ and $\langle j, i \rangle$ in all arguments. Generally, a positive PMI value means that there is a high semantic correlation between two words. Thus, we only build edges between words with positive PMI values, and use the PMI value as the weight of the "word-word" edge.

Arg-Word Edge. We establish an edge between the argument node and the word nodes it contains. We construct "argument-word" edges based on the importance of words in arguments, and use the TF-IDF values as the weight of the "argument-word" edges. TF-IDF is similar to prior attention, which can make the model focus on important words of arguments. TF is the frequency of occurrence of words in the argument; IDF is the frequency of the inverse document after log normalization. When counting IDF, we treat each argument as a document. In the way, we not only retain all word information in the argument, but also increase the proportion of important words in the argument node representation.

Self-loop Edge. Following previous work [15, 17], we add self-loop edges to the argument nodes *arg1*, *arg2* and the word node *w*. In this way, the nodes not only pay attention to the information transmitted by the surrounding nodes, but also retain the information they have learned.

Graph Construction. We extend the single-text graph construction method of Yao et al. [17] in the argument pair task, and establish a large heterogeneous text graph G named Discourse Argument Pair Graph on the entire corpus. We use a notation χ to represent the dataset contains t samples: $\chi = \{x_1, x_2, x_3, \ldots\ldots x_t\}$. Formally, the adjacency matrix A of the graph G is defined as follows, where i, j are nodes.

$$A_{ij} = \begin{cases} PMI(i, j) & word\ i,\ j\ and\ PMI(i, j) > 0 \\ TF \cdot IDF_{ij} & arg\ i,\quad word\ j \\ 1 & i == j,\ self\ loop \\ 0 & other \end{cases} \tag{4}$$

The argument nodes can pay more attention to the important word nodes through the "argument-word" edges with TF-IDF value. These words with higher TF-IDF values reflect a certain extent to the topic of the argument. Besides, word nodes gather information of words with similar semantics and provide global semantic clues about the topic behind arguments, thereby better capture the connections and differences between arguments. Finally, the total number of nodes in graph G is the sum of twice the total number of samples and the size of the vocabulary in the corpus.

3.2 GCN-Based Discourse Relation Recognition

In this paper, we propose a GCN-based neural network model on discourse argument pair graph (i.e., DAGGNN) for the task of discourse relation recognition and its framework is shown in Fig. 2. This framework includes three layers: input layer, encoding layer and classification layer.

Input Layer. We construct the discourse argument pair graph to obtain the adjacency matrix A and initial node feature matrix H^0 of the graph. They are the input of the model and fed into the encoding layer.

Encoding Layer. The graph convolutional operation [15] is used to extract local neighborhood information. The feature representation of the node is updated by gathering information from its adjacent nodes. In this paper, two graph convolutional layers are used to process the graph G constructed above.

After the first graph convolutional layer encoding, the argument node aggregates the information of its connected word nodes and obtains its own semantic representation; the word node aggregates information from the semantically similar word nodes connected to it, and obtain global word co-occurrence features, as shown in Eq. 5. After the second graph convolutional layer encoding, the argument node combines its own semantic representation with the global semantic clues brought by its word nodes as shown in Eq. 6.

$$H^1 = \text{ReLU}\left(\tilde{A}H^0W_0\right) \tag{5}$$

$$H^2 = \text{ReLU}\left(\tilde{A}H^1W_1\right) \tag{6}$$

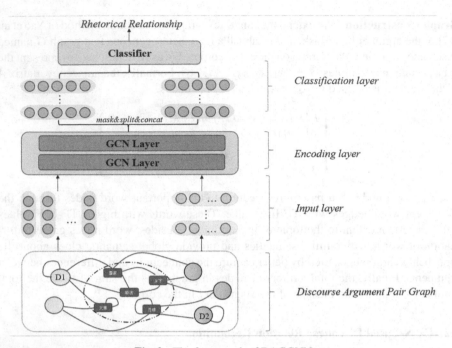

Fig. 2. The framework of DAGGNN.

Classification Layer. The semantic representations of the two arguments in the sample x_i do not directly correspond to each other in the node representation matrix H^2. Thus, we use a mask operation and a slice split operation on H^2 to obtain h_{arg1} and h_{arg2}, which are the semantic representations of the two arguments in the sample x_i as shown in Eq. 7. We concatenate all h_{arg1}, h_{arg2} as H_{arg1}, H_{arg2}, respectively, as shown in Eq. 8 and 9.

$$h_{arg1}, h_{arg2} = mask\&split\left(H^2\right) \tag{7}$$

$$H_{arg1} = concat\left(h^1_{arg1}, h^2_{arg1}, \ldots, h^t_{arg1}\right) \tag{8}$$

$$H_{arg2} = concat\left(h^1_{arg2}, h^2_{arg2}, \ldots, h^t_{arg2}\right) \tag{9}$$

After obtaining all arguments representation H_{arg1} and H_{arg2}, we concatenate them as H and feed it into a classifier consisting of two fully connected layers, as shown in Eq. 10, 11 and 12., where W_2, W_3, b_2 and b_3 are trainable parameters.

$$H = concat\left(H_{arg1}, H_{arg2}\right) \tag{10}$$

$$Z = Tanh(W_2H + b_2) \tag{11}$$

$$\hat{Y} = Softmax(W_3Z + b_3) \tag{12}$$

We use cross-entropy loss function to optimize our model, as shown in Eq. 13, where N is the total number of train samples, y_i is the indicator variable and $\hat{y}_i$ is the predicted probability.

$$L = -\frac{1}{N} \sum_{i=1}^{N} y_i \log(\hat{y}_i) \tag{13}$$

4 Experimentation

4.1 Dataset and Experimental Setting

In this paper, we verify our model DAGGNN on MCDTB [7] consisting of 720 articles with macro information, including the discourse structure, nuclearity and relation. The distribution of relation in MCDTB is shown in Table 1. In order to be more objective, we use the same dataset division as Jiang et al. [14] and use five-fold cross-validation for experiments. Following previous work, we also report the metrics micro-F1 and Macro-F1 to evaluate the performance.

Table 1. The distribution of relation in MCDTB

Elaboration	Causality	Coordination
2406	828	3296

All experimental parameters are adjusted on the validation set (20% of the training set), as shown in Table 2.

Table 2. Experimental parameter settings.

Name	Value
Embedding dim	300
Hidden size	200
The number of graph convolutional layer	2
Dropout	0.5
Learning-rate	0.002

4.2 Experimental Results

To evaluate our model DAGGNN in the task of discourse relation recognition, we use the following models for comparison:

LSTM [14]. A Bi-LSTM was used to encode the word sequence of the argument, and an attention layer was applied to all hidden states to obtain the semantic representation of the argument. Finally, a multi-layer perceptron was used to identify the discourse relation between two arguments.

MSRM [6]. It proposed a macro semantic representation method based on the difference in information between *word2vec* [16] and *glove* [18] word vectors, and this method combined two kinds of word vectors with some structural features, which were helpful to relation recognition.

STGSN [14]. It proposed a semantic network model based on structure and topic gating, which introduced the structure information and the topic information in arguments. The model controlled the flow of semantic representation by gated linear unit and the two kinds of information.

Table 3 shows the results of our model DAGGNN and all three baselines. Following Jiang et al. [14], we use the three types (*Elaboration*, *Causality* and *Coordination*) for evaluation in relation recognition. As expected, our DAGGNN outperforms all baselines and achieves the best Micro-F1 and Macro-F1 score. Specifically, it got 70.01 and 55.38 on micro-F1 and macro-F1, which are 3.56% and 0.95% higher than the state-of-the-art baseline STGSN, respectively.

Table 3. The performance comparison between DAGGNN and baselines.

Model	Relation	
	Micro-F1	Macro-F1
LSTM	65.15	49.83
MSRM	66.29	51.55
STGSN	66.45	54.43
DAGGNN (ours)	**70.01**	**55.38**

When encoding the argument, MSRM fused the global information (from *glove*) but ignored the inconsistency of the importance of words in the sentence. Due to building "arg-word" edges based on TF-IDF that highlights keywords, our model DAGGNN is conducive to modeling long texts and makes the semantic representation of arguments more accurate. STGSN used a sequence-learning model and attention mechanism to calculate the semantic representation of the argument. There are some flaws in this approach. First, sequence models such as LSTM, CNN, etc. cannot capture complex inter-word dependencies in long text well. Second, the attention mechanism does not perform well when encountering long texts. In addition, STGSN ignores global information, which results in ignoring the topical consistency between discourse arguments.

Compared with STGSN, our model DAGGNN considers the global information and important information in the argument through the graph neural network, achieving better performance. As a priori attention, TF-IDF increases the importance of keywords in the argument representation; PMI brings global information into our model by the "word-word" edges constructed in the graph because the PMI value represents the semantic correlation between words and reflect global word co-occurrence. Besides, the argument node can learn better semantic representations by these edges, due to some "word-word" edges that represent the inter-word dependence in the same argument.

4.3 Analysis on Different Relations

Table 4 shows the performance of different models on different relations. Compared with MSRM, DAGGNN has greatly improved the performance on *Causality* (+13.42%). This is due to that recognizing *Causality* relation requires not only the argument understanding, but also the certain logical reasoning, while MSRM cannot reflect the process of logical reasoning. Besides, DAGGNN can capture the implicit relationship between the arguments after encoding, if the nodes *arg*1 and *arg*2 contain some same words. During the semantic matching stage, our model can explicitly capture the interaction between the arguments. Thus obtaining a better result. Moreover, it should point out that DAG-GNN has obtained weaker results in terms of *Elaboration* and *Coordination*, because MSRM uses *word2vec* and *glove* for initialization while DAGGNN only uses *word2vec*. Compared with STGSN, DAGGNN has improved in all relations (+0.51%, +1.55%, +0.78%) that prove the effectiveness of graph-based text modeling. Moreover, the F1-score of the relation *Causality* is much lower than other two relations and the main reason is due to the data sparsity where only 12.7% of relations in the corpus are *Causality*.

Table 4. Performance of all models in each relation.

Model	Elaboration			Causality			Coordination		
	P	R	F1	P	R	F1	P	R	F1
LSTM	64.63	**68.81**	66.53	14.04	1.86	3.25	73.45	87.29	79.70
MSRM	66.45	68.16	**67.30**	**62.50**	3.62	6.85	73.29	**89.26**	**80.49**
STGSN	66.12	65.41	65.59	37.95	12.79	18.72	73.22	85.86	78.99
Ours	66.19	66.04	66.10	42.62	**14.43**	**20.27**	**73.87**	86.74	79.77

4.4 Analysis on Different Edges

We further analyze the importance of two types of edges in the recognition of discourse relations and the results are shown in Table 5. We obtained two ablated models: the w/o PMI model excludes word-word edges; the w/o TF-IDF model excludes TF-IDF in initializing the weight of "arg-word" edges but keeps the reciprocal of the argument length for initialization. It should be noted that we did not remove the "arg-word" edges, because such edges are needed to learn the complete argument semantic representation.

It can be seen that the performance of the model is reduced when removed from "word-word" edges with PMI values. This result is consistent with Zhou et al. [6], which proves the importance of global information. Besides, the performance of the model also decreases when replacing TF-IDF with the normalized argument length to

Table 5. The ablation experiments of DAGGNN.

Model	Relation	
	Micro-F1	Macro-F1
DAGGNN	70.01	55.38
w/o PMI	−1.10	−3.31
w/o TF-IDF	−2.36	−6.76

initialize "arg-word" edges. It shows that the priori attention information such as TF-IDF is very important for the semantic representation of macro discourse arguments. Therefore, our model DAGGNN considering the two kinds of information achieves the best result.

5   Conclusion

In this paper, we propose a graph neural network based on discourse argument pair graph (DAGGNN) for macro Chinese discourse relation recognition. We are the first to introduce graph neural network into Chinese discourse relation recognition and treat this task as a node classification task. First, we build a discourse argument pair graph that considering the important keywords in arguments and global information to represent discourse arguments better. Then, we adopt a graph-based learning method to learn paragraph-level semantic representation from macro discourse arguments, which can be transferred to other sentence pair or multi sentences tasks. The experimental results on MCDTB show that our model achieves the best performance. In the future, we will study how to build better graphs to represent macro discourse arguments.

Acknowledgments. The authors would like to thank three anonymous reviewers for their comments on this paper. This research was supported by the National Natural Science Foundation of China (No. 61836007, 61772354 and 61773276.), and the Priority Academic Program Development of Jiangsu Higher Education Institutions.

References

1. Xu, F., Zhu, Q., Zhou, G.: Survey of discourse analysis methods. J. Chin. Inf. Process. **27**(3), 20–33 (2013)
2. Liakata, M., Dobnik, S., Saha, S., Batchelor, C., Rebholz-Schuhmann, D.: A discourse-driven content model for summarising scientific articles evaluated in a complex question answering task. In: Proceedings of the 21st Conference on Empirical Methods in Natural Language Processing, pp. 747–757 (2018)
3. Cohan, A., Goharian, N.: Scientific article summarization using citation-context and article's discourse structure. In: Proceedings of the 23rd Conference on Empirical Methods in Natural Language Processing, pp. 390–400 (2015)

4. Zhou, L., Li, B., Gao, W., Wei, Z., Wong, K.: Unsupervised discovery of discourse relations for eliminating intra-sentence polarity ambiguities. In: Proceedings of the 19th Conference on Empirical Methods in Natural Language Processing, pp. 162–171 (2011)
5. Zou, B., Zhou, G., Zhu, Q.: Negation focus identification with contextual discourse information. In: Proceedings of the 52nd Annual Meeting of the Association for Computational Linguistics, pp. 522–530 (2014)
6. Zhou, Y., Chu, X., Zhu, Q., Jiang, F., Li, P.: Macro discourse relation classification based on macro semantics representation. J. Chin. Inf. Process. **33**(3), 1–7
7. Jiang, F., Xu, S., Chu, X., Li, P., Zhu, Q. Zhou, G.: MCDTB: a macro-level Chinese discourse treebank. In: Proceedings of the 27th International Conference on Computational Linguistics, pp. 3493–3504 (2018)
8. Xu, S., Li, P., Kong, F., Zhu, Q., Zhou, G.: Topic tensor network for implicit discourse relation recognition in Chinese. In: Proceedings of the 57th Annual Meeting of the Association for Computational Linguistics, pp. 608–618 (2019)
9. Carlson, L., Marcu, D., Okurowski, M.E.: RST discourse treebank. Linguistic Data Cponsortium, University of Pennsylvaia (2002)
10. Prasad, R., et al.: The Penn Discourse Treebank 2.0. In: Proceedings of the 6th International Conference on Language Resources and Evaluation (2008)
11. Li, Y., Kong, F., Zhou, G.: Building Chinese discourse corpus with connective-driven dependency tree structure. In: Proceedings of the 14th Conference on Empirical Methods in Natural Language Processing, pp. 2105–2114 (2014)
12. Li, Q., Li, T., Chang, B.: Discourse parsing with attention-based hierarchical neural networks. In: Proceedings of the 24th Conference on Empirical Methods in Natural Language Processing, pp. 362–371 (2016)
13. Bai, H., Zhao, H.: Deep enhanced representation for implicit discourse relation recognition. In: Proceedings of the 27th International Conference on Computational Linguistics, pp. 571–583 (2018)
14. Jiang, F., Li, P., Zhu, Q.: Joint modeling of recognizing macro chinese discourse nuclearity and relation based on structure and topic gated semantic network. In: Tang, J., Kan, M.-Y., Zhao, D., Li, S., Zan, H. (eds.) NLPCC 2019. LNCS (LNAI), vol. 11839, pp. 276–286. Springer, Cham (2019). https://doi.org/10.1007/978-3-030-32236-6_24
15. Kipf, T.N., Welling, M.: Semi-supervised classification with graph convolutional networks. In: Proceedings of 5th International Conference on Learning Representations (2017)
16. Mikolov, T., Chen, K., Corrado, G., Dean, J.: Efficient estimation of word representations in vector space. In: The 1st International Conference on Learning Representations Workshop
17. Yao, L., Mao, C., Luo, Y.: Graph convolutional networks for text classification. In: Proceedings of the 33rd Association for the Advancement of Artificial Intelligence Conference on Artificial Intelligence, pp. 7370–7377 (2019)
18. Pennington, J., Socher, R., Manning, C.: GloVe: global vectors for word representation. In: Proceedings of the 22nd Conference on Empirical Methods in Natural Language Processing, pp. 1532–1543 (2014)
19. Peters, M., et al.: Deep contextualized word representation. In: Proceedings of the 2018 Conference of the North American Chapter of the Association for Computational Linguistics, pp. 2227–2237 (2018)
20. Devlin, J., Chang, M.W., Lee, K., Toutanova, K.: BERT: pre-training of deep bidirectional transformers for language understanding. In: Proceedings of the 2019 Conference of the North American Chapter of the Association of Computational Linguistics, pp. 4171–4186 (2019)

Dependency Parsing with Noisy Multi-annotation Data

Yu Zhao, Mingyue Zhou, Zhenghua Li[(✉)], and Min Zhang

Institute of Artificial Intelligence, School of Computer Science and Technology,
Soochow University, Suzhou, China
zhaoyu9067@live.cn, 20194227026@stu.suda.edu.cn,
{zhli13,minzhang}@suda.edu.cn

Abstract. In the past few years, performance of dependency parsing has
been improved by large margin on closed-domain benchmark datasets.
However, when processing real-life texts, parsing performance degrades
dramatically. Besides the domain adaptation technique, which has made
slow progress due to its intrinsic difficulty, one straightforward way is to
annotate a certain scale of syntactic data given a new source of texts.
However, it is well known that annotating data is time and effort consuming, especially for the complex syntactic annotation. Inspired by the
progress in crowdsourcing, this paper proposes to annotate noisy multi-
annotation syntactic data with non-experts annotators. Each sentence is
independently annotated by multiple annotators and the inconsistencies
are retained. In this way, we can annotate data very rapidly since we can
recruit many ordinary annotators. Then we construct and release three
multi-annotation datasets from different sources. Finally, we propose and
compare several benchmark approaches to training dependency parsers
on such multi-annotation data. We will release our code and data at
http://hlt.suda.edu.cn/~zhli/.

Keywords: Dependency parsing · Multi-annotation · Chinese
treebank

1 Introduction

As a fundamental NLP task, dependency parsing aims to convert the input
word sequence into a tree structure representing the syntax information. Given
a sentence $S = w_0 w_1 w_2 ... w_n$, dependency parsing aims to find a dependency tree
$d = \{(i, j, l), 1 \leq i \leq n, 1 \leq j \leq n, l \in \mathcal{L}\}$, as depicted in Fig. 1, where (i, j, l) is a
dependency arc from head word w_i to the modifier word w_j and l is the label of
its relation type. Dependency parsing has been found to be extremely useful for

This work was supported by National Nature Science Foundation of China (Grant No.
61876116, 61525205) and a project funded by the Priority Academic Program Development of Jiangsu Higher Education Institutions. We thank the anonymous reviewers
for the helpful comments.

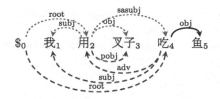

Fig. 1. An example of multi-annotation dependency tree. It's a full tree of a Chinese sentence with 5 words. Dotted lines and dashed lines are different annotations from two annotators. English translation: "I eat the fish with a fork."

a wide range of NLP tasks, such as event extraction [11], semantic parsing [13] and sentiment analysis [1].

In recent years, dependency parsing has achieved great progress thanks to the strong capability of deep neural networks in context representation. The deep biaffine graph-based parser has achieved the state-of-the-art accuracy on a variety of datasets and languages [5]. However, parsing performance drops dramatically when processing texts are different from the training data. In fact, the main challenge of dependency parsing is how to improve the performance on real-life data which is usually cross-domain. But the research progress in this field is slow because of its extreme difficulty.

A direct and effective solution is annotating a certain amount of data for the target domain. With such extra domain-specific training data, dependency parsers can handle the texts of this domain much better. However, it is well known that data annotation is highly time- and money-consuming, especially for complex tasks like dependency parsing. As far as we know, previous works on treebanking usually rely on very few linguistic experts annotating, such as PTB [21] and CTB [2], since it is very difficult to recruit many annotators with linguistic background.

In this paper, we propose to annotate syntactic trees with non-experts annotators, which is efficient and effective. To verify our approach in the dependency parsing scenario, we launched a treebanking project and recruited annotators without linguistic background to annotate independently after simple training. In this way we created three noisy multi-annotation parsing datasets. Following previous practice, as discussed in Sect. 2, multi-annotation data means that annotations from multiple annotators are available but there is no actual ground truth. Compared with annotation from experts, annotations from non-experts may be of lower quality and inconsistency. In order to make effective use of multi-annotation syntactic data, the parser need to eliminate inconsistencies of training data. We proposed and compared several benchmark approaches to training dependency parsers with these noisy multi-annotation data. We conducted experiments based on the state-of-the-art biaffine parser, and found the weighted ambiguous-labeling approach achieved a better performance.

In summary, this paper makes two major contributions: 1) releasing three multi-annotation parsing datasets; 2) proposing and comparing several benchmark approaches for learning from such multi-annotation data.

2   Related Work

There has been an intense research interest in using non-experts multi-annotation data. Following Rodrigues et al. (2014) [17], we distinguish the concepts of multi-annotation data and multi-label data. Multi-label data describes the situation that an instance may have multiple gold-standard labels at the same time. For example, a picture contains many objects in the object detection task. Multi-annotation data means that annotations from multiple annotators are available but there is only one unknown ground-truth label.

The first work to accommodate multi-annotation data can be traced back to Dawid and Skene (1979) [3]. They proposed an EM-based algorithm to resolve disagreement of patient's medical records taken by different clinicians. Following them, Raykar and Yu (2009) [15,16] proposed an algorithm for image and text classification. They modeled the annotators by introducing the concepts of sensitivity and specificity. Demartini et al. (2012) [4] described the annotators' reliability with a binary parameter to avoid estimation bias caused by data sparseness.

Many works endeavoured to investigate and compare the quality of multi-annotation data. Snow et al. (2008) [20] demonstrated that learning from the non-experts multi-annotation data can be as good as the data annotated by one expert. They compared the results on five NLP tasks: affect recognition, word similarity, recognizing textual entailment, event temporal ordering, and word sense disambiguation. Sheng et al. (2008) [19] showed how to improve label quality through repeated annotating. Gurari et al. (2015) [9] compared the accuracy between expert annotation and non-experts multi-annotation for image segmentation.

In terms of learning from the multi-annotation data, most works in the NLP field focus on the relatively simpler sequence labeling task, especially named entity recognition (NER). Dredze et al. (2009) [6] proposed a multi-CRF model to eliminate ambiguous labels in the sequence labeling task. Following their work, Rodrigues et al. (2014) [17] took annotator identities into account and assumed that only one annotator tagged the label correctly. Nguyen et al. (2017) [12] introduced a crowd CRFs model in which they used the crowd vectors to represent the annotators' reliability.

For the more complicated parsing task, research works on the multi-annotation data are rare due to the lack of data. In this paper, we propose three multi-annotation parsing datasets to facilitate future research. So far, we have only proposed and compared several simple benchmark approaches. However, the models and the algorithms proposed for other tasks may also apply to the parsing task and may achieve good performance. We leave this issue as future work.

3   Data Annotation

We launched a non-experts Chinese treebanking project and recruited some annotators to participate in it. We focused on dependency parsing, so we only annotated the dependency information of a sentence that had been well segmented. At the same time, we adopt the active learning (AL) based partial annotating method, i.e., only a few most valuable words of a sentence should be annotated [7,10,18].

Annotation Flow. We built an annotating system for our project, which could assign tasks for annotators automatically. As shown in Fig. 2, every sentence was assigned to two independent annotators randomly. The private communication during annotation process was prohibited. Each annotator was asked to give the answer alone without any reference. The only help for them was a guideline [8] which gave the basic knowledge of Chinese syntax and some annotation principles. Meanwhile, we had our experts check and correct sentences and determine the ground truth for evaluation. With a view to facilitate the research, we kept both the original annotations and the ground truth.

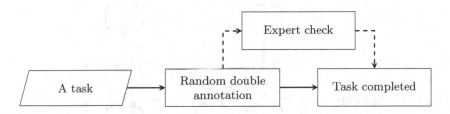

Fig. 2. The workflow for annotating a task.

Annotator. We recruited part-time annotators from our university and trained them through three steps: 1) a two-hour face-to-face meeting to explain job content, some basic concepts of syntax and the dependency tree formalism; 2) give them several days to learn the guidelines; 3) practice and evaluation. We only kept applicants with reasonable accuracy as our annotators. For the three datasets, we had 69 annotators in total. CTB, HIT and PMT were completed by 20, 26 and 44 annotators respectively. The number of annotated sentences of individual annotators was not equal and some of the annotators participated in more than one dataset. There were 13 annotators take part in both CTB and HIT, 6 annotators take part in both CTB and PMT, 6 annotators take part in both HIT and PMT, and 4 annotators take part in all the three.

4   The Basic Biaffine Parser

There are two paradigms of dependency parsing, i.e., graph-based and transition-based approaches. In this work, we adopt the state-of-the-art deep biaffine parser proposed by Dozat and Manning [5] as our basic parsing framework, which belongs to the graph-based paradigm.

Figure 3 shows the basic framework of the biaffine parser. Considering a sentence $S = w_0 w_1 w_2 w_3 ... w_n$, where w_0 is the the pseudo root. The input layer maps each input word w_i into a vector x_i, which is the concatenation of the word embedding and the Char-BiLSTM embedding. The encoder layer is a multi-layer BiLSTMs. The concatenated outputs of both directions of the former layer BiLSTM is the input of the latter one. Then the MLP representation layer takes the context-aware word representation h_i outputted from encoder layer as input. Finally, the biaffine scoring layer computes scores of all dependencies via a biaffine operation.

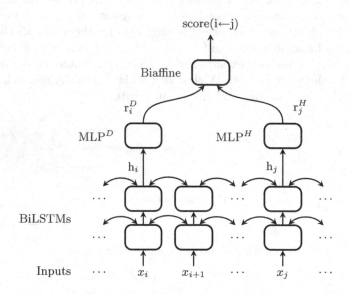

Fig. 3. Framework of biaffine attention model

5   Approaches to Learning from Multi-annotation Data

In this section, we introduce some approaches to train a dependency parser with multi-annotation data.

5.1   Discarding Inconsistent Submissions

A straightforward approach is discarding the sentences that have inconsistent answers to get a training set with no inconsistent data. Then the training set can be treated as ground truth approximately, which can be fed to the parser directly. This approach requires that the inter-consistency of annotators is not very low, or it will lose information. It works in most multi-annotation scenarios.

5.2   Concatenating

If a sentence has inconsistent answers, we can think of it as different valid annotations with the same word sequence (described in Fig. 4). In this way, all the
annotation information has been retained. But the wrong answers may give negative effects to the parser at the same time. Actually, every valid annotation
affect the result with the same weight.

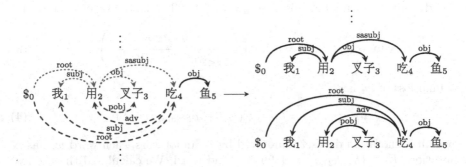

Fig. 4. An example of concatenating. Left is a double-label annotation sentence of a
dataset. The right is the concatenating dataset correspondingly.

5.3   Weighted Voting

The most common method is majority voting which based on an intuitive
assumption, that is, the more annotators give the same answer the higher probability this answer is right if we have no any other information about these
annotators. Furthermore, we can weight the annotators by their capabilities,
which is weighted voting. We describe an annotator's capability by calculating
his consistency rate with others. The annotators with a higher consistency rate
have a higher weight. If there are N annotators $\{a_1, a_2, ..., a_N\}$, $s(a_i)$ is the
number of all the words that a_i has annotated, $w(a_i)$ is the number of words
annotated by a_i for which there is another annotator gives the same answer,
$w(a_i)/s(a_i)$ is the consistency rate of a_i. Then normalize the consistency rate to
get the weight. The weight of annotator a_i is described as:

$$weight(a_i) = \frac{e^{\frac{w(a_i)}{s(a_i)}}}{\sum_j e^{\frac{w(a_j)}{s(a_j)}}} \tag{1}$$

5.4   Ambiguous-Labeling Learning

Another approach is that we make the model fit the data. We try to modify the
loss function of the model slightly to make use of the answers of every annotator.
In the biaffine attention parser, we usually use cross entropy as loss function.

Consider a word w_i in an input sequence $W = \{w_0, w_1, w_2, ..., w_d\}$. The head word of w_i is w_j. It's output score of this arc is $score_{arc}(i, j)$. Then the arc loss of word w_i is calculated as:

$$loss_{arc}(w_i) = -log\left(\frac{e^{score_{arc}(i,j)}}{\sum_{j' \leq d} e^{score_{arc}(i,j')}}\right) \tag{2}$$

If there are T labels for every arc $L = \{l_1, l_2, ..., l_T\}$. The label score of arc w_i to its head word w_j with label l_t is $score_{label}(i, j, l_t)$. The label loss of word w_i is:

$$loss_{label}(w_i, L) = -log\left(\frac{e^{score_{label}(i,j,l_t)}}{\sum_{t' \leq T} e^{score_{label}(i,j,l_{t'})}}\right) \tag{3}$$

The final loss of w_i is:

$$loss(w_i, L) = loss_{arc}(w_i) + loss_{label}(w_i, L) \tag{4}$$

In a multi-annotation dataset annotated by N annotators, each word w_i has N annotations $H = \{h_1, h_2, ..., h_N\}$ for its head word. We calculated the arc loss as:

$$loss_{arc\_m}(w_i, H) = -log\left(\sum_{k \leq N} \frac{e^{score_{arc}(i,h_k)}}{\sum_{j' \leq d} e^{score_{arc}(i,j')}}\right)$$

$$= -log\left(\sum_{k \leq N} e^{score_{arc}(i,h_k)}\right) + log\left(\sum_{j' \leq d} e^{score_{arc}(i,j')}\right) \tag{5}$$

Also, there are N labels for each arc $Y = \{y_1, y_2, ..., y_N\}$. According the biaffine model, we can get the label score vector for each arc annotation h_k in Y and the corresponding label annotation y_k in Y [5]. We use formula (3) to calculate the label loss for each annotation pair (h_k, y_k) and sum them up. The final loss is:

$$loss_m(w_i, L, H, Y) = loss_{arc\_m}(w_i, H) + \sum_{(h_k, y_k) \in (H, Y)} loss_{label}(w_i, L) \tag{6}$$

5.5   Weighted Ambiguous-Labeling Learning

When considering the weight of annotators, i.e. weighted ambiguous-labeling learning, the loss function should be written as:

$$loss_{arc\_m\_w}(w_i, H) = -log\left(\sum_{k \leq N} \frac{weight_k e^{score_{arc}(i,h_k)}}{\sum_{j' \leq d} e^{score_{arc}(i,j')}}\right)$$

$$= -log\left(\sum_{k \leq N} weight_k e^{score_{arc}(i,h_k)}\right) + log\left(\sum_{j' \leq d} e^{score_{arc}(i,j')}\right) \tag{7}$$

The $weight_k$ means the weight of the answers of annotator k, which can be calculated by formula (1) in the front section. It should be noted that the label scores are calculated based on the arc scores in the biaffine attention model. So we don't weight the label loss any more, the final loss is:

$$loss_{m\_w}(w_i, L, H, Y) = loss_{arc\_m\_w}(w_i, H) + \sum_{(h_k, y_k) \in (H, Y)} loss_{label}(w_i, L) \quad (8)$$

In this paper, the N is 2 for our datasets, and these methods also work when $N > 2$.

6 Data

As shown in Table 1, We annotated three datasets named CTB, HIT and PMT for experiments in this paper. CTB includes about 11K sentences chosen from Penn CTB [21] and contains 198K tokens among which 50K tokens are selected for annotation according to the annotation methodology described in Sect. 3. Similarly, HIT includes about 10K sentences chosen from HIT-CDT [2] and PMT includes about 10K sentences from PKU-CDT [14]. The number of tokens and annotated tokens of HIT and PMT are listed in Table 1. Each datasets was divided to TRAIN set, DEV set and TEST set by 7:1:2 for experiments.

Table 1. Statistics of annotated data. For each domain, we list the number (K means thousand) of "All" annotated sentences. Among "All" tokens, "Anno" gives the number of annotated tokens.

Domain	Dataset(K Sent)			#Sent (K)	#Token (K)	
	Train	Dev	Test		Anno	All
CTB	8	1	2	11	50	198
HIT	7	1	2	10	51	164
PMT	7	1	2	10	35	173

Table 2, 3 and 4, show consistency rate of the top 10 annotators who annotated most chosen from CTB, HIT and PMT. The last column means the annotator's overall consistency rate with others. The "anno1" to "anno10" is sorted in reverse order of annotation quantity. The consistency rate of annotators who has too little data (less than 100) was ignored and replaced by "–". The inter-annotator consistency is affected by multiple factors: capability of annotators, difficulty of sentences (such as sentence length, degree of normalization in language use), maturity degree of the guideline, etc. In our work, the annotator's overall consistency rate is used to evaluate the capability of annotators, shown in Sect. 5.3.

7 Experiments

7.1 Hyperparameter Settings

In this section, we give the hyperparameters in our model. As described in Sect. 4, a biaffine attention parser contains an Embedding layer, a multi BiLSTM layer, a MLP representation layer and a biaffine scoring layer.

In the embedding layer, we use a BiLSTM for the character embedding and concatenate it to the word embedding as the input sequence. The dimension of character embedding is 50 and the dimension of output from Char-BiLSTM is 100. The dimension of word embedding is 100 so the final dimension of output from the whole embedding layer is 200. We add a dropout layer with 67% keep probability.

After embedding layer, we choose triple 400 dimensional BiLSTMs and one 100 dimensional MLP layer with the Leaky ReLU function after that. The dropout of BiLSTM is 67% keep probability and the same number is used for MLP dropout.

We use the Adam optimizer with $\beta_1 = \beta_2 = 0.9$, learning rate $2e^{-3}$, annealed continuously at a rate of 0.75 every 5000 iterations, with batches of 5000 tokens. These hyperparameters were selected based on the suggestion of [5].

7.2 Results and Analysis

In this section, we compare the methods mentioned in Sect. 5 on our three datasets. Each dataset was divided to TRAIN set, DEV set and TEST set by 7:1:2 as described in Sect. 6. We kept expert-checked ground-truth of DEV set and TEST set for testing. Table 5 reports UAS and LAS on test data of parsers trained from CTB, HIT and PMT. From the table, we can find that the weighted ambiguous-labeling learning performs better than discarding, concatenating and weighted voting on all the three datasets. The results of normal

Table 2. Annotator consistency of CTB

%	anno2	anno3	anno4	anno5	anno6	anno7	anno8	anno9	anno10	overall
anno1	80	84	77	71	78	75	74	71	83	77
anno2	–	80	78	70	77	74	72	78	76	78
anno3	–	–	76	72	75	72	76	74	–	79
anno4	–	–	–	71	75	77	70	74	78	76
anno5	–	–	–	–	68	70	65	64	–	70
anno6	–	–	–	–	–	–	67	75	–	75
anno7	–	–	–	–	–	–	71	–	–	77
anno8	–	–	–	–	–	–	–	–	–	71
anno9	–	–	–	–	–	–	–	–	–	72
anno10	–	–	–	–	–	–	–	–	–	80

Table 3. Annotator consistency of HIT

%	anno2	anno3	anno4	anno5	anno6	anno7	anno8	anno9	anno10	overall
anno1	80	75	80	84	83	74	83	72	78	77
anno2	–	76	77	80	86	81	78	76	80	78
anno3	–	–	76	77	82	79	79	64	73	76
anno4	–	–	–	76	83	77	–	69	77	76
anno5	–	–	–	–	87	75	76	66	74	76
anno6	–	–	–	–	–	78	73	78	–	81
anno7	–	–	–	–	–	–	70	79	66	77
anno8	–	–	–	–	–	–	–	76	75	76
anno9	–	–	–	–	–	–	–	–	69	72
anno10	–	–	–	–	–	–	–	–	–	74

Table 4. Annotator consistency of PMT

%	anno2	anno3	anno4	anno5	anno6	anno7	anno8	anno9	anno10	overall
anno1	64	64	67	68	64	65	–	64	55	60
anno2	–	60	64	62	63	51	63	57	–	59
anno3	–	–	69	65	62	–	70	67	52	60
anno4	–	–	–	67	–	67	71	65	54	63
anno5	–	–	–	–	–	68	65	68	–	63
anno6	–	–	–	–	–	–	–	–	–	60
anno7	–	–	–	–	–	–	59	65	–	59
anno8	–	–	–	–	–	–	–	–	–	64
anno9	–	–	–	–	–	–	–	–	–	62
anno10	–	–	–	–	–	–	–	–	–	53

ambiguous-labeling learning is closed to the weighted one. We think the reason is that the annotators are more distributed and their inner consistency rate is close (Sect. 6). The weighted voting ranks the last place. One explanation is that the model for annotator weight is too simple and the wrong annotations gives too many negative effects when voting. It simply discards the annotations with low weight which magnifies the weight of the chosen one.

Figure 5 shows the LAS convergence curves of each approach on the three datasets. The convergence efficiency of the parsers on CTB, HIT is better than one on PMT. The reason may be the quality difference between corpora. As shown in Table 4, the average of consistency rate of PMT is lower, which means lower accuracy of each annotator. The advantage of ambiguous-labeling learning is more obvious when processing on PMT.

Table 5. Results of each method on the three datasets.

	CTB		HIT		PMT	
	UAS	LAS	UAS	LAS	UAS	LAS
Golden-standard	66.43	60.85	68.22	62.13	50.91	40.27
Discarding	65.50	59.64	68.01	61.51	47.81	37.32
Concatenating	66.51	61.13	67.96	61.71	49.51	38.83%
Weighted voting	63.59	58.02	66.33	59.85	47.39	37.07
Ambiguous-labeling	65.59	60.40	**68.89**	61.91	**50.63**	**39.57**
Weighted ambiguous-labeling	**66.78**	**61.34**	68.78	**62.53**	49.77	39.39

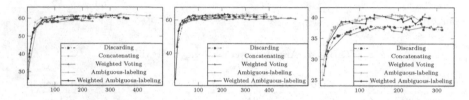

Fig. 5. Convergence curves(LAS vs. training epoches) on dev set from CTB, HIT, PMT

8   Conclusions

This paper targets at the problem of dependency parsing with noisy multi-annotation data. On the one hand, we introduced the process of creating multi-annotation data using non-experts annotators. We obtain three datasets from different sources for further experiments. On the other hand, we introduced how to train a dependency parser with multi-annotation data. Following the state-of-the-art biaffine attention model, we compared results with five benchmark approaches, i.e., discarding, concatenating, weighted voting, ambiguous-labeling learning, and weighted ambiguous-labeling learning. The experiments showed that the ambiguous-labeling and weighted ambiguous-labeling performed better than some baseline approaches on our datasets.

In the future, there are several interesting issues to be addressed. First, we would like to expand our datasets to cover more domains. Second, we also plan to explore more sophisticated approaches for utilizing multi-annotation data. For example, there may be better ways than using consistency rates to model abilities of annotators.

References

1. Caro, L.D., Grella, M.: Sentiment analysis via dependency parsing. Comput. Stand. Interfaces **35**(5), 442–453 (2013)
2. Che, W., Li, Z., Liu, T.: Chinese dependency treebank 1.0 (LDC2012T05). Website. Linguistic Data Consortium (2012). https://catalog.ldc.upenn.edu/LDC2012T05

3. Dawid, A.P., Skene, A.M.: Maximum likelihood estimation of observer error-rates using the EM algorithm. J. Roy. Stat. Soc.: Ser. C (Appl. Stat.) **28**(1), 20–28 (1979)
4. Demartini, G., Difallah, D.E., Cudré-Mauroux, P.: ZenCrowd: leveraging probabilistic reasoning and crowdsourcing techniques for large-scale entity linking. In: Proceedings of WWW, pp. 469–478 (2012)
5. Dozat, T., Manning, C.D.: Deep biaffine attention for neural dependency parsing. In: Proceedings of ICLR (2017)
6. Dredze, M., Talukdar, P.P., Crammer, K.: Sequence learning from data with multiple labels. In: Proceedings of ECML/PKDD Workshop Co-Chairs, p. 39 (2009)
7. Flannery, D., Miayo, Y., Neubig, G., Mori, S.: Training dependency parsers from partially annotated corpora. In: Proceedings of 5th IJCNLP, pp. 776–784 (2011)
8. Guo, L., Li, Z., Peng, X., Zhang, M.: Annotation guideline of Chinese dependency treebankfrom multi-domain and multi-source texts. J. Chin. Inform. Process. **32**(10), 28–35 (2018)
9. Gurari, D., et al.: How to collect segmentations for biomedical images? A benchmark evaluating the performance of experts, crowdsourced non-experts, and algorithms. In: Proceedings of WACV, pp. 1169–1176. IEEE (2015)
10. Li, Z., et al.: Active learning for dependency parsing with partial annotation. In: Proceedings of ACL, pp. 344–354 (2016)
11. Mcclosky, D., Surdeanu, M., Manning, C.D.: Event extraction as dependency parsing. In: Proceedings of ACL, pp. 1626—1635 (2011)
12. Nguyen, A.T., Wallace, B.C., Li, J.J., Nenkova, A., Lease, M.: Aggregating and predicting sequence labels from crowd annotations. In: Proceedings of ACL, vol. 2017, p. 299. NIH Public Access (2017)
13. Oepen, S., et al.: SemEval 2014 task 8: broad-coverage semantic dependency parsing. In: Proceedings of the 8th International Workshop on Semantic Evaluation. (SemEval 2014), pp. 63–72 (2014)
14. Qiu, L., Zhang, Y., Jin, P., Wang, H.: Multi-view Chinese treebanking. In: Proceedings of COLING, pp. 257–268 (2014)
15. Raykar, V.C., et al.: Supervised learning from multiple experts: whom to trust when everyone lies a bit. In: Proceedings of ICML, pp. 889–896 (2009)
16. Raykar, V.C., et al.: Learning from crowds. J. Mach. Learn. Res. **11**, 1297–1322 (2010)
17. Rodrigues, F., Pereira, F., Ribeiro, B.: Sequence labeling with multiple annotators. Mach. Learn. **95**(2), 165–181 (2013). https://doi.org/10.1007/s10994-013-5411-2
18. Sassano, M., Kurohashi, S.: Using smaller constituents rather than sentences in active learning for Japanese dependency parsing. In: Proceedings of ACL, pp. 356–365 (2010)
19. Sheng, V.S., Provost, F., Ipeirotis, P.G.: Get another label? Improving data quality and data mining using multiple, noisy labelers. In: Proceedings ACM SIGKDD, pp. 614–622 (2008)
20. Snow, R., O'connor, B., Jurafsky, D., Ng, A.Y.: Cheap and fast-but is it good? Evaluating non-expert annotations for natural language tasks. In: Proceedings of EMNLP, pp. 254–263 (2008)
21. Xue, N., Xia, F., Chiou, F., Palmer, M.: The penn Chinese treebank: phrase structure annotation of a large corpus. Nat. Lang. Eng. **11**(2), 207–238 (2005)

Joint Bilinear End-to-End Dependency Parsing with Prior Knowledge

Yunchu Gao, Ke Zhang, and Zhoujun Li[(✉)]

State Key Lab of Software Development Environment,
Beihang University, Beijing, China
{gaoyunchu,zhangke,lizj}@buaa.edu.cn

Abstract. Dependency parsing aims to identify relationships between words in one sentence. In this paper, we propose a novel graph-based end-to-end dependency parsing model, including POS tagger and Joint Bilinear Model (JBM). Based on prior POS knowledge from dataset, we use POS tagging results to guide the training of JBM. To narrow the gap between edge and label prediction, we pass the knowledge hidden in label prediction procedure in JBM. Motivated by success of deep contextualized word embeddings, this work also finetunes BERT for dependency parsing. Our model achieves 96.85% UAS and 95.01% LAS in English PTB dataset. Moreover, experiments on Universal Dependencies dataset indicates our model also reaches state-of-the-art performance on dependency parsing and POS tagging.

Keywords: Dependency parsing · Joint Bilinear Model · Prior POS knowledge · Deep contextualized word embedding

1 Introduction

Dependency parsing is a tree-structured method to capture semantic relationships between words in one sentence, which is important to other NLP tasks as a downstream task. Existing approaches in dependency parsing can be classified as graph-based and transition-based approaches.

In this paper, we present a novel graph-based end-to-end model with prior POS knowledge. Recent successful parsers often need word embeddings and POS (part-of-speech) tagging embeddings as input. However, pretrained POS tagging embeddings from external POS tagger may lead deviation to the training process of dependency parser. Our approach combines dependency parsing with POS tagging, receiving segmented words as input, then producing both parsing tree and POS tagging result simultaneously. During the process of dependency parsing, we focus on relationships between POS and parsing label through prior POS knowledge based on statistics result from training data. Through prior POS knowledge, POS tagging results are used in a more explicit way for dependency parsing. In parsing part, most of the existing graph-based approaches calculate edge and label scores independently. However, label should be predicted for high

© Springer Nature Switzerland AG 2020
X. Zhu et al. (Eds.): NLPCC 2020, LNAI 12431, pp. 132–143, 2020.
https://doi.org/10.1007/978-3-030-60457-8_11

potential edge. To narrow the gap between edge and label prediction, we present Joint Bilinear Model (JBM) to combine edge parsing with label parsing.

Experiments show that our approach achieves state-of-the-art performance on Penn Treebank 3.0 [1] and Universal Dependencies Treebank 2.4 in CoNLL 2018 multilingual parsing shared-task [2].

2 Related Work

In recent years, some graph-based approaches achieved state-of-the-art performance. Dozat and Manning's [3,4] presented a simple and accurate biaffine dependency parser by using multilayer perceptron (MLP) or feedforward networks (FNN) to split word representations into its head and dependent representation. These representations are applied to deep biaffine transformation, and predict scores of edge and label matrix. Based on Dozat's approaches, Xinyu Wang [5] proposed a graph-based second-order semantic parser. Second-order relation can be handled by trilinear function. This model use Conditional Random Field(CRF) to decode and achieved higher performance. Tao Ji [6] used graph neural networks (GNN) to capture high-order information concisely and efficiently.

Transformer and self-attention mechanism are effective in many NLP tasks. Inspired by this point, Ying Li [7] applied self-attention-based encoder to dependency parsing as the replacement of BiLSTMs. They also tried to ensemble self-attention encoder and BiLSTMs for parsing. As for word embeddings, they employed external contextualized word representations ELMo and BERT [8,9], which can further improve parsing performance.

Deep contextualized word embeddings are effective in many tasks. In the field of dependency parsing, Kulmizev [10] investigated the impact of deep contextualized word representations on transition-based parser and graph-based parser. Experiments showed that ELMo and BERT provided significant improvements on both of these parsers. Deep contextualized representations can overcome difficulties on dependency length, non-projective dependencies, and sentence length. Yuxuan Wang [11] applied BERT on cross-lingual dependency parser transformation. Their approach learned a linear transformation from mBERT to word alignments, which is a zero-shot cross-lingual transfer parsing approach. These works show deep contextualized models significantly benefit the dependency parsing task.

3 Approach

Our model architecture is shown in Fig. 1. Given an input sentence, our model computes word representations through fine-tuned BERT. Word-level representations will be applied to POS tagger and Joint Bilinear Model (JBM), generating POS tagging and parsing scores. Differs from Dozat's [3,4] approaches, JBM applies prior POS knowledge and narrows the gap between edge and label prediction. These two scores are decoded by Chu-Liu-Edmonds algorithm, producing a dependency parsing tree.

3.1   Word Representation

The input of our model is segmented words. These words will be fed into BERT. In BERT tokenization process, word which is not in vocabulary will be divided into subwords. As dependency parsing needs word-level input, we need to align those subwords vector to a word-level vector. We tried two method: taking word's first subword vector and calculating average subword vectors of one word. Finally we take the averaging method to align subword as in Eq. (1), feeding these vectors into BiLSTM as in Eq. (2). Word-level representations will be applied to POS tagger and JBM.

$$x_i = \frac{\sum_{j=1}^{N} BERT(W_{ij})}{N} \tag{1}$$

$$R = BiLSTM(X) \tag{2}$$

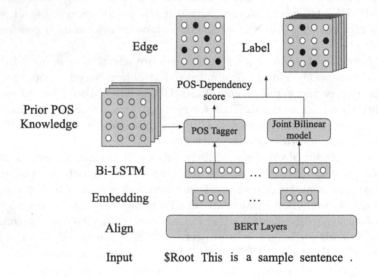

Fig. 1. Illustration of our model architecture.

3.2   Prior POS Knowledge

POS tagging is an important feature for dependency parsing. Most of previous approaches concatenate word and POS tagging embeddings and feed them into the model. As pretrained POS tagging embeddings from external POS tagger may lead deviation to training process, we arrange POS tagger into our model and produce POS tagging result. We calculate probabilities between POS tagging and dependency label in training data, which constitute prior POS knowledge. Based on tagging result and prior POS knowledge, POS-Dependency scores will be introduced to JBM.

We apply simple and effective multi-class POS tagger. Word representations from outputs of BiLSTM are fed into 2-layers FNN, which is a multi-class classifier, producing POS tagging result, as shown in Eq. (3,4,5). Every POS tagging of words is transmitted to one-hot vector, and these vector are stacked to P which is tagging result for the whole sentence, as shown in Eq. (6,7).

$$h_i^{(tag)} = BiLSTM^{(tag)}(X) \tag{3}$$

$$v_i = FNN(h_i^{(tag)}) \tag{4}$$

$$P(y_{ik}^{(tag)}|X) = Softmax_k(Wv_i) \tag{5}$$

$$p_i = argmax(y_{ik}) \tag{6}$$

$$P = Stack(p_i^{(one-hot)}) \tag{7}$$

Prior POS knowledge is statistical result from training data. We traverse all dependency relationships in training data, combining following three elements as a 3-tuple: POS tagging of head word in dependency arc, POS tagging of tail word in this arc, and the dependency label of this arc. From all these 3-tuples, we calculate prior probabilities of dependency label from two given POS information. Prior POS knowledge will be filled by top-n 3-tuples with highest probability and generate *KnowledgeEdge* and *KnowledgeLabel* matrix. The shape of *KnowledgeEdge* matrix is (p,p), and the shape of *KnowledgeLabel* matrix is (p,p,c), where p is the total number of POS tagging, c is the number of dependency labels. $KnowledgeEdge(i,j)$ indicates the probability of a directed arc from word with p_i to word with p_j. $KnowledgeLabel(i,j,k)$ indicates the probability of a fixed-class arc d_k from word with p_i to word with p_j. Those two matrices are statistical results from training data. For example, in English PTB training data, there are 97 relations of *PRP* word to *NNS* word. Among these relations, there are 68 relations with *nsubj* label. Therefore, the initial score of *PRP* word to *NNS* word with label *nsubj* in *KnowledgeLabel* is 0.701. If this edge score is in the top-n scores, it will be set at initial score 1.0 in *KnowledgeEdge*. Scores in these two matrices are not constant, they requires backpropagation of parsing errors in training process.

Both *KnowledgeEdge* and *KnowledgeLabel* matrix multiply with tagging matrix P of the whole sentence, generating POS-Dependency scores E and L, as in Eq. (8,9). Figure 2 illustrates the calculation process of E. $E(i, j)$ indicates the edge score of word$_i$ to word$_j$ in this sentence based on POS tagging and prior POS knowledge. while $L(i,j,k)$ indicates the dependency label$_k$ score of word$_i$ to word$_j$. Those two matrices are sparse as the large amount of p and c and small number of prior POS knowledge selected. Most of probabilities in matrix are zero. The advantage of applying POS tagger and prior POS knowledge is to avoid deviation by pretrained POS embeddings in intuitively method. In addition, we can apply new rules based on the feedback of practical application.

$$E = P \times KnowledgeEdge \times P^T \tag{8}$$

$$L = P \times KnowledgeLabel \times P^T \tag{9}$$

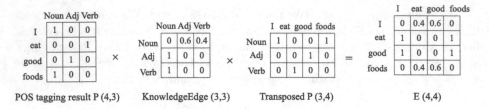

Fig. 2. Prior POS knowledge calculation process.

POS-Dependency scores E and L will be introduced to JBM parsing process. As Chu-Liu-Edmonds althorithm decodes graph based on relative scores, adding those two matrices will improve a small amount of scores in matrix, enable these relationships corresponding to prior POS knowledge are more likely to be selected as dependency arcs.

3.3   Joint Bilinear Model (JBM)

In parsing module, we select Dozat's deep biaffine model as baseline. In their model, top recurrent states from BiLSTM will feed into MLP to split it into head and dependent representation, as in Eq. (10,11). Biaffine classifiers will calculate multiplicative interactions between head and dependent representations, generating edge and label scores, as in Eq. (12,13,14). Original deep biaffine model calculate edge and label scores sequentially and independently. However, label should be predicted for high potential edge. To narrow the gap between edge and label prediction, we present Joint Bilinear Model (JBM).

$$h_i^{(arc-dep)} = MLP^{(arc-dep)}(r_i) \tag{10}$$

$$h_i^{(arc-head)} = MLP^{(arc-head)}(r_i) \tag{11}$$

$$Biaffine(x_1, x_2) = x_1^T U x_2 + W(x_1 \oplus x_2) + b \tag{12}$$

$$s_{ij}^{(edge)} = Biaffine^{(edge)}(h_i^{(arc-dep)}, h_i^{(arc-head)}) \tag{13}$$

$$s_{ij}^{(label)} = Biaffine^{(label)}(h_i^{(arc-dep)}, h_i^{(arc-head)}) \tag{14}$$

JBM integrates edge and label prediction, combining with POS-Dependency scores E and L in 3.2. Through FNN, word representation is splitted into d-dimensional head and dependent representation vector, as in Eq. (15,16). We use bilinear function to calculate Edge, where $U^{(edge)}$ is a $(d,1,d)$-dimensional diagonal matrix, which predicts whether a directed edge exists between two words or not. Label prediction is joined with edge prediction results. Once two words' edge score is at low rate, their label score will reduce. Label score will increase with high credit edge score accordingly. The score of edge and label combine with POS-Dependency scores through a interpolation coefficient α, as in Eq. (17,18), where $U^{(label)}$ is (d,c,d)-dimensional. JBM narrows the gap between edge and label prediction, which can further improve UAS and LAS performance simultaneously.

$$head_i = FNN^{(head)}(r_i) \tag{15}$$

$$dep_i = FNN^{(dep)}(r_i) \tag{16}$$

$$Edge_{ij} = \alpha \times head_i \times U^{(edge)} \times dep_j^T + (1 - \alpha) \times E \tag{17}$$

$$Label_{ij} = \alpha \times head_i \times U^{(label)} \times Softmax(Edge_{ij}) \times dep_j^T + (1 - \alpha) \times L \tag{18}$$

3.4   Learning

Based on cross entropy loss, we define the following loss. These loss variables will be used in maximizing accuracy for both edge and label. As mentioned above, calculation of label loss takes edge prediction into consideration, back-propagating error to labels in gold edges. Therefore, when the prediction of edge meets gold parse graph and this label prediction misses, the penalty of loss will increase. Relatively, when the prediction of edge misses, label loss of word pairs will decrease, as in Eq. (19,20,21,22). We even out edge and label losses through a interpolation coefficient $\lambda_{parsing}$, as in Eq. (23).

$$P(y_{ij}^{(edge)})|w) = Softmax(Edge_{ij}) \tag{19}$$

$$P(y_{ij}^{(label)})|w) = Softmax(Label_{ij}) \tag{20}$$

$$\mathcal{L}^{(edge)}(\theta) = \sum_{i,j} -LogSoftmax(P_\theta(y_{ij}^{*(edge)}|w)) \tag{21}$$

$$\mathcal{L}^{(label)}(\theta) = \sum_{i,j} -LogSoftmax(P_\theta(y_{ij}^{*(label)}|w)) \times Softmax(P_\theta(y_{ij}^{*(edge)}|w)) \tag{22}$$

$$\mathcal{L}^{(parsing)} = \lambda_{parsing} \times \mathcal{L}^{(edge)} + (1 - \lambda_{parsing}) \times \mathcal{L}^{(label)} \tag{23}$$

Finally, we even out parsing loss and POS tagging loss through λ, as in shown in Eq. (24, 25).

$$\mathcal{L}^{(POS)}(\theta) = \sum_{i,j} -LogSoftmax(P_\theta(y_{ij}^{*(tag)}|w)) \tag{24}$$

$$\mathcal{L} = \lambda \times \mathcal{L}^{(parsing)} + (1 - \lambda) \times \mathcal{L}^{(POS)} \tag{25}$$

4   Experiments

We evaluate our model on English Penn Treebank (PTB 3.0) and Universal Dependencies (UD 2.4) from CoNLL 2018 shared task. We use standard splits of PTB (train 02–21, dev: 22, test : 23), while for Universal Dependencies we use official splits.

For evaluation metrics, we use labeled attachment score (LAS) and unlabeled attachment score (UAS) as well as accuracy of UPOS. In PTB evaluation, we ignore all punctuation marks in evaluation. In Universal Dependencies evaluation, we use official evaluation script.

4.1 Hyperparameters Setting

Table 1. Final hyperparameter configuration.

BiLSTM hidden size	4 @ 600
Bilinear hidden size	600
BiLSTM dropout rate	25%
Bilinear dropout rate	33%
Interpolation($\lambda_{parsing}$)	0.6
Interpolation(λ)	0.6
Interpolation(α)	0.9
L_2 regularization	$3e^{-9}$
Learning rate	$3e^{-3}$
BERT learning rate	$1e^{-5}$
LR decay	0.8
Adam β_1	0.9
Adam β_2	0.99

We tune hyperparameters for our model on development data. The hyperparameter configuration of our final model is shown in Table 1. For English dataset, we select bert-large-cased model for input. For Chinese dataset, we use bert-base-chinese model. While for other languages, we use bert-base-multilingual-uncased model. We apply the last layer of BERT output as BiLSTM input. The BiLSTM is 4 layers deep with 600-dimensional hidden size. Output from BERT and BiLSTM is dropped at rate 20%, and in joint bilinear process, head and dependent representations are dropped at rate 33%. Following Dozat [4], we use Adam for optimizing model, annealing the learning rate by 0.8 for every 10,000 steps. The model is trained with batch size of 16 sentences for up to 75000 training steps, terminating early after 10,000 steps pass with no improvement in validation accuracy.

4.2 Performance

We compare our model performance in PTB dataset with previous approaches in Table 2. Chen and Manning [12], Dyer [13] and Andors'[14] models are transition-based model. Kiperwasser and Goldberg's [15] model is graph-based model. Ji's [6] model apply GNN. Li's [7] model applied self-attention-based encoder to parsing, we use their single self-attention with BERT version to compare. The baseline is Dozat's Biaffine parser with BERT model as input instead of pre-trained word embeddings.

Dozat's biaffine parser with BERT achieves 96.18% UAS and 94.48% LAS. With more prior POS knowledge added, our model achieves higher improvements

Table 2. Results on English PTB dataset.

Model	UAS	LAS
Chen and Manning 2014 [12]	91.8	89.6
Dyer et al. 2015 [13]	93.1	90.9
Kiperwasser 2016 [15]	93.1	91.0
Andor et al. 2016 [14]	94.61	92.79
Dozat and Manning 2017 [3]	95.74	94.08
Ji et al. 2019 [6]	95.97	94.31
Clark et al. 2018 [16]	96.60	95.00
Li et al. 2019 [7]	96.67	**95.03**
Baseline	96.18	94.48
Ours (Knowledge 0)	96.28	94.32
Ours (Knowledge 50)	96.42	94.77
Ours (Knowledge 200)	96.60	94.89
Ours (Knowledge 500)	**96.85**	95.01

and finally reaches 96.85% UAS and 95.01% LAS with 500 prior POS knowledge, matching the state-of-the-art models, indicating the proper amount of prior POS knowledge brings considerable improvement.

Table 3. Results on UD English EWT dataset.

Model	UAS	LAS	UPOS
Dozat et al. 2018 [17]	86.40	83.87	94.47
Lim et al. 2018 [18]	86.90	84.02	93.98
Che et al. 2018 [19]	86.79	84.57	95.22
Ahmad et al. 2019 [20]	90.83	89.07	–
He et al. 2019 [21]	91.82	–	94.02
Baseline	92.17	89.60	–
Ours (Knowledge 200)	**92.62**	**89.98**	**96.76**

We compare model performances over UD English-EWT dataset on Table 3. Dozat [17], Lim [18] and Che's [19] model are CoNLL-2018 shared task submitted approaches. Ahmad [20] and He's [21] models are cross-lingual approaches. They trained model on English-EWT dataset and applied their model on other languages. We apply our model with 200 prior POS knowledge and achieves 92.62% UAS and 89.98% LAS. As for other languange in UD dataset, we compare our model with Ji's GNN parser [6] and achieve average 92.64% UAS and 89.46% LAS, as is shown in Table 4. Both UAS and LAS reach state-of-the-art performance as well.

Table 4. Parsing results on other languages in UD dataset.

Dataset	GNN parser		Ours	
	UAS	LAS	UAS	LAS
Bulgarian	91.64	88.28	**94.43**	**90.96**
Chinese	–	–	**90.25**	**86.82**
Czech	92.00	**89.85**	**92.66**	89.83
France	86.82	83.73	**93.71**	**91.90**
German	86.47	81.96	**88.68**	**83.79**
Italian	90.81	88.91	**94.52**	**92.20**
Spanish	91.28	88.93	**93.46**	**90.63**
Romanian	89.11	84.44	**91.93**	**86.82**
Russian	88.94	86.62	**94.12**	**92.16**
Avg.	89.63	86.59	**92.64**	**89.46**

As an end-to-end model, our model produces both dependency parsing tree and POS prediction. We compare accuracy of UPOS in Universal Dependencies with two successful POS tagger in CoNLL 2018 shared task, as is shown in Table 5. Experiment results show that our model reach state-of-the-art in POS prediction as well, bringing average 0.64% improvement on UPOS accuracy.

Table 5. UPOS accuracy on UD dataset.

Dataset	Dozat [17]	Che [19]	Ours
Bulgarian	98.68	**99.03**	99.00
Chinese	88.51	91.94	**96.96**
Czech	98.71	**99.22**	98.75
France	**96.97**	96.42	96.61
German	93.98	94.50	**95.35**
Italian	97.97	98.13	**98.51**
Spanish	98.70	**98.80**	98.31
Romanian	97.66	97.63	**97.81**
Russian	98.25	98.60	**98.72**
Avg.	96.60	97.14	**97.78**

Table 6. The performance comparasion on prior knowledge and JBM on PTB dataset.

Model	UAS	LAS
Baseline	96.18	94.48
+ prior knowledge	96.23	94.58
+ JBM	**96.37**	**94.62**

4.3 Ablation Study

We study how prior POS knowledge and JBM affect the performance of our parser. We trained our model with only prior POS knowledge without JBM. And we trained our JBM model without prior POS knowledge on English PTB dataset. The result is shown in Table 6. While both prior POS knowledge and JBM can improve the parsing performance over the baseline, JBM leads to larger performance gain on both LAS and UAS.

4.4 Error Analysis

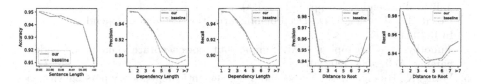

Fig. 3. Parsing performance of baseline and our parser in length and graph factors.

Following Ji [6],we analyze errors from Dozat's baseline (BERT+Biaffine) and our model in PTB dataset as is shown in Fig. 3. Results show that our parser improve performances in difficult cases.

Sentence Length. We evaluate models performance in different sentence lengths. Our model improves the performance in middle and long sentences, but is slightly worse in short sentences.

Dependency Length. Dependency length is the length between $word_i$ and $word_j$ which have dependency relation. Our model improves the performance in longer dependency length in both precision and recall than baseline.

Root Distance. Root distance is measured by the number of arcs in the path from the root. Our model improves the performance in long root distance compared with the baseline model in both precision and recall as well.

5   Conclusion

We propose a joint bilinear end-to-end model with prior knowledge, taking POS tagging into concern. POS tagging result calculate with prior POS knowledge which is statistical result from training data, emphasizing POS as a strong feature for dependency parsing. Joint Bilinear Model brings relationship between edge and label into consideration. Experiments on PTB and UD show the effectiveness of our model. we will explore high-order joint parsing method and search other type of prior knowledge in future work.

Acknowledgement. This work was supported in part by the National Natural Science Foundation of China (Grant Nos. U1636211, 61672081, 61370126), the Beijing Advanced Innovation Center for Imaging Technology (Grant No. BAICIT-2016001), and the Fund of the State Key Laboratory of Software Development Environment (Grant No. SKLSDE-2019ZX-17).

References

1. Marcus, M.P., Santorini, B., Marcinkiewicz, M.A.: Building a large annotated corpus of English: the Penn treebank. Comput. Linguist. **19**(2), 313–330 (1993)
2. Zeman, D., et al.: CoNLL 2018 shared task: multilingual parsing from raw text to universal dependencies, pp. 1–21 (2018)
3. Dozat, T., Manning, C.D.: Deep biaffine attention for neural dependency parsing. In ICLR (2017)
4. Timothy, D., Christopher, D.M.: Simpler but more accurate semantic dependency parsing. ACL, 484–490 (2018)
5. Wang, X., Huang, J., Tu, K.: Second-order semantic dependency parsing with end-to-end neural networks. In: ACL, pp. 4609–4618 (2019)
6. Ji, T., Wu, Y., Lan, M.: Graph-based dependency parsing with graph neural networks. In: ACL, pp. 2475–2485 (2019)
7. Li, Y., Li, Z., Zhang, M., Wang, R., Li, S., Si, L.: Self-attentive biaffine dependency parsing. In: IJCAI, pp. 5067–5073 (2019)
8. Peters, M.E., et al.: Deep contextualized word representations. In: NAACL-HLT, pp. 2227–2237 (2018)
9. Devlin, J., Chang, M.-W., Lee, K., Toutanova, K.: BERT: pre-training of deep bidirectional transformers for language understanding. In: NAACL-HLT, pp. 4171–4186 (2019)
10. Kulmizev, A., de Lhoneux, M., Gontrum, J., Fano, E., Nivre, J.: Deep contextualized word embeddings in transition-based and graph-based dependency parsing - a tale of two parsers revisited. In: EMNLP-IJCNLP, pp. 2755–2768 (2019)
11. Wang, Y., Che, W., Guo, J., Liu, Y., Liu, T.: Cross-lingual BERT transformation for zero-shot dependency parsing. In: EMNLP-IJCNLP, pp. 5720–5726 (2019)
12. Danqi, C., Christopher, M.: A fast and accurate dependency parser using neural networks. EMNLP **2014**, 740–750 (2014)
13. Dyer, C., Ballesteros, M., Ling, W., Matthews, A., Smith, N.A..: Transition-based dependency parsing with stack long short-term memory. In: ACL, pp. 334–343 (2015)
14. Andor, D., et al.: Globally normalized transition-based neural networks. In: ACL (2016)

15. Eliyahu, K., Yoav, G.: Simple and accurate dependency parsing using bidirectional LSTM feature representations. Trans. Assoc. Comput. Linguist. **4**, 313–327 (2016)
16. Clark, K., Luong, M.-T., Manning, C.D., Le, Q.V.: Semi-supervised sequence modeling with cross-view training. In: Proceedings of the 2018 Conference on Empirical Methods in Natural Language Processing, pp. 1914–1925 (2018)
17. Qi, P., Dozat, T., Zhang, Y., Manning, C.D.: Universal dependency parsing from scratch. In: Proceedings of the CoNLL 2018 Shared Task: Multilingual Parsing from Raw Text to Universal Dependencies, pp. 160–170 (2018)
18. Lim, K., Park, C.-E., Lee, C., Poibeau, T.: SEx BiST: a multi-source trainable parser with deep contextualized lexical representations. In: Proceedings of the CoNLL 2018 Shared Task: Multilingual Parsing from Raw Text to Universal Dependencies, pp. 143–152 (2018)
19. Che, W., Liu, Y., Wang, Y., Zheng, B., Liu, T.: Towards better UD parsing: deep contextualized word embeddings, ensemble, and treebank concatenation. In: Proceedings of the CoNLL 2018 Shared Task: Multilingual Parsing from Raw Text to Universal Dependencies, pp. 55–64 (2018)
20. Ahmad, W.U., Zhang, Z.., Ma, X., Hovy, E.H., Chang, K.-W., Peng, N.: On difficulties of cross-lingual transfer with order differences: a case study on dependency parsing. In: NAACL-HLT, pp. 2440–2452 (2019)
21. He, J., Zhang, Z., Berg-Kirkpatrick, T., Neubig, G.: Cross-lingual syntactic transfer through unsupervised adaptation of invertible projections. ACL **2019**, 3211–3223 (2019)

Multi-layer Joint Learning of Chinese Nested Named Entity Recognition Based on Self-attention Mechanism

Haoru Li, Haoliang Xu, Longhua Qian$^{(\boxtimes)}$, and Guodong Zhou

School of Computer Science and Technology, Soochow University, Suzhou, China
20185227001@stu.suda.edn.cn, 20175227009@stu.suda.edu.cn,
{qianlonghua,gdzhou}@suda.edu.cn

Abstract. Nested named entity recognition attracts increasingly attentions due to their pervasiveness in general domain as well as in other specific domains. This paper proposes a multi-layer joint learning model for Chinese named entities recognition based on self-attention aggregation mechanism where a series of multi-layered sequence labeling sub-models are joined to recognize named entities in a bottom-up fashion. In order to capture entity semantic information in a lower layer, hidden units in an entity are aggregated using self-attention mechanism and further fed into the higher layer. We conduct extensive experiments using various entity aggregation methods. The results on the Chinese nested entity corpus transformed from the People's Daily show that our model performs best among other competitive methods, implying that self-attention mechanism can effectively aggregate important semantic information in an entity.

Keywords: Nested named entity · LSTM-CRF model · Entity aggregation · Self-attention mechanism

1 Introduction

Named Entity Recognition (NER) aims to recognize words or phrases with particular meaning in a sentence, such as persons (PER), locations (LOC), and organizations (ORG). Many machine learning approaches based on sequence labeling [1–4] have been proposed to improve NER performance on different corpora. There is one particular type of entities with overlapping structure called nested named entities, where an entity is completely contained in another entity. For example, the Chinese entity "[[[中共]$_{ORG}$[北京]$_{LOC}$市委]$_{ORG}$宣传部]$_{ORG}$" (Publicity Department of Beijing Municipal Committee of the Communist Party of China) contains three internal entities, i.e. "[中共]$_{ORG}$" (the Communist Party of China), "[北京]$_{LOC}$" (Beijing) and "[中共北京市委]$_{ORG}$" (Beijing Municipal Committee of the Communist Party of China). Nested named entities entail rich entities and relationships between them, therefore, the recognition of nested named entities [5–7] has become an important research direction.

Methods for recognizing nested entities are mainly divided into rule-based ones and machine learning-based ones. In early years, after flat entities are recognized, rule-based

© Springer Nature Switzerland AG 2020
X. Zhu et al. (Eds.): NLPCC 2020, LNAI 12431, pp. 144–155, 2020.
https://doi.org/10.1007/978-3-030-60457-8_12

post-processing is performed to obtain nested entities [8, 9], design of rules requires human labor and lacks flexibility. Machine learning methods usually take a hierarchical approach, regarding nested entities as a series of separate entities at different levels, the problem is then cast as a multi-layer fundamental sequential labeling tasks. This hierarchical perspective can be refined in three ways: 1) Label Hierarchization [10]: instead of a single label, each word has a combined label which indicates all entity labels layer by layer in a bottom-up fashion. However, this will lead to a large number of labels and small-scale training instances for high-level entities; 2) Model Hierarchization [10, 11]: separate sequence labeling models are trained at and applied to different levels sequentially from bottom to top. Its disadvantages are that there are multiple models and the training/test time might be long; 3) Corpus Hierarchization [12]: the entity instances are generated up to n consecutive words, and each instance can be given an entity type, so we can recognize nested entities with different lengths. The deficiency is that there will be a huge amount of training and testing instances. In addition to these sequential labeling models [13, 14], syntactic tree [15] and hynpergraph [5, 6] are also used to model the task of nested entity recognition. The former uses a syntactic tree to find out the structure of internal or external entities as well as the dependency relationship between them in a sentence; the latter finds different levels of nested entities by using different paths in a directed graph, nevertheless, the training and prediction are computation-intensive due to its complex model structure.

At present there are several corpora available for nested named entity recognition using supervised learning. GENIA V3.02 [16] is an English corpus that is widely used in the biomedical field, and it has been used to nested entities recognition in related research [5, 6, 13–15]. For Chinese named entity recognition there are two corpora available, i.e. ACE2005 [17] and People's Daily [18]. The ACE2005 corpus contains nested entity mentions and People's Daily has been developed into a fully functioned corpus of Chinese nested named entities in a semi-automatic way [19].

Inspired by the success of applying a multi-layer sequential labeling model to nested named entity recognition in biomedical domain [14], we follow the same path to deal with Chinese nested entity recognition. We propose to use a self-attention mechanism to aggregate the entity information and in turn feed the aggregated information to the upper layer. Our self-attention mechanism takes full advantage of different importance from different units in an entity mention and achieves promising experimental results in a Chinese nested entity corpus.

Section 2 illustrates our multi-layer joint learning model for Chinese named entity recognition, and details self-attention aggregation mechanism; In Sect. 3, the experiment setting is described and experimental results are compared and analyzed among different entity aggregation methods; Sect. 4 concludes the paper with future work.

2 Model

2.1 Chinese Nested Entity Recognition Based on Multi-layer Joint Learning

Figure 1 is our multi-layer model for recognizing Chinese nested entities, including an input layer and multiple bottom-up BiLSTM-CRF sub-models, where each sub-model consists of an LSTM layer, an entity aggregation layer and a CRF output layer. The input layer transforms the characters in a sentence into vectors, which are then fed into the first BiLSTM-CRF sub-model. On one hand, the model outputs the first layer of entity labels through its CRF output layer, on the other hand, the LSTM hidden units belonging to an entity are aggregated in the aggregation layer and are further fed into the upper-layer sub-model, and again we will obtain the second-layer entity labels and hidden units. In this way, we will ultimately get highest-level entity labels.

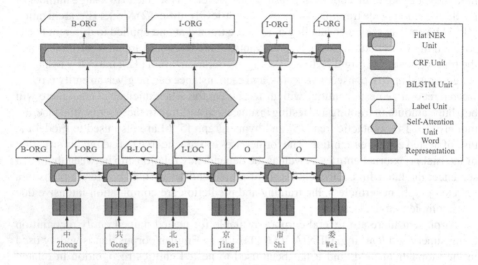

Fig. 1. The multi-layer joint learning model for Chinese nested entity recognition

Input Layer

Similar to other sequence labeling models, our model first converts the Chinese characters in a sentence into a sequence of continuous dense vectors. Formally, for a Chinese sentence $X = \{c_1, c_2, c_3, \ldots, c_n\}$ with n characters, the vector $e_i \in \mathbb{R}^{d_e}$ corresponding to the i-th character c_i can be obtained through a pre-trained character embedding matrix, where d_e is the dimension of the character vector, i.e.:

$$e_i = Lookup(c_i) \tag{1}$$

We use a 200-dimensional embedding matrix which was based on the Word2Vec [20] and pre-trained on Gigaword and Chinese Wikipedia corpora.

LSTM Layer

Bidirectional long-term short-term memory network (BiLSTM) [21] is a variant of recurrent neural network (RNN) [22]. Its advantage is that it can effectively capture the long-distance information in both directions in sequence labeling. In the BiLSTM-CRF model of the j-th layer, the hidden vectors in the forward and backward directions can be expressed as follows:

$$\vec{h}_i^j = \begin{cases} \overrightarrow{LSTM}\left(\vec{h}_{i-1}^j, \vec{h}_i^{j-1}\right) & j > 1 \\ \overrightarrow{LSTM}\left(\vec{h}_{i-1}^j, e_i\right) & j = 1 \end{cases} \tag{2}$$

$$
\overleftarrow{h}_i^j =
\begin{cases}
\overleftarrow{LSTM}\left(\overleftarrow{h}_{i-1}^{j}, \overleftarrow{h}_i^{j-1}\right) & j > 1 \\
\overleftarrow{LSTM}\left(\overleftarrow{h}_{i-1}^{j}, e_i\right) & j = 1
\end{cases}
\tag{3}
$$

$$
h_i^j = \overrightarrow{h}_i^j \oplus \overleftarrow{h}_i^j
\tag{4}
$$

Where e_i is the *i-th* character vector. The final output vector h_i^j of the hidden layer at the i-th moment of the *j-th* layer is composed of the forward vector $\overrightarrow{h}_i^j$ and the backward vector $\overleftarrow{h}_i^j$ and will be fed as input into the next layer.

CRF Output Layer

The conditional random field (CRF) is used to decode the hidden vector output from each LSTM layer to obtain the entity labels. Assume that the hidden units in the *j-th* LSTM layer of is $H^j = \left\{h_1^j, h_2^j, h_3^j, \ldots, h_n^j\right\}$, and the label sequence is $Y^j = \left\{y_1^j, y_2^j, y_3^j, \ldots, y_n^j\right\}$, the output score can be expressed as:

$$
s\left(H^j, Y^j\right) = \sum_{i=0}^{n} A_{y_i^j, y_{i+1}^j} + \sum_{i=1}^{n} P_{i,y_i^j}
\tag{5}
$$

$$
P_{i,y_i^j} = W_p h_i^j + b_p
\tag{6}
$$

Where A denotes the label transition matrix, $A_{y_i^j, y_{i+1}^j}$ represents the transition score from label y_i^j to label y_{i+1}^j. P is the state output matrix, and P_{i,y_i^j} represents the score that the output of the i-th unit is label y_i^j, which is linearly transformed from the i-th output vector h_i^j in the j-th layer. W_p and b_p are the weight and bias matrices respectively. Ultimately, the probability of label sequence in the j-th layer can be calculated as:

$$
p\left(Y^j | H^j\right) = \frac{e^{s(H^j, Y^j)}}{\sum_{\tilde{y} \in Y_{Hj}} e^{s(H^j, \tilde{y})}}
\tag{7}
$$

Where Y_{Hj} is the set of all possible label sequences in the *j-th* layer.

During training, the multi-layer joint learning model sums the loss functions from each LSTM-CRF model. Assume the number of layers is L, then the whole loss function for a training instance (X, y) is:

$$
Loss(X, y) = -log(p(y|X)) = -\sum_{j=1}^{L} log\left(p\left(Y^j | H^j\right)\right)
\tag{8}
$$

Therefore, the overall training objective function can be expressed as:

$$J(\theta) = -\frac{1}{m} \sum_{i=1}^{M} Loss(X_i, y_i) + \lambda ||\theta||^2 \tag{9}$$

When predicting, each LSTM-CRF model uses the Viterbi algorithm to decode independently, and the optimal label sequence for that layer is obtained by:

$$y^* = argmax_{\tilde{y} \in Y_H} s(H, \tilde{y}) \tag{10}$$

Entity Aggregation Layer

The entity aggregation layer aggregates the hidden unit vectors belonging to the same entity in the LSTM layer into a single vector. Then, these entity vectors and other non-entity hidden unit vectors are reassembled in the original order into a new sequence, and the sequence is input into the upper LSTM-CRF model. These same operations are performed until all levels of nested entities are recognized.

2.2 Self-attention-Based Entity Aggregation

A simple method for entity aggregation is the average method [13], which takes the average value of the consecutive hidden units belonging to an entity in the LSTM layer as the entity representation as shown below:

$$m_j = \frac{1}{end - start + 1} \sum_{i=start}^{end} z_i \tag{11}$$

Where start and end indicate the start and end positions of the entity in the LSTM sequence, and the z_i denotes the i-th hidden vector. While j indicates the entity position in the newly formed sequence fed to the upper LSTM-CRF submodel, and m_j represents its corresponding vector. The average method has achieved good performance in the recognition of nested entities on the GENIA corpus [13].

The disadvantage of the average method is that it does not consider the different contributions from different words in an entity to its meaning. For example, in the Chinese nested entities "[[中共]ORG[安徽]LOC[宿州]LOC市委]ORG" (Anhui Suzhou Municipal Party Committee of the Communist Party of China), after the first level of entities such as "中共 (the Communist Party of China)", "安徽(Anhui)" and "宿州 (Suzhou)" were recognized, these three entities need to be merged into their respective units. Among three entities, the meaning of the second entity is evenly distributed on two characters, while those of the first and third entities are mainly focused on the last characters, i.e. the last characters determine their semantic types.

Attention mechanism is a selective mechanism for allocating the importance of each unit in a sequence. It can selectively focus on some important units while ignoring others [23, 24], so it has been widely used in various NLP tasks. However, its disadvantage is that it does not take the syntactically structured information in a sentence into account. To solve this problem, self-attention mechanism [24] is proposed and has been widely used in recent years. Self-attention mechanism can evaluate the importance of other units to each unit in a sequence, and this importance information can be regarded in some degree as a kind of syntactic structure information. Formally, the self-attention function Attention (Q, K, V) can be described as a mapping relationship between a query to a series of key-value pairs in a sequence. Within a nested entity, if the query, key and value in a sequence of continuous units belonging to the same entity, are denoted as Q, K and V respectively, its aggregated vector m_j can be expressed as:

$$\begin{bmatrix} Q \\ K \\ V \end{bmatrix} = \begin{bmatrix} W_Q \\ W_K \\ W_V \end{bmatrix} Z \tag{12}$$

$$M = \text{Attention}(Q, K, V) = softmax\left(\frac{QK^T}{\sqrt{d_k}}\right) V \tag{13}$$

$$m_j = MaxPooling(M) \tag{14}$$

Where $Z = \{z_{start} \ldots z_{end}\}$ is a sequence of hidden units within an entity, and d_k is the input hidden vector dimension, j is the sequence number of the entity in the newly merged sequence. W_Q, W_K, and W_V denote the transformation matrices for Q, K, and V, respectively.

3 Experimentation

This section mainly introduces the compared methods, the corpus used in the experiment, the model parameter settings and the analysis of experimental results.

3.1 Compared Methods

From the perspective of entity aggregation methods, we explore their performance impact on Chinese nested entity recognition. The following methods are compared:

- **No Aggregation**: On the basis of the current LSTM layer, the units directly go to the upper LSTM-CRF sub-model.
- **Average Aggregation**: As described in Sect. 2, the hidden vectors of the entities recognized by the current LSTM-CRF sub-model are fed to the upper sub-model after averaging [14].
- **CNN Aggregation**: A window with a size of 3 is used for convolution operation on the hidden vectors within each entity in the current LSTM layer, and then maximum pooling operation is performed to output the entity vectors to the upper submodel.
- **LSTM Aggregation**: A Bi-LSTM model is used to aggregate each entity and its last units are fed to the upper sub-model.
- **Attention Aggregation**: the attention mechanism as in [25] are used for entity aggregation.
- **Self-attention Aggregation**: the method we used as described in Subsect. 2.2.

3.2 Corpus

We use the Chinese nested entity corpus transformed from the "People's Daily" [19] as the training and test corpus, which contains more than 40,000 sentences and more than 60,000 entities. The entity statistics in each layer are shown in Table 1. There are three types of entities, i.e. person (PER), location (LOC) and organization (ORG). Nested entities in layers 2–5 are called high-level entities, while those in the layer 1, no matter whether they are nested in the upper entities, are called bottom-level ones.

Table 1. Entity statistics in different layers.

Layer	PER		LOC		ORG		Total	
	#	%	#	%	#	%	#	%
1	19,808	100.0	28,174	97.4	5,779	45.7	53,761	87.6
2	0	0.0	723	2.5	6,107	48.3	6,830	11.1
3	0	0.0	13	0.0	715	5.7	728	1.2
4	0	0.0	1	0.0	40	0.3	41	0.1
5	0	0.0	1	0.0	1	0.0	2	0.0
High-level	0	0.0	738	2.6	6,863	54.3	7,601	12.4
Total	19,808	100.0	28,912	100.0	12,642	100.0	61,362	100.0

It can be seen from the table that all the person entities are at bottom level, while the organization entities have most of the high-level entities, which account for over 12% in all entities.

3.3 Evaluation

The corpus is randomly divided into three parts: training, development, and test sets according to the ratio of 8:1:1. The model are trained on the training set and validated on the development set in order to select the best model, and finally tested on the test set. In order to verify the stability of the model, we run 5 times to get the average performance score as the overall score.

The standard precision P, recall R and the harmonic F1 to evaluate nested entity recognition performance [15].

3.4 Hyper-parameters

The dimension of word-embedding we take is 200. During training, we set the batch size to 100, and the learning rate to 0.005, together with 0.5 dropout. The optimization we take is Adam. It should be noted that during training, a random dropout process is performed before entity aggregation, however it is not performed during testing.

3.5 Experimental Results

Performance Impact of Different Entity Aggregation Methods
Table 2 compares the nested entity recognition performance of different entity aggregation methods. The performance scores are divided into bottom-level entities, high-level entities and all entities. The values in parentheses on the right side of the F1 scores indicate the standard deviations across 5 runs, and the highest values in each column are indicated in bold. It can be seen from the table:

Table 2. Performance comparison of various entity aggregation methods

Aggregation methods	Bottom-level entities			High-level entities			All entities		
	P(%)	R(%)	F1(%)	P(%)	R(%)	F1(%)	P(%)	R(%)	F1(%)
No	93.2	92.0	92.6(0.9)	78.4	84.4	81.2(4.4)	91.9	91.8	91.9(1.0)
Average	**94.7**	92.3	93.5(0.7)	81.8	82.9	82.4(5.9)	93.4	91.5	92.4(1.2)
Attention	93.4	92.2	92.8(0.7)	83.2	79.0	81.0(2.1)	92.8	91.0	91.9(0.6)
Self-attention	94.0	**93.2**	**93.6(0.4)**	84.6	**86.3**	**85.4(1.5)**	93.2	**92.6**	**92.9(0.4)**
CNN	94.4	92.1	93.2(0.2)	84.8	84.7	84.7(1.7)	**93.5**	91.6	92.6(0.4)
BiLSTM	94.1	93.1	**93.6(0.5)**	**86.5**	83.8	85.1(2.2)	93.2	92.6	92.9(0.8)

(1) From an overall perspective, various entity aggregation methods except the vanilla attention perform better than the one without aggregation. Self-attention and LSTM perform comparably, which are about 0.5 units higher than the average one. However, the standard deviation of self-attention is smaller than LSTM, implying the former performs more stable than the latter.

(2) From the perspective of high-level entity recognition, self-attention performs slightly better than LSTM, and both have reached over 85% of F1. We believe that entity aggregation plays an important role in the process of high-level entity recognition. While the average aggregation treats each character in an entity equally and the LSTM aggregation selects the last unit, the self-attention mechanism can effectively select the most important information across different units and therefore improves the recognition performance for high-level entities.

Performance Comparison Between Entities at Different Levels
We compare the performance of entity recognition at different levels with the self-attention aggregation method in Table 3. Since there is no entity recognized at all in the 4th and 5th layers, there are omitted in the table. For reference, the number and ratio of entities at different layers are also reported in the 1st and 2nd data columns. It can be seen from the table:

Table 3. Performance of named entity recognition on various layers.

Layers	#	%	P(%)	R(%)	F1(%)
1	53,761	87.6	**94.0**	**93.2**	**93.6(0.4)**
2	6,830	11.1	84.3	86.4	85.3(1.0)
3	728	1.2	74.1	73.1	73.1(5.4)
High-level	7,601	12.4	84.6	86.3	85.4(1.5)
Overall	61,362	100.0	93.1	92.7	92.9(0.4)

(1) With the level of layer increases, the performance of entity recognition consistently and drastically decreases, and the standard deviation increases as well. The reason for this phenomenon is that with the level of layer increases, the number of entities in that level decreases at a rate of approximate 1/8–1/9. Reasonably, the F1 scores for the 2nd and 3rd layers are roughly 8–12 units lower than their lower lays.

(2) Counter-intuitively, the overall F1 score of the high-level layers is slightly higher than the weighted average F1 score of the 2nd and 3rd layers. This is due to the phenomenon called "mis-layered recognition", which occurs when an entity at a higher level is recognized in advance at a lower level. This entity is regarded as a false positive in the lower layer, but is a true positive in overall high-level layers. For example, "[[[中共]$_{ORG}$ [北京]$_{LOC}$ 市委]$_{ORG}$ 宣传部]$_{ORG}$" (Publicity Department of Beijing Municipal Committee of the Communist Party of China) is a three-layered nested entity, however, the entity "[中共北京市委]$_{ORG}$"(Beijing Municipal Committee of the Communist Party of China) is not recognized in the 2nd layer, but instead the outmost entity is recognized.

Performance Comparison Between Different Entity Types

Table 4 reports the performance scores on different types of entities on the test set using self-attention for entity aggregation, where all entities are divided into bottom-level and high-level. Also, the maximal score in each data column are indicated in bold.

Table 4. Performance on different types of named entities.

Type	Bottom-level entities			High-level entities			All entities		
	P(%)	R(%)	F1(%)	P(%)	R(%)	F1(%)	P(%)	R(%)	F1(%)
PER	**94.9**	93.2	**94.1(0.2)**	0.0	0.0	0.0(0.0)	**94.9**	**93.2**	**94.1(0.2)**
LOC	93.8	**93.7**	93.7(0.6)	68.7	66.0	67.1(1.8)	93.4	93.2	93.3(0.6)
ORG	91.5	90.4	90.9(0.6)	**86.4**	**88.7**	**87.5(1.8)**	89.7	90.6	90.2(1.3)
Avg.	94.0	93.2	93.6(0.4)	84.6	86.3	85.4(1.6)	93.1	92.7	92.9(0.4)

It can be seen from the table:

(1) For the bottom-level entities, the type of PER achieves the highest F1 score and the ORG kind gets the lowest F1 scores. This is no surprise since the person entities are simplest in entity composition while the organization entities are the most complicated.

(2) From the high-level entities, the type of ORG performs better than LOC. The main reason is that it has about 10 times more instances that LOC, so the former F1 score is ~10 units higher than that for LOC.

(3) Overall, the type of PER achieves the highest F1 score which ORG gets the lowest one. The reason is that there is no person entity at high levels where the recognition performance will be significantly lower than that at the bottom level. For LOC, though the F1 score at high levels are significantly lower than that for ORG, the smaller number of high-level entities decreases the overall performance in less degree than for ORG.

3.6 Error Analysis

We mainly analyzed 100 recognition errors in entities randomly selected from the test set. They are roughly divided into the following 4 cases:

Long Entities
High-level entities contain internal entities; they are usually longer that flat entities. Long entities with a length of 8–15 Chinese characters are often erroneously recognized by the model, accounting for about 40% of all false negative instances. It seems clear that there are fewer training examples for long entities and furthermore, long entities are often complex and hard to be recognized. For example, in the instance "[[北京]$_{LOC}$产品质量监督检测所]$_{ORG}$" (Beijing Product Quality Supervision and Inspection Institute), the outer entity is not recognized by the model.

Cascaded Errors
Many high-level entities are mis-recognized caused by erroneously recognized internal entities, accounting for about 27% of all high-level recognition mistakes. For example, for the entity "[[江苏省]$_{LOC}$[南京]$_{LOC}$火车站]$_{LOC}$" (Jiangsu Nanjing Railway Station), the model mistakenly recognizes "[火车站]$_{LOC}$" (Railway Station) as an entity, leading to leave out the outmost entity.

Generic Entities
Nearly 50% of the false positives are related to generic nouns recognized as named entities. For example, although the phrase "人民检察院" (People's Procuratorate) might be regarded as an entity of ORG, it is not labeled as an entity in the corpus due to its unspecific reference.

Keywords Misleading
Some highly informative keywords plus infrequent characters may lead to false positives, accounts for about 20% of false positives instances. For example, in the sentence "翻

翩委屈地哇哇大哭" (Pianpian cries in grievances), the model mis-recognized "翩翩委(Pianpian wei)" as an organization probably because the character "委" (committee) is highly indicative of an organization and "翩翩" (pianpian) is an infrequent word.

4 Conclusion

This paper casts Chinese nested entity recognition as a multi-layer sequence labeling task and proposes a joint learning model based on self-attention aggregation mechanism. Various aggregation methods are explored and compared with self-attention mechanism in terms of their performance scores on a Chinese nested entity corpus. Experiments demonstrate the efficacy of our model. We also point out the existing problems with Chinese nested named entity recognition via error analysis. Future work can be focused on the augmentation of training data for long entities by semi-supervised learning and reduce the impact of misleading keywords by introducing semantically powerful pre-trained language models like BERT [26].

Acknowledgments. Sincere appreciation to anonymous reviewers for their helpful and insightful comments that greatly improve the manuscript.

Funding. Publication of this article was sponsored by National Natural Science Foundation of China [61976147; 2017YFB1002101; 61373096].

References

1. Lample, G., Ballesteros, M., Subramanian, S., Kawakami, K., Dyer, C.: Neural architectures for named entity recognition. In: Proceedings of the 2016 Conference of the North American Chapter of the Association for Computational Linguistics: Human Language Technologies, pp. 260–270 (2016)
2. Ma, X., Hovy, E.: End-to-end sequence labeling via bi-directional LSTM-CNNs-CRF. In: Proceedings of the 54th Annual Meeting of the Association for Computational Linguistics (Long Papers), vol. 1, pp. 1064–1074 (2016)
3. Gridach, M.: Character-level neural network for biomedical named entity recognition. J. Biomed. Inform. **70**, 85–91 (2017)
4. Strubell, E., Verga, P., Belanger, D., McCallum, A.: Fast and accurate entity recognition with iterated dilated convolutions. In: Proceedings of the 2017 Conference on Empirical Methods in Natural Language Processing, pp. 2670–2680 (2017)
5. Muis, A.O., Lu, W.: Labeling gaps between words: recognizing overlapping mentions with mention separators. In: Proceedings of the 2017 Conference on Empirical Methods in Natural Language Processing, pp. 2608–2618 (2017)
6. Lu, W., Roth, D.: Joint mention extraction and classification with mention hypergraphs. In: Proceedings of the 2015 Conference on Empirical Methods in Natural Language Processing, pp. 857–867 (2015)
7. Xu, M.B., Jiang, H., Watcharawittayakul, S.: A local detection approach for named entity recognition and mention detection. In: Proceedings of the 55th Annual Meeting of the Association for Computational Linguistics (Long Papers), vol. 1, pp. 1237–1247 (2017)

8. Zhou, G.D., Zhang, J., Su, J., Shen, D., Tan, C.L., et al.: Recognizing names in biomedical texts: a machine learning approach. Bioinformatics **20**, 1178–1190 (2004)
9. Zhou, G.D.: Recognizing names in biomedical texts using mutual information independence model and SVM plus sigmoid. Int. J. Med. Inform. 456–467 (2006)
10. Alex, B., Haddow, B., Grover, C.: Recognising nested named entities in biomedical text. In: Proceedings of the Workshop on BioNLP 2007, pp. 65–72 (2007)
11. Fu, C.Y.: Research on Chinese Nested Named Entity Recognition Method. Heilongjiang University, Harbin (2011)
12. Byrne, K.: Nested named entity recognition in historical archive text. In: Proceedings of International Conference on Semantic Computing, pp. 589–596 (2007)
13. Sohrab, M.G., Miwa, M.: Deep exhaustive model for nested named entity recognition. In: Proceedings of the 2018 Conference on Empirical Methods in Natural Language Processing, pp. 2843–2849 (2018)
14. Ju, M., Miwa, M., Ananiadou, S.: A neural layered model for nested named entity recognition. In: Proceedings of the 2018 Conference of the North American Chapter of the Association for Computational Linguistics: Human Language Technologies (Long Papers), vol. 1, pp. 1446–1459 (2018)
15. Finkel, J.R., Manning, C.D.: Nested named entity recognition. In: Proceedings of the 2009 Conference on Empirical Methods in Natural Language Processing, vol, pp. 141–150 (2009)
16. Ohta, T., Tateisi, Y., Kim, J.D.: The GENIA corpus: an annotated research abstract corpus in molecular biology domain. In: Proceedings of the Second International Conference on Human Language Technology Research, pp. 82–86. Morgan Kaufmann Publishers Inc. (2002)
17. Walker, C., Strassel, S., Medero, J., Maeda, K.: ACE 2005 Multilingual Training Corpus. Linguistic Data Consortium, Philadelphia (2006)
18. Hu, J.H.: Statistics and analysis of data in people's daily 1998. In: Proceedings of the First Symposium on Computational Linguistics for Students, pp. 323–329 (2002)
19. Li, Y.Q., He, Y.Q., Qian, L.H., Zhou, G.D.: Chinese nested named entity recognition corpus construction. J. Chin. Inform. Process. 19–26 (2018)
20. Mikolov, T., Sutskever, I., Chen, K., Corrado, G., Dean, J.: Distributed representations of words and phrases and their compositionality. In: Proceedings of the 26th International Conference on Neural Information Processing Systems, Advances in neural information processing systems, vol. 2, pp. 3111–3119 (2013)
21. Hochreiter, S., Schmidhuber, J.: Long short-term memory. Neural Comput. 1735–1780 (1997)
22. Elman, J.L.: Distributed representations, simple recurrent networks, and grammatical structure. Mach. Learn. **7**, 195–225 (1991)
23. Feng, H.: Research on visual attention mechanism and its application. North China Electric Power University (Beijing) (2011)
24. Vaswani, A., et al.: Attention is all you need. In: Proceedings of the 31st International Conference on Neural Information Processing, pp. 6000–6010 (2017)
25. Zhu, Y.Y., Wang, G.X.: CAN-NER: convolutional attention network for chinese named entity recognition. In: Proceedings of the 2019 Conference of the North American Chapter of the Association for Computational Linguistics: Human Language Technologies (Long and Short Papers), vol. 1, pp. 3384–3393 (2019)
26. Devlin, J., Chang, M.W., Lee, K., Toutanova, k.: BERT: pre-training of deep bidirectional transformers for language understanding. In: Proceedings of the 2019 Conference of the North American Chapter of the Association for Computational Linguistics: Human Language Technologies (Long and Short Papers), vol. 1, pp. 4171–4186 (2019)

Adversarial BiLSTM-CRF Architectures for Extra-Propositional Scope Resolution

Rongtao Huang[1], Jing Ye[1], Bowei Zou[1,2(✉)], Yu Hong[1], and Guodong Zhou[1]

[1] Natural Language Processing Lab, Soochow University, Suzhou, China
`rthuang.suda@gmail.com`, `jye.scu@gmail.com`, `tianxianer@gmail.com`,
`gdzhou@suda.edu.cn`
[2] Institute for Infocomm Research, Singapore, Singapore
`zou_bowei@i2r.a-star.edu.sg`

Abstract. Due to the ability of expressively representing narrative structures, proposition-aware learning models in text have been drawing more and more attentions in information extraction. Following this trend, recent studies go deeper into learning fine-grained extra-propositional structures, such as negation and speculation. However, most of elaborately-designed experiments reveal that existing extra-proposition models either fail to learn from the context or neglect to address cross-domain adaptation. In this paper, we attempt to systematically address the above challenges via an adversarial BiLSTM-CRF model, to jointly model the potential extra-propositions and their contexts. This is motivated by the superiority of sequential architecture in effectively encoding order information and long-range context dependency. On the basis, we come up with an adversarial neural architecture to learn the invariant and discriminative latent features across domains. Experimental results on the standard BioScope corpus show the superiority of the proposed neural architecture, which significantly outperforms the state-of-the-art on scope resolution in both in-domain and cross-domain scenarios.

Keywords: Scope resolution · Domain adaptation · Adversarial BiLSTM-CRF

1 Introduction

So far previous studies mainly focus on modeling intra-propositional contents, such as that in information extraction. Recently, there is an increasing interest in the study of extra-propositional aspects in narratives, in general, including negation and speculation. As two kinds of fascinating grammatical phenomena due to the potential contribution of understanding the deep meanings of a sentence, negation reverses the true value of a proposition, while speculation refers

Supported by National Natural Science Foundation of China (Grants No. 61703293, No. 61672368, No. 61751206).

to a statement at a specific certainty level, or that of reliability, subjectivity and perspective [13]. According to the statistics on the biomedical literature genre [23], about 13.45% and 17.69% narrative sentences contain negative and speculative expressions, respectively. Therefore, their resolution has become extremely crucial for deep semantic analysis.

In principle, negation and speculation scope resolution aims to determine the text fragment affected by a given negative or speculative keyword in a sentence. Consider following two sentences as examples. The negative keyword *"not"* and the speculative keyword *"possible"* dominate their corresponding scopes of *"not expensive"* and *"the possible future scenarios"*, respectively.

(S1) [*The chair is **not** expensive*] *but comfortable.*
(S1) *Considering we have seen, what are now* [*the **possible** future scenarios*]?

In the literature, most of existing models recast scope resolution as a classification problem, determining each token in a sentence as being either inside or outside a specific scope. This undoubtedly enables a wide range of use of various machine learning models as the solutions, such as neural networks. Though it also raises a challenging question: *how to model context.* On the one hand, the existing learning models are difficult to capture long-distance syntactic features, even if they have put into use the dependency parsing tree [16]; On the other hand, the models heavily rely on highly-engineered features, such as the syntactic path between the words inside and outside a candidate scope [24].

Another challenge for scope resolution is *cross-domain adaptation.* A robust learning model generally has comparable performances over different domains of data. On the contrary, a model is of less adaptation if it exhibits decreasing performance when being transferred to other domain. This problem hasn't yet been completely overcome in the field of scope resolution, although ad-hoc heuristics [22] and cross-domain universal feature representations [3] have been used.

In this paper, to well address the challenge in context modeling, we alternatively treat the scope resolution as a sequence labeling problem, and thus turn to the use of a bidirectional LSTM network integrated with a sequential CRF layer, namely BiLSTM-CRF, to extract the long-distance contexts at sentence level. Moreover, we replace the sophisticated syntactic features with the shallow ones, which have been proven more suitable for a sequence-to-sequence model. Besides, to well address the challenge in cross-domain adaptation, we come up with an adversarial domain adaptation framework to transfer latent features from the source domain to the target. Using such a framework, we attempt to enable the learning model to be aware of both domain-specific discriminative features and shareable ones among different domains.

Our experimentation is carried out on the BioScope corpus. For in-domain scope resolution, our sequence-to-sequence model achieves 81.87% on negation, while 87.43% on speculation, yielding an improvement of 4.73% and 1.68% respectively than the state-of-the-art. In the cross-domain scenario, our adversarial model also outperforms the benchmarks on two different genres. This suggests the great effectiveness of our approach in both in-domain and cross-domain negation and speculation scope resolution.

2   Related Work

Extra-Propositional Scope Resolution. Earlier studies on extra-propositional scope resolution mainly focused on developing various heuristic rules with syntactic structures to identify scopes [14,21]. With the release of the BioScope corpus [23], machine learning-based methods began to dominate this task [11,12,22,24]. However, these models rely extensively on feature engineering.

In recent years, deep neural networks are alternative models that can learn latent features automatically. Qian et al. [16] employ a CNN-based model with syntactic path features to identify the negative and speculative scopes. Fancellu et al. [3] introduce BiLSTM networks by only word embeddings and PoS embeddings for scope resolution. Different from their studies, we add a CRF layer on the BiLSTM model and investigate the effects of various features. Moreover, to the best of our knowledge, our work is the first to utilize the adversarial adaptation framework for cross-domain scope resolution.

BiLSTM-CRF for NLP. BiLSTM-CRF is one of deep neural sequence models, where a bidirectional long short-term memory (BiLSTM) layer [6] and a conditional random fields (CRF) layer [8] are stacked together for sequence learning. Currently, it has obtained certain successes on various NLP tasks, e.g., sentiment analysis [1] and named entity recognition [9]. We utilize such model to learn bidirectional features at sentence level.

Adversarial Domain Adaptation. Recently, adversarial training have become increasingly popular [5,10]. For domain adaptation, Ganin et al. [4] propose DANN to learn discriminative but invariant representations, transferring features from the source domain to the target. In the NLP community, there are a couple of studies in sentiment classification [2], dependency parsing [19], and relation classification [17]. In this paper, we propose an adversarial framework to represent invariant features across domains, and gain discrimination of features, which allows our model to generalize better.

3   Extra-Propositional Scope Resolution

Figure 1 illustrates the architecture of BiLSTM-CRF networks for scope resolution. Regarding it as a sequence labeling problem, the sequence of embeddings (x_i) is given as input to BiLSTM networks, which generates a representation of the left context (l_i) and the right context (r_i) for each token in a sentence. These representations are then concatenated (c_i) and linearly projected onto a CRF layer to take into account neighboring tags, yielding the final prediction for every token (y_i).

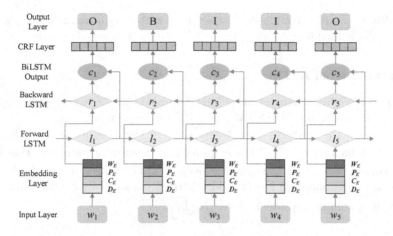

Fig. 1. Architecture of BiLSTM-CRF networks for scope resolution.

3.1 Label Scheme

We apply the BIO label scheme.

- **B:** The token is inside the scope and occurs before the negative or speculative keyword.
- **I:** The token is inside the scope and occurs after the keyword (inclusive).
- **O:** The token is outside of the scope.

Under such scheme, our model tags each word a label and decodes the scope.

3.2 Embedding Layer

We build an embedding layer to encode words, relative positions, constituency nodes, and dependency relations by real-valued vectors. Given an input sentence $S = (w_1, w_2, ..., w_n)$, we first transform each word into a real-valued vector $\boldsymbol{x}_w \in \mathbb{R}^{d_w}$ by using a word embedding matrix $\boldsymbol{W} \in \mathbb{R}^{d_w \times |V|}$, where V is the input vocabulary.

To capture the informative features of the relationship between words and the negative or speculative keyword, we map the relative distance from keyword to each word to a real-valued vector $\boldsymbol{x}_p \in \mathbb{R}^{d_p}$ by using a position embedding matrix $\boldsymbol{P} \in \mathbb{R}^{d_p \times |P|}$, where P is the set of relative distances which are mapped to a vector initialized randomly [18].

Instead of complicated features, such as parsing trees [24] and syntactic paths [16], we only employ a syntactic tag of the current token. For constituency parsing, we map the direct syntactic categories of each word to a real-valued vector $\boldsymbol{x}_c \in \mathbb{R}^{d_c}$ by using a constituency embedding matrix $\boldsymbol{C} \in \mathbb{R}^{d_c \times |C|}$, where C is the set of syntactic category. With the same manner, we can obtain the dependency real-valued vector $\boldsymbol{x}_d \in \mathbb{R}^{d_d}$. We utilize the father node of the current word in dependency tree as input.

Finally, we represent a input sentence as a vector sequence $x = \{x_1, x_2, ..., x_n\}$ with the embedding dimension $d = (d_w + d_p + d_c + d_d)$.

3.3 Bidirectional LSTM

Inspired by the work Huang et al. [7] and Lample et al. [9], we present a hybrid tagging architecture with BiLSTM and CRF for scope resolution.

Considering the contexts of each token x_t in vector sequence x, a forward LSTM and a backward LSTM are employed to generate a representation $\overrightarrow{h_t}$ of the left context and $\overleftarrow{h_t}$ of the right, respectively. The representation of a token using such bidirectional LSTM (BiLSTM). h_t is obtained by concatenating the left and right context representations $\left[\overrightarrow{h_t}; \overleftarrow{h_t}\right]$.

3.4 CRF Layer

As a scope is the text fragment in sentence governed by a negative or speculative keyword, there are some strong dependencies across output labels. For instance, the tag B cannot follow the tag I in our label scheme. It is difficult to learn these constraints by BiLSTM. Therefore, we model them jointly using a conditional random field (CRF) layer [8].

For an input sentence x, we denote C as the matrix of the output by BiLSTM. C is of size $n \times k$, where k is the number of distinct tags, and $c_{i,j}$ corresponds to the score of the jth tag of the ith token in a sentence. For a sequence of predictions y, we define its score to be

$$s(x, y) = \sum_{i=0}^{n} A_{y_i, y_{i+1}} + \sum_{i=1}^{n} c_{i, y_i}, \tag{1}$$

where $A_{i,j}$ denotes the score of a transition from the tag i to the tag j. y_0 and y_{n+1} are the additional tags of $START$ and END, respectively. A softmax layer over all possible tag sequences yields a probability for the sequence y:

$$p(y|x) = \frac{1}{Z(x)} \exp(s(x, y)), \tag{2}$$

where $Z(x) = \sum_Y \exp(s(x, Y))$, and Y denotes all possible tag sequences. During training, we maximize the log-probability of the correct tag sequence:

$$\mathcal{L}_c = \max \log(p(y|x)) \tag{3}$$

While decoding, we predict the output sequence that obtains the maximum score given by

$$y^* = \arg \max_Y s(x, Y). \tag{4}$$

3.5   Domain Adaptation via Adversarial Training

The BiLSTM-CRF networks learn the latent feature representations which are discriminative for scope resolution, while the adversarial domain adaptation framework aims to make these feature representations invariant across domains. To this end, we add a domain discriminator that takes the feature representations (output of the BiLSTM-CRF networks) as input, and tries to discriminate between the source domain and the target domain.

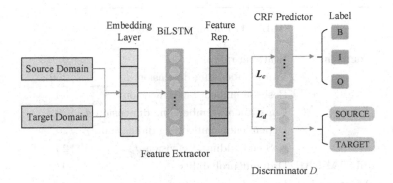

Fig. 2. Architecture of the adversarial framework for cross-domain scope resolution.

Figure 2 shows the architecture of our cross-domain adversarial framework, containing three main components: a *feature extractor* that encodes an input sentence S in shared feature space, a *CRF predictor* that labels the scope tags ("BIO") for S given the feature representations, and a *domain discriminator* that indicates whether S is from "SOURCE" or "TARGET".

We introduce BiLSTM networks as the feature extractor and a CRF layer as the scope predictor, respectively. The domain discriminator D is a binary classifier which is implemented as a fully-connected neural network. The training objective of D is to distinguish the input source of feature representations as far as possible:

$$\mathcal{L}_d = \mathbb{E}_{(\boldsymbol{x}_s, \boldsymbol{x}_t) \sim data} \left[D(H(\boldsymbol{x}_s)) - D(H(\boldsymbol{x}_t)) \right], \tag{5}$$

where $\mathbb{E}_{(\boldsymbol{x}_s, \boldsymbol{x}_t) \sim data} [\cdot]$ denotes the expectation in terms of the data distribution, $D(\boldsymbol{H})$ denotes the output of discriminator D to estimate the probability that $\boldsymbol{H}$ comes from the source domain rather than the target, and $\boldsymbol{x}_s$ and $\boldsymbol{x}_t$ are instances from the source domain and the target domain, respectively.

Finally, the feature extractor strives to minimize both the scope predictor loss $\mathcal{L}_c$ (Eq. (3)) and the domain discriminator loss $\mathcal{L}_d$ (Eq. (5)):

$$\mathcal{L}_f = -\mathcal{L}_c + \lambda \mathcal{L}_d. \tag{6}$$

Algorithm 1 illustrates the adversarial training procedure. First, we initialize the parameters by uniform distribution (step line 1). Then we interleave the

---

Algorithm 1. Adversarial Training Procedure

Require: Training sets $\mathcal{D}_{sou}$, $\mathcal{D}_{tar}$
Ensure: BiLSTM-CRF model for target domain
1: Initialize model parameters.
2: **repeat**
3:    Randomly sample each 50% instances from $\mathcal{D}_{sou}$ and $\mathcal{D}_{tar}$, respectively
4:    Train discriminator D through Eq. (5)
5:    Train BiLSTM-CRF model through Eq. (6)
6: **until** convergence

Table 1. Parameter settings.

Common	Learning rate η	0.015
	Word embedding dimension d_w	200
	Position embedding dimension d_P	50
	Constituency embedding dimension d_C	20
	Dependency embedding dimension d_D	20
	PoS embedding dimension d_{pos}	20
BiLSTM-CRF	Dropout probability d_1	0.5
Adversarial	Dropout probability d_2	0.3
Framework	Adversarial balance λ	0.01

following steps at each iteration: (1) forming a mini-batch set by randomly sampling each 50% instances from source domain and target domain, respectively (step line 3), (2) optimizing the adversarial loss function by all of instances (step line 4), and (3) optimizing the CRF loss function by only the instances of source domain (step line 5). Note that, for the instances from source domain, both $\mathcal{L}_c$ and $\mathcal{L}_d$ are active, while only the $\mathcal{L}_d$ is active for the instances from target domain. Upon successful training, the feature representations generated by the BiLSTM networks are thus encouraged to be both discriminative for scope resolution and invariant across domains.

4   Experimentation

4.1   Experimental Settings

We conduct our experiments on the commonly used BioScope corpus [23], which is a widely used and freely available resource consisting of sentences annotated with negative and speculative scopes in biomedical domain. We evaluate all of the systems by using precision, recall, and F1-score over the number of tokens correctly classified as part of the scope. Moreover, the Percentage of Correct Scopes (PCS) is adopted to report the scope-based performance, which considers a scope correct if all of the tokens in the sentence have been assigned the correct scope types. Obviously, PCS can better describe the overall performance for the task.

We employ trained word vectors induced from 230M sentences in biomedical domain[1] [15]. In addition, both the constituency and dependency parsing trees are produced by Stanford Parser[2] automatically. All of the models are optimized using the stochastic gradient descent (SGD). We pick the parameters showing the best performance via early stopping. Table 1 shows the best settings of parameters in our experiments.

We compare with the following systems for negative and speculative scope resolution.

- **CNN_C** and **CNN_D**. The CNN-based models are proposed by Qian et al. [16], which cast scope resolution as a classification problem. The features are extracted by the path between the keyword and the current token in both constituency (CNN_C) and dependency (CNN_D) parse trees. The CNN_C represents the state-of-the-art for in-domain scope resolution.
- **CRF**. The CRF-based model is proposed by Tang et al. [20], using PoS, chunks, NERs, and dependency relations as features.
- **BiLSTM_PoS**. This model is proposed by Fancellu et al. [3], which is a sequence-to-sequence model with word embeddings and part-of-speech (PoS) embeddings.
- **BiLSTM-CRF_PoS**. To verify the effectiveness of the CRF layer, we directly add it on the BiLSTM_PoS system.
- **BiLSTM-CRF_P**. For comparison of the effectiveness of PoS features and position features, we replace the PoS embeddings with the position embeddings (_P). Note that this system only employs the simple features in the word sequence with no syntactic features.
- **BiLSTM-CRF_ALL**. To measure the best performance of our approach for scope resolution, we utilize all features, including tokens, relative position, constituency tag, and dependency tag. This system excludes the PoS embeddings due to the descent of performance when adding it.

4.2 Experimental Results

In-domain Scope Resolution. Following the previous work [16,24], we divide the Abstracts sub-corpus into 10 folds to perform cross-validation. Table 2 shows the comparisons of our approach with the state-of-the-art systems and some proper baselines for in-domain scope resolution.

First, our BiLSTM-CRF_ALL system achieves PCS scores of 81.87% with an improvement of 4.73% for negation scope resolution, and 87.43% with an improvement of 1.68% for speculation, compared to the state-of-the-art (CNN_C /CNN_D). Besides, it is worth noting that the CNN_* systems heavily rely on highly-engineered features, such as constituency and dependency parsing

---

[1] http://evexdb.org/pmresources/vec-space-models/.
[2] http://nlp.stanford.edu/software/lex-parser.shtml.

Table 2. Performances on the Abstract sub-corpus for in-domain negation and speculation scope resolution. Besides the word embeddings that utilized in all of systems, it also involves other types of embeddings. "C": Constituency path; "D": Dependency path; "P": Position; "ALL": All types of embeddings except the PoS.

	System	P	R	F1	PCS
Negation	CNN_C [16]	85.10	92.74	89.64	70.86
	CNN_D [16]	89.49	90.54	89.91	77.14
	CRF [20]	75.36	81.84	78.47	68.24
	BiLSTM_PoS [3]	85.37	89.86	87.56	75.37
	BiLSTM-CRF_PoS	91.06	85.10	87.98	78.03
	BiLSTM-CRF_P	90.16	89.71	89.94	80.45
	BiLSTM-CRF_ALL	86.71	95.10	**90.71**	**81.87**
Speculation	CNN_C [16]	95.95	95.19	95.56	85.75
	CNN_D [16]	92.25	94.98	93.55	74.43
	CRF [20]	81.30	72.13	76.88	74.14
	BiLSTM_PoS [3]	91.83	96.62	94.16	80.78
	BiLSTM-CRF_PoS	95.71	94.24	94.97	83.92
	BiLSTM-CRF_P	94.02	95.89	94.95	85.86
	BiLSTM-CRF_ALL	97.30	94.67	**95.97**	**87.43**

tree, while our system without any syntactic information (BiLSTM-CRF_P) has already outperformed theirs.

Second, compared with the sequence-to-sequence models (CRF system and BiLSTM_Pos system), it can be observed that our model (BiLSTM-CRF_PoS) outperforms on both negation and speculation datasets. The reason might be that the BiLSTM-CRF network has more complicated hidden units, and offers better composition capability. It indicates that combining CRF and BiLSTM models can improve the performance. In addition, we see that CRF with a lot of hand-crafted features gives comparable performance to CNN, but lower performance than more complex DNN models.

Finally, comparing BiLSTM-CRF_PoS with BiLSTM-CRF_P, it is observed that both PoS embeddings and position embeddings are effective, and the latter improves more. Moreover, the BiLSTM-CRF_P system (with only position features) and the BiLSTM-CRF_ALL system (with additional syntactic features) achieve similar performances. This indicates that the position embeddings could better capture and represent the information of relationship between tokens and the negative and speculative keywords.

We manually analyzed each 50 of incorrect scopes predicted by BiLSTM-CRF_ALL for negation and speculation, respectively. Table 3 summaries the error patterns. For the error pattern #1, if there are more than one negative or speculative keywords in a sentence, the system might be interfered by other confused keywords. For instance, when identifying the scope of "suggest", it is

Table 3. Main error patterns of the BiLSTM-CRF_ALL system for in-domain scope resolution. "Neg" and "Spe" denote negation and speculation, respectively; Ground truth (keyword: in **bold**, scope: in square brackets); System prediction (scope: underlined); Confused keyword: in round brackets.

#	Error pattern	Examples	Number
1	Multi-keyword	Neg: ... [***not*** *discriminate the stages,* *(with the exception of) the M-CSF receptor*]	Neg: 8
		Spe: ... [***suggest*** *that it regulates iNOS expression*], *and (indicate) a regular role of nNOS*	Spe: 23
2	Subject missing	Neg: ..., [*the transcription factor* *is* ***not*** *required for promoter activity*]	Neg: 17
		Spe: ..., *and* [*this* ***may*** *be related to* *scavenging of endogenously produced NO*]	Spe: 11
3	Annotation Err.	Spe: *A putative function of BHRF1* [***may*** *be* *to protect infected cells from death*] *in order to* ...	Spe: 6

difficult to block the effects of the other speculative keyword "*indicate*" in the same sentence. For the error pattern #2, when a scope includes a subject in sentence, the system sometimes misses it. The reason is probably the lack of such samples in the training set. Thus we have counted the number of the sentences (or clauses) including at least one subject in a scope, and find there are about 12% and 14% of instances in negation and speculation, respectively. Moreover, we also noticed that a certain of instances are not consistent with the annotation guideline of the BioScope corpus. Compared the error pattern #2 with #3, it does not agree on whether include the subject into the scope of keyword "*may*".

To further provide an empirical insight into the affects of the data size of training set for our BiLSTM-CRF-based scope resolution model, we start from only 10% of the preceding dataset for training, and keep adding 10% of dataset

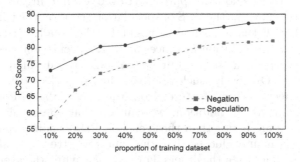

Fig. 3. Comparison of the PCS when adding different sizes of training set from 10% to 100%. The experiments is employ the BiLSTM-CRF_ALL system on the Abstract sub-corpus. (Color figure online)

each time until 100%. As shown in Fig. 3, when decreasing the size of training set from 100% to 30%, the performances of our model do not decline dramatically, with about 9% and 7% of PCS for negation (the red dashed curve) and speculation (the blue solid curve), respectively. It indicates that our BiLSTM-CRF-based scope resolution model can efficiently utilize the supervision from a smaller training dataset.

Table 4. Performances on the Full Paper and the Clinical Report sub-corpora for cross-domain scope resolution. "AT" denotes Adversarail Training. [†]For cross-domain comparison, we only highlight the best performances of the transfer learning systems in this table, excluding the in-domain systems trained on the corresponding sub-corpus.

System	Full paper				Clinical report			
	Negation		Speculation		Negation		Speculation	
	F1	PCS	F1	PCS	F1	PCS	F1	PCS
CNN [16]	75.62	43.12	85.25	45.45	94.86	86.70	88.45	60.69
CNN+AT	75.76	44.79	85.67	47.48	95.16	87.69	88.74	61.65
BiLSTM_PoS [3]	82.74	52.91	87.49	53.52	95.63	88.42	89.51	60.16
BiLSTM_PoS+AT	82.33	53.44	87.55	53.81	95.72	89.56	88.84	61.30
BiLSTM-CRF_ALL	82.54	57.67	88.47	59.24	95.98	90.83	90.20	67.72
BiLSTM-CRF_ALL+AT	**83.41**	**60.32**	**89.05**	**61.49**	**96.33**	**91.51**	**90.69**	**69.66**
BiLSTM-CRF_ALL (in-domain)	69.30	50.01	83.25	59.12	94.46	84.39	90.63	75.49[†]

Cross-domain Scope Resolution. Table 4 shows the experimental results for our cross-domain scope resolution. The systems without the tag "+AT" (Rows 1, 3, and 5) train on the Abstract sub-corpus, and test on the other two sub-corpora, i.e., Full Paper and Clinical Report. We can see that all of the systems' performances are boosted by the adversarial domain adaptation framework with the unlabeled target domain samples. Moreover, compared with the in-domain system (Row 7), our cross-domain approach (Row 6) obtains higher performances than it in all metrics, except the PCS of speculation scope on the Clinical Report sub-corpus. Although the main reason might be the smaller sizes of training datasets (e.g., only 376 negation instances and 672 speculation instances in the Full Papers sub-corpus), note that our system utilizes only unlabeled data on the target domain. Obviously, such approach has provided a flexible manner to transfer the effective latent features from the richly-labeled domains to the poorly-labeled domains. In addition, we can see that the results on Clinical Reports sub-corpus are better than those on Full Papers sub-corpus (especially on negation). It is mainly due to that the syntactic structures of the clinical report texts are simpler than the others. For instance, while the average sentence length on Clinical Report sub-corpus is 8.19 tokens, that on Full Paper sub-corpora is 30.49.

5   Conclusion

This paper presents an adversarial BiLSTM-CRF network for negation and speculation scope resolution. First, we develop a BiLSTM neural network with a CRF layer to jointly modeling the extra-propositional clues and their contexts. Experimental results on the BioScope corpus indicate that such model achieves a performance of 81.87% with an improvement of 4.73% on negation, and 87.43% with an improvement of 1.68% on speculation, compared with the state-of-the-art system. Second, we come up with an adversarial neural architecture to learn the invariant and discriminative latent features across domains. In the cross-domain scenario, our approach also achieves the state-of-the-art. The datasets and source code of this paper are publicly available at —. For future work, we intend to apply our adversarial domain adaptation framework to learn the shared latent feature representations in cross-language settings.

References

1. Chen, T., Xu, R., He, Y., et al.: Improving sentiment analysis via sentence type classification using BiLSTM-CRF and CNN. ESA **72**, 221–230 (2017)
2. Chen, X., Sun, Y., Athiwaratkun, B., et al.: Adversarial deep averaging networks for cross-lingual sentiment classification. arXiv:1606.01614 (2016)
3. Fancellu, F., Lopez, A., Webber, B.: Neural networks for negation scope detection. In: ACL, pp. 495–504 (2016)
4. Ganin, Y., Ustinova, E., Ajakan, H., et al.: Domain-adversarial training of neural networks. J. Mach. Learn. Res. **17**(1), 2030–2096 (2015)
5. Goodfellow, I.J., Pouget-Abadie, J., Mirza, M., et al.: Generative adversarial nets. In: NIPS, pp. 2672–2680 (2014)
6. Graves, A., Mohamed, A.R., Hinton, G.: Speech recognition with deep recurrent neural networks. In: ICASSP, pp. 6645–6649 (2013)
7. Huang, Z., Xu, W., Yu, K.: Bidirectional LSTM-CRF models for sequence tagging. arXiv:1508.01991 (2015)
8. Lafferty, J., Mccallum, A., Pereira, F.: Conditional random fields: probabilistic models for segmenting and labeling sequence data. In: ICML, pp. 282–289 (2001)
9. Lample, G., Ballesteros, M., Subramanian, S., et al.: Neural architectures for named entity recognition. In: NAACL, pp. 260–270 (2016)
10. Makhzani, A., Shlens, J., Jaitly, N., et al.: Adversarial autoencoders. arXiv:1511.05644 (2016). Version 2
11. Morante, R., Daelemans, W.: A metalearning approach to processing the scope of negation. In: CoNLL, pp. 21–29 (2009)
12. Morante, R., Liekens, A., Daelemans, W.: Learning the scope of negation in biomedical texts. In: EMNLP, pp. 715–724 (2008)
13. Morante, R., Sporleder, C.: Modality and negation: an introduction to the special issue. Comput. Linguist. **38**(2), 223–260 (2012)
14. Özgür, A., Radev, D.R.: Detecting speculations and their scopes in scientific text. In: EMNLP, pp. 1398–1407 (2009)
15. Pyysalo, S., Ginter, F., Moen, H., et al.: Distributional semantics resources for biomedical text processing. In: LBM, pp. 39–44 (2013)

16. Qian, Z., Li, P., Zhu, Q., et al.: Speculation and negation scope detection via convolutional neural networks. In: EMNLP, pp. 815–825 (2016)
17. Qin, L., Zhang, Z., Zhao, H., et al.: Adversarial connective-exploiting networks for implicit discourse relation classification. In: ACL, pp. 1006–1017 (2017)
18. dos Santos, C.N., Xiang, B., Zhou, B.: Classifying relations by ranking with convolutional neural networks. In: ACL, pp. 626–634 (2015)
19. Sato, M., Manabe, H., Noji, H., et al.: Adversarial training for cross-domain universal dependency parsing. In: CoNLL, pp. 71–79 (2017)
20. Tang, B., Wang, X., Wang, X., et al.: A cascade method for detecting hedges and their scope in natural language text. In: CoNLL, pp. 13–17 (2010)
21. Velldal, E., Oepen, S.: Syntactic scope resolution in uncertainty analysis. In: COLING, pp. 1379–1387 (2010)
22. Velldal, E., Øvrelid, L., Read, J., et al.: Speculation and negation: rules, rankers, and the role of syntax. Comput. Linguist. **38**(2), 369–410 (2012)
23. Vincze, V., Szarvas, G., Farkas, R., et al.: The BioScope corpus: biomedical texts annotated for uncertainty, negation and their scopes. BMC Bioinform. **9**(Suppl 11), 1–9 (2008)
24. Zou, B., Zhou, G., Zhu, Q.: Tree kernel-based negation and speculation scope detection with structured syntactic parse features. In: EMNLP, pp. 968–976 (2013)

Analyzing Relational Semantics of Clauses in Chinese Discourse Based on Feature Structure

Wenhe Feng, Xi Huang, and Han Ren[✉]

Laboratory of Language Engineering and Computing, Guangdong University of Foreign Studies, Guangzhou 510420, China
{wenhefeng,hanren}@gdufs.edu.cn

Abstract. The discourse clause relational semantics is the semantic relation between discourse clause relevance structures. This paper proposes a method to represent the discourse clause relational semantics as a multi-dimensional feature structure. Compared with the simple classification mechanism of discourse relations, it can reveal the discourse semantic relations more deeply. Furthermore, we built Chinese discourse clause relational semantic feature corpus, and study the clause relational semantic feature recognition. We Transfer the clause relational semantic feature recognition into multiple binary classification problems, and extract relevant classification features for experiment. Experiments show that under the best classifier (SVM), the overall semantic feature recognition effect of F1 value reaches 70.14%; each classification feature contributes differently to the recognition of different clause relational semantic features, and the connectives contributes more to the recognition of all semantic features. By adding related semantic features as classification features, the interaction between different semantic features is studied. Experiments show that the influence of different semantic features is different. The addition of multiple semantic features has a more significant effect than a single semantic feature.

Keywords: Correlate structure of clause · Discourse semantics · Relational semantic feature · Multi-label learning

1 Introduction

Discourse structure analysis is one of the main issues in discourse understanding. Current research on discourse structure analysis mainly represents discourse structures via hierarchical frameworks [2–4], in which clauses or elementary discourse units are connected by upper discourse units or concepts. However, it is very challenging to represent semantic relations of clauses within discourse texts having complex discourse hierarchy or multiple structure layers. Alternatively, clause correlation structure (hereafter CCS) [1, 6, 7] characterizes semantic relations among clauses by connecting them directly, making discourse relations and structures more clear and easier to be analyzed.

This paper explores discourse relation representation in CCS, which is also called relational semantics of clause (hereafter RSC). Current discourse structure frameworks

© Springer Nature Switzerland AG 2020
X. Zhu et al. (Eds.): NLPCC 2020, LNAI 12431, pp. 169–180, 2020.
https://doi.org/10.1007/978-3-030-60457-8_14

[2–6] often utilize exclusionary taxonomies for discourse relation, that is, two correlated clauses have and only have one semantic relation. However, such assumption is unrealistic, since two clauses may have multiple discourse relations. For example, two clauses having the relation of causality may also have the relation of continuity, and the reason lies in that, such two clauses are viewed based on different aspects, i.e., logical and temporal one. In fact, such two relations are compatible in most cases. On the other hand, different viewpoints lead to ambiguity of categorization, such as Penn Discourse Treebank [7], which allows one-to-many phenomena between an implicit relation and multiple discourse relation classes.

This paper proposes a discourse relation representation framework for RSC. By regarding discourse relation as a combination of multiple relation aspects [8], each of which represents a single discourse relation from a specific perspective, a discourse relation is characterized as a multidimensional feature structure. In comparison with exclusionary taxonomies, such feature structure helps represent discourse relation with multiple aspects, which makes the analysis of discourse relation entirely and deeply.

The contribution of this paper lies in three folds:

1) We propose a relation representation framework for RSC, which includes a ten-dimension feature space, representing ten discourse relation aspects. Every dimension is non-exclusive so that such framework is easy to be expanded.
2) We build the annotation scheme for the framework. We also annotate a dataset having 5,212 correlated clause pair, each of which is represented by a multidimensional feature structure with ten relation aspects.
3) We make a preliminary recognition experiment to testify the validation of the dataset. Such recognition method can be employed by downstream tasks.

2   Related Work

2.1   Discourse Structure and Relation Semantics Representation

Discourse Structure and RSC. Currently, there are three main discourse structure schemes: the Rhetorical Structure Theory (RST) [2], Penn Discourse Treebank scheme (PDTB) [3] and the fusion of the two schemes [4]. RST maps a text-level discourse to a hierarchical tree, while PDTB scheme decomposes it to discourse connectives with arguments, which are roughly equivalent to elementary discourse units (EDU). Essentially, both of such two schemes are hierarchical structure, which, however, is hard to represent the direct semantic relation of two EDUs, not to mention semantic relations between discrete or cross-level EDUs. Meanwhile, the discourse semantics framework CCS [1] tends to solve the problem by focusing on the direct semantic relation between two clauses. In fact, a discourse relation connects two clauses or EDUs by CCS, which is more direct and clear than the representation by hierarchical discourse structure ones. Although dependency-based discourse theories such as discourse dependency structure [5, 6] can also represent direct semantic relations between two EDUs, they still consider the problem of centroid, which impact the analyzing performance of discourse relation [9]. In this paper, we study the discourse relationship semantics based on CCS.

Relational Semantic Representation. Discourse relation schemes in most discourse structure frameworks are a hierarchical taxonomy. For example, the RST Discourse Treebank involves 78 relations belong to 16 groups [2, 10], while PDTB define a three-level structure with 23 sub relations [3, 7]. However, relations in these systems are always exclusive, meaning that two correlated clauses have and only have one relation. In fact, two clauses may have multiple discourse relations since language objects are multidimensional semantic units, as mentioned earlier. Since semantic understanding is a task containing subjective judgment, it may not be suitable to employ exclusionary taxonomies to represent discourse relations.

2.2 Feature Structure and Multi-label Learning

Feature Structure. In this paper, the relational semantics in a text-level discourse is represented as a multidimensional feature structure of relational semantics. Such feature-based representation have been successfully applied in phonological and word meaning analysis [11]. Based on it, an analyzing target can be featured to discriminative aspects, each of which profiles the target from a specific perspective and non-exclusive to each other. Such characteristics also exist in discourse relation representation: discourse relations often contain different aspects, some of them may be correlated, and all of them represent discourse relations. The characteristics make the feature structure suitable for representing discourse relation.

Multi-label Learning. Essentially, the recognition of relational semantic feature in this paper can be cast as a multi-label learning problem. Given a target sample, the task of multi-label learning is to associates it with multiple correct category tags. Typical strategies for multi-label learning are: 1) bi-categorization [12], that is, to judge if a target sample belongs to each category, which can be viewed as a multi-classification problem, 2) classifier chain [13], that is, to build a classifier pipeline, by which a target sample is sequentially tagged if it belongs to a class or not and, 3) label ensembling method [14], that is, to ensemble multiple labels as a new one in order to make the original problem as a single-label learning task. Being preliminary experiments, we utilize single-label learning, which is also adopted in current discourse semantic relation analysis tasks [15, 16].

3 Representation and Annotation of RSC

3.1 RSC and Its Feature Structure Representation

In CCS, a clause is the minimum or elementary discourse unit [17], and two clauses can be viewed as a compound sentence with semantic coherence and formal articulation. Figure 1 gives an example described by CCS. Here the numeric superscripts represent sequence numbers for clauses, while the lines with tags represent their semantic relations.

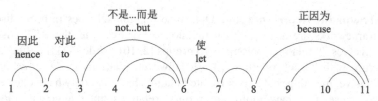

Fig. 1. RSC for the above example.

¹浦东开发开放是一项振兴上海，建设现代化经济、贸易、金融中心的跨世纪工程，²因此大量出现的是以前不曾遇到过的新情况、新问题。³对此，浦东不是简单的采取"干一段时间，等积累了经验以后再制定法规条例"的做法，⁴而是借鉴发达国家和深圳等特区的经验教训，⁵聘请国内外有关专家学者，⁶积极、及时地制定和推出法规性文件，⁷使这些经济活动一出现就被纳入法制轨道。⁸去年初浦东新区诞生的中国第一家医疗机构药品采购服务中心，正因为一开始就比较规范，⁹运转至今，¹⁰成交药品一亿多元，¹¹没有发现一例回扣。

The development and opening up of Pudong is a cross-century project to revitalize Shanghai and build a modern economy, trade and financial center. Accordingly, a large number of new situations and new problems that have never been encountered before have emerged. To address this issue, Pudong is not simply to adopt the practice of "working for a period of time, then making regulations after accumulating experience", but to learn from the experience and lessons from developed countries and special economic zones such as Shenzhen as well as employ domestic and foreign experts and scholars to actively and timely formulate and launch laws and regulations, so that economic activities in such district are incorporated into the legal track as soon as they appear. Early last year, the first medical institution drug procurement service center in China was born in Pudong New Area. Just because the regularizing operation at the beginning according to such laws and regulations, the drug turnover of the center achieves a total amount of more than 100 million Chinese yuan without any case of kickback since it opens.

Compared with the hierarchical discourse structure frameworks, the semantic targets in the framework for RSC are more precise and specific. For example, connectives in the framework are utilized to represent semantic relations directly, such as the relation "not…but" that reflects the relation of clause 3 and 6. Such relation, however, does not appear directly according to the hierarchical analysis, which may increase the complexity of semantic parsing in discourse.

In the framework for RSC, a discourse relation is characterized as a multidimensional feature structure, and each dimension in it represents one discourse relation aspect (hereafter DRA), such as causality and continuity. Each DRA is a boolean value (+positive or −negative), showing whether such DRA exists in two clauses or not. Accordingly, an RSC can be represented by a series of DRAs. We also define a primary DRA in the feature structure, indicating the uppermost relation between two clauses. For example, causality is the primary DRA between clause 1 and 2, while reversibility between clause 3 and 6. In most cases, connectives indicate primary DRAs, e.g., the word because means a causality relation, while the word but suggests the relation of reversibility. Table 1 shows part of DRAs among clauses of the example text.

Table 1. Feature structure representation for the RSC of the above example.

Clause pair	Primary DRA	DRA						
		Causality	Purpose	Condition	Reversibility	Sequence	Coordination	Illustration
1–2	Causality	+	–	–	–	+	–	–
2–3	Causality	+	–	–	+	+	–	–
3–6	Reversibility	–	–	–	+	–	+	–
4–6	Condition	+	+	+	–	+	–	–
5–6	Condition	+	+	+	–	+	–	–
6–7	Purpose	+	+	+	–	+	–	–
7–8	Illustration	–	–	–	–	–	–	+
8–11	Causality	+	–	+	–	+	–	–
9–11	Reversibility	+	–	–	+	+	–	–
10–11	Reversibility	+	–	–	+	+	–	–

Such feature structure has some advantages, compared with simple discourse relation taxonomies: 1) it helps represent the discourse relationship semantics more comprehensively. One is that, it is able to reveal small distinction between discourse relations. For example, the clause pair (1,2) and (2,3) have the same discourse relation of causality, but actually they are different because the pair (1,2) has another DRA reversibility. The other is that, it helps uncover those relational indications that are usually overlooked. For example, the clause pair (9,10) has the relation of reversibility, but they also has the relation of causality and continuity. 2) It is an elastic and flexible scheme, because a DRA can be appended or removed without affecting other DRAs, and the judgment of DRAs is unaffected with each other.

3.2 Data Annotation

3.2.1 Annotation Scheme

We have defined 10 DRAs for the annotation experiments. In this subsection, we give the explanation of 4 relations that are most occurred in text-level discourse.

Causality. From abstraction of the traditional Causal relation, if the situation presented in clause A is recognized as a cause or an outcome for the action or situation presented in B, the relation feature is annotated as positive, otherwise it is negative. In the example, besides the clause pair 3–6 and 7–8, all other clauses are positive.

Condition. From abstraction of the traditional Condition relation, [conditional] is a sub-feature of [causality]. When the necessity or adequacy of the causation is stressed, it is annotated as the relation of condition. In the example, the clause pair 4–6, 5–6 and 6–7 have the relation of condition, while the other clauses have not.

Purpose. Abstracted from the traditional Purpose relation, the relation of purpose is a sub-feature of the relation causality. When the activity is initiated in order to realize, it is annotated as the relation of purpose. In the example, the clause pair 4–6, 5–6 and 6–7 have the relation of purpose.

Reversibility. Abstracted from the traditional Transition and Comparative relations, if there are opposite or reverse relationships between the situations presented in clause A and B, then the relation feature is annotated as the relation of reversibility. In the example, the clause pair 3–6, 9–11 and 10–11 have the relation of reversibility.

3.2.2 Annotation Evaluation

We labeled relational semantics in a dataset, which has been annotated with correlated structure of clauses [1]. Two students were trained to label 20 news texts in the Chinese Penn Treebank [18]. Two metrics are employed to measure the annotation performance: the agreement rate was 96.84% and the result of Kappa evaluation was 84.49%, which shows the feasibility of the annotation scheme. Then we extracted and labeled 300 news texts from the Chinese Penn Treebank, and built a dataset containing 5,212 correlated clause pairs. Table 2 shows the number of each DRA in the dataset.

Table 2. Number of positive data for each DRA

DRA	Number
Coordination	1272
Reversibility	156
Explanation	1387
Illustration	545
Purpose	211
Commentary	718
Sequence	1436
Condition	153
Supposition	296
Casuality	1285

4   Preliminary Experiment for DRA Recognition

4.1   Experiment Setting

The task of DRA recognition is to identify the relational signatures contained in a given pair of known sentences. Formally, the input is a clause pair with two clauses, the output should be a vector with 12 dimensions, each of which is a boolean value representing whether the specific DRA is positive or negative. Such problem can be cast as a bi-categorization or multi-categorization task. Although the former strategy needs multiple steps than the latter one, it still achieves a better performance. Based on it, we adopt bi-categorization method for recognition.

The labeled dataset includes 300 news articles from Chinese Penn Treebank. We randomly select 80% articles as training data, and the other 20% as test data.

The aim of the preliminary experiment is to investigate the performances of classifiers to this task, the contribution of features for DRAs and the impact of each DRA recognition to the overall performance. To this end, we adopt accuracy, precision, reall and F1 score [14] as the evaluation metrics. Micro-averaging metrics are adopted to evaluate the overall performance of each feature to DRA recognition in order to avoid the data bias by imbalanced classes.

4.2 Features

There are 8 kinds of features that are employed in our experiment:

F1: connectives and their related DRA categories. Connectives are clue words for recognizing discourse relation. For example, the connective word therefore indicates the class causality. In this paper, we classify connectives into 10 DRA categories, and make a heuristics based on the labeling data.

F2: the first word (not the connective) and its part-of-speech of the latter clause. The first word is usually a notional word (noun, verb, adjective or adverb), and it may indicate the relation between two clauses. For example, if the latter clause starts with a verb, it probably means that the subject constituent, which is as same as that of the former clause, is omitted. Therefore, the two clauses may have the relation of coordination.

F3_1: predicate; F3_2: relation of predicates in two clauses; F3_3: the similarity of predicate; F3_4: grammatical class of predicate. Such features are derived from the assumption that relation of clauses is always reflected by the relation of their predicates. We use CTB tool [18] to parse each clause and select the first VP node of the clause as its predicate. There are three relations of predicate: accordant, synonymous, and non-relative one. Tongyici Cilin is employed to judge the synonyms.

F4_1: the grammatical class of the former word of a predicate; F4_2: the former word of a predicate; F4_3: the similarity of such two words in two clauses; F4_4: the latter word of a predicate; F4_5: the similarity of such two words in two clauses. In fact, if such two words in two clauses are same or synonymous, the clause pair often has the relation of coordination.

F5_1: the number of identical words in the two clauses; F5_2: the part-of-speech of the most common word in two clauses; F5_3: number of synonyms in two clauses. Generally, the greater the number of the common words or synonyms is, the more likely the topics of the clauses is. In other words, they may have the relation of coordination.

F6: sentence similarity of two clauses. The assumption is that, the more similar the clauses are, the closer the meaning of the clauses, which means the relation of coordination. The similarity of two clauses is computed by cosine similarity.

F7: punctuation at the end of the former clause. In most cases, a colon means the following explanation, while a semicolon indicates a coordination relation.

F8: the distance of correlated clauses. A close distance always hints some specific relations, such as explanation or coordination.

4.3 Experimental Results and Analysis

4.3.1 DRA Recognition Performance

We employ three classifiers: support vector machine (SVM), decision tree and naive bayes (NB). Table 3 show their overall performance of relation recognition.

Table 3. The overall performance of three classifiers (%).

Classifier	Accuracy	Precision	Recall	F1
SVM	86.43	72.60	68.42	70.14
Decision Tree	86.03	71.06	66.04	67.97
Naive Bayes	75.08	62.51	70.77	63.57

As shown in Table 3, the SVM model outperforms the other classifiers. The result is reasonable, since SVM can solve the high-dimensional feature problem and handle the interaction of non-linear features. By contrast, decision tree is prone to yield the problem of overfitting, while NB model assumes that each feature is independent to each other, which is inappropriate to this experiment. The following experiments are based on the SVM model.

Table 4 shows the recognition performance for each DRA. We can see that, the recognition of reversibility achieves the best performance (80.29% of F1), while the recognition of explanation gets the lowest score (63.83% of F1). Although there are much few positive examples on the relation of reversibility, most of them have explicit connectives such as "but" and "however", which are much conducive to recognizing such relation. On the contrary, relations that have rich positive examples have low recognition performance, and the reason is the that few of them have explicit connectives, which increases the difficulty of recognition.

4.3.2 The Ablation Test

We also run some ablation tests to investigate the impact of each feature to the classification. A feature or a feature group is removed at one time, and each negative value is the decreasing value to the baseline, which is the recognition performance of the classifier using all the features.

Table 5 show the impact of each feature to the overall performance. We can see that, the feature F1 has the greatest influence to the classifier, since F1 score decreases by 3.7% after removing it from the feature set. Obviously, the feature F1 provides important information for classification. On the other hand, the recall performances drop when removing other features, indicating that our features are helpful for finding discourse relations.

Table 6 shows a more detailed ablation test to survey the impact of each feature to each DRA. It can be seen from the table that: 1) The feature F1 has positive effect on the

Table 4. Detailed recognition results for each DRA (%).

DRA	Accuracy	Precision	Recall	F1
Coordination	79.70	72.26	67.96	70.04
Reversibility	98.06	93.58	70.30	80.29
Explanation	73.93	65.50	62.24	63.83
Illustration	89.98	75.00	63.19	68.59
Purpose	97.28	91.72	69.60	79.14
Commentary	90.98	85.83	73.17	79.00
Sequence	73.62	66.36	62.67	64.46
Condition	97.77	87.66	64.82	74.53
Supposition	94.70	83.32	58.37	68.31
Casuality	77.91	70.34	66.16	68.19

Table 5. The impact of each feature to the overall performance (%).

	Accuracy	Precision	Recall	F1
Baseline	**86.43**	**72.60**	**68.42**	**70.14**
w/o F1	−0.73	−1.79	−4.23	−3.7
w/o F2	0.66	2.01	−2.01	−0.94
w/o F3	0.32	0.93	−1.25	−0.61
w/o F4	−0.15	−0.16	−0.88	−0.67
w/o F5, F6	0.46	1.91	−1.92	−0.91
w/o F7	−0.08	−1.21	−0.32	−0.63
w/o F8	−0.01	−0.19	−0.56	−0.44

recognition of all DRAs, and has the biggest effect on the recognition of reversibility; 2) One feature has different impact on the recognition of different DRA, and different features have different impacts on the recognition of one DRA. For example, the recognition of the relation coordination mainly depends on the similarity of connectives (F1) and syntactic structures (F3 and F4) rather than lexical similarity (F5 and F6). It suggests that the further work can be carried out to build general and specific features for discourse relation recognition, that is, the aim of general features is to find whether two clauses has a relation, while the specific features are employed to classify the discourse relation.

This final experiment investigates the impact of the relevance between DRAs to their recognition. Each time the gold standard for one DRA recognition is given and are added

Table 6. The impact of each feature to each DRA (%).

DRA	Baseline	w/o F1	w/o F2	w/o F3	w/o F4	w/o F5, F6	w/o F7	w/o F8
Coordination	70.04	−4.46	−0.11	−2.95	−1.91	0.62	−1.97	0.03
Reversibility	80.29	−18.39	−0.68	4.03	2.48	2.35	1.51	0.84
Explanation	63.83	−2.25	0.79	0.12	−0.77	2.22	0.61	1.98
Illustration	68.59	−1.48	−0.49	−1.85	−3.93	1.08	−1.33	0.24
Purpose	79.14	−4.62	2.47	0.68	1.32	−0.55	0.70	0.45
Commentary	79.00	−3.74	−1.80	−3.31	−2.41	0.23	0.13	0.23
Sequence	64.46	−2.99	−1.06	1.20	−2.43	−0.60	0.05	−0.22
Condition	74.53	−3.96	−3.53	−2.57	−4.19	−2.86	−3.96	−1.17
Supposition	68.31	−2.22	−0.62	−1.16	−1.68	−1.60	−0.50	0.27
Casuality	68.19	−4.82	−1.89	−2.32	−2.80	−1.63	−2.12	−1.07

to the classifier as an additional feature. Table 7 shows the changing performance for each DRA.

Table 7. The impact of the relevance between DRAs(%).

DRA	Coordination	Reversibility	Explanation	Illustration	Purpose	Commentary	Sequence	Condition	Supposition	Casuality
Baseline	**70.04**	**80.29**	**63.83**	**68.59**	**79.14**	**79.00**	**64.46**	**74.53**	**68.31**	**68.19**
Coordination		0.05	5.47	2.7	0.43	0.65	−0.66	−1.83	2.56	2.18
Reversibility	−0.6	−	1.23	0.27	1.39	0.94	−0.27	−1.24	0.16	−1.63
Explanation	2.68	1.6	−	0.08	2.7	0.25	1.23	−1.68	−1.1	0.59
Illustration	1.69	2.06	2.88	−	1.43	0.19	−0.71	−3.3	1.23	0.59
Purpose	−0.11	0.69	1.49	−0.45	−	−1.13	0.07	−4.23	−0.32	2.36
Commentary	−0.09	2.62	3.19	0.16	−0.24	−	−0.11	−0.65	0.12	0.2
Sequence	−0.44	1.65	2.78	0.56	0.24	0.32	−	−1.31	−2.76	−1.09
Condition	0.3	2.58	1.57	−0.9	1.43	−1.14	0.43	−	−0.68	2.33
Supposition	−0.09	1.4	1.45	0.39	−0.23	−0.42	−0.19	−2.11	−	−1.61
Casuality	2.58	−2.22	3.79	2.54	1.85	−0.38	0.52	−1.97	−1.36	−
All others	20.08	3.01	20.2	15.01	2.71	7.07	2.32	1.24	−0.93	17.79

Table 7 shows that, multiple features are more instructive than a single feature. For example, for the identification of the relation coordination, the increasing performance is 2.68% after appending the feature of the explanation relation, while the performance sharply increases by 20.08% after appending all the other features of DRA. In addition, not all of the DRAs promote the performance of recognition. For example, the performance of recognizing the supposition relation decreases after adding other DRAs as features. The reason lies in to two folds: 1) the less influenced relational semantics are themselves less relevant to other relational semantics, such as the relation supposition and other DRAs; 2) discourse relations with balanced data have slight influence by other DRAs, while discourse relation with imbalanced data have significant influence by others.

5 Conclusion

This paper propose a relation representation framework for relation structure of clause, which includes a ten-dimension feature space, representing ten discourse relation aspects. Compared with the current classification mechanism of discourse relation, all the discourse relation aspects are compatible and the proposed framework is easy to be expanded. We build a dataset having 5,212 correlated clause pair, and make a recognition system for the preliminary experiments. The experiments show that the overall performance of DRA recognition achieves 70.14%, showing the availability of our data and the recognition approach for downstream applications.

Further work will focuses on enlarging our labeled dataset. In order to achieve a better performance, sophisticated models such as deep neural networks will be considered, and targeted features to identify the discourse relation should be designed as well.

Acknowledgement. This work is supported by Basic and Applied Basic Research Foundation Project of Guangdong Province (2020A1515011056), Foundation of the Guangdong 13th Five-year Plan of Philosophy and Social Sciences (GD19CYY05), General Project of National Scientific and Technical Terms Review Committee (YB2019013), Special innovation project of Guangdong Education Department (2017KTSCX064), Bidding Project of GDUFS Laboratory of Language Engineering and Computing (LEC2019ZBKT002).

References

1. Feng, W., Chen, Y., Ren, Y., Ren, H.: Representation and recognition of clauses relevance structure in Chinese text. Acta Scientiarum Naturalium Universitatis Pekinensis **56**(1), 23–30 (2020)
2. Carlson, L., Marcu, D., Okurowski, M.E.: Building a discourse-tagged corpus in the framework of rhetorical structure theory. In: van Kuppevelt, J., Smith, R.W. (eds.) Current and New Directions in Discourse and Dialogue. Text, Speech and Language Technology, vol. 22, pp. 85–112. Springer, Dordrecht (2003). https://doi.org/10.1007/978-94-010-0019-2_5
3. Prasad, R., Dinesh, N., Lee, A., et al.: The Penn Discourse Treebank 2.0. In: Proceedings of the 6th International Conference on Language Resources and Evaluation (LREC), Marrakech, pp. 2961–2968 (2008)
4. Li, Y., Feng, W., Kong, F., et al.: Building Chinese discourse corpus with connective-driven dependency tree structure. In: Proceedings of the Conference on Empirical Methods in Natural Language Processing (EMNLP), Doha, pp. 2105–2114(2014)
5. Li, S., Wang, L., Cao, Z., Li, W.: Text-level discourse dependency parsing. In: Proceedings of the 52nd Annual Meeting of the Association for Computational Linguistics (ACL), Baltimore, pp. 25–35 (2014)
6. Yang, A., Li, S.: SciDTB: discourse dependency TreeBank for scientific abstracts. In: Proceedings of the 56th Annual Meeting of the Association for Computational Linguistics (ACL), Melbourne, pp. 444–449 (2018)

7. The PDTB Research Group: The Penn Discourse Treebank 2.0 Annotation Manual (2007)
8. Feng, W.: Feature structure for relationship of Chinese complex sentence. J. Chin. Inf. Process. **29**(6), 13–21 (2015)
9. Iruskieta, M., De Ilarraza, A.D., Lersundi, M.: The annotation of the central unit in rhetorical structure trees: a key step in annotating rhetorical relations. In: Proceedings of the 25th International Conference on Computational Linguistics: Technical Papers, pp. 466–475 (2014)
10. Carlson, L., Marcu, D.: Discourse tagging reference manual. Technical Report ISI-TR-545, University of Southern, California (2001)
11. Hu, Y.: Modern Chinese, vol. 6. Shanghai Educational Press, Shanhai (1995)
12. Boutell, M.R., Luo, J., Shen, X., et al.: Learning multi-label scene classification. Pattern Recognit. **37**(9), 1757–1771 (2004)
13. Read, J., Pfahringer, B., Holmes, G., et al.: Classifier chains for multi-label classification. Mach. Learn. **85**(3), 333–359 (2011)
14. Read, J., Pfahringer, B., Holmes, G.: Multi-label classification using ensembles of pruned sets. In: Proceedings of ICDM 2008, 8th IEEE International Conference on Data Mining, pp. 995–1000 (2008)
15. Pitler, E., Louis, A., Nenkova, A.: Automatic sense prediction for implicit discourse relations in text. In: Proceedings of the ACL-IJCNLP 2009. Association for Computational Linguistics, Stroudsburg, pp. 683–691 (2009)
16. Marcu, D., Echihabi, A.: An unsupervised approach to recognizing discourse relations. In: Proceedings of the 40th Annual Meeting of the Association for Computational Linguistics, Morristown, pp. 368–375 (2002)
17. Li, Y., Feng, W., Zhou, G., Zhu, K.: Research of Chinese clause identification based on comma. Acta Scientiarum Naturalium Universitatis Pekinensis **49**(1), 7–14 (2013)
18. Xue, N., Xia, F., Chiou, F.D., et al.: the Penn Chinese TREEBANK: phrase structure annotation of a large corpus. Nat. Lang. Eng. **11**(2), 207–238 (2005)

Efficient Lifelong Relation Extraction with Dynamic Regularization

Hangjie Shen[1], Shenggen Ju[1(✉)], Jieping Sun[1], Run Chen[1], and Yuezhong Liu[2]

[1] College of Computer Science, Sichuan University, Chengdu 610065, China
jsg@scu.edu.cn
[2] Enterprise Service, Commonwealth Bank of Australia,
Sydney, NSW 2000, Australia

Abstract. Relation extraction has received increasing attention due to its important role in natural language processing applications. However, most existing methods are designed for a fixed set of relations. They are unable to handle the lifelong learning scenario, i.e. adapting a well-trained model to newly added relations without catastrophically forgetting the previously learned knowledge. In this work, we present a memory-efficient dynamic regularization method to address this issue. Specifically, two types of powerful consolidation regularizers are applied to preserve the learned knowledge and ensure the robustness of the model, and the regularization strength is adaptively adjusted with respect to the dynamics of the training losses. Experiment results on multiple benchmarks show that our proposed method significantly outperforms prior state-of-the-art approaches.

Keywords: Relation extraction · Lifelong · Dynamic regularization

1 Introduction

Relation extraction (RE) aims to identify relational facts for pairs of entities in text, which can be applied to many NLP applications such as knowledge base construction [3] and question answering [17]. Compared with traditional approaches which focus on manually designed features, neural methods based on either CNN [18,21] or RNN [9,20] have achieved impressive improvement in this area. However, previous neural models assume a pre-identified set of relations, which do not always exist in real-world RE scenarios.

Dealing with lifelong learning [14,15] (also called continual learning) for neural networks is a non-trivial problem, as the demand is usually dynamic and evolving, that is, the set of relations that need predicting could be changed or enlarged over time. Given such scenarios, a straight-forward solution would be re-training. Nevertheless, this heuristic approach requires to store all previous training data as well as new data to train a completely new model, which is expensive and time-consuming.

© Springer Nature Switzerland AG 2020
X. Zhu et al. (Eds.): NLPCC 2020, LNAI 12431, pp. 181–192, 2020.
https://doi.org/10.1007/978-3-030-60457-8_15

Therefore, the goal of lifelong learning is to enrich a model's ability of handling such a case, by trying to perform well on the entire set of tasks in an online way that avoids revisiting all previous data at each stage. It is challenging because of catastrophic forgetting [4] which refers to the significant drop in performance when switching from a trained task to a new one. To alleviate forgetting problem, recent work suggests to either use a regularizer that prevents the parameters from drastic changes in their values yet still enables to find a good solution for the new task [7], or augment the model with an episodic memory module [2,8].

These methods have resulted in considerable gains in performance on simple image classification datasets, but they are proved to perform poorly in the context of NLP [16]. In fact, limited literature has discussed achieving lifelong learning for NLP tasks such as RE. To remedy this, [16] proposed a method to overcome the forgetting problem for RE models. They introduced an explicit alignment model to mitigate the sentence embedding distortion of the learned model when training on new data, and achieved state-of-the-art performances.

Although [16]'s method is able to work effectively, it relies on the use of an alignment model which introduces additional parameters to already over-parameterized RE models. This leads to an increase in the quantity of supervision, computing resources and memory required for training.

In view of these issues, we propose a dynamic regularization method for lifelong RE. We model RE as a matching problem. Given an entity pair, the input is a sentence-relation pair and the output is the corresponding matching score. For knowledge preservation, our method maintains an episodic memory for each old task, which is much smaller than the original dataset, and shows the memory data to the deep learning model every time there is a new task coming in. In this way, the model can review the representatives of the old tasks while learning new information. To further retain the old knowledge, we utilize two types of consolidation regularizers, the EWC regularizer and the feature regularizers, to slow down updates on important weights and constrain the model to produce fixed representation. The key problem is that current task learning and old knowledge preservation often conflict with each other, so it's challenging to find the optimal trade-off. Instead of using fixed hyperparameters, we propose that the regularization factors keep updating to follow the dynamics of the training losses. This dynamic balance strategy can provide a comparable or better trade-off between learning and forgetting.

We compare our approach with previous state-of-the-art methods on two benchmark RE datasets. And extensive experiments show that our approach achieves significant and consistent improvement over all baseline methods. Moreover, in a condition of no memory module, the accuracy of our model is also competitive without any changes to the model.

2 Related Work

Relation Extraction. Early works on supervised RE employ feature-based methods, which heavily depend on feature engineering and require many manual efforts. To reduce manual work, recent studies have investigated neural methods for RE. Both CNN and RNN have been well applied to RE [9,18,20,21]. Furthermore, RE can be improved by integrating attention mechanism [21], parser tree [9], etc. However, all the previous neural models simply assume a closed set of relations which has been specified during training, whereas the realistic demand is usually dynamic, thus cannot be used directly in the real world.

Lifelong Learning. Recent lifelong learning work mainly falls into three categories: (1) Regularization methods [7,19]: In this setting, the loss function is augmented with extra regularization terms to protect the consolidated knowledge. Elastic weight consolidation (EWC) [7] is a representative work of this category, which minimizes changes in parameters that are crucial for previous tasks by correspondingly adjusting the learning rate. (2) Memory-based methods [2,8]: The core idea is to partially keep samples from previous tasks to help the network retain its old representations. For example, Gradient Episodic Memory (GEM) [8] stores previous data and constrains gradient updates from deviating away from their original values. (3) Dynamic architectural methods [12,13]: These methods dynamically allocate neural resources such as additional layers or nodes to learn the new knowledge, but they suffer from scalability issues.

In this paper, we focus on the RE task in a lifelong setting. The exploration of lifelong learning has produced impressive results for image classification. However, these have not yet been well-studied in the NLP domain. [16] propose a lifelong RE method that employs an explicit alignment model to overcome forgetting, but such a method strongly relies on the alignment module and introduces additional parameters to the network. Different from their approach, our method adopts to the regularization methods and memory-based methods without introducing extra parameters.

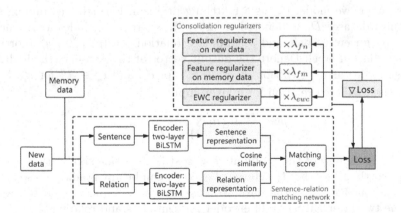

Fig. 1. An overview of our framework. The basic idea is to incrementally train a neural model efficiently using the current task data and the memory data of the old tasks. We apply two types of consolidation regularizers to the network to retain the learned knowledge. $\nabla Loss$ denotes the backward difference of the training losses. The dynamic regularization aims to make a self-adaptive schedule throughout training by adjusting the strength of the regularization factors λ_{fn}, λ_{fm} and λ_{ewc}.

3   Method

Our goal is to sequentially learn a deep RE neural network, that could not only quickly adapt to a new task but also retain its performance on the old tasks. The framework of our method is shown in Fig. 1. In the following, we will define the problem setup and introduce our approach for lifelong RE in details.

3.1   Problem Setup

Let us consider a lifelong learning setup where a model needs to learn from a sequence of datasets $\{D_1, D_2, \ldots, D_N\}$, where each dataset corresponds to a task. The data for task k includes observation and label pairs $D_k = \{(x_i^k, y_i^k)\}_{i=1}^{|D_k|}$. We assume that all relation sets in each dataset are disjoint from the others. The goal of learning is to train a single neural network f_θ parameterized by $\theta \in \mathbb{R}^p$ to perform well on both previous and new tasks. Consequently, the objective is to find parameters θ that minimize the empirical risk of all training datasets under our model:

$$Loss = \sum_{k=1}^{N} \sum_{i=1}^{|D_k|} \ell(f_\theta(x_i^k), y_i^k) \tag{1}$$

where N is the total number of datasets and $\ell(\cdot, \cdot)$ denotes the loss function which could be ranking loss in our RE.

3.2   Architecture

In this paper, we model RE as a matching problem. Formally, a training sample from a dataset D_k is denoted as (x_i^k, y_i^k), where x_i^k includes a sentence s_i^k containing an entity pair and a candidate relation set $\{c_{ij}^k\}_{j=1}^{N_c}$, y_i^k represents the true relation label. Denote the output vector of the encoder (the high level representation) as $o_i^k \in \mathbb{R}^n$ for s_i^k, $v_{ij}^k \in \mathbb{R}^n$ for c_{ij}^k and $r_i^k \in \mathbb{R}^n$ for y_i^k. In our model, the predicted relation for a given input x_i^k is:

$$pred = \underset{j \in \{1, \ldots, N_c\}}{\arg\max} \; cos(o_i^k, v_{ij}^k) \tag{2}$$

where N_c is the size of the candidate set, $cos(\cdot, \cdot)$ is cosine similarity distance.

It is worth noting that the choice of encoder can be any gradient-based model that could encode sequential data. To ensure a fair comparison to [16], we use the same two-layer BiLSTM [6] encoder for sentences and relations.

Our model aims to predict well on all tasks $1, \ldots, N$, despite training in a sequential manner. The main obstacle is the catastrophic forgetting problem, which occurs because trained parameters on the initial task need changing in favor of fitting new objectives.

To alleviate this problem, we adopt the memory-based methods which keep a memory containing data from previous tasks and perform experience replay in new task training. Obviously, it is not scalable to store every example in memory. In practice, we consider each previous task to store an episodic memory with an equal number of B examples. When training for task k, we keep a memory module $\mathcal{M} = \{\mathcal{M}_t\}_{t=1}^{k-1}$, where $\mathcal{M}_t$ contains selected examples from task t, such that $t \leq k - 1$. In experience replay, we follow Episodic Memory Replay (EMR) [16] and use examples retrieved from memory to be trained alongside the current examples. The loss function associated with memory while learning task k can be written as:

$$Loss = L_k + L_m$$
$$= \sum_{i=1}^{|D_k|} \ell(f_\theta(x_i^k), y_i^k) + \sum_{t=1}^{k-1} \sum_{i=1}^{B} \ell(f_\theta(x_i^t), y_i^t) \tag{3}$$

where $\ell(\cdot, \cdot)$ denotes the ranking loss function. We call the first term L_k as **Current Loss** and the second term L_m as **Memory Loss**.

3.3 Consolidation Regularizers

After a new dataset was trained with the current model, a subset representative examples is selected based on the vectors produced by the sentence encoder and stored in memory. The problem is that when we optimize the loss function for new data, the representations of old data would definitely be affected by the shared parameters in the single model. As a result, old data previously stored in memory may no longer be representative, which invalidates the memory data. We argue that the high level representations should not be distorted much in order to make the model work consistently on previous tasks. To address the issue, we add two types of consolidation regularizers to retain the old knowledge, as described below.

Feature Regularizers. We use the following feature regularizer to force the high level representations of the old data to remain stable during the new training process. Following the setting in Sect. 3.2, o_i^t and r_i^t depend on the parameters of the model. The **Feature Loss** on memory data is:

$$L_{fm} = \sum_{t=1}^{k-1} \sum_{i=1}^{B} (\|o_i^t(\theta_{new}) - o_i^t(\theta_{old})\| + \|r_i^t(\theta_{new}) - r_i^t(\theta_{old})\|) \tag{4}$$

where θ_{new} is the parameters for the deep learning model trained with the old data from memory and the new data from the new dataset; and θ_{old} is the parameters for the trained model using the old data.

To further reduce forgetting, we also apply a feature regularizer to current dataset. First we freeze the weights of the entire model before training. Then we propagate the current training data (x_i^k, y_i^k) through the encoders and get the output vectors o_i^k and r_i^k. The **Feature Loss** on current task data is:

$$L_{fn} = \sum_{i=1}^{|D_k|} (\|o_i^k(\theta_{new}) - o_i^k(\theta_{old})\| + \|r_i^k(\theta_{new}) - r_i^k(\theta_{old})\|) \tag{5}$$

In this way, we can force the new trained model to maintain the old behavior as the previously model, so that we could keep the memory of the old tasks.

EWC Regularizer. EWC [7] is an algorithm that modifies online learning where the loss is regularized to overcome catastrophic forgetting by applying a quadratic penalty on the difference between the new parameters and the old ones. The core idea of this regularizer is to prevent drastic changes in the parameters that contributed a lot for old tasks, but allows other parameters to change more freely. Specifically, EWC regularizes the model parameter at each step with the model parameter at the previous iteration via the Fisher information matrix for the current task, which enables us to find a good solution for both tasks. Denote the Fisher information matrix calculated from the old parameters as F_{old}, the EWC regularizer can be formulated as Eq. (6). We call it as **EWC Loss**.

$$L_{ewc} = \sum_i F_{old,i}(\theta_{new,i} - \theta_{old,i})^2 \tag{6}$$

where i denotes the indexes of the parameters.

We include the EWC regularizer in our method. As the model train through the sequence of tasks, the learning is slowed down for parameters that are important to the old tasks, which can lead to less forgetting.

Loss Function. After adding the feature regularizers and the EWC regularizer, the total loss function is given as:

$$Loss = L_k + L_m + \lambda_{fm}L_{fm} + \lambda_{fn}L_{fn} + \lambda_{ewc}L_{ewc} \tag{7}$$

where the lambdas are hyperparameters which balance current task k learning and previous tasks forgetting. As we can see, the bigger lambdas are, the stronger knowledge preservation and less knowledge update can be achieved. The key problem is how to set proper hyperparameters lambdas to get a good trade-off.

3.4   Dynamic Balance Strategy

There are five terms in Eq. (7). The first term $L_k := \sum_{i=1}^{|D_k|} \ell(f_\theta(x_i^k), y_i^k)$ drives the model toward current task learning. The rest terms preserve the previous task knowledge. The fixed hyperparameters lambdas are applied to strike a balance between adapting to new data and retaining knowledge from old data. This simple balance strategy is commonly used in many previous model regularization methods like [7,19]. However, as the gradients of those terms are unstable, the fixed hyperparameters may not be able to give a good compromise between L_k and the last three regularization terms in the entire data stream.

To overcome this problem, we propose a dynamic regularization for lifelong RE which adaptively adjusts hyperparameters with respect to the dynamics of the training losses. Specifically, at the beginning of training, the learner has not yet acquired new knowledge from the current task, which means that the network should have less regularization strength to facilitate current task learning. However, through a certain number of iterations, the network may overemphasize the current task learning, causing a rapid increase of regularization losses (including Feature Loss and EWC Loss). The design of our method needs to follow these dynamics. If the Current Loss drops in an iteration, the regularization strength should increase to prevent the ignorance of retaining old knowledge in the next iteration due to the bias to the current task; otherwise, the regularization strength should decrease against insufficient learning of the current task. If the regularization loss (L_{fm}, L_{fn} or L_{ewc}) rises in an iteration, the corresponding regularization strength should increase to consolidate the old knowledge. Otherwise, leave that regularization strength unchanged.

The dynamic characteristic of the training loss can be model as the difference of the training loss between successive iterations. For example, the backward difference between the Current Loss at two successive iterations is defined as:

$$\nabla L_k^i = L_k^i - L_k^{i-1} \tag{8}$$

where L_k^i denotes the smoothed Current Loss at the ith iteration. Since the loss may fluctuate when feeding sequential mini-batches, we performed exponential smoothing with an attenuation coefficient of 0.9 to eliminate the noise.

Our dynamic balance strategy is inspired by a previous deep learning model optimizer, gradient descent of momentum described in [11]. We take λ_{ewc} as an example to illustrate the update of the regularization strength. To obtain λ_{ewc} in the next $i+1$ iteration, we first calculate a vector to record the magnitude and direction that should be updated, which is analogous to the concept of gradient. The value of $\Delta\lambda_{ewc}^{i+1}$ is obtained via the backward difference of the Current Loss and EWC Loss, which is calculated by the following two steps:

$$step\ 1 : \Delta\lambda_{ewc}^{i+1} = \begin{cases} -\Delta\lambda_{ewc} & \nabla L_k^i \geq 0 \\ +\Delta\lambda_{ewc} & \nabla L_k^i < 0 \end{cases}$$

$$step\ 2 : \Delta\lambda_{ewc}^{i+1} = \begin{cases} \Delta\lambda_{ewc}^{i+1} + \gamma\Delta\lambda_{ewc} & \nabla L_{ewc}^i \geq 0 \\ \Delta\lambda_{ewc}^{i+1} & \nabla L_{ewc}^i < 0 \end{cases} \tag{9}$$

where $\Delta\lambda_{ewc}$ is a small constant step for changing the regularization amplitude, $\Delta\lambda_{ewc}^{i+1}$ is a vector indicating the direction and magnitude that λ_{ewc} will update and γ is used to weigh the impact of Current Loss and EWC Loss.

Then we introduce an iterative variable v_{ewc} that takes into account both the direction and magnitude of current and early updates, given as:

$$v_{ewc}^{i+1} = \beta v_{ewc}^i + (1 - \beta)\Delta\lambda_{ewc}^{i+1} \tag{10}$$

where $\beta \in [0, 1]$ is an attenuation coefficient that allows earlier updates to have less impact on the current update. Otherwise, the update of the regularization strength tends to oscillate or even diverge.

Finally, we sum up the vector v_{ewc}^{i+1} in Eq. (10) and the regularization factor of the previous iteration, given as:

$$\lambda_{ewc}^{i+1} = \lambda_{ewc}^i + v_{ewc}^{i+1} \tag{11}$$

where λ_{ewc}^{i+1} is the final dynamic factor for the $(i+1)st$ iteration. From Eq. (11), it can be observed that the update of the dynamic factor combines history and current updates and follows the dynamics of the training losses in each iteration of the training procedure.

4 Experiments

4.1 Datasets and Evaluation Metrics

We evaluate our model on *Lifelong FewRel* and *Lifelong SimpleQuestions* datasets, both proposed in [16]. *Lifelong FewRel* consists of 10 tasks which are obtained by dividing the *FewRel* [5] dataset into 10 disjoint clusters. *Fewrel* has a total of 80 relations, so each cluster contains 8 relations, and each sample in the cluster includes a sentence containing the target relation and a candidate set selected by random sampling. *Lifelong SimpleQuestions* is built similarly, which consists of 20 tasks derived from the *SimpleQuestions* [1] dataset.

Following [16], we adopt two metrics including ACC_{avg} and ACC_{whole} to evaluate our model. ACC_{avg} measures the average test accuracy of the observed tasks. If we define $a_{i,j}$ as the testing accuracy on task j after sequentially training the model from task 1 to i, ACC_{avg} on task i can be calculated by $\frac{1}{i}\sum_{j=1}^{i} a_{i,j}$. ACC_{whole} is performing on the whole test set of all N tasks that measures the overall performance of the model on both observed and unobserved tasks, and ACC_{whole} on task i can be calculated by $\frac{1}{N}\sum_{j=1}^{N} a_{i,j}$.

4.2 Baselines

For comparison, we select several public models as baselines including: (1) **Origin**, which simply trains on new tasks based on the previous model; (2) **EWC** [7], which slows down learning on parameters that are important to previous tasks; (3) **GEM** [8], which yields positive transfer of knowledge to previous tasks with an episodic memory; (4) **AGEM** [2], an improved version of GEM, which makes GEM orders of magnitude faster at training time while maintaining similar performance; (5) **EA-EMR** [16], the previous state-of-the-art method, which performs lifelong learning in the embedding space.

And we also compare our model with its other versions, which do not have a memory module to store old data but work with only one single consolidation regularization term. We name our model as "Our+FULL", the version that applies only the dynamic feature regularizer to the current task data as "Our+DF" and the version that uses only the dynamic EWC regularizer as "Our+DE".

4.3 Experimental Settings

The following settings are used throughout the experiments. For pre-trained word embeddings, we use the 300-dimensional GloVe word embeddings [10]. On both *FewRel* and *SimpleQuestions*, the attenuation coefficient β is set to 0.9

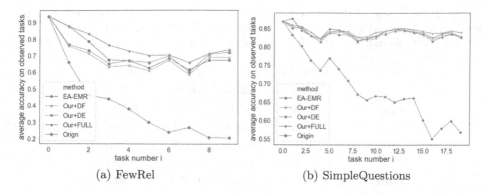

(a) FewRel   (b) SimpleQuestions

Fig. 2. The average accuracy of all the observed tasks on the benchmarks of *Lifelong FewRel* and *Lifelong SimpleQuestions* during the lifelong learning process.

and the hyperparameter γ is set to 0.2. For the dynamic regularization, we set all initial dynamic factors λ_{fm}^0, λ_{fn}^0 and λ_{ewc}^0 to 0, and $\Delta\lambda_{fm} = 0.05$, $\Delta\lambda_{fn} = 2 \times 10^{-5}$, $\Delta\lambda_{ewc} = 5$ for *FewRel* dataset and $\Delta\lambda_{fm} = 0.002$, $\Delta\lambda_{fn} = 0.06$, $\Delta\lambda_{ewc} = 0.03$ for *SimpleQuestions* dataset.

The settings of other hyperparameters, such as candidate set size, learning rate, hidden size of LSTM and batch size, etc., are consistent with [16]. All experimental results are presented by the average of 5 runs.

4.4 Main Results

The performance of our models at the last time step is shown in Table 1. Except for ours, other models' results come from [16]. From the results, we can observe that Our+FULL achieves better results on both two datasets as compared to other baselines. The reason is that our full model uses three powerful consolidation regularization terms and can dynamically control the regularization strength based on the training losses during the lifelong learning process to balance current task learning and old knowledge preservation, while other baseline models only consider the fixed balance strategy.

Figure 2 shows the average accuracy of all observed tasks during the whole learning process. From Fig. 2, we can see that Origin performs poorly, which only remembers the information of the current task batch. The results show that our methods could overcome catastrophic forgetting and achieve superior performance over Origin. In addition, we noted that EA-EMR performs better than the rest methods, so we list it and compare it with our method. We conclude that our dynamic regularizers are effective for lifelong RE. Overall, Our+FULL performs best, Our+DE and Our+DF have good performance without storing old data in memory.

Table 1. Accuracy on the whole test data ("ACC_{whole}" column) and average accuracy on all observed tasks ("ACC_{avg}" column) on the *Lifelong FewRel* and *Lifelong SimpleQuestions* datasets after the last time step. Best results are marked in bold.

Method	FewRel		SimpleQuestions	
	ACC_{whole}	ACC_{avg}	ACC_{whole}	ACC_{avg}
Origin	0.189	0.208	0.632	0.569
GEM	0.492	0.598	0.841	0.796
AGEM	0.361	0.425	0.776	0.722
EWC	0.271	0.302	0.672	0.590
EMR	0.510	0.620	0.852	0.808
EA-EMR(Full)	0.566	0.673	0.878	0.824
Our+FULL	**0.608**	**0.736**	**0.880**	**0.839**
Our+DF	0.563	0.689	0.872	0.829
Our+DE	0.591	0.721	0.870	0.826
Fixed style	0.589	0.718	0.865	0.831

4.5   Results Without Memory Support

Equipped with a memory module can significantly alleviate the catastrophic forgetting problem, but it also needs to preserve the data of the old tasks, which could lead to potential memory overhead. In addition, in some scenarios, such as data streams, the model may not be able to access the data of old tasks at all. Therefore, we also test the accuracy of our model without memory support. For Our+DF, set $\Delta\lambda_{fn} = 0.0001$ for *FewRel* and $\Delta\lambda_{fn} = 0.02$ for *SimpleQuestions*, for Our+DE, set $\Delta\lambda_{ewc} = 10$ for *FewRel* and $\Delta\lambda_{ewc} = 0.01$ for *SimpleQuestions*.

From Table 1, we can see that the accuracy of the Our+DF model is much better than the EMR model, and it is not much different from the EA-EMR model. Our + DE model performs similarly to the EA-EMR model on the *SimpleQuestions* dataset and has about 3% ACC_{whole} increment and 5% ACC_{avg} increment as compared to the EA-EMR model on the *FewRel* dataset. Figure 2 also shows that Our + DE and Our + DF work well without the help of memory.

4.6   Effectiveness of Dynamic Balance Strategy

As shown in Table 1, the accuracy of Our+DE model is greatly improved as compared to the EWC model, which proves that our dynamic regulrization effectively achieves a better trade-off between learning and forgetting.

Apart from the proposed dynamic balance strategy, the regularization strength can be fixed which is the case in many previous methods. That is, keep the network structure unchanged and fix the hyperparameters in Eq. (7). We compared our dynamic method with such a fixed schedule. Set $\lambda_{fm} = 0.3$, $\lambda_{fn} = 0.005$ and $\lambda_{ewc} = 500$ for *FewRel*. Set $\lambda_{fm} = 60$, $\lambda_{fn} = 40$ and $\lambda_{ewc} = 2$

for *SimpleQuestions*. Table 1 illustrates a comparison of regularization strategies between fixed style and ours. Compared with them, the dynamic setting achieves the best performance, which shows the effectiveness of our dynamic balance strategy.

4.7 Comparison of the Number of Parameters

One of the motivations of adopting dynamic regularization is to reduce the memory cost in [16] where 36% parameters are used to anchor the sentence embedding space, due to its extra alignment model. However, our method does not require the use of additional alignment layers, and instead uses consolidation regularizers to dynamically prevent distortion of the embedding space.

If we denote d, h, n to be the word embedding size, hidden size of LSTM and alignment layer size respectively ($n = 2h$), then the total number of parameters for [16] and our method can be calculated as follows:

$$EA - EMR[16] : 2 \times d \times h + 4 \times h^2 + 4 \times h + 2 \times h \times n + n = 441,200$$

$$Our + FULL : 2 \times d \times h + 4 \times h^2 + 4 \times h = 280,800$$

We can find that our total parameter space is 64% large as that in [16], and the alignment model needs more $2hn + n = 160,400$ parameters. Without introducing more parameters, our method still outperforms theirs.

5 Conclusion

In this paper, we aim to deal with the scenario of lifelong relation extraction. We propose two types of consolidation regularizers to handle the catastrophic forgetting problem and a dynamic schedule to adjust the regularization strength to fit the learning process. Our dynamic regularization is self-adaptive with the change of the training loss, thus can provide a better compromise between learning and forgetting. In the experiments, our method achieves remarkable results compared with the cutting edge methods. Furthermore, we demonstrate that the performance of our model is still competitive without the memory module.

Acknowledgements. The work was partially supported by the Sichuan Science and Technology Program under Grant Nos. 2018GZDZX0039 and 2019YFG0521.

References

1. Bordes, A., Usunier, N., Chopra, S., Weston, J.: Large-scale simple question answering with memory networks. arXiv preprint arXiv:1506.02075 (2015)
2. Chaudhry, A., Ranzato, M., Rohrbach, M., Elhoseiny, M.: Efficient lifelong learning with A-GEM. arXiv preprint arXiv:1812.00420 (2018)
3. Dai, Z., Li, L., Xu, W.: CFO: Conditional focused neural question answering with large-scale knowledge bases. arXiv preprint arXiv:1606.01994 (2016)

4. Goodfellow, I.J., Mirza, M., Xiao, D., Courville, A., Bengio, Y.: An empirical investigation of catastrophic forgetting in gradient-based neural networks. arXiv preprint arXiv:1312.6211 (2013)
5. Han, X., et al.: FewRel: a large-scale supervised few-shot relation classification dataset with state-of-the-art evaluation. arXiv preprint arXiv:1810.10147 (2018)
6. Hochreiter, S., Schmidhuber, J.: Long short-term memory. Neural Comput. **9**(8), 1735–1780 (1997)
7. Kirkpatrick, J., et al.: Overcoming catastrophic forgetting in neural networks. Proc. Nat. Acad. Sci. **114**(13), 3521–3526 (2017)
8. Lopez-Paz, D., Ranzato, M.: Gradient episodic memory for continual learning. In: Advances in Neural Information Processing Systems, pp. 6467–6476 (2017)
9. Miwa, M., Bansal, M.: End-to-end relation extraction using LSTMs on sequences and tree structures. arXiv preprint arXiv:1601.00770 (2016)
10. Pennington, J., Socher, R., Manning, C.: GloVe: global vectors for word representation. In: Proceedings of the 2014 Conference on Empirical Methods in Natural Language Processing (EMNLP), pp. 1532–1543 (2014)
11. Polyak, B.T.: Some methods of speeding up the convergence of iteration methods. USSR Comput. Math. Math. Phys. **4**(5), 1–17 (1964)
12. Roy, D., Panda, P., Roy, K.: Tree-CNN: a deep convolutional neural network for lifelong learning. CoRR abs/1802.05800 (2018). http://arxiv.org/abs/1802.05800
13. Rusu, A.A., et al.: Progressive neural networks. arXiv preprint arXiv:1606.04671 (2016)
14. Thrun, S.: A lifelong learning perspective for mobile robot control. In: Intelligent Robots and Systems, pp. 201–214. Elsevier (1995)
15. Thrun, S.: Lifelong learning algorithms. In: Thrun, S., Pratt, L. (eds.) Learning to Learn. Springer, Boston (1998). https://doi.org/10.1007/978-1-4615-5529-2_8
16. Wang, H., Xiong, W., Yu, M., Guo, X., Chang, S., Wang, W.Y.: Sentence embedding alignment for lifelong relation extraction. arXiv preprint arXiv:1903.02588 (2019)
17. Wu, F., Weld, D.S.: Open information extraction using Wikipedia. In: Proceedings of the 48th Annual Meeting of the Association for Computational Linguistics, pp. 118–127. Association for Computational Linguistics (2010)
18. Zeng, D., Liu, K., Chen, Y., Zhao, J.: Distant supervision for relation extraction via piecewise convolutional neural networks. In: Proceedings of the 2015 Conference on Empirical Methods in Natural Language Processing, pp. 1753–1762 (2015)
19. Zenke, F., Poole, B., Ganguli, S.: Continual learning through synaptic intelligence. In: Proceedings of the 34th International Conference on Machine Learning, vol. 70, pp. 3987–3995. JMLR.org (2017)
20. Zhang, D., Wang, D.: Relation classification via recurrent neural network. arXiv preprint arXiv:1508.01006 (2015)
21. Zhu, J., Qiao, J., Dai, X., Cheng, X.: Relation classification via target-concentrated attention CNNs. In: Liu, D., Xie, S., Li, Y., Zhao, D., El-Alfy, E.S. (eds.) ICONIP 2017. LNCS, pp. 137–146. Springer, Cham (2017). https://doi.org/10.1007/978-3-319-70096-0_15

Collective Entity Disambiguation Based on Deep Semantic Neighbors and Heterogeneous Entity Correlation

Zihan He, Jiang Zhong[✉], Chen Wang, and Cong Hu

Chongqing University, Chongqing 400044, People's Republic of China
zhongjiang@cqu.edu.cn

Abstract. Entity Disambiguation (ED) aims to associate entity mentions recognized in text corpus with the corresponding unambiguous entry in knowledge base (KB). A large number of models were proposed based on the topical coherence assumption. Recently, several works have proposed a new assumption: topical coherence only needs to hold among neighboring mentions, which proved to be effective. However, due to the complexity of the text, there are still some challenges in how to accurately obtain the local coherence of the mention set. Therefore, we introduce the self-attention mechanism in our work to capture the long-distance dependencies between mentions and quantify the degree of topical coherence. Based on the internal semantic correlation, we find the semantic neighbors for every mention. Besides, we introduce the idea of "simple to complex" to the construction of entity correlation graph, which achieves a self-reinforcing effect of low-ambiguity mention towards high-ambiguity mention during collective disambiguation. Finally, we apply the graph attention network to integrate the local and global features extracted from key information and entity correlation graph. We validate our graph neural collective entity disambiguation (GNCED) method on six public datasets and the results demonstrate a better performance improvement compared with state-of-the-art baselines.

Keywords: Entity disambiguation · Local topical coherence · Long-distance dependencies · Entity correlation graph

1 Introduction

As the key technology of multiple natural language processing tasks, such as knowledge graph construction, information extraction, and so on, entity disambiguation (ED) has gained increasing attention. Formally, it aims to associate

Supported by National Key Research and Development Program of China Grant 2017YFB1402400, in part by the Key Research Program of Chongqing Science and Technology Bureau No. cstc2019jscx-fxyd0142, in part by the Key Research Program of Chongqing Science and Technology Bureau No. cstc2019jscx-mbdxX0012.

X. Zhu et al. (Eds.): NLPCC 2020, LNAI 12431, pp. 193–205, 2020.
https://doi.org/10.1007/978-3-030-60457-8_16

entity mentions recognized in unstructured text with the corresponding unambiguous entry in a structured knowledge base (KB) (e.g.., Wikipedia). However, this task is challenging due to the inherent ambiguity between surface form mentions. A unified form of mention in different context may refer to different entities, and different surface form mentions may refer to the same entity in some cases. For example, the mention "Titanic" can refer to a movie, a ship, or a shipwreck in different contexts.

To solve the problem, current ED methods have been divided into local disambiguation models and global disambiguation models. The former focus on the local information around the mention and related candidate entity. The latter additionally consider the correlation between entity mentions in the same document. Generally, based on the assumption that the mentions in the same document shall be on the same topic, large numbers of global models have been proposed. In particular, the work [1,18] claimed that topical coherence only need to hold among mention neighbors, which we called "local topical coherence" in this paper. They calculated sequence distance and syntactic distance respectively to determine the mention neighbors, which may lead to inconsistent mention sets due to insufficient mining of deep semantic associations between entities. In fact, our paper will be developed based on the same assumption.

To solve the above problems, our paper tries to calculate the semantic distance between mention pairs and select a set of mention neighbors with the closest semantic distance for each mention. Then, we introduce the self-attention mechanism into our model to model the text deeply and better capture the internal relevance of entity mentions.

Besides, we introduce the simple to complex (S2C) idea to the construction of entity correlation graph. We fully exploit the key information brought by the low-ambiguity mentions and the supplementary information obtained from the external KB to promote the disambiguation of the high-ambiguity mentions, to achieve the self-reinforcing of the collective process. In particular, we build a heterogeneous entity correlation graph based on the correlation information between mentions, and further aggregate the feature data.

Therefore, the main contributions of our ED method can be summarized as:

(1) We propose a semantic-information based mention neighbors selection method to capture the semantic relevance between mentions and find top-k closest semantic distance mention neighbors for each mention to disambiguate.
(2) We construct a new collective disambiguation entity correlation graph and introduce the idea of simple to complex to dig the disambiguation effect of the low-ambiguity mentions on the high-ambiguity mentions.
(3) We evaluate our method on several public datasets. The experimental results compared with existing state-of-the-art ED baselines verify the efficiency and effectiveness of our model.

2   Related Work

Entity Disambiguation. Entity disambiguation in nature language processing tasks, has gained increasing attention in recent years. Many research work has been proposed based on two main disambiguation models: local models and global models. Early local ED models mainly extracted string features between candidate entities and the local context of current mention to find the optimal solution for each mention [1,3,13]. Since the increasing popularity of deep learning, recent ED approaches had fully used neural network, such as CNN/LSTM-encoders [4,8], to learn the representation of context information and model the local features. By contrast, a large number of collective disambiguation models have been proposed based on the hypothesis: all mentions in a document shall be on the same topic. However, the maximization of coherence between all entity disambiguation decisions in the document is NP-hard. [11] had firstly tried to solve it by turning it into a binary integer linear program and relaxing it to a linear program (LP). [9] proposed a graph-pruned method to compute the dense sub-graph that approximated the best joint mention-entity mapping. [7,12,15,19] applied the Page Rank, Random Walk, Loop Belief Propagation algorithm respectively to quantify the topical coherence for finding the optimal linking assignment. Recently, [1,10,18] applied graph neural network into the calculation of global coherence, such as GCN/GAT.

Self-attention. The self-attention mechanism was firstly proposed in the task of machine translation [16], which caused a great of focus. Self-attention mechanism can associate any two words in a sequence to capture the long distance dependency between them. And, it had been cited by a large number of studies and generalized to many NLP tasks [2,17,21]. In our paper, we apply the self-attention mechanism to capture the dependencies between distant mentions to hold the topical coherence assumption.

3   Graph Neural Collective Entity Disambiguation

3.1   Overview of Framework

As with most entity disambiguation work, we take a document collection as input where all the candidate entity mentions have been identified. Formally, we define the collective disambiguation task as follows: given a set of mentions $M(D)$ in a document D and the candidate entities generated, $C(m_i) = \{e_{i1}, e_{i2}, \cdots, e_{ij}\}$, the goal of our model is to find an optimal linking assignment. As the Fig. 1 shown, our model mainly includes the mainly two modules: feature extraction module and graph neural disambiguation module. The details are as follows:

Embedding of Word, Mention and Entity: In the first step, we need to get the embedding vector to avoid manual features and better encode the semantics of words and entities. Following the work of [6], we train the embedding of each

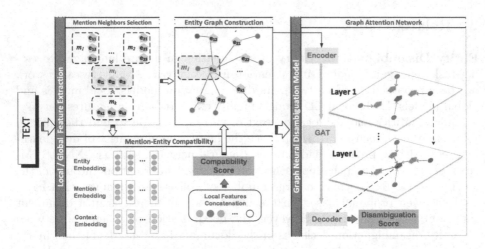

Fig. 1. Overview of framework.

word and related entity at the same time (the mention embedding can calculate from related word embedding).

Candidate Generation: As the essential procedure, the candidate generation step affect the accuracy of entity disambiguation and the recall rate directly. Generally, we generate candidate entities for each entity mention in document based on the mapping dictionary built by [1,9,14], noted as $C(m_i) = \{e_{i1}, e_{i2}, \cdots, e_{ij}\}$, where each entity corresponds to a specific entity entry in the knowledge base (Wikipedia in our paper).

Feature Extraction: Disambiguation is the key step in the entity disambiguation task. In this part, we consider extract two types of evidence to support the final decision: local features and global features. The features include there parts: string compatibility between the string of mention and candidate entities; contextual similarity between the text surrounding the mention and the candidate entity; entity relatedness for all mentions in the document. Following the work of [20], we construct the string compatibility features using the edit distance, noted as Sim_{str}. To make full use of the context and external information, we extract word level and sentence level contextual similarity evidence. On the basis of above features, we come to extract the global features. In particular, considering the local topical coherence, we propose a selection strategy based on semantic information to select most relevant mention neighbors for each mention. Then, we build the entity semantic correlation graph $G = (V, E)$ for each mention to characterize the relatedness between entities with the introduction of the idea of simple to complex (S2C) and dig deep into the contextual information and external KB, which achieves a self-reinforcing effect. The details will be explained in Sect. 3.2–3.4.

Neural Network Disambiguation Model: After the process of feature extraction, we can get a set of local similarity representation, and entity correlation graph G for each mention. Considering the special representation of structured graph, Graph Attention Network (GAT) will be used in our paper to better aggregate feature data and ensure the validity of feature information transmission. The detailed implementation of the model will be explained in Sect. 3.5.

3.2 Word and Sentence Level Contextual Compatibility

To extract local features, we first get the surrounding context of a mention and the textual representation (from external KB) of the given candidate entity. For mention m_i, we can get a c-word context $C(m_i) = \{w_1, w_2, \cdots, w_{C_1}\}$, where C_1 is the context window size. For every candidate entity, we can get the complete description page from the knowledge base. To obtain more accurate keywords and reduce information processing complexity, we focus on the first two paragraph of the description page as the textual representation and extract the top C_2 terms with the highest TF-IDF score for given candidate entity e, noted as $C(e) = \{w_1, w_2, ..., w_{C_2}\}$. To represent the local context information mentioned and the description information of the candidate entity more accurately, we design our model in word and sentence level.

Firstly, based on pre-trained word embedding, we can directly obtain the context representation at the word level [1]. The word level contextual compatibility $Sim(m, e)$ is defined as follows:

$$Sim(m_i, e)_{word} = \frac{D_m \cdot D_e}{\|D_m\| \|D_e\|} \tag{1}$$

where D_m and D_e are the weighted average of context vectors corresponding to the mention's and entity's textual representations.

Secondly, we try to use the Bi-LSTM model to encode sentence-level evidence. Differently, the evidence at sentence level takes the positional relation between words into consideration, which is more conducive to retaining the deep meaning of language. Feeding the sentence containing the mention m and the entity description information (contains several sentences) into the model respectively, we can obtain the final hidden state $< h_m, h_e >$ as the sentence level vectors of the mention and entity. Then, the sentence level similarity is defined as follows:

$$Sim(m_i, e)_{sen} = \frac{H_m \cdot H_e}{\|H_m\| \|H_e\|} \tag{2}$$

3.3 Semantic Information Based Mention Neighbors Selection

In this section, we introduce our mention neighbors selection strategy based on the assumption of local topical coherence. The whole process is shown in Fig. 2.

We use the self-attention mechanism [16] to obtain the relevant features of the text from multiple angles. The self-attention mechanism is to do the attention inside the sequence and find the connection of the inner part of the sequence. We apply self attention mechanism to the entire document to catch the key

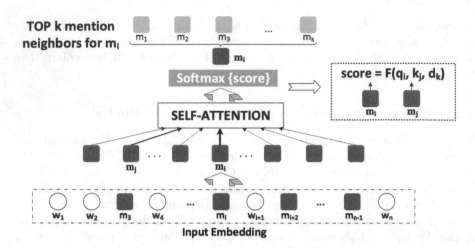

Fig. 2. Mention neighbors selection

semantic information among entity mentions. Considering that there are many words other than the mentions in the document and the needs of the problem, we only calculate the attention value with other mentions and the context words for every m_i, which is used to measure the semantic correlation between each mention pairs, which we called semantic distance α_{sd}.

To calculate the α_{sd}, we construct a basic multi-layer self-attention module to model mentions in the entire document. We use $\{X_1, X_2, \cdots, X_n\}$ to represent the entire document, including all mentions X_{m_i} and their context words X_w. For the calculation of each self-attention layer, the embedding of mention m_i will be updated by encoding the context information and the associated information between mention pairs. The calculation process is as follows:

$$X'_{m_i} = \sum_{j,q} w_{ij}X_{m_j} + w_{iq}X_{w_q}; \quad w = \frac{Q \cdot K^T}{\sqrt{d_K}} \tag{3}$$

In the last layer of self-attention, we directly output the normalized attention value between mention pairs.

$$[\alpha_{sd}]_{ij} = X'_{m_i}{}^T X'_{m_j} \tag{4}$$

$$[\alpha_{sd}]'_{ij} = \frac{\exp[\alpha_{sd}]_{ij}}{\sum_j \exp[\alpha_{sd}]_{ij}} \tag{5}$$

After the above calculation, the semantic correlation between any two mentions in the document D can be represented as $[\alpha_{sd}]'_{ij}$. The larger the semantic correlation value, the closer the semantic distance between mention pairs. For mention m_i, we select mentions with the top-k minimum semantic distance as neighbors of the current mention m_i, $N(m_i) = \{m_1, m_2, ..., m_k\}$.

3.4 Construction of S2C Entity Correlation Graph

The entity correlation graph is the key module of feature extraction as the structure of carrying and transmitting local and global information. To model the global semantic relationships, we construct a heterogeneous entity semantic graph for each mention m_i based on its neighbor mentions $N(m_i)$.

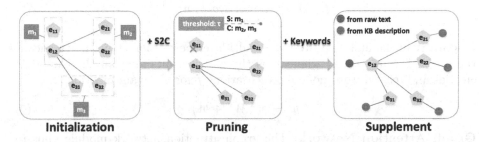

Fig. 3. Illustration of entity graph construction

As shown in Fig. 3, the process is divided into three steps: (1) **Initialization of the entity graph:** Take the candidate entities of mention m_i and its neighbor mentions as the initial nodes of the graph, and build graph G_1, and establish edges between the candidate entities mentioned by different mentions. (2) **Pruning of the entity graph:** Introduce the idea of S2C. First, we will divide the entire mention set into simple and complex parts according to the threshold setting τ. In this setting, we make full use of local features to preferentially link (Simple) mentions with low ambiguity. Once the final entity referred to by Simple mention is identified, the redundant candidate entity nodes that mention has and the corresponding edges connected to these nodes are removed from the initial diagram G_2. (3) **Supplement of the entity graph:** Introduce evidence nodes other than entity nodes. To maintain the influence of text context, we introduce two kinds of evidence nodes into entity graph G_2: one is the top S_1 surrounding words of the simple mention selected from the document; another is the top S_2 key words for entity selected from the description page. We connect these evidence nodes with corresponding entity nodes to form new edges. Then, the construction of the entity correlation graph G is completed.

For every entity node, we initialize the representation with the concentration of pre-trained entity embedding and obtained local features, including Sim_{str}, Sim_{word}, Sim_{sen}. For every keyword node, we initialize the representation with the concentration of pre trained word embedding and weights between keywords and corresponding entities. The initial representation have been expressed as f.

3.5 Disambiguation Model on Entity Correlation Graph

Our model adopts a Graph Attention Network to deal with the document-specific S2C entity semantic graph. In particular, the input of the neural model is the sub-graph structure $G = \{V, E\}$, where contains all the entity and keyword nodes we need. All nodes in the graph G represented by the entity and word embedding are in the same space, so that the information between different nodes can be directly calculated. The overall goal of our model is to maximize the value in Eq. 6, where $Score(m, e_i)$ is a scoring function that our network model learns from multi-features for mention m and its candidate entities.

$$\Gamma(m) = \arg\max_{e_i \in \phi(m)} Score(m, e_i) \tag{6}$$

Encoder: In the first step, we use a multi-layer perception structure to encode the initial feature vector, where F is the matrix containing all the candidate entities and related word node representations f for a certain mention.

$$h^1 = \sigma(FW^1 + b^1) \tag{7}$$

Graph Attention Network: The graph attention network module aims to extract key features from the hidden state of the mention and its neighbor mentions. Then, we can derive the new representation for each mention as:

$$h^l = \sigma(Ah^{l-1}W^{l-1}) + h^{l-1} \tag{8}$$

where A is the symmetric normalized adjacent matrix of the input graph with self-connections. We normalize A such that all rows sum to one, avoiding the change in the scale of the feature vectors. To enable the model to retain information from the previous layer, we add residual connections between hidden layers.

Decoder: After going through multi-layer graph attention network, we will get the final hidden state of each mention in the document-specific entity graph, which aggregate semantics from their neighbor mentions in the entity semantic graph. Then, we can map the hidden state to the number of candidates as follows:

$$Score = W^L h^L + b^L \tag{9}$$

Training: To train the graph neural disambiguation model, we aim to minimize the following cross-entropy loss, where $P(\Delta)$ is a probability function calculated by $Score(m, e_i)$.

$$L_m = -\sum_{j=1}^{n} y_j \log(P(\hat{y} = e_j; f, \tilde{A}, w)) \tag{10}$$

4   Experiments

In this section, we compared with existing state-of-the-art methods on six standard datasets to verify the performance of our method.

4.1 Setup

Datasets: We conducted experiments on the following sets of publicly-available datasets used by previous studies: (1) AIDA-CoNLL: annotated by [9], this dataset consists of there parts: AIDA-train for training, AIDA-A for validation, and AIDA-B for testing; (2) MSNBC, AUIAINT, ACE2004: cleaned and updated by [7]; (3) WNED-CWEB, WNED-WIKI: two larger but less reliable datasets that are automatically extracted from ClueWeb and Wikipedia respectively [5,7]. The composition scale of the above datasets can be seen in Table 1.

Table 1. Statistics of datasets in this experiment.

Dataset	AIDA(B)	MSNBC	AQUAINT	ACE2004	WIKI	CWEB
Total documents	213	20	50	36	320	320
Total mentions	4486	656	699	248	6821	11154

We train the model on AIDA-train and validate on AIDA-A. For in-domain and out-domain testing, we test on AIDA-B and other datasets respectively.

Baselines: We compare our model with the following state-of-the-art methods:

– AIDA [9]: built a weighted graph of mentions and candidate entities and computed a dense sub-graph that maps the optimal assignment.
– Random-Walk [7]: proposed a graph-based disambiguation model, and applied iterative algorithm based on random-walk.
– DeepEL [6]: applied a deep learning architecture combining CRF for joint disambiguation and solved the global training using truncated fitting LBP.
– NCEL [1]: first introduced Graph Neural Network into the task of NED to integrate local and global features.
– MulRel [12]: designed a collective disambiguation model based on the latent relations of entities and obtained a set of optimal linking assignments by modeling the relations between entities.
– CoSimTC [18]: applied a dependency parse tree method to drive mention neighbors based on the topical coherence assumption.
– GNED [10]: proposed a heterogeneous entity-word graph and applies GCN on the graph to fully exploit the global semantic information.

Experimental Settings: Our experiments are carried out on the PyTorch framework. For fair comparison, we train and validate our model on AIDA-A, and test on other benchmark datasets (including AIDA-B). We use standard micro F1 score (aggregates over all mentions) as measurement. Following the work [6], we get the initial word embedding and entity embedding with size $d = 300$, $\gamma = 0.1$ and window size of 20 for the hyperlinks. Before training, we have removed the stop words. We use Adam with a initial learning rate of 0.01 for optimization. For the over fitting problem, we use the early stopping to avoid it. Then, we set epoch = 50 and batch size = 64 to train our model. Besides, we set top 10 candidate entities for every mention and the context window size to 20 to extract the local features. For other hyper-parameters, we set different values according to the situation.

4.2 Experimental Results

Overall Results: In this section, we compare our model with precious state-of-the-art baselines on six public datasets. The results of the comparison are listed in Table 2. It can be seen that our proposed model outperformed the current SOTA baselines on more than half datasets. Our proposed method has achieved the highest micro F1 score on AIDA(B), AQUAINT, ACE2004, and WIKI. On average, we can see that our model has achieved a promising overall performance compared with state-of-the-art baselines. For in-domain testing, our proposed model reaches the performance of Micro F1 of 93.57%, which is a 0.5% improvement from the current highest score. For out-domain testing, our method has achieved relatively high-performance scores on three datasets of MSNBC, AQUAINT, and ACE2004, which the best is achieved on the AUQAINT and ACE2004 datasets. However, the improvement of our model on WIKI and CWEB datasets is not obvious. We analyze the data and think that the reason for this result may have a lot to do with the noise problem of the data itself.

Table 2. The micro F1 scores on six public datasets.

Model	AIDA(B)	MSNBC	AQUAINT	ACE2004	WIKI	CWEB	AVG
AIDA [9]	–	79.00	56.00	80.00	58.60	63.00	67.32
Random-Walk [7]	89.00	92.00	87.00	88.00	77.00	84.50	86.25
DeepEL [6]	92.22	93.70	88.50	88.50	77.90	77.50	86.39
NCEL [1]	87.20	–	87.00	88.00	–	**86.00**	87.05
MulRel [12]	93.07	93.90	88.30	89.90	77.50	78.00	86.78
CoSimTC [18]	–	94.16	90.90	92.92	76.96	75.02	86.00
GNED [10]	92.40	**95.50**	91.60	90.14	77.50	78.50	87.61
GNCED (our model)	**93.57**	95.00	**92.40**	**93.92**	**78.03**	82.67	**89.27**

Table 3. The comparison of mention neighbors selection strategy.

Model	AIDA(B)	WIKI
Basic ED + all mentions	74.16	89.41
Basic ED + sequence distance	76.30	90.44
Basic ED + syntactic distance	76.55	90.80
Basic ED + self-attention	**78.22**	**92.27**

Impact of Mention Neighbors Selection Strategy: In this part, we designed experiments to verify the performance improvement brought by our self-attention based mention neighbors selection strategy in the whole ED model. Specifically, we compared our selection strategy with the adjacency strategy [1] and the syntactic distance strategy [18] respectively. To facilitate observation and explanation, we implement experiments on two testing datasets, WIKI, and AIDA(B). The results are shown in Table 3. We can see that for the document-level disambiguation, our semantic-based mention neighbors selection strategy can effectively improve the performance of collective disambiguation by selecting a set of most semantically relevant subsets for each mention.

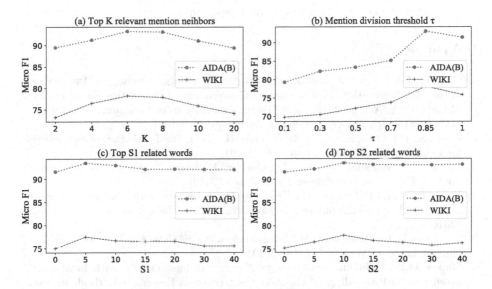

Fig. 4. The impact of hyper-parameters.

Impact of Hyper-Parameters: We analyzed the impact of three hyper-parameter settings in the model on the performance of the entire model. As in the last experiment, we completed this experiment on datasets, WIKI and AIDA(B). The parameters include the number K of top relevant mention neighbors for current mention m, the threshold parameter τ for mention division, the number S_1 of top related keywords for the entity of simple mentions, and the number S_2 of top related keywords for the entity of complex mentions. From Fig. 4, we can see that the parameters of K and τ have an obvious impact on the performance. Besides, the effects of parameters S_1, S_2 are big only when the values are between zero and non-zero but gradually become small as the values increase, which shows that the keywords selected from context and external KB improve the performance of our model. Generally, with the increasing of these parameters, the value of micro $F1$ will increase incrementally but decrease slightly after reaching a certain maximum value. After a large number of experiments, we found that the model performance can be the best when $K = 6, \tau = 0.85, S_1 = 5, S_2 = 10$.

5   Conclusion

In this paper, we propose a semantic based mention neighbors selection strategy for collective entity disambiguation. We use the self-attention mechanism to find the optimal mention neighbors among all mentions for the collective disambiguation. We also propose an entity graph construction method. We introduce the S2C idea to add more sufficient evidence information for the disambiguation process of high ambiguity mention and achieve a self-reinforcing effect in the disambiguation process. The results of experiments and module analysis have demonstrated the effectiveness of our proposed model.

References

1. Cao, Y., Hou, L., Li, J., Liu, Z.: Neural collective entity linking. In: Proceedings of the 27th International Conference on Computational Linguistics, Santa Fe, New Mexico, USA, August 2018, pp. 675–686. Association for Computational Linguistics (2018). https://www.aclweb.org/anthology/C18-1057
2. Chen, S., Hu, Q.V., Song, Y., He, Y., Wu, H., He, L.: Self-attention based network for medical query expansion, pp. 1–9 (2019)
3. Dredze, M., Mcnamee, P., Rao, D., Gerber, A., Finin, T.: Entity disambiguation for knowledge base population, pp. 277–285 (2010)
4. Francislandau, M., Durrett, G., Klein, D.: Capturing semantic similarity for entity linking with convolutional neural networks. arXiv: Computation and Language (2016)
5. Gabrilovich, E., Ringgaard, M., Subramanya, A.: FACC1: Freebase annotation of clueweb corpora. Version 1, 2013 (2013)
6. Ganea, O.E., Hofmann, T.: Deep joint entity disambiguation with local neural attention. In: Proceedings of the 2017 Conference on Empirical Methods in Natural Language Processing, Copenhagen, Denmark, September 2017, pp. 2619–2629. Association for Computational Linguistics (2017). https://doi.org/10.18653/v1/D17-1277. https://www.aclweb.org/anthology/D17-1277
7. Guo, Z., Barbosa, D.: Robust named entity disambiguation with random walks. Sprachwissenschaft **9**(4), 459–479 (2017)
8. Gupta, N., Singh, S., Roth, D.: Entity linking via joint encoding of types, descriptions, and context, pp. 2681–2690 (2017)
9. Hoffart, J., et al.: Robust disambiguation of named entities in text. In: Proceedings of the Conference on Empirical Methods in Natural Language Processing, pp. 782–792. Association for Computational Linguistics (2011)
10. Hu, L., Ding, J., Shi, C., Shao, C., Li, S.: Graph neural entity disambiguation. Knowl. Based Syst. **195**, 105620 (2020)
11. Kulkarni, S.V., Singh, A.K., Ramakrishnan, G., Chakrabarti, S.: Collective annotation of wikipedia entities in web text, pp. 457–466 (2009)
12. Le, P., Titov, I.: Improving entity linking by modeling latent relations between mentions. In: Proceedings of the 56th Annual Meeting of the Association for Computational Linguistics, Melbourne, Australia, July 2018 (Volume 1: Long Papers), pp. 1595–1604. Association for Computational Linguistics (2018). https://doi.org/10.18653/v1/P18-1148. https://www.aclweb.org/anthology/P18-1148
13. Liu, X., Li, Y., Wu, H., Zhou, M., Wei, F., Lu, Y.: Entity linking for tweets, vol. 1, pp. 1304–1311 (2013)

14. Spitkovsky, V.I., Chang, A.X.: A cross-lingual dictionary for English wikipedia concepts. In: Conference on Language Resources and Evaluation (2012)
15. Usbeck, R., et al.: AGDISTIS - graph-based disambiguation of named entities using linked data. In: Mika, P., et al. (eds.) ISWC 2014. LNCS, vol. 8796, pp. 457–471. Springer, Cham (2014). https://doi.org/10.1007/978-3-319-11964-9_29
16. Vaswani, A., et al.: Attention is all you need, pp. 5998–6008 (2017)
17. Wang, X., Girshick, R., Gupta, A., He, K.: Non-local neural networks, pp. 7794–7803 (2018)
18. Xin, K., Hua, W., Liu, Yu., Zhou, X.: Entity disambiguation based on parse tree neighbours on graph attention network. In: Cheng, R., Mamoulis, N., Sun, Y., Huang, X. (eds.) WISE 2020. LNCS, vol. 11881, pp. 523–537. Springer, Cham (2019). https://doi.org/10.1007/978-3-030-34223-4_33
19. Xue, M., et al.: Neural collective entity linking based on recurrent random walk network learning. arXiv: Computation and Language (2019)
20. Yamada, I., Shindo, H., Takeda, H., Takefuji, Y.: Joint learning of the embedding of words and entities for named entity disambiguation. In: Proceedings of The 20th SIGNLL Conference on Computational Natural Language Learning, Berlin, Germany, August 2016, pp. 250–259. Association for Computational Linguistics (2016). https://doi.org/10.18653/v1/K16-1025. https://www.aclweb.org/anthology/K16-1025
21. Zukovgregoric, A., Bachrach, Y., Minkovsky, P., Coope, S., Maksak, B.: Neural named entity recognition using a self-attention mechanism, pp. 652–656 (2017)

Boosting Cross-lingual Entity Alignment with Textual Embedding

Wei Xu, Chen Chen, Chenghao Jia, Yongliang Shen, Xinyin Ma,
and Weiming Lu[✉]

College of Computer Science and Technology, Zhejiang University, Hangzhou, China
luwm@zju.edu.cn

Abstract. Multilingual knowledge graph (KG) embeddings have attracted many researchers, and benefit lots of cross-lingual tasks. The cross-lingual entity alignment task is to match equivalent entities in different languages, which can largely enrich the multilingual KGs. Many previous methods consider solely the use of structures to encode entities. However, lots of multilingual KGs provide rich entity descriptions. In this paper, we mainly focus on how to utilize these descriptions to boost the cross-lingual entity alignment. Specifically, we propose two textual embedding models called Cross-TextGCN and Cross-TextMatch to embed description for each entity. Our experiments on DBP15K show that these two textual embedding model can indeed boost the structure based cross-lingual entity alignment model.

Keywords: Cross-lingual entity alignment · Graph Convolutional Networks · Entity embedding.

1 Introduction

Knowledge graphs (KGs) organize human knowledge in a structured form, providing a data foundation for various AI-related applications, such as question answering systems, recommender systems, relation extraction, synonym extraction, and so on. With the development of monolingual KG, many multilingual KGs have been constructed, such as DBpedia [12], Yago [13], BabelNet [14], and ConceptNet [17]. KGs usually represent knowledge in the form of triples (*subject*, *property*, *object*). Besides, KGs often provide rich descriptions of entities. For multilingual KGs, there are also cross-lingual links referring to the equivalent real-world entities in different languages. In Fig. 1, we show an aligned entity pair in DBpedia with its associated triples and descriptions. However, not all the equivalent entities are connected in most multilingual KGs, since these multilingual KGs are built based on the existing cross-lingual links in Wikipedia. But the cross-lingual links in Wikipedia are still far from complete, as they are edited by human collectively.

Traditional cross-lingual entity alignment methods are typically based on machine translation, which greatly depend on the quality of the translation.

© Springer Nature Switzerland AG 2020
X. Zhu et al. (Eds.): NLPCC 2020, LNAI 12431, pp. 206–218, 2020.
https://doi.org/10.1007/978-3-030-60457-8_17

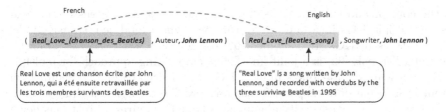

Fig. 1. Example of an aligned entity pair with their triples and descriptions.

In recent years, a series of embedding-based methods have been proposed for cross-lingual entity alignment tasks, such as JE [8], MtransE [2], ItransE [22], JAPE [18] and GCN-Align [21]. However, most of these methods only use the structural information of KGs, but ignore the descriptions of entities.

In fact, most entities in real-world KGs have literal descriptions to describe the entity shortly. Taking DBpedia for example, we observe that it provides $5,045,732$ short abstracts for English entities in DBpedia (2016-04)[1]. Since the descriptions of an entity in different languages often share a lot of semantic information, thus they would be utilized to boost cross-lingual entity alignment.

In this paper, we mainly focus on how to utilize the description of each entity in the cross-lingual entity alignment task. On one hand, we build a cross-lingual textual graph among KGs and then use Graph Convolutional Networks (GCNs) to encode entities by transferring semantics among KGs through words and entities. On the other hand, we use pre-trained cross-lingual aligned word embeddings to encode the descriptions of entities, and then train a cross-lingual entity matching model. Finally, these two textual embedding models can be jointly trained with structure-based models to promote the performance of the cross-lingual entity alignment.

2   Related Work

2.1   Monolingual Entity Alignment

Most entity alignment involves in the same language, and traditional entity alignment techniques mainly focus on pairwise entity matching, especially for records in database, such as DeepER [4], EMLC [19], GML [9] and ExplainER [3], but they rely on the high-quality schema.

For entity matching between knowledge graphs, due to the heterogenity and loose-schema of KGs, many works utilized the structural information (subject-predicate-object triples). For example, HolisticEM [16] computes attributes overlapping to construct a graph of potential entity pairs and uses personalized page rank to gather local and global information for aligning instances. HolE [15] uses tensor-based factorization and represent relationships with matrices. MinoanER [5] proposed schema-agnostic similarity metrics that consider

---

[1] http://wiki.dbpedia.org/downloads-2016-04.

both the content and the neighbors of entities. JE [8] jointly learns the embeddings of multiple KGs in a uniform vector space via a modified TransE model to align entities in KGs. It combines the loss function with the loss of entity alignments. ITransE [22] is a joint knowledge embedding approach for multiple KGs. It first learns embeddings in each KG, then learns to join embeddings of different KGs into a unified space. It also uses predicted entities with high confidence to perform iterative entity alignment. ITransE requires all relations being shared among KGs. Much of the work is done on multiple heterogeneous KGs in the same language, but it only relies on its structural information, so it can also be applied to cross-lingual KG alignment tasks.

2.2   Multilingual Entity Alignment

With the construction of cross-lingual KGs, more and more attention has been focused on cross-lingual KG alignment tasks.

MtransE [2] is a multilingual KG embedding model, which consists of a knowledge model based on TransE and an alignment model learning the transition of entities and relations between different embedding spaces.

JAPE [18] jointly embed relational triple embeddings and attribute triple embeddings, using TransE and Skip-gram model respectively. The embeddings can effectively maintain the structural features and attribute correlation of the KG. While training, It needs aligned relations and entity attributes.

KDCoE [1] jointly trains multilingual KG embeddings and entity description embeddings. In the former, it combines triples loss with cross-lingual entity distance loss. For the latter, it needs to train cross-lingual word vectors based on machine translation and uses GRU and self-attention. KDCoE also adopts iterative training to expand the training set for better performance.

GCN-Align [21] constructs models to encode relational embedding and attribute embedding of multilingual KGs via GCNs. The approach does not require pre-aligned relations. And is only based on a small number of aligned entity pairs. It achieves the state-of-art performance on the cross-lingual entity alignment task.

MtransE, JAPE, and KDCoE are based on the TransE method, and the GCN-Align [21] and our Cross-TextGCN are trained via GCNs. Besides pre-aligned entiteis, MtransE, JAPE, and KDCoE also need pre-aligned relationship information which we do not need.

3   The Proposed Approach

In this section, we define the cross-lingual alignment with textual information task in Sect. 3.1. Then, we elaborate two cross-lingual entity embedding models with textual information: Cross-TextGCN and Cross-TextMatch in Sect. 3.2 and Sect. 3.3. Finally, we integrate Cross-TextGCN and Cross-TextMatch into GCN-Align for cross-lingual entity alignment.

3.1 Problem Formulation

Knowledge graph $\mathcal{G}$ consists of a collection of triples $T = (h, r, t) \subset E \times R \times E$, where E and R denote entity set and relation set respectively. We use D to denote the textual descriptions of all entities. For two KGs in different languages L_1, L_2, we have $G_{L_1} = (E_{L_1}, R_{L_1}, T_{L_1}, D_{L_1})$ and $G_{L_2} = (E_{L_2}, R_{L_2}, T_{L_2}, D_{L_2})$. Therefore, the task of cross-lingual KG alignment is to find more entity alignments between G_{L_1} and G_{L_2} when giving some pre-aligned entity pairs between KGs.

3.2 Cross-TextGCN

For Cross-TextGCN, we firstly construct a unified heterogeneous cross-lingual textual graph G_T from G_{L_1} and G_{L_2} and then use GCN to obtain semantic representations of entities. Figure 2 shows the framework of our Cross-TextGCN.

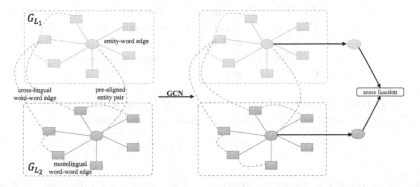

Fig. 2. Framework of Cross-TextGCN, where circles and squares denote entities and words respectively.

G_T has two types of nodes, including entities and words from entity descriptions, and it has three types of edges, including entity-word edges, monolingual word-word edges and cross-lingual word-word edges, which cover the information of each entity description, the co-occurrence of two words in the same language, and the cross-lingual word interaction between G_{L_1} and G_{L_2}.

For entity-word edges, we use term frequency-inverse document frequency (TF-IDF) to calculate the edge weight. In our approach, the term frequency is the number of times the word appears in the entity description, and the inverse document frequency is the logarithmically scaled inverse fraction of the number of entity descriptions that contain the word.

For monolingual word-word edges, we first calculate global word co-occurrence in a fixed-size sliding window and then calculate their point-wise mutual information (PMI). PMI is a measure for indicating whether two variables have a relationship and the strength of the relationship. Only when the PMI value is positive indicates that there is a strong correlation between two words, so we only keep the positive PMI value as the weight of monolingual word-word edges. Formally, for the word pair (i, j), PMI is calculated as:

$$PMI(i, j) = \log \frac{p(i, j)}{p(i)p(j)}, \ p(i, j) = \frac{\#W(i, j)}{\#W}, \ p(i) = \frac{\#W(i)}{\#W}$$

where $\#W$ denotes the total number of sliding windows in descriptions, $\#W(i)$ denotes the number of sliding windows that contains word i, and $\#W(i, j)$ denotes the number of sliding windows that contain both word i and j.

For cross-lingual word pairs, we can not directly calculate their co-occurrence. Since we have partial cross-lingual aligned entity pairs, we connect each word of an entity to each word of its aligned entity (if there is) as word pairs, and then count the co-occurrence among all aligned entities. We use $X - DF(i, j)$ to denote the co-occurrence of the cross-lingual word pair (i, j).

Thus, the adjacency matrix A of the cross-lingual textual graph

$$A_{ij} = \begin{cases} \text{TF-IDF}(i, j) & i \text{ is an entity, } j \text{ is a word} \\ \text{PMI}(i, j) & i \text{ and } j \text{ are monolingual words} \\ & \text{and PMI}(i, j) > 0 \\ \text{X-DF}(i, j) & i \text{ and } j \text{ are cross-lingual words} \\ 0 & \text{otherwise} \end{cases}$$

Then, we train a two-layer GCN on G_T. Let $H^{(l)}$ denote embeddings of nodes in the l-th layer, and then $H^{(l+1)}$ can be computed as follows:

$$H^{(l+1)} = \sigma \left(\hat{D}^{-\frac{1}{2}} \hat{A} \hat{D}^{-\frac{1}{2}} H^{(l)} W^{(l)} \right)$$

where $\hat{A} = A + I$ is the adjacency matrix A of the graph with diagonal elements set to 1. $\hat{D}$ is the diagonal node degree matrix of $\hat{A}$. $W^{(l)}$ is the weight matrix of the l-th layer. σ is an activation function, and we use $ReLU(\cdot) = \max(0, \cdot)$. Given pre-aligned entity pairs $S = \{(e_1, e_2)|e_1 \in G_{L1}, e_2 \in G_{L2}\}$, we can construct a negative set $S' = \{(e_1, e'_2)\} \cup \{(e'_1, e_2)\}$, where e'_1 or e'_2 is replaced by other entities in G_{L_1} or G_{L_2}. Finally, we use the standard pairwise loss as follows.

$$\mathcal{L}_{gcn} = \sum_{p \in S, p' \in S'_p} [f_{gcn}(p) - f_{gcn}(p') + \gamma_{gcn}]_+$$

where $f_{gcn}(p) = \|H^L(e_1), H^L(e_2)\|_1$ is the score function, $p = (e_1, e_2)$ is an element of S or S', $H^L(e)$ is the textual embedding of entity e from GCN, and γ_{gcn} is the margin.

3.3 Cross-TextMatch

In order to better reflect the semantic information of entity descriptions in different languages, we use BiLSTM (Bidirectional Long Short-Term Memory) with

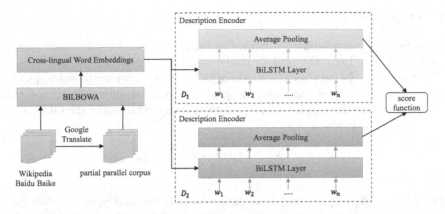

Fig. 3. Framework of Cross-TextMatch, where cross-lingual word embeddings are pre-trained.

pre-trained cross-lingual word embeddings to encode the description. The framework is shown in Fig. 3.

BILBOWA [7] is used to pre-train the cross-lingual word embeddings, since it can induce bilingual distributed word representations from monolingual raw text and a limited amount of parallel data, without requiring word-alignments or dictionaries. In order to obtain the training data, we can download the latest Wikipedia pages[2] in English, French, and Japanese, and crawl articles from Baidu Baike[3], and then use *Google Translate* to obtain the partial parallel corpus between Chinese-English, English-French, and English-Japanese.

Thus the description of an entity e can be represented as a sequence of cross-lingual word embeddings $T_d = [\boldsymbol{w}_1, \boldsymbol{w}_2, ..., \boldsymbol{w}_d]$. Then, T_d is fed to a BiLSTM, and the output is a set of vectors $(\boldsymbol{h}_1, \boldsymbol{h}_2, ..., \boldsymbol{h}_d)$, where $\boldsymbol{h}_i$ is a concatenation $\boldsymbol{h}_i = [\overrightarrow{h}_i, \overleftarrow{h}_i]$ of a forward and backward LSTMs:

$$\overrightarrow{h}_i = \overrightarrow{LSTM}_i(\boldsymbol{w}_1, \boldsymbol{w}_2, ..., \boldsymbol{w}_d)$$
$$\overleftarrow{h}_i = \overleftarrow{LSTM}_i(\boldsymbol{w}_1, \boldsymbol{w}_2, ..., \boldsymbol{w}_d).$$

Thus, the entity e can be represented as $\boldsymbol{v}_e = \frac{1}{d} \sum_{i=1}^{d} \boldsymbol{h}_i$. We also use the standard pairwise loss as in Sect. 3.2.

$$\mathcal{L}_{match} = \sum_{p \in S, p' \in S'_\mu} [f_{match}(p) - f_{match}(p') + \gamma_{match}]_+$$

where $f_{match}(p) = \|\boldsymbol{v}_{e_1}, \boldsymbol{v}_{e_2}\|_1$, and γ_{match} is the margin.

---

[2] https://dumps.wikimedia.org/.
[3] https://baike.baidu.com.

3.4   Model Integration

We can boost structure-based approaches for cross-lingual entity alignment by integrating Cross-TextGCN and Cross-TextMatch.

In this paper, we employ GCN-Align [21] as the structure-based approach, where an entity graph is built according to it structural information, and then GCN is applied on the graph to represent each entity. The loss of the GCN-Align can be defined as follows.

$$\mathcal{L}_s = \sum_{p \in S, p' \in S'_p} [f_s(p) - f_s(p') + \gamma_s]_+$$

where $f_s(p) = \|\boldsymbol{h}_s(e_1), \boldsymbol{h}_s(e_2)\|_1$ is the score function, and γ_s is the margin.

Therefore, when integrating Cross-TextGCN to GCN-Align, we can calculate the distance between entity $e_1 \in G_{L_1}$ and $e_2 \in G_{L_2}$ as:

$$f(e_1, e_2) = \alpha \frac{f_s(e_1, e_2)}{d_s} + (1 - \alpha) \frac{f_{gcn}(e_1, e_2)}{d_{gcn}}$$

When integrating both Cross-TextGCN and Cross-TextMatch to GCN-Align, the distance between entity $e_1 \in G_{L_1}$ and $e_2 \in G_{L_2}$ can be calculated as:

$$f(e_1, e_2) = \alpha \frac{f_s(e_1, e_2)}{d_s} + \beta \frac{f_{gcn}(e_1, e_2)}{d_{gcn}} + (1 - \alpha - \beta) \frac{f_{match}(e_1, e_2)}{d_{match}}$$

where α and β are the hyper-parameters to tune the effect of GCN-Align, Cross-TextGCN and Cross-TextMatch. d_s, d_{gcn} and d_{match} are dimensions of the entity embeddings in GCN-Align, Cross-TextGCN and Cross-TextMatch.

Our model can integrate both structural and textual information of entities, so we call it **STGCN** when integrating GCN-Align and Cross-TextGCN. When further integrating Cross-TextMatch, the model is denoted as **STGCN+**.

4   Experiment

In this section, we first describe the datasets and experimental setup, and then evaluate the performance of Cross-TextGCN and Cross-TextMatch.

4.1   Dataset and Experimental Settings

We conduct our experiments on DBP15K [18]. DBP15K contains three cross-lingual subsets built from DBpedia (2016-04), including Chinese-English (ZH-EN), Japanese-English (JA-EN) and French-English (FR-EN), and each has 15 thousand pre-aligned entity links. The details of all subsets are shown in Table 1. In order to introduce the descriptions for entities, we obtain short abstracts from DBpedia (2016-04), and they cover 98.2%–99.6% of entities in each language of the datasets.

Table 1. Details of the DBP15K

Datasets		Entities	Relations	Attributes	Rel. triples	Attr. triples
$DBP15K_{ZH-EN}$	Chinese	66,469	2,830	8,113	153,929	379,684
	English	98,125	2,317	7,173	237,674	567,755
$DBP15K_{JA-EN}$	Japanese	65,744	2,043	5,882	164,373	354,619
	English	95,680	2,096	6,066	233,319	497,230
$DBP15K_{FR-EN}$	French	66,858	1,379	4,547	192,191	528,665
	English	105,889	2,209	6,422	278,590	576,543

We compare our method with the aforementioned methods JE, MTransE, JAPE, and GCN-Align, and the results of these approaches are obtained from [21].

To be the same with the compared approaches, we also use 30% of pre-aligned entity pairs for training by default, and the rest 70% for testing. We use $Hits@k$ to evaluate the performance of the approaches, which indicates the probability that the top k entities hit the aligned entity. Vectors we used are all randomly initialized by truncated normal function. We choose the parameters of the models through experiments, and set $d_s = 300, d_{gcn} = d_{match} = 100$, $\gamma_s = 3$, $\gamma_{gcn} = \gamma_{match} = 1$, the window size $w_s = 10$ in the textual graph. We use Adam with the learning rate of 0.1 to do optimization.

4.2 Results

Evaluation on Cross-TextGCN. In this experiments, we mainly evaluate that whether Cross-TextGCN can boost cross-lingual entity matching, and the results are shown in Table 2.

From the table, we can see that our model can achieve the best performance in the cross-lingual entity alignment task in all scenarios. Since French and English are much more similar, the $Hits$ on FR-EN are higher than that on other datasets, and Cross-TextGCN makes more improvement on FR-EN.

In addition, we also conduct experiments for Cross-TextGCN in different settings, and the results are shown in Table 3.

From the table, we can see that (1) Both smaller and larger sliding window size will degrade the performance, since smaller sliding window size may lose word co-occurrence information, and larger size may introduce noise. (2) All types of edges are useful and complementary in Cross-TextGCN. For example, only using entity-word edges can achieve 27.19% in $Hits@1$ on ZH-EN, and monolingual and cross-lingual word-word edges can increase 1.29% and 0.89% in $Hits@1$ respectively.

Moreover, we also study how our approach will perform with varied proportions of training data. We set the proportions from 10% to 50%, and the results of STGCN with two strong baselines are showed in Fig. 4.

From the figure, we can see that all approaches get better performance with the increasing size of training data, and our approach performs best at all datasets all the time. Thus, our approach can be more suitable to a circumstance with less training data.

Table 2. Results of cross-lingual entity alignment. Here, JAPE denotes its variants as Structure Embedding without negative triples (SE w/o neg.), Structure Embedding (SE), Structure and Attribute joint embedding (SE + AE). GCN-Align (SE) and GCN-Align (SE + AE) denote GCN-Align with only the relational triples and with both relational triples and attributional triples respectively. We set $\alpha = 0.6$ in STGCN.

$DBP15K_{ZH-EN}$		$ZH \rightarrow EN$			$EN \rightarrow ZH$		
		Hits@1	Hits@10	Hits50	Hits@1	Hits@10	Hits50
JE		21.27	42.77	56.74	19.52	39.36	53.25
MTransE		30.83	61.41	79.12	24.78	52.42	70.45
JAPE	SE w/o neg.	38.34	68.86	84.07	31.66	59.37	76.33
	SE	39.78	72.35	87.12	32.29	62.79	80.55
	SE + AE	41.18	74.46	**88.90**	40.15	71.05	**86.18**
GCN-Align	SE	38.42	70.34	81.24	34.43	65.68	77.03
	SE + AE	41.25	74.38	86.23	36.49	69.94	82.45
STGCN		**46.54**	**77.91**	87.71	**40.62**	**71.81**	82.53
$DBP15K_{JA-EN}$		$JA \rightarrow EN$			$EN \rightarrow JA$		
		Hits@1	Hits@10	Hits50	Hits@1	Hits@10	Hits50
JE		18.92	39.97	54.24	17.80	38.44	52.48
MTransE		27.86	57.45	75.94	23.72	49.92	67.93
JAPE	SE w/o neg.	33.10	63.90	80.80	29.71	56.28	73.84
	SE	34.27	66.39	83.61	31.40	60.80	78.51
	SE + AE	36.25	68.50	85.35	38.37	67.27	82.65
GCN-Align	SE	38.21	72.49	82.69	36.90	68.50	79.51
	SE + AE	39.91	74.46	86.10	38.42	71.81	83.72
STGCN		**45.38**	**75.91**	**86.27**	**43.61**	**74.48**	**84.50**
$DBP15K_{FR-EN}$		$FR \rightarrow EN$			$EN \rightarrow FR$		
		Hits@1	Hits@10	Hits50	Hits@1	Hits@10	Hits50
JE		15.38	38.84	56.50	14.61	37.25	54.01
MTransE		24.41	55.55	74.41	21.26	50.60	69.93
JAPE	SE w/o neg.	29.55	62.18	79.36	25.40	56.55	74.96
	SE	29.63	64.55	81.90	26.55	60.30	78.71
	SE + AE	32.39	66.68	83.19	32.97	65.91	82.38
GCN-Align	SE	36.51	73.42	85.93	36.08	72.37	85.44
	SE + AE	37.29	74.49	86.73	36.77	73.06	86.39
STGCN		**52.07**	**82.68**	**90.44**	**51.40**	**82.25**	**90.76**

Evaluation on Cross-TextMatch. First, we show some examples of words and their corresponding top 5 similar words in the pre-trained cross-lingual word embedding space by BILBOWA in Table 4. From the table, we can see that

Table 3. Ablation study for Cross-TextGCN.

$DBP15K_{ZH-EN}$	$ZH \rightarrow EN$			$EN \rightarrow ZH$		
	Hits@1	Hits@10	Hits50	Hits@1	Hits@10	Hits50
$w_s = 5$	27.77	55.66	72.53	27.94	54.51	71.01
$w_s = 15$	22.61	50.35	69.08	23.19	59.31	67.67
Entity-word edge	27.19	54.12	71.55	27.63	53.12	69.11
e-w and monolingual w-w edge	28.48	57.75	75.41	28.91	56.61	73.35
Cross-TextGCN	29.37	58.04	74.75	29.96	57.14	73.28

Table 4. Examples of words and their top 5 similar words in Chinese and English in the pre-trained cross-lingual word embedding space, where the words in the parentheses are the translated English words.

Word	The top 5 similar words in the pre-trained cross-lingual word embedding space
苹果 (apple)	草莓 (strawberry), 樱桃(cherry), 树莓(raspberry), 甜瓜(muskmelon), 芒果(mango)
	apple, strawberry, cherry, frooti, banana
fruit	水果 (fruit), 百香果(passion fruit), 柑橘类(citrus fruits), 坚果(nut), 果实(fruit)
	fruitarian, melon, berry, vine, strawberry
春天(spring)	秋天(autumn), 春季(spring), 初秋(early autumn), 秋季(autumn), 初夏(early summer)
	spring, springtime, autumn, blossom, fall
rain	下雨(rain), 大雨(heavy rain), 雨水(rainwater), 暴雨(rainstorm), 刮风(wind blowing)
	wind, downpour, rainstorm, sleet , snow

BILBOWA can efficiently learn the bilingual distributed word embeddings for encoding description.

Table 5 presents the results of BILBOWA, Cross-TextMatch, STGCN and STGCN+. From the table, we can see that (1) Cross-TextMatch can achieve a better performance than BILBOWA, which only average the word embeddings in description as the entity embedding. (2) With the help of Cross-TextMatch, STGCN+ can obtain a much better performance against STGCN, which will obtain about 10% more on all *Hits*.

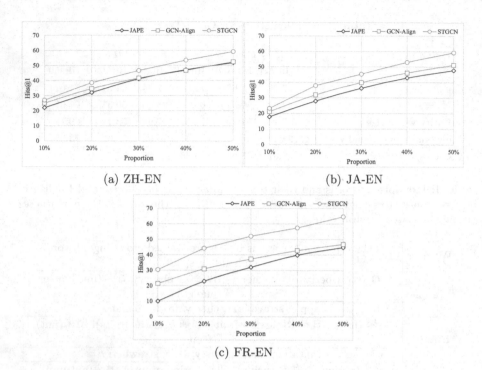

(a) ZH-EN   (b) JA-EN

(c) FR-EN

Fig. 4. Hits@1 with different proportions of training data

Table 5. Evaluation on Cross-TextMatch, where $\alpha = 0.4$, $\beta = 0.3$ in STGCN+.

$DBP15K_{ZH-EN}$	$ZH \rightarrow EN$			$EN \rightarrow ZH$		
	Hits@1	Hits@10	Hits50	Hits@1	Hits@10	Hits50
BILBOWA	27.73	54.78	63.87	22.54	45.94	62.84
Cross-TextMatch	32.31	67.34	87.37	31.77	65.85	87.08
STGCN	46.54	77.91	87.71	40.62	71.81	82.53
STGCN+	**56.10**	**86.07**	**94.10**	**50.32**	**80.90**	**91.10**

5   Conclusion and Future Work

In this paper, we verify that textual information of entities can be used to boost cross-lingual entity alignment, and propose two textual embedding models Cross-TextGCN and Cross-TextMatch. In our experiments, we integrate them into structure-based cross-lingual entity alignment model GCN-Align, and the results show the effectiveness of our models.

In future, we will integrate our textual embedding models to other cross-lingual entity alignment approaches. Moreover, we will explore more sophisticated deep learning models to the task of cross-lingual entity matching, such as pretrained cross-lingual models, e.g. Unicoder [10] and XLM [11], and more sophisticated GCN-like models such as R-GCN [6] and GAT [20] to model the complex cross-lingual textual graph.

Acknowledgments. This work is supported by the National Key Research and Development Project of China (No. 2018AAA0101900), the Fundamental Research Funds for the Central Universities (No. 2019FZA5013), the Zhejiang Provincial Natural Science Foundation of China (No. LY17F020015), the Chinese Knowledge Center of Engineering Science and Technology (CKCEST) and MOE Engineering Research Center of Digital Library.

References

1. Chen, M., Tian, Y., Chang, K.W., Skiena, S., Zaniolo, C.: Co-training embeddings of knowledge graphs and entity descriptions for cross-lingual entity alignment. In: IJCAI (2018)
2. Chen, M., Tian, Y., Yang, M., Zaniolo, C.: Multilingual knowledge graph embeddings for cross-lingual knowledge alignment. In: IJCAI (2017)
3. Ebaid, A., Thirumuruganathan, S., Aref, W.G., Elmagarmid, A., Ouzzani, M.: Explainer: entity resolution explanations. In: ICDE, pp. 2000–2003. IEEE (2019)
4. Ebraheem, M., Thirumuruganathan, S., Joty, S., Ouzzani, M., Tang, N.: Distributed representations of tuples for entity resolution. Proc. VLDB Endow. **11**(11), 1454–1467 (2018)
5. Efthymiou, V., et al.: MinoanER: schema-agnostic, non-iterative, massively parallel resolution of web entities. In: Advances in Database Technology - 22nd International Conference on Extending Database Technology (2019)
6. Schlichtkrull, M., Kipf, T.N., Bloem, P., van den Berg, R., Titov, I., Welling, M.: Modeling relational data with graph convolutional networks. In: Gangemi, A., et al. (eds.) ESWC 2018. LNCS, vol. 10843, pp. 593–607. Springer, Cham (2018). https://doi.org/10.1007/978-3-319-93417-4_38
7. Gouws, S., Bengio, Y., Corrado, G.: BilBOWA: fast bilingual distributed representations without word alignments (2015)
8. Hao, Y., Zhang, Y., He, S., Liu, K., Zhao, J.: A joint embedding method for entity alignment of knowledge bases. In: Chen, H., Ji, H., Sun, L., Wang, H., Qian, T., Ruan, T. (eds.) CCKS 2016. CCIS, vol. 650, pp. 3–14. Springer, Singapore (2016). https://doi.org/10.1007/978-981-10-3168-7_1
9. Hou, B., et al.: Gradual machine learning for entity resolution. In: The World Wide Web Conference, pp. 3526–3530. ACM (2019)
10. Huang, H., et al.: Unicoder: a universal language encoder by pre-training with multiple cross-lingual tasks. In: EMNLP/IJCNLP (2019)
11. Lample, G., Conneau, A.: Cross-lingual language model pretraining. In: NeurIPS (2019)
12. Lehmann, J., et al.: DBpedia-a large-scale, multilingual knowledge base extracted from wikipedia. Semantic Web **6**(2), 167–195 (2015)
13. Mahdisoltani, F., Biega, J., Suchanek, F.M.: YAGO3: a knowledge base from multilingual wikipedias. In: CIDR (2013)
14. Navigli, R., Ponzetto, S.P.: BabelNet: the automatic construction, evaluation and application of a wide-coverage multilingual semantic network. Artif. Intell. **193**, 217–250 (2012)

15. Nickel, M., Rosasco, L., Poggio, T.: Holographic embeddings of knowledge graphs. In: AAAI (2016)
16. Pershina, M., Yakout, M., Chakrabarti, K.: Holistic entity matching across knowledge graphs. In: 2015 IEEE International Conference on Big Data, pp. 1585–1590. IEEE (2015)
17. Speer, R., Chin, J., Havasi, C.: ConceptNet 5.5: an open multilingual graph of general knowledge. In: AAAI (2017)
18. Sun, Z., Hu, W., Li, C.: Cross-lingual entity alignment via joint attribute-preserving embedding. In: d'Amato, C., et al. (eds.) ISWC 2017. LNCS, vol. 10587, pp. 628–644. Springer, Cham (2017). https://doi.org/10.1007/978-3-319-68288-4_37
19. Tao, Y.: Massively parallel entity matching with linear classification in low dimensional space. In: 21st International Conference on Database Theory (ICDT), pp. 20:1–20:19 (2018)
20. Velickovic, P., Cucurull, G., Casanova, A., Romero, A., Liò, P., Bengio, Y.: Graph attention networks. In: ICLR (2018)
21. Wang, Z., Lv, Q., Lan, X., Zhang, Y.: Cross-lingual knowledge graph alignment via graph convolutional networks. In: EMNLP, pp. 349–357 (2018)
22. Zhu, H., Xie, R., Liu, Z., Sun, M.: Iterative entity alignment via joint knowledge embeddings. In: IJCAI, pp. 4258–4264 (2017)

Label Embedding Enhanced Multi-label Sequence Generation Model

Yaqiang Wang[1,2(✉)], Feifei Yan[1], Xiaofeng Wang[1], Wang Tang[3,4],
and Hongping Shu[1,2(✉)]

[1] College of Software Engineering,
Chengdu University of Information Technology, Chengdu 610225, Sichuan, China
{yaqwang,cqshp}@cuit.edu.cn
[2] Sichuan Key Laboratory of Software Automatic Generation and Intelligent Service,
Chengdu 610225, Sichuan, China
[3] School of Electronic Engineering,
Chengdu University of Information Technology, Chengdu 610225, Sichuan, China
[4] Sunsheen Inc., Chengdu 610225, Sichuan, China

Abstract. Existing sequence generation models ignore the exposure bias problem when they apply to the multi-label classification task. To solve this issue, in this paper, we proposed a novel model, which disguises the label prediction probability distribution as label embedding and incorporate each label embedding from previous step into the current step's LSTM decoding process. It allows the current step can make a better prediction based on the overall output of the previous prediction, rather than simply based on a local optimum output. In addition, we proposed a scheduled sampling-based learning algorithm for this model. The learning algorithm effectively and appropriately incorporates the label embedding into the process of label generation procedure. Through comparing with three classical methods and four SOTA methods for the multi-label classification task, the results demonstrated that our proposed method obtained the highest F1-Score (reaching 0.794 on a chemical exposure assessment task and reaching 0.615 on a clinical syndrome differentiation task of traditional Chinese medicine).

Keywords: Multi-label classification · Sequence generation model · Label embedding · Exposure bias problem

1 Introduction

Multi-label classification studies the problem where one real-world object might have multiple semantic meanings by assigning a set of labels to the object in order to explicitly represent its semantics. Multi-label classification has a wide range of real-world application scenarios, and the labels of one object often have correlations. For example, a medical paper often has a set of correlated keywords, which summarizes the topics of the paper's content [1]; a traditional Chinese medicine (TCM) practitioner often uses

---

Y. Wang and F. Yan—These authors contributed equally to this work.

© Springer Nature Switzerland AG 2020
X. Zhu et al. (Eds.): NLPCC 2020, LNAI 12431, pp. 219–230, 2020.
https://doi.org/10.1007/978-3-030-60457-8_18

multiple correlated syndromes to summarize the chief complaint in a clinical record of TCM for one patient [2].

The multi-label classification task is usually solved by two types of methods. One type is the problem transformation methods, such as the Label Powerset (LP) [3], the Classifier Chain (CC) [4], and another type is the algorithm adaptation methods, such as the ML-kNN [5], the Collective Multi-Label Classifier [6]. In recent years, deep learning has shown excellent performance in various applications, including the multi-label classification task. Researchers attempt to convert the multi-label classification task into a multi-label sequence generation problem through applying the encoder-decoder framework. This approach has yielded satisfactory results [7–9].

The exposure bias problem is often raised when the encoder-decoder framework is applied to the sequence generation task [10]. However, it is ignored when researchers build the multi-label sequence generation models. In consequence, we proposed a novel model in this paper to solve this issue. The model disguises the label prediction probability distribution as label embedding and incorporates each label embedding from previous step into the current step's LSTM decoder process. Furthermore, we proposed a scheduled sampling-based learning algorithm for this model. The experimental results demonstrate that our method outperforms three classical methods, including Binary Relevance (BR), LP and CC, and four SOTA methods, including TextCNN, RCNN, Transformer and SGM, on two representative datasets of the multi-label classification task.

2   Related Work

Considering the label correlation during designing multi-label classification models has attracted much attention. Some work is done by introducing prior knowledge, e.g. the hierarchical relationship among labels [11–14]. Others are done by mining and utilizing the correlations of labels during model training procedure [15–17]. Inspired by the researches of deep learning for machine translation and text summarization, Jinseok et al. [18] proposed to treat the multi-label classification task as a multi-label sequence generation problem and attempted it by using recurrent neural networks. Recently, multi-label sequence generation models based on the encoder-decoder framework have been proposed. Jonas et al. [7] believed that conventional word-level attention mechanism could not provide enough information for the label prediction making, therefore they proposed a multiple attention mechanism to enhance the feature representation capability of input sequences. Li et al. [8] proposed a Label Distributed sequence-to-sequence model with a novel loss function to solve the problem of making a strong assumption on the labels' order. Yang et al. [9] further reduced the sensitivity of the sequence-to-sequence model to the pre-defined label order by introducing reward feedback strategy of reinforcement learning into the model training procedure. However, the exposure bias problem has not been considered, although it is a common issue when the encoder-decoder framework is used to solve the sequence generation problem.

The exposure bias problem is caused by an inconsistency in the training and the inference procedures of the sequence generation models based on the encoder-decoder framework. The inconsistency is reflected in the difference between the input of the next time-step's encoding process in the training procedure and in the inference procedure. One is from the data distribution, and another is from the model distribution. Consequently, when the sequence generation models are applied to the multi-label classification task, the inconsistency would in turn lead to error accumulation during the inference procedure. There are some studies trying to solve the exposure bias problem. Bengio et al. [10] proposed a scheduled sampling algorithm to choose an input for the next time-step from the ground truth word and the predicted word according to a probability change during the sequence generation process. Sam et al. [19] attempted to solve the exposure bias problem through improving the beam search algorithm. Zhang et al. [20] addressed the exposure bias problem by randomly selecting the ground truth word and the predicted word of the previous time-step. An important idea for solving the exposure bias problem is to introduce the predicted words instead of the ground truth words in the training procedure to improve the robustness of the model. How to introduce the predicted words, i.e. the predicted labels, effectively for the multi-label sequence generation models is still an open question.

3 Our Proposed Model

Formally, the multi-label classification task is to assign a label subset y, which contains n labels from the label set $\mathcal{L} = \{l_1, l_2, \ldots, l_L\}$, to a sequence $x = \{x_1, x_2, \ldots, x_m\}$, where x_i is the ith word in x. From the perspective of a sequence generation model, this multi-label-label classification task can be modeled as finding an optimal label sequence y^* which can maximize the conditional probability:

$$p(y|x) = \prod_{t=1}^{n} p(y_t|y_{<t}, x) \tag{1}$$

We apply a sequence-to-sequence model with the attention mechanism for the multi-label sequence generation task. The model in this paper consists of three components, including the XLNet encoder, the attention mechanism and the LSTM decoder. The framework of the model is shown in Fig. 1. h, c and s in Fig. 1 represent the hidden states of the encoder, the context vector, and the hidden states of the decoder, respectively, and the subscript t in the figure represent the time-step.

3.1 The XLNet Encoder

Different from Jonas et al. [7], we apply the generalized autoregressive language model, XLNet [21], to replace the commonly used Bidirectional LSTM and GRU encoders in this paper. The XLNet will output the hidden state vector h_i for each word.

$$h_i = \text{XLNet}(x_i) \tag{2}$$

3.2 The Attention Mechanism

Different words in one sequence often have different contributions when the model predicts the labels. The attention mechanism can make the model have ability to give

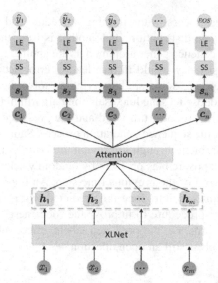

Fig. 1. Framework of our proposed model. LE denotes the label embedding method and SS denotes the scheduled sampling process.

different weights to different words of a sequence according to the contributions of the words to the label prediction task. The weight α_{ti} of a word x_i in a sequence x at time-step t is calculated by

$$\alpha_{ti} = v^T \tanh(W_1 s_{t-1} + U_1 h_i), \tag{3}$$

where s_{t-1} is the hidden state of the decoder at time-step $t-1$ and v^T, W_1 and U_1 are the weighting parameters. The weights will be normalized by using the SoftMax function

$$w_{ti} = \frac{\exp(\alpha_{ti})}{\sum_{j=1}^{m} \exp(\alpha_{tj})}, \tag{4}$$

and then the final context vector c_t is computed as follows:

$$c_t = \sum_{i=1}^{m} w_{ti} h_i \tag{5}$$

3.3 The LSTM Decoder

LSTM models the correlations between labels at different time-steps in the generated label sequence. The context vector c_t, the hidden state s_{t-1} of the decoder at time-step $t-1$ and the label embedding, which will be introduced in Sect. 4, form the input to the hidden state s_t of the decoder at time-step t as follows

$$s_t = \text{LSTM}(s_{t-1}, [c_t; g(P_{t-1}^y)]), \tag{6}$$

where P_{t-1}^y represents the label prediction probability distribution for the labels outputted by the LSTM decoder at time-step $t-1$, [;] is the vector concatenation operation, and $g(\cdot)$ is used to disguise the label prediction probability distribution as a label embedding, which will be introduced in the next section.

4   Label Embedding Method

Inspired by the Global Embedding [22] and the LSTM gating mechanism [23], we proposed a label embedding method which is used to disguises the label prediction probability distribution of the labels outputted by the LSTM decoder at time-step $t - 1$. The label embedding outputted from $g\left(P_t^y\right)$ is formed by an expected label embedding $\bar{e}_t$ at time-step t and a label embedding $\hat{e}_t$ of which label with the highest probability in P_t^y.

$$g\left(P_t^y\right) = \left[o_t \odot \bar{e}_t; (1 - o_t) \odot \hat{e}_t\right] \tag{7}$$

$$\bar{e}_t = P_t^y E, \tag{8}$$

$$P_t^y = \text{SoftMax}\left(\frac{s_{t-1} W_2}{\gamma}\right) \tag{9}$$

$$o_t = \sigma\left(W_3 \bar{e}_t + W_4 \hat{e}_t\right) \tag{10}$$

where $\odot$ is the element-wise multiplication operation, $\hat{e}_t$ is selected from $E \in \mathbb{R}^{k \times L}$, which is a learnable embedding matrix, k is the dimension of the label embeddings, $W_2 \in \mathbb{R}^{d \times L}$ is a weight matrix, d is the dimension of the hidden state of the LSTM decoders. The large L is, the more elements in P_t^y tend to be zero. It would, consequently, causes the back-propagation process having the vanishing gradient problem. This is why we define P_t^y in terms of Eq. (9), and the Eq. (9) is inspired by the Scaled Dot-Product Attention method [24], where γ is a scaling factor used to solve the aforementioned problem. $\sigma(\cdot)$ is the sigmoid function, and $W_3, W_4 \in \mathbb{R}^{k \times k}$. The range of the values of o_t are in $(0, 1)$. o_t and $(1 - o_t)$ define the contributions of $\bar{e}_t$ and $\hat{e}_t$, and o_t will be automatically determined by the learning algorithm.

5   Learning Algorithm

In this section, we designed the learning algorithm for the proposed model based on a scheduled sampling process. The cross-entropy loss function is used in this paper, and it is defined as follows:

$$loss_{CE} = -\sum_{t=1}^{n} \log p_\theta (y_t | y_{t-1}; x), \tag{11}$$

$$\hat{y}_t = \text{argmax}_y p_\theta \left(y | \hat{y}_{t-1}\right), \tag{12}$$

where θ is the set of parameters to be learned, $\hat{y}_t$ represents the predicted label at time-step t. In order to learn the parameters based on variable length sequences, following the method used in [22], we also added a special token, <EOS> , at the end of each sequence.

The scheduled sampling approach has been proven to be effective for solving exposure bias problem [10]. Therefore, we followed this idea and proposed a scheduled sampling-based algorithm for our proposed multi-label sequence generation model. The pseudo code is described in Algorithm 1.

Algorithm 1 Algorithm Combining Label Embedding and Scheduled Sampling

Input: $(x, y = \{y_1, y_2, \cdots, y_n\})$, *threshold*, k
Output: $\{\hat{y}_1, \hat{y}_2, \cdots, \hat{y}_n\}$
 1: **for** i in epoch **do**
 2:    $t \leftarrow 1$
 3:    **if** $i \leq threshold$ **then**
 4:       $\hat{e}_t = y_t$
 5:       $g(P_t^y)$
 6:    **else**
 7:       $\epsilon_i = k^{(i-threshold)}$
 8:       $\hat{e}_t = ScheduledSampling(\epsilon_i, \hat{y}_t, y_t)$
 9:       $g(P_t^y)$
10:    **end if**
11:    $t \leftarrow t + 1$
12: **end for**

If the label embedding method introduced in Sect. 4 is utilized in the early stages of the training procedure, it may bring too much uncertainty to the loss leading to loss fluctuation and may even cause the curve of the loss function to not converge. Therefore, we designed a function of the number of the iteration index i, $\epsilon_i = k^{(i-threshold)}$, which is used to control that only the ground labels will be used in the early stages of the training procedure, and after a period of training time, the label embedding will be incorporated. In ϵ_i, k is a hyperparameter which is ranging from 0 to 1, and *threshold* is the number of iterations that the algorithm starts using the scheduled sampling algorithm to get $\hat{e}_t$. It is clear that the value of ϵ_i begins to decay exponentially after the number of iterations reaching the *threshold*.

6 Experiments

In this paper, we compared our proposed method with three classical multi-label classification methods and four SOTA methods on two biomedical domain datasets. One is in Chinese, and another is in English. The datasets, the evaluation measurements, the compared methods and the results will be introduced in following sections.

6.1 Datasets

We used two biomedical domain datasets in the experiments. Both of the datasets are typically used to validate the multi-label classification methods. Detailed information of these datasets is shown in Table 1. CEA (a Chemical Exposure Assessments dataset) is an English dataset, and TCM (a syndrome differentiation dataset of traditional Chinese medicine) is a Chinese dataset.

CEA: PubMed [28] provides a large amount of biochemical exposure information, which is of vital research value for the study of human health. Larsson et al. [25] constructed the CEA dataset relying on the domain experts based on part of PubMed literature. The CEA dataset contains 32 labels which are keywords described from the perspectives of biological detection and exposure pathway.

Table 1. Detailed statistics information of the datasets CEA and TCM.

Dataset	Number of labels	Number of instances	Number of words in one instance			Number of labels in one instance		
			Avg	Max	Min	Avg	Max	Min
CEA	32	3661	233.6	622	49	2.0	8	0
TCM	1127	10000	8.84	35	1	1.85	5	1

TCM: The TCM dataset is composed of chief complaints and syndromes. The chief complaints are noted by TCM experts during their daily work, and they are short and concise texts. The syndromes are descriptive and positional order sensitive, and they are the labels. The dataset is obtained from a real-world medical information system. An example is list as follows:

A chief complaint: "心悸, 胸闷, 气短, 口干, 不渴, 左胁略胀, 饮食正常 , 二便正常, 舌暗红, 形体胖 苔薄, 脉时快时慢, 节律不齐". (Palpitation, chest distress, breathe hard, dry mouth, hydroadipsia, left rib-side distention, normal diet, bowel function is normal, dark red and swollen tongue, thin tongue fur, pulse waxes and wanes, rhythm not neat).

Syndrome labels: "痰热内扰, 心气不足". (Phlegm hot inside, heart qi insufficient).

6.2 Evaluation Measurements

There are two types of evaluation measurements for the multi-label classification task. They are sample-based measure and label-based measure. In this paper, we used the label-based measurements, including $Precision_{micro}$ (P_{micro}), $Recall_{micro}$ (R_{micro}), and $F1_{micro}$, to evaluate the performance of different methods. The calculating methods of P_{micro}, R_{micro} and $F1_{micro}$ are shown in Eq. (13), (14) and (15), respectively.

$$P_{micro} = \frac{TP}{TP + FP} \tag{13}$$

$$R_{micro} = \frac{TP}{TP + FN} \tag{14}$$

$$F1_{micro} = \frac{2 \times P_{micro} \times R_{micro}}{P_{micro} + R_{micro}} \tag{15}$$

6.3 Experimental Settings

CEA and TCM datasets are randomly divided into three parts, including a training dataset, a validation dataset and a test dataset, with a ratio of 7:1:2. The learning rate of XLNet is set to $3e-5$, the learning rate of other layers in the model is set to 0.001, we used the Adam optimizer, $\beta_1 = 0.9$, and $\beta_2 = 0.999$. The batch size is set to 16, the hyperparameter k in the learning algorithm is set to 0.85, and the dropout and L2 regularizer are used to avoid overfitting. The dimension of pre-trained XLNet word embedding is 768.

Three classical multi-label classification models, i.e. BR, LP and CC, are implemented by using Scikit-Multilearn [26], and LinearSVM is used in these models as the base classifier. The descending order of label's frequencies is used in CC. TextCNN and RCNN are implemented based on an open source tool, named NeuralNLP [27]. We used the SGM code published by Yang et al. [21] in this paper, and the default parameter setting, which can yield the best result, is used.

6.4   Results

The best $F1_{micro}$ results achieved by different methods under different settings are listed in Table 2.

Table 2. Comparison of different results of various methods.

Algorithms	CEA			TCM		
	P_{micro}	R_{micro}	$F1_{micro}$	P_{micro}	R_{micro}	$F1_{micro}$
BR	0.896	0.555	0.685	**0.843**	0.402	0.544
CC	**0.897**	0.547	0.679	0.764	0.460	0.574
LP	0.669	0.483	0.561	0.606	0.609	0.608
TextCNN	0.740	0.643	0.688	0.800	0.487	0.605
RCNN	0.757	0.669	0.710	0.667	0.489	0.564
Transformer	0.629	0.590	0.609	0.713	0.484	0.576
SGM	0.590	0.584	0.586	0.559	0.566	0.552
SGM+XLNet	0.792	0.781	0.787	0.588	0.600	0.594
Our	0.796	0.776	0.786	0.610	0.597	0.604
+SS	0.788	**0.788**	0.788	0.614	0.603	0.608
+LE	0.801	0.776	0.789	0.628	0.593	0.610
+LE+SS	0.813	0.777	**0.794**	0.620	**0.611**	**0.615**

"Our" represents our proposed method, LE = Label Embedding, SS = Scheduled Sampling

In general, it vividly shows in Table 2 that the proposed method outperforms other methods. On the CEA dataset, the best $F1_{micro}$ (Our+LE+SS) obtained by our method can reach 0.794, which is 0.149 higher than other methods on average. On the TCM dataset, the best $F1_{micro}$ (Our+LE+SS) can reach 0.615, which is also higher than other methods, but is a little bit lower than on the CEA dataset, it is because the label set size of the TCM dataset is much larger than the CEA dataset.

The P_{micro} and R_{micro} results of SGM and our proposed method listed in Table 2 show that converting the multi-label classification tasks into a multi-label sequence generation problem can achieve more balanced P_{micro} and R_{micro} results. Almost all other methods have the problem of high P_{micro} and low R_{micro}.

Compared with SGM, our proposed method is much better. On one hand, XLNet used in our method has a stronger encoding capacity than bidirectional LSTM used in SGM, and XLNet can achieve good results with only limited sample fine-tuning. On the other hand, our proposed label embedding method and the scheduled sampling-based learning algorithm further improve the performance.

Through a further in-depth analysis of the results, we found that the unseen domain-specific terms are a potential negative factor for the performance improvement. Taking the results on the TCM dataset as an example, the dataset contains a large number of domain-specific terms, e.g. "脉细" (pulse fine), "神疲" (mental fatigue), etc., which are usually unseen in the vocabulary used in XLNet, because the XLNet is pre-trained on a general domain corpus. Consequently, it would result in many inaccurate semantic representations for these domain-specific terms and lead to a negative impact on the performance.

Comparison of the Label Generation Results with Different Granularity.
The labels (i.e. the syndromes) in the TCM dataset are often composed of fine-grained semantic units (characters or syndrome factors), e.g. syndrome factors "筋脉" (tendons), "瘀" (stasis) and "滞" (stagnation) making up the syndrome "筋脉瘀滞" (tendons stasis and stagnation). Therefore, we attempt to reduce the label set size by fine-grained labels. With this approach, we expect to further improve the performance. The results are listed in Table 3.

Table 3. Comparison of different granularity label generation results on the TCM dataset.

Granularity	P_{micro}	R_{micro}	$F1_{micro}$
Character level	0.513	0.322	0.396
Syndrome factor level	0.572	0.479	0.522

The results in Table 3 are worse than in Table 2. Character level's results are worse than syndrome factor level's results, and both are worse than syndrome level's results. This result is mainly due to the fact that our proposed method cannot accurately generate complete syndrome labels based on the fine-grained labels. This issue presents us a new challenge that how to generate coarse-grained labels accurately based on the fine-grained labels. This is our future work.

Comparison of the Loss Convergence Results. In order to verify the contribution of the label embedding, we further examined the loss convergence results during training procedure (shown in Fig. 2).

In Fig. 2, TCM and CEA represent that label embedding and scheduled sampling are used during training. TCM+LE (truth) and CEA+LE (truth) represent just use the label embedding of the ground truth from previous time-step. TCM+LE (predict) and

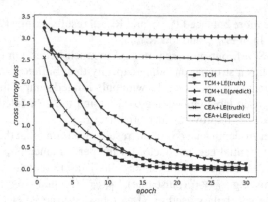

Fig. 2. Comparison of the loss convergence results with and without the label embedding.

CEA+LE (predict) represent just use the label embedding of the prediction with highest probability from previous time-step. It is clear that our proposed method has better loss convergence results on both datasets.

Qualitative Evaluation Results of Attention in Our Method. Figure 3 visualizes four examples of the attention results. The left is examples of TCM, and the right is examples of CEA. The results show that the attention mechanism is able to accurately make use of corresponding key informative words in the sequence when predicting labels.

血虚:	Food:
冲 热 时有时无，时眠 差，便秘 显好，疲倦 消失，舌脉 如上	Certain types of dietary habits such as seafood and noodle consumption were significantly associated with pcband ocp .
肝气亢:	
冲 热 时有时无，时眠 差，便秘 显好，疲倦 消失，舌脉 如上	The exposure of korean infants to chlordanes via breast milk had a potential health risk which deserves further investigation .
血虚:	Drinking water:
偏头痛，前额 和 眼眶，头昏，抑郁，欲 吐，发病 前，阵 热汗 出，疲倦，心悸，眠 差，手足 发麻 其	The large volume of water they consume relative to body mass .
	protein:
夹风:	The beta-2 microglobulin excretion rate remained elevated
偏头痛，前额 和 眼眶，头昏，抑郁，欲 吐，发病 前，阵 热汗 出，疲倦，心悸，眠 差，手足 发麻 其	(> 40 microg/mmol creatinine) only in the youngest child.

Fig. 3. Four examples of the attention results visualized based on heatmaps.

7 Conclusion

Multi-label classification has a wide range of real-world application scenario. It is an effective way to treat the multi-label classification as a multi-label sequence generation task, and it is of great significance to use other auxiliary information (such as the label embedding) to enhance the ability of multi-label sequence generation. The experimental results show that our proposed label embedding method and the scheduled sampling-based learning algorithm are effective and outperform the compared method.

Acknowledgement. The research work is partially supported by the Sichuan Major Science and Technology Special Program under Grant (2017GZDZX0002), the Sichuan Science and Technology Program under Grant (2018GZ207), the Sichuan Province Science and Technology Support Program under Grant (2020YFG0299, 2020YFSY0067), and the National Natural Science Foundation of China under Grant (61801058, 61501063).

References

1. Pratt, W., Yetisgen-Yildiz, M.: LitLinker: capturing connections across the biomedical literature. In: 2nd International Conference on Knowledge Capture, New York, pp. 105–12. Association for Computing Machinery (2003)
2. Zhang, L., Yu, D.L., Wang, Y.G.: Selecting an appropriate interestingness measure to evaluate the correlation between Chinese medicine syndrome elements and symptoms. Chin. J. Integr. Med. **18**(2), 93–99 (2012)
3. Tsoumakas, G., Vlahavas, I.: Random k-labelsets: an ensemble method for multilabel classification. In: Kok, J.N., Koronacki, J., de Mantaras, R.L., Matwin, S., Mladenič, D., Skowron, A. (eds.) ECML 2007. LNCS (LNAI), vol. 4701, pp. 406–417. Springer, Heidelberg (2007). https://doi.org/10.1007/978-3-540-74958-5_38
4. Read, J., Pfahringer, B., Holmes, G., et al.: Classifier chains for multi-label classification. Mach. Learn. **85**(3), 333 (2011)
5. Zhang, M.L., Zhou, Z.H.: ML-KNN: a lazy learning approach to multi-label learning. Pattern Recognit. **40**(7), 2038–2048 (2007)
6. Ghamrawi, N., McCallum, A.: Collective multi-label classification. In: 14th ACM International Conference on Information and Knowledge Management, New York, pp. 95–200. Association for Computing Machinery (2005)
7. Gehring, J., Auli, M., Grangier, D., Yarats, D., Dauphin, Y.N.: Convolutional sequence to sequence learning. In: 34th International Conference on Machine Learning, Sydney, pp. 1243–1252 (2017)
8. Li, W., Ren, X.C., Dai, D., et al.: Sememe prediction: learning semantic knowledge from unstructured textual wiki descriptions. arXiv preprint arXiv:1808.05437 (2018)
9. Yang, P.C., Luo, F.L., Ma, S.M., et al.: A deep reinforced sequence-to-set model for multi-label classification. In: 57th Annual Meeting of the Association for Computational Linguistics, Florence, pp. 5252–5258. Association for Computational Linguistics (2019)
10. Bengio, S., Vinyals, O., Jaitly, N., et al.: Scheduled sampling for sequence prediction with recur-rent neural networks. In: Advances in Neural Information Processing Systems, Montreal, pp. 1171–1179. Neural Information Processing Systems (2015)
11. Kowsari, K., Brown, D.E., Heidarysafa, M., et al.: HDLTex: hierarchical deep learning for text classification. In: 16th IEEE International Conference on Machine Learning and Applications (ICMLA), Cancun, pp. 364–371. IEEE (2017)
12. Baker, S., Korhonen, A.L.: Initializing neural networks for hierarchical multi-label text classification. In: 16th Biomedical Natural Language Processing Workshop, Vancouver, pp. 307–315. Association for Computational Linguistics (2017)
13. Peng, H., Li, J., He, Y., et al.: Large-scale hierarchical text classification with recursively regularized deep graph-CNN. In: 2018 World Wide Web Conference, Lyon, France pp. 1063–1072. International World Wide Web Conferences Steering Committee (2018)
14. Cerri, R., Barros, R.C., De Carvalho, A.C.: Hierarchical multi-label classification using local neural networks. J. Comput. Syst. Sci. **80**(1), 39–56 (2014)

15. Yang, Y.Y., Lin, Y.A., Chu, H.M., et al.: Deep learning with a rethinking structure for multi-label classification. In: Asian Conference on Machine Learning, Nagoya, pp. 125–140. Proceedings of Machine Learning Research (2019)
16. Fu, D., Zhou, B., Hu, J.: Improving SVM based multi-label classification by using label relationship. In: 2015 International Joint Conference on Neural Networks (IJCNN), Killarney, pp. 1–6. IEEE (2015)
17. Aly, R., Remus, S., Biemann, C.: Hierarchical multi-label classification of text with capsule networks. In: 57th Annual Meeting of the Association for Computational Linguistics, Florence, pp. 323–330. Association for Computational Linguistics (2019)
18. Nam, J., Mencía, E.L., Kim, H.J., et al.: Maximizing subset accuracy with recurrent neural networks in multi-label classification. In: Advances in Neural Information Processing Systems, Long Beach, pp. 5413–5423. Neural Information Processing Systems (2017)
19. Wiseman, S., Rush, A.M.: Sequence-to-sequence learning as beam-search optimization. In: 2016 Conference on Empirical Methods in Natural Language Processing, Austin, pp. 1296–1306 (2016)
20. Zhang, W., Feng, Y., Meng, F., et al.: Bridging the gap between training and inference for neural machine translation. arXiv preprint arXiv:1906.02448 (2019)
21. Yang, Z., Dai, Z., Yang, Y., et al.: XLNet: generalized autoregressive pretraining for language understanding. In: Advances in Neural Information Processing System, Vancouver, pp. 5753–5763. Neural Information Processing Systems (2019)
22. Yang, P., Sun, X., Li, W., et al.: SGM: sequence generation model for multi-label classification. In: 27th International Conference on Computational Linguistics, Santa Fe, pp. 3915–3926. Association for Computational Linguistics (2018)
23. Hochreiter, S., Schmidhuber, J.: Long short-term memory. Neural Comput. 9(8), 1735–1780 (1997)
24. Vaswani, A., Shazeer, N., Parmar, N., et al.: Attention is all you need. In: Advances in Neural Information Processing Systems, Long Beach, pp. 5998–6008. Neural Information Processing Systems (2017)
25. Larsson, K., Baker, S., Silins, I., et al.: Text mining for improved exposure assessment. PLoS ONE 12(3), e0173132 (2017)
26. Szymański, P., Kajdanowicz, T.: A scikit-based Python environment for performing multi-label classification. arXiv preprint arXiv:1702.01460 (2017)
27. Liu, L., Mu, F., Li, P., et al.: NeuralClassifier: an open-source neural hierarchical multi-label text classification toolkit. In: 57th Annual Meeting of the Association for Computational Linguistics: System Demonstrations, Florence, pp. 87–92. Association for Computational Linguistics (2019)
28. PubMed Homepage. https://pubmed.ncbi.nlm.nih.gov. Accessed 20 Mar 2020

Ensemble Distilling Pretrained Language Models for Machine Translation Quality Estimation

Hui Huang[1], Hui Di[2], Jin'an Xu[1(✉)], Kazushige Ouchi[2], and Yufeng Chen[1]

[1] Beijing Jiaotong University, Beijing, China
{18112023,jaxu,chenyf}@bjtu.edu.cn
[2] Toshiba (China) Co., Ltd, Beijing, China
{dihui,kazushige.ouchi}@toshiba.com.cn

Abstract. Machine translation quality estimation (Quality Estimation, QE) aims to evaluate the quality of machine translation automatically without golden reference. QE can be implemented on different granularities, thus to give an estimation for different aspects of machines translation output. In this paper, we propose an effective method to utilize pretrained language models to improve the performance of QE. Our model combines two popular pretrained models, which are Bert and XLM, to create a very strong baseline for both sentence-level and word-level QE. We also propose a simple yet effective strategy, ensemble distillation, to further improve the accuracy of QE system. Ensemble distillation can integrate different knowledge from multiple models into one model, and strengthen each single model by a large margin. We evaluate our system on CCMT2019 Chinese-English and English-Chinese QE dataset, which contains word-level and sentence-level subtasks. Experiment results show our model surpasses previous models to a large extend, demonstrating the effectiveness of our proposed method.

Keywords: Machine translation · Quality estimation · Pretrained language model · Knowledge distillation

1 Introduction

In recent years, with the development of deep learning, machine translation systems made a few major breakthroughs and were wildly applied. The performance of machine translation (MT) systems is usually evaluated by the metric BLEU based on golden references, but there are many scenarios where golden references are unavailable or hard to get. Besides, reference-based metrics completely ignore the source segment, and are unable to capture lexical or word-order synonymy [1].

Machine translation quality estimation (Quality Estimation, QE) aims to evaluate the quality of machine translation automatically without golden reference [2].The goal

---

H. Huang—Work was done when Hui Huang was an intern at Research and Develop Center, Toshiba (China) Co., Ltd., China.

X. Zhu et al. (Eds.): NLPCC 2020, LNAI 12431, pp. 231–243, 2020.
https://doi.org/10.1007/978-3-030-60457-8_19

of the word-level QE task is to assign quality labels (OK or BAD) for each machine translated word, and the goal of the sentence-level QE is to predict the quality of the whole translated sentence, based on how many edit operations are required to fix it in terms of HTER (Human Translation Error Rate) [3].

The construction of QE dataset is based on human corrected machine translation outputs, which needs translation experts to post-edit the translated results, and then calculate the discrepancy between translation results and post-edited results. Since post-editing is expensively available, current QE datasets normally contain only 10–20K sentence-pairs, making QE a highly data-scarce task [4].

In this paper, we propose an effective method to utilize pretrained language models to improve the performance of QE. Our model combines two different models, Bert [5] and XLM [6], to create very strong baselines for both granularities. We also introduce a few functional strategies, namely further-pretraining for bilingual input, multi-task learning for multi-granularities and weighted loss for unbalanced word labels. We also propose a simple yet effective strategy, ensemble distillation, to further improve the accuracy of QE system.

We evaluate our system on CCMT2019 Chinese-English and English-Chinese QE dataset, which contains word-level and sentence-level subtasks. Experiment results show our model surpasses previous models to a large ex-tend, demonstrating the effectiveness of our proposed method.

2 Related Work

Early methods referred to QE as a machine learning problem [7]. Their model could be divided into the feature extraction module and the classification module. Highly relied on heuristic artificial feature designing, these methods did not manage to provide reliable estimation results.

During the trending of deep learning in the field of natural language processing, there were also a few works aiming to integrate deep neural network into QE systems. Kreutzer [8] used neural networks to obtain sentence representations, combined with some manually extracted features, and was applied to word-level quality assessment tasks. Specia [9] employed a neural network model formed by stacking several bidirectional LSTM and feedforward neural networks. Since QE is highly data-scarce, these methods still needed manually extracted features as a part of their input.

Kim [10] proposed for the first time to leverage massive parallel machine translation data to improve QE results. They applied RNN-based machine translation model to extract high-quality feature vectors for each word, and predicted different-level QE scores on top of the machine translation system. Fan [11] replaced the RNN-based MT model with Transformer, and achieved strong performance without the help of manually-designed features, which is the current state-of-the-art model.

After the emerge of Bert, there were a few tries on leveraging pretrained models on the task of QE [12], but they just applied simple fine-tuning for Bert on QE data. The potential of pretrained models on QE has not been thoroughly explored.

3 Model Description

3.1 Pretrained Models for Quality Estimation

Pre-trained sentence encoders such as Bert and XLM have rapidly improved the state of the art on many NLP tasks. There are many different pre-trained language models after the emerge of Bert, and different models are trained with different strategies. The diversity of pretraining strategies endow different models the ability to capture different information for the same input text.

Our method is based on two recent proposed pretrained models, Bert and XLM. Both of these two models are based on multi-layer Transformer architecture with different training procedures.

For both word-level and sentence-level QE task, we concatenate source sentences and machine translated sentences following the way these two models treat sentence pairs, and do prediction on the top of the pretrained models, as demonstrated in Fig. 1. For sentence-level prediction, we directly use the first token accords to the special token [CLS] to perform prediction, as we believe this logit integrates sentence-level information. For word-level prediction, we use each logit accords to each token in the sentence to generate word-quality label.

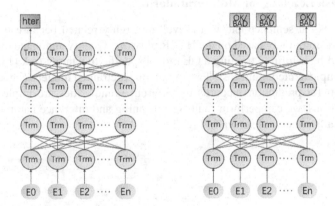

Fig. 1. Pretrained models for QE. Left is for sentence-level, and right is for word-level.

The loss functions for word and sentence-level are as follows:

$$L_{word} = \sum_{s \in D} \sum_{x \in s} -(p_{OK} \log p_{OK} + p_{BAD} \log p_{BAD}) \tag{1}$$

$$L_{sent} = \sum_{s \in D} \|sigmoid(W_s h(s)) - hter_s\| \tag{2}$$

where s and x denote each sentence and word in the dataset, p_{OK} and p_{BAD} denote the probability for each word to be classified as OK/BAD, $h(s)$ denotes the hidden representation for each sentence, and w_s and w_w denote the transformation matrices for sentence and word level prediction.

3.2 Further Pretraining for Bilingual Input

Despite the shared multilingual vocabulary, Bert is originally a monolingual model [13], treating the input as either being from one language or another. To help Bert adapts to sentence pairs from different languages, we implement a further pretraining step, training Bert model with massive parallel machine translation data.

For our task of QE, we combine bilingual sentence pairs from large-scale parallel dataset, and randomly mask sub-word units with a special token, and then train Bert model to predict masked tokens. Since our input are two parallel sentences, during the predicting of masked words given its context and translation reference, Bert can capture the lexical alignment and semantic relevance between two languages.

After this further pretraining step, Bert model is familiar with bilingual inputs, and acquires the ability to capture translation errors between different languages. This method is similar to the pretraining strategy mask-language-model in [5], while its original implementation is based on only sentences from monolingual data.

In contrast, XLM is a multilingual model which receives two sentences from different languages as input, which means further pretraining is likely to be redundant. This is verified by our experiment results demonstrated in the following section.

3.3 Multi-task Learning for Multi-granularities

The QE subtasks at sentence and word-level are highly related because their quality annotations are commonly based on the HTER measure. Quality annotated data of other subtasks could be helpful in training a QE model specific to a target task [14].

We also implemented multi-task learning on our pretrained models. Since the linear transformation for predictions accords to different granularities are implemented on different positions, we can perform multi-task training and inference naturally without any structure adjustment, as shown in Fig. 2.

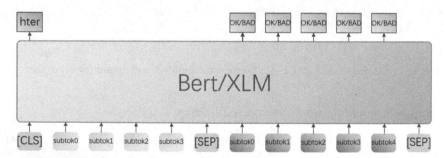

Fig. 2. Multi-task learning combining word-level and sentence-level QE.

During training, predictions for different granularities are generated at the same time on different positions, and losses are combined and back-propagated simultaneously. The loss function is as follows:

$$L_{join} = \sum_{s \in D} \sum_{x \in s} cross\_entropy(W_w h(x), y_x) + \|sigmoid(W_s h(s)) - hter_s\| \quad (3)$$

where $h(x)$ and $h(s)$ denote the hidden representations for each word and sentence.

Most model components are common across sentence-level and word-level tasks except for the output matrices of each task, which is especially beneficial for sentence-level prediction, since the training objective for sentence QE only consists of one single logit containing limited information.

3.4 Weighted Loss for Unbalanced Word Labels

The quality of machine translated sentences in QE data is very high [4], which means a huge proportion of the sentences do not need post-editing at all. This leads to an unbalanced label distribution where most of the word labels are BAD, which makes it very likely to give a skewed prediction with a very low F1 score for BAD words.

To improve the overall performance, we add up to the weight for BAD words when calculating cross-entropy loss, enabling the model emphasize more on the incorrectly translated words. The word-level loss function is as follows:

$$L_{word} = \sum_{s \in D} \sum_{x \in s} -(p_{OK} \log p_{OK} + \lambda p_{BAD} \log p_{BAD}) \tag{4}$$

where λ is a hyper-parameter larger than 1.

We also tried other data augmentation skills to balance word labels, which is demonstrated in the next section.

4 Ensemble Distilling

4.1 Ensemble Distilling via Unlabeled Data

Till now, we have built two different QE models trained with different strategies, and can capture different information from the same text. Instead of simply ensemble multiple models when doing inference which is heavy to implement, we want to strengthen single models with the combination of multiple models. For that purpose, we come up with a novel method to integrate ensembled knowledge into a single model, which is ensemble distillation.

The objective of distilling is to enhance a student network by matching its predictions to the ones of a stronger teacher network [15, 16]. In our work, the teacher network is the ensemble of two different models. Despite the predicted results are not hundred-percent accurate, the output logits contain rich knowledge which could be helpful for strengthening single models.

More importantly, despite the scarcity of post-edited data, parallel data with source text and machine translated text is readily accessible. Since knowledge distilling is exerted on the output logits rather than human annotated labels, our method is not constrained by the data-scarcity nature of QE task.

Our Ensemble Distilling method contains the following steps:

1. Train two different models following the strategies explained in the former section.
2. Train a machine translation system on public-available parallel dataset.

3. Infer monolingual data with the trained MT system, and refer to the original monolingual text as the source sentence, and the machine translated text as the target
   sentence, henceforth attain a huge amount of unlabeled QE data.
4. Infer the unlabeled QE data at different granularities with our two models, and then
   ensemble word and sentence logits together. In this paper, we simply take the average
   of logits on the same positions from different models.
5. Train the original single models with massive distilling data from scratch. Notice in
   this step, no manually labeled data is needed, and the training of student model is
   guided with only ensembled logits.
6. Finally, fine-tune each single model on the artificial labeled QE data, to further
   improve the prediction performance.

After these steps, our model can learn from both ensembled logits and labeled data.
The training objectives vary on different granularities, which is explained in the next
section.

4.2 Soft Label vs Hard Label

The cross-entropy loss for word-level classification in Equation 3 is computed over hard
labels (binary OK/BAD). Prior works on knowledge distillation in the computer vision
community show that the logits on the other hand, contains more information and allow
the student to train on difficult targets [15].

Therefore, when incorporating word-level logits, we try two different training strategies on both hard labels (binary OK/BAD) and soft labels (namely the logits). Different
loss functions are as follows:

$$L_{soft} = \sum_{x \in D} \|h(x) - logit_x\| \tag{5}$$

$$L_{hard} = \sum_{x \in D} cross\_entropy(W_w h(x), y_x) \tag{6}$$

where $h(x)$ refer to the output state of the student model, y_x and $logit_x$ denote the hard
label and soft label for input x generate by the teacher model, respectively.

For sentence-level, the distilling objective is heuristic. Since sentence-level QE is a
regression problem, the output is a contagious real-value number, and the student model
can be trained to fit this contagious output following Eq. 2.

As mentioned in the former section, multi-task training on multi-granularities is
especially helpful for sentence-level QE, so the final training objective for sentence-level
distillation also consists of two transformations.

4.3 Iterative Ensemble Distillation

After the ensemble distillation step, each model is enhanced by a large margin, which
means the ensembled model based on these two models are also strengthened. It is natural
to think that the strengthened ensemble model can generate better distillation logits, and

the single models further strengthened can generated an even better ensemble model, which can be implemented in an iterative manner.

The final algorithm is described as follows:

Iterative Ensemble Distillation
1   Train a neural machine translation model
2   Infer monolingual data with the MT model from step 1 and generate source-target sentence pairs
3   Fine-tune different pretrained language models on real-world QE data
4   *Repeat:*
5   Ensemble multiple models to infer source-target pairs and generate logits on different granularities
6   Distill different pretrained language models on the logits from step 5
7   Fine-tune different models from step 6 on real-world QE data
8   *Until* single models are converged

5   Experiment

5.1   Setup

Baseline. We mainly compare our system with [11], which is the state-of-the-art architecture on QE tasks. We reimplement their experiment with open-source hyper-parameters, and for the purpose of fair comparison, we constrain all experiments on one single GPU, including their predictor part (which is basically a machine translation system). And the data we use to train their predictor and further pretrain our models is also the same.

We also compare with the winning system in CCMT2019 evaluation contest [17], which is an extension of [11]. They replace the normal Transformer encoder in [11] with deeper-layer and pre-norm architecture. Since their system is trained on eight GPUs, we refer to this comparison as unfair.

Dataset. We use the QE data from CCMT2019 Machine Translation Quality Estimation tasks. CCMT QE tasks contain two different language directions (Chinese-English and English-Chinese) on both sentence-level and word-level. The amount of data provided on both language pairs and levels are very small (no more than 15 k triples on all directions), which makes QE a highly data-sparse task.

To train the predictor for [11] and further pretrain our models, we use the parallel dataset for Chinese-English Translation task in CCMT2019, which contains nearly 10 million sentence pairs. We filter too long or too short sentences, and the sentence-pairs with a too low alignment score provided by fast-align[1], which leaves us rough 7 million sentence pairs.

---

[1] https://github.com/clab/fast_align.

5.2 Experiment Results

The experiment results on both directions and granularities are shown in Table 1 and Table 2, where *postech*[2] and *bi-expert*[3] denotes the models in [10] and [11], and *transformer-dlcl* [17] and *CCNN* were the top2 systems in CCMT 2019 QE task.

Table 1. Experiment results on CCMT2019 sentence-level QE dev set

Language direction	System	Pearonr	Spearman	MSE
Chinese-English	postech	0.5052	–	–
	bi-expert	0.4781	–	–
	CCNN	0.50	0.45	–
	transformer-dlcl	0.5831	–	–
	Bert (distill)	0.6196	0.5426	0.5811
	XLM (distill)	0.6147	0.5395	0.5784
	Bert (iterative)	**0.6248**	0.5438	0.5855
	XLM (iterative)	0.6173	0.5442	0.5820
English-Chinese	postech	0.3491	–	–
	bi-expert	0.3542	–	–
	CCNN	0.53	0.41	–
	transformer-dlcl	0.5537	–	–
	Bert (distill)	0.5483	0.4127	0.4805
	XLM (distill)	0.5497	0.4132	0.4817
	Bert (iterative)	**0.5576**	0.4194	0.4887
	XLM (iterative)	0.5523	0.4179	0.4842

For sentence-level QE, we surpass all baselines on both directions with limited computation resource. Especially on Chinese-English sentence-level QE, we surpass [11] by 4 points on development set with the same data and much smaller computation overhead.

For word-level QE, we do not release our results of iterative ensemble distillation, since ensemble distillation seems not effective on word-level training. On Chinese-English direction, we surpass all baselines by a large margin with limited computation resource, but we fail to overtake the result of [17] on English-Chinese direction.

Notice on word-level task, we do not apply further pretraining step on both models before finetuning, so the computation overhead is very low with just a few hours finetuning on one single GPU.

---

[2] https://github.com/Unbabel/OpenKiwi.
[3] https://github.com/lovecambi/qebrain.

Table 2. Experiment results on CCMT2019 word-level QE dev set

Language direction	System	F1-Multi	F1-BAD	F1-OK
Chinese-English	postech	0.4490	0.5369	0.8364
	bi-expert	0.4257	0.5308	0.8021
	transformer-dlcl	0.4739	0.5673	0.8353
	Bert	0.4749	0.5543	0.8568
	XLM	0.4939	0.5719	0.8636
	Bert (distill)	0.4797	0.5656	0.8481
	XLM (distill)	**0.4976**	0.5769	0.8702
English-Chinese	postech	0.3524	0.4124	0.8544
	bi-expert	0.3453	0.4013	0.8604
	transformer-dlcl	**0.4217**	0.4695	0.8980
	Bert	0.3916	0.4486	0.8728
	XLM	0.3959	0.4478	0.8841
	Bert (distill)	0.3769	0.4412	0.8541
	XLM (distill)	0.3629	0.4222	0.8595

In a word, the pretrained language model can be a very strong baseline for QE at both sentence-level and word-level. It requires no complicated architecture engineering and massive training data, and can provide reliable performance.

5.3 Ablation Study

In this section, we will discuss the influence of different strategies on our model. Notice although we described a lot of strategies to boost QE system in former sections, their influence on different granularities are different.

Further Pre-training for Bilingual Input. As shown in Table 3, for XLM, a further pretraining step could not lead to any improvement. On the contrary, it causes catastrophic forgetting and makes the results decline by a large margin.

On the other hand, Bert is only trained with monolingual input, so it is reasonable to believe further pre-training could help Bert adapted to multilingual input. But astonishingly, we find further pre-training can only improve the sentence-level QE, and is harmful for word-level QE on Bert, which needs our future investigation.

Multi-task Learning for Multi-granularities. As shown in Table 4, after joint trained with different granularities, the results of sentence-level QE increase a lot, which verifies our conjecture that word-level labels can help the training of sentence-level QE. For word-level QE, the avail of multi-task learning seems limited.

Table 3. Further pre-training for bilingual input

Language direction	System	Level	Further pretrain	Pearsonr/F1-multi
English-Chinese	Bert	Sentence	No	0.4230
			Yes	0.5169
		Word	No	0.3902
			Yes	0.3837

Table 4. Multi-task learning for multi-granularities

Language direction	Level	Model	Multi-task	Pearsonr/F1-multi
English-Chinese	Sentence	Bert	No	0.4893
			Yes	0.5169
	Word	Bert	No	0.3962
			Yes	0.3902

Label Balancing for Word-Level QE. We try three different strategies including up-sampling sentence-pairs with high HTER values and down-sampling sentence-pairs with low HTER values, and find that weight balancing when calculating loss is a simple yet effective strategy, as shown in Table 5. Although data sampling can also help the model to emphasize more on the bad words when training, but it will damage the natural distribution of sentence-pairs, and thus harmful to final performance. We try different values for λ ranging from 5 to 20, and finally set λ as 10 in Eq. 4.

Table 5. Label balancing for word QE

Language direction	Level	Model	Balancing strategy	F1-multi
English-Chinese	Word	Bert	No	0.3227
			Up sampling	0.3847
			Down sampling	0.3357
			Weight balancing	0.3962

Ensemble Distillation. We try two different strategies when distilling ensemble models to a single model, as explained in the former section.

As we can see from Table 6, for sentence level QE, the improvement introduced by ensemble distillation is evident, especially when conducting multi-task training with soft labels. And after several rounds' iteration, distilled models can be further improved.

Since improvement introduced by more iterations is marginal, and too many iterations would occupy to much computational resource with no significant benefit, so we only conduct iterative ensemble distillation for no more than three rounds.

Table 6. Ensemble distillation in iterative manners

Language direction	Level	Model	Label	Round	Pearsonr/F1-multi
English-Chinese	Sentence	Bert	No	0	0.5313
			Hard	1	0.5316
			Soft (no finetune)	1	0.5357
			Soft	1	0.5483
			Soft	3	0.5576
	Word	Bert	No	0	0.3916
			Hard	1	0.3769
			Soft	1	0.3748

More interestingly, even before the fine-tuning step on real-world QE data, with only the distilling data on our predicted logits, our model can still surpass the original single model. We hypothesize that for the task of sentence-level QE, the prior knowledge contained in pretrained models is more important than artificial annotated data, which deserves our further exploration.

For word level QE, it seems ensemble distillation is not helpful. We believe it is because the unbalanced word-level labels, which make output logits unable to represent the accurate state for each sub-word. How to cater for the unbalanced word labels when distilling remains a challenging problem.

6 Conclusion

Machine translation quality estimation (Quality Estimation, QE) aims to evaluate the quality of machine translation automatically on different granularities. Since its reference-free nature, QE can be applied in universal scenarios and attracts a lot of research interest in recent years.

In this paper, we explore the application of pre-trained models on both sentence-level and word-level quality estimation. We implement the QE system based on two popular pretrained models, Bert and XLM, and study different applicable strategies on QE task, i.e. further pretraining on bilingual input, multi-task training on multi-granularities and weighted loss for word labels. We also come up with a novel training paradigm, ensemble distillation, which can improve sentence-level QE of a single model by a large margin when multiple models are available. We perform experiments on CCMT2019 QE data, and our model achieve strong performance on both sentence-level and word-level QE tasks with limited computation resource.

Massive linguistic knowledge contained in pretrained models is very helpful for the QE task even when there is limited training data. In the future, we will continue our research on the application of pretrained models on different QE tasks.

Acknowledgement. This work is supported by the National Natural Science Foundation of China (Contract 61976015, 61976016, 61876198 and 61370130), and the Beijing Municipal Natural Science Foundation (Contract 4172047), and the International Science and Technology Cooperation Program of the Ministry of Science and Technology (K11F100010), and Toshiba (China) Co., Ltd.

References

1. Lucia, S.: Exploiting objective annotations for measuring translation post-editing effort. In: Proceedings of the 15th Conference of the European Association for Machine Translation, pp. 73–80 (2011)
2. John, B., et al.: Confidence estimation for machine translation. In: Proceedings of the International Conference on Computational Linguistics, p. 315 (2004)
3. Snover, M., Dorr, B., Schwartz, R., Micciulla, L., Makhoul, J.: A study of translation edit rate with targeted human annotation. In: Proceedings of Association for Machine Translation in the Americas, vol. 200, no. 6 (2006)
4. Specia, L., Blain, F., Logacheva, V., Astudillo, R., Martins, A.F.: Findings of the WMT 2018 shared task on quality estimation. In: Proceedings of the Third Conference on Machine Translation: Shared Task Papers, pp. 689–709 (2018)
5. Devlin, J., Chang, M.W., Lee, K., Toutanova, K.: BERT: pre-training of deep bidirectional transformers for language understanding. arXiv preprint arXiv:1810.04805 (2018)
6. Lample, G., Conneau, A.: Cross-lingual language model pretraining. arXiv preprint arXiv: 1901.07291 (2019)
7. Bojar, O., et al.: Findings of the 2017 conference on machine translation. In: Proceedings of the Second Conference on Machine Translation, pp. 169–214 (2017)
8. Julia, K., Shigehiko, S., Stefan, R.: Quality estimation from ScraTCH (QUETCH): deep learning for word-level translation quality estimation. In: Proceedings of the Tenth Workshop on Statistical Machine Translation, pp. 316–322 (2015)
9. Martins, A.F., Junczys-Dowmunt, M., Kepler, F.N., Astudillo, R., Hokamp, C., Grundkiewicz, R.: Pushing the limits of translation quality estimation. Trans. Assoc. Comput. Linguist. **5**, 205–218 (2017)
10. Kim, H., Jung, H.-Y., Kwon, H., Lee, J.H., Na, S.-H.: Predictor-estimator: neural quality estimation based on target word prediction for machine translation. ACM Trans. Asian Low-Resour. Lang. Inf. Process. (TALLIP) **17**(1), 3 (2017)
11. Kai, F., Bo, L., Fengming, Z., Jiayi W.: "Bilingual expert" can find translation errors. arXiv preprint arXiv:1807.09433 (2018)
12. Kepler, F., et al.: Unbabel's PARTICIPATIOn in the WMT19 translation quality estimation shared task. arXiv preprint arXiv:1907.10352 (2019)
13. Pires, T., Schlinger, E., Garrette, D.: How multilingual is multilingual BERT? arXiv preprint arXiv:1906.01502 (2019)
14. Hyun, K., Jong-Hyeok, L., Seung-Hoon, N.: Predictor-estimator using multilevel task learning with stack propagation for neural quality estimation. In: Proceedings of the Second Conference on Machine Translation, Volume 2: Shared Task Papers, pp. 562–568 (2017)

15. Geoffrey, H., Oriol, V., Jeff, D.: Distilling the knowledge in a neural network. arXiv preprint arXiv:1503.02531 (2015)
16. Kim, Y., Rush, A.M.: Sequence-level knowledge distillation. arXiv preprint arXiv:606.07947 (2016)
17. Wang, Z., et al.: NiuTrans submission for CCMT19 quality estimation task. In: Huang, S., Knight, K. (eds.) CCMT 2019. CCIS, vol. 1104, pp. 82–92. Springer, Singapore (2019). https://doi.org/10.1007/978-981-15-1721-1_9

Weaken Grammatical Error Influence in Chinese Grammatical Error Correction

Jinggui Liang and Si Li[✉]

School of Artificial Intelligence, Beijing University of Post and Telecommunications,
Beijing, China
{liangjinggui,lisi}@bupt.edu.cn

Abstract. Chinese grammatical error correction (CGEC), a task of correcting grammatical errors in text, is treated as a translation task, where error sentences are "translated" to correct sentences. However, some grammatical errors in the training data can confuse the CGEC models and have negative influence in the "translating" process. In this paper, we propose a Grammatical Error Weakening Module (GEWM) to impair the negative influence of grammatical errors in CGEC task. The grammatical error weakening module first extracts contextual features for each word in an error sentence via context attention mechanism. Then the proposed module uses learnable error weakening factors to control the proportion of contextual features and word features in the final representation of each word. As such, features from grammatical error words can be suppressed. Experiments show that our approach has better performance compared with the baseline models in CGEC task.

Keywords: Chinese grammatical error correction · Grammatical error weakening · Attention mechanism

1 Introduction

Grammatical error correction (GEC) is a task of automatically correcting grammatical errors in text. Grammatical error correction models are helpful for facilitating the progress of language learners and improving the grammaticality of machine generated text in natural language generation [6]. In recent years, some English [11,12] and Chinese [25] shared tasks are devoted to promote the research on grammatical error correction. In this paper, we focus on Chinese grammatical error correction (CGEC).

Table 1 shows an example of error-correct sentence pair in CGEC task. Chinese grammatical error correction is usually considered as a translation task [23], where sentences with grammatical errors are translated to correct sentences. Recent works on CGEC [3,9,13,15] adopt sequence to sequence architecture [19], and achieve impressive performance. In their CGEC models, the encoder is used to extract word features from error sentences. The decoder simply uses the features extracted by the encoder to generate the correct sentences. However, simply

X. Zhu et al. (Eds.): NLPCC 2020, LNAI 12431, pp. 244–255, 2020.
https://doi.org/10.1007/978-3-030-60457-8_20

using these features could confuse the CGEC models since the information of grammatical error words is mixed up in it, which leads to a failure in correcting these grammatical errors.

Table 1. An example of error-correct sentence pair.

Error Sentence	听他母亲说他是副经历。 (His mother said he was a deputy *experience.*)
Correct Sentence	听他母亲说他是副经理。 (His mother said he was a deputy *manager.*)

To suppress the mixed grammatical error information extracted by the encoder, we present a novel encoder-decoder model with a Grammatical Error Weakening Module (GEWM). The grammatical error weakening module is embedded in each layer of the encoder. For an error sentence, firstly, the grammatical error weakening module extracts contextual features for each word. Secondly, the module learns to assign different weights named error weakening factor to different words in the sentence. These weights are then used to control the proportion of the contextual features and word features extracted by multi-head attention in the final representation of each word. As such, the decoder in our model gains features with weak influence of grammatical error words. The contributions of our work are summarized as follows:

1) We propose a novel architecture for CGEC task, which uses a grammatical error weakening module to weaken the grammatical errors influence in error sentences.
2) We evaluate the proposed architecture on NLPCC-2018 shared task test set, the result shows that our proposed architecture has better performance compared with baseline models in CGEC task.

2   Related Work

As grammatical error correction task is one of the most important tasks in natural language processing, a lot of work have been done in it, especially in the field of English grammatical error correction. Xiang et al. [21] proposed to combine machine learning and rule-based methods to correct five types of grammatical errors in English. Yuan and Briscoe [23] first used an encoder-decoder architecture, which is similar to neural machine translation, to translate the error sentences into the correct ones. In the work of Sakaguchi et al. [16], they trained grammatical error correction model with reinforcement learning. Later, the researchers noticed that the scarcity of training data deeply hinder the development of grammatical error correction. To address this problem, Ge et al. [5] presented a fluency boosting method to generate additional error-contained data for grammatical error correction. Xu et al. [22] obtained erroneous data for English grammatical error correction by randomly generating several of five types of errors in a sentence. Motivated by the task of quality estimation in machine translation, Chollampatt and Ng [1] proposed the first neural approach to automatic quality estimation of grammatical error correction output sentences that did not employ any hand-crafted features. Moreover, Chollampatt and Ng [2] discovered that some errors can be corrected reliably using cross-sentence context, they further improved the strong grammatical error correction model by incorporating cross-sentence context from previous sentence. Recently, Zhao et al. [24] first presented a copy-augmented architecture in grammatical error correction, which allowed the grammatical error correction model to copy the unchanged words from input sentence.

Compared with English, there are much fewer studies on Chinese grammatical error correction. Since the great success of NLPCC-2018 [25] and NLPTEA shared task [14], the researchers started to pay more attention to CGEC task. Shiue et al. [18] corrected the grammatical errors by translating erroneous Chinese into well-formed Chinese. The work of Fu et al. [4] contained two models. They first detected the location and the type of errors in sentence via a bidirectional Long Short-Term Memory model with a conditional random field layer (BiLSTM-CRF), and then they used a correction model based on ePMI values and sequence to sequence model to correct the detected grammatical errors. In the work of Fu et al. [3], they rescored the output sentence corrected by five different models thought a 5-gram language model and their approach won the first place in NPLCC-2018 shared task. Zhou et al. [8] combined statistical models and neural models for the CGEC task. Different from others that used multiple models, Ren et al. [15] built a single CGEC model based entirely on convolutional neural network and applied a BPE-based algorithm to handle the problem of out-of-vocabulary words in CGEC task. More recently, Qiu et al. [13] presented a two-stage model to solve the CGEC problem. Li et al. [9] proposed two optimization methods, shared embedding and policy gradient, to optimize the CGEC model.

3   Background

Transformer [20] is a sequence to sequence framework based on attention mechanism, which has been demonstrated to be effective in grammatical error correction task [3,13]. Therefore, we use the Transformer as one of our baseline systems. Recently, Copy-Augmented Transformer [24] achieved state-of-the-art performance in grammatical error correction. We also use the Copy-Augmented Transformer as another one of our baseline systems. In this section, we will introduce the Transformer architecture and copying mechanism that are adopted in grammatical error correction task.

3.1   Transformer Architecture

The Transformer is a new sequence to sequence architecture that relies heavily on the attention mechanism. Both the encoder and the decoder of a Transformer are stacks of Transformer blocks, each of which consists two sub-layers: a multi-head self-attention layer and a feed-forward network. The key component in the multi-head self-attention layer is the scaled dot-product mechanism, which maps a query and a set of key-value pairs to an output vector as below:

$$Attention(Q, K, V) = softmax\left(\frac{QK^T}{\sqrt{d_k}}\right)V \tag{1}$$

where d_k is the dimension of the key vector. $\{Q, K, V\}$ represent the query, key and value vectors and all of them come from the output of the previous layer.

Instead of performing a single attention function, multi-head self-attention mechanism applies scaled dot-product attention mechanism to extract h different representations of query, key and value vectors. These different representations are concatenated and once again projected as the final output representation. This can be expressed as follows:

$$head_i = Attention(QW_i^Q, KW_i^K, VW_i^V) \tag{2}$$

$$MultiHead(Q, K, V) = Concat(head_1, ..., head_h)W^O \tag{3}$$

where W_i^Q, W_i^K and W_i^V are parameters matrices for the i_{th} attention head, W^O is the final output projection matrix.

Each Transformer decoder block also attends to the encoder outputs through an additional sub-layer between the two sub-layers mentioned above. The third sub-layer is a modified multi-head self-attention based layer that receives previous decoder layer output as its query vector and the output of the encoder as its key vector and value vector. By doing this, the third sub-layer enables every position in the decoder to attend to all positions in the input sentence.

3.2 Copying Mechanism

Copying mechanism is an important mechanism of enabling neural model to select words to be copied from the input. Copying mechanism has been proved effective in many natural language processing task, such as text summarization [17] and semantic parsing [7].

Recently, Zhao et al. [24] observed that more than 80% of the words were unchanged in the input sentence, they applied the copying mechanism to grammatical error correction task to directly copy the unchanged words from the input sentence. The copying mechanism used in grammatical error correction can be described as follows: At each output position t, the model generates a final distribution $P(y_t)$ for the output token y_t. Since the output tokens of the grammatical error correction model come from a predefine vocabulary or the words appearing in the input sentence, the final output distribution $P(y_t)$ is a dynamic mixture of model generation distribution $P^{gen}(y_t)$ and copy distribution $P^{copy}(y_t)$. The mixture can be described as below:

$$P(y_t) = (1 - \alpha_t^{copy}) \cdot P^{gen}(y_t) + \alpha_t^{copy} \cdot P^{copy}(y_t) \tag{4}$$

where $\alpha_t^{copy} \in [0, 1]$ is a mixture weight parameter that controls the dynamic combination of these two distribution at each decoding step.

4   Approach

In this section, we present a novel encoder-decoder model with a grammatical error weakening module to weaken the negative influence of grammatical errors in CGEC task. As show in Fig. 1, the grammatical error weakening module is embedded in each layer of encoder and consists of two components: context attention and combination module. To weaken the negative influence of the grammatical error words, we first extract the contextual features for each word in the sentence. Then we use the word features and their contextual features to learn the error weakening factors for different words. These error weakening factors are finally used to control the proportion of the word features and the contextual features in the final representation of each word. Under the control of the error weakening factors, the negative influence of the grammatical errors is weakened. In the following subsection, we will introduce the context attention and the combination module in details.

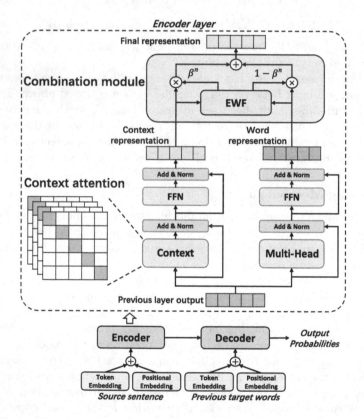

Fig. 1. The encoder-decoder model with grammatical error weakening module: context refers to the context attention mechanism. Multi-Head is the multi-head self-attention mechanism. FFN represents the feed-forward network. EWF refers to the network that used to learn the error weakening factors. β^n means the error weakening factors in the n_{th} encoder layer.

4.1   Context Attention

The context attention is used to extract contextual information for each word in the input sentence. The context attention is a variant of the original multi-head self-attention. Different from the original multi-head attention that allows a word to attend to arbitrary words in the input sentence, in context attention, the word has a limited vision that can only connect with its surrounding words. The context attention is achieved by adding a hard mask to each head. By this way, we can redefine Eq. (1) as follows:

$$Attention(Q, K.V) = softmax \left(\frac{QK^T}{\sqrt{d_k}} + M_{(i,j)} \right) V \qquad (5)$$

where $M_{(i,j)}$ is the hard masking function. For i_{th} word, we add a hard mask $M_{(i,j)}$ to the position j. The results of the soft-max function will be influenced by the value of $M_{(i,j)}$. If $M_{(i,j)} = -\infty$, it means that the result of the soft-max function equals to 0 and there is no attention of the i_{th} word to position j. On the contrary, if $M_{(i,j)} = 0$, it means that the i_{th} word can capture information from the position j without any limitation. The masking function we employ in the context attention mechanism can be described as below:

$$M_{(i,j)} = \begin{cases} -\infty, & i = j \\ \\ 0, & otherwise \end{cases} \qquad (6)$$

4.2   Combination Module

After extracting word information and contextual information via multi-head attention and context attention, we obtain two features for each word: word features and contextual features. The combination module learns to assign different weights, named error weakening factor, to different words in the sentence. These error weakening factors are real values between 0 and 1, which indicate that the word features receive different degrees of suppression. Different from copy mechanism that directly influence the output probabilities in the final decoding process, error weakening factors aim to reduce the proportion of grammatical error words features in the final representation of each encoder layer output, which can also help the copy mechanism to focus more on the original correct words (unchanged words). These error weakening factors are learned from word features and contextual features. For the n_{th} layer of the encoder stack, the error weakening factor can be calculated as below:

$$\beta^n = \text{sigmoid} \left(\tanh(H_c^n \cdot W_c^n + H_w^n \cdot W_w^n) \cdot T^n \right) \qquad (7)$$

where β^n are the error weakening factors in the n_{th} layer of the encoder stack, $W_c^n \in R^{d_{model} \times d_{model}}$, $W_w^n \in R^{d_{model} \times d_{model}}$, $T^n \in R^{d_{model} \times 1}$ are parameters matrices and d_{model} is the dimension of the feature vectors. H_c^n and H_w^n are the contextual features and word features.

These error weakening factors are then used to control the proportion of word features and contextual features in the final representation of each word. The combination function can be described as follows:

$$H^n_{final} = (1 - \beta^n) \otimes H^n_w + \beta^n \otimes H^n_c \qquad (8)$$

where H^n_{final}, H^n_w, H^n_c are the final representation, word features and contextual features for each word in the input sentence. As shown in Eq. (8), by combining these two features, we gain the final representation with weak influence of grammatical errors for each word.

5   Experiments

In this section, we will introduce the dataset, the evaluation method and the experiment settings used in our experiments. Then, we will list our experiment results on the dataset to show the effectiveness of the proposed approach in CGEC task. Finally, we will analyze some study cases in our experiments.

Table 2. Information of corpus: correct means the number of sentences which do not contain grammatical errors. Error refers to the number of grammatical error sentences in the corpus. All the data comes from the NLPCC-2018 shared task 2. NLPCC-2018 refers to the training corpus and Test is the standard test set.

Corpus	Num of pairs	Correct	Error
NLPCC-2018	1,220,069	123,500	1,096,569
Test	2,000	17	1,983

5.1   Datasets

We conduct our experiments on the dataset that comes from NLPCC-2018 shared task [25]. Table 2 shows the detailed information about the dataset.

The corpus provided by NLPCC-2018 is derived from lang-8 website, which collects corrections for grammatical error sentences from the netizens who use Chinese as their native language. To gain the high quality sentence pairs for model training, we filter the corpus as follows:

1) The length of error sentence and correct sentence do not exceed 75 characters.
2) Sentence pair where the length of corrected sentence exceeds 1.5 times the length of the error sentence will be removed.
3) The traditional Chinese are converted to simplified Chinese by wiki.

After filtration, our final experiment data is a collection over 1.17 million sentence pairs. We randomly split our whole experiment data into two parts: a validation set with 5,000 sentence pairs and a training set with the remaining 1,167,014 sentence pairs. The test set used in our experiments is the standard test set in NLPCC-2018 CGEC shared task, which contains 2,000 sentence pairs.

5.2   Evaluation

We use Max-Match (M_2) algorithm, which is widely used in grammatical error correction, to evaluate the results of our experiments. In grammatical error correction, M_2 algorithm computes Precision, Recall and $F_{0.5}$ for the outputs of the grammatical error correction models to choose the hypothesis that holds the highest overlap with the gold edits from annotators. Since the accuracy of CGEC models corrections is profundly valued to gain the acceptance of users, the $F_{0.5}$ that emphasizes precision twice as much as recall is usually regarded as the most important score in evaluating the performance of CGEC models.

Herein, we define $\{g_1, g_1, ..., g_n\}$ as the gold edit set from annotator and $\{e_1, e_1, ..., e_n\}$ as the system edit set. The Precision, Recall and $F_{0.5}$ can be calculated as follows:

$$P = \frac{\sum_{i=1}^{n} |g_i \cap e_i|}{\sum_{i=1}^{n} |e_i|} \tag{9}$$

$$R = \frac{\sum_{i=1}^{n} |g_i \cap e_i|}{\sum_{i=1}^{n} |g_i|} \tag{10}$$

$$F_{0.5} = 5 \times \frac{P \times R}{P + 4 \times R} \tag{11}$$

where the intersection between e_i and g_i is defined as:

$$e_i \cap g_i = \{e \in e_i | \exists g \in g_i(match(e, g))\} \tag{12}$$

5.3   Settings

For the proposed models in our experiments, we set the dimensions of word embedding to 512. The encoder and decoder stacks consist of 6 layers. The attention heads in both multi-head attention and context attention is set to 8. And we set the inner layer size of the feed-forward network to 4,096. Moreover, in the Copy-Augmented Transformer with grammatical error weakening module, we set the copying attention head to 1.

For model optimization, we use Nesterovs Accelerated Gradient (NAG) [10] optimizer to optimize both two models. The initial learning rate is set to 0.002 and the weight decay is 0.5 together with 0 patience. The momentum is 0.99 and minimum learning rate is 0.0001.

5.4   Experiment Results

We compare our approach with the following famous systems in grammatical error correction task. The detailed information about these systems is listed in the below:

1) Zhou et al. [8]: The system combines rule-based model, SMT-based model and NMT-based model.
2) Fu et al. [3]: The winning solution to the NLPCC-2018 shared task 2 challenge, which is based on spelling error correction model and NMT model.

3) Ren et al. [15]: A seq2seq model that bases entirely on convolutional neural network.
4) Qiu et al. [13]: A two-stage model that combines spelling check and Transformer for Chinese grammatical error correction.
5) Zhao et al. [24]: A Transformer architecture that enhanced by copying mechanism.

Table 3. Comparison of grammatical error correction systems on NLPCC-2018 test set. Transformer-only and Copy-Augmented Transformer (Zhao et al. [24]) are our two baseline systems. +GEWM refers to the grammatical error weakening module.

Model	P	R	$F_{0.5}$
Zhou et al. [8]	41.00%	13.75%	29.36%
Fu et al. [3]	35.24%	18.64%	29.91%
Ren et al. [15]	47.63%	12.56%	30.57%
Qiu et al. [13]	36.88%	18.94%	31.01%
Zhao et al. [24]	41.84%	16.49%	32.00%
Transformer-only	40.82%	15.25%	30.57%
Transformer-only+GEWM	41.65%	15.38%	31.04%
Copy-Augmented Transformer [24]	41.84%	16.49%	32.00%
Copy-Augmented Transformer+GEWM	42.40%	17.06%	**32.69%**

Table 3 presents the experiment results of our models and other different grammatical error correction models on NLPCC-2018 test set. From the Table 3, we can observe that:

Our basic CGEC model (Transformer-only) achieves 30.57% in $F_{0.5}$. The value of $F_{0.5}$ increases to 32.00% with the application of copying mechanism in Transformer model (Copy-Augmented Transformer, Zhao et al. [24]). Both two baseline CGEC models in our experiments reach competitive results compared with previous CGEC systems, which indicates that our baseline models are strong CGEC systems.

For the Transformer-only+GEWM model, the precision increases 0.83% and achieves 41.65% while the recall has slightly improvement from 15.25% to 15.38% compared with the Transformer-only model. The $F_{0.5}$ value has 0.47% improvement in the Transformer-only+GEWM model. For the Copy-Augmented Transformer+GEWM model, all the evaluating metrics have better performance compared with Copy-Augmented Transformer model. The precision and recall increase by 0.56% and 0.57%. The $F_{0.5}$ improves 0.69% and achieves a result of 32.69% in the Copy-Augmented Transformer+GEWM model.

The best performance on the NLPCC-2018 test set is achieved by the Copy-Augmented Transformer+GEWM ($F_{0.5} = 32.69\%$). It can not only reach a high precision in CGEC task, but also maintain a high recall at the same time, compared to the current grammatical error correction systems. All the experiment results demonstrate that our approach is effective in CGEC task.

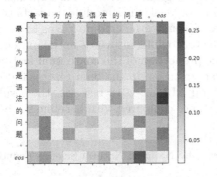

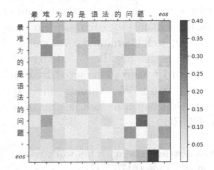

(a) Copy-Augmented Transformer attention weights

(b) Copy-Augmented Transformer +GEWM attention weights

Fig. 2. Visualization of attention weights in Copy-Augmented Transformer and Copy-Augmented Transformer+GEWM model. The grammatical sentence is "最难为的是语法的问题。" (meaning "The hardest part is grammar.")

5.5 Cases Analysis

To further analyze the behavior of our proposed grammatical error weakening module, we visualized the attention distributions in Copy-Augmented Transformer and Copy-Augmented Transformer+GEWM model and show an example of grammatical sentence as plotted in Fig. 2.

In this example, the correction of this grammatical sentence is directly deleting the word "为" ("for"). Figure 2(a) shows that Copy-Augmented Transformer focuses their attention weights on every word in the sentence. The information from the grammatical error word "为" confuses the Copy-Augmented Transformer, which leads to a failure in deleting the word "为". From the Fig. (2b), we can notice that the Copy-Augmented Transformer+GEWM model reduces the attention weight on the grammatical error word "为" compared with the Copy-Augmented Transformer. It means that the Copy-Augmented Transformer model assigns a high error weakening factor to the grammatical error word "为" and the features of word "为" is suppressed in the final representation. Meanwhile, from the Fig. (2b), we can also observe that the attention weights of some original correct words (such as "是" ("is"), "语" ("language")) are slightly lowered. This suggests that the Copy-Augmented Transformer+GEWM can better utilize the contextual features to understand the meaning of these original correct words during the correcting process. The analysis mentioned above indicates that our CGEC model can effectively utilize the contextual features and weaken the negative influence of the grammatical errors.

6   Conclusion

In this paper, we propose a novel architecture for CGEC task, which uses a grammatical error weakening module to weaken the grammatical errors influence in error sentences. Firstly, the grammatical error weakening module extracts contextual features for each word in sentences. Secondly, the module learns to assign different weights named error weakening factor to different words in the sentence. These weights are then used to control the proportion of the contextual features and word features extracted by multi-head attention in the final representation of each word. We evaluate our approach on NLPCC-2018 test set, the results show that our approach has better performance compared with baseline systems in CGEC task.

Acknowledgment. This work was supported by National Natural Science Foundation of China (61702047) .

References

1. Chollampatt, S., Ng, H.T.: Neural quality estimation of grammatical error correction. In: Proceedings of EMNLP, Brussels, Belgium, 31 October–4 November 2018, pp. 2528–2539 (2018)
2. Chollampatt, S., Wang, W., Ng, H.T.: Cross-sentence grammatical error correction. ACL **2019**, 435–445 (2019)
3. Fu, K., Huang, J., Duan, Y.: Youdao's winning solution to the NLPCC-2018 task 2 challenge: a neural machine translation approach to Chinese grammatical error correction. In: Proceedings of NLPCC 2018, pp. 341–350 (2018)
4. Fu, R., et al.: Chinese grammatical error diagnosis using statistical and prior knowledge driven features with probabilistic ensemble enhancement. In: Proceedings of the 5th Workshop on Natural Language Processing Techniques for Educational Applications, pp. 52–59 (2018)
5. Ge, T., Wei, F., Zhou, M.: Fluency boost learning and inference for neural grammatical error correction. In: Proceedings of the 56th Annual Meeting of the Association for Computational Linguistics, ACL 2018, Melbourne, Australia, 15–20 July 2018, vol. 1: Long Papers, pp. 1055–1065 (2018)
6. Ge, T., Zhang, X., Wei, F., Zhou, M.: Automatic grammatical error correction for sequence-to-sequence text generation: an empirical study. In: ACL 2019, pp. 6059–6064 (2019)
7. Jia, R., Liang, P.: Data recombination for neural semantic parsing. arXiv preprint arXiv:1606.03622 (2016)
8. Li, C., Zhou, J., Bao, Z., Liu, H., Xu, G., Li, L.: A hybrid system for Chinese grammatical error diagnosis and correction. In: Proceedings of the 5th Workshop on Natural Language Processing Techniques for Educational Applications, pp. 60–69 (2018)
9. Li, S., et al.: Chinese grammatical error correction based on convolutional sequence to sequence model. IEEE Access **7**, 72905–72913 (2019)
10. Nesterov, Y.E.: A method for solving the convex programming problem with convergence rate o $(1/k^2)$. Dokl. akad. nauk Sssr. **269**, 543–547 (1983)

11. Ng, H.T., Wu, S.M., Briscoe, T., Hadiwinoto, C., Susanto, R.H., Bryant, C.: The CoNLL-2014 shared task on grammatical error correction. In: Proceedings of CoNLL, pp. 1–14 (2014)

12. Ng, H.T., Wu, S.M., Wu, Y., Hadiwinoto, C., Tetreault, J.R.: The CoNLL-2013 shared task on grammatical error correction. In: Proceedings of CoNLL, pp. 1–12 (2013)

13. Qiu, Z., Qu, Y.: A two-stage model for Chinese grammatical error correction. IEEE Access **7**, 146772–146777 (2019)

14. Rao, G., Gong, Q., Zhang, B., Xun, E.: Overview of NLPTEA-2018 share task Chinese grammatical error diagnosis. In: Proceedings of the 5th Workshop on Natural Language Processing Techniques for Educational Applications, pp. 42–51 (2018)

15. Ren, H., Yang, L., Xun, E.: A sequence to sequence learning for Chinese grammatical error correction. In: Zhang, M., Ng, V., Zhao, D., Li, S., Zan, H. (eds.) NLPCC 2018. LNCS (LNAI), vol. 11109, pp. 401–410. Springer, Cham (2018). https://doi.org/10.1007/978-3-319-99501-4_36

16. Sakaguchi, K., Post, M., Van Durme, B.: Grammatical error correction with neural reinforcement learning. arXiv preprint arXiv:1707.00299 (2017)

17. See, A., Liu, P.J., Manning, C.D.: Get to the point: summarization with pointer-generator networks. arXiv preprint arXiv:1704.04368 (2017)

18. Shiue, Y., Huang, H., Chen, H.: A Chinese writing correction system for learning Chinese as a foreign language. IN: COLING 2018, pp. 137–141 (2018)

19. Sutskever, I., Vinyals, O., Le, Q.V.: Sequence to sequence learning with neural networks. CoRR abs/1409.3215 (2014)

20. Vaswani, A., et al.: Attention is all you need. CoRR abs/1706.03762 (2017)

21. Xiang, Y., Yuan, B., Zhang, Y., Wang, X., Zheng, W., Wei, C.: A hybrid model for grammatical error correction. In: Proceedings of CoNLL, pp. 115–122 (2013)

22. Xu, S., Zhang, J., Chen, J., Qin, L.: Erroneous data generation for grammatical error correction. In: Yannakoudakis, H., Kochmar, E., Leacock, C., Madnani, N., Pilán, I., Zesch, T. (eds.) Proceedings of the Fourteenth Workshop on Innovative Use of NLP for Building Educational Applications, pp. 149–158 (2019)

23. Yuan, Z., Briscoe, T.: Grammatical error correction using neural machine translation. In: NAACL HLT 2016, pp. 380–386 (2016)

24. Zhao, W., Wang, L., Shen, K., Jia, R., Liu, J.: Improving grammatical error correction via pre-training a copy-augmented architecture with unlabeled data. In: Proceedings of NAACL-HLT 2019, pp. 156–165 (2019)

25. Zhao, Y., Jiang, N., Sun, W., Wan, X.: Overview of the NLPCC 2018 shared task: grammatical error correction. In: Zhang, M., Ng, V., Zhao, D., Li, S., Zan, H. (eds.) NLPCC 2018. LNCS (LNAI), vol. 11109, pp. 439–445. Springer, Cham (2018). https://doi.org/10.1007/978-3-319-99501-4_41

Encoding Sentences with a Syntax-Aware Self-attention Neural Network for Emotion Distribution Prediction

Chang Wang and Bang Wang[✉]

Huazhong University of Science and Technology (HUST), Wuhan, China
{wang_chang,wangbang}@hust.edu.cn

Abstract. Emotion distribution prediction aims to simultaneously identify multiple emotions and their intensities in a sentence. Recently, neural network models have been successfully applied in this task. However, most of them have not fully considered the sentence syntactic information. In this paper, we propose a *syntax-aware self-attention neural network* (SynSAN) that exploits syntactic features for emotion distribution prediction. In particular, we first explore a syntax-level self-attention layer over syntactic tree to learn the syntax-aware vector of each word by incorporating the dependency syntactic information from its parent and child nodes. Then we construct a sentence-level self-attention layer to compress syntax-aware vectors of words to the sentence representation used for emotion prediction. Experimental results on two public datasets show that our model can achieve better performance than the state-of-the-art models by large margins and requires less training parameters.

Keywords: Self-attention · Syntax-aware · Emotion prediction

1 Introduction

Most of previous work about emotion analysis is to classify the text emotion into one or multiple categories. However, it is also important to simultaneously identify emotion classes and their intensities in a sentence (i.e., emotion distribution prediction), such as for social media analysis, public opinion analysis and etc. [21].

Some early strategies of label distribution prediction have appeared in the image recognition field. They can be generally divided into three categories: problem transformation (e.g., PT-Bayes), algorithm adaptation (e.g., AA-KNN) and specialized algorithms (e.g., SA-IIS) [4]. These approaches are based on machine learning algorithms or parametric models. The drawback is the lack of exploring textual semantics if directly applying them to emotion distribution prediction.

Recently, some neural network-based methods have been proposed for emotion distribution prediction [19,21]. For example, Zhang et al. [21] uses a convolutional neural network to compose the sentence semantic representation and

© Springer Nature Switzerland AG 2020
X. Zhu et al. (Eds.): NLPCC 2020, LNAI 12431, pp. 256–266, 2020.
https://doi.org/10.1007/978-3-030-60457-8_21

predicts emotion distribution with multi-task learning. However, existing methods have not fully considered the sentence syntactic information that has shown advantages in some other natural language processing tasks [17].

To this end, we exploit syntactic information in our model. Specifically, we learns dependency syntactic features with a self-attention network. Various self-attention mechanisms have been adopted in many neural models because of their flexibility in sentence encoding and time efficiency [14,18].

In this paper, we propose a *syntax-aware self-attention network* (SynSAN) for emotion distribution prediction. First, we explore a syntax-level self-attention layer to learn a syntax-aware vector for each word by encoding the dependency syntactic features from its parent and child nodes over the syntactic tree. Then a sentence-level self-attention layer is constructed to compute the importance weight of each word and compose the final sentence representation for emotion prediction from weighted syntax-aware vectors of words. Experimental results on two public datasets show that our proposed model outperforms the state-of-the-art ones on most evaluation metrics and also requires less training parameters.

2 Related Work

2.1 Emotion Distribution Prediction

The early methods of label distribution prediction have been proposed for image recognition. They can be mainly categorized into three types: problem transformation (e.g., PT-Bayes), algorithm adaptation (e.g., AA-KNN) and specialized algorithms (e.g., SA-IIS) [4]. These methods usually adopt machine learning algorithms or parametric models. For example, PT-Bayes has constructed a Bayes classifier to predict the probability of each label. The disadvantage is that textual semantics can not be considered if applying these methods to emotion distribution prediction. Later on, topic-based methods have been proposed [12,13]. They construct a latent topic model with emotion layer to leverage the association of the document topics and the emotions. Recently, many neural network-based methods have been presented for emotion distribution prediction [10,11,21,22]. They usually compose a semantic vector representation for the document based on convolutional neural networks or recurrent neural networks. For example, Li et al. [10] have developed a phrase-level convolutional neural network to learn word-phrase and phrase-sentence relations for reader emotion prediction. Zhang et al. [21] have constructed a convolutional neural network to encode sentence semantics and predicts emotion distributions with multi-task learning.

2.2 Attention Mechanisms

Attention Mechanisms can adaptively learn different weights for different components of the input sequence. There have been various attention mechanisms proposed and they have been successfully applied in many natural language processing tasks, e.g., text classification [9,20], machine translation [2].

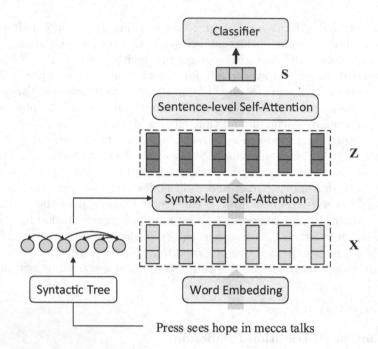

Fig. 1. The overall framework of the proposed SynSAN model. **X** denotes the word embeddings. **Z** denotes the syntax-aware vectors of words. **s** denotes the sentence representation.

Recently, self-attention networks have widely attracted research interest. Compared with traditional neural models, they are more flexible in learning long-distance relations between words and more time efficient [14,18]. Different from the existing self-attention networks that consider the temporal feature, we incorporate the syntactic knowledge into self-attention and construct a syntax-aware self-attention network.

3   The SynSAN Model

The overall framework of the SynSAN model is presented in Fig. 1. It consists of a syntax-level self-attention layer and a sentence-level self-attention.

3.1   Syntax-Level Self-attention

In this layer, we learn the syntax-aware vector of each word. Given a sentence containing N words, we first transform each word into the hidden state through a fully connected layer, which is calculated as:

$$\mathbf{h}_n = tanh(\mathbf{W}^{(h)}\mathbf{x}_n + \mathbf{b}^{(h)})$$

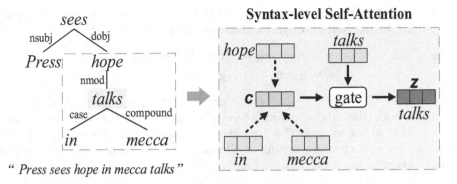

c : syntactic context vector   **z** : syntax-aware vector

Fig. 2. The left part is the dependency syntactic tree. The right part is the illustration of the syntax-level self-attention layer.

where $\mathbf{h}_n \in \mathbb{R}^{d_h}$ is the hidden state of the n-th word, and $\mathbf{x}_n \in \mathbb{R}^{d_w}$ is the word embedding, which is a real-valued vector obtained by a pre-trained word2vec model.[1]

We adopt a syntactic parser to obtain the dependency tree of the sentence, where each node represents a word and each edge represents a dependency syntactic relation. As shown in the left part of Fig. 2, each word is connected with its parent and child nodes (we call them syntactic context). For each word, a syntax-aware vector is learned by the syntax-level self-attention layer. We first calculate the alignment scores between the word and its syntactic context with the multi-dimensional alignment function which generates a feature-wise score vector [14]:

$$\mathbf{a}_{ij} = sigmoid(\mathbf{W}^{(c)}\mathbf{h}_i + \mathbf{U}^{(c)}\mathbf{h}_j + \mathbf{b}^{(c)}), j \in C(w_i)$$

where $C(w_i)$ denotes the syntactic context of the ith word w_i, and $\mathbf{W}^{(c)}, \mathbf{U}^{(c)} \in \mathbb{R}^{d_h \times d_h}, \mathbf{b}^{(c)} \in \mathbb{R}^{d_h}$ are learnable parameters. Based on the alignment score vector $\mathbf{a}_{ij}$, the syntactic context vector $\mathbf{c}_i$ can be calculated as follows:

$$\mathbf{c}_i = \sum_j \frac{exp(\mathbf{a}_{ij})}{\sum_{k \in C(w_i)} exp(\mathbf{a}_{ik})} \odot \mathbf{h}_j$$

where $\mathbf{c}_i \in \mathbb{R}^{d_h}$ is the syntactic context vector of w_i, and $\odot$ denotes the point-wise product. The syntax-level self-attention allows the network to assign larger weights for the context words with important dependency relations (like subject-predicate relation) and smaller weights for unimportant context words (like preposition). Therefore, we argue that the generated syntactic context vector $\mathbf{c}_i$ captures effective dependency syntactic features about the word w_i.

---

[1] https://code.google.com/archive/p/word2vec/.

We then fuse the hidden state $\mathbf{h}_i$ and the syntactic context vector $\mathbf{c}_i$ with a gate function to obtain the syntax-aware vector $\mathbf{z}_i$ of the word w_i:

$$\mathbf{g} = sigmoid(\mathbf{W}^{(g)}\mathbf{h}_i + \mathbf{U}^{(g)}\mathbf{c}_i + \mathbf{b}^{(g)})$$
$$\mathbf{z}_i = \mathbf{g} \odot \mathbf{h}_i + (\mathbf{1} - \mathbf{g}) \odot \mathbf{c}_i$$

where $\mathbf{W}^{(g)}, \mathbf{U}^{(g)} \in \mathbb{R}^{d_h \times d_h}, \mathbf{b}^{(g)} \in \mathbb{R}^{d_h}$ are learnable parameters. And $\mathbf{z}_i \in \mathbb{R}^{d_h}$ contains both the original word information of w_i and the syntactic context information about w_i over the dependency syntactic tree. Following the same process, the syntax-aware vectors of all words can be easily computed, and we denote them as $[\mathbf{z}_1, \mathbf{z}_2, \ldots, \mathbf{z}_N]$.

3.2   Sentence-Level Self-attention

Considering that words are not equally important for sentence encoding, we construct a sentence-level self-attention layer to calculate the importance weight for each word and compose the fixed-length sentence representation:

$$\mathbf{m}_i = \mathbf{V}^T sigmoid(\mathbf{W}^{(s)}\mathbf{z}_i + \mathbf{b}^{(s)}) + \mathbf{b}^{(v)}$$
$$\mathbf{s} = \sum_{i=1}^{N} \frac{exp(\mathbf{m}_i)}{\sum_{j=1}^{N} exp(\mathbf{m}_j)} \odot \mathbf{z}_i$$

where $\mathbf{V}, \mathbf{W}^{(s)} \in \mathbb{R}^{d_h \times d_h}, \mathbf{b}^{(s)}, \mathbf{b}^{(v)} \in \mathbb{R}^{d_h}$ are learnable parameters. And $\mathbf{m}_i$ is a weight vector rather than a scalar in the multi-dimensional attention. Through this layer, the dependency syntactic information is incorporated into the final sentence representation $\mathbf{s} \in \mathbb{R}^{d_h}$.

3.3   Emotion Distribution Prediction

We feed the obtained sentence representation $\mathbf{s}$ into a linear layer, generating a label vector whose dimension is the number of the emotion labels E. Then a softmax layer transforms the label vector to the predicted probability vector $\hat{\mathbf{y}}$:

$$\hat{\mathbf{y}} = softmax(\mathbf{W}^{(l)}\mathbf{s} + \mathbf{b}^{(l)})$$

where $\mathbf{W}^{(l)} \in \mathbb{R}^{E \times d_h}$ and $\mathbf{b}^{(l)} \in \mathbb{R}^{E}$ are learnable parameters. Each value in $\hat{\mathbf{y}}$ means the predicted probability intensity of each emotion.

For training, we adopt the Kullback-Leibler divergence between the gold emotion distribution $\mathbf{y}$ and the predicted one $\hat{\mathbf{y}}$ as the loss function:

$$Loss(\hat{\mathbf{y}}, \mathbf{y}) = \frac{1}{E} \sum_{k=1}^{E} y_k(\log(y_k) - \log(\hat{y}_k))$$

4   Experiment

We evaluate the performance of the proposed SynSAN model on two public datasets and report the experimental results in this section.

Table 1. Experimental results of distribution prediction on SemEval. The first group is existing traditional methods. The second group is existing neural network-based models. The third group is neural sentence encoders implemented by ourselves.

Models	Euclidean	Sϕrensen	Squaredχ^2	KL divergence	Cosine	Intersection
PT-Bayes	0.7724	0.7036	1.1776	2.5013	0.3798	0.2964
AA-KNN	0.5483	0.5457	0.8006	1.3988	0.5897	0.4543
SA-IIS	0.5175	0.5277	0.7324	0.8047	0.6447	0.4723
BCPNN	0.5207	0.5281	0.7399	0.8377	0.6383	0.4719
MT-CNN	0.4438	0.4196	0.5519	0.7306	0.7291	0.5804
BiLSTM	0.3617	0.3338	0.3982	0.5462	0.7904	0.6663
TreeLSTM	0.3427	0.3176	0.3743	0.4876	0.8086	0.6825
DiSAN	0.3363	0.3178	0.3652	**0.4211**	0.8179	0.6822
SynSAN	**0.3355**	**0.3147**	**0.3619**	0.4369	**0.8199**	**0.6853**

4.1 Experiment Settings

Datasets: SemEval is a multi-label dataset provided by the SemEval-2007 task 14 [16]. It contains 1,250 English news headlines with 6 emotion labels: anger, disgust, fear, joy, sadness and surprise. Each label is annotated by an intensity score of [0, 100]. FairyTales is a single-label dataset consisting of 185 children's stories [1], each sentence of which is annotated with one of five emotion classes: angry, fearful, happy, sad and surprised. All experimental results on the two datasets are the mean of tenfold cross validation.

Parameter Settings: We obtain word embeddings based on the 300-dimensional English word2vec model provided by Google.[2] The dimension of hidden layers is set to $d_h = d_w = 300$. Stanford Parser [8] is used to construct dependency trees. The whole network is trained by the Adam optimizer [7] with a learning rate of 0.005. Consistent with baselines, we use the dropout rate [15] of 0.5 and the batch size of 50.

Evaluation Metrics: Six metrics including Euclidean, Sϕrensen, Squaredχ^2, KL divergence, Cosine and Intersection are used to evaluate the quality of predicting emotion distribution [3]. Four metrics including Precision, Recall, F1-score, and Accuracy are used for the evaluation of classification performance. On the single-label dataset FairyTales, only the classification indicators are adopted.

Comparison Models: The following distribution prediction methods are used as baselines on the multi-label dataset SemEval. PT-Bayes, AA-KNN, SA-IIS [4], BCPNN [19] and Multi-Task CNN (MT-CNN) [21]. The following classification models including NMF [6], CNN and MT-CNN [21], are the baselines on the single-label dataset FairyTales.

For more comprehensive analysis of our proposed SynSAN, we also implement three effective neural models for comparison: Bidirectional LSTM (BiLSTM)

---

[2] https://code.google.com/archive/p/word2vec/.

Table 2. Classification performance on SemEval. The first group is existing traditional methods. The second group is existing neural network-based models. The third group is neural sentence encoders implemented by ourselves.

Models	Classification			
	P(%)	R(%)	F1(%)	Acc(%)
PT-Bayes	11.28	16.60	12.67	22.00
AA-KNN	26.67	19.01	18.33	24.40
SA-IIS	6.90	15.94	9.44	28.00
BCPNN	18.13	22.40	18.44	30.00
MT-CNN	48.33	42.23	41.41	51.60
BiLSTM	49.23	47.34	47.29	54.96
TreeLSTM	55.78	**52.44**	51.62	57.84
DiSAN	57.78	50.04	51.72	58.08
SynSAN	**58.23**	50.79	**51.91**	**58.72**

Table 3. Classification performance on FairyTales. The first group is existing traditional methods. The second group is existing neural network-based models. The third group is neural sentence encoders implemented by ourselves.

Models	P	R	F1	Acc
NMF	74.70	73.10	73.30	-
CNN	76.68	77.28	76.27	76.82
MT-CNN	78.21	**79.23**	78.72	79.21
BiLSTM	74.63	69.97	72.30	69.83
TreeLSTM	78.50	74.79	75.96	79.67
DiSAN	80.02	75.97	76.87	80.25
SynSAN	**80.70**	78.51	**79.22**	**82.04**

[5]: a widely-used sentence encoding network; Tree-structured LSTM (TreeL-STM) [17]: a LSTM network based on syntactic tree; Directional Self-Attention Network (DiSAN) [14]: a fully attention network that considers temporal order information.

4.2   Experimental Results

The results on the two datasets are presented in Table 1, 2 and 3. We can see that the proposed SynSAN achieves better performance by a large margin than the existing methods. Specifically, our SynSAN increases F1, Acc by 10.50%, 7.12% than the best existing model (i.e., MT-CNN) on SemEval, and increases F1, Acc by 0.5%, 2.83% on FairyTales. Our SynSAN also performs best compared with the other strong sentence encoder baselines (i.e., BiLSTM, TreeLSTM and DiSAN).

Table 4. The comparison of the number of model parameters $|\theta|$. dim means the dimension of sentence representation.

Models	dim	$|\theta|$
BiLSTM	600	1.45M
TreeLSTM	300	0.72M
DiSAN	600	1.63M
SynSAN	300	0.63M

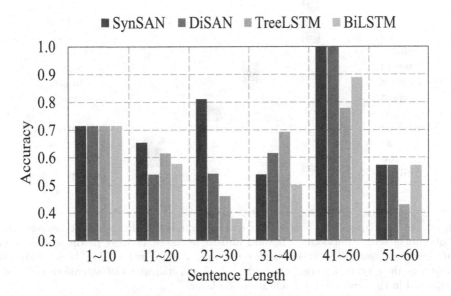

Fig. 3. The accuracy performance of BiLSTM, TreeLSTM, DiSAN and our SynSAN against the sentences with different lengths.

Three traditional methods based on machine learning algorithms or parametric models (i.e., PT-bayes, AA-KNN, SA-IIS) on SemEval, and the non-negative matrix factorization-based model NMF on FairyTales perform worse than neural network-based models (e.g., BCPNN, MT-CNN, etc.), as the latter can capture more effective textual semantics.

The DiSAN and our SynSAN are both fully attention-based models. It can be observed that they obtain better results than the two LSTM-based models (i.e. BiLSTM, TreeLSTM) because self-attention mechanism is more flexible in learning long-distance relations among words. Moreover, different from DiSAN that utilizes temporal order information, our proposed SynSAN learns the syntax-aware vector for each word by syntax-level self-attention and incorporates the syntactic features into the final sentence representation. Experimental results show that our SynSAN outperforms DiSAN on the two datasets, which indicates the effectiveness of encoding sentences with syntactic information for emotion distribution prediction.

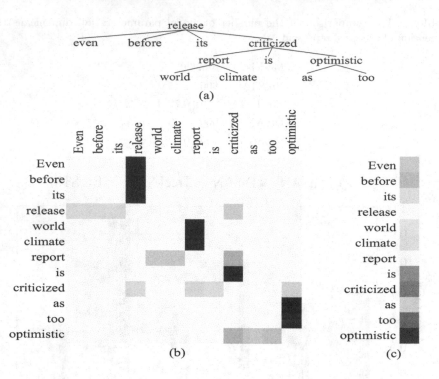

Fig. 4. (a) The dependency syntactic tree of the sample sentence. (b) The visualization of alignment scores between each word and its syntactic context in the syntax-level self-attention layer. The vertical axis represents original words. The horizontal axis represents their syntactic context words. (c) The visualization of attention weight of each word in the sentence-level self-attention layer.

Table 4 presents the number of network parameters to be trained. It can be seen that compared with the three strong sentence encoders BiLSTM, TreeLSTM and DiSAN, our SynSAN is also a light network model requiring much less training parameters.

4.3   The Influence of Sentence Length

We also study the prediction performance of different models on the sentences with different lengths. Taking the dataset FairyTales as an example, Fig. 3 plots the accuracy performance of BiLSTM, TreeLSTM, DiSAN and our SynSAN against varying sentence lengths. We observe that the SynSAN significantly outperforms the other models when the sentence length is in the range of [11, 30]. It does not show superiority when the sentence is longer than 30, whose reason may be that syntactic parsing performs worse on long sentences than short ones and thus reduces the effectiveness of syntax-aware self-attention in SynSAN. The similar trend can also be seen in the comparison of TreeLSTM and BiLSTM.

4.4   Case Study and Visualization

In Fig. 4, we visualize the alignment scores between each word and its syntactic context in the syntax-level self-attention layer and the attention weight of each word in the sentence-level self-attention layer. As the alignment scores and attention weights are both vectors, we average each of them along the vector dimension to get a scalar value. The example sentence is from SemEval: "*Even before its release, world climate report is criticized as too optimistic*".

Figure 4(a) presents the dependency syntactic tree of the sample sentence. It can be seen from Fig. 4(b) that the syntax-level self-attention layer successfully captures the important parent or child words to compose the syntax-aware vector for each word. For example, "*criticized*" and "*too*" are more important than "*as*" for the word "*optimistic*", and "*criticized*" is more important than "*word*", "*climate*" for the word "*report*". Meanwhile, as Fig. 4(c) shows, in the sentence-level self-attention layer, the important emotional words usually obtain lager attention weights (e.g., "criticized", "optimistic") than the other non-affective words (e.g., "its", "report", "as"). These observations reveal that our SynSAN can learn an effective sentence representation for emotion prediction.

5   Conclusion

In this paper, we have proposed a SynSAN model for emotion distribution prediction. It contains a syntax-level self-attention mechanism to leverage the dependency syntactic information and constructs a sentence-level self-attention layer to compose the final sentence representation. Experiments on two public datasets show that the proposed SynSAN can achieve better performance than the state-of-the-art models and also requires much less training parameters. In the future, we would like to study how to further consider more features such as the prior relations between emotions into our methods.

References

1. Alm, C.O., Sproat, R.: Emotional sequencing and development in fairy tales. In: Tao, J., Tan, T., Picard, R.W. (eds.) ACII 2005. LNCS, vol. 3784, pp. 668–674. Springer, Heidelberg (2005). https://doi.org/10.1007/11573548_86
2. Bahdanau, D., Cho, K., Bengio, Y.: Neural machine translation by jointly learning to align and translate. arXiv preprint arXiv:1409.0473 (2014)
3. Deyu, Z., Zhang, X., Zhou, Y., Zhao, Q., Geng, X.: Emotion distribution learning from texts. In: Proceedings of the 2016 Conference on Empirical Methods in Natural Language Processing, pp. 638–647 (2016)
4. Geng, X.: Label distribution learning. IEEE Trans. Knowl. Data Eng. **28**(7), 1734–1748 (2016)
5. Graves, A., Jaitly, N., Mohamed, A.R.: Hybrid speech recognition with deep bidirectional LSTM. In: 2013 IEEE Workshop on Automatic Speech Recognition and Understanding, pp. 273–278. IEEE (2013)

6. Kim, S.M., Valitutti, A., Calvo, R.A.: Evaluation of unsupervised emotion models to textual affect recognition. In: Proceedings of the NAACL HLT 2010 Workshop on Computational Approaches to Analysis and Generation of Emotion in Text, pp. 62–70. Association for Computational Linguistics (2010)
7. Kingma, D.P., Ba, J.: Adam: a method for stochastic optimization. arXiv preprint arXiv:1412.6980 (2014)
8. Klein, D., Manning, C.D.: Accurate unlexicalized parsing. In: Proceedings of the 41st Annual Meeting on Association for Computational Linguistics, vol. 1, pp. 423–430. Association for Computational Linguistics (2003)
9. Kokkinos, F., Potamianos, A.: Structural attention neural networks for improved sentiment analysis. arXiv preprint arXiv:1701.01811 (2017)
10. Li, X., Rao, Y., Xie, H., Lau, R.Y.K., Yin, J., Wang, F.L.: Bootstrapping social emotion classification with semantically rich hybrid neural networks. IEEE Trans. Affect. Comput. 8(4), 428–442 (2017)
11. Li, X., Rao, Y., Xie, H., Liu, X., Wong, T.L., Wang, F.L.: Social emotion classification based on noise-aware training. Data Knowl. Eng. 123, 101605 (2017)
12. Rao, Y.: Contextual sentiment topic model for adaptive social emotion classification. IEEE Intell. Syst. 1, 41–47 (2016)
13. Rao, Y., Li, Q., Wenyin, L., Wu, Q., Quan, X.: Affective topic model for social emotion detection. Neural Netw. 58, 29–37 (2014)
14. Shen, T., Zhou, T., Long, G., Jiang, J., Pan, S., Zhang, C.: DISAN: directional self-attention network for RNN/CNN-free language understanding. In: Thirty-Second AAAI Conference on Artificial Intelligence (2018)
15. Srivastava, N., Hinton, G., Krizhevsky, A., Sutskever, I., Salakhutdinov, R.: Dropout: a simple way to prevent neural networks from overfitting. J. Mach. Learn. Res. 15(1), 1929–1958 (2014)
16. Strapparava, C., Mihalcea, R.: Semeval-2007 task 14: affective text. In: Proceedings of the 4th International Workshop on Semantic Evaluations (SemEval-2007), pp. 70–74 (2007)
17. Tai, K.S., Socher, R., Manning, C.D.: Improved semantic representations from tree-structured long short-term memory networks. In: Proceedings of the 53rd Annual Meeting of the Association for Computational Linguistics and the 7th International Joint Conference on Natural Language Processing, vol. 1: Long Papers), pp. 1556–1566. Association for Computational Linguistics (2015)
18. Vaswani, A., et al.: Attention is all you need. Adv. Neural Inf. Process. Syst. 30, 5998–6008 (2017)
19. Yang, J., Sun, M., Sun, X.: Learning visual sentiment distributions via augmented conditional probability neural network. In: Proceedings of the Thirty-First AAAI Conference on Artificial Intelligence (2017)
20. Yang, Z., Yang, D., Dyer, C., He, X., Smola, A., Hovy, E.: Hierarchical attention networks for document classification. In: Proceedings of the 2016 Conference of the North American Chapter of the Association for Computational Linguistics: Human Language Technologies, pp. 1480–1489 (2016)
21. Zhang, Y., Fu, J., She, D., Zhang, Y., Wang, S., Yang, J.: Text emotion distribution learning via multi-task convolutional neural network. In: Proceedings of the Twenty-Seventh International Joint Conference on Artificial Intelligence, pp. 4595–4601 (2018)
22. Zhao, X., Wang, C., Yang, Z., Zhang, Y., Yuan, X.: Online news emotion prediction with bidirectional LSTM. In: Cui, B., Zhang, N., Xu, J., Lian, X., Liu, D. (eds.) WAIM 2016. LNCS, vol. 9659, pp. 238–250. Springer, Cham (2016). https://doi.org/10.1007/978-3-319-39958-4_19

Hierarchical Multi-view Attention for Neural Review-Based Recommendation

Hongtao Liu[1], Wenjun Wang[1,4], Huitong Chen[1], Wang Zhang[1], Qiyao Peng[1],
Lin Pan[2(✉)], and Pengfei Jiao[3]

[1] College of Intelligence and Computing, Tianjin University, Tianjin, China
{htliu,wjwang,chtcs,wangzhang,qypeng}@tju.edu.cn
[2] School of Marine Science and Technology, Tianjin University, Tianjin, China
linpan@tju.edu.cn
[3] Center for Biosafety Research and Strategy, Law School, Tianjin University,
Tianjin, China
pjiao@tju.edu.cn
[4] State Key Laboratory of Communication Content Cognition, Beijing, China

Abstract. Many E-commerce platforms allow users to write their opinions towards products, and these reviews contain rich semantic information for users and items. Hence review analysis has been widely used in recommendation systems. However, most existing review-based recommendation methods focus on a single view of reviews and ignore the diversity of users and items since users always have multiple preferences and items always have various characteristics. In this paper, we propose a neural recommendation method with hierarchical multi-view attention which can effectively learn diverse user preferences and multiple item features from reviews. We design a review encoder with multiview attention to learn representations of reviews from words, which can extract multiple points of a review. In addition, to learn representations of users and items from their reviews, we design a user/item encoder based on another multi-view attention. In this way, the diversity of user preference and item features can be fully exploited. Compared with the existing single attention approaches, the hierarchical multi-view attention in our method has the potential for better user and product modeling from reviews. We conduct extensive experiments on four recommendation datasets, and the results validate the advantage of our method for review based recommendation.

Keywords: Recommender system · Attention · Review mining

1 Introduction

Recommendation System (RS) is an information filtering system that can learn user preferences according to historical behaviors of users and predict items that user would like or purchase [7]. RS is now widely used on e-commerce platforms such as Amazon and Netflix [7]. Traditional recommendation methods

X. Zhu et al. (Eds.): NLPCC 2020, LNAI 12431, pp. 267–278, 2020.
https://doi.org/10.1007/978-3-030-60457-8_22

are usually based on Collaborative Filtering (CF), which decomposes the user-item rating matrix into latent factors to model the user preference and the item features for rating prediction [6,13,14]. For example, Mnih et al. [13] proposes to learn user and item latent factor from the rating matrix via a probabilistic matrix factorization method. However, these methods only based on rating matrix would suffer from the natural sparsity of the rating data due to the large numbers of users and items [2,5,19].

Therefore, in order to alleviate this problem, many works begin to exploit reviews posted by users to capture user preference and item features. These text reviews contain rich semantic information about users and products, which is useful to learn representations of users and items [2,4,5,8,11]. These methods usually extract features from the reviews to enhance the recommendation phase. For example, DeepCoNN [19] utilizes Convolutional Neural Networks (CNN) to learn the features from reviews as the latent features of users and items. After-wards, Factorization Machine is used to predict the user rating towards the target item. D-Attn [15] introduces the word-level attention to focus on more impor-tant words in reviews and NARRE [2] utilizes the review-level attention and takes review usefulness into consideration. Although the attentions in existing works could help find out the important words or reviews, they usually ignore the diversity of user preference and item features for that these methods based on single attention mechanism would be incapable of capturing the complex semantic information from reviews.

Thus, our approach is motivated by the following observations towards the review influence on user and item representations. First, the same word in a review would be of different informativeness while focusing on different views. For example, suppose there is a review "I like this package, although it is expensive, but the quality is very good", the word "expensive" would be more important than the word "quality" for users who care product price, and less important for users who focus on item quality. Likewise, when representing users or items from their reviews, a review should be differently treated since the user preference and item features are always of diversity. However, existing attention-based methods always learn a single weight for words or reviews, which would be insufficient to explore the complex rating behaviors between users and items.

To this end, we propose a Neural Recommendation model with hierarchical Multi-view Attention (NRMA) to fully exploit diverse features of users and items from reviews. Firstly, we design a review encoder to extract semantic features of a review from words, and propose a multi-view attention model over word level to learn different weights for a word when focusing on multiple views. Afterwards, we propose a user/item encoder to learn the representations of users/items from their reviews. We utilize another multi-view attention network over review level to focus on diverse user preference and item features, and aggregate all repre-sentations of reviews according to the diverse weights of reviews to model users and items. The core of our method is that the query vectors are multiple in both word- and review-level attention modules, which is inspired by the superior abil-ity to capture the multiple semantic meaning of multi-head mechanism in self attention [18]. Different query vectors would indicate different attention points of reviews, users and items. The experimental results on benchmark datasets show that our method can achieve a superior performance in terms of rating prediction compared to recent competitive baseline methods.

2 Related Works

There are many review-based recommendation works proposed. In this section we will introduce the related works in the following two categories.

2.1 Recommendation Models with Reviews

Traditional approaches utilized topic modelling technology such as Latent Dirichlet Allocation (LDA) to extract the semantic feature of reviews [1,12,16]. For example, McAuley et al. [12] learn the latent factors of users and items from reviews via a LDA-like technique. Tan et al. [16] propose a effective rating-boosted method RBLT which integrates the rating-boosted reviews and rating scores together for recommendation. However, the methods suffer from the limitation that the topic modelling ignore the word order and hence is incapable of fully extracting the semantic information in reviews. With the development of deep learning, many works utilize neural network to learn representations of users and items from reviews [4,5,10]. For example, Kim et al. [5] propose to use convolutional neural network to extract features from item reviews, and then combine matrix factorization together (ConvMF) to learn representations of users and items. DeepCoNN [19] adopts a parallel CNN to obtain the features of users and items from their reviews simultaneously.

2.2 Attention-Based Neural Recommendation with Review

The above neural recommendation methods have achieved significant performance, nevertheless they most treat words or reviews equally, and ignore that the reviews contain noise information. Hence, it is necessary to indicate those important words or reviews separately. D-Attn [15] use word-level local and global attention mechanism to select more informative words in the reviews. NARRE [2] utilizes review-level attention to find useful reviews automatically since different reviews are of different importance for users and items. Liu et al. [9] uses a rating-guided attention method to enhance the review learning procedure. Tay et al. [17] propose to use an attention-based pointer network to indicate those useful words and reviews explicitly. Recently, Liu et al. [8] design a mutual attention layer between users and items to learn the relevant semantic information, which could demonstrate the importance words under the user-item pair. However, these attention-based approaches most focus on a single view about a word or a review, which would be difficult to interpret the diversity of user preference and item features as denoted in Sect. 1. Hence in this paper we propose to apply multiple views attention in both word and review level to help select more important words and reviews under different views for users and items.

3   Proposed Method

In this section, we will introduce our method NRMA in detail, which contains three components, a review encoder to learn representations from words, a user/item encoder to learn latent factor from reviews, and a rating prediction module for recommendation. Since the structures of modelling users and items are similar, we will describe the user modelling in the following part. The whole framework of our approach is shown in Fig. 1.

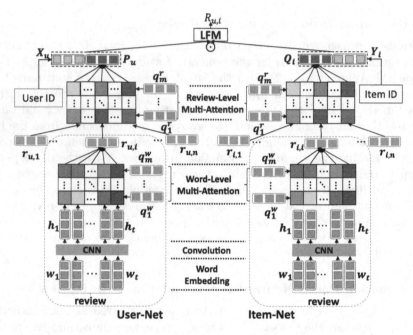

Fig. 1. The framework of our approach *NRMA*.

3.1   Problem Definition

Give the user set U, item set I and the rating matrix $\mathbf{R} \in \mathcal{R}^{|U| \times |I|}$, the entry $R_{u,i}$ denotes that the rating user $u \in U$ has given item $i \in I$. Besides, the review $d_{u,i} = \{w_1, \cdots, w_t\}$ denotes there are t words in the review posted by user u towards item i. The goal in recommendation is to predict the ratings that users would score towards unobserved items.

3.2   Review Encoder

We use the review encoder to learn review representations from words. We firstly utilize word-embedding to map each word in the review into a low-dimensional vector and use Convolutional Neural Networks (CNN) to extract the semantic features from review. Then, we introduce a hierarchical multi-view attention into review encoder to make use of the various information of user preference and item features.

Word Embedding and Convolution Layer. Given a review $d_{u,i}$, we map each word w_k in $d_{u,i}$ into a d_w dimensional vector $\mathbf{w_k}$ via the word embedding technology. Thus, we convert the review text $d_{u,i}$ into a matrix $\mathbf{T_{u,i}} = [\mathbf{w_1}, \mathbf{w_2}, \cdots, \mathbf{w_t}]$. Afterwards, we extract the semantic features from the embedding matrix $\mathbf{T_{u,i}}$ of the review $d_{u,i}$ by convolutional operation:

$$\mathbf{c_f} = \sigma(\mathbf{W_f} * \mathbf{T_{u,i}} + \mathbf{b_f}), 1 \le f \le K, \tag{1}$$

where $*$ is the convolutional operator, K is the number of filters, $\mathbf{W_f}$ and $\mathbf{b_f}$ are the parameters of the f-th filter.

Then we stack the outputs of all filters, denoted as $\mathbf{H} = [\mathbf{c_1}, \mathbf{c_2}, \cdots, \mathbf{c_K}]$. Since we have conduct zero padding on the before convolution layer, the j-th column of $\mathbf{H}$ is the semantic representation of the j-th word in the review $d_{u,i}$, denoted as $\mathbf{h_j}, 1 \le j \le t$.

Multi-view Attention Over Word Level. As each review would contain different aspects, such as price, quality, etc., hence, the same word would output different meanings under different views. Hence inspired by the multi-head mechanism in self attention [18], we adopt the similar attention mechanism to learn representations of multiple views for each review from their words.

As shown in User-Net of Fig. 1, there are m attention view query vectors instead of only one, to indicate the different views of words in review, denoted as:

$$\mathbf{q^w} = [\mathbf{q_1^w}, \mathbf{q_2^w}, \cdots, \mathbf{q_m^w}]^\mathbf{T}. \tag{2}$$

Each view query vector could help point one aspect of words. We define the attention weight of the i-th word in the review under the j-th query vector q_j^w by $\alpha_{i,j}$:

$$\alpha_{i,j} = \frac{\exp(M_{i,j})}{\sum_{i=1}^{t} \exp(M_{i,j})}, \ \alpha_{i,j} \in (0,1), j \in \{1,2,...,m\}, \tag{3}$$

$$M_{i,j} = \mathbf{h_i} \odot \mathtt{FC}(\mathbf{q_j^w}), i \in \{1,2,...,t\}, j \in \{1,2,...,m\}, \tag{4}$$

where $\odot$ is the inner product operator, $\mathtt{FC}$ is a linear transformation for dimension reduction and $\mathbf{h_i}$ is the feature vector of the i-th word.

Afterwards, we utilize weighted summation to obtain the representation of the review under the j-th attention query vector:

$$\mathbf{O}_j^r = \sum_{i=1}^{t} \alpha_{i,j} \mathbf{h_i}, j \in \{1,2,...,m\}. \tag{5}$$

To obtain the more comprehensive representation of the review, we concatenate all the features of the review under different views, denoted as:

$$\mathbf{r}_{u,i} = \mathbf{O_1^r} \oplus \mathbf{O_2^r} \oplus \cdots \oplus \mathbf{O_m^r}, \tag{6}$$

where $\oplus$ is the concatenation operation, $\mathbf{r}_{u,i} \in \mathcal{R}^{m \times K}$ is the final feature of the review $r_{u,i}$ derived from multi-view attentions, which can reflect different views of the review.

3.3   User/Item Encoder

We have obtained the representations of all reviews of the user u via the review encoder:$\mathbf{r}_u = \mathbf{r}_{u,1}, \mathbf{r}_{u,2}, \cdots, \mathbf{r}_{u,n}$, n is the review number of user u, and in the proposed user/item encoder, we aim to learn latent features of users according to their reviews via another attention module.

As users always have various preferences, hence the reviews of a user would have multiple importance when learning user representation from reviews. Similar with the multi-view word-level attention, we apply another multi-view attention network over review level to capture the review importances under different views. Similarly, we define another m query vectors for m views:

$$\mathbf{q}^r = [\mathbf{q}_1^r, \mathbf{q}_2^r, \cdots, \mathbf{q}_m^r]^T . \tag{7}$$

These attention vectors are used to indicate different weights of a review with respect to different preference of the user u. The attention weight $\beta_{i,j}$ of the i-th review of the user u under j-the query vector $\mathbf{q}_j^r$ is denoted as:

$$\beta_{i,j} = \frac{\exp(N_{i,j})}{\sum_{i=1}^n \exp(N_{i,j})}, \; \beta_{i,j} \in (0,1) \, , j \in \{1, 2, ..., m\} \, , \tag{8}$$

$$N_{i,j} = \mathbf{r}_{u,i} \odot \mathrm{FC}(\mathbf{q}_j^r) \, , i \in \{1, 2, ..., n\} \, , j \in \{1, 2, ..., m\} \, . \tag{9}$$

Afterwards, we utilize weighted summation to aggregate all review representations under the j-th attention vector, which is defined as the j-th feature of the user u:

$$\mathbf{O}_j^u = \sum_{i=1}^n \beta_{i,j} \mathbf{r_i} \, , j \in \{1, 2, ..., m\} \, . \tag{10}$$

Then we combine all the m representations derived from multi-view attentions which can reflect user diverse preference as the final representation of the user u, denoted as $\mathbf{P_u}$:

$$\mathbf{P_u} = \mathbf{O}_1^u \oplus \mathbf{O}_2^u \oplus \cdots \oplus \mathbf{O}_m^r . \tag{11}$$

Likewise, we can obtain the representation of item i as $\mathbf{Q_i}$. In this way, the representations $\mathbf{P_u}$ and $\mathbf{Q_i}$ could indicate the multiple latent features of users and items derived from reviews.

3.4   Rating Prediction

In this section we will introduce how to predict the ratings that users would score items based on $\mathbf{P_u}$ and $\mathbf{Q_i}$. Considering that some users or items would have very few or no reviews, motivated by Latent Factor Model (LFM) [6], we introduce the User-ID embedding $\mathbf{X_u}$ and the Item-ID embedding $\mathbf{Y_i}$ as the extra latent factors of user and item. ID embeddings are widely used in recommendation models, which can be viewed as the features of users and items to characterize their own intrinsic properties.

Then we combine the ID embedding and features from reviews of users and items as the final interaction latent feature

$$\hat{O} = (X_u + P_u) \odot (Y_i + Q_i) \,, \tag{12}$$

where $\odot$ is the element-wise sum operator, and the vector $\hat{O}$ is the final representation that integrates the user and item feature.

Based on LFM, the predicted rating $R_{u,i}$ that user u would score towards item i is computed by

$$R_{u,i} = f(W_1^T \hat{O}) + b_u + b_i + \mu \,, \tag{13}$$

where $f()$ is a non-linear activation function (e.g., ReLU in this paper), b_u is the user bias, b_i is the item bias, μ is the global bias and W_1^T is the parameter matrix in LFM.

3.5 Training

We adopt squared loss function to train our rating prediction model:

$$L_{sqr} = \sum_{u,i \in \Omega} (\hat{R}_{u,i} - R_{u,i})^2 \,, \tag{14}$$

where Ω denotes the set of instances for training, and $\hat{R}_{u,i}$ is the ground truth rating assigned by the user u to the item i.

4 Experiments

4.1 Datasets and Experimental Settings

Datasets. We adopt four widely used recommendation datasets from Amazon Review[1] to evaluate the performance, i.e., **Digital Music**, **Office Products**, **Tools Improvement** and **Video Games**. Each dataset contains reviews along with ratings (from 1 to 5) for user-item pairs. Note that all users and items have at least five ratings in the datasets. Besides, following [2], we keep the length and the number of reviews covering 85% percent users and items respectively since there would be a long tail effect. The details of the datasets are shown in Table 1.

We randomly split each dataset into training (80%), validation (10%) and testing sets (10%), and the validation dataset is to tune the hyperparameters.

---

[1] http://jmcauley.ucsd.edu/data/amazon/.

Table 1. Statistical details of the datasets.

Dataset	#users	#items	#ratings	density(%)
Digital Music	5,540	3,568	64,666	0.327
Office Products	4,905	2,420	53,228	0.448
Tools Improvement	16,638	10,217	134,345	0.079
Video Games	24,303	10,672	231,577	0.089

Hyperparameter Setting. In our experiments, the word embedding is pretrained via GloVe, and its dimension is 300. The dimension of the query vectors are set 32. The filter number in CNN is 100 and the window size is set to 3. Besides, the optimal view number of attention in both word and review level is set to 5 among all datasets. We use Adam optimizer to update parameters in our model, and the learning rate is 0.001.

Evaluation Metric. Following previous works, we use Mean Square Error (MSE) as the evaluation metric:

$$MSE = \frac{\sum_{u,i \in \Omega} (\hat{R}_{u,i} - R_{u,i})^2}{|\Omega|} , \tag{15}$$

where $\hat{R}_{u,i}$ is the ground truth rating and $R_{u,i}$ is the predicted rating. The lower MSE, the better performance of the methods.

4.2 Performance Comparison

In this section, we compare our method with recent competitive baseline methods including:

- PMF [13] uses probabilistic matrix factorization to learn user and item latent factor only based on rating matrix.
- DeepCoNN [19] learns users and items representations from their reviews via CNN.
- D-Attn [15] uses word-level attention mechanism to learn representations of users and items from review.
- ANR [3] utilizes aspect-level attention in review documents to point aspect importance for users and items.
- NARRE [2] introduces the review-level attention mechanism to help select useful reviews for modeling users and items.
- MPCN [17] designs a pointer-based network to learn important words and reviews.
- DAML [8] adopts local attention and mutual attention layer to select informative words.

Table 2. MSE comparison of all methods among all datasets.

Methods	Digital Music	Office Products	Tools Improvement	Video Games
PMF	1.206	1.092	1.566	1.672
DeepCoNN	1.056	0.860	1.061	1.238
D-Attn	0.911	0.825	1.043	1.145
ANR	0.867	0.742	0.975	1.182
NARRE	0.812	0.732	0.957	1.112
MPCN	0.903	0.769	1.017	1.201
DAML	0.913	0.705	0.945	1.165
NRMA	**0.792**	**0.699**	**0.943**	**1.104**

The experimental results of MSE are summarized in Table 2. Note that the difference of baselines to our NRMA is statistically significant at 0.05 level. We can have the following observations. First, the review-based methods always outperform PMF, which is only based on rating matrix. The reason is that the reviews contain rich information about users and items. Second, for the neural network approaches, the methods with attention mechanisms (i.e., NRMA, MPCN, DAML, NARRE, ANR, D-Attn) perform better than DeepCoNN. This is because attention mechanism can help select more informative words or reviews for users and items.

Third, our NRMA method achieves the best performance among all datasets and outperforms other state-of-the-art attention-based baselines. These baselines do not take the diversity of users and items into consideration and the single attention model could not fully exploit the rich semantic information of reviews. Our approach utilizes multi-view attention to learn the more comprehensive representations of users/items, which can improve recommendation performance.

Table 3. The effect of the number of views.

Number of Views	Digital Music	Office Products	Tools Improvement	Video Games
1	0.815	0.728	0.968	1.128
5	**0.792**	**0.699**	**0.943**	**1.104**
7	0.829	0.711	0.947	1.204

4.3 Analysis of NRMA

The Effect of Multi Views. Since the core of our method is hierarchical multi-view attention, we further analyze the effect of different numbers of the views, i.e., the number of view query vectors defined in Eq. (2) and Eq. (8). From the results in Table 3, we can find that when the optimal number of views is 5. The reason would be that multi-view attention can capture the multiple aspects of reviews, users and items while single attention models can only focus one aspect for users and items. When the number becomes more larger, the performance will decrease a little, this may because the model of larger size with more parameters would result in overfitting problem.

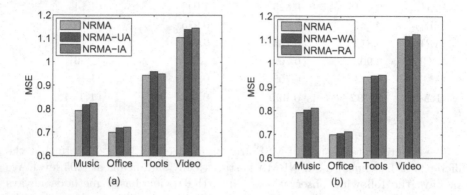

Fig. 2. The effect of our multi-view attention in different components.

Ablation Study. To further explore the effect of our model, we conduct ablation study by removing different attention parts in our NRMA.

We design four variants:

- NRMA-UA: remove the word- and review-level multi-view attention in User Net.
- NRMA-IA: remove the word- and review-level multi-view attention in Item Net.
- NRMA-WA: remove word-level attention in User and Item Net.
- NRMA-RA: remove review-level attention in User and Item Net.

Note that when we remove the attention part, we adopt a normalized constant weight to all words or reviews.

From the results in Fig. 2, we can find that NRMA-UA and NRMA-IA both perform worse than NRMA. This indicates that the multi-view attentions in both User-Net and Item-Net are useful and could improve the performance in recommendation tasks. In addition, we find NRMA outperforms both NRMA-WA and NRMA-RA, which shows that the multi-view attention in word- and review- level can both improve the experimental performance. This is because that the different words and reviews are of different informativeness to represent users and items, and attention mechanism could help select more important words and reviews, which meets the conclusion of previous attention-based approaches.

Our method NRMA composed of UA, IA, WA, and RA can perform best, which indicates the effectiveness of our multi-view attention in recommendation.

4.4   Case Study

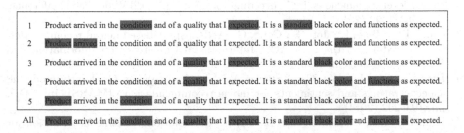

Fig. 3. The multi-view attention weight visualization of a review from Office Products dataset in the User Net.

In this section, we conduct a case study to demonstrate the effectiveness of multi-views attention intuitively. We show an example review from Amazon Office Product in Fig. 3. There are 5 query vectors in our word-level attention, and we select 3 words with the highest weight in the review under each query vector. From the visualization result, we can find that different query vectors can help indicate different important words of the review, which could express different preference of the user. Besides, combining the results of all the query vectors can select more informative words, hence our multi-view attention could learn more comprehensive representations of reviews from words, which would benefit the feature learning of users and items.

5   Conclusion

In this paper, we propose a Neural Recommendation method with Hierarchical Multi-view Attention (NRMA) to learn representations of users and items from review texts. We design a review encoder to learn representations of reviews, and a user/item encoder to learn representations of users and items. We propose two multi-view attention modules both on review encoder and user/item encoder to exploit the rich information of reviews and diversity of users and items. Extensive experimental results verify that our method can effectively improve the performance of neural recommendations, and our multi-view attention could learn more comprehensive representations of users and items.

Acknowledgement. This work was supported by the National Key R&D Program of China (2018YFC0832101), the Tianjin Science and Technology Development Strategic Research Project under Grant (18ZXAQSF00110), National Social Science Foundation of China (15BGL035) and the Science and Technology Project for Livelihood of Qingdao (18-6-1-106-nsh).

References

1. Bao, Y., Fang, H., Zhang, J.: TopicMF: simultaneously exploiting ratings and reviews for recommendation. In: Twenty-Eighth AAAI Conference on Artificial Intelligence (2014)
2. Chen, C., Zhang, M., Liu, Y., Ma, S.: Neural attentional rating regression with review-level explanations. In: Proceedings of the 2018 World Wide Web Conference, pp. 1583–1592 (2018)
3. Chin, J.Y., Zhao, K., Joty, S., Cong, G.: ANR: aspect-based neural recommender. In: Proceedings of the 27th ACM International Conference on Information and Knowledge Management, pp. 147–156. ACM (2018)
4. Diao, Q., Qiu, M., Wu, C.Y., Smola, A.J., Jiang, J., Wang, C.: Jointly modeling aspects, ratings and sentiments for movie recommendation (JMARS). In: KDD, pp. 193–202 (2014)
5. Kim, D., Park, C., Oh, J., Lee, S., Yu, H.: Convolutional matrix factorization for document context-aware recommendation. In: RecSys, pp. 233–240. ACM (2016)
6. Koren, Y., Bell, R., Volinsky, C.: Matrix factorization techniques for recommender systems. Computer **8**, 30–37 (2009)
7. Linden, G., Smith, B., York, J.: Amazon.com recommendations: item-to-item collaborative filtering. IEEE Internet Comput. **7**(1), 76–80 (2003)
8. Liu, D., Li, J., Du, B., Chang, J., Gao, R.: DAML: dual attention mutual learning between ratings and reviews for item recommendation. In: ACM SIGKDD, pp. 344–352. ACM (2019)
9. Liu, H., et al.: Hybrid neural recommendation with joint deep representation learning of ratings and reviews. Neurocomputing **374**, 77–85 (2020)
10. Liu, H., et al.: NRPA: neural recommendation with personalized attention. In: Proceedings of the 42nd International ACM SIGIR Conference on Research and Development in Information Retrieval, pp. 1233–1236 (2019)
11. Lu, Y., Dong, R., Smyth, B.: Coevolutionary recommendation model: mutual learning between ratings and reviews. In: WWW, pp. 773–782 (2018)
12. McAuley, J., Leskovec, J.: Hidden factors and hidden topics: understanding rating dimensions with review text. In: RecSys, pp. 165–172. ACM (2013)
13. Mnih, A., Salakhutdinov, R.R.: Probabilistic matrix factorization. In: NIPS, pp. 1257–1264 (2008)
14. Rendle, S.: Factorization machines. In: ICDM, pp. 995–1000 (2010)
15. Seo, S., Huang, J., Yang, H., Liu, Y.: Interpretable convolutional neural networks with dual local and global attention for review rating prediction. In: ACM Conference on Recommender Systems, pp. 297–305. ACM (2017)
16. Tan, Y., Zhang, M., Liu, Y., Ma, S.: Rating-boosted latent topics: understanding users and items with ratings and reviews. IJCAI **16**, 2640–2646 (2016)
17. Tay, Y., Luu, A.T., Hui, S.C.: Multi-pointer co-attention networks for recommendation. In: Proceedings of the 24th ACM SIGKDD International Conference on Knowledge Discovery & Data Mining, pp. 2309–2318. ACM (2018)
18. Vaswani, A., et al.: Attention is all you need. In: Advances in Neural Information Processing Systems, pp. 5998–6008 (2017)
19. Zheng, L., Noroozi, V., Yu, P.S.: Joint deep modeling of users and items using reviews for recommendation. In: WSDM, pp. 425–434 (2017)

Negative Feedback Aware Hybrid Sequential Neural Recommendation Model

Bin Hao[1], Min Zhang[1(✉)], Weizhi Ma[1], Shaoyun Shi[1], Xinxing Yu[2],
Houzhi Shan[2], Yiqun Liu[1], and Shaoping Ma[1]

[1] Department of Computer Science and Technology, Beijing National Research
Center for Information Science and Technology, Tsinghua University,
Beijing 100084, China
`haob15@mails.tsinghua.edu.cn, z-m@tsinghua.edu.cn`
[2] Zhihu, Beijing, China

Abstract. Content-based (CB) and collaborative filtering (CF) are two classical types of recommendation methods that widely applied in various online services. Recently, sequential based recommender systems achieved good performance. However, how to integrate the advantages of these recommendation systems has not been well studied yet. Besides, most previous algorithms conduct negative sampling for each user based on items the user has not interacted with for model training, while it is unreasonable when there is known users' negative feedback over items. We believe that a user's negative feedback is valuable and should be used to better model users' preferences. In this study, we propose a novel negative feedback aware hybrid sequential recommendation model (NFHS) to take the advantages of these three types of recommendation systems and to directly utilize negative feedback. There are two modules in our algorithm: 1) a static module to model the interaction history and the content features of the user and the current item. 2) a sequence module to distill a user's interaction sequence features, negative feedback has also been directly introduced into this module. The experimental results on two real-world datasets from distinct scenarios demonstrate our model significantly outperforms various state-of-the-art approaches.

Keywords: Neural recommendation model · Negative feedback aware · Hybrid model

This work is supported by the National Key Research and Development Program of China (2018YFC0831900), Natural Science Foundation of China (Grant No. 61672311, 61532011) and Tsinghua University Guoqiang Research Institute. This project is also funded by China Postdoctoral Science Foundation and Dr Weizhi Ma has been supported by Shuimu Tsinghua Scholar Program.

X. Zhu et al. (Eds.): NLPCC 2020, LNAI 12431, pp. 279–291, 2020.
https://doi.org/10.1007/978-3-030-60457-8_23

1   Introduction

Nowadays, information is highly overloaded, and recommendation systems have been widely used in many online web applications, such as E-commerce, job recommendation, and movie platforms.

There are mainly two types of classical recommendation systems: collaborative filtering (CF) and content-based (CB). CF algorithms usually conduct matrix factorization to get user & item embeddings based on user-item interactions. While content based methods often utilize features such as user profiles and item attributes to get items that similar to the ones the user preferred in the past [9]. The two types of recommender systems contribute to the recommendation, and there are many studies try to combine them together. Besides, sequential based recommendation methods achieve good performance recently, as they consider the time-order of user-item interactions and focus on the sequential relationship among the items. Each of the three types of recommendation algorithms has its own advantages, while to the best of our knowledge, most of existing studies integrate two of them. The combination of all the three types of recommendation systems has not been well studied yet.

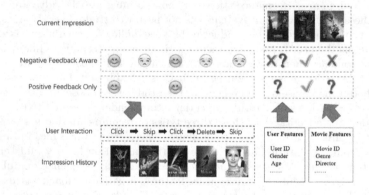

Fig. 1. User interaction sequence and feedback information in recommendation system (taking movies as example).

On the other side, user feedback, which shows user preferences, is very important in system training for the recommendation. For example, a lot of work have been done in recommendation with user implicit feedback [11], which takes some types of user interactions (e.g.: user click, forwarding) as positive feedback. When negative feedback of the users is already recorded in the dataset, it should be directly introduced as negative feedback for model training. While these methods often face the problem of lacking negative feedback (users will not show which items they dislike), so negative sampling is applied to randomly sample some items as negative items. However, though explicit negative feedback is unavailable, we argue that implicit negative feedback (e.g.: user's skip behavior in browsing) should be taken into consideration instead of random sampling.

Figure 1 shows an example of user-item interaction sequence and user feedback in movie recommendation. When the system try to generate a recommendation list for the user with current context, the features of both the user and movies, the user's interaction with the past impression list should be taken into consideration.

Motivated by above findings, we propose a Negative Feedback aware Hybrid Sequence neural recommendation model (NFHS) to combine CF, content-based, and sequential recommender systems with user implicit negative feedback in this study. Firstly, a two-module framework is designed to take advantages from the three types of recommender systems. CF and content-based features are used in static module and sequential features are applied at sequence module. Secondly, to better utilize different types of one-hot features (user/item IDs, user demographic features, item attributes) [3,7], we adopt a Bi-Interaction pooling method [6] to transfer the one-hot embeddings into dense embeddings, which is similar to factorization machine (FM) [12]. Thirdly, different from previous studies, users' implicit negative feedback is adopted as negative samples in model training. Our main contributions are as follows:

- A novel recommendation model named NFHS is proposed in this study. NFHS is able to take the advantages of CF, CB, and sequential recommender systems, which combine user's static preferences and dynamic item sequence features for the prediction task.
- We propose to adopt user implicit negative feedback (such as: skip) as negative samples in model training, which is also used in NFHS model.
- Experimental results on two real-world datasets from Zhihu and Xing demonstrate that our model outperforms various of state-of-the-art approaches significantly.

2 Related Work

2.1 Traditional Recommendation Models

CF and CB are two types of classical methods in recommender systems. CF methods [13] try to predict the utility of items for a particular user based on his/her interaction history. Matrix factorization (MF) [8] is the most popular latent vector-based CF algorithm, which projects users and items into vectors of latent features. The utility of a item to a user is modeled by the inner product result of their latent factors. Koren et al. [8] propose a recommendation model named SVD++, it integrates implicit feedback with explicit feedback to leverage multiple sorts of user feedback for improving user profiling, which improves its accuracy on rating prediction task. He et al. [7] propose a neural CF model which constitute the inner product of the user and the item to a non-linear transformation. Manotumruksa et al. [10] propose a model to capture user-venue interactions in a Collaborative Filtering (CF) manner with users' positive interaction sequence, which enhance the performance of CF. While it does not take user and item content information into consideration.

On another line of research, CB algorithms conduct recommendation based on user/item content features [9]. Some hybrid recommendation models [1] combines CF and content-based methods achieved many progresses. Many hybrid recommendation models use both user ID, item ID, and their content features as inputs and combine CF with content-based model adaptively to take advantage of both recommendation models. For example, Google [3] proposes Wide & Deep model in 2016, which combines the deep neural network and linear model. It works very well but largely rely on manually crafting combinational features. Shi et al. [14] proposes ACCM model in 2018, which can unify both content and historical feedback information in the recommendation. He et al. [6] point out that FM's performance has been limited due to its linearity, they devised a new operation called Bi-linear Interaction (Bi-Interaction) pooling to conduct feature interaction.

Some hybrid methods try to combine CF and CB together, while these models usually ignore the time-order of items user consumed/liked and unable to capture user dynamic preference change from his/her interaction sequences.

2.2 Sequential Interactions in Recommendation System

Sequential interactions of users (e.g. sequences of clicks) play an important role in improving the performance of many recommendation tasks, as they reveal user's dynamic preference. A lot of work focus on sequential recommendation now, such as next-basket [2], next-item [16], and session-based [15] recommendations.

Deep learning techniques, such as recurrent neural network (RNN), are designed to better utilize time-ordered features. Many approaches have been proposed to capture users' interaction history for recommendation. Gated Recurrent Unit network (GRU) [4] is a special kind of RNN and capable of learning long-term dependencies and it requires less computation than Long Short-Term Memory network (LSTM) [5] and achieved state of art performance. However, existing work usually only focuses on user's positive feedback (e.g. click), neglecting user's negative feedback (e.g. impression, delete).

The differences between sequential recommendation models and our NFHS model is that content features, especially user features, are applied in our model. Besides, both positive and negative feedback are taken into consideration.

3   Negative Feedback Aware Hybrid Sequence Neural Recommendation Model

In this section, we will give the problem definition and introduce the proposed NFHS model, which takes all types of features (IDs, content features and interaction sequences) to predict user's feedback toward an item. NFHS model mainly consists of two parts (namely static part and sequence part) to model users' long-term and short-term preferences, respectively.

3.1   Problem Definition

If a user u interacted with a item i, the feedback score of u towards i is defined in Eq. 1. Positive feedback means user u shows interest towards item i, which is reflected in the user's bookmark, click, etc. And negative feedback means user u skipped or deleted item i.

$$r_{ui} = \begin{cases} 1, & positive\ feedback\ happened \\ 0, & negative\ feedback\ happened \end{cases} \tag{1}$$

Given a user set U, an item set I, their content features, and each user's interaction item sequence $S^u = \left\{ S_{i1}^u, S_{i2}^u, ..., S_{|S^u|}^u \right\}$, where $S_i^u \in I$ denotes a user u interacted with an item i. Our target is to predict the feedback score of users towards different items. Formally, this problem is to learn $\hat{r} = f(u, i|\Theta)$, where $\hat{r}$ denotes the predicted score of the feedback r_{ui}, Θ denotes the model parameters, and f denotes the function which maps the parameters to the predicted score.

3.2   Model Overview

The framework of NFHS is illustrated in Fig. 2. The two parts are surrounded by dashed lines in the figure. User and item embeddings are the input of static part and the output is noted as e_{st}, in which content features are applied. The sequential feature is used in sequence part and the output is denoted as e_{seq}. Then, the concatenation of e_{st} and e_{seq} is applied to predict the feedback score p with a hidden layer, as shown in Eq. 2.

$$p = h^T(e_{st} \oplus e_{seq}) \tag{2}$$

where h denotes the hidden layer, $\oplus$ denotes concatenation operation. Besides, several biases (global bias b_g, user bias b_u and item bias b_i) are taken into consideration, so the final predict value of NFHS is calculated by Eq. 3

$$r = p + b_g + b_u + b_i \tag{3}$$

where user bias b_u is the summation of user ID bias b_{uid} and user feature bias b_{uf} as Eq. 4, item bias b_i is the summation of item ID bias b_{iid} and item feature bias b_{if} as Eq. 5.

$$b_u = b_{uid} + b_{uf} \tag{4}$$

$$b_i = b_{iid} + b_{if} \tag{5}$$

3.3   Static Part of NFHS

The input of static part of NFHS is the content features of the user and the item which the user currently interacts with. To better model the interactions between features, we adopt Bi-interaction pooling here [6], which can be regarded as a pooling operation that converts a batch of embedding vectors into one vector.

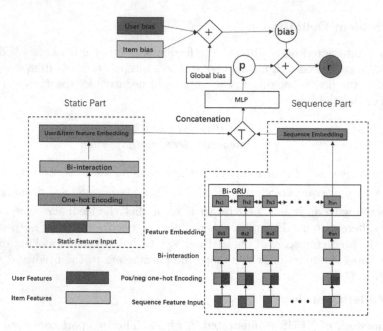

Fig. 2. The architecture of negative feedback aware hybrid sequence neural recommendation model (NFHS).

Bi-interaction calculates the summation of element-wise dot product of every two embedding vectors, as Eq. 6.

$$f_{BI}(V_x) = \sum_{i=1}^{n} \sum_{j=i+1}^{n} x_i v_i \odot x_j v_j \tag{6}$$

Where V_x denotes the set of all feature embedding vectors, $v_i \in V_x$ denotes the ith embedding vector of the features and $x_i \in \{0, 1\}$ denotes the value of the ith value of the one-hot encoding sparse feature vector. $\odot$ means the operation of element-wise production of two vectors, n is the dimension of the one-hot encoding sparse feature vector.

Besides, Bi-interaction pooling method is able to calculate f_{BI} efficiently in linear time [6], and Eq. 6 can be reformulated as Eq. 7:

$$f_{BI}(V_x) = \frac{1}{2} \left[\left(\sum_{i=1}^{n} x_i v_i \right)^2 - \sum_{i=1}^{n} (x_i v_i)^2 \right] \tag{7}$$

As denoted in Eq. 6, Bi-interaction is used for features embedding: The content features of user u and current item i can be turned to very sparse vectors after one-hot encoding. Embedding vectors V_x are generated from the sparse vector, then the sum vector e_{st} of the element-wise product of every two embedding vectors is calculated via Eq. 7 and the sum vector e_{st} can be viewed as the embedding of the content features of the user and current item. Notice that the user ID and item ID are not treated as input feature, since when the user number and item number are huge, the IDs of the user and the item are too sparse to make model underfitting. Instead we use ID biases in Eq. 4 and Eq. 5 to combine the benefits of collaborative filtering.

3.4 Sequence Part of NFHS

The recent n items which the user has recently interacted with are kept in the sequence part of NFHS. n is a hyperparameter of the model. We use the content features of each item i_{sj}, and combine them with the content features of the user u as the input sequence. The features of each node in the sequence are turned into a sparse vector via one-hot encoding. Notice that the same item with positive feedback and negative feedback are treated as different items in the model. By this way, negative feedback is directly introduced to NFHS model. We also use Bi-interaction pooling mentioned in Sect. 3.3 to generate the feature embedding of each node. E_s denotes the total sequence embedding set, $e_{si} \in E_s$ is the embedding of the i-th node of the sequence. Then we treat them as input and use a Bi-directional GRU [4] to generate the final embedding of the sequence part. The final Bi-directional GRU state h_{sn} is treated as the embedding of sequence part e_{eq}.

3.5 Model Learning

Squared loss is chosen as loss function here. In Eq. 8, χ denotes all the training examples, $r^{gt}(x)$ is the ground truth of instance x, $\|\cdot\|$ denotes the l_2-norm, $\lambda \|W\|$ is the regularization term, and W denotes all the variables to be learned from the model.

$$L = \sum_{x \in \chi} (r(x) - r^{gt}(x))^2 + \lambda \|W\|^2 \tag{8}$$

Though neural network models have strong representation ability, they are easy to over-fit the training dataset. So dropout, which is known to be a regularization technique to avoid over fitting, is used in the process of Bi-interaction during feature embedding. Batch normalization is also used in model training.

4   Experiments

In this section, we conduct experiments to answer the following research questions:

1. *Does our proposed NFHS model outperform the state-of-the-art approaches?*
2. *What is the impact of using negative feedback in model training?*
3. *Are all types of input (IDs, contents, sequences) helpful to the performance of NFHS?*
4. *What is the impact of different interaction sequence length?*

Table 1. Statistics of the datasets.

Statistics	Zhihu	Xing
# users	135,089	1,193,996
# items	296,634	613,824
# feedback	13,546,369	26,614,334
Avg. feedbacks per user	100.28	22.29
# positive feedback	3,413,462	5,102,175
# negative feedback	10,132,907	21,512,159
# pos:# neg (feedbacks)	1:2.969	1:4.216

4.1 Experimental Settings

DataSet. Experiments are on two real-world datasets: Zhihu and Xing. Some statistical information is shown in Table 1.

1. Zhihu dataset. This dataset[1] is used for the evaluation challenge of the 24th China conference on information retrieval (CCIR2018). Zhihu is an online knowledge-sharing community. In this dataset, we take click as user's positive feedback and impression (without click) as negative feedback. User and item have abundant features in this dataset.
2. Xing dataset. This dataset[2] is used for recsys challenge 2017 and Xing is a job sharing and recommendation German social networking site. We take impression and delete as negative feedback and other interactions as positive feedback. User and item also have abundant features in this dataset.

For both dataset, we remove the users whose interaction number is less than 20 and sort all the items interacted by each user according to the interaction time. 70%, 10%, and 20% data are divided as training, validation, and test set.

Baselines and Variations of Our Model. We compare our proposed NFHS model with the following state-of-the-art algorithms. Each has been trained and optimized on each dataset. We use the same hidden factor and loss function between NFHS and the baselines.

- **Wide & Deep** [3]: It is proposed by Google in 2016, which combines the deep neural network and linear model. One-hot vectors are directly fed into the wide linear part and embedded in the deep neural part.
- **NFM** [6]: It is Neural Factorization Machine proposed by He and Chua in 2017. A generalized factorization machine which use bi-linear interaction to capture pairwise feature interactions and use deep learning to model higher-order and non-linear feature interactions.

---

[1] https://biendata.com/competition/CCIR2018/.
[2] http://www.recsyschallenge.com/2017/.

- **ACCM** [14]: It is an attentional collaborate & content model proposed by Shi and Zhang in 2018, which can unify both content and historical feedback information in the recommendation.
- **DRCF** [10]: It is a deep recurrent collaborative filtering framework proposed by Manotumruksa in 2017, which can capture user's static and dynamic preferences.

Table 2 shows the comparisons between NFHS and baselines. Our NFHS model takes all features into account, especially directly introduces negative feedback in the model.

Table 2. Comparisons between NFHS, baselines and its variations

Method	ID	Content	Pos sequence	Neg sequence
NFM	✓	✓		
WideDeep	✓	✓		
ACCM	✓	✓		
DRCF	✓		✓	
NFHS	✓	✓	✓	✓

Besides, to better understand the structure of NFHS model, we did ablation study and tested some variations of our model, including **NFHS - ID** (without ID features), **NFHS - sequence** (without sequence features), **NFHS - neg** (without negative sequence features), **NFHS - pos** (without positive sequence features), and **NFHS + ID Emb** (ID features are used in bi-interaction pooling).

Metric and Parameter Settings. AUC (Area Under Curve) and RMSE (Root Mean Squared Error) are chosen as the evaluation metrics in our task. We implemented our NFHS model based on tensorflow. To ensure the usability of the model, the maximum length of sequence N is set to 5 in Zhihu dataset and 1 in Xing dataset. The size of hidden factor of NFHS and baselines is 8 in two datasets, and the batch size of NFHS is 10,240 in both datasets. L2 regularization coefficient is 1e−4 to prevent over-fitting. Besides, the dropout ratio is 0.2 and batch Normalization is conducted in training.

4.2   Model Performance

Overall Performance (RQ1). Table 3 shows the overall performance of NFHS and baselines. From the results, we have following observations:

Our proposed NFHS model outperforms all the baselines significantly, and the reason is that NFHS makes use of all the information contained in Table 2. User and item IDs are used to capture user's interaction history, user and item content features are used to find the content relationship between the user and the current interaction item, both positive and negative feedback is used to help NFHS capture the interacted items sequence features. The NFHS model makes better use of all information than other baselines.

Table 3. The performances of all methods in terms of AUC and RMSE. The best performing result is highlighted in bold. *Denotes the improvement over the baseline is significant (P-value < 0.01)

Algorithm	Zhihu dataset		Xing dataset	
	AUC	RMSE	AUC	RMSE
NFM	0.6909 (+2.95%)*	0.4243 (−3.34%)*	0.8756 (+7.82%)*	0.3215(−21.09%)*
Wide & Deep	0.6938 (+2.52%)*	0.4240 (−3.28%)*	0.8772 (+7.63%)*	0.3233 (−21.53%)*
ACCM	0.6740 (+5.53%)*	0.4281 (−4.20%)*	0.8599 (+9.79%)*	0.3515 (−27.82%)*
DRCF	0.6960 (+2.20%)*	0.4261 (−3.75%)*	0.9168 (+2.98%)*	0.3208 (−20.92%)*
NFHS	**0.7113**	**0.4101**	**0.9441**	**0.2537**

The Impacts of Negative Feedback (RQ2). As mentioned above, NFHS model directly introduces negative feedback to model training. We removed the items with negative feedback in the items sequence input and trained the modified NFHS model (NFHS - neg), the result comparing with the primary one is recorded in Table 4.

From the table, NFHS - neg's performance decreased significantly comparing with NFHS. The reason is that items with negative feedback in the sequence contain more information about what the user dislike.

Table 4. Performance in terms of AUC and RMSE between NFHS and its ablations. The best performing result is highlighted in bold. *Denotes the improvement over the ablation of NFHS is significant (P-value < 0.01)

Algorithm	Zhihu dataset		Xing dataset	
	AUC	RMSE	AUC	RMSE
NFHS-ID	0.6781 (+4.90%)*	0.4269 (−3.94%)*	0.9141 (+3.28%)*	0.2558 (−0.82%)
NFHS-sequence	0.6927 (+2.69%)*	0.4241 (−3.30%)*	0.8932 (+5.70%)*	0.3097 (−18.08%)*
NFHS-neg	0.6947 (+2.39%)*	0.4243 (−3.35%)*	0.9063 (+4.17%)*	0.3090 (−17.90%)*
NFHS-pos	0.6941 (+2.48%)*	0.4240 (−3.28%)*	0.8897 (+6.11%)*	0.3100 (−18.16%)*
NFHS+ID Emb	0.7093 (+0.28%)	0.4203 (−2.43%)*	0.9425 (+0.17%)	0.2555 (−0.70%)
NFHS	**0.7113**	**0.4101**	**0.9441**	**0.2537**

Ablation Study (RQ3). Table 4 shows the performance of NFHS and all its ablation variations. From the results, following observations can be made:

Our proposed NFHS model outperforms all its ablation models. It clearly shows that all these input data contains valuable information which could help

NFHS model to improve its performance. It can also be found that treating user and item IDs the same as content features doesn't improve model performance. The reason is that user and item ID embeddings are very sparse and the model is very easy to under-fitting. It is also very space consuming when the user and item numbers are huge. Besides, we can see that user and item IDs are the most important features in the model, which indicates that personalization is the most important factor in the recommendation.

Impact of Variational Items Sequence Length (RQ4). As the input of the sequence part of NFHS is the recent n items sequence which the user has recently interacted with, and n is a hyper-parameter of NFHS model. We train NFHS model with different n (from 1 to 10). The experiment result is shown in Fig. 3. The black polyline represents NFHS model. The blue polyline represents the best performing baseline.

The results show that the performance of NFHS model becomes better as n increases in Zhihu dataset and the performance of NFHS model has remained stable in Xing dataset. The reason is that the users and items in zhihu dataset have a lot more content features and items sequence in zhihu dataset carries more information to fit the NFHS model as n increases. It is valuable to find that even the items sequence is short (5 in Zhihu dataset and 1 in Xing dataset), NFHS model can already achieve good performance.

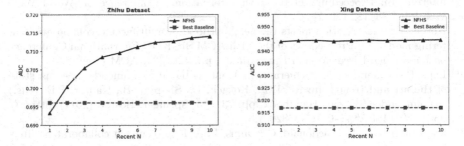

Fig. 3. AUC w.r.t. the max sequence length of recently interacted N items on Zhihu dataset and Xing dataset. The blue polyline represents the best performing baseline (DRCF).

5   Conclusions

In this work, we propose a new negative feedback aware hybrid sequential model that combines the user's static preferences from user & item features and dynamic preferences from user's feedback sequences. We use both positive and negative feedback in our model, and the results reveal that introducing negative feedback can improve the performance of NFHS. We also find when the feedback sequence's length is very short, it can still effectively improve our model performance. The experimental results on two real-world datasets demonstrate the effectiveness of our model by outperforming various state-of-the-art approaches. In the future, we will try different feature embedding method such as BERT and try to model long and short term preference in item sequence. We will also try to introduce new auxiliary information as knowledge graph to our model.

References

1. Burke, R.: Hybrid web recommender systems. In: Brusilovsky, P., Kobsa, A., Nejdl, W. (eds.) The Adaptive Web. LNCS, vol. 4321, pp. 377–408. Springer, Heidelberg (2007). https://doi.org/10.1007/978-3-540-72079-9_12
2. Chen, X., et al.: Sequential recommendation with user memory networks. In: WSDM, pp. 108–116. ACM (2018)
3. Cheng, H.T., et al.: Wide & deep learning for recommender systems. In: Proceedings of the 1st Workshop on Deep Learning for Recommender Systems, pp. 7–10. ACM (2016)
4. Chung, J., Gulcehre, C., Cho, K., Bengio, Y.: Empirical evaluation of gated recurrent neural networks on sequence modeling. arXiv preprint arXiv:1412.3555 (2014)
5. Gers, F.A., Schmidhuber, J., Cummins, F.: Learning to forget: continual prediction with LSTM (1999)
6. He, X., Chua, T.S.: Neural factorization machines for sparse predictive analytics. In: Proceedings of the 40th International ACM SIGIR conference on Research and Development in Information Retrieval, pp. 355–364. ACM (2017)
7. He, X., Liao, L., Zhang, H., Nie, L., Hu, X., Chua, T.S.: Neural collaborative filtering. In: Proceedings of the 26th International Conference on World Wide Web, pp. 173–182 (2017)
8. Koren, Y.: Factorization meets the neighborhood: a multifaceted collaborative filtering model. In: Proceedings of the 14th ACM SIGKDD International Conference on Knowledge Discovery and Data Mining, pp. 426–434. ACM (2008)
9. Lops, P., de Gemmis, M., Semeraro, G.: Content-based recommender systems: state of the art and trends. In: Ricci, F., Rokach, L., Shapira, B., Kantor, P.B. (eds.) Recommender Systems Handbook, pp. 73–105. Springer, Boston (2011). https://doi.org/10.1007/978-0-387-85820-3_3
10. Manotumruksa, J., Macdonald, C., Ounis, I.: A deep recurrent collaborative filtering framework for venue recommendation. In: Proceedings of the Conference on Information and Knowledge Management, pp. 1429–1438 (2017)
11. Oard, D.W., Kim, J., et al.: Implicit feedback for recommender systems. In: Proceedings of the AAAI Workshop on Recommender Systems, vol. 83 (1998)
12. Rendle, S.: Factorization machines. In: IEEE 10th International Conference on Data Mining (ICDM), pp. 995–1000. IEEE (2010)
13. Sarwar, B., Karypis, G., Konstan, J., Riedl, J.: Item-based collaborative filtering recommendation algorithms. In: Proceedings of the 10th International Conference on World Wide Web, pp. 285–295. ACM (2001)
14. Shi, S., Zhang, M., Liu, Y., Ma, S.: Attention-based adaptive model to unify warm and cold starts recommendation. In: Proceedings of the 27th ACM International Conference on Information and Knowledge Management, pp. 127–136. ACM (2018)

15. Wu, S., Tang, Y., Zhu, Y., Wang, L., Xie, X., Tan, T.: Session-based recommendation with graph neural networks. In: Proceedings of the AAAI Conference on Artificial Intelligence, vol. 33, pp. 346–353 (2019)
16. Yuan, F., Karatzoglou, A., Arapakis, I., Jose, J.M., He, X.: A simple convolutional generative network for next item recommendation. In: Proceedings of the Twelfth ACM International Conference on Web Search and Data Mining, pp. 582–590. ACM (2019)

MSReNet: Multi-step Reformulation for Open-Domain Question Answering

Weiguang Han[1(✉)], Min Peng[1(✉)], Qianqian Xie[1], Xiuzhen Zhang[2], and Hua Wang[3]

[1] School of Computer Science, Wuhan University, Wuhan, China
{han.wei.guang,pengm,xieq}@whu.edu.cn
[2] School of Science, RMIT University, Melbourne, Australia
xiuzhen.zhang@rmit.edu.au
[3] Centre for Applied Informatics, Victoria University, Melbourne, Australia
hua.wang@vu.edu.au

Abstract. Recent works on open-domain question answering (QA) rely on retrieving related passages to answer questions. However, most of them can not escape from sub-optimal initial retrieval results because of lacking interaction with the retrieval system. This paper introduces a new framework MSReNet for open-domain question answering where the question reformulator interacts with the term-based retrieval system, which can improve retrieval precision and QA performance. Specifically, we enhance the open-domain QA model with an additional multi-step reformulator which generates a new human-readable question with the current passages and question. The interaction continues for several times before answer extraction to find the optimal retrieval results as much as possible. Experiments show MSReNet gains performance improvements on several datasets such as TriviaQA-unfiltered, Quasar-T, SearchQA, and SQuAD-open. We also find that the intermediate reformulation results provide interpretability for the reasoning process of the model.

Keywords: Open-domain QA · Question reformulation · Neural network

1 Introduction

Due to recent advances in reading comprehension systems, there has been a revival of interest in open-domain Question Answering(QA), where the supporting passages must be retrieved from an open corpus rather than the given inputs. To tackle the scalable open-domain QA problem, one can leverage a retrieval-reader paradigm to make a system [2], in which the answer span can be extracted by a Machine Reading Comprehension(MRC) model. However, the accuracy of the final QA system is bounded by the ability of the search engine in finding the relevant passages for the MRC model [9]. Therefore, an open-domain QA model needs to have the ability to recover from sub-optimal results returned

© Springer Nature Switzerland AG 2020
X. Zhu et al. (Eds.): NLPCC 2020, LNAI 12431, pp. 292–304, 2020.
https://doi.org/10.1007/978-3-030-60457-8_24

Fig. 1. An example of 1 step question reformulation and answer is in boldface. At first, passages retrieved by the search engine don't contain an answer. After one step reformulation, the passages containing answers appear in the returned passage set.

from the search engine since it adopts search engine to tackle a large collection of passages. An example of this problem shows in Fig. 1.

Based on the above observations, we think a general open-domain QA system should have features as follows: **(1) Scalable**, i.e., the scale of the corpus can be arbitrarily expanded without retraining the model. **(2) Interactive**, i.e., inspired by the human QA process, if the initial search results are sub-optimal, a human will iteratively modify the question to increase the appearing probability of answer in search results. **(3) Interpretability**, i.e., the process of question modification should be human-readable. Previous open-domain QA systems do not meet above principles more or less. **(a)** DrQA [2] and BERTserini [28] rely non-parametric TF-IDF retriever, which performs worse than retriever based on neural network. R^3 [24], DocumentQA [4], Multi-Passage BERT [26], DS-QA [16], HASQA [20] and RE^3QA [10] have sophisticated retriever and reader models jointly trained. However, the retriever-reader framework has not introduced interactive design so that they can not recover from initial mistakes. Moreover, the neural retriever has to rank a lot of passages, which limits its application to the larger corpus. **(b)** Lee et al. [15] and Seo et al. [22] introduced fully trainable models that retrieve a few candidates directly from large-scale corpus. These methods find documents independently and match passages in latent space. These methods are scalable but rely on latent space matching thus lack human-readable intermediate output. Moreover, they do not have multi-step interactions with the retriever. **(c)** Das et al. [5] proposed a multi-step retriever-reader interaction model, which re-ranks passages in latent space multiple times. Nevertheless, the process of multi-step interaction is still only understandable by the model.

In this paper, we aim to propose a framework which addresses the above three features simultaneously. We introduce an open-domain QA architecture, MSReNet, in which the reformulator reformulates question and interacts with the search engine to improve the retriever precision and the reader performance. Our model first retrieves and ranks passages related to the question. Whereas the answer might not exist in the initially retrieved passage set, the model would have to combine information across multiple passages [25]. We equip the retriever-reader framework with an additional reformulator based on Gated Recurrent Unit(GRU) [3]. It takes in the ranked passages and generates a new question. Then the retriever uses the new question to create a new passage set, which allows the model to read new passages and combine evidence across multiple passages. After several interactions, the passage set reaches optimal state and the passage reader is triggered to extract answer in the passage set.

To summarize, our paper makes the following contributions: **(1)** We introduce a new framework for open-domain QA in which the reformulator reformulates question and interacts with the search engine in a multi-step manner, which allows it to retrieve and combine information across multiple passages. Thus, our model can be easily integrated with an existing search engine. **(2)** The intermediate reformulation results are human-readable, which provides interpretability for the model's reasoning process. **(3)** Lastly, experiments show improvements in performance and interpretability on various open-domain QA datasets such as TriviaQA-unfiltered, Quasar-T, SearchQA, and SQuAD-open.

2   Related Work

Open-Domain QA is a well-established task that widely attracts researchers' attention. In many open-domain systems [2,28], the retriever is a simple information retrieval pipeline without trainable parameters and recovering from mistakes. Recent works such as R^3 [24], DocumentQA [4], Multi-Passage BERT [26], DS-QA [16], HASQA [20] and RE^3QA [10] using a sophisticated trained retriever have shown improvement on performance. However, they can not scale to full open-domain settings because they only re-rank on a small closed set, and neither do their support multi-step reformulation to recover from initial mistakes due to the pipelined nature of the search process. Lee et al. [15] and Seo et al. [22] introduced fully end-to-end models to retrieve from Wikipedia collections. The work most related to ours is Das et al. [5] which trains a multi-step retriever-reader model using the GRU [3] to regenerate query vector multiple times. Nevertheless, it retrieves passage in a latent space which is not human-readable and is hard to integrate with an existing search engine.

Query Reformulation can date back to days when search engine became popular. Previous works [13,27] augment original query with terms from top-k retrieved documents, which has proven to be an effective search engine artefact. Instead of using handcraft query reformulation methods, Rodrigo and Kyunghyun [19] trains a neural query reformulation model to maximize the recall of information retrieval results by Reinforcement Learning (RL). The most related to our work is Active Question Answering (AQA) [1], which reformulates the question sent to downstream MRC model and aggregates the downstream answers to the user. The main difference between AQA and our work is that our model reformulates question interactively and selects words in documents to query search engine rather than generating sentence using a Seq2Seq [3] model to query the MRC model.

3   Methodology

In this section, we will introduce our framework in details. We first retrieve passages related to the question from the open-domain corpus using **term-based retriever** to narrow the scope to the initial passage set (Sect. 3.1). Next, we rank each passage in the initial passage set and continue to narrow the scope from the initial passage set to ranked passage set by **passage ranker** (Sect. 3.2). At the final step, to recover from initial mistakes, we adopt **multi-step reformulator** to reformulate the question and extract the answer from the refined passage set using **passage reader** (Sect. 3.3 and Sect. 3.4). These components form our open-domain QA pipeline which is illustrated in Fig. 2.

Formally, our model takes a natural language question $Q = (q^1, ..., q^{|Q|})$ consisting of $|Q|$ tokens and a passage collective $\mathbb{P}^c = (P_1, ..., P_i, ..., P_m)$ containing m passages where $P_i = (p_i^1, ..., p_i^{|p_i|})$ is i-th passage consisting $|p_i|$ tokens. Our model extracts a span of text a as an answer to the question from the passage set in $\mathbb{P}^c$.

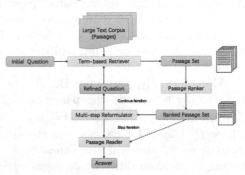

Fig. 2. An overview of our framework. Our framework first retrieves passages related to the question, followed by the passage ranker to generate ranked passage set, which is then adopted in multi-step reformulator to conduct multi-step reformulation. After several iterations, the termination gate sends the "STOP" signal and the passage reader returns the answer span with the highest score.

3.1 Term-Based Retriever

The term-based retriever is a standard procedure in open-domain QA literature [2,14,18]. It can efficiently find relevant passages from a very large corpus without expensive computing overhead. Given a question Q, it is leveraged to retrieve the initial passage set $\mathbb{P}^0(\mathbb{P}^0 \subset \mathbb{P}^c)$ to keep the size of passage set computable for downstream processing.

3.2 Passage Ranker

To narrow the initial passage set $\mathbb{P}^0$, we rank each passage in $\mathbb{P}^0$ with input question using BERT-base [6] model. Under distantly supervised setting, passages containing answer are regarded as positive samples while others are regards as negative samples. Therefore, we feed the question and passage into BERT-base model as $[CLS]Q[SEP]P_i^0$. We then apply an affine layer and a sigmoid activation on the last layer of BERT-base model of the $[CLS]$ token, which outputs a scalar value $\hat{y}_p$. The parameters are updated by the objective function:

$$loss_{ranker} = -\sum_{i \in T_{pos}} \log(\hat{y}_p) - \sum_{i \in T_{neg}} \log(1 - \hat{y}_p) \tag{1}$$

Where T_{pos} is the positive set and T_{neg} is the negative set.

The scalar value $\hat{y}_p$ is regarded as the relatedness score between question and passage, which will be used to sort all upstream passages in $\mathbb{P}^0$. Then, $\mathbb{P}^1$ ($\mathbb{P}^1 \subset \mathbb{P}^0$) will be a narrowed new passage set by selecting top k_p passages having relatedness score higher than threshold value h_p.

3.3 Multi-step Reformulator

To recover from initial sub-optimal retrieval results, we conduct multi-step reformulation on passage set. To be specific, multi-step reformulator takes question Q and passage set $\mathbb{P}_t^1$ as input and outputs a new question Q_t and a termination signal t_t, which facilitates iterative interaction between reformulator model and retrieval model. The reformulated question Q_t is sent back to the term-based retriever which adopts it to retrieve a new passage set $\mathbb{P}_{t+1}^0$ in the corpus, while the termination signal t_t is an indicator of whether the passage reader will execute at the t time step. The architecture of multi-step reformulator is illustrated in Fig. 3.

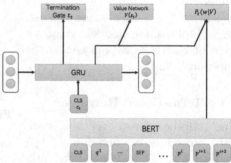

More formally, we apply BERT-base model to encode the passages, $[CLS]Q_{t-1}[SEP]P_1^1 + P_2^1 + ... + P_{|P^1|}^1$, where P_i^1 stands for passage i in the passage set $\mathbb{P}_t^1$ and $+$ means concatenating texts from different passages, and Q_{t-1}(we set $Q_0 = Q$) is the reformulated question at a previous time step. We deem that last layer output of the $[CLS]$ token $c_t \in \mathbb{R}^d$ captures the state information of $\mathbb{P}_t^1$ and feed it into GRU. Thus, we have a new GRU output $o_t = GRU(c_t, h_{t-1})$ $(o_t \in \mathbb{R}^d)$, where h_{t-1} is the hidden state of GRU at the last time step. We avoid normalizing over a large vocabulary by only using terms from the retrieved passages. To be specific, we map o_t to a vocabulary space V which is constructed by passage words in $\mathbb{P}_t^1$, question words in Q_{t-1} and an artefact token <EOS>. And then we sum the attention value which occurs in different place of the text sequence $Q_{t-1} + P_1^1 + P_2^1 + ... + P_{|P^1|}^1$ but shares the same word.

Fig. 3. The architecture of multi-step reformulator.

$$\alpha_j^t = \frac{\exp(o_t \cdot m_j^t)}{\sum\limits_{j'} \exp(o_t \cdot m_{j'}^t)}$$

$$P_t(w|V) = \sum_{i \in I(w,t)} \alpha_i^t, w \in V \tag{2}$$

Where m_j^t is the representation of the last layer of BERT-base encoder at jth word, excluding $[CLS]$ token and $[SEP]$ token, and $I(w,t)$ indicates the positions that word w appears in text sequence $Q_{t-1} + P_1^1 + P_2^1 + ... + P_{|P^1|}^1$. Finally, we sample $P_t(w|V)$ k_w times to formulate a new question Q_t.

Besides, the termination gate t_t is computed by an affine layer and a sigmoid activation on the current GRU state o_t. If t_t is greater than a threshold h_a, the multi-step reformulation will stop, and the passage reader will execute at the t

time step; otherwise, the multi-step reformulator will continue generating a new question Q_t.

Training: To train the parameters, we consider the reformulation as Partially Observable Markov Decision Process (POMDP) [12]. We model the multi-step reformulation under POMDP as follows:

(1) *State*: a state s_t in the state space consists of the entire corpus, the reformulated question trajectory, the term-based retriever, the passage ranker, and the passage reader.

(2) *Observation*: to get the representation of the current state and the memory of last states, we map c_t and h_{t-1} to o_t by GRU.

(3) *Action*: the action is denoted as a_t and the policy π_t which generates question Q_t (a_t in RL literature) can be described by multinomial distribution, where the generation procedure of each unique word is modelled as a $|V|$-side die rolled k_w times.

$$\pi(a_t|s_t;\theta) = Multinomial(P_t(w|V), k_w) \tag{3}$$

(4) *Reward*: at every step, the reward r_{t+1} is measured by how well the passages containing answer are retrieved by the term-based retriever. We use the improvement of the precision score as the reward at each step.

$$r_{t+1} = precision(\mathbb{P}_{t+1}^0) - precision(\mathbb{P}_t^0) \tag{4}$$

(5) *Transition*: the environment evolves deterministically after getting Q_t sent by the multi-step reformulator. Specifically, the term-based retriever and passage ranker will retrieve passage set $\mathbb{P}_{t+1}^1$ for Q_t.

(6) *Termination condition*: to avoid infinite reformulations, we set a lucky step count c_l, which allows the multi-step reformulator to continue reformulating the question when the precision c_l steps after the current maximum precision is equal or greater than current maximum precision. The maximum precision step is termination step T, and we train the termination gate t_t with the supervision of T. Especially, the non-termination steps are regarded as negative samples and termination steps are regarded as positive samples.

Our policy is parameterized by the neural networks. To stabilize training dynamics and strengthen sample efficiency, we maximize the expected return by the PPO algorithm [21]. We treat the reward at each step equally and no discounting is applied.

$$loss_{reform} = loss_{actor} + \alpha_c loss_{critic} - \alpha_p \mathbb{E}_{\pi_{\theta_{old}}}(Entropy(\pi))$$

$$loss_{actor} = \mathbb{E}_{\pi_{\theta_{old}}}[-\min(r_t(\theta)\hat{A}_t, clip(r_t(\theta), 1+\varepsilon, 1-\varepsilon)\hat{A}_t)] \tag{5}$$

$$loss_{critic} = \mathbb{E}_{\pi_{\theta_{old}}}[\frac{1}{2}\hat{A}_t^2]$$

Where $\hat{A}_t = -V_\theta(s_t) + r_t + r_{t+1} + ... + r_{T-1} + V_{\theta_{old}}(s_{\hat{T}})$. $\hat{A}_t$, which is calculated by a two layer value network $V(s_t)$ with RELU activation, is an advantage estimator that does not look beyond time step $\hat{T}$, $r_t(\theta)$ denotes the ratio $r_t(\theta) = \frac{\pi(a_t|s_t;\theta)}{\pi(a_t|s_t;\theta_{old})}$, and $Entropy(\pi)$ is an entropy bonus which encourages the policy network exploring action space sufficiently.

3.4 Passage Reader

To extract the answer span from $\mathbb{P}_T^1$, we follow [6] for answer span prediction modelling. Specifically, we feed question Q and passage set $\mathbb{P}_T^1$ into BERT-base model as $[CLS]Q[SEP]P_1^1 + P_2^1 + ... + P_{|P^1|}^1$, where P_i^1 stands for passage i in passage set $\mathbb{P}_T^1$ and $+$ means concatenating texts from different passage.

$$loss_{reader} = -(\log(\sum_i \hat{y}_i^s) + \log(\sum_i \hat{y}_i^e)) \quad (6)$$

Where $\hat{y}_i^s$ and $\hat{y}_i^e$ are the predicted probability on the distantly supervised start and end positions for the ith passage. For passages without any answers, we set start and end positions to the $[CLS]$ token.

3.5 MSReNet

Training. During training, we first pretrain passage ranker and passage reader by distantly supervised data. To pretrain multi-step reformulator, we set the number of multi-step reformulation steps to 1 and construct pseudo training data by forcing model reconstructing question and answer texts, discarding stop words in constructed texts. After the pretraining coverages, we train our model using PPO. The entire process is summarized in Algorithm 1.

Inference. During inference, we apply greedily policy to decode the reformulated question. The initial question Q_0 is first used to retrieve initial passage set, followed by the passage ranker to generate ranked passage set, which is then adopted in multi-step reformulator to conduct multi-step reformulation. After several iterations, the termination gate sends the "STOP" signal and the passage reader returns the answer span with the highest score.

Algorithm 1. Training

Input: Question text Q, the passage collection $\mathbb{P}^c$, hyperparameters k_p, h_p, h_a, k_w, c_l, α_c, α_p and ε. Experience replay poll E.

Output: Model parameters Θ.

1: Pretrain passage ranker.
2: Pretrain passage reader.
3: Pretrain multi-step reformulator.
4: **for** iteration=1, 2, 3, ... **do**
5:   **for** actor=1, 2, 3, ... **to** N **do**
6:     sample Q in the dataset.
7:     Let $t = 0$, $Q_t = Q$.
8:     **while** not reach termination condition **do**
9:       Retrieve $\mathbb{P}_{t+1}^0$ using Q_t.
10:       Rank $\mathbb{P}_{t+1}^0$ to get $\mathbb{P}_{t+1}^1$.
11:       Randomly sample $\pi(a_{t+1}|s_{t+1}; \theta)$ to get Q_{t+1}.
12:       Computer r_{t+2}.
13:       Let $t = t + 1$.
14:       Store $< Q_t, \mathbb{P}_{t+1}^0, \mathbb{P}_{t+1}^1, Q_{t+1}, r_{t+2} >$ in E.
15:     **end while**
16:   **end for**
17:   Sample minibatch in E and optimize $loss_{ranker}$, $loss_{reform}$ and $loss_{reader}$.
18:   Optimize the termination gate t_t according to the termination condition.
19: **end for**

---

4 Experiments

4.1 Datasets

(1) Quasar-T [7] consists of 43k open-domain trivia questions and their answers obtained from various internet sources.

(2) SQuAD-open [2] is an open-domain version of the SQuAD dataset. We use the 2016-12-21 English Wikipedia dump. 5,000 QA pairs are randomly selected from the original training set as our validation set, and the remaining QA pairs are taken as our new training set. The original development set is used as our test set.

(3) TriviaQA-unfiltered [11] is a version of TriviaQA built for open-domain QA. We randomly hold out 10,000 QA pairs from the original training set as our validation set and take the remaining pairs as our new training set. The original development set is used as our test set.

(4) SearchQA [8] is another open-domain dataset which consists of question-answer pairs crawled from the J! archive. The passages are obtained from 50 web snippets retrieved using the Google search API.

Table 1. Performance on test sets of various datasets. The metric is rounded one decimal place and * indicates the result is obtained from [5].

	Quasar-T		SearchQA		TrivalQA-unfiltered		SQuAD-open	
	EM	F1	EM	F1	EM	F1	EM	F1
AQA [1]			40.5	47.4				
R^3 [24]	35.3	41.7	49.0	55.3	47.3	53.7	29.1	37.5
DS-QA* [16]	37.3	43.6	58.5	64.5	48.7	56.3	28.7	36.6
Dr.QA* [2]	36.9	45.5	51.4	58.2	48.0	52.1	27.1	
Multi-step reasoner [5]	40.6	47.0	56.3	61.4	55.9	61.7		
DocumentQA* [4]					61.6	68.0		
Multi-Passage BERT (Base) [26]	51.3	59.0	**65.2**	**70.6**	62.0	67.5	51.2	59.0
ORQA [15]					45.0		20.2	
DENSPI-Hybrid [22]							36.2	44.4
BERTserini [28]							38.6	46.1
HASQA [20]					63.6	68.9		
RE^3QA (base) [10]					**64.1**	**69.8**	40.1	48.4
Ours	**52.2**	**60.1**	63.1	68.3	61.7	67.3	**51.7**	**60.5**

4.2 Basic Settings

For simplicity, we use Elasticsearch as our term-based retriever and BM25 as ranking function. For each dataset, the articles are pre-segmented into segments by sliding window with windows size 100 words and stride 50 words, and each segment is indexed and treated as a "passage".

If not specified, the pre-trained BERT-base model with default hyper-parameters is adopted. We set k_p to 5, h_p to 0.6, h_a to 0.8, k_w to 7, c_l to 2, α_c to 0.5, α_p to 0.01 and ε to 0.2. The optimizer is AdamW [17] with learning rate of 3e−5 and learning rate warmup is applied over the first 10% steps, and linear decays of the learning rate until converges. We use batch size of 32. The sequences longer than 512 are truncated to 512. For multi-step reformulator, we employ truncated backpropagation through time [23] to train the model. We restrict our max reformulation steps up to 5. During training, the passage ranker ranks top 10 passages. During testing, the passage ranker ranks top 20 passages. Following Chen et al. [2], we adopt EM and F1 as our evaluation metrics.

4.3 Overall Performance

Table 1 compares the performance of our model with various competitive base-lines on four open-domain datasets. One of main observation is that our model performs better than ORQA and DENSPI-Hybrid, which indicates that retrieval in latent space is inferior to lexical matching and multi-step reformulation. More-over, on the SQuAD-open and Quasar-T datasets, our model improves at least 0.5 EM and 1.1 F1 scores than the state-of-art. On the SearchQA and TrivalQA-unfiltered datasets, our methods also yield competitive performance.

4.4 Model Analysis

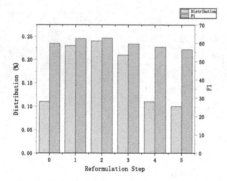

Fig. 4. Distribution of reformulation step and associated F1 score of each step on SQuAD-open dataset. We limit the maximum reformulation step to 5.

Table 2. Retrieval performance on Quasar-T. For our retriever (initial), we report precision after passage ranking, and for our retriever (multi-step), we report precision on the last reformulation step.

Model	P@1	P@3	P@5
R^3 [24]	40.3	51.3	54.5
Multi-step reasoner [5]	42.9	55.5	59.3
Our retriever (initial)	45.1	57.8	63.7
Our retriever (multi-step)	**47.7**	**61.3**	**64.2**

Large Scale Experiment. Although there are average 100 passages for each question in the benchmark datasets, it is still not adequate for real open-domain applications since the size of the evidence corpus is much bigger. To test the

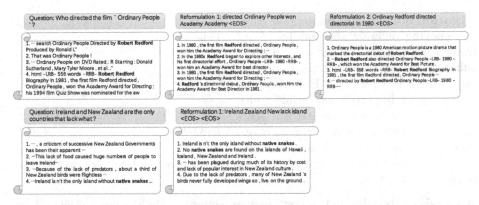

Fig. 5. Examples of how multi-step reformulator iteratively modifies the question by reading passages to find more evidence (discarding overlapping segments) and answers are in boldface. Figure (top) shows an example where the reformulator recovers from a partially correct answer. Figure (bottom) shows an example where the initially retrieved passages containing answer are ranked at the bottom of the results. After reformulation, golden passages are ranked at top of the results.

ability of manipulating search engine, we create Trivia-QA-open setting. For any question, we combine all evidence passages in the development set, resulting in a passage set containing about 1.6M passages for each question. Our model achieves a score of EM $-$ 41.3 and F1 $-$ 45.6. This indicates that: **(1)** our model is capable to deal with large scale corpus with an existing search engine. **(2)** the overall performance decreases compared to closed passage set setting (from 67.3 to 45.6 F1), which indicates that the open-domain QA under open setting is more complicated than the closed setting.

Retrieval Performance. We investigate the performance of our retrieval model. Our retriever is based on term-based retriever, passage ranker and multi-step reformulator. Results in Table 2 demonstrate that our retriever performs better than other models. Moreover, we also measure the performance of our reformulator reformulating the question after a few steps. As shown in Table 2, the question reformulation results in better P@k than the initial model. It proves that reformulation can benefit the overall performance of our model.

Number of Reformulation Steps. We analyze the multi-step reformulation ability of our model on SQuAD-open dataset. Figure 4 shows the distribution of reformulation step associated with the F1 score of each step. We find that our model prefers to stop at 2nd step, at which the model gains the best F1 score, while a greater or less step will yield a worse result. We conjecture that when the reformulation step is less than 2, the model has not collected enough evidence to answer the question. Whereas when reformulation step is greater than 2, there is too much noise in reformulated question to retrieve the passages, which undermines the F1 score.

Ablation Study. Table 3 shows the effect of removing different submodules of our framework and the importance of these submodules. We can find that our passage ranker gives us 16.5 EM score and 15.0 F1 score improvements, while multi-step reformulator gives us 2.0 EM score and 1.4 F1 score improvements. This verifies that passage ranker is an indispensable submodule in our framework, while multi-step reformulator ices on the cake of our framework.

Table 3. Retrain ablations on Quasar-T dataset.

Model	EM	F1
w/o multi-step reformulator	50.2	58.7
w/o passage ranker	35.7	45.1
Full model	52.2	60.1

Analysis of Results. In this section, we are interested in how our model gathers evidence and reformulates the question. We conduct this study on Quasar-T test set. The retrieved results are then ranked by passage ranker. As depicted in Fig. 5, the results improve after several reformulations. Although correct answers are not ranked at top of the results at first, our method can retrieve more evidence passages once words related to answers are fetched.

5   Conclusion

This paper introduces a new framework for open-domain QA in which the reformulator reformulates question and interacts with the search engine, to improve the retriever precision and the reader performance. We also show our model can be easily integrated with an existing search engine. Moreover, we investigate the intermediate reformulated question to show the interpretability of the reasoning process in our model. Finally, our model brings an increase in performance to popular and widely used open-domain QA datasets. In the future, we plan to consider inter-correction among passages for open-domain QA and integrate query-agnostic [15,22] model into our framework.

Acknowledgement. We thanks anonymous reviewers for their precious comments. This research is supported by the National Key R&D Program of China (Grant No. 2018YFC1604000 and No. 2018YFC1604003) and Natural Science Foundation of China (NSFC) (Grant No. 71950002 and No. 61772382).

References

1. Buck, C., et al.: Ask the right questions: active question reformulation with reinforcement learning. arXiv preprint arXiv:1705.07830 (2017)
2. Chen, D., Fisch, A., Weston, J., Bordes, A.: Reading wikipedia to answer open-domain questions. arXiv preprint arXiv:1704.00051 (2017)
3. Cho, K., et al.: Learning phrase representations using RNN encoder-decoder for statistical machine translation. arXiv preprint arXiv:1406.1078 (2014)
4. Clark, C., Gardner, M.: Simple and effective multi-paragraph reading comprehension. arXiv preprint arXiv:1710.10723 (2017)

5. Das, R., Dhuliawala, S., Zaheer, M., McCallum, A.: Multi-step retriever-reader interaction for scalable open-domain question answering. arXiv preprint arXiv:1905.05733 (2019)
6. Devlin, J., Chang, M.W., Lee, K., Toutanova, K.: Bert: pre-training of deep bidirectional transformers for language understanding. arXiv preprint arXiv:1810.04805 (2018)
7. Dhingra, B., Mazaitis, K., Cohen, W.W.: Quasar: datasets for question answering by search and reading. arXiv preprint arXiv:1707.03904 (2017)
8. Dunn, M., Sagun, L., Higgins, M., Guney, V.U., Cirik, V., Cho, K.: SearchQA: a new Q&A dataset augmented with context from a search engine. arXiv preprint arXiv:1704.05179 (2017)
9. Htut, P.M., Bowman, S.R., Cho, K.: Training a ranking function for open-domain question answering. arXiv preprint arXiv:1804.04264 (2018)
10. Hu, M., Peng, Y., Huang, Z., Li, D.: Retrieve, read, rerank: towards end-to-end multi-document reading comprehension. In: Proceedings of the 57th Annual Meeting of the Association for Computational Linguistics, Florence, Italy, pp. 2285–2295. Association for Computational Linguistics, July 2019. https://doi.org/10.18653/v1/P19-1221, https://www.aclweb.org/anthology/P19-1221
11. Joshi, M., Choi, E., Weld, D.S., Zettlemoyer, L.: TriviaQA: a large scale distantly supervised challenge dataset for reading comprehension. arXiv preprint arXiv:1705.03551 (2017)
12. Kaelbling, L.P., Littman, M.L., Cassandra, A.R.: Planning and acting in partially observable stochastic domains. Artif. Intell. **101**(1–2), 99–134 (1998)
13. Lavrenko, V., Croft, W.B.: Relevance-based language models. In: ACM SIGIR Forum, vol. 51, pp. 260–267. ACM, New York (2017)
14. Lee, J., Yun, S., Kim, H., Ko, M., Kang, J.: Ranking paragraphs for improving answer recall in open-domain question answering. arXiv preprint arXiv:1810.00494 (2018)
15. Lee, K., Chang, M.W., Toutanova, K.: Latent retrieval for weakly supervised open domain question answering. arXiv preprint arXiv:1906.00300 (2019)
16. Lin, Y., Ji, H., Liu, Z., Sun, M.: Denoising distantly supervised open-domain question answering. In: Proceedings of the 56th Annual Meeting of the Association for Computational Linguistics (Volume 1: Long Papers), pp. 1736–1745 (2018)
17. Loshchilov, I., Hutter, F.: Fixing weight decay regularization in Adam (2018)
18. Nie, Y., Chen, H., Bansal, M.: Combining fact extraction and verification with neural semantic matching networks. In: Proceedings of the AAAI Conference on Artificial Intelligence, vol. 33, pp. 6859–6866 (2019)
19. Nogueira, R., Cho, K.: Task-oriented query reformulation with reinforcement learning. arXiv preprint arXiv:1704.04572 (2017)
20. Pang, L., Lan, Y., Guo, J., Xu, J., Su, L., Cheng, X.: Has-QA: hierarchical answer spans model for open-domain question answering. In: Proceedings of the AAAI Conference on Artificial Intelligence, vol. 33, pp. 6875–6882, June 2019. https://doi.org/10.1609/aaai.v33i01.33016875
21. Schulman, J., Wolski, F., Dhariwal, P., Radford, A., Klimov, O.: Proximal policy optimization algorithms. arXiv preprint arXiv:1707.06347 (2017)
22. Seo, M., Lee, J., Kwiatkowski, T., Parikh, A.P., Farhadi, A., Hajishirzi, H.: Real-time open-domain question answering with dense-sparse phrase index. arXiv preprint arXiv:1906.05807 (2019)
23. Sutskever, I.: Training recurrent neural networks. University of Toronto Toronto, Ontario, Canada (2013)

24. Wang, S., et al.: R3: reinforced ranker-reader for open-domain question answering. In: Thirty-Second AAAI Conference on Artificial Intelligence (2018)
25. Wang, S., et al.: Evidence aggregation for answer re-ranking in open-domain question answering. arXiv preprint arXiv:1711.05116 (2017)
26. Wang, Z., Ng, P., Ma, X., Nallapati, R., Xiang, B.: Multi-passage Bert: a globally normalized bert model for open-domain question answering. arXiv preprint arXiv:1908.08167 (2019)
27. Xu, J., Croft, W.B.: Quary expansion using local and global document analysis. In: ACM SIGIR Forum, vol. 51, pp. 168–175. ACM, New York (2017)
28. Yang, W., et al.: End-to-end open-domain question answering with BERTserini. arXiv preprint arXiv:1902.01718 (2019)

ProphetNet-Ads: A Looking Ahead Strategy for Generative Retrieval Models in Sponsored Search Engine

Weizhen Qi[1]([✉]), Yeyun Gong[2], Yu Yan[3], Jian Jiao[3], Bo Shao[4], Ruofei Zhang[3], Houqiang Li[1], Nan Duan[2], and Ming Zhou[2]

[1] University of Science and Technology of China, Hefei, China
{weizhen,lihq}@mail.ustc.edu.cn
[2] Microsoft Research Asia, Beijing, China
{yegong,nanduan,mingzhou}@microsoft.com
[3] Microsoft, Redmond, USA
{yyua,jian.jiao,bzhang}@microsoft.com
[4] Sun Yat-sen University, Guangzhou, China
shaobo2@mail2.sysu.edu.cn

Abstract. In a sponsored search engine, generative retrieval models are recently proposed to mine relevant advertisement keywords for users' input queries. Generative retrieval models generate outputs token by token on a path of the target library prefix tree (Trie), which guarantees all of the generated outputs are legal and covered by the target library. In actual use, we found several typical problems caused by Trie-constrained searching length. In this paper, we analyze these problems and propose a looking ahead strategy for generative retrieval models named ProphetNet-Ads. ProphetNet-Ads improves the retrieval ability by directly optimizing the Trie-constrained searching space. We build a dataset from a real-word sponsored search engine and carry out experiments to analyze different generative retrieval models. Compared with Trie-based LSTM generative retrieval model proposed recently, our single model result and integrated result improve the recall by 15.58% and 18.8% respectively with beam size 5. Case studies further demonstrate how these problems are alleviated by ProphetNet-Ads clearly.

Keywords: Sponsored search engine · Generative retrieval model · Keywords extension · Information retrieval · Natural language generation

1 Introduction

In a sponsored search engine, search queries from the user are expanded to appropriate advertisements (Ads) keywords. Advertisers bid on triggered keywords to display their ads and pay by click. The primary income for a sponsored search

Work is done during internship at Microsoft Research Asia.

engine is to provide ads that users potentially need. Therefore the applications of keywords extension from queries to relevant keywords in the ads library are deeply concerned. At the beginning, search engines trigger ads when the queries are identical with an ads keyword. Then, methods like Information retrieval (IR) with quality filter [4] are commonly used to recall more relevant keywords. However, traditional IR techniques are unable to fill the semantic gap between queries and ads keywords. Thus sponsored search engines pay much attention on how to excavate more semantic-related keywords. A solution is to re-write the initial user queries to a range of intermediate queries and then combine all the outcomes retrieved from them, such as [5] from Yahoo, [11] from Google, and [1] from Microsoft. Re-writing strategies are widely used because directly extending queries to keywords will lead to the low-efficiency problem: very few extensions are included in the keywords library. Recently [9] used Trie-based LSTM model to address this problem by constraining the generation searching space. Trie means a prefix tree. Trie-based NLG models generate tokens on paths of a Trie to make sure outputs are covered by the keywords library.

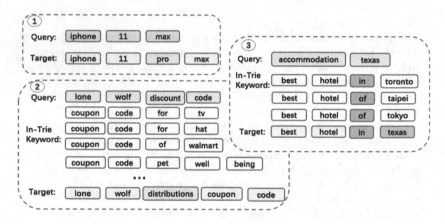

Fig. 1. In example 1, "pro" is a noise word with low generation score if NLG model is not trained on this data. In example 2, generative retrieval models will be easily trapped into the common prefix "coupon code xxx". In example 3, both "in" and "of" have high generation scores but "of" has no desired suffix "texas".

However, simply adding a Trie constraint to a natural language generation (NLG) model is not enough, and we found several common problems in daily use. The biggest problem of Trie-based generative retrieval model is that it cannot utilize global information. We list three examples in Fig. 1. The first problem is that noise tokens will have a very low generation score thus lead to a wrong searching path. A second common problem is called "common prefix has no target object in the future tokens", which implies that the entire beam search space is filled with common prefixes. Although these prefixes may compose good keywords, sometimes expected suffixes are not in the Trie to compose desired keywords. We cannot simply throw these sequences from beam search unfinished queue as these prefixes are really "common" and take a portion of good results. The last problem is that models are hard to decide which one is better when several tokens have similar high generation scores. For keywords extension, models have no idea which suffix will lead to desired keywords in a Trie.

Inspired by ProphetNet [15], which is able to predict next several tokens simultaneously, we propose ProphetNet-Ads to alleviate above problems with the future information. ProphetNet is proposed as a new pre-training architecture to predict next n-grams. ProphetNet-Ads employs the future tokens' scores to look ahead several steps in the Trie, which directly optimizes the searching space. With Trie-based beam search, the next token to generate is constrained to possible suffixes of the decoded hypothesis according to the Trie. ProphetNet-Ads is proposed for better selection of the suffixes. ProphetNet-Ads modifies the predicting tokens' scores as a weighted sum of its generation score and future information scores to optimize the searching space. We rank the decoding hypothesis with the modified scores, but store the unchanged sentence scores, which optimizes searching space and meantime keeps the scores consistent to original NLG model. The experimental results show that our proposed strategies recall more relevant keywords with an obvious improvement. Case studies further demonstrate how ProphetNet-Ads alleviates these typical problems.

2   Background

ProphetNet
ProphetNet [15] is recently proposed as a new pretraining NLG architecture. To alleviate strong local correlations such as bi-gram combination and enhance the hidden states to contain more global information, next n-grams are trained to predict. ProphetNet employs n-stream self-attention to support next n-grams from any starting positions in a given output are trained to predict simultaneously. Although next n-grams are explicitly used in the training procedure, only the next first token is predicted in the inference procedure like traditional NLG models. These future tokens' scores can be used to point out whether the next first token has desired information in a Trie.

Trie-Based NLG
A Trie is a prefix tree, and a path from the starting token to an internal node denotes a prefix of a sequence, a path from the starting token to a leaf node denotes a complete sequence. Suppose the already decoded token sequence is a prefix of a legal keyword sequence, then it must be a route in Trie, and we generate next tokens from the suffix nodes of this route. In this manner, all of the generated outputs are in-library. Trie-based inference have been successfully used in NLG tasks in recent years [6,7,9,16]. [6] firstly used Trie to constrain the model output candidates for email replying task. It can also been seen as picking responses from already given sentences in a Trie for any given email.

Keywords Extension for Sponsored Search Engine

Sponsored search engine service providers are deeply concerned with the task of extending users' input queries into ads keywords. Researches are carried out to fill the semantic gap between queries and ads keywords. One solution is to re-write the initial user queries to intermediate queries to retrieve keywords, such as [1,5,11]. With the improvement of NLG techniques, [3] used LSTM to train the re-writing model, utilizing the deep learning network for better semantic modeling ability. [8] from Microsoft directly trained a NLG model to generate candidate ads keywords. Even though the NLG model's outputs are highly qualified, however, they have a high likelihood to be out of the target set. Recently [9] used Trie-based NLG model to overcome the low-efficiency barrier by restricting the search space, and this methodology brought a considerable enhancement for their system with an additional 10% revenue each year.

3   ProphetNet-Ads

Based on ProphetNet which is able to predict more future tokens, we propose an explicit looking ahead strategy named ProphetNet-Ads as a possible solution for problems discussed in the introduction. ProphetNet-Ads modifies the scores of the next first predicting tokens by looking ahead future tokens' scores and directly optimizes the searching space. Figure 2 shows an illustration of ProphetNet-Ads generation procedure.

ProphetNet-Ads modifies the in-Trie suffix tokens' scores with the information of its future tokens when beam searching on a Trie. We look ahead ℓ steps, where ℓ is usually $n-1$ for a ProphetNet n-gram generation model, since we can generate n tokens simultaneously, the next first predicting token, and $n-1$ future tokens to look ahead for this suffix. A residual weight λ is set to control the weight of next token's generation score and its looking ahead score.

As shown in Fig. 2, a Bi-gram ProphetNet is able to generate next two tokens' generation scores at each time step, and we can call them g_1, g_2. We refer the previous decoded sequence as seq, and next first suffixes of seq as $s1$. For each node ρ_1 in $s1$, one step further suffixes of ρ_1 are noted as $s2$. The generation score of next first token ρ_1 is modified as:

$$g_1[\rho_1] = \lambda \times g_1[\rho_1] + (1 - \lambda) \times max(g_2[s_2]) \tag{1}$$

For example, the step scores for the suffixes we are predicting from Fig. 2 are modified as:

$$g_1[\text{``}in\text{''}] = \lambda \times g_1[\text{``}in\text{''}] + (1 - \lambda) \times max(g_2[\text{``}toronto\text{''}], g_2[\text{``}texas\text{''}])$$
$$g_1[\text{``}of\text{''}] = \lambda \times g_1[\text{``}of\text{''}] + (1 - \lambda) \times g_2[\text{``}tokyo\text{''}] \tag{2}$$

Similarly, a n-gram generation model could output the probability distributions of next n tokens as $g_1, g_2, ...g_n$. We use a recursive function to modify their scores from the furthest to the nearest next first tokens' scores. Scores of g_{n-1} are modified with their highest children nodes' scores in g_n, and then be used

---

Algorithm 1: N-gram ProphetNet-Ads Trie-based Searching

---

input : Beam Size b, n-gram ProphetNet $\mathcal{P}$, Trie T, Residual weight λ, Input query X, max output token length l

output: Keywords extensions π

alive buffer: $\mathcal{H} \leftarrow \emptyset$; finished buffer: $\pi \leftarrow \emptyset$; // with [hypothesis, scores]

put [bos, score_bos] in $\mathcal{H}$;   // Initialize the alive buffer

while $best\_alive\_score \geq worst\_alive\_score$ and $decoded\_length < l$ **do**

    $\mathcal{O}_{sen} \leftarrow \emptyset$;   // Original sentence scores to be stored in $\mathcal{H}$

    $\mathcal{M}_{sen} \leftarrow \emptyset$;   // Modified sentence scores to be ranked temporarily

    for seq in $\mathcal{H}$ **do**

        $[g_1, g_2, ..., g_n] \leftarrow \mathcal{P}(seq, X)$;   // Next future n tokens' scores

        $s_1, m_1 \leftarrow T(seq)$;   // $s1$: suffix tokens, $m1$: mask vector

        $\mathcal{O}_{token} = \mathcal{M}_{token} = g_1 + m_1$;   // Mask the tokens out of Trie

        for ρ_1 in s_1 ;   // Start looking ahead

        do

            $s_2, m_2 \leftarrow T(seq + \rho_1)$;

            for ρ_2 in $s2$;   // Could be replaced with recursive function

            do

                $s_3, m_3 \leftarrow T(seq + \rho_1 + \rho_2)$;

                for $\rho_{...}$ in $s_{...}$ **do**

                    ...;

                    for ρ_{n-1} in s_{n-1} **do**

                        // Modify scores from the farthest nodes

                        $s_n, m_n \leftarrow T(seq + \rho_1 + \rho_2 + ... + \rho_{n-1})$;

                        $g_{n-1}[\rho_{n-1}] = \lambda \times g_{n-1}[\rho_{n-1}] + (1 - \lambda) \times max(g_n + m_n)$;

                    end

                ...;

            end

            $g_2[\rho_2] = \lambda \times g_2[\rho_2] + (1 - \lambda) \times max(g_3 + m_3)$;

        end

        // Modify scores until the next first token

        $\mathcal{M}_{token}[\rho_1] = \lambda \times \mathcal{O}_{token}[\rho_1] + (1 - \lambda) \times (max(g2 + m2))$;

        end

        // Calculate new sentence scores with previous decoded score

            and next first tokens' step score

        $\mathcal{O} \leftarrow func(seq.score, \mathcal{O}_{token})$ put $\mathcal{O}$ into $\mathcal{O}_{sen}$;   // Original scores

        $\mathcal{M} \leftarrow func(seq.score, \mathcal{M}_{token})$ put $\mathcal{M}$ into $\mathcal{M}_{sen}$ // Modified scores

    end

    // Rank with modified scores but store their original scores

    $new\_seqs, id \leftarrow top\_b\_of(\mathcal{M}_{sen})$,

    $new\_finished\_seqs, id\_f \leftarrow top\_b\_of(\pi.socres, \mathcal{M}_{sen}.eos)$;

    $\mathcal{H} \leftarrow new\_seqs, \mathcal{O}_{sen}[id]$;

    $\pi \leftarrow new\_finished\_seqs, \mathcal{O}_{sen}[id\_f]$;

end

return π;

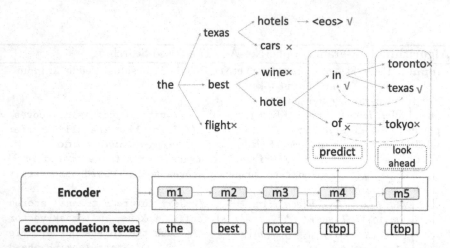

Fig. 2. An example of Bi-gram ProphetNet-Ads. When generating next token for "the best hotel", "in" and "of" are its suffix tokens according to the Trie. Though both of them are good suffixes to generate, "of" has no future tokens with high score, while future tokens of "in" cover desired token "texas". Thus "in" is generated.

to modify g_{n-2}, until next first tokens' scores g_1 are modified. Then, the best token in g_1 is chosen. Considering a high-confidence suffix before explicit looking ahead strategy, if it has no good tokens steps further, a low future score will be passed backward. On the opposite if there are any noise tokens in suffix but with expected tokens in the future, further high-confidence scores will also be passed across the noise to give a bonus for the token we are predicting.

However, if we directly use the modified generation tokens' score g_1 to calculate decoded sequence scores in beam search, results are inconsistent with the generation model as it modifies the output sequences scores, which could bring error accumulation. Thus, we only use the modified scores to rank and pick the best sequences, but store their original scores. ProphetNet-Ads not only optimizes the searching space but also keeps the scores consistent to the generation model. The algorithm of ProphetNet-Ads is described in Algorithm 1.

4   Experiment

In this section, we introduce the dataset and implementations of models to validate ProphetNet-Ads. Since ProphetNet only releases its Bi-gram uncased pretrainied checkpoint[1] for now, for fair comparison, in this paper the Uni-gram to Tri-gram ProphetNet or ProphetNet-Ads are finetuned in ProphetNet architecture but without pretraining.

---

[1] https://github.com/microsoft/ProphetNet.

4.1   Dataset

The keywords extension dataset is collected from Bing search engine keywords extension library, formed as "query, triggered ads keyword" pairs. They are collected from advertisers, human labelling, searching log history, high quality extensions from old algorithms, etc. 260 million keywords are used to build a Trie as the searching space. After a quality model and Trie-filtering, we randomly select one million high-qualified training data and ten thousand testing data. The average length for target keywords after WordPiece tokenization is 6.69 and the average length for training data query input is 4.47. Each query from the testing data has at least one associated ads keyword, but we are unsure of how many other related keywords it has in the Trie. In actual use for a sponsored search engine, a number of relevant keywords are generated for a given query for further filtering and subsequent processing. More relevant keywords are recalled is concerned. Under this setting, we use recall rate to compare different models. MAP (mean average precision) is also included for comparison in the main results Table 1.

4.2   Model Settings

We implement both traditional IR algorithm BM25 and a list of generative retrieval models as our baseline. Okapi BM25 [12] is a traditional IR strategy, with the word tokenization of nltk [10] and parameters as $k_1 = 1.2, b = 0.75, \epsilon = 0.25$. Second type baseline is Trie based LSTM models as proposed by [9]. A 4-layer encoder, 4-layer decoder uni-directional LSTM+Trie model is implemented according to the complex model for offline use of [9]. Improvements are added based on it. We change the uni-directional LSTM encoder to bi-directional LSTM encoder to validate the effects of encoding bi-directional information. Copy mechanism [2,13] gives a bonus to generation scores of those words appear in the input sequence. Output keywords often have some overlap with the input queries, and copy mechanism allows model to directly pick some tokens from the input to compose the answer, which improves the generation ability for overlapped tokens. We train ProphetNet_large [15] models with copy mechanism as the third baselines. ProphetNet-Ads shares the same checkpoint as ProphetNet baselines, with additional proposed optimization by looking ahead.

All generative retrieval models use a same 30,000 words vocabulary with WordPiece [14] tokenization and share the same Trie. The LSTM based models are implemented according to [13], and trained for 10 epochs. ProphetNet and ProphetNet-Ads are implemented according to [15], trained with learning rate 3e−4, 5 epochs. Other hyper-parameters are same to the referenced models. Training batch sizes are all set to 36, with a maximum input token length of 20 and a maximum output length of 20.

4.3   Results Analyze

Table 1. Comparison with traditional IR algorithm BM25 and generative retrieval models. Results include recently proposed Trie-based LSTM model and its enhanced variants, ProphetNet generative retrieval model and ProphetNet-Ads. ProphetNet-Ads uses same checkpoint as Tri-gram ProphetNet, with looking ahead optimization. Merged Tri+Tri-Ads means the results merged with Tri-gram ProphetNet and ProphetNet-Ads. R@x for generation model means recall of generation procedure with beam size x, for BM25 means recall of top x of the IR results.

Model	R@5	R@10	R@15	R@20	MAP@5	MAP@10	MAP@15	MAP@20
BM25	27.86	33.40	37.30	39.13	0.2051	0.2125	0.2156	0.2166
LSTM	62.47	71.81	75.63	77.76	0.5716	0.6267	0.6442	0.6534
Bi-LSTM	63.28	72.28	76.21	78.13	0.5770	0.6292	0.6479	0.6563
Bi-LSTM+Copy	67.37	76.12	79.40	83.37	0.6114	0.6616	0.6755	0.6811
Uni-gram ProphetNet	75.00	82.50	84.90	86.50	0.6929	0.7362	0.7461	0.7526
Tri-gram ProphetNet	75.48	83.08	85.45	86.68	0.6974	0.7426	0.7518	0.7565
ProphetNet-Ads	78.05	84.28	86.24	87.54	0.7133	0.7472	0.7542	0.7580
Merged Tri+Tri-Ads	81.34	86.83	88.45	89.39	/	/	/	/
Merged above	86.56	90.11	91.34	92.15	/	/	/	/

We analyze different keywords extension models according to the results in Table 1. Firstly, we can easily draw the idea that traditional IR algorithm like BM25 is not suitable for keywords extension task, since it cannot fill the semantic gap. Compared with LSTM with the beam size 5, replacing encoder with bi-directional LSTM could improve the recall by 0.81% and adding copy mechanism could improve the recall by 4.09% further. Copy mechanism enhances the results obviously, because the keywords are likely to cover some same words as the input query, copy mechanism enables model to directly fetch some words or word pieces from the input, which is a strong assistant to our model. Compared to the LSTM variants, Uni-gram ProphetNet which is similar to Transformer, improves recall by 7.63%. This is mainly because the stacked Transformer architecture are deeper and keywords extension task has a big training corpus, with a large amount of features and information for the generation model to capture and learn. Tri-gram ProphetNet improves the recall by 0.48%, which shows that trained to predict more future tokens helps NLG ability even the future tokens are not explicitly used. ProphetNet-Ads uses the same trained model as Tri-gram ProphetNet, and improves the recall by 2.57% further. This shows that optimizing searching space in the inference procedure could help a generative retrieval model a lot, and our proposed looking ahead strategy can optimize it effectively by incorporating future information. Merged result is more concerned by sponsored search engine for offline use. From the merged results we observe that, with the same one million training data, integrating different searching space optimization models can generate more satisfactory results.

With the comparison between our models and the baseline models, we see that our proposed looking ahead strategies improve the results obviously. It shows that simply using Trie to constrain the searching space is not enough, and our looking ahead strategies can optimize the searching space and help the keywords extension task effectively.

4.4   Ablation Analyze

In this part, we will analyze the choice of how many tokens to predict as the n for n-gram ProphetNet-Ads and the choice of residual weight λ.

Firstly, we discuss the choice of n with Fig. 3. Compared with the Uni-gram model, we obverse that looking ahead one future token significantly improves the results and the benefit of looking further is limited. It is due to the short length of target keywords. Most of the problems could be alleviated even with one token to look ahead. We can also see in the case study Sect. 4.5 that one length noise token is common for keywords extension. Thus we do not carry experiments for $n \geq 4$.

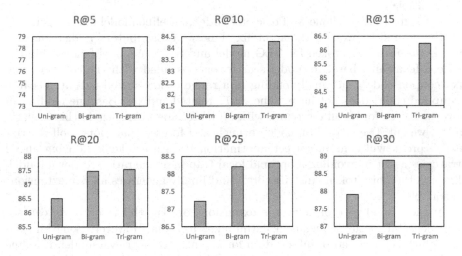

Fig. 3. Results of different grams to predict. Improvement is significant by looking ahead one token, but benefit is limited by looking ahead more.

Secondly, we discuss options for the residual weight of λ. We conduct results for a Bi-gram model with λ equals 0.4, 0.6, 0.8. Results can be seen from Table 2. We observe that using $\lambda = 0.6$ or $\lambda = 0.8$ reaches comparable results. This result is reasonable. Firstly, $\lambda = 0.6$ or 0.8 reaches the balance between maintaining sufficient representation for the decoding token and using future information to assist. Further, no matter what value λ is, it is used to modify the ranking score rather than real sentence score, thus as long as one sequence is put into the alive buffer, the same NLG model-consistent sentence score is recorded. Thus our strategy is robust to the choice of hyper-parameter λ. In other chapters of the paper, explicit n-gram strategies uses λ as 0.8.

Table 2. Results for different residual weight λ for a Bi-gram model.

λ	R@5	R@10	R@15	R@20	R@25	R@30
0.4	76.31	82.03	84.23	85.54	86.22	86.89
0.6	78.13	84.09	86.07	87.23	87.89	88.65
0.8	77.54	84.14	86.15	87.44	88.17	88.88

4.5 Case Study

In this section, we discuss on how ProphetNet-Ads helps to solve the problems in the generative retrieval model with actual cases. We list three examples that the best baseline model, Tri-gram ProphetNet, failed to find golden ads keywords with the beam size 30 and our model could successfully generate with the beam size 5 (Table 3).

In the first case of "lone wolf discount code", baseline model fails on generating the desired keyword with the prefix "lone wolf distributors". "distributors" in this case is a noise token for NLG model and baseline model fails to skip the noise. Meanwhile, baseline model search space is filled with the common prefix "coupon code" and finally ending in a range of low-scored outputs because "coupond code" does not have "lone wolf" related suffixes. Baseline model will never achieve "lone wolf discount" with an increasing beam size in this scenario unless we cut Trie's "coupon code" brunch and foresee that "lone wolf distributors" prefix will contain correct information in future tokens. Looking ahead strategies assist in avoiding a optimal local trap in a generative retrieval model, skipping the noise token "distributors", and finally generates all five extensions reasonable.

In the second case of keywords extensions of "kalathil resort", we can see that "kalathil" actually means "kalathil lake" in India. However, "kalathil" is a lake which is an unknown information for a generative retrieval model. Baseline method generates a lot of extensions resembling the input query, but most of them are wrong. Our model implicitly knows the combination of "kalathil lake", by looking ahead. Looking ahead strategies allow generative retrieval model to find a proper path with golden target information to go.

In the last case of keywords extensions of "workmans car insurance", two difficulties are there for generative retrieval models: "workmen" is misspelled as "workmans" and synonym words "car" and "auto" used in the query and outputs. Both of the models are powerful enough to learn that "car" and "auto" are synonymous, but baseline model fails in generating "workmen". It is because no sufficient data about misspelled "workmans" and correct "workmen" are provided in the training corpus. But our model successfully generate it by looking ahead future information. Other extensions are also more reasonable than

Table 3. Extensions of queries from ProphetNet-Ads and baseline model.

input: lone wolf discount code	Baseline: lone wolf coupon code
golden: lone wolf distributors coupon code	lone wolfs coupon code discount
Ours: lone wolf coupon code lone wolf distributors coupon code lone wolf distributors discount code lone wolf distributors promotional code lone wolf distributors promotional codes	lone wolf car rentals coupon code coupon code coupon code contact ... coupon code pet well being coupon code athleta yoga
input: kalathil resort	Baseline: kalathil resort
golden: kalathil lake resort	kalamata resort kalahari hotel
Ours: kalathil resort kalathil lake resort kalathi lake resorts kalathil lake kalathil lake resort india	resort kalahari khao resort koh samui resorts ... khao lak resort khao lak hotel koh samui all inclusive holiday
input: workmans car insurance	Baseline: workmans auto insurance quote
golden: workmen auto insurance	worx products walmart car insurance rates
Ours: workmen auto insurance workmens auto car insurance car insurance man car insurance driver women workmans auto insurance quote	workman islington walmart auto insurance quote walmart auto insurance toronto ... worxs website call worx warranty registration usa

baseline ones, with diverse prefix "workmen", "workmans" and "car insurance", which also show the strong retrieval ability of our model.

5   Conclusion

In this work, we investigate the weakness of present generative retrieval models and propose ProphetNet-Ads to improve the retrieval ability. For the experiments, we collect a keywords extension dataset from a real-world search engine.

We carry experiments on the recently proposed Trie-based LSTM generation model and other variants of generative retrieval models to analyze generative retrieval models in keywords extension task. Experimental results show that ProphetNet-Ads brings significant improvement over the recall and MAP metrics.

References

1. Gao, J., He, X., Xie, S., Ali, A.: Learning lexicon models from search logs for query expansion. In: Proceedings of the 2012 Joint Conference on Empirical Methods in Natural Language Processing and Computational Natural Language Learning, pp. 666–676. Association for Computational Linguistics (2012)
2. Gu, J., Lu, Z., Li, H., Li, V.O.: Incorporating copying mechanism in sequence-to-sequence learning. arXiv preprint arXiv:1603.06393 (2016)
3. He, Y., Tang, J., Ouyang, H., Kang, C., Yin, D., Chang, Y.: Learning to rewrite queries. In: Proceedings of the 25th ACM International on Conference on Information and Knowledge Management, pp. 1443–1452. ACM (2016)
4. Hillard, D., Schroedl, S., Manavoglu, E., Raghavan, H., Leggetter, C.: Improving ad relevance in sponsored search. In: Proceedings of the Third ACM International Conference on Web Search and Data Mining, pp. 361–370. ACM (2010)
5. Jones, R., Rey, B., Madani, O., Greiner, W.: Generating query substitutions. In: Proceedings of the 15th International Conference on World Wide Web, pp. 387–396. ACM (2006)
6. Kannan, A., et al.: Smart reply: automated response suggestion for email. In: Proceedings of the 22nd ACM SIGKDD International Conference on Knowledge Discovery and Data Mining, pp. 955–964. ACM (2016)
7. Laddha, A., Hanoosh, M., Mukherjee, D.: Understanding chat messages for sticker recommendation in hike messenger. arXiv preprint arXiv:1902.02704 (2019)
8. Lee, M.C., Gao, B., Zhang, R.: Rare query expansion through generative adversarial networks in search advertising. In: Proceedings of the 24th ACM SIGKDD International Conference on Knowledge Discovery & Data Mining, pp. 500–508. ACM (2018)
9. Lian, Y., et al.: An end-to-end generative retrieval method for sponsored search engine-decoding efficiently into a closed target domain. arXiv preprint arXiv:1902.00592 (2019)
10. Loper, E., Bird, S.: NLTK: the natural language toolkit. arXiv preprint cs/0205028 (2002)
11. Riezler, S., Liu, Y.: Query rewriting using monolingual statistical machine translation. Comput. Linguist. **36**(3), 569–582 (2010)
12. Robertson, S.E., Walker, S., Jones, S., Hancock-Beaulieu, M.M., Gatford, M., et al.: Okapi at TREC-3. NIST Special Publication Sp, vol. 109, p. 109 (1995)
13. See, A., Liu, P.J., Manning, C.D.: Get to the point: summarization with pointer-generator networks. arXiv preprint arXiv:1704.04368 (2017)
14. Wu, Y., et al.: Google's neural machine translation system: bridging the gap between human and machine translation. arXiv preprint arXiv:1609.08144 (2016)

15. Yan, Y., et al.: Prophetnet: predicting future n-gram for sequence-to-sequence pre-training. arXiv preprint arXiv:2001.04063 (2020)
16. Ye, N., Fuxman, A., Ramavajjala, V., Nazarov, S., McGregor, J.P., Ravi, S.: PhotoReply: automatically suggesting conversational responses to photos. In: Proceedings of the 2018 World Wide Web Conference, pp. 1893–1899. International World Wide Web Conferences Steering Committee (2018)

LARQ: Learning to Ask and Rewrite Questions for Community Question Answering

Huiyang Zhou[1(✉)], Haoyan Liu[2], Zhao Yan[1], Yunbo Cao[1], and Zhoujun Li[2]

[1] Tencent Cloud Xiaowei, Beijing, China
{huiyangzhou,zhaoyan,yunbocao}@tencent.com
[2] State Key Lab of Software Development Environment, Beihang University, Beijing, China
{haoyan.liu,lizj}@buaa.edu.cn

Abstract. Taking advantage of the rapid growth of community platforms, such as Yahoo Answers, Quora, etc., Community Question Answering (CQA) systems are developed to retrieve semantically equivalent questions when users raise a new query. A typical CQA system mainly consists of two key components, a retrieval model and a ranking model, to search for similar questions and select the most related, respectively. In this paper, we propose **LARQ**, **L**earning to **A**sk and **R**ewrite **Q**uestions, which is a novel sentence-level data augmentation method. Different from common lexical-level data augmentation progresses, we take advantage of the Question Generation (QG) model to obtain more accurate, diverse, and semantically-rich query examples. Since the queries differ greatly in a low-resource code-start scenario, incorporating the QG model as an augmentation to the indexed collection significantly improves the response rate of CQA systems. We incorporate LARQ in an online CQA system and the Bank Question (BQ) Corpus to evaluate the enhancements for both the retrieval process and the ranking model. Extensive experimental results show that the LARQ enhanced model significantly outperforms single BERT and XGBoost models, as well as a widely-used QG model (NQG).

Keywords: Question generation · Data augmentation · Community Question Answering

1 Introduction

The developments of community platforms bring various Frequently Asked Questions (FAQ) pages on the web [26]. When users raise a question on the platform, Community Question Answering (CQA) systems retrieve the relevant question-answer (Q-A) pairs from these FAQ pages to make a response or suggestion [12].

H. Zhou and H. Liu—Equal Contributions.
H. Liu—Work done during an internship at Tencent.

© Springer Nature Switzerland AG 2020
X. Zhu et al. (Eds.): NLPCC 2020, LNAI 12431, pp. 318–330, 2020.
https://doi.org/10.1007/978-3-030-60457-8_26

Retrieving high-quality comprehensive answers is challenging as the queries which are semantically equivalent may differ greatly, especially in a low-resource cold-start scenario.

It is noticeable that retrieving from more existing Q-A pairs results in more comprehensive and accurate candidates, but sacrifices more efficiency. Therefore, the basis of an online CQA system contains a retrieval model, which not only constructs a large indexed collection containing existing Q-A pairs, but also yield a candidate set of relevant questions for a certain user query efficiently. Under the performance requirements, search engines - such as Elasticsearch and Lucene - are utilized to effectively seek a relative high-quality candidate set. Afterwards, a powerful ranking model, e.g. a sentence similarity model, picks out answers of the most relevant questions as the final responses.

Existing approaches mainly improve CQA models in both components. For the retrieval model, some researchers [3,13,17,18,29,33] propose a complicated and precise answer selection method, e.g. using pre-trained language models fine-tuned on human-labeled datasets. Others [23,26–28] create a novel ranking model considering many features. Nonetheless, large-scale manually constructed training data for each new domain is extremely expensive and practically infeasible, and training a ranking model with limited data inevitably results in a low performance [21,24].

Original Query A:
Lowest point in Norway?

Generated Query B:
What is the lowest point in Norway?

User Query C:
What is the lowest elevation of Norway?

Fig. 1. Narrow the gap from $A \to C$ to $A \to B \to C$.

Instead of designing deep sophisticated models to measure query similarities, we propose to narrow the gaps between the relevant queries. For example, as shown in Fig. 1, supposing that we generate a query B which is semantically equivalent to the query A, we can straightforwardly determine answers for the query C because it is similar to the query B. The data for relevant queries can be easily crawled abundantly from community platforms such as Yahoo Answers, Quora, and Stack Overflow. Finally, we propose to generate semantically-equivalent queries for existing query-answer (Q-A) pairs as an augmentation, which is denotes as Question Rewriting (QR).

In this paper, we propose a novel data augmentation method **LARQ**, **L**earning to **A**sk and **R**ewrite **Q**uestions for Community Question Answering. The intuition behind LARQ is that, given a search query, we can generate various similar queries that have the same meaning as the original one.

Therefore, the CQA system may seek out the correct answer which is related to a query with scarce rhetorical modes. Our major contributions can be summarized as follows,

- We propose LARQ, a QG model to effectively generate query-query relevant pairs, which are accurate, diverse, and semantically-rich.
- We introduce the queries generated from LARQ into the retrieval process of an online task-specific CQA system and achieve an impressive response accuracy in cold-start scenarios.
- We leverage LARQ into Bank Question (BQ) Corpus and demonstrate the effectiveness of enhancing the training set for the ranking model.

We conduct LARQ enhanced CQA system in comparison with single BERT [11] and XGBoost [6] based CQA baselines, and extensive experimental results show that LARQ achieves significantly better performances, which demonstrates the effectiveness of incorporate QG models into the CQA systems as a sentence-level data augmentation component.

2   LARQ Model

The relevant query-query pairs generation can be formulated as a sequence-to-sequence process. We construct the LARQ model utilizing BERT as the encoder and the Transformer [30] decoder, as shown in Fig. 2.

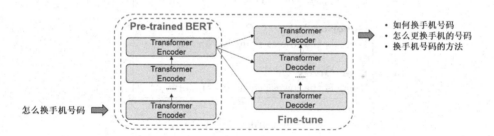

Fig. 2. LARQ is constructed by BERT as encoder and Transformer decoder.

2.1   Question Generation Structure

BERT Encoder. The input text of the BERT model is tokenized into Word-Pieces [32], and two special tokens [CLS] and [SEP] are utilized as the representation and separation tokens for input sentences, respectively. We use BERT as the encoder of LARQ. The final hidden state of the special token [CLS] is treated as the representation of Q, which is the input of the generation module.

Transformer Decoder. We employ a multi-layer Transformer decoder as the decoder of LARQ. We feed the hidden state of token [CLS] as the input and add a mask matrix for the relevance query Q' to preserve the auto-regressive property. We apply a copy mechanism [14] to address the out-of-vocabulary (OOV) issue. Given the Transformer decoder state s_t and the attentive vector c_t on source sequence at time t together with the source Q, the probability of generating any target word y_t is given by the mixture of probabilities as follows:

$$p(y_t|s_t, y_{t-1}, c_t, Q) = p(y_t, g|s_t, y_{t-1}, c_t, Q) + p(y_t, c|s_t, y_{t-1}, c_t, Q), \qquad (1)$$

where g stands for the generate mode, and c the copy mode. Sharing the normalization term, the two modes are basically competing through a softmax function.

2.2 Training

BERT Pre-training. BERT proposes the masked language model (MLM) objective to represent the input text without the unidirectional constraints. Additionally, the next sentence prediction (NSP) task is introduced to jointly pre-train text-pair representations. We utilize the Whole Word Masking pre-trained Chinese BERT checkpoints[1] [8] for LARQ. They fine-tune the official Chinese BERT$_{BASE}$ checkpoint using the Chinese Wikipedia (13.6M lines) after obtaining word segmentation by LTP[2].

Fine-Tuning. We fine-tune the whole model using corpus described in Sect. 4.1. We exploit the log-likelihood objective as the loss function. Given a set of training examples $\{(Q_i, Q'_i)\}|_{i=1}^K$, the loss function $\mathcal{L}$ can be defined as $\mathcal{L} = \sum_i^K \log P(Q'_i|Q_i)$.

We use the Adam algorithm to optimize the final objective with all the parameters described in Sect. 4.1. Furthermore, we employ a beam-search mechanism to obtain more relevant diversity results.

3   Question Answering

We leverage the relevant query-query (Q-Q') pairs generated from LARQ as an augmentation for CQA systems, including 1) enlarging the indexer for the retrieval model of an online CQA system, and 2) extending the training examples for a sentence-matching based ranking model.

3.1   General CQA System

As illustrated in Fig. 3, the CQA system is typically an end-to-end structure and takes query-answer (Q-A) pairs as inputs and outputs. An online CQA system consists of two key components - a retrieval model and a ranking model, and utilizes a trigger model to determine the final response.

---

[1] https://github.com/ymcui/Chinese-BERT-wwm.
[2] http://ltp.ai/.

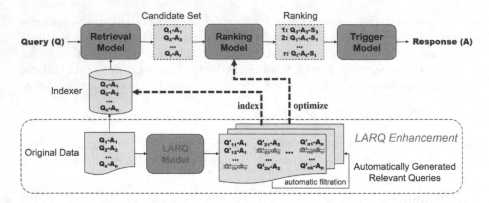

Fig. 3. General CQA system. We incorporate LARQ as an augmentation for both the indexer of the retrieval model and the training data for the ranking model.

Retrieval Model. For an online CQA server, there is a pre-constructed indexer contains frequently asked Q-A pairs. When a user question coming, the retrieval model seeks relevant queries in the indexer and presents a candidate set for further judgments. Since a larger indexer provides more comprehensive answers, the efficiency of retrieval methods become particularly important. Therefore, rule-based matching methods, e.g. search engines, are widely-used to effectively seek relatively high-quality candidates.

Ranking Model. Taking the relatively high-quality Q-A candidates as inputs, a ranking model is usually constructed by a sophisticated and precise sentence-matching models to evaluate the real semantic relevance between user query and each query of the candidates. The sentence-matching based ranking model takes two sentences as inputs and output a similarity score based on their semantic relevance. Hence, in line with similarity scores between the user question and each query in the candidate set, the ranking model presents a list of sorted Q-A pairs for the final response.

Trigger Model. Receiving the sorted candidate Q-A pairs, the trigger model controls the final response based on specific pre-defined policies:

- *Reply:* The answers in this mode should have a high precision. Given a relative-high threshold a, if the *Top* 1 candidate answer has a higher similarity with the user query, the CQA system responds it as a directly reply.
- *Suggest:* A CQA model should suggest potential answers balancing the precision and recall. Given a relative-soft threshold b $(b < a)$, the CQA system presents *Top* K results with higher scores in candidates as suggestions;
- *NoAns:* There would be no response or respond by chat skills if the scores of *Top* K are less than b.

We focus on incorporating duplicate questions crawled from the web community platform into both the retrieval and ranking models in the CQA system, described as follows.

3.2   Improving Retrieval Process

We evaluate the enhancement of the relevant Q-Q' pairs generated from LARQ in the retrieval process of the CQA system. It inevitably performs poorly with limited datasets in a new cold-start domain. Therefore, we propose to augment the limited user data by the relevant Q-Q' pairs generated from LARQ to establish the indexed collection as:

$$\begin{aligned}
\mathcal{R}_{QA} &= \{Q, A\}, \\
\mathcal{R}_{Q'A} &= \mathcal{R}_{QA} \cup \{(Q', A) | Q' \in \mathbf{LARQ}(Q)\},
\end{aligned} \tag{2}$$

where $\mathcal{R}_{QA}$ represents the original Q-A pairs; Q is the query and A is the corresponding answer; $\mathbf{LARQ}(Q)$ represents relevant queries of Q generated by LARQ. We use $\mathcal{R}_{Q'A}$ as the new indexed collection, and $\mathcal{R}_{Q'A}$ contains much more different expressions than $\mathcal{R}_{QA}$ while they are semantically-equivalent. It is valuable when users express the same query in various ways.

3.3   Improving Ranking Model

We evaluate the relevant Q-Q' pairs on two widely-used ranking models, BERT and XGBoost based sentence similarity models, which focus on the semantic-level and character-level information of pairs respectively. A ranking model takes Q - the original query, and Q_i - from the candidate pair (Q_i, A_i), as inputs, and predicts a similarity score S_i. We demonstrate the enhancement for the BERT based model, which is the same as XGBoost.

Formally, a ranking model is trained on a set of triples:

$$\mathcal{R}_{QQ} = \{(Q_{1i}, Q_{2i}, L_i)\} |_{i=1}^{N}, \tag{3}$$

where N denotes the total number of training examples; Q_{1i} and Q_{2i} are two queries; and L_i equals 1 if two queries have the same semantic, otherwise 0.

We propose to extend the training set of the ranking model using LARQ as,

$$\mathcal{R}_{QQ'} = \{(Q'_{1i}, Q_{2i}, L_i) | Q'_{1i} \in \mathbf{LARQ}(Q_1)\} \\ \cup \{(Q_{1i}, Q'_{2i}, L_i) | Q'_{2i} \in \mathbf{LARQ}(Q_2)\} \Big|_{i=1}^{N}, \tag{4}$$

where $\mathbf{LARQ}(Q)$ represents the generated queries of Q from LARQ, which creates arbitrarily large, yet noisy, query-query relevance pairs in a target domain.

We introduce a similarity filter model to denoise the low-confidence relevant pairs generated from LARQ. And the final enhanced training set of the ranking model is constructed as:

$$\begin{aligned}
\mathcal{R}_{QQ'+} &= \mathcal{R}_{QQ} + f(\mathcal{R}_{QQ'}), \\
f(\mathcal{R}_{QQ'}) &= \{(Q_{1i}, Q_{2i}, L_i) | \cos(\mathbf{BAS}(Q_{1i}), \mathbf{BAS}(Q_{2i})) > \mathcal{T}\},
\end{aligned} \tag{5}$$

where f is the filter function; $\mathcal{T}$ denotes the filter threshold; $\mathbf{BAS}$ stands for the bert-as-service[3] tool to encode a query text using the BERT model.

---

[3] https://github.com/hanxiao/bert-as-service.

4   Experiments

To demonstrate the effectiveness of incorporating the relevant Q-Q' for CQA systems, we evaluate LARQ over several tasks, namely 1) question generation rewriting, 2) improving the retrieval process, and 3) improving the ranking model.

4.1   Question Generation Rewriting

Setup. We construct the encoder using the BERT$_{BASE}$ model and form the decoder using the Transformer decoder with the same size as the encoder. Both the encoder and decoder are with 12 layers, a hidden size of 768, a filter size of 3072, and 12 attention heads. The lengths of the queries are limited to 64 tokens, and the max decode step is also 64. We set batch size as 32, learning rate as 3e−4, and fine-tune 3 epochs using Adam optimizer with datasets below. We combine a copy mechanism with beam size 5 during decoding. The encoder is warm-start using public Chinese BERT [8], leaving parameters of the decoder as randomly initialized.

Dataset and Evaluation. The training data for LARQ consists of two parts: the Phoenix Paraphrasing datasets[4] (75.6%) and the Large-scale Chinese Question Matching Corpus (LCQMC) [20] (23.5%). 1) The **Phoenix Paraphrasing** is a public Chinese paraphrasing dataset of Baidu broad that contains 450K high-quality commercial synonymous short text pairs with a precision of 95%. 2) The **LCQMC** is more general as it focuses on intent matching rather than paraphrase, so we select the pairs labeled positive to ensure the semantic quality, resulting in 138K question pairs. Finally, the average sentence lengths of the source and target queries in our dataset are 8.92 and 8.91 tokens, respectively.

We apply LARQ to an education customer service scenario, with a total of 866 Q-A pairs that users actually met and asked before. After generating the 4330 (beam size 5) relevant Q-Q' pairs by LARQ, we perform a human judgment to determine the quality of all these pairs. For each Q-Q' pair, 3 participants give scores in i) "good", ii) "not bad", and iii) "bad", in order of *informativeness* - capturing important information, *fluency* - written in well-formed Chinese, and *relevance* - having the same semantics with the original. A pair is treated as "good" or "bad" if more than one participants give "good" or "bad" scores, otherwise, it is determined as "not bad". We take NQG [36] for comparison with the same queries and human evaluation.

Results. As shown in Fig. 4a, 63.07% of the generated queries are regarded as "good", 19.86% as "not bad", and only 17.07% as "bad". The useful ratio is up to 82.93% ("good" & "not bad"), which presents that LARQ has a quite competitive performance.

Besides, 25% of the NQG generated queries are the same as the original query, while the rest also has a low editing distance. As seen in Fig. 4b, the

---

[4] https://ai.baidu.com/broad/introduction.

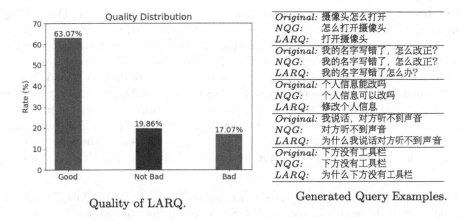

| Quality of LARQ. | Generated Query Examples. |

Fig. 4. The quality of LARQ and comparisons with NQG.

queries generated from NQG are just omitting some words or change the order of the tokens. This demonstrates that LARQ has a relatively strong ability to generate more accurate, diverse, and semantically-rich queries.

4.2 Improving Retrieval Process

Dataset and Evaluation. The retrieval model of the online CQA system utilizes the Elasticsearch (ES)[5] whose default retrieval algorithm is BM25 [25]. We initialize the indexer with 866 real Q-A pairs to form a *cold-start* scenario. Then we collect another 866 real queries (Q') as the test set, each of which is corresponding to an answer (A) with the original queries (Q) one-by-one. This is a 100% answerable and 100% coverage dataset for this CQA system. There are practically 80% answerable queries in the real CQA scenario, therefore we add 141 (13%) queries without correct answers in the indexer, and 76 (7%) chat sentences to construct a variant test set.

As shown in Sect. 4.1, there are around 17.07% queries unavailable after generated from LARQ. We heuristically filter out the low-confidence Q-Q' pairs by a cosine similarity of $\mathbf{BAS}(Q)$ and $\mathbf{BAS}(Q')$ with a threshold 0.1. Finally, we obtain 3513 (81.13%) among the total 4330 relevant queries and feed them into the indexer as an augmentation.

In line with Sect. 3.1, the final end-to-end CQA system would respond in 3 kinds of results:

- **Top 1:** the top 1 candidate if satisfied the *Reply* policy;
- **Top 5:** a maximum of top 5 candidates for the *Suggest* policy;
- **NoAns:** no response if all the candidate results are below the suggestion threshold.

---

[5] https://github.com/elastic/elasticsearch.

Results. As shown in Table 1, for the 100% answerable test set, the LARQ augmentation gains a 4.62% improvement of the reply and suggestion accuracy. The *NoAns* examples decrease from 31 to 20, and we gain 39 more accurate answer in Top 1 correct numbers. For the 80% answerable scenario, we also obtain a 3.79% gain. The significant improvement in both Top 1 and Top 5 accuracy demonstrates the effectiveness of introducing LARQ generated queries into the indexer of the CQA system. The *NoAns* examples decrease from 65 to 43, and we gain 38 more accurate answer in Top 1 correctness. The significant improvements in both Top 1 and Top 5 accuracy demonstrate the effectiveness of introducing LARQ generated queries into the indexer of the CQA system.

Table 1. Accuracy of the *cold start* end-to-end CQA model with LARQ. Numbers inside brackets denote the correct while those outside denote the total.

	Index	Test	Top 1	Top 5	NoAns	Acc@5
100% answerable test set						
cold-start	866	866	196 (103)	835 (307)	31	35.45%
cold-start$_{+LARQ}$	866 + 3513	866	281 (142)	846 (347)	20	40.07%
80% answerable test set, including out of index set and chat sentences						
cold-start	866	866 + 141 + 76	215 (106)	1018 (308)	65	28.44%
cold-start$_{+LARQ}$	866 + 3513	866 + 141 + 76	316 (144)	1040 (349)	43	32.23%

Table 2. F1 score of the *cold start* end-to-end CQA model with LARQ.

	Precision	Recall	F1	Correct
Top 1				
cold-start	52.55%	11.89%	19.39%	103
cold-start$_{+LARQ}$	50.53%	16.40%	24.76%	142
Δ	−2.02%	**+4.50%**	**+5.37%**	**+37.86%**
Top 5				
cold-start	36.77%	35.45%	36.10%	307
cold-start$_{+LARQ}$	41.02%	40.07%	40.54%	347
Δ	**+4.25%**	**+4.62%**	**+4.44%**	**+13.03%**

Table 2 gives F1-score and correct number on the 100% answerable dataset. In the Top 1 scenario, we get 4.50% and 5.37% increment of *Recall* and *F1*, respectively, while only a minor decrement of *Precision* due to the noise. In the Top 5 scenario, we have 4.25%, 4.62% and 4.44% increment of *Precision*, *Recall* and *F1*, respectively. The results present that the LARQ augmentation promotes the whole probability of the CQA system instead of simply increasing the recall.

4.3   Improving Ranking Model

Setup. As illustrated in Sect. 3.3, both BERT$_{BASE}$ and XGBoost models take Q-Q' pairs as inputs and predict a similarity score, and we introduce LARQ to enlarge the training data described below. For the BERT model, we set batch size as 32, learning rate as $3e-4$, and fine-tune 3 epochs using Adam optimizer. And for the XGBoost model, we set learning rate as 0.1, max depth as 15, and train 800 rounds in total. Similar to it in Sect. 4.2, we propose to find a low-confidence filter threshold for LARQ. And we also conduct experiments on different training data size to simulate low-resource scenarios.

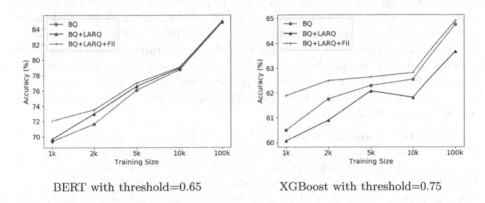

BERT with threshold=0.65   XGBoost with threshold=0.75

Fig. 5. Ranking model performance on BQ corpus with different filter thresholds and different training sizes.

Dataset and Evaluation. We evaluate our model on the Bank Question (BQ) corpus [5], a Chinese corpus for Sentence Semantic Equivalence Identification (SSEI). The BQ corpus contains 120K question pairs from 1-year online bank custom service logs. It is split into three parts: 100K pairs for training, 10K pairs for validation, and 10K pairs for test. There is no sentence overlap among training, validation, and test sets.

Results. Figure 5 shows that the LARQ augmentation works for both BERT and XGBoost models in all different data settings. It's remarkable that when the training data contains 1K examples (in Fig. 5a and 5b), the BERT and XGBoost models achieve 2.67% and 1.40% performance promotion respectively. The LARQ augmentation also has a slightly better or comparable accuracy than the original model in the training set of 100K examples, which demonstrates that the LARQ augmentation is indispensable in a low-resource scenario.

Besides, the best filter thresholds for BERT and XGBoost are 0.65 and 0.75, respectively. As the higher threshold means less diversity while lower contains more noise, we notice that the XGBoost model is more sensitive to bad cases than Bert model. The slight performance drop of the XGBoost model without filter function also verifies this appearance, while BERT still obtains a slight gain without filtration (the blue and red lines in Fig. 5a and 5b). Both models achieve significant increment after filtering the bad generation cases, which proves the indispensable of the LARQ augmentation for the ranking model.

5   Related Work

Our approach is related to 1) the community question answering tasks, and 2) the data augmentation methods, especially the question generation approaches.

Community Question Answering. The CQA systems consist of two components: a retrieval model and a ranking model. Recent works [9,15,22,34] have shown that deep neural scoring models significantly improve the ranking quality. However, these approaches rely on the candidates generated by ad-hoc retrieval systems and they require large supervised training sets [35]. Besides, weakly supervised data achieves a competitive performance and can be developed from raw corpora, e.g., click data [4,10]. Nevertheless, even weakly supervised data is scarce for many domains [7,16].

Question Generation. To tackle the issue that even no (weakly-)supervised data is available, data augmentation [31] approaches are proposed to leverage public domain question-answer pairs or high-quality human-annotated datasets [1]. Additionally, question generation [2,19] has been employed to increase training data for CQA tasks. However, such task-specific objectives have not been distinctly introduced to the retrieval and ranking processes in ad-hoc retrieval systems [21].

6   Conclusion

In this paper, we propose LARQ, a novel sentence-level data augmentation method for Community Question Answering systems, based on a Question Generation model. We demonstrate that LARQ, constructed with the BERT as the encoder and the Transformer decoder, produces more accurate, diverse, and semantically-rich relevant query pairs, which significantly enhance both the retrieval and ranking processes in CQA models. Experimental results on an online task-specific CQA system and the Bank Question Corpus show that our approach effectively improves the *Reply* and *Suggest* accuracy in a *cold-start* scenario, especially for the low-resource domain.

References

1. Ahmad, A., Constant, N., Yang, Y., Cer, D.: ReQA: an evaluation for end-to-end answer retrieval models. In: EMNLP 2019 MRQA Workshop (2019). https://doi.org/10.18653/v1/d19-5819

2. Alberti, C., Andor, D., Pitler, E., Devlin, J., Collins, M.: Synthetic QA corpora generation with roundtrip consistency. In: ACL (2019). https://doi.org/10.18653/v1/p19-1620
3. Bonadiman, D., Kumar, A., Mittal, A.: Large scale question paraphrase retrieval with smoothed deep metric learning. In: W-NUT Workshop (2019). https://doi.org/10.18653/v1/d19-5509
4. Borisov, A., Markov, I., de Rijke, M., Serdyukov, P.: A neural click model for web search. In: WWW. ACM (2016). https://doi.org/10.1145/2872427.2883033
5. Chen, J., Chen, Q., Liu, X., Yang, H., Lu, D., Tang, B.: The BQ corpus: a large-scale domain-specific Chinese corpus for sentence semantic equivalence identification. In: EMNLP (2018). https://doi.org/10.18653/v1/d18-1536
6. Chen, T., Guestrin, C.: Xgboost: a scalable tree boosting system. In: SIGKDD. ACM (2016). https://doi.org/10.1145/2939672.2939785
7. Chirita, P.A., Nejdl, W., Paiu, R., Kohlschütter, C.: Using ODP metadata to personalize search. In: SIGIR. ACM (2005). https://doi.org/10.1145/1076034.1076067
8. Cui, Y., et al.: Pre-training with whole word masking for Chinese BERT. arXiv:1906.08101 (2019)
9. Dai, Z., Xiong, C., Callan, J., Liu, Z.: Convolutional neural networks for soft-matching N-grams in ad-hoc search. In: WSDM. ACM (2018). https://doi.org/10.1145/3159652.3159659
10. Dehghani, M., Zamani, H., Severyn, A., Kamps, J., Croft, W.B.: Neural ranking models with weak supervision. In: SIGIR. ACM (2017). https://doi.org/10.1145/3077136.3080832
11. Devlin, J., Chang, M.W., Lee, K., Toutanova, K.: BERT: pre-training of deep bidirectional transformers for language understanding. In: NAACL-HLT (2019)
12. Dietz, L., Verma, M., Radlinski, F., Craswell, N.: TREC complex answer retrieval overview. In: TREC (2017)
13. Feng, M., Xiang, B., Glass, M.R., Wang, L., Zhou, B.: Applying deep learning to answer selection: a study and an open task. In: Workshop on ASRU. IEEE (2015). https://doi.org/10.1109/asru.2015.7404872
14. Gu, J., Lu, Z., Li, H., Li, V.O.: Incorporating copying mechanism in sequence-to-sequence learning. In: ACL (2016). https://doi.org/10.18653/v1/p16-1154
15. Guo, J., Fan, Y., Ai, Q., Croft, W.B.: A deep relevance matching model for ad-hoc retrieval. In: CIKM. ACM (2016). https://doi.org/10.1145/2983323.2983769
16. Hawking, D.: Challenges in enterprise search. In: ADC, vol. 4. Citeseer (2004)
17. Jing, F., Zhang, Q.: Knowledge-enhanced attentive learning for answer selection in community question answering systems. arXiv:1912.07915 (2019)
18. Kumar, A., Dandapat, S., Chordia, S.: Translating web search queries into natural language questions. In: LREC (2018)
19. Lewis, P., Denoyer, L., Riedel, S.: Unsupervised question answering by cloze translation. In: ACL (2019). https://doi.org/10.18653/v1/p19-1484
20. Liu, X., et al.: LCQMC: a large-scale Chinese question matching corpus. In: COLING (2018)
21. Ma, J., Korotkov, I., Yang, Y., Hall, K., McDonald, R.: Zero-shot neural retrieval via domain-targeted synthetic query generation. arXiv:2004.14503 (2020)
22. MacAvaney, S., Yates, A., Cohan, A., Goharian, N.: CEDR: contextualized embeddings for document ranking. In: SIGIR. ACM (2019). https://doi.org/10.1145/3331184.3331317
23. Nguyen, M.T., Phan, V.A., Nguyen, T.S., Nguyen, M.L.: Learning to rank questions for community question answering with ranking SVM. arXiv:1608.04185 (2016)

24. Rücklé, A., Moosavi, N.S., Gurevych, I.: Neural duplicate question detection without labeled training data. In: EMNLP-IJCNLP (2019). https://doi.org/10.18653/v1/d19-1171
25. Robertson, S.E., Walker, S., Jones, S., Hancock-Beaulieu, M.M., Gatford, M., et al.: Okapi at TREC-3. NIST Special Publication 109 (1995)
26. Sakata, W., Shibata, T., Tanaka, R., Kurohashi, S.: FAQ retrieval using query-question similarity and BERT-based query-answer relevance. In: SIGIR. ACM (2019). https://doi.org/10.1145/3331184.3331326
27. Sen, B., Gopal, N., Xue, X.: Support-BERT: predicting quality of question-answer pairs in MSDN using deep bidirectional transformer. arXiv:2005.08294 (2020)
28. Simpson, E., Gao, Y., Gurevych, I.: Interactive text ranking with Bayesian optimisation: a case study on community QA and summarisation. arXiv:1911.10183 (2019)
29. Tan, M., Santos, C.D., Xiang, B., Zhou, B.: LSTM-based deep learning models for non-factoid answer selection. arXiv:1511.04108 (2015)
30. Vaswani, A., et al.: Attention is all you need. In: NeurIPS (2017)
31. Wong, S.C., Gatt, A., Stamatescu, V., McDonnell, M.D.: Understanding data augmentation for classification: when to warp? In: DICTA. IEEE (2016). https://doi.org/10.1109/dicta.2016.7797091
32. Wu, Y., et al.: Google's neural machine translation system: bridging the gap between human and machine translation. arXiv:1609.08144 (2016)
33. Xue, X., Jeon, J., Croft, W.B.: Retrieval models for question and answer archives. In: SIGIR. ACM (2008). https://doi.org/10.1145/1390334.1390416
34. Yang, W., Zhang, H., Lin, J.: Simple applications of BERT for Ad Hoc document retrieval. arXiv:1903.10972 (2019)
35. Zamani, H., Dehghani, M., Croft, W.B., Learned-Miller, E., Kamps, J.: From neural re-ranking to neural ranking: learning a sparse representation for inverted indexing. In: CIKM. ACM (2018). https://doi.org/10.1145/3269206.3271800
36. Zhou, Q., Yang, N., Wei, F., Tan, C., Bao, H., Zhou, M.: Neural question generation from text: a preliminary study. In: Huang, X., Jiang, J., Zhao, D., Feng, Y., Hong, Yu. (eds.) NLPCC 2017. LNCS (LNAI), vol. 10619, pp. 662–671. Springer, Cham (2018). https://doi.org/10.1007/978-3-319-73618-1_56

Abstractive Summarization via Discourse Relation and Graph Convolutional Networks

Wenjie Wei, Hongling Wang$^{(\boxtimes)}$, and Zhongqing Wang

Natural Language Processing Laboratory, School of Computer Science and Technology,
Soochow University, Suzhou, Jiangsu 215006, China
wjwei@stu.suda.edu.cn, hlwang@suda.edu.cn, wangzq@gmail.com

Abstract. Currently, the mainstream abstractive summarization method uses a machine learning model based on encoder-decoder architecture, and generally utilizes the encoder based on a recurrent neural network. The model mainly learns the serialized information of the text, but rarely learns the structured information. From the perspective of linguistics, the text structure information is effective in judging the importance of the text content. In order to enable the model to obtain text structure information, this paper proposes to use discourse relation in text summarization tasks, which can make the model focus on the important part of the text. Based on the traditional LSTM encoder, this paper adds graph convolutional networks to obtain the structural information of the text. In addition, this paper also proposes a fusion layer, which enables the model to pay attention to the serialized information of the text while acquiring the text structure information. The experimental results show that the system performance is significantly improved on ROUGE evaluation after joining discourse relation information.

Keywords: Abstractive summarization · Text structure · Discourse relation

1 Introduction

As an important field of natural language processing, text summarization has aroused a lot attention [1, 2] from researchers in the past few decades. By compressing and refine the text, it generates concise sentences to form a summary for users. From the method of realization, text summarization can be divided into: extractive summarization [1] and abstractive summarization [2]. Compared with the extractive methods, abstractive summarization can utilize the words not in document to generate more novelty summary, which is closer to our human. Currently, mainstream abstractive summarization is usually based on Encoder-Decoder framework [3], which generally uses Recurrent Neural Networks (RNN) for encode and decode. However, traditional neural networks can only use the serialized information of text, while ignoring the structured information, such as discourse relation. From the perspective of linguistics, the discourse relation is effective to the judgment of the text content. For example, for the transition relation, we will automatically focus on the part after the transitional word. And for the juxtaposition relation, we will regard the sentences on both sides of the juxtaposition word as equally important.

© Springer Nature Switzerland AG 2020
X. Zhu et al. (Eds.): NLPCC 2020, LNAI 12431, pp. 331–342, 2020.
https://doi.org/10.1007/978-3-030-60457-8_27

The same is true for the model that discourse relation can allow it to understand the text better.

In this paper, we propose an abstractive summarization model based on discourse relation and graph convolutional networks (GCN) [4]. It has made the following improvements on the traditional sequence-to-sequence framework: (I) At the encoder part, graph convolutional network is added on the basis of bidirectional LSTM [5] to obtain the structural information of the text. (II) Discourse relation is integrated into the model by the identification of connecting words. (III) A fusion layer is proposed, which aims to enable the model to pay attention to the serialized information of the text while acquiring the text structure information, by integrating the LSTM representation into the target sequence.

2   Related Work

Since the birth of the text summarization in the 1950s, it has been widely concerned by researchers. Early text summarization methods were mainly extractive and based on statistical machine learning, such as Naive Bayes algorithm, Hidden Markov Model. These methods all treat the text summarization tasks as a binary classification problem, train it with a suitable classifier, and then obtain candidate summary sentences. However, with the development of deep learning, abstractive summarization based on neural networks has received more attention, especially the methods of encoder and decoder architecture.

Rush et al. [6] applied the encoder and decoder framework to the text summarization for the first time, and utilized the attention mechanism to generate the summaries. It has achieved good results on summarization tasks. Based on encoder and decoder model, Gu et al. [7] proposed the CopyNet mechanism, which copies the rare words in the source text with a certain probability to solve the problem of OOV words that are not covered in the vocabulary. A similar point has been made by Gulcehre et al. [8], using a selection gate to control whether a word is coped from the text or selected from the vocabulary. As an extension to the traditional model, Cohan et al. [9] proposed a hierarchical encoder, which takes the output of the previous neural network layer as the input of the subsequent neural network layer and aims to obtain the hierarchical information of the text. The experimental results show that the model has achieved high scores on long text summarization tasks, which makes up for the shortcomings of recurrent neural networks that are not good at processing long sequences.

With the development of discourse theory and the construction of large-scale English corpora, discourse-level research has received more attention. In recent years, algorithms based on discourse analysis have been widely used in various tasks in the NLP field. Farzi et al. [10] used phrasal dependency tree to solve the word reordering problem, and has achieved good experimental results on machine translation. In addition to supervised learning, discourse analysis is also widely used in unsupervised learning. Jernite et al. [11] exploited signals from paragraph-level discourse coherence to train these models to understand text, which speeds up the convergence of models. Inspired by these works, this paper uses discourse relation to assist in the generation of summaries. On the basis of encoder, we utilize graph convolutional network to encode the input sequence. Besides, we propose a fusion layer, which integrates the LSTM representation into the target sequence, so that the model can also pay attention to the serialized information of the text while acquiring the text structure information.

3 Model Description

In this section, we firstly give an overview of our model. We then discuss various type of discourse relation in English and their impact on model. Finally, we elaborate on each part of the model.

3.1 Overview of the Model

The abstractive summarization model based on discourse relation and graph convolutional networks proposed in this paper mainly contains three parts: discourse-based encoder, fusion layer and decoder which equipped with Multi-Head attention [12]. The discourse-based encoder is composed of a bidirectional LSTM and discourse-based GCN, which aims to gain the representation that contains text structure by incorporate the discourse relation. The task of the fusion layer is to pool and normalize the sequence representation, then fuse the serialized semantic representation and the target sequence, which allows the model to refocus on the serialized information of the text after LSTM. The decoder layer is responsible for generating summaries through semantic representation.

Figure 1 depicts the overview of our model. At the encoding end, the input word vectors pass through the bidirectional LSTM and discourse-based GCN in turn to obtain serialized semantic representations and text structure semantic representations, respectively. Here, we incorporate the discourse relation into the GCN, in order to make the model focus on the important parts of the text, so as to better understand the meaning of the document. It should be noted that only serialized semantic representation enters the fusion layer and merges with the target sequence because the model also needs the serialized information obtained by LSTM. We also add relative position embedding to the target sequence, which is the same as used by Raffel et al. [13]. Then the target sequence fused with serialized semantic features is taken as input, and the Multi-Head attention are used on representation obtained by the discourse based encoder for attention distribution. At last, the final output probability distribution is obtained through the dense layer and softmax function.

3.2 Discourse Relation in English

Discourse relation refers to the semantic connections between sentences or clauses within the same discourse. In English, discourse relation can be divided into four categories: causality, juxtaposition, transition and interpretation, as shown in Table 1.

For causality, the model needs to focus on the clauses after conjunctions such as "to", "as" and "because", for the purpose and conditions are generally the parts containing important information. The same is true for the transitional relation. The model should be focus on the transitional part, such as the information after the words "but", "however", etc. For interpretational relation, the model needs to pay attention to the entity being interpreted, because the interpretation part usually only plays an auxiliary role. For the special relation of juxtaposition, the model needs to pay attention to the information on both sides of the parallel conjunction at the same time. We use the existing relational conjunctions recognition tool to recognize the discourse relations in the text, and assign

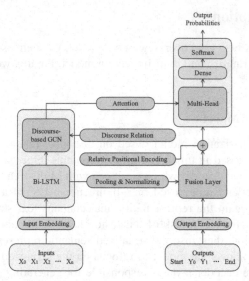

Fig. 1. Overview of the model based on discourse relation and GCN

Table 1. Division of discourse relation in English.

Category	Relation	Example
Causality	causality, inference, assumption, purpose, condition, background, etc.	thus, to, as, because, etc.
Juxtaposition	juxtaposition, comparison, progression, etc.	and, while, etc.
Transition	transition, concession, etc.	however, but, etc.
Interpretation	interpretation, illustration, comment, etc.	all this shows, etc.

different weights to words and clauses accordingly, which achieves the purpose of integrating the discourse relation in the model. According to our statistics, we can find that the integration of discourse relation has an impact on the summaries generated. That is, the more frequently a relation appears in the source text, the higher the probability of the relation in the summary.

3.3 Discourse-Based Encoder

Figure 2 shows the structure of the discourse-based encoder. As we can see, it consists of two parts: bidirectional LSTM and discourse-based GCN. The bidirectional LSTM is well-known to the researches, so it will not be elaborated. The following mainly interprets discourse-based GCN.

Discourse-Based GCN. From Fig. 2, it can be noted that the text is divided into a set of sentence sequences, and then put into the tree-GCN. Each sentence corresponds to a GCN in the tree-GCN, which means that the model treats each sentence as a graph

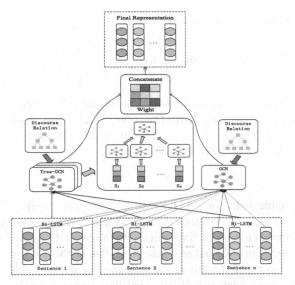

Fig. 2. Overview of the discourse-based encoder

structure, and uses GCN to learn the structure information of its sequence. As we know the main algorithm of GCN is as follows:

$$H^{i+1} = \sigma(AH^iW^i) \tag{1}$$

Where W^i refers to the trainable matrix, H^i indicates the ith hidden layer, and A is the adjacency matrix, which is a square matrix of order N. From here we can see that how to construct the adjacency matrix becomes the key of the model. From a linguistic point of view, in most cases, there is a connection between each word in a sentence. They can be transition, condition, causality, progression, etc. From this perspective, we consider constructing an adjacency matrix of related words, that is, the previous word and the next word in each sentence are related. We set the value of each relevant position in the adjacency matrix to 1. At the same time, we also consider that each word is related to itself, that means, the diagonal elements of the adjacency matrix are set to 1. Then the output of the GCN corresponding to each sentence is concatenated as the input of another GCN to further integrate the relationship between sentences into the model. When initializing the adjacency matrix of this GCN, we use discourse relation to assign values. 14 kinds of relation are used among the four categories of discourse relation listed in Table 1 to initialize this GCN's adjacency matrix. The central sentence judged by these discourse relations will be given a high weight in the corresponding position of the adjacency matrix, which is usually a number between 3–5 according to experimental results. For non-central sentences, we generally set the corresponding values in the matrix to a decimal between 0 and 1. For the special case of juxtaposition, which without a central sentence, we set the relative weights of the clauses to be equal, and when the value is between 2–3, the model has the best performance. For the weights that are not related to these discourse relations, we use the similarity between sentences to assign values, which is calculated as follows:

$$f(i \rightarrow j) = sim_{\text{cosine}}(v_i, v_j) = \frac{\vec{v_i} \cdot \vec{v_j}}{\left|\vec{v_i}\right| \times \left|\vec{v_j}\right|} \quad (2)$$

The smaller the calculated angle, the higher the similarity between sentences, that is, the more relevant the two sentences are. The resulting adjacency matrix is no longer of type 0–1, but decimal type. Besides, in order to make the adjacency matrix trainable in learning, we connect a dense layer to it as follows:

$$\hat{A} = g(W * A + b) \quad (3)$$

Where W is a trainable matrix, b is a bias vector, and $g(\cdot)$ is the sigmoid function.

Besides, we also use a GCN on the original text sequence (not divided by sentences), whose adjacency matrix is constructed similarly to the tree-GCN. Here, the relationship is considered between previous and next sentences, that is, the last word of the previous sentence is related to the first word of the following sentence. Each central sentence judged by the discourse relation will be added with appropriate weight to reflect its importance. For example, when the previous one of the two adjacent sentences is determined to be the central sentence, a larger weight will be added to the corresponding position of the adjacency matrix of the GCN. Then, the output of the GCN and the tree-GCN are concatenated to obtain the final semantic representation of the encoder through the linear layer:

$$R = linear([G_{tree}; G]) \quad (4)$$

Note that we have also used addition and dot product methods, but the result is not as good as the linear transformation after concatenating.

3.4 Fusion Layer

The purpose of adding the fusion layer is to enable the model to show solicitude for the original serialized information of the text. The main functions of the fusion layer are pooling, normalization and fusion. Here we choose Max-Pooling [14] as the pooling method to remove redundancy and use Layer-Normalization [15] to normalize the representation of a layer. The so-called fusion is to combine the representation of bidirectional LSTM with the target sequence after passing through the pooling layer and normalization layer. Since the semantic representation finally obtained at the encoding end is based on GCN, considering the output of the model may pay too much attention to the structural information of the text, and ignore the serialized information. Therefore, we fuse the serialized representation of the text extracted by bidirectional LSTM into the target sequence, and the calculation method is as follows:

$$Y_i = y_i * W_1 * h_T + W_2 * h_T \quad (5)$$

Where y_i is the target sequence, W_1 and W_2 are trainable parameter matrices, h_T denotes the representation of the text obtained by bidirectional LSTM. Here, we are not using the linear transformation like conventional fusion layer, because the dot product method can fuse the information more thorough. Experiments have also proved that this method is more effective. As shown in formula (5), in order to prevent the loss of presentation after fusion, we also add $W_2 * h_T$ to it, which is similar to the residual network [16].

3.5 Decoder Layer

We implement a unidirectional LSTM decoder equipped with Multi-Head attention mechanism to read the representation of the text and generate the summary word by word. Different from traditional attention, the Multi-Head attention mechanism splits the representation into N tensors with the same dimension. The tensor divided here is usually called the head. For each head, the attention distribution is calculated by scaling and dot product. It is described below:

$$Attention(Q, K, V) = soft \max(\frac{QK^T}{\sqrt{d_k}})V \qquad (6)$$

Where Q (Query) refers to the hidden layer matrix for the target sequence, K (Key) and V (Value) denote the hidden layer matrix for the input sequence. d_k is the last dimension of each matrix. Each head needs to be scaled and dot product, and then the results are concatenated to obtain the final attention distribution. It is described below:

$$head_i = Attention(QW_i^Q, KW_i^K, VW_i^V) \qquad (7)$$

$$MultiHead(Q, K, V) = Concat(head_1, \dots, head_N)W^O \qquad (8)$$

4 Experiments

In this section, we first introduce the experimental settings. Then we report the results of our experiments and compare the performance of our model with some state-of-the-art models and classic methods. Finally, we discuss the impact of different components on the model.

4.1 Experimental Settings

Dataset. We conduct our experiments on CNN/Daily Mail dataset [2], which has been widely used for long document summarization tasks. The corpus is constructed by collecting online news articles and human-generated summaries on CNN/Daily Mail website. We use the non-anonymized version [17], which is not replacing named entity with the unique identifier. Table 2 shows the statistics of the dataset.

Training Details. We use Tensorflow learning framework, and conduct our experiments with 1 NVIDIA 1080Ti GPU. During training and testing time, we limit the vocabulary size to 10k and truncate the source text to 600 words. For word embedding, we use pre-trained case-sensitive GloVe embeddings [18] for the task and set its dimension to 256. The number of LSTM hidden units is 512, and we set the number of LSTM layers to 1 in both the encoder and the decoder. The batch size is set to 32. We use Adam optimizer [19] with the default settings: $\alpha = 0.001$, $\beta_1 = 0.9$, $\beta_2 = 0.999$.

Table 2. The statistics of CNN/Daily Mail dataset.

CNN/Daily Mail	Numbers	Avg-token-len (article)	Avg-token-len (abstract)
Train	287726	790	55
Vaild	13368	768	61
Test	11490	777	58

Evaluation Metrics. This paper utilizes ROUGE [20] as the evaluation standard for the generated summaries. We use F-measures of ROUGE-1, ROUGE-2 and ROUGE-L metrics which respectively represent the overlap of N-gram and the longest common sequence between the gold summaries and the generated summaries.

4.2 Comparison of Results

To evaluate the performance of our model, we compare it with following baselines: **LEAD-3** [2], which takes the first three sentences as the summary; **PG + Coverage** [17], which uses a pointer-generator network and a coverage mechanism to generate the summaries; **S2S-ELMo** [21], which uses the pre-trained ELMo [22] representations; **Bottom-Up** [23], which implements a bottom-up content selector based on Seq2Seq model; **Aggregation Transformer** [24], which uses the history aggregation based on transformer model; **ProphetNet** [25], which each time step predicts the next several tokens instead of one.

Table 3 shows the experimental results on the CNN/Daily Mail test set. We can see that our model(DGF) performs slightly better than ProphetNet, but far better than other comparative experiments. The results confirm that our model is effective, and the theory of incorporating discourse relation is feasible.

Table 3. Results on CNN/Daily Mail test set.

Model	ROUGE-1	ROUGE-2	ROUGE-L
LEAD-3	40.42	17.62	36.67
PG + Coverage	39.53	17.28	36.38
S2S-ELMo	41.56	18.94	38.47
Bottom-Up	41.22	18.68	38.34
Aggregation Transformer	41.06	18.02	38.04
ProphetNet	43.68	20.64	40.72
DGF	**44.39**	**21.03**	**41.14**

4.3 Influence of Different Components on the Model

In order to explore the contribution of each part of the model, we decompose the model into the following four types: **Baseline**, its encoder uses only bidirectional LSTM and the decoder is equipped with a Multi-Head attention mechanism; **GM**, which adds GCN to the encoder on the basis of the Baseline model; **GM-DR**, based on GM model, it integrates discourse relation into the model; **DGF**, the model proposed in this paper, which adds a fusion layer to the GM-DR model.

Table 4 demonstrates the experimental results of the above models on the CNN/Daily Mail test set. It can be seen that after joining the GCN, the performance of the model has improved by 1.42, 0.90 and 1.48 points on ROUGE-1, ROUGE-2 and ROUGE-L, respectively. This shows that it is effective to use the GCN to obtain the text structure information. After merging discourse relation in GM, the model has been significantly improved, which is increased by 1.66, 1.38 and 1.96 points on ROUGE-1, ROUGE-2 and ROUGE-L respectively. This shows that the theory of integrating the discourse relation into the model is feasible; it can improve the quality of the generated summaries. Similarly, after the adding of the fusion layer, the model has also been improved by 0.89, 0.81 and 0.91 points on ROUGE-1, ROUGE-2 and ROUGE-L, respectively. This confirms that the fusion layer is effective, but also illustrates the disadvantages of using GCN from the side, that is, the model will pay too much attention to the text structure information, and ignore the linear information.

Table 4. Experimental results with different component models.

Model	ROUGE-1	ROUGE-2	ROUGE-L
Baseline	40.42	17.94	36.79
GM	41.84	18.84	38.27
GM-DR	43.50	20.22	40.23
DGF	**44.39**	**21.03**	**41.14**

As an extension of the traditional evaluation standard ROUGE method, the following will compare and analyse the summaries generated by the above models from the aspects of generality and readability, using manual evaluation.

For a given text sample, the summaries generated by each model is shown in Table 5. In order to facilitate the comparison of the generated summaries, the important information in the source text is bold and underlined. For the generated summaries, the part that contains the important information of the source text or similar to the standard summary, are also bold and underlined to highlight.

It can be seen from the table that the summary generated by the Baseline model has the following two problems: first, it covers less important information of the source text; second, it is poor language readability. After adding the GCN, the summary generated by the GM model obviously covers more important information, that is, the generality is enhanced. This confirms that the encoder composed of GCN can output representations with text structure information, to enable the model to capture important information

Table 5. Comparison of summaries generated by each model.

*Text(truncated):***The Palestinian authority officially became the 123rd member of the international criminal court on Wednesday, a step that gives the court jurisdiction over alleged crimes in Palestinian territories.** The formal accession was marked with a ceremony at the Hague, in the Netherlands, where the court is based. The Palestinians signed the ICC's founding Rome statute in January, **when they also accepted its jurisdiction over alleged crimes committed "in the occupied Palestinian territory, including east Jerusalem, since June 13, 2014."** Later that month, the ICC opened a preliminary examination into the situation (…)
Gold(standard):Membership gives the ICC jurisdiction over alleged crimes committed in Palestinian territories since last June.
*Baseline:*The accession mark at Netherlands, in the **Palestinian territories, gives the court jurisdiction over crimes.**
GM: **Palestinian gives the jurisdiction over alleged crimes in territories, over alleged crimes in Palestinian, since June.**
GM-DR: **Palestinian gives the jurisdiction over alleged crimes in territories, since June.**
DGF: **Palestinian officially became the member, that gives the jurisdiction over alleged crimes in Palestinian territories.**

in the source text. After incorporating the discourse relation, the repetitiveness of the generated summary is reduced and the readability is enhanced. This shows that the discourse relation can make the model understand the text better, thereby improving the quality of the generated summaries. Similarly, after joining the fusion layer, the summary generated by the DGF model is obviously more readable. This also confirms that after adding the fusion layer, the model will refocus on the serialized information of the text, making the generated summaries more logical, and greatly improve the readability.

5 Conclusion

The model proposed in this paper, based on the traditional Seq2Seq abstractive summarization framework, has made the following improvements: first, we incorporate discourse relation into the model, to make it focus on the important part of the source text; second, on the basis of LSTM encoder, we join the GCN, which can output the representations with text structure information; last, a fusion layer is proposed, which aims to enable the model to pay attention to the serialized information of the text. Experimental results show that compared with classic abstractive summarization models and some SOTA methods, this model has a significant improvement in ROUGE evaluations, and the generated summaries have better generality and readability. As a future work, we will consider joint learning of text summarization tasks and discourse relation recognition.

Acknowledgments. This research is supported by National Natural Science Foundation of China (Grant No. 61976146, No. 61806137, No. 61702149, No. 61836007 and No. 61702518), and Jiangsu High School Research Grant (No. 18KJB520043).

References

1. Gupta, V., Lehal, G.S.: A survey of text summarization extractive techniques. J. Emerg. Technol. Web Intell. **2**(3), 258–268 (2010)
2. Nallapati, R., Zhou, B., Santos, C.N., Gulcehre, C., Xiang, B.: Abstractive text summarization using sequence-to-sequence rnns and beyond. In: Conference on Computational Natural Language Learning, pp. 280–290 (2016)
3. Cho, K., et al.: Learning phrase representations using rnn encoder-decoder for statistical machine translation. arXiv Computation and Language. arXiv:1406.1078 (2014)
4. Kipf, T., Welling, M.: Semi-supervised classification with graph convolutional networks. arXiv Learning arXiv:1609.02907 (2016)
5. Elman, J.L.: Finding structure in time. Cogn. Sci. **14**(2), 179–211 (1990)
6. Rush, A.M., Chopra, S., Weston, J.: A neural attention model for abstractive sentence summarization. arXiv Computation and Language. arXiv:1509.00685 (2015)
7. Gu, J., Lu, Z., Li, H., Li, V.O.: Incorporating copying mechanism in sequence-to-sequence learning. In: Meeting of the association for Computational Linguistics, pp. 1631–1640 (2016)
8. Gulcehre, C., Ahn, S., Nallapati, R., Zhou, B., Bengio, Y.: Pointing the unknown words. arXiv Computation and Language. arXiv:1603.08148 (2016)
9. Cohan, A., et al.: A discourse-aware attention model for abstractive summarization of long documents. North American Chapter of the Association for Computational Linguistics, pp. 615–621 (2018)
10. Farzi, S., Faili, H., Kianian, S.: A neural reordering model based on phrasal dependency tree for statistical machine translation. Intell. Data Anal. **22**(5), 1163–1183 (2018)
11. Jernite, Y., Bowman, S.R.: Discourse-based objectives for fast unsupervised sentence representation learning. arXiv Computation and Language. arXiv:1705.00557 (2017)
12. Vaswani, A., Shazeer, N., Parmar, N., Uszkoreit, J., Jones, L., Gomez, A.N., et al.: Attention is all you need. arXiv Computation and Language. arXiv:1706.03762 (2017)
13. Raffel, C., Shazeer, N., Roberts, A., Lee, K., Narang, S., Matena, M.: Exploring the limits of transfer learning with a unified text-to-text transformer. arXiv Computation and Language. arXiv:1910.10683 (2019)
14. Graham, B.: Fractional max-pooling. arXiv Computer Vision and Pattern Recognition. arXiv: 1412.6071 (2014)
15. Kim, T., Song, I., Bengio, Y., et al.: Dynamic layer normalization for adaptive neural acoustic modeling in speech recognition. arXiv Computation and Language. arXiv:1707.06065 (2017)
16. He, K., Zhang, X., Ren, S., Sun, J.: Deep residual learning for image recognition. In: Computer Vision and Pattern Recognition, pp. 770–778 (2016)
17. See, A., Liu, P. J., Manning, C.D.: Get to the point: summarization with pointer-generator networks. In: Meeting of the Association for Computational Linguistics, pp. 1073–1083 (2017)
18. Pennington, J., Socher, R., Manning, C.: Glove: global vectors for word representation. In: Proceedings of the 2014 Conference on Empirical Methods in Natural Language Processing (EMNLP), pp. 1532–1543 (2014)
19. Kingma, D.P., Ba, J.: Adam: a method for stochastic optimization. arXiv Learning. arXiv: 1412.6980 (2014)
20. Lin, C.: ROUGE: a package for automatic evaluation of summaries. In: Meeting of the Association for Computational Linguistics, pp. 74–81 (2004)
21. Edunov, S., Baevski, A., Auli, M.: Pre-trained language model representations for language generation. arXiv Computation and Language. arXiv:1903.09722 (2019)
22. Peters, M.E., et al.: Deep contextualized word representations. In: North American Chapter of the Association for Computational Linguistics, pp. 2227–2237 (2018)

23. Gehrmann, S., Deng, Y., Rush, A.M.: Bottom-up abstractive summarization. Empirical Methods in Natural Language Processing, pp. 4098–4109 (2018)
24. Liao, P., Zhang, C., Chen, X., Zhou, X.: Improving abstractive text summarization with history aggregation. arXiv Computation and Language. arXiv:1912.11046 (2019)
25. Yan, Y., et al.: ProphetNet: predicting future n-gram for sequence-to-sequence pre-training. arXiv Computation and Language. arXiv:2001.04063 (2020)

Chinese Question Classification Based on ERNIE and Feature Fusion

Gaojun Liu[1,2], Qiuxia Yuan[1], Jianyong Duan[1,2]([✉]), Jie Kou[1], and Hao Wang[1,2]

[1] School of Information Science, North China University of Technology,
Beijing 100144, China
`duanjy@ncut.edu.cn`
[2] CNONIX National Standard Application and Promotion Laboratory,
North China University of Technology, Beijing 100144, China

Abstract. Question classification (QC) is a basic task of question answering (QA) system. This task effectively narrows the range of candidate answers and improves the operating efficiency of the system by providing semantic restrictions for the subsequent steps of information retrieval and answer extraction. Due to the small number of words in the question, it is difficult to extract deep semantic information for the existing QC methods. In this work, we propose a QC method based on ERNIE and feature fusion. We approach this problem by first using ERNIE to generate word vectors, which we then use to input into the feature extraction model. Next, we propose to combine the hybrid neural network (CNN-BILSTM, which extracts features independently), highway network and DCU (Dilated Composition Units) module as the feature extraction model. Experimental results on Fudan university's question classification data set and NLPCC(QA)-2018 data set show that our method can improve the accuracy, recall rate and F1 of the QC task.

Keywords: Chinese question classification · ERNIE · Highway network · Feature fusion

1 Introduction

QA is a hot research topics in the field of information retrieval. It is a more intelligent form than traditional search engines. It does not require users to input keywords to be retrieved, but allows users to ask questions in natural language, and the system returns accurate answers instead of a document or web page related to the answer. The question answering system mainly consist of three modules: question analysis, information retrieval and answer extraction [1]. QC is the most basic tasks, which can effectively reduce the range of the candidate answers. It can influence the answer extraction strategy, and adopt different answer selection strategies according to different categories of questions [2].

Different from the general text classification, the corpus of question classification has the following two characteristics:

© Springer Nature Switzerland AG 2020
X. Zhu et al. (Eds.): NLPCC 2020, LNAI 12431, pp. 343–354, 2020.
https://doi.org/10.1007/978-3-030-60457-8_28

- The text of the question is usually short so that the information of the feature is insufficient.
- Natural language questions presented by users are often colloquial and ambiguous, which is mainly due to the different cultural levels and expressions of users.

Current methods on QC are mainly based on machine learning [3] or deep learning [4–7]. Zhou et al. [8] proposed a novel combined model (C-LSTM) by combining the convolutional neural network with the long short-term memory model, which makes the convolutional neural network and the long short-term memory model complement each other. Good performance has been achieved in both sentiment classification and question classification tasks. In 2016, Ying Wen et al. [9] proposed a hierarchical hybrid model combining a recurrent convolutional neural network (RCNN) with the highway layer, which is superior to ordinary neural network models in sentiment analysis task. Jin Liu et al. [10] combined the advantages of convolutional neural network, bidirectional GRU and attention mechanism to classify questions, and achieved good classification results.

Despite such impressive achievements, it is still challenging to Q&A with short text, due to problems such as insufficient semantic representation and textual ambiguity. In this paper, we combine the deep learning model with a pre-training model, and present a method based on ERNIE and feature fusion. Specifically, we propose to embed words using ERNIE to get dynamic word vectors with enhanced semantic information in order to eliminate ambiguity to the greatest extent. However, this also requires us to increase some parameters of the neural network, resulting in a certain degree of training difficulties. To tackle this challenge, we implement a novel framework (HCNN-HDBILSTM) that combines the advantages of CBILSTM, highway network and DCU modules to extract features from the questions.

2   Related Work

Most of the traditional deep learning methods are based on non-dynamic character or word vectors as input. The non-dynamic character or word vectors contain relatively single information and cannot be changed according to its context. The methods in Word2Vec [11] and Glove [12] represent words as vectors, where similar words have similar word representations. Recently, lots of works such as BERT [13] improved word representation via different strategies, which has been shown to be more effective for down-stream natural language processing tasks. Yu Sun et al. [14] present a language representation model enhanced by knowledge called ERNIE (Enhanced Representation through Knowledge Integration).

ERNIE improved two mask strategies based on the phrase and entity (like names, locations, organizations, products, etc.). It treats a phrase or entity composed of multiple words as a unified unit, and all of the words in this unit are uniformly masked during training. Compared with the way of mapping the query of knowledge classes directly into vectors and then adding them directly, the way of unifying mask can learn knowledge dependence and longer semantic dependence more potentially, which makes the model more generalized. Figure 1 shows the different mask strategies of BERT and ERNIE. Knowledge (such as phrases, proper nouns, etc.) learned in the pre-training process helps ERNIE realize the transformation from question text to dynamic word vector better than BERT. The obtained dynamic word vector is more closely related to the context information, and it contains richer semantic information to distinguish ambiguity.

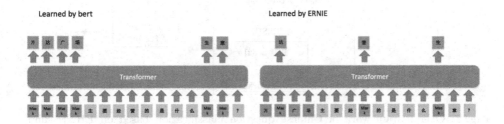

Fig. 1. The different mask strategy between BERT and ERNIE.

In recent years, deep learning has achieved excellent performance in natural language processing fields. There are many scholars use deep learning technology to solve natural language processing tasks. Srivastava et al. [15] propose a new architecture designed to ease gradient-based training of very deep networks. It allows unimpeded information flow across several layers on information highways, thus alleviating the problem of obstructed flow of gradient information as the network deepens. Yi Tay et al. [16] proposed a new combined encoder DCU (didactic composite units) for reading comprehension (RC). It explicitly models across multiple granularities using a new dilated composition mechanism. In this approach, gating functions are learned by modeling relationships and reasoning over multi-granular sequence information, enabling compositional learning that is aware of both long and short term information.

3   Method

Our method involves three main modules: question representation, feature extraction and feature fusion. A key aspect of this method is to accurately extract the needed feature from the question corpus. The method structure is shown in Fig. 2. In this section, we introduce this method in detail.

3.1   Question Representation Based on ERNIE

Traditional deep learning methods are based on non-dynamic character or word vectors as input. For example, the word vectors learned by Word2Vec or Glove

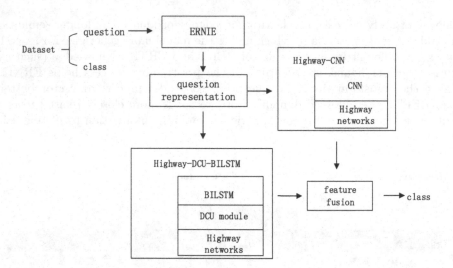

Fig. 2. Overall framework of Chinese question classification based on ERNIE and HCNN-HDBILSTM.

are fixed non-dynamic word vectors, and there is only one-word vector in a word. Its relatively simple information coverage makes it difficult to distinguish ambiguity and provide deeper semantic information for subsequent steps. In order to solve the above problems, we use ERNIE to represent the question corpus.

Firstly, the input original question text data set T is preprocessed to ensure the standardization of the question text, and finally the question text data set T' is obtained, where $len(T')$ is the number of question texts, and t'_b is the bth question text in T'::

$$T' = \left\{t'_1, t'_2, \cdots, t'_{len(T')}\right\} \tag{1}$$

The question text data set T' is vectorized by ERNIE: unify the question text t'_b into a fixed length L_{MAX} (short complement and long cut); then each text t'_b in T' is tokenized and Converted into the form of token, and a token sequence T'' is obtained, where t''_c represents the cth text, and $c \in [1, len(T')], d \in [1, len(L_{MAX})]$, W_d represents the dth token representation in each text:

$$T'' = \left\{t''_1, t''_2, \cdots, t''_c, \cdots, t''_{len(T')},\right\} \tag{2}$$

$$t''_c = \{W_1, W_2, \cdots, W_d, \cdots, W_{L_{MAX}}\} \tag{3}$$

Then, each token in t''_c is sent to the Token Embedding layer, Position Embeddings layer and dialogue embedding layer of ERNIE respectively to obtain three vector codes $V1$, $V2$ and $V3$; add the three and input them into ERNIE's bidirectional Transformer to get a word vector sequence, where $V(W_e)$ represents the vector representation of the eth token:

$$s_i = \{V(W_1), V(W_2), \cdots, V(W_e), \cdots, V(W_{L_{MAX}})\} \tag{4}$$

The final output is a word vector sequence S composed of $len(T')$ s_i, where s_i is the output vector representation of the ith text:

$$S = \left\{ s_1, s_2, \cdots, s_i, \cdots, s_{len(T')} \right\} \tag{5}$$

3.2 Question Feature Extraction

In feature extraction, our model deeply encodes the word vector sequence obtained in the previous section twice to extract feature information. In this process, we implement Highway-CNN that extracts local features. At the same time, we combine the DCU module with Highway-BILSTM to extract sequences features. we refer to this network as Highway-DCU-BILSTM. This section will describe some details of Highway-CNN and Highway-DCU-BiLSTM.

3.2.1 Highway-CNN

In the Highway-CNN network layer, taking s_i as an example, the word vector sequence s_i obtained in the previous section is used as the input of the Highway-CNN layer to extract features. As shown in Fig. 3, compared with the traditional convolutional neural network, the Highway-CNN network adds two non-linear conversion layers, a transform gate and a carry gate.

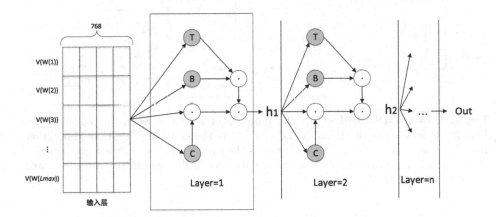

Fig. 3. Highway-CNN. The input layer is the word vector obtained by ERNIE, B represents the CNN network, T is the transform gate in the highway layer, C is the carry gate, $Layer = n$ represents the nth layer network, and the output of n-1th layer in the entire network is used as the input of the nth layer

After the input information of the word vector sequence s_i passes through the transform gate T and the CNN network, part of the information is converted, and the relevant local features are obtained while some original information is still retained through the carry gate C:

$$y = T \cdot H_{CNN} + x \cdot C \tag{6}$$

$$T = \sigma\left(W_T x + b\right) \tag{7}$$

$$H_{CNN} = \sigma\left(W_{CNN} x + b\right) \tag{8}$$

Where T represents the output vector of the "transform gate", W_T is the weight, and b is the bias term; H_{CNN} is the output obtained by the convolutional pooling operation; C is the output of the carry gate; x is the network input and y is the output. Finally, the output feature vector $F^1 = \{y_1, y_2, \cdots, y_n\}$ of the Highway-CNN is obtained.

3.2.2 Highway-DCU-BiLSTM

We use the Highway-DCU-BILSTM network to extract the sequence features of the question text. As shown in Fig. 4, we embed the DCU module into the Highway BiLSTM network to form Highway-DCU-BILSTM.

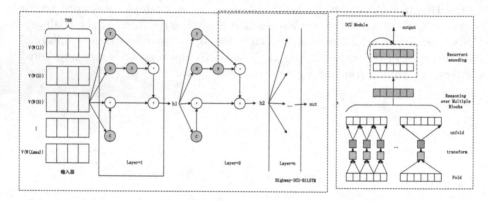

Fig. 4. Highway -DCU-BiLSTM. The input layer is the word vector obtained by ERNIE, B represents the BiLSTM network, D is the embedded DCU module, T is the transform gate in the highway layer, C is the carry gate, $Layer = n$ represents the nth layer in the highway network, and the output of n–1th layer in the entire network is used as the input of nth layer.

We use the Highway-DCU-BILSTM model which integrates the respective advantages of various network modules to extract contextual information for Chinese questions. The specific calculation flow is as follows: firstly, the word vector sequence s_i is used as the input of the model, and part of the information is calculated by BiLSTM for forward and reverse semantic information, and then the output vector H_B is obtained. Then H_B is used as the input sequence of the DCU module. Through the unique structure of the DCU module, a series of hidden vectors $H_D = \{h_1, h_2, \cdots, h_l\}$ are obtained from the input sequence by folding, transforming, unfolding, reasoning over multiple blocks and recurrent encoding operations. Other operations are similar to the Highway-CNN layer. H_D and the output of transform gate T are the final outputs of the information transform. At the same time, part of the original information is retained through the carry gate C.

$$y = T \cdot H_D + x \cdot C \tag{9}$$

where T represents the output vector of the "transform gate", C is the output of the carry gate; x is the network input and y is the output. Finally, the output feature vector $F^2 = \{y_1, y_2, \cdots, y_n\}$ of the entire Highway-DCU-BiLSTM layer is obtained.

3.3 Feature Fusion and Probability Output

Connect the output vector F^1 of the Highway-CNN layer with the output vector F^2 of the Highway-DCU-BiLSTM network to obtain a new feature vector F^3:

$$F^3 = F^1 + F^2 \tag{10}$$

Then F^3 is linearly dimensionalized through the full connection layer, and the following results are obtained:

$$F^4 = \left\{ F_1^4, F_2^4, \cdots, F_c^4 \right\} \tag{11}$$

Where c is the number of question categories. Input the F^4 into the softmax layer so that each real number in the input vector is mapped between 0 and 1, and the sum of all real numbers in the output vector is 1. These real numbers represent the probabilities of the corresponding categories, and the final output is the probability prediction vector:

$$P = \{p_1, p_2, \cdots, p_f, \cdots, p_c\} \tag{12}$$

Among them, p_f represents the probability that the question text is the fth category, search for the maximum value in the vector P, and use the classification result corresponding to the maximum value as the final output, that is, the result of the question classification is Y_{out}.

4   Experiment and Analysis

4.1   Selection and Processing of Data Sets

In order to verify the effectiveness of this method, we conducted experiments on two data sets, including the Q&A data set of the NLPCC2018 QA evaluation of CCF International Natural Language Processing and Chinese Computing Conference and Chinese Question Classification Data Set of Fudan University[1] (hereinafter referred to as FUDAN). The Fudan contains 17,243 questions and 13 categories. For categories with significantly more samples, we randomly delete some samples. For the categories with a small number of samples, we use Python

---

[1] http://code.google.com/p/fudannlp/w/edit/QuestionClassification.

to crawl questions on Baidu Know and Sogou Ask and filter them. Finally, each category and its actual example are shown in Table 1 (top). In this paper, the NLPCC data set with only question answer pairs was manually labeled with the question classification system proposed by the Information Retrieval and Social Computing Center of Harbin Institute of Technology [5], and the questions are divided into six categories: description type (DES), human type (HUM), location type (LOC), number type (NUM), time type (TIME) and entity type (OBJ). Each question was independently labeled by four people, and the data with objections was finally negotiated and labeled. After marking, each category and its actual example are shown in Table 1 (below).

Table 1. Categories and examples of datasets.

FUDAN	
Categories	Examples
比较类	管片模具固定式和流水线式区别?
表示类	Daniel Powter 译音成中文是什么?
不作处理	大家来领悟《领悟》这首歌?
方法类	怎样才可以把钢琴弹得更好?
关系类	陶晶莹和郑华娟什么关系?
枚举类	陈楚生的新歌有哪些?
描述类	对中国现存古典园林的分析?
评价类	最爱还是你这首歌好听吗?
事实类	其实你懂我这首歌是什么时候的?
是非类	LA IS LA BONITA 这首歌有中文版的吗?
推荐类	周董走红以来，他出的哪首专辑里的歌最好听?
需求类	什么频道可以收听鬼故事的电台?
原因类	伊甸园之东里的红豆为什么有两个人唱的?
NLPCC(QA)-2018	
Categories	Examples
描述类	万达广场主要经营的是什么生意?
人物类	《机械设计基础》这本书的作者是谁?
地点类	安德烈是哪个国家的人呢?
数字类	合肥地铁一号线总投资额是多少?
时间类	华严寺何时建造的?
实体类	中国第二大民族是什么族?

4.2 Comparative Experiment

To verify the effectiveness of our method, we carry out comparative experiments on the two data sets processed in the previous section. **Text-CNN**. The basic convolutional neural network model proposed by Kim et al. [17] It consists of the convolutional layer, pooling layer and fully connected layer. **LSTM**. Simple long short-term memory model for QC task. **C-LSTM**. Zhou et al. [8] combined the convolutional neural network with the LSTM, characterized text sequences by the convolution layer, and input them into the LSTM, using a novel vector rearrangement mode. **AB-BIGRU-CNN**. Jin Liu et al. [10] proposed a model combining CNN, bidirectional GRU and attention mechanism. **Our method:** Combines the advantages of Highway networks, DCU module and ERNIE to classify the questions.

Accuracy, precision, recall and F1 are used as evaluation indicators. The best model parameter settings obtained after model tuning is shown in Table 2.

Table 2. Parameter settings.

Parameter	Epoch	Batch size	Dropout	Padding size	Learning rate	Initialize weight of highway
Value	50	128	0.1	32	5e−5	5

4.3 Comparative Experiment Results and Analysis

By comparing with different models to verify the applicability and superiority of this method in the question classification task, the results obtained on the two data sets are shown in Table 3.

Table 3. Classification results of different models on two data sets.

Model	FUDAN				NLPCC(QA)-2018			
	acc	P	recall	F1	acc	P	recall	F1
Text-CNN	0.7430	0.7420	0.7575	0.7424	0.8366	0.7956	0.8621	0.8041
LSTM	0.7479	0.7675	0.7677	0.7477	0.8333	0.8027	0.8710	0.8033
C-LSTM	0.7550	0.7872	0.7898	0.7769	0.8689	0.8291	0.8905	0.8330
AB-BIGRU-CNN	0.7598	0.8012	0.7778	0.7775	0.9450	0.9141	0.9274	0.9192
Our method	0.8379	0.8703	0.8600	0.8598	0.9741	0.9452	0.9734	0.9573

Our method is superior to other models in the scores of each indicator on the two data sets. As shown in Fig. 5, the F1 score of this method is higher than the five baseline methods by 11.74%, 11.21%, 8.29%, 8.23% and 2.21% on Fudan, and higher by 15.32%, 15.4%, 12.43%, 3.81% and 0.26% on NLPCC(QA)-2018. Experimental results show that this method not only solves the problem of insufficient semantic information obtained by traditional methods, but also improves the performance of the model in the feature extraction stage to a certain extent.

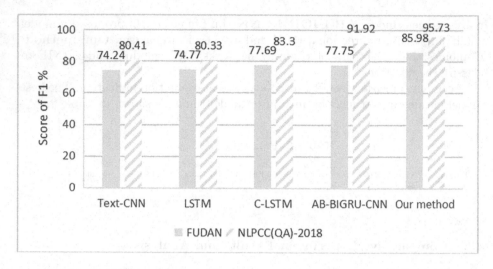

Fig. 5. Comparison of F1 scores of different methods.

4.4 Ablation Experiment

Convolutional neural network and the bidirectional long short-term memory model in deep learning have a strong ability to capture local information and extract sequence features. We use a hybrid neural network model CBILSTM as the benchmark model (CNN-BILSTM, which are independent of each other). The experimental results after adding the highway networks, DCU module, ERNIE and BERT to the benchmark model are shown in Table 4.

Table 4. Comparison of model performance after adding different modules.

Model	FUDAN				NLPCC(QA)-2018			
	acc	P	recall	F1	acc	P	recall	F1
CBILSTM	0.7030	0.7575	0.6919	0.6949	0.8414	0.8020	0.8790	0.8034
CBILSTM + highway	0.7479	0.7675	0.7677	0.7477	0.8916	0.8511	0.9209	0.8595
CBILSTM + DCU	0.7491	0.7938	0.7740	0.7759	0.8689	0.8161	0.8885	0.8301
CBILSTM + Bert	0.8201	0.8488	0.8362	0.8377	0.9660	0.9396	**0.9759**	0.9547
CBILSTM + ERNIE	0.8272	0.8507	0.8510	0.8457	0.9676	0.9294	0.9544	0.9401
Our method	**0.8391**	**0.8666**	**0.8552**	**0.8580**	**0.9741**	**0.9452**	0.9734	**0.9573**

The results in Table 4 prove that the different modules added in this method can have a positive impact, optimize the performance of the model. Figure 6 shows the cross entropy loss in the training process.

The loss curve of the model after adding the Highway Layer tends to be smoother and more stable, while also decreasing. Embedding the DCU into the model gives the model excellent reasoning and representation capabilities for a

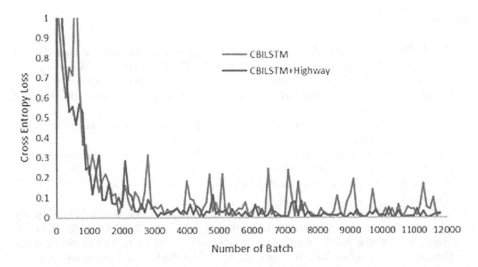

Fig. 6. Cross entropy loss in training process.

single granular block and multiple granular blocks when extracting timing features, and effectively solves the time-consuming and laborious shortcomings of BiLSTM for processing long text sequences. Use ERNIE to complete the conversion of question text to dynamic word vector. This method not only enhances the contextual semantics, but also allows the parameters of the neural network to be increased appropriately.

5   Conclusion

In this paper, we have presented a novel method for Chinese QC by considering the semantic information as well as feature fusion. The empirical study shows the effectiveness of each components of our architecture. This method not only solves the problem of difficulty in extracting deep semantic information, but to a certain extent alleviates the disappearance of gradients caused by the network being too deep, and finally improves the performance of the model. The current QC task still faces the problem of lack of corpus. Besides the idea of continuing to collect and label new data, it is also a feasible direction to use a large number of unlabeled corpora for semi-supervised learning. Besides, how to better feature fusion is also the research direction of the next step.

Acknowledgements. This research work has been partially supported by two NSFC grants, No. 61972003 and No. 61672040.

References

1. Xu, J., Zhang, D., Li, S., Wang, H.: Research on question classification via bilingual information. J. Chin. Inf. Process. **31**(05), 171–177 (2017). ISBN 1003-0077
2. Zhang, D., Li, S., Wang, J.: Semi-supervised question classification with jointly learning question and answer representations. J. Chin. Inf. Process. **31**(01), 1–7 (2017). ISBN 1003-0077
3. Barigou, F.: Impact of instance selection on kNN-based text categorization. J. Inf. Process. Syst. **14** (2018)
4. Fan, Z., Su, L., Liu, X., Wang, S.: Multi-label Chinese question classification based on word2vec. pp. 546–550 (2017)
5. Yu, B., Xu, Q., Zhang, P.: Question classification based on MAC-LSTM, p. 75 (2018)
6. Yang, S., Gao, C.: Enriching basic features via multilayer bag-of-words binding for Chinese question classification. CAAI Trans. Intell. Tech. **2**(3), 133–140 (2017)
7. Wang. D., Nyberg, E.: A long short-term memory model for answer sentence selection in question answering. In: Meeting of the Association for Computational Linguistics & the International Joint Conference on Natural Language Processing (2015)
8. Zhou, C., Sun, C., Liu, Z., Lau, F.C.M.: A C-LSTM neural network for text classification. Comput. Sci. **1**(4), 39–44 (2015)
9. Wen, Y., Zhang, W., Luo, R., Wang, J.: Learning text representation using recurrent convolutional neural network with highway layers (2016)
10. Liu, J., Yang, Y., Lv, S., Wang, J., Chen, H.: Attention-based BiGRU-CNN for Chinese question classification. J. Ambient Intell. Hum. Comput. (2) (2019). https://doi.org/10.1007/s12652-019-01344-9
11. Mikolov, T., Chen, K., Corrado, G., Dean, J.: Efficient estimation of word representations in vector space. Computer Science (2013)
12. Pennington, J., Socher, R., Manning, C.: Glove: global vectors for word representation. In: Conference on Empirical Methods in Natural Language Processing (2014)
13. Devlin, J., Chang, M.-W., Lee, K., Toutanova, K.: BERT: pre-training of deep bidirectional transformers for language understanding (2018)
14. Sun, Y., Wang, S., Li, Y., Feng, S., Wu, H.: ERNIE: enhanced representation through knowledge integration (2019)
15. Srivastava, R.K., Greff, K., Schmidhuber, J.: Training very deep networks. Computer Science (2015)
16. Yi, T., Tuan, L.A., Hui, S.C.: Multi-granular sequence encoding via dilated compositional units for reading comprehension. In: Proceedings of the 2018 Conference on Empirical Methods in Natural Language Processing (2018)
17. Kim, Y.: Convolutional Neural Networks for Sentence Classification. Eprint Arxiv (2014)

An Abstractive Summarization Method Based on Global Gated Dual Encoder

Lu Peng[1,2], Qun Liu[1,2(✉)], Lebin Lv[1,2], Weibin Deng[1], and Chongyu Wang[1,2]

[1] School of Computer Science and Technology, Chongqing University of Posts and Telecommunications, Chongqing, China
liuqun@cqupt.edu.cn
[2] Chongqing Key Laboratory of Computational Intelligence, Chongqing, China

Abstract. The sequence-to-sequence model based on the RNN attention mechanism has been well applied in abstractive summarization, but the existing models generally cannot capture long-term information because of the defects of RNN. So an abstractive text summarization method is proposed in this paper, which is based on global gated double encoding (GDE). Combined with Transformer to extract global semantics, a global gating unit based on dual encoder is designed that can filter the key information to prevent the redundant information, and the problem of insufficient semantics is compensated dynamically. Many experiments on the LCSTS Chinese and CNN/Daily Mail English datasets show that our model is superior to the current advanced generative methods.

Keywords: Abstractive summarization · Seq2Seq · Global semantics · Global gating unit · Pointer generator

1 Introduction

Automatic text summarization is the process of compressing and streamlining a long text to a short text. The short text can simply and accurately express the meaning of the original text and retain key information. In the era of information overload, automatic text summarization technology is more important. It not only accurately expresses the author's intention, but also effectively reduces the user's reading cost.

Recently, there are two broad approaches of summarization: extractive and abstractive. Extractive summarization directly extracts the element information from the original text to form summarization. This method is easy to produce redundancy of information and semantic incoherence between sentences. Abstractive summarization expresses the original text information with concise words by understanding the key contents. This process is similar to the mode of manual summarization, so abstractive summarization has become a hot spot in the text summarization.

This paper is Supported by the National Key Research and Development Program of China under Grant No. 2018YFC0832102 and National Natural Science Foundation of China (Grant No. 61936001).

X. Zhu et al. (Eds.): NLPCC 2020, LNAI 12431, pp. 355–365, 2020.
https://doi.org/10.1007/978-3-030-60457-8_29

With the successful application of deep learning, thanks to the advantages of Recurrent Neural Network (RNN) in processing sequence data, sequence-to-sequence (seq2seq) models are widely applied in abstractive summarization. However, RNN mainly focuses on current information and is easy to forget the previous memory information. Moreover seq2seq model is prone to generate numerous Out-Of-Vocabulary (OOV) and repeated words, which affects the readability of the generated summary and reduces the quality of the summarization.

To solve the above problems, in this paper, the long-short-term memory (LSTM) is introduced to make up for the defects that RNN forgets semantic information and the Transformer structure proposed by Vaswani [1] is used to obtain the global semantics. To avoid redundancy caused by semantics extraction by Transformer, we design a global gating unit to filter key information. At the same time, a pointer generator network with coverage mechanism is used to directly copy the words in accord with semantics from the original text. It makes the semantics of the generated summarization more completely and accurately.

2 Related Work

Text summarization is a typical task in natural language processing, which is very similar to machine translation. Therefore, many machine translation methods were applied to generate summarizations. To solve the problem of insufficient sequence annotation data in machine translation, Sutskever et al. [2] proposed an end-to-end seq2seq model. The model includes encoder and decoder. The encoder is responsible for obtaining the semantic vector of input information and the decoder is responsible for transforming the semantic vector into output information. Bahdanau et al. [3] and Luong et al. [4] improved seq2seq model. Enlightened by the thinking mode that people's attention will be focused on the keyword part while reading, they improved the soft attention mechanisms that significantly enhanced the effect of machine translation.

Then many natural language processing tasks have introduced seq2seq model based on the attention mechanism. Rush et al. [5] first applied the attention-based seq2seq model in abstractive summarization task, and achieved good results on the DUC2004 and Gigaword datasets. Hu et al. [6] proposed the first Chinese large-scale text summarization dataset LCSTS, which used characters or words as units to train a neural network model, then produced a baseline model for Chinese text summarization evaluation that promoted the development of the Chinese text summarization field. By using the seq2seq model based on RNN, Nallapati et al. [7] constructed an abstractive summarization in which both encoder and decoder used Bi-GRU.

With the development of abstractive text summarization research based on seq2seq model, researchers found that the quality of text summarization obtained once was not high. Hence, Zeng et al. [8] proposed a rereading mechanism to simulate the reading process of human beings, and just confirmed which words are the key points after finishing reading. Since the vocabulary list cannot completely cover all words, OOV words are inevitably appeared in the process of summary generation. Gu et al. [9] proposed to directly copy OOV words into the output sequence. A pointer generator network is proposed to solve the problems of direct generation, direct copy, and copy position of the decoder in [10]. In [11], the authors designed coverage mechanism on the pointer generator network, which solved the problem of repeated words better when generating summary.

Due to the lack of structural characteristics of the article in abstractive text summarization, combined the latent structure vector with the variational auto-encoder (VAE), Li et al. [12] proposed to add the structural vector into the end-to-end model. In [13], by evaluating the semantic relevance between the target summary and the source text, the authors proposed a function that maximized the similarity between the original text and the generated summary. To improve the performance of the encoder, an adversarial learning was introduced to measure the supervision strength of encoder in [14]. The authors found that the more relevant the original text and summary were, the stronger the supervision learning was, and the better the quality of generating summary was.

3 Proposed Model

In this section, we will illustrate our model in detail. The framework of our proposed model is shown in Fig. 1. Dual encoders read input text and extract global semantic information; Global gating unit further filters the semantic information obtained above and deliveries it to the decoder to generate the context semantic vector; Pointer generator and Coverage mechanism directly copy the unregistered words to avoid OOV words while generating summarization via obtained semantic vector. The first contribution of our model is using dual encoders to extract more abundant global semantic information to make up for the lack of Bi-LSTM. The second is using the global gating unit to distinguish more global key information to avoid redundant information extracted by dual encoders.

3.1 Dual Encoder

Our model is based on pointer-generator network [11]. The tokens of the input text $X = \{x_1, x_2, \ldots, x_n\}$ are fed into the encoder, where n represents the length of the input text. The purpose of task is to output summarization text $Y = \{y_1, y_2, \ldots, y_m\}$, where $m(m < n)$ represents the length of the output text.

Since Bi-LSTM must rely on the input of the previous unit and process the input sequence word by word, it cannot better represent the global information. We use dual encoder model (Bi-LSTM + Transformer) to model summarization task. The introduction of the Transformer encoder can improve the performance of Bi-LSTM by obtaining more global semantic information. Then the word embedding matrix W_x is used to convert the word x_t of the input text into a word embedding representation E, where $t \in (0, n)$. The conversion formula is as following:

$$E = \sum_0^n W_x x_t \tag{1}$$

After obtaining the word embedding representation E, it is sent to the two encoders for encoding separately. Bi-LSTM encoder is composed of forward and backward networks,

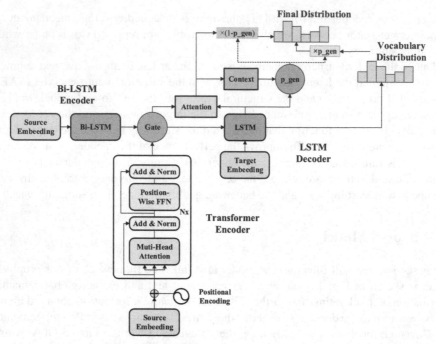

Fig. 1. An overview of GDE which mainly includes Bi-LSTM Encoder, Transformer Encoder, Global Gating Unit, Pointer Generator and Coverage Mechanism, and LSTM Decoder with Contextual Semantic Vector.

and its output is $H_1 = \{h_1, h_2, \ldots, h_n\}$, in which every output includes two directions of hidden states ($h_i = [\overrightarrow{h}_i, \overleftarrow{h}_i]$) at each moment. It can be calculated as following:

$$H_1 = \text{BiLSTM}(E) \tag{2}$$

To collect more global semantic information, the Transformer encoder is composed of multiple Transformer Blocks, each block is composed of a multi-head self-attention mechanism and a fully connected feedforward network. The self-attention formula is denoted:

$$\text{Attention}(Q, K, V) = \text{softmax}\left(\frac{QK^T}{\sqrt{d_k}}\right)V \tag{3}$$

The multi-head self-attention mechanism is used to calculate the attention weight of each word in the sequence. Through increasing the number of Transformer block layers, the self-monitoring ability of the multi-head self-attention is strengthened, and the word weight of each head will be adjusted so that some heads can get global semantic information. Then the output of Transformer encoder H_2 can be get.

3.2 Global Gating Unit

As the length of text sequence increases, although the combination of Transformer and Bi-LSTM can capture more global semantic information, it still contains too many redundant words, and only a few words can become the key information of input sequence. Since the key information is the essential information for the text summarization. A global gating unit is designed to filter the result of the above-mentioned dual encoders structure.

To enhance the global semantic information expression of the input sequence, the semantic vectors H_1 and H_2 output by the dual encoders are spliced into H firstly, then the screening probability g_t is generated after they passed through the gating unit. Finally, the semantic vector O_t containing the global key information is obtained. It can help the decoder to effectively use key information to generate summary. The specific formulas are as follows:

$$H = \text{concat}(H_1, H_2) \tag{4}$$

$$g_t = \sigma\left(W_g H\right) \tag{5}$$

$$O_t = \left(1 - g_t\right)H_1 + g_t H_2 \tag{6}$$

Where concat($\cdot$) is the splicing function, σ is the *sigmoid* function, and W_g is learnable parameter.

3.3 Pointer-Generator Network and Coverage Mechanism

Pointer-Generator Network. In the decoding process, the model may generate new words. If some new words are not in the vocabulary, it will cause OOV problems. We use a pointer generator network, which can not only copy words directly from the original text, but also generate words directly from the vocabulary to avoid OOV words. Assuming at time t of decoding, the probability $p_{gen} \in [0, 1]$ of word selection in the vocabulary list can be calculated by the following formula with the input x_t of decoder, hidden layer status s_t, and context semantic vector c_t at the current moment:

$$p_{gen} = \sigma\left(W_c c_t + W_s s_t + W_x x_t + b_{gen}\right) \tag{7}$$

Where vector W_c, W_s, W_x and scalar b_{gen} are learnable parameters, and σ is the *sigmoid* function.

$1 - p_{gen}$ is the probability of copying words from the original text through attention distribution a_t. The calculation formula for generating the target word w at time t of decoding is as follows:

$$P(w) = p_{gen}P_{vocab}(w) + \left(1 - p_{gen}\right)\sum_{i:w_i=w} a_i^t \tag{8}$$

Note that if w is an OOV word, then $P_{vocab}(w)$ is zero; similarly if w does not appear in the source text, then $\sum_{i:w_i=w} a_i^t$ is zero.

Coverage Mechanism. To address the repetitive problem in text summarization, a coverage vector is set. The value of this vector is the sum of the attention distributions computed by all previous prediction steps. Based on the coverage vector, our model (GDE) has already paid attention to each word of the source text. Meanwhile, the loss function is designed by the authors in [11] to punish the attention on the repeated words. Summarization generated by seq2seq model often brings about repetition in a sentence. Then we introduce a coverage mechanism to overcome this problem. In the experimental verification, the coverage mechanism is only used for the CNN/Daily Mail dataset, and not be used in the LCSTS dataset, because the training process on LCSTS is dealt with characters and the coverage mechanism has no usage.

3.4 Training and Inference

In the training process, given the input text X, for making the generated summary Y_d closer to the target summary Y_t, i.e. maximizing the probability of the generated summary sequence Y_d, the following negative log likelihood function needs to be minimized.

$$L_{GDE}(\theta) = -\frac{1}{N} \sum_{i=1}^{N} \log p(y|x) \qquad (9)$$

Where θ represent the set of are all learnable parameters, N is the training set, and $p(y|x)$ is the probability of obtaining the summary sequence y after inputting a given x sequence.

In the decoding process, we use beam search method to generate the summary vocabulary, to find the optimal solution in a relatively limited search space at the lowest cost.

4 Experiments

4.1 Datasets

To verify the effectiveness of our model (GDE), the LCSTS and CNN/Daily Mail datasets are used in the experiment.

LCSTS. A large-scale Chinese short text summary dataset, which mainly contains three parts. Part I contains 2,400,591 (short text, summary) training data for real news; Part II includes 10,666 pairs of artificially labeled short texts and summaries randomly sampled from the training data; Part III is different from Part I, a total of 1106 pairs of data are annotated manually. Each pair of statements in PART II and PART III is scored 1–5 by manual scoring, and the score is used to judge the degree of relevance between the short text and the abstract. As suggested by Hu *et al.* [6], we use PART I as the training set and the 725 statement pairs with scores above 3 (including 3 points) in PART III as the test set.

CNN/Daily Mail. Alarge-scale English text summary dataset, including more than 280,000 pairs for training, 13,000 pairs for validation, and 11,000 pairs for testing. Each source text corresponds to multiple summary sentences. On average, Each source document in the training set contains 766 words and 29.74 sentences, the corresponding summary also contains 53 words and 3.72 sentences.

4.2   Evaluation and Parameter Settings

We employ ROUGE [15] as our evaluation metric. ROUGE evaluates the quality of summary based on the co-occurrence information of n-grams in a summary, which is an evaluation method oriented to the recall rate of n-grams. Its core idea means the artificial summaries generated by many experts separately form a standard summary set. Automatic summary generated by different method is compared with the above standard summary set. The number of overlapping basic units (n-grams, word sequences and the number of word pairs) is counted to assess the quality of the generated summary.

For LCSTS, we use a dictionary with 5000 vocabulary, the dimension of word vector is 300, the LSTM hidden layer unit is 600, and the batch size is set to 64. For CNN/Daily Mail, the dictionary has 50000 vocabulary, the batch size is set to 16, the maximum length of input article tokens is 400, and the maximum length of output article tokens is 100. During the decoding process, coverage mechanism is used to reduce content duplication. During the training process, the word vectors in encoder and decoder share parameters, and a global gated network and Adagrad optimizer are used. The initial learning rate is set to 0.15, the beam search width is set to 4 and the discard rate of neural network is set to 0.1.

4.3   Comparison with State-of-the-Art Methods

We implement our experiments on the LCSTS Chinese dataset and the CNN/Daily Mail English dataset. The performance of different models is evaluated by the F1 values of ROUGE-1, ROUGE-2, and ROUGE-L.

As shown in Table 1, there are seven baselines are compared on Chinese LCSTS dataset. **RNN** [6] is the RNN-based seq2seq model without using context during decoding. **RNN-Context** [6] is the RNN-based seq2seq model using context during decoding and all information of encoder are input into decoder. **CopyNet** [9] is the attention-based seq2seq model with the copy mechanism. **SRB** [13] is a model that improves semantic relevance between source text and summary. **DGRD** [12] is the attention-based seq2seq model that introduce the latent structure vectors to learn structure information of the target summary. **R-NET** [16] is gated-based network model with reading comprehension thinking mode. **S2S + superAE** [14] is LSTM-based seq2seq model with the autoencoder as an assistant supervisor.

Compared with **S2S + superAE** [14], the results of our model GDE raised by 1.0 and 0.3 for ROUGE-1 score and ROUGE-L score on the LCSTS respectively, but slightly lower in ROUGE-2. Because the value of ROUGE-2 is calculated depending on the global semantic information of words, it shows that our model cannot capture the global key information well dynamically. However, it is significantly better than other models on all metrics. It depicts that abstractive text summarization method based on the global dual encoder better solves the problem of using only single RNN encoder, it can not only obtain more semantic features of the original text, but also effectively integrate more key global information.

As shown in Table 2, four advanced baseline methods are compared on English CNN/Daily Mail dataset. **words-lvt2k-temp-att** [17] is the attention-based seq2seq

Table 1. Automatic summarization result on LCSTS

MODEL	ROUGE-1	ROUGE-2	ROUGE-L
RNN	21.5	8.9	18.6
RNN-context	29.9	17.4	27.2
CopyNet	34.4	21.6	31.3
SRB	33.3	20.0	30.1
DGRD	37.0	24.2	34.2
R-NET	37.8	25.3	35.0
S2S + superAE	39.2	**26.0**	36.2
GDE	**40.2**	25.0	**36.5**

model with incorporating semantic features. **graph-based attention** [18] take advantage of the graph attention into the seq2seq to improve the quality of summary. **pointer-generator** [11] is the LSTM-based seq2seq with pointer generator to prevent the generation of OOV words. **pointer-generator + coverage** [11] uses coverage mechanism under the pointer generator to prevent repeated words during summary generation.

Table 2. Automatic summarization result on CNN/Daily Mail

MODEL	ROUGE-1	ROUGE-2	ROUGE-L
words-lvt2k-temp-att	35.46	13.3	32.65
graph-based attention	38.01	13.9	34
pointer-generator	36.44	15.66	33.42
pointer-generator + coverage	39.53	17.28	36.38
GDE	37.19	16.15	34.01
GDE + coverage	**40.43**	**17.80**	**37.15**

From the F1 value of the ROUGE indicators given in Table 2, our model GDE has a significant improvement. Compared with the pointer-generator, the score of ROUGE-1, ROUGE-2 and ROUGE-L are increased by 0.75, 0.49 and 0.59 respectively, which is slightly worse than the **pointer-generator + coverage** model. However, when GDE add the coverage mechanism, the results score increased by 0.9, 0.52 and 0.77 respectively.

4.4 Comparison with Different Global Semantic Information

To analyze the impact of different global semantic information on abstractive summary, three typical baselines are compared which adopt two different ways to capture the global semantic information on the LCSTS dataset. Both of the **seq2seq** and the **pointer-generator** models use Bi-LSTM encoder, but the latter uses pointer generator network to be decoder. The **transformer** uses the Transformer encoder, and the rest is consistent with the seq2seq model.

Table 3 describes the impact of different global semantic information generation methods on text summarization. It can be seen that the transformer performs better and indicate that the transformer has higher ability to grasp the global key information of sequence data. Compared with pointer-generator model, GDE increases the evaluation index values of ROUGE-1, ROUGE-2 and ROUGE-L by 1.9, 1.4 and 2.8 respectively, which indicates that GDE can capture more global information. Generally, under the same premise of the decoder, the more global key information collected by the encoder, the more complete the summary generated by the decoder.

Table 3. Performance of models with different global information on LCSTS

Model	ROUGE-1	ROUGE-2	ROUGE-L
seq2seq	35.1	22.7	32.5
transformer	35.5	23.2	33.0
pointer-generator	38.3	23.6	34.7
GDE	**40.2**	**25.0**	**36.5**

4.5 Case Analysis

To verify the performance of the GDE on the real cases, we select some real samples from the LCSTS dataset. As shown in Table 4, from the comparison between the correctness and robustness of the summary, GDE can well grasp key information and accurately express the original meaning. In Text 1, seq2seq model gave an error expression because of misunderstanding semantics. "The U.S. Air Force will encircle China like the Soviet Union". The original meaning is that the United States will encircles China as they do with the Soviet Union. GDE express the same meaning as the reference. It depicts that GDE can effectively integrate the key global information. In Text 2, Seq2Seq model caught the wrong point and only stayed at what Premier Li Keqiang said, but the core of the GDE highlighting text was "scoring the reform of the free trade zone". Compared with reference, "Shanghai " was not found in original text, GDE can not only retain the key information of source text, but also prevent the generation of unnecessary words.

Table 4. Some examples of LCSTS abstractive summarization

Text 1:美国太平洋空军司令透露，美国空军将像当年对苏联那样，将精锐部队轮流部署在中国周边，以包围中国。空军将派大量的 F-22 猛禽、F-35 闪电 II 和 B-2 隐身轰炸机到该地区，卡莱尔还说，F-35 的第一个海外永久性基地将位于太平洋地区。 The commander of the U.S. Pacific Air Force revealed that the U.S. Air Force will deploy its elite troops in turns around China to encircle China as it did to the Soviet Union. The Air Force will send a large number of F-22 Raptors, F-35 Lightning II and B-2 stealth bombers to the area. Carlisle also said that F-35's first overseas permanent base will be located in the Pacific.
Reference:美军司令：美军精锐将像包围苏联一样包围中国 US Commander: The elite of the US military will encircle China like the Soviet Union
Seq2Seq:美国空军司令：美国空军将像苏联那样包围中国 US Air Force Commander: The US Air Force will encircle China like the Soviet Union
GDE:美军司令：美军将像当年对苏联那样包围中国 Commander of the U.S. Army: The U.S. Army will encircle China as it did with the Soviet Union
Text 2:李克强总理 18 日在美药典公司餐厅与 10 家进驻自贸区的中外企业家座谈，请他们给自贸区各项改革"打分"。他对 10 位参会企业家说："希望我们在留有饭菜余香中进行的座谈会，不仅 friendly（友好），而且 frankly（坦率），有什么问题直来直去讲出来。" On the 18th, Premier Li Keqiang met with 10 Chinese and foreign entrepreneurs stationed in the free trade zone in the American Pharmacopoeia restaurant, and asked them to "rate" various reforms in the free trade zone. He said to 10 entrepreneurs participating in the conference: "I hope that the symposium we will hold while leaving the food is not only friendly (friendly), but also frankly (frankly). If you have any questions, just go straight to it."
Reference:李克强邀 10 企业给上海自贸区打分 Li Keqiang invited 10 companies to score Shanghai Free Trade Zone
Seq2Seq:李克强：希望我们在留有饭菜余香中进行座谈会 Li Keqiang: I hope we will have a symposium while leaving the fragrance of food
GDE:李克强请 10 家企业家给自贸区改革打分 Li Keqiang asked 10 entrepreneurs to rate the reform of the free trade zone

5 Conclusion

In this paper, we propose an abstractive text summarization method based on global gated dual encoders. By using dual encoders, more global semantic information can be obtained. Then the global gated unit is designed to filter the key information so that the more accurate text summary can be generated. In the future work, prior knowledge and element extract will be introduced to enhance the quality of text summary generation.

References

1. Vaswani, A., Shazeer, N., Parmar, N., et al.: Attention is all you need. In: Advances in Neural Information Processing Systems, 5998–6008 (2017)
2. Sutskever, I., Vinyals, O., Le, Q.V.: Sequence to sequence learning with neural networks. In: Advances in Neural Information Processing Systems, pp. 3104–3112 (2014)
3. Bahdanau, D., Cho, K., Bengio, Y.: Neural machine translation by jointly learning to align and translate. arXiv preprint arXiv:1409.0473 (2014)
4. Luong, M.T., Pham, H., Manning, C.D.: Effective approaches to attention-based neural machine translation. In: Proceedings of the 2015 Conference on Empirical Methods in Natural Language Processing, pp. 1412–1421 (2015)
5. Rush, A.M., Chopra, S., Weston, J.: A neural attention model for abstractive sentence summarization. In: Proceedings of the 2015 Conference on Empirical Methods in Natural Language Processing. ACL Press, Lisbon, pp. 379–389 (2015)

6. Hu, B., Chen, Q., Zhu, F.: LCSTS: a large scale chinese short text summarization dataset. In: Proceedings of the 2015 Conference on Empirical Methods in Natural Language Processing, pp. 1967–1972 (2015)
7. Nallapati, R., Zhou, B., Santos, C., et al.: Abstractive text summarization using sequence-to-sequence RNNs and beyond. In: Proceedings of the 20th SIGNLL Conference on Computational Natural Language Learning. ACL Press, Berlin, pp. 280–290 (2016)
8. Zeng, W., Luo, W., Fidler, S., et al.: Efficient summarization with read-again and copy mechanism. arXiv preprint arXiv:1611.03382 (2016)
9. Gu, J., Lu, Z., Li, Hang, et al.: Incorporating copying mechanism in sequence-to-sequence learning. In: Proceedings of the 54th Annual Meeting of the Association for Computational Linguistics. ACL Press, Berlin, pp. 1631–1640 (2016)
10. Gulcehre, C., Ahn, S., Nallapati, R., et al.: Pointing the unknown words. In: Proceedings of the 54th Annual Meeting of the Association for Computational Linguistics (Long Papers), vol. 1, pp. 140–149 (2016)
11. See, A., Liu, P.J., Manning, C.D.: Get to the point: summarization with pointer-generator networks. In: Proceedings of the 55th Annual Meeting of the Association for Computational Linguistics (Long Papers), vol. 1, pp. 1073–1083 (2017)
12. Li, P., Lam, W., Bing, L., et al.: Deep recurrent generative decoder for abstractive text summarization. In: Proceedings of the 2017 Conference on Empirical Methods in Natural Language Processing, pp. 2091–2100 (2017)
13. Ma, S., Sun, X., Xu, J., et al.: Improving semantic relevance for sequence-to-sequence learning of chinese social media text summarization. In: Proceedings of the 55th Annual Meeting of the Association for Computational Linguistics (Short Papers), vol. 2, pp. 635–640 (2017)
14. Ma, S., Sun, X., Lin, J., et al.: Autoencoder as assistant supervisor: improving text representation for chinese social media text summarization. In: Proceedings of the 56th Annual Meeting of the Association for Computational Linguistics (Short Papers), vol. 2, pp. 725–731 (2018)
15. Lin, C.: Rouge: a package for automatic evaluation of summaries. In: Proceedings of the ACL Workshop: Text Summarization Braches Out, Barcelona, pp. 74–81 (2004)
16. Wang, W., Yang, N., Wei, F., et al.: Gated self-matching networks for reading comprehension and question answering. In: Proceedings of the 55th Annual Meeting of the Association for Computational Linguistics (Long Papers), vol. 1, pp. 189–198 (2017)
17. Nallapati, R., Zhou, B., Santos, C.N.D., et al.: Abstractive text summarization using sequence-to-sequence RNNs and beyond. In: SIGNLL Conference on Computational Natural Language Learning, pp. 280–290 (2016)
18. Tan, J., Wan, X., Xiao, J.: Abstractive document summarization with a graph-based attentional neural model. In: Proceedings of the 55th Annual Meeting of the Association for Computational Linguistics (Long Papers), vol. 1, pp. 1171–1181 (2017)

Rumor Detection on Hierarchical Attention Network with User and Sentiment Information

Sujun Dong[1], Zhong Qian[1(✉)], Peifeng Li[1,2], Xiaoxu Zhu[1], and Qiaoming Zhu[1,2]

[1] School of Computer Science and Technology, Soochow University, Suzhou, China
1820766741@qq.com, {qianzhong,pfli,xiaoxzhu,qmzhu}@suda.edu.cn
[2] AI Research Institute, Soochow University, Suzhou, China

Abstract. Social media has developed rapidly due to its openness and freedom, and people can post information on Internet anytime and anywhere. However, social media has also become the main way for rumors to spread largely and quickly. Hence, it has become a huge challenge to automatically detect rumors among such a huge amount of information. Currently, there are many neural network methods, which mainly considered text features but did not pay enough attention to user and sentiment information that are also useful clues for rumor detection. Therefore, this paper proposes a hierarchical attention network with user and sentiment information (HiAN-US) for rumor detection, which first uses the transformer encoder to learn the semantic information at both word-level and tweet-level, then integrates user and sentiment information via attention mechanism. Experiments on the Twitter15, Twitter16 and PHEME datasets show that our model is more effective than several state-of-the-art baselines.

Keywords: Rumor detection · User and sentiment information · Hierarchical attention network

1 Introduction

Rumors, usually used to spread panic and confusion, are untrue or inaccurate information breed on public platforms and Rumor Detection (RD) is to judge whether the information is true or false. Our work focuses on using relative public information to detect the false information spreading on social media. The key behind this work is that users on social media can express their opinions on the information disseminated on social media, and can provide evidence and speculation on false information [1].

In recent years, it has become increasingly popular to use neural network models to detect rumors. By modeling text information on social media, for example, Ma et al. [6–10] proposed a series of RNN-based methods, and these methods can automatically obtain a high-level text representation to detect the true degree of information. However, they only focused on how to use the text information of the rumor, and did not pay enough attention to user information, or even ignored it. Moreover, these methods hardly considered the role of sentiment information. Different users hold different degrees of credibility, and the sentiment expressed by them is directly related to their opinions.

© Springer Nature Switzerland AG 2020
X. Zhu et al. (Eds.): NLPCC 2020, LNAI 12431, pp. 366–377, 2020.
https://doi.org/10.1007/978-3-030-60457-8_30

Table 1. An example of a rumor source tweet and its user features

Source tweet	*Breaking! A four meter long Cobra with three heads was found in Myanmar!*
User Features	**username:** ABCD_1234 **verified:** False **description:** **follower:** 15 **listed_count:** 300 **user_creat_time:** 2011/10/4 9:36:17 **tweet_creat_time:** 2011/10/4 17:52:36 … …

Table 1 shows an example of a rumor source tweet and its user features. User *ABCD_1234* posted a tweet: *A 4 m long cobra with three heads was found in Myanmar.* The tweet sounds appalling, but considering the characteristics of many snakes in Myanmar, it is difficult to identify *true* or *false* of the tweet, and may eventually be predicted as *Unverified*. However, combined with user information, the authenticity of this tweet can be predicted more accurately. First, in terms of user name, "*ABCD_1234*" is composed of "*ABCD*" and "*1234*" that is just a sequence of letters and digits without any actual meanings, indicating that this is probably not a normal user. Next, the user's verified property is *False*, showing that the user has not been verified who may spread false information maliciously. Finally, the user had no user description and posted 300 tweet in less than 24 h of user creations. Based on the above information, it is easy to determine that this is probably a user who specializes in spreading rumors, so the source tweet is identified as a rumor. Table 1 shows that user information plays an important role in RD.

In Table 2, the majority of users expressed fear of the source tweet, such as "*breaking*", "*terrify*", "*fear*", "*crying*", "*scared*" and so on, whose main purpose is to spread fear. Of course, there are users who express different sentiment information, such as "*fake*", "*don't believe*", etc. These sentimental information plays an important role in exposing rumors. Therefore, we think that considering sentiment information can effectively describe the sentiment features of a rumor in the process of spreading, so as to obtain more accurate high-level representation.

According to the above analysis, this paper proposes a novel hierarchical attention network with user and sentiment information (HiAN-US), which uses the hierarchical structure model to learn features from the word-level and tweet-level, respectively, and considers user and sentiment information via attention mechanism. Khoo et al. [1] showed that propagation tree structure on social media does not reflect the process of information propagation well. Therefore, the model uses linear structure to model text based on post time. In addition, the corresponding user and sentiment information are also used through word-level and tweet-level attention to improve the performance of rumor detection. The experimental results on Twitter15, Twitter16 and PHEME prove that our model HiAN-US is superior to the state-of-the-art baselines. The contributions of this paper can be summarized as the following two points:

Table 2. An example of a rumor source tweet and its reply tweets

Source tweet	*Breaking! A four meter long Cobra with three heads was found in Myanmar!*
Reply tweet	*Oh my god! It's terrify...*
	I'm fear! Crying...
	...
	Really? It is scared me!
	...
	Fake! I don't believe.
	It is fake! I know it at first sight.

- We propose a hierarchical model HiAN-US for RD to integrate the word-level and tweet-level information;
- Our model integrates user and sentiment information via attention at word-level and tweet-level.

The rest of the paper is organized as follows: Sect. 2 draws related research work in this field; Sect. 3 introduces the model proposed in the paper; Sect. 4 presents the experimental results and analysis; Sect. 5 summarizes the paper and proposes direction of future research work.

2   Related Work

Recently, rumor detection (RD) on social media has become a more popular topic, attracting more attention than before. Compared with the traditional machine learning methods, the neural network methods can more accurately learn the representation of text information, and does not require too many artificial labeling features. Therefore, more and more neural network methods are applied to rumor detection.

Chen et al. [2] proposed unsupervised rumor detection model based on user behavior, which combined RNN and AutoEncoder (AE) to obtain more features, in which user features encoded by RNN and then transmitted to AE. Do et al. [3] proposed a DRRD model based on text information and user information. The model used GRU to encode text information and user information, and then obtained a high-level text representation and user information representation through the maximum pooling layer. Finally, the two types of information were stitched together to predict whether the information to be tested is a rumor through the softmax classifier. Li et al. [5] used user information, attention mechanism and multi-task learning to detect rumors. After splicing user information and text information, they used LSTM to encode, and finally used the attention mechanism and softmax classifier to predict the true degree of information. Khoo et al. [1] proposed a rumor detection model named PLAN based on self-attention mechanism focusing on user interaction, in which only texts were considered, and user interaction was achieved by using self-attention mechanism. The above methods of using user information will be compared with the methods proposed by this paper:

- Compared with those studies that did not utilize self-attention in Transformer model (e.g., Chen et al. [2] and Do et al. [3]), our model uses a transformer encoder to encode user information. A large number of experiments prove that the transformer encoder is more effective than RNN. And our model uses attention to model user information, which highlights the impact of important users.
- Compared with those studies that only focused on text and user information (e.g., Li et al. [5]), first, the coding model we used is superior to LSTM; second, when using the attention mechanism, our method puts more emphasis on the role of users.
- Compared with those studies that only consider the propagation structure of tweets (e.g., Khoo et al. [1]), our model integrates user and sentiment information via attention, which is the main novelty of this paper.

As far as we know, previous work did not consider the effect of sentiment information for rumor detection. As shown in Table 2 above, sentiment information in tweets can also help to detect rumors. Therefore, we propose a hierarchical neural network with both user and sentiment attention for rumor detection.

3 Model for Rumor Detection

3.1 Problem Definition

We define each thread as $t_i = \{t_{i,1}, t_{i,2}, t_{i,3}, \ldots\ldots, t_{i,n}\}$, where $t_{i,1}$ is source tweet, $t_{i,j}$ is the j-th tweet in chronological order, and there are n tweets in the thread, whose user information and sentiment information is $u_i = \{u_{i,1}, u_{i,2}, u_{i,3}, \ldots\ldots, u_{i,n}\}$ and $s_i = \{s_{i,1}, s_{i,2}, s_{i,3}, \ldots\ldots, s_{i,n}\}$, respectively. The RD task is to assign a label y to each (t_i, u_i, s_i), where $y = \{False, True, Unverified, Non\text{-}Rumor\}$. In this paper, rumor means that a text may be true or false and should be identified furtherly. Therefore, *False* rumor means the text contains and spreads false information, while *True* rumor means the text contains true information, and *Non-Rumor* is true information without further identification. *Unverified* means it is difficult to judge whether the text is true or false due to the lack of the related information.

3.2 Hierarchical Attention Network with User and Sentiment Information

We propose a Hierarchical Attention Network with User and Sentiment information (HiAN-US) for RD and our model consists of five parts: word encoder layer, word attention layer, tweet encoder layer, tweet attention layer, and output layer. The encoder layers use transformer encoder to learn more semantic information on word-level and tweet-level, and use attention to integrate user and sentiment information between different levels. The architecture of our model is displayed in detail in Fig. 1.

Word Encoder Layer. We map each word of text information $(t_{i,j})$, user information $(u_{i,j})$ and sentiment information $(s_{i,j})$ in tweet to the vectors $w_{i,j}^k$, $u_{i,j}^k$, and $s_{i,j}^k$, respectively. After stitching them together, they are fed to the word encoder layer for encoding. In

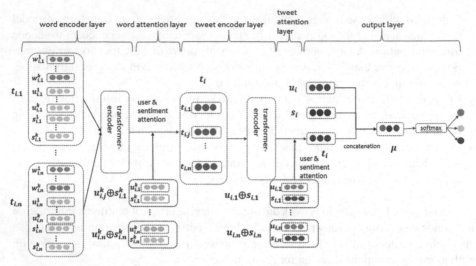

Fig. 1. Hierarchical attention network with user and sentiment information (HiAN-US)

this way, three types of information can be fused and encoded to improve the accuracy of the final text representation.

$$I_{i,j}^k = w_{i,j}^k \oplus u_{i,j}^k \oplus s_{i,j}^k \tag{1}$$

Attention Layer. In the sentiment analysis task, Yu et al. [11] have proved that the sentimental words in a text can express the author's sentiment to some extent. Therefore, we think that these sentimental words or sentences have an important role in improving the performance of rumor detection. Moreover, Li et al. [5] and Chen et al. [2] have proved that user features can significantly improve the performance of rumor detection. Hence, we introduce the attention mechanism based on user and sentiment information to our model at word-level and tweet-level, respectively.

1) **Word-level Attention.** We encode $I_{i,j}^k$ through the word-level transformer encoder to obtain the vector $I_{i,j}^{ka}$, and then feed it to the word-level attention based on user and sentiment information to obtain a high-level representation as follows.

$$m_{i,j}^k = tanh\left(w_w I_{i,j}^{ka} + w_u u_{i,j}^k + w_s s_{i,j}^k + b_w\right) \tag{2}$$

$$\alpha_{i,j}^k = softmax\left(m_{i,j}^k\right) \tag{3}$$

$$t_{i,j} = \sum_k \alpha_{i,j}^k I_{i,j}^{ka} \tag{4}$$

where w_w, w_u, w_s, b_w are the parameters of the attention mechanism. $\alpha_{i,j}^k$ indicates the importance of $I_{i,j}^k$ to $u_{i,j}^k$ and $s_{i,j}^k$. $t_{i,j}$ is a high-level learned representation of a tweet.

2) **Tweet-level Attention.** After obtaining the word-level representation vector $t_{i,j}$, the transformer encoder is also used to encode tweets to obtain the vector $t_{i,j}^a$. Different

sentiments play different roles in determining the true value of source tweets similarly, different users have different credibility for information disclosure. Therefore, similarly, a tweet-level attention mechanism based on user and sentiment information is adopted. The formula is expressed as follows.

$$m_{i,j} = tanh\left(w_t t_{i,j}^a + w_u u_{i,j} + w_s s_{i,j} + b_t\right) \tag{5}$$

$$\alpha_{i,j} = softmax\left(m_{i,j}\right) \tag{6}$$

$$t_i = \sum_j \alpha_{i,j} t_{i,j}^a \tag{7}$$

where w_t, w_u, w_s, b_t are the parameters of the attention mechanism. $\alpha_{i,j}$ indicates the importance of $t_{i,j}$ to $u_{i,j}$ and $s_{i,j}$. t_i is high-level representation of a set of tweets after learning.

Output Layer. The finally vector μ consists of the vectors t_i, u_i and s_i as follows.

$$\mu = t_i \oplus u_i \oplus s_i \tag{8}$$

where u_i represents the global user vector, which contains all the user information in t_i; s_i represents the global sentiment vector, which contains all the sentiment information in t_i . u_i, s_i are obtained by average pooling of $u_{i,j}$ and $s_{i,j}$. μ is the feature vector of a set of tweets, which contains the semantic information of tweets, the corresponding user and sentiment information of each tweet. After that, we will classify it through a softmax layer as follows.

$$p(t_i) = softmax\left(w_\mu \mu + b_\mu\right) \tag{9}$$

Finally, the loss function of our model is designed as follows.

$$L = -\sum_i y(t_i) \log(p(t_i)) \tag{10}$$

where $y(t_i)$ is the ground truth, $p(t_i)$ is the predicted probability of rumor for t_i.

4 Experimentation

This section details the datasets, data preprocessing, implementation details, and experimental results. We evaluate the model based on two datasets collected from social media. Experimental results prove that our model can achieve more satisfactory performance than several state-of-the-art baselines.

4.1 Experimental Setup

In this paper, two publicly available datasets, i.e., PHEME and Twitter (including Twitter15 and Twitter16), are used to evaluate our model. The PHEME is an expanded version of PHEME 5events and consists of 9 events. This dataset has two levels of annotation information: 1) annotation of thread as rumor or Non-Rumor; 2) comment rumor to true, false, or unverified. In Table 3, we give statistics on the data distribution of PHEME. For PHEME, our preprocess approach is different from Kumar and Carley et al. [4]: we divide the data randomly rather than based on events. For Twitter15 and Twitter16, we use the same processing methods as Khoo et al. [1]. The dataset annotates threads as true, false, unverified and Non-Rumor. Table 4 shows the data distribution of Twitter15 and Twitter16.

Table 3. Data distribution of PHEME

Events	Treads	Rumors	Non-Rumor	True	False	Unverified
Charlie Hebdo	2079	458	1621	193	116	149
Sydney Siege	1221	522	699	382	86	54
Ferguson	1143	284	859	10	8	266
Ottawa Shooting	890	470	420	329	72	69
Germany Crash	469	238	231	94	111	33
Putin Missing	238	126	112	0	9	117
Prince Toronto	238	229	4	0	222	7
Gurritt	138	61	77	59	0	2
Ebola Essien	14	14	0	0	14	0
Total	6425	2402	4023	1067	638	697

Table 4. Data distribution of Twitter15 and Twitter16

Dataset	Threads	True	False	Unverified	Non-Rumor
Twitter15	1413	350	334	358	371
Twitter16	756	189	172	190	275

According to the analysis on Twitter15 and Twitter16, we find that the proportion of retweeting source tweets in each thread is larger. We think that these retweets have little impact on RD and remove them. In the process of unified data processing, we replace all URLs with "URL". All "@XXX" and "#XXX" are divided into two words, i.e., "@nycaviation" is divided into "@" and "nycaviation".

Our model uses user and sentiment information. PHEME contains user information, while twitter15 and twitter16 not. So we only consider sentiment information for twitter15 and twitter16. The user and sentiment information used in PHEME are shown in Table 5.

Table 5. User and sentiment information

Information	Features
User	User name
	Verified
	Description
	Followers_count
	Follow_count
	Favorite_count
	Create_time
	List_count
Sentiment	Sentiment words
	Polarity(positive/negative)

4.2 Experimental Result

For the experiments on PHEME, Twitter15, and Twitter16, we used the same parameters while the word embeddings are initialized by GloVe. The following models are selected as the baselines.

- **RvNN** is a tree-based recursive neural network model proposed by Ma et al. [9].
- **PLAN** is one of the models proposed by Khoo et al. [1]. The model uses the maximum pooling layer at the word-level to obtain the tweet representation and the transform encoder to encode at tweet-level, and finally obtains a high-level representation of the entire thread through the attention.
- **HiAN-S** is our model, and only sentiment information is considered via attention at the word and tweet-level.
- **HiAN-U** is our model, only user information is considered via word-level and tweet-level attention.
- **HiAN-US** is our model, considering both user and sentiment information via attention at both word-level and tweet-level.

For the Twitter15 and Twitter16 datasets, we compare with RvNN and PLAN, while for the PHEME dataset, we compare with PLAN since RvNN only reported their results on the Twitter15 and Twitter16 datasets. Table 6 shows the results among different models on the three datasets.

For Twitter15 and Twitter16, as mentioned in 4.1, we only consider sentiment information to the model (HiAN-S). It can be seen from the experimental results that the performance of HiAN-S is higher than baseline systems on both datasets. On the Twitter15, the model is 11.3 higher than RvNN and 1.6 higher than PLAN on accuracy; on the Twitter16 dataset, the model is 8.5 higher than RvNN and 1.4 higher than PLAN on accuracy.

Table 6. Results of comparison with different methods

Dataset	Model	Accuracy
Twitter15	RvNN	72.3
	PLAN	82.0
	HiAN-S	**83.6**
Twitter16	RvNN	73.7
	PLAN	80.8
	HiAN-S	**82.2**
PHEME	PLAN	70.6
	HiAN-U	73.5
	HiAN-S	74.5
	HiAN-US	**77.7**

For PHEME, we can incorporate two information into the model: user information and sentiment information, which can produce three variants of the model: HiAN-U, HiAN-S, and HiAN-US. The experimental results show that the performance is significantly higher than the baseline system on this dataset, i.e., HiAN-U, HiAN-S and HiAN-US are 2.9, 3.9 and 7.1 higher than PLAN, respectively.

4.3 Analysis

Table 7 reports the experimental results of various models on four labels (FR, TR, UR, NR) on Twitter15, Twitter16, and PHEME. Form Table 7, we can find that our HiAN-S (with sentiment information) outperforms the other two baselines on NR on all three datasets, which shows that sentiment information is helpful to detect the tweets with NR. Our model HiAN-U (with user information) almost outperforms PLAN on three types except UR. This result further ensures the effectiveness of user information in RD. Combining the sentiment and user information into our model, HiAN_US can take the advantages from two aspects and further improve the performance. Especially, in comparison with HiAN-S and HiAN-U, HiAN-US improves the accuracies on FR and UR significant, with the gains of 6.0, 15.2, 8.8, and 13.1, respectively. This indicates that user information and sentiment information can complement each other to improve the performance of RD.

For different datasets, the performance of our model on each category is not always better than the baselines, but our model can achieve the best results on NR. We counted the average number of sentiment words contained in each tweet in different categories on each dataset as shown in Table 8. We can find that sentiment words contained in NR tweets of Twitter15, Twitter16 and PHEME are the majority, which are 4.83, 4.36 and 4.42 respectively. This explains why the performance of our model is higher than the baselines on NR. On Twitter15, the FR tweets contains an average of 4.28 sentiment words per tweet, which is relatively large, so the performance of HiAN-S in this category

Table 7. Performance on four types on Twitter15, Twitter16 and PHEME (FR: False Rumor; TR: True Rumor; UR: Unverified Rumor; NR: Non-Rumor)

Dataset	Model	Accuracy	FR	TR	UR	NR
Twitter15	RvNN	72.3	75.8	82.1	65.4	68.2
	PLAN	82.0	75.5	**90.2**	**82.2**	79.1
	HiAN-S	**83.6**	**83.3**	88.1	78.8	**84.2**
Twitter16	RvNN	73.7	74.3	83.5	70.8	66.2
	PLAN	80.8	**82.9**	88.4	77.5	72.7
	HiAN-S	**82.2**	77.6	**90.9**	**78.2**	**80.6**
PHEME	PLAN	70.6	56.3	62.8	62.7	77.1
	HiAN-U	73.5	57.6	**69.0**	52.4	81.8
	HiAN-S	74.5	60.4	63.3	50.3	84.9
	HiAN-US	**77.7**	**76.4**	58.9	**65.5**	**85.7**

can be higher than the baselines. On Twitter16, the FR tweets only contains an average of 1.60 sentiment words per tweet. Therefore, the sentiment information used by HiAN-S in this category is insufficient to improve performance.

Table 8. Statistics of sentiment words contained in each tweet

Dataset	FR	TR	UR	NR
Twitter15	4.28	4.03	2.70	4.83
Twitter16	1.60	2.67	2.71	4.36
PHEME	3.35	3.67	2.69	4.42

Table 9 shows an example of Non-Rumor in PHEME, while Table 10 shows an example of Non-Rumor user information in PHEME, including *username, verified, description, followers_count, list_count, follow_count*, etc. From the perspective of user information, source user is a verified news media with a large number of followers, relevant descriptions, and analysis of the information of reply users also shows that all users are in a normal state. From the perspective of sentiment information, source tweets do not contain sentiment words. There are panic words in reply users, such as "*awful*", "*very dark*", "*upsetting*", "*tragical*", etc., but there is no sentiment against source tweet. Our model can combine these two kinds of information to give source tweet and source user higher weight, so that it is easier to detect source tweet as Non-Rumor.

Based on the above analysis, the following conclusions can be drawn: 1) Our model can effectively improve the performance of Non-Rumor detection, thereby improve the overall performance; 2) Both user and sentiment information play an important role in

Table 9. An example of Non-Rumor in PHEME

Source tweet	• *french interior ministry: debris from #germanwings airbus a320 #4u9525 at 2,000m altitude http://t.co/8upmsinqkx http://t.co/miu94nhnbr*
Reply tweets	• *@skynews oh god.* 😩 • *@skynews a very dark day in the aviation industry .#germanwings* • *" @skynews: debris from #germanwings airbus a320 #4u9525 http://t.co/gzsw4yj6s2 http://t.co/sggsmujkly" awful, awful news. really upsetting*😩 • *@skynews man this sucks. and i'm flying to barcelona in 2 weeks.* • *@leonhenry16 @skynews so? have u ever heard about such a tragical event happening twice within 2 weeks on the same route?*

Table 10. An example of Non-Rumor user information in PHEME

Source user	Sky news	True	True	1964051	15444	17
Reply user	Carly Marie	False	True	671	6	455
	Joseph Muiruri	False	True	540	20	1770
	Zia Lombardi	False	True	647	20	1362
	Leon Henry	False	True	12	0	66
	Screenwriting girl	False	True	1102	42	917

improving rumor detection performance; 3) User and sentiment information can form a complementary role to jointly improve the accuracy of rumor detection.

5 Conclusion

In this paper, a hierarchical attention network with user and sentiment information (HiAN-US) is proposed for RD. The model uses a transformer encoder to obtain semantic information at word-level and tweet-level. Different from previous research, we incorporate user information and sentiment information at both word-level and tweet-level via attention to capture more important components. Experiments on the PHEME, Twitter15 and Twitter16 datasets show that our proposed model is more effective than state-of-the-arts.

At present, most platforms can share messages in the form of text, pictures and short videos at the same time, and rumors can also be spread more quickly through these three ways. We consider how to combine three completely different information for multi-modal RD in future.

Acknowledgments. The authors would like to thank the three anonymous reviewers for their comments on this paper. This research was supported by the National Natural Science Foundation of China (No. 61772354, 61836007 and 61773276.), and the Priority Academic Program Development of Jiangsu Higher Education Institutions (PAPD).

References

1. Khoo, L., Chieu, H., Qian, Z., Jiang, J.: Interpretable rumor detection in microblogs by attending to user interactions. In: 34th AAAI Conference on Artificial Intelligence, AAAI 2020, New York, pp. 8783–8790 (2020)
2. Chen, W., Zhang, Y., Yeo, C., Lee, B., Lau, C.: Unsupervised rumor detection based on users' behaviors using neural networks. Pattern Recogn. Lett. **105**, 226–233 (2018)
3. Do, T., Luo, X., Nguyen, D., Deligiannis, N.: Rumour detection via news propagation dynamics and user representation learning. In: IEEE Data Science Workshop, DSW 2019, Minneapolis, MN, USA, pp. 196–200 (2019)
4. Kumar, S., Carley, K.: Tree LSTMs with convolution units to predict stance and rumor veracity in social media conversations. In: 57th Conference of the Association for Computational Linguistics, Florence, pp. 5047–5058 (2019)
5. Li, Q., Zhang, Q., Si, L.: Rumor detection by exploiting user credibility information, attention and multi-task learning. In: 57th Conference of the Association for Computational Linguistics, Florence, pp. 1173–1179 (2019)
6. Ma, J., Gao, W., Wei, Z., et al.: Detect rumors using time series of social context information on microblogging websites. In: 24th ACM International Conference on Information and Knowledge Management, Melbourne, pp. 1751–1754 (2015)
7. Ma, J., Gao, W., Mitra, P., et al.: Detecting rumors from microblogs with recurrent neural networks. In: 25th International Joint Conference on Artificial Intelligence, New York, pp. 3818–3824 (2016)
8. Ma, J., Gao, W., Wong, K.F.: Detect rumors in microblog posts using propagation structure via kernel learning. In: 55th Annual Meeting of the Association for Computational Linguistics, Vancouver, pp. 708–717 (2017)
9. Ma, J., Gao, W., Wong, K.-F.: Rumor detection on twitter with tree-structured recursive neural networks. In: The Meeting of the Association for Computational Linguistics, Australia, pp. 1980–1989 (2018)
10. Ma, J., Gao, W., Wong, K.F.: Detect rumor and stance jointly by neural multi-task learning. In: The Web Conference Companion, Lyon, pp. 585–593 (2018)
11. Yu, J., Jiang, J.: Learning sentence embeddings with auxiliary tasks for cross-domain sentiment classification. In: The 2016 Conference on Empirical Methods in Natural Language Processing, Austin, pp. 236–246 (2016)

Measuring the Semantic Stability
of Word Embedding

Zhenhao Huang[1] and Chenxu Wang[1,2](✉)

[1] School of Software Engineering, Xi'an Jiaotong University, Xi'an, China
huangzhenhao@stu.xjtu.edu.cn, cxwang@mail.xjtu.edu.cn
[2] MOE Key Lab of Intelligent Network and Network Security, Xi'an, China

Abstract. The techniques of word embedding have a wide range of applications in natural language processing (NLP). However, recent studies have revealed that word embeddings have large amounts of instability, which affects the performance in downstream tasks and the applications in safety-critical fields such as medical diagnosis and financial analysis. Further researches have found that the popular metric of Nearest Neighbors Stability (NNS) is unreliable for qualitative conclusions on diachronic semantic matters, which means NNS cannot fully capture the semantic fluctuations of word vectors. To measure semantic stability more accurately, we propose a novel metric that combines the Nearest Senses Stability (NSS) and the Aligned Sense Stability (ASS). Moreover, previous studies on word embedding stability focus on static embedding models such as Word2vec and ignore the contextual embedding models such as Bert. In this work, we propose the SPIP metric based on Pairwise Inner Product (PIP) loss to extend the stability study to contextual embedding models. Finally, the experimental results demonstrate that CS and SPIP are effective in parameter configuration to minimize embedding instability without training downstream models, outperforming the state-of-the-art metric NNS.

Keywords: Static word embeddings · Contextual word embeddings · Semantic stability

1 Introduction

Word embeddings are dense and low-dimensional vectors that can capture the lexical semantics of words [1–3]. In order to extract the representation of words better, various kinds of word embedding models are proposed, which can be classified as static and contextual embedding models. For example, Word2vec [4] and Glove [5] are static embedding models which learn a fixed vector to represent each word. In contrast, contextual embedding models such as EMLo [6] and Bert [7] extract word representations dynamically with the input context. These models have significantly boosted the application of word embeddings in many fields, from sentiment analysis [8] to entity alignment [9]. However, subsequent studies have found that word embeddings have significant amounts

© Springer Nature Switzerland AG 2020
X. Zhu et al. (Eds.): NLPCC 2020, LNAI 12431, pp. 378–390, 2020.
https://doi.org/10.1007/978-3-030-60457-8_31

of instability [10, 11], i.e., a word has different nearest neighbors in different instances of a model. The instability could significantly affect the robustness and performance of word embeddings in downstream tasks [10]. Investigating the stability of the word embedding models could benefit the design of novel models and the interpretability of existing models.

Previous studies universally employ the variance of nearest neighbors (e.g., NNS) to measure the stability of word embeddings [10, 12]. Nevertheless, Hellrich and Hanh [13] observed that Nearest Neighbors Stability (NNS) as a metric for qualitative conclusions on diachronic semantic matters is unreliable. It is not reliable enough to measure the stability of word embeddings in downstream tasks. To address the problem, we propose a combined metric, including Nearest Senses Stability (NSS) and Aligned Sense Stability (ASS), to quantify the stability of word embeddings. As a variant of NNS, NSS uses WordNet [14] to calculate the overlap ratio of neighbors' senses as embedding stability. Therefore, NSS can solve the problem that the stability calculated by NNS is lower than the actual stability if different neighborhood words of a certain word are synonyms, such as "erase" and "delete". It is inaccurate that the synonyms are considered to be completely different in NNS. In contrast, NSS calculates the similarity of the synonyms by their senses to measure stability more accurately.

Different from the above neighbors-based metrics, ASS measures the stability with the numerical variances of word vectors in the embedding space. Nevertheless, The original word embeddings cannot be used directly to measure stability because of the stochastic nature of the static embedding model. Levy and Goldberg prove that Word2vec is equivalent to implicit factorization of the word-context matrix [15]. An important side-effect of this essence is that the obtained embeddings are arbitrarily rotated by an orthogonal matrix without affecting the objective of the embedding model. Since the embeddings are unconstrained, and the only error signal comes from the orthogonally-invariant objective, the entire embedding space is free to arbitrary orthogonal transform during training [16, 17]. The arbitrary orthogonal transformations are not problematic in most scenarios because it does not affect the relative positions of nodes in the embedding space. However, the transformations indeed result in the inconsistency of coordinate axes of word embeddings in different instances of an embedding model. We call this phenomenon as word sense misalignment. In order to measure the numerical variances of word embeddings from different instances, we must ensure that the vectors are aligned to the same coordinate axes. For this purpose, we map the word embeddings obtained in different instances to a super-sense space whose features in each dimension has explicit meaning [18].

Furthermore, previous studies on the stability of word embeddings focus on static embedding models, while the contextual embedding model has been neglected. The metrics for static embedding models are not suitable for contextual embedding models because word vectors in the contextual embedding model are dynamic. To tackle this difficulty, we propose a novel metric SPIP which is defined as the similarity of the matrices consisting of vectors of words in the same context from different instances to measure the stability of contextual embedding models. Here, we use the Pairwise Inner Product (PIP) loss [19] to calculate the similarity.

Finally, we empirically validate that the proposed metrics are effective in selecting parameters for a model to generate stable embeddings, without having to train downstream models. Experiments show that our novel metrics correlate strongly with the performance stability of downstream tasks.

2   Word Embedding Models

In this section, we briefly review the word embedding models, including static and contextual embedding models.

Skip-Gram with Negative Sampling (SGNS). Skip-gram (SG) is a three-layered fully connected network model [4] to predict the context of the inputting word. To reduce the computational complexity of the model, Mikolov et al. [20] also proposed an optimization method named Negative sampling (NS) and a more straightforward loss function based on Noise Contrastive Estimation (NCE) [21].

GloVe. GloVe [5] is an unsupervised model to extract representations of words from an aggregated global word-word co-occurrence matrix. The obtained representations combine the advantages of global matrix factorization and local context window methods.

EMLo. EMLo [6] is a deep bidirectional language model which extracts word representations dynamically with the input context. This model overcomes the disadvantages of the above two static embedding models which use a static vector to represent all the senses of a word.

Bert. Similar to EMLo, Bert [7] is a contextual embedding model whose word vectors are based on the input context. By taking advantage of transformer encoders [22], Bert can jointly combine both the left and right context in all layers.

3   The Word Embedding Stability Metrics

3.1   Task Result Stability

We first define Task Result Stability (TRS), which acts as a basic metric to reflect the ability of other task-free stability metrics. Leszczynski et al. [23] define the instability as disagreement ratio in downstream predictions. As shown in Table 1, the measurement method cannot measure the stability of downstream task well when the predictions are the same while the probability values vary dramatically. To address the problem, we propose to compute the cosine similarity of the result vectors to quantify the stability of the downstream task. Let $X_1, \ldots, X_m \in \mathbb{R}^{n \times d}$

be m embedding matrices, where n is the size of the vocabulary and d is the dimension of the embedding. Denote f_{X_i} as the i-th instance of a t-classification model $\mathcal{M}_t$ trained by X_i. Given a test data θ, the result vector of f_{X_i} is $f_{X_i}(\theta) = [p_1, \ldots, p_t]$ where p_j is the probability of θ being the j-th category predicted by f_{X_i}. Then TRS is defined as:

$$TRS = \frac{2\sum_{1 \leq i < j \leq m} \text{Cos}\left(f_{X_i}(\theta), f_{X_j}(\theta)\right)}{m(m-1)} \tag{1}$$

where Cos is a function to calculate the cosine similarity between two result vectors.

Table 1. The predictions of f_{E_1} and f_{E_2} are same, but their result vectors have changed considerably. Clearly, TRS can measure the variation of the predicted results more accurately.

	f_{E_1}			f_{E_2}			TRS	Disagreement
	Prob. A	Prob. B	Pred.	Prob. A	Prob. B	Pred.		
1	0.98	0.02	A	0.56	0.44	A	0.799	No
2	0.93	0.07	A	0.79	0.21	A	0.983	No
3	0.77	0.23	A	0.73	0.27	A	0.998	No
4	0.43	0.57	B	0.47	0.53	B	0.997	No
5	0.08	0.92	B	0.18	0.82	B	0.992	No

3.2 Stability Metrics for Static Embedding Models

Given a training corpus $\mathcal{D}$ which contains a mass of documents, we could extract a vocabulary V which contains all distinct words in $\mathcal{D}$. For each word $w \in V$, an embedding model $\mathcal{M}$ learns a mapping $f : w_i \to \mathbf{x}_i \in \mathbb{R}^d$ from a word to a d-dimensional vector based on the training corpus $\mathcal{D}$. Accordingly, the learned vector space can be denoted by a matrix $\mathbf{X}^{|V| \times d}$, where the i-th row $\mathbf{x}_i$ represent the learned vector of $w_i \in V$. For each metric, we first generate m embedding spaces by applying a specific embedding model $\mathcal{M}$ to the same corpus $\mathcal{D}$ with identical parameters for m times. Consequently, we will obtain a set of embedding spaces $\mathcal{X} = \{\mathbf{X}_1, \mathbf{X}_2, \ldots, \mathbf{X}_m\}$. Then, we calculate the top k nearest neighbors $N_i^{(j)} = \{w'_1, w'_2, \ldots, w'_k\}$ of word w_i in j-th embedding space $\mathbf{X}_j$. Here, We evaluate the distances between two words w_s and w_t by the cosine similarity of their corresponding embedding vector:

$$sim(w_s, w_t) = \frac{\mathbf{x}_s \mathbf{x}_t}{|\mathbf{x}_s||\mathbf{x}_t|} \tag{2}$$

where $\mathbf{x}_s$ and $\mathbf{x}_t$ are the embedding vectors of w_s and w_t, respectively. Higher similarity scores indicate closer distances between two words.

Nearest Neighbors Stability. Nearest Neighbors Stability (NNS) is used to measure the intrinsic stability of word embedding in recent works [10–13]. The metric is defined as the overlap ratio between nearest neighbors of $w_i \in V$ in different embedding spaces:

$$NNS = \frac{\sum_{i=1}^{|V|} \left| \bigcap_{1 \leq j \leq m} N_i^{(j)} \right|}{|V| \left| \bigcup_{1 \leq j \leq m} N_i^{(j)} \right|} \tag{3}$$

Nearest Senses Stability. Different from nearest neighbors stability (NNS), nearest senses stability (NSS) measures invariance of sense neighbors rather than word neighbors. We gain certain word's sense neighbors from WordNet [14], which divides nouns, verbs, adjectives and adverbs into sets of cognitive synonyms (synsets). For each word $w \in N_i^{(j)}$, we retrieve the senses of w in the WordNet. Denoting the senses set of w as $SN(w)$, we define the sense-based nearest neighbors of $w_i \in V$ in j-th embedding space $\mathbf{X}_j$ as follows:

$$NS_i^{(j)} = \bigcup_{w' \in N_i^{(j)}} SN(w'). \tag{4}$$

We then quantify the stability of w_i in the models through the Jaccard coefficient of the m sets of sense-based nearest neighbors:

$$SB_i = \frac{\left| \bigcap_{\mathbf{X}_j \in \mathcal{X}} NS_i^{(j)} \right|}{\left| \bigcup_{\mathbf{X}_j \in \mathcal{X}} NS_i^{(j)} \right|} \tag{5}$$

Finally, NSS is defined as the average stability of all words:

$$NSS = \frac{\sum_{j=1}^{|V|} SB_j}{|V|} \tag{6}$$

In this paper, we set $k = 10$ and $m = 3$ to make a tradeoff between calculation efficiency and measurement accuracy [10].

Aligned Sense Stability. Word embeddings are arbitrarily rotated because the objective does not constrain the orientation of the obtained embeddings. Therefore, it is hard to interpret the semantics of each individual feature dimension. NSS can measure relative position invariance of words in the latent space. However, this metric fails to capture the invariance of dimensional semantics. To address this issue, we propose aligned senses stability (ASS), which measures the stability of word embeddings which are aligned to a super-sense space [18].

We employ a human-annotated super-sense space based on the corpus of SemCor[1] [24]. Super-sense[2] consists of 41 semantic categories, including 26

---

[1] http://moin.delph-in.net/SemCor.
[2] http://wordnet.princeton.edu/man/lexnames.5WN.html.

nouns and 15 verbs in WordNet [14]. The super-sense vector [25,26] contains the normalized occurrence frequency of words which appear at least five times in SemCor [18]. Specifically, a super-sense vector of a word w_i is denoted as $\mathbf{s}_i = [d_1, d_2, \ldots, d_{41}]$. The i-th dimension d_i is defined as:

$$d_i = \frac{\#(w, i)}{\#(w)}, i = 1, 2, \ldots, 41 \tag{7}$$

where $\#(w, i)$ is the number of w that is marked as the i-th supersense in SemCor and $\#(w)$ is the total number of occurrences of w in SemCor.

The SemCor corpus contains a vocabulary of 4,199 nouns and verbs. Denote the vocabulary set of SemCor as V_s. To align an embedding space $\mathbf{X} \in \mathcal{X}$ to the super-sense space, we extract the words that appear both in our corpus and SemCor. Denote the set of these common words as $I = V \cap V_s$. Then, we construct the super-sense space as a matrix $\mathbf{S} = [\mathbf{s}_1, \mathbf{s}_2, \ldots, \mathbf{s}_{|I|}] \in \mathbb{R}^{41 \times |I|}$. Similarly, we extract the aligning word embedding matrix $\mathbf{W} = \mathbf{X}_{[I]}^T = [\mathbf{x}_1, \mathbf{x}_2, \ldots, \mathbf{x}_{|I|}] \in \mathbb{R}^{d \times |I|}$.

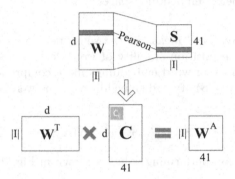

Fig. 1. Supersense-based alignment method maps the original embeddings matrix $\mathbf{W}$ to the super-sense space with the correlation matrix $\mathbf{C}$. Each entry c_{ij} of $\mathbf{C}$ is the pearson correlation coefficient between the i-th row of $\mathbf{W}$ and the j-th row of the super-sense matrix $\mathbf{S}$.

We then align the extracted word embeddings $\mathbf{X} \in \mathcal{X}$ to the common super-sense space $\mathbf{S}$ by the Pearson correlation of the aligned dimensions [18]. Figure 1 illustrates the calculation of the super-sense alignment. Particularly, we calculate a correlation matrix $\mathbf{C}_p \in \mathbb{R}^{d \times 41}$ for the p-th embedding space $\mathbf{X}_p$. Each entry of $\mathbf{C}_p$ is calculated as follows:

$$c_{ij} = Pearson(\mathbf{r}_i^{\mathbf{W}}, \mathbf{r}_j^{\mathbf{S}}) \tag{8}$$

where $\mathbf{r}_i^{\mathbf{S}}$ and $\mathbf{r}_j^{\mathbf{W}}$ are the i-th row of $\mathbf{S}$ and the j-th row of $\mathbf{W}$, respectively. The j-th dimension of aligned embeddings $\mathbf{r}_j^A$ is defined as the weighted sum of all dimensions of original embeddings with the weights $c_{.j}$:

$$\mathbf{r}_j^A = \sum_{i=1}^{d} c_{ij} \cdot \mathbf{r}_i^w \tag{9}$$

As shown in Fig. 1, we can calculate each dimension of aligned embeddings and obtain the aligned matrix of word embeddings as follows:

$$\mathbf{W}_p^A = \mathbf{W}_p^T \cdot \mathbf{C}_p \tag{10}$$

For each aligned matrix pair $(\mathbf{W}_i^A, \mathbf{W}_j^A), 1 \leq i < j \leq m$, we quantify their similarity with the Frobenius norm:

$$SM\left(\mathbf{W}_i^A, \mathbf{W}_j^A\right) = \frac{2\left\|\mathbf{W}_i^A - \mathbf{W}_j^A\right\|_F}{\left\|\mathbf{W}_i^A\right\|_F + \left\|\mathbf{W}_j^A\right\|_F} \tag{11}$$

Finally, ASS is defined as the mean of similarity between the aligned matrices:

$$ASS = \frac{2\sum_{1 \leq i < j \leq m} SM\left(\mathbf{W}_i^A, \mathbf{W}_j^A\right)}{m(m-1)} \tag{12}$$

where m is the number of embedding spaces.

Combined Stability. NSS measures the sense neighbors stability of words, and ASS measures the position stability of word vectors in super-sense space. To measure the stability of word embeddings more comprehensively, we define the combined stability (CS) of word embeddings as the weighted average of NSS and ASS:

$$CS = \alpha NSS + (1 - \alpha)ASS \tag{13}$$

where $\alpha = 0.3$ is the top-performing value as shown in Fig. 2.

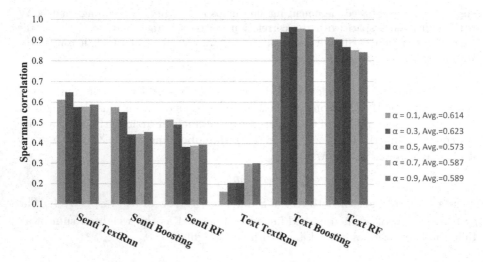

Fig. 2. The Spearman correlation for TRS and the Combined Stability (CS) with different values of α. In general, we observe $\alpha = 0.3$ is the top-performing value.

3.3 Stability Metric for Contextual Embedding Models

Unlike the static embedding models, the word vectors in the contextual embedding model change with their context so that the above metrics are no longer applicable. So, we propose the SPIP to measure the stability of the contextual embedding model, which is defined as the PIP loss between the matrixes consisting of vectors of words in same context from different instances. Given two word embedding matrix $\mathbf{X}_1 \in \mathbb{R}^{n \times d}$ and $\mathbf{X}_2 \in \mathbb{R}^{n \times d}$ trained on corpora D, where n is the size of the vocabulary and d is the dimension of the embedding. The PIP loss between $\mathbf{X}_1$ and $\mathbf{X}_2$ is defined as Frobenius norm between their PIP matrices:

$$PIP(\mathbf{X}_1, \mathbf{X}_2) = \left| \mathbf{X}_1\mathbf{X}_1^T - \mathbf{X}_2\mathbf{X}_2^T \right|_F \tag{14}$$

Similarly, we train m instances by applying the certain contextual embedding model $\mathcal{M}$ on the same corpus $\mathcal{D}$ with identical parameters. Given a context dataset $\mathcal{C}$, we can obtain n contexts $T_{1 \leq i \leq n} = \{w_1^{(i)}, w_2^{(i)}, \ldots, w_{L_i}^{(i)}\}$ where L_i is the length of i-th context. We then denote the word embedding matrix of i-th context from j-th instance as $\mathbf{X}_i^{(j)} = [\mathbf{x}_1^{(i)}, \mathbf{x}_2^{(i)}, \ldots, \mathbf{x}_{L_i}^{(i)}]$. The SPIP is defined as:

$$SPIP = -\frac{2 \sum_{1 \leq i < j \leq m} \sum_{1 \leq q \leq n} PIP(\mathbf{X}_q^{(i)}, \mathbf{X}_q^{(j)})}{n(m^2 - m)} \tag{15}$$

Intuitively, the metric captures how different the word embedding matrixes are of the same context from different instances. It will be equal to zero when these matrices are exactly the same (i.e., the model has the highest stability).

4 Experiments

4.1 Pre-trained Models Setup

Parameters Initialization. In the experiments, we employ a popular python library Gensim[3] to train Skip-gram with negative sampling (SGNS) and Glove[4], EMLo[5] and Bert[6] with their original implementation. For SGNS and GloVe, all vectors are also trained with dimensionality of 50,100,...,500 and other parameters are the default values in [4,5,20]. For EMLo and Bert, we also train the models with different dimensionality of 128, 256,... ,768 and other parameters are the default values in [6,7].

Corpus. We use two standard corpus: 1 Billion Word Language Model Benchmark[7] (BWLMB) and TEXT8[8]. BWLMB is pre-processed by a combination of

---

[3] http://www.radimrehurek.com/gensim/.
[4] https://github.com/stanfordnlp/GloVe.
[5] https://github.com/allenai/bilm-tf.
[6] https://github.com/google-research/bert.
[7] http://www.statmt.org/lm-benchmark/.
[8] http://mattmahoney.net/dc/text8.zip.

Bash shell and Perl scripts[9] from the WMT 2011 News Crawl data[10]. TEXT8 contains a large amount of text for different topics and 210k tokens of an English Wikipedia dump collected on March 3, 2006.

4.2   Word Embedding Performance Evaluation Benchmarks

Existing schemes for evaluating the performance of word embeddings fall into two major categories: extrinsic and intrinsic evaluation. Extrinsic evaluations use word embeddings as input features to a downstream task and measure the performance of the task. Intrinsic evaluations directly test for syntactic or semantic relationships between words [27]. In this paper, we select two intrinsic tasks and two extrinsic tasks [28] to exploring the relationship between word vector stability and task result stability and performance. Next, we describe these benchmarks in detail.

Word Similarity. We measure the cosine similarity between two words and quantify the performance of word embeddings as Spearman correlation between the rankings produced by word embeddings and golden scores which are in the standard database SimLex-999 [29], which contains 999 pairs of English words that have been marked similarity.

Word Analogy. This metric uses the Google Analogy[11] dataset developed by Mikolov et al. [20], which contains 8,869 semantic correlated items and 10,675 morphological correlated items. Each item has four words which are formatted as: $w_a \sim w_b :: w_c \sim w_d$ where the similarity relation is expressed as '$\sim$' and the analogy relation is expressed as '::'. The vector of word w_* is denoted as $*$. For each item, we we calculate a vector $\mathbf{e} = \mathbf{a} - \mathbf{b} + \mathbf{c}$ and obtain the nearest word w_e to $\mathbf{e}$. If w_e is w_d, the analogy of this item is correct, otherwise is wrong. The accuracy of these analogies is taken as the performance of word embeddings.

Sentiment Analysis (Senti). The metric is a binary classification task to determine whether the text is positive or negative using standard database IMDB[12]. The database contains 50,000 highly polarized comments from the Internet movie database which is divided equally into a training set and a test set. Both sets contain 50% positive and 50% negative comments. The model for the task contains two layers, including an embedding layer initialized with pre-trained word embeddings and a classifier layer [30]. Recently, Wendlandt et al. [10] found that the weight values of the embedding layer vary significantly after model training. Therefore, we freeze the embedding layer to make the task result reflect the performance of the word embeddings itself.

---

[9] https://code.google.com/p/1-billion-word-language-modeling-benchmark.
[10] http://www.statmt.org/wmt11/translation-task.html.
[11] http://download.tensorflow.org/data/questions-words.txt.
[12] http://ai.stanford.edu/~amaas/data/sentiment/.

Text Classification (Text). The metric is a multiclass classification task to judge the topic of text using the Reuters[13] database which contains 11,228 news texts on 46 topics. Similarly, the model for the task has an embedding layer which is initialized by the pre-trained word embeddings. We also froze the embedding layer.

Baseline Models. For the Sentiment analysis and Text classification task, we choose three baseline models, including TextRnn model [31], random forest model [32] and Boosting model [33]. TextRnn is a BiLSTM model witch can capture variable-length and bidirectional context information. Both random forest and boosting are ensemble learning models based on decision trees, but they adopt different ensemble strategies. Boosting combines decision trees one by one, which means it adaptively changes the data set's distribution based on the result of previous decision trees. Different from Boosting, random forest trains decision trees independently and combines the classifiers using majority or average rule.

4.3   Results and Discussion

To test the effectiveness of CS and SPIP in measuring the stability of word embeddings, we measure the Spearman correlation coefficients between the metrics and downstream task stability (TRS) for each of two tasks and three models. The Spearman correlation quantifies the similarity between the scores of stability metric and the actual stability of downstream tasks, with a maximum value of 1.0. As shown in Table 2, CS is the top-performing metric for static embedding models, with the CS attaining much higher Spearman correlations than current state-of-the-art metric NNS on most tasks. Moreover, SPIP also has a strong correlation (more than 0.45) with the TRS across the six downstream tasks and two contextual embedding models. Therefore, CS and SPIP are effective selection criteria for stable embedding models without training downstream tasks.

Table 2. Results for Spearman correlation between stability metrics and TRS. Three baseline models are chosen in the experiment, including TextRnn model [31], random forest model [32] (RF), Boosting model [33].

Model		SGNS				GloVe				EMLo	Bert
Metric		ASS	NSS	CS	NNS	ASS	NSS	CS	NNS	SPIP	SPIP
Senti	TextRnn	0.59	0.56	0.65	0.45	0.71	0.72	0.72	0.73	0.59	0.48
	Boosting	0.46	**0.71**	0.55	0.51	**0.96**	0.95	0.95	0.86	0.49	0.45
	RF	0.40	**0.66**	0.49	0.45	**0.90**	0.89	0.89	0.79	0.50	0.45
Text	TextRnn	**0.31**	0.21	0.21	0.07	0.75	**0.76**	0.75	0.70	0.67	0.60
	Boosting	0.95	0.80	**0.95**	0.84	**0.97**	0.95	0.96	0.83	0.68	0.58
	RF	0.84	0.78	**0.90**	0.82	0.95	0.95	**0.96**	0.86	0.64	0.58

---

[13] https://www.kaggle.com/nltkdata/reuters.

Table 3. Results for Spearman correlation of the word embedding models stability and performance. Here CS and SPIP are used to evaluate the stability of static and contextual embedding models, respectively. Because the intrinsic evaluations, Simlex-999 and Analogy, only apply to static embedding models, we only measure the performance of contextual embedding models with extrinsic evaluations, Senti and Text.

Task	SimLex-999	Analogy	Senti			Text			Average
			TextRnn	Boosting	RF	TextRnn	Boosting	RF	
SGNS	0.88	0.44	0.81	0.83	0.84	0.60	0.82	0.90	0.77
GloVe	0.87	0.56	0.88	0.89	0.72	0.74	0.86	0.88	0.80
EMLo	–	–	0.48	0.46	0.35	0.58	0.53	0.47	0.48
Bert	–	–	0.43	0.38	0.42	0.53	0.62	0.60	0.50

In contrast, training and evaluating downstream tasks to find a stable embedding model parameter setting is fairly expensive and slow because the contextual embedding model is large and consumes a lot of computational resources.

Stability (i.e., robustness) and performance are two of the most critical metrics for a model. Although the stability of word embeddings is a popular research field, there is still a lack of research on the relationship between the stability and performance of the word embedding model. In other words, whether selecting a robust model will have an impact on the performance of the model is unknown so far. To fully understand the stability of word embeddings, we quantitatively analyze the relationship between word vector stability and performance. Namely, we calculate the Spearman correlation coefficients between the stability metrics and the word embedding performance benchmarks. In Table 3, we observe the strong positive correlation of at least 0.48 between stability metrics and performance scores of benchmarks. Namely, we also get better performance when we choose a more stable model.

5   Conclusion

In this work, we propose two novel metrics, Combined Stability (CS) and SPIP, to measure the stability of word embeddings. CS is the top-performance stability metric for static embedding models, with the CS attaining higher Spearman correlation with downstream task stability (TRS) than previous state-of-the-art metric Nearest Neighbors Stability (NNS). SPIP also correlates strongly with TRS, which means the metric can be used to measure the stability of contextual embedding models. In contrast, previous stability metrics only apply to static embedding models. Furthermore, we observe the stability of word embeddings is positively correlated with its performance. To summarize, CS and SPIP are effective criteria in parameter selections for stable static and contextual embedding models without training downstream tasks, respectively.

Acknowledgement. The research presented in this paper is supported in part by National Natural Science Foundation (No. 61602370, 61672026, 61772411, U1736205,

61922067, 61902305), Shenzhen Basic Research Grant (JCYJ20170816100819428), Postdoctoral Foundation (No.201659M2806, 2018T111066), MoE-CMCC Artifical Intelligence Project (MCM20190701), Fundamental Research Funds for the Central Universities (No. 1191320006), Natural Science Basic Research Plan in Shaanxi Province of China (2019JM-159).

References

1. Harris, Z.S.: Distributional Structure. Word **10**(2–3), 146–162 (1954)
2. Deerwester, S., Dumais, S.T., Furnas, G.W., Landauer, T.K., Harshman, R.: Indexing by latent semantic analysis. JASIS **41**(6), 391–407 (1990)
3. Levy, O., Goldberg, Y., Dagan, I.: Improving distributional similarity with lessons learned from word embeddings. TACL **3**, 11–225 (2015)
4. Mikolov, T., Chen, K., Corrado, G., Dean, J.: Efficient estimation of word representations in vector space. In: ICLR, Scottsdale, Arizona, May 2013
5. Pennington, J., Socher, R., Manning, C.D.: GloVe: global vectors for word representation. In: EMNLP, Doha, Qatar, pp. 1532–1543, October 2014
6. Peters, M.E., et al.: Deep contextualized word representations. In: NAACL, pp. 2227–2237 (2018)
7. Devlin, J., Chang, M.W., Lee, K., Toutanova, K.: BERT: pre-training of deep bidirectional transformers for language understanding. In: NAACL-HLT, pp. 4171–4186 (2019)
8. Socher, R., et al.: Recursive deep models for semantic compositionality over a sentiment treebank. In: EMNLP, pp. 1631–1642 (2013)
9. Xu, K., et al.: Cross-lingual knowledge graph alignment via graph matching neural network. In: ACL, pp. 3156–3161. Association for Computational Linguistics, Florence, July 2019
10. Wendlandt, L., Kummerfeld, J.K., Mihalcea, R.: Factors influencing the surprising instability of word embeddings, New Orleans, USA. In: ACL, pp. 2092–2102, June 2018
11. Pierrejean, B., Tanguy, L.: Predicting word embeddings variability. In: JCLCS, New Orleans, USA, pp. 154–159, June 2018
12. Antoniak, M., Mimno, D.: Evaluating the stability of embedding-based word similarities. TACL **6**, 107–119 (2018)
13. Hellrich, J., Hahn, U.: Bad company–neighborhoods in neural embedding spaces considered harmful. In: ICCL, Osaka, Japan, pp. 2785–2796, December 2016
14. Kilgarriff, A., Fellbaum, C.: WordNet: an electronic lexical database. Language **76**(3), 06 (2000)
15. Levy, O., Goldberg, Y.: Neural word embedding as implicit matrix factorization. In: NeurIPS, Montreal, Canada, pp. 2177–2185, December 2014
16. Hamilton, W.L., Leskovec, J., Jurafsky, D.: Diachronic word embeddings reveal statistical laws of semantic change. In: AC, Berlin, Germany, pp. 1489–1501, August 2016
17. Thompson, D.M.L.: The strange geometry of skip-gram with negative sampling. In: EMNLP, Copenhagen, Denmark, pp. 2863–2868, September 2017
18. Tsvetkov, Y., Faruqui, M., Ling, W., Lample, G., Dyer, C.: Evaluation of word vector representations by subspace alignment. In: EMNLP, Lisbon, Portugal, pp. 2049–2054, September 2015
19. Yin, Z., Shen, Y.: On the dimensionality of word embedding. In: NeurIPS, vol. 2018-December, pp. 887–898 (2018)

20. Mikolov, T., Sutskever, I., Chen, K., Corrado, G.S., Dean, J.: Distributed representations of words and phrases and their compositionality. In: NeurIPS, Lake Tahoe, USA, pp. 3111–3119, December 2013
21. Gutmann, M.U., Hyvärinen, A.: Noise-contrastive estimation of unnormalized statistical models, with applications to natural image statistics. JMLR **13**, 307–361 (2012)
22. Vaswani, A., et al.: Attention is all you need. In: NeurIPS, vol. 2017-December, pp. 5999–6009 (2017)
23. Leszczynski, M., May, A., Zhang, J., Wu, S., Aberger, C., Ré, C.: Understanding the downstream instability of word embeddings. In: MLSys, February 2020
24. Miller, G.A., Leacock, C., Tengi, R., Bunker, R.T.: A semantic concordance. In: ACL, Plainsboro, USA, pp. 303–308, March 1993
25. Altun, M.C.Y.: Broad-coverage sense disambiguation and information extraction with a supersense sequence tagger. In: EMNLP, Sydney, Australia, pp. 594–602, July 2006
26. Nastase, V.: Unsupervised all-words word sense disambiguation with grammatical dependencies. In: IJCNLP, Hyderabad, India, pp. 7–12, January 2008
27. Schnabel, T., Labutov, I., Mimno, D., Joachims, T.: Evaluation methods for unsupervised word embeddings. In: EMNLP, Lisbon, Portugal, pp. 298–307, September 2015
28. Baroni, M., Dinu, G., Kruszewski, G.: Don't count and predict! a systematic comparison of context-counting vs context-predicting semantic vectors. In: ACL, Baltimore, USA, pp. 238–247, June 2014
29. Hill, F., Reichart, R., Korhonen, A.: SimLex-999: evaluating semantic models with (genuine) similarity estimation. Comput. Linguist. **41**(4), 665–695 (2015)
30. Hochreiter, S., Schmidhuber, J.: Long short-term memory. Neural Comput. **9**(8), 1735–1780 (1997)
31. Lai, S., Xu, L., Liu, K., Zhao, J.: Recurrent convolutional neural networks for text classification. In: AAAI (2015)
32. Tsvetkov, Y., Boytsov, L., Gershman, A., Nyberg, E., Dyer, C.: Metaphor detection with cross-lingual model transfer. In: ACL, pp. 248–258 (2014)
33. Kowsari, K., Meimandi, K.J., Heidarysafa, M., Mendu, S., Barnes, L., Brown, D.: Text classification algorithms: a survey. Information **10**(4), 150 (2019)

Task-to-Task Transfer Learning
with Parameter-Efficient Adapter

Haiou Zhang[1], Hanjun Zhao[1], Chunhua Liu[2], and Dong Yu[1(✉)]

[1] Beijing Language and Cultural University, Beijing, China
{hozhangel,xk18zhj,yudong_blcu}@126.com
[2] The University of Melbourne, Melbourne, Australia
chunhualiu596@gmail.com

Abstract. Many existing pre-trained language models have yielded strong performance on many NLP tasks. They depend on enough labeled data of downstream tasks, which are difficult to be trained on tasks with limited data. Transfer learning from large labeled task to narrow task based on the pre-trained language models can solve this problem. However, it always suffers from catastrophic forgetting. In this paper, we propose an effective task-to-task transfer learning method with parameter-efficient adapter based on pre-trained language model, which can be trained on new tasks without hindering the performance of those already learned. Our experiments include transfer learning from MNLI or SQUAD (as the source task) to some related small data tasks based on Bert. Experimental results show large gains in effectiveness over previous approaches on transfer learning and domain adaptation without forgetting. By adding less than 2.1% of the parameters, our method matches or outperforms vanilla fine-tuning and can overcome catastrophic forgetting.

Keywords: Transfer learning · Domain adaptation · Language model

1 Introduction

There are a large scale research about transfer learning from unlabeled data to annotated data. Many existing state-of-the-art pre-trained models, are first pre-trained on a large text corpus and then fine-tuned on specific downstream tasks. They yield strong performance on many NLP tasks [2,6,10,16,28]. But all the performance depends on the enough labeled data of downstream task, as these models often have a large number of parameters to training. It is difficult to train these modern comprehension systems on narrow domain data or task with limited data.

Many NLP tasks share common knowledge about language. For the better performance on low resources target task, how to combine the pre-trained language model and related task which has large training data is important. There are main two methods. One is multitask learning, such as Multi-Task Deep

© Springer Nature Switzerland AG 2020
X. Zhu et al. (Eds.): NLPCC 2020, LNAI 12431, pp. 391–402, 2020.
https://doi.org/10.1007/978-3-030-60457-8_32

Neural Network (MT-DNN) [9]. It incorporates a pre-trained Bert model [2] and learns text representations across multiple Natural language understanding tasks. But Multi-task learning (MTL) involves training on tasks simultaneously. Another is task-to-task transfer learning (TL) or domain adaptation. It allows training tasks separately. In [25], they show that employing domain adaptation on neural systems trained on large-scale, open-domain datasets can yield good performance in domains where large datasets are not available. This method can be applied to pre-trained language model. Transfer learning first trains a pre-trained language model on a large source task and continues training it on target task with a limited data. One of the greatest challenges in transfer learning is that model often performs poorly when it is re-applied to the source task, a phenomenon known as catastrophic forgetting [4,12,13].

The issue of catastrophic forgetting task-to-task in transfer learning has received attention. A method introduced by [27] can overcome catastrophic forgetting during domain adaptation. It first pretrains the model on large out-of-domain source data and then finetune them with the limited target data. They experiment with a number of auxiliary penalty terms to reduce catastrophic forgetting for comprehension systems during domain adaption. However, a major problem with this kind of application is that it restricts the adaptation for the target data. We are inspired by adapter [19]. Adapter is a small modular and can be attached to an existing network. In paper [5], adapters are new layers added between layers of a pre-trained transformer network. When training a new task, only the parameters of adapter are trained. It is parameter-efficient. But this adapter-model only focuses on tuning a large text model on the downstream tasks. It is not considered to do transfer learning or domain adaptation between tasks based on pre-trained language model.

In this paper, we focus on task-to-task transfer learning based on pre-trained language model using adapter and assume have no access to data from the previous task. The model we propose uses related tasks with sufficient data to assist in solving target tasks with limited data. It can overcome catastrophic forgetting and the knowledge of a certain task learned by the model can be used to solve a target task through transfer learning. Adapter used in our model includes two feedforward layers and a non-linear layer. When doing a transfer learning from a large labeled $task_i$ to a $task_j$ with limited data, the method first adds $adapter_i$ for $task_i$ and trains it on $task_i$. Then adds $adapter_j$ for $task_j$. Parameters of $adapter_i$ will be fixed when trained on $task_j$, but its output will flow into the next layer with the output of $adapter_j$. Our method trains $adapter_j$ only on $task_j$. The parameters of the previously trained adapter are fixed, so it will not be overwritten.

The contributions of this paper can be summarized as follows:

- We introduce an effective task-to-task transfer learning method, that can do transfer learning and domain adaptation based on the pre-trained language model. Experiments show that our model consistently performs better than Bert on limited data.

- Our transfer learning method can avoid catastrophic forgetting and is parameter-effective in task-to-task transfer learning and question answering domain adaptation.
- We compare our proposed task-to-task transfer learning method to other transfer learning and domain adaptation methods and demonstrate its efficacy.

2 Relate Work

The relevant work part mainly involves the field of NLP. Multi-Task Learning (MTL) aims to leverage useful information contained in multiple related tasks to help improve the generalization performance of all the tasks [29]. It is practical when there are multiple related tasks each of which have limited training samples [14]. In multitask learning, all the tasks learned simultaneously. MT-DNN [9] proposed a model to combine multi-task learning and language model pre-training. It leverages large amounts of cross-task data, and leads to more general representations to help adapt to new tasks and domains. MULTIQA [23], a Bert-based model, trained on multiple reading comprehension datasets, which leads to state-of-the-art performance on five RC datasets. The two models mentioned above assume accessing all the data of tasks simultaneously. It is not practical as accessing all the relate task data is difficult.

Transfer learning can improve the performance of a target task with the help of source tasks [20]. Transferring information or reusing previously learned tasks for the learning of new tasks has the potential to significantly improve the efficiency of model. Transfer learning by first training a pre-trained model on a data from a large source task and continues finetune it with examples from the small target task, is a common method to transfer knowledge. But a fine-tuned model often forgets the source task and suffers catastrophic forgetting [7,13].

There are some trails to try to solve catastrophic forgetting problem. These approaches can be divided into three main methods [15]. The first are regularization approaches, via additional regularization terms that penalize changes in the mapping function of a neural network. In [8], the predictions of the previous task's network and the current network are encouraged to be similar when applied to data from the new task. EWC [7] remembers old tasks by selectively slowing down learning on the weights important to those tasks. The method we mentioned before, introduce new auxiliary penalty terms and combine auxiliary penalty terms to regularise the fine-tuning process for adapting comprehension models. The second is complementary learning systems and memory replay. LAMAL [22], which is a language model learning to solve the task and generate training samples at the same time based on GPT [17]. The model generates some pseudo samples of previous tasks to train alongside the data of the new task. But it can't be applied to language model that can't tackle generation task. [11] proposed the Gradient Episodic Memory (GEM) model. The main feature of GEM is an episodic memory used to store a subset of the observed examples from a given task. It requires considerable more memory than other regularization approaches such as EWC [7]. A lifelong language learning setup introduced

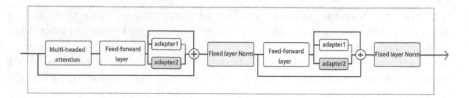

Fig. 1. The transfer learning method we proposed. (Color figure online)

by [1], presents an episodic memory model that performs sparse experience replay and local adaptation to continuously learn and reuse previously acquired knowledge. But tasks in the stream are essentially just the same task. The third is dynamic architectures, like PNN, every column will add to next [21]. But for transfer learning, our model only selects column that is useful for the target task.

3   Model

We proposed a simple and effective method to do task-to-task transfer learning or domain adaptation based on pre-trained language model using adapter. It is a new transfer learning method which can overcome catastrophic forgetting, and assume that the model can't get the data of the previous task.

3.1   Adapter for Task-to-Task Transfer Learning

What the adapter module does is equivalent to making a slight general modification to the original model structure to reuse the pre-trained network for downstream tasks. We can choose a variety of different architectural adapters. For convenience, we use a similar adapter that has proven to perform well on many tasks in [5]. It includes two feedforward layers and a non-linear layer. The first feedforward projects the input into a smaller dimensional, and the second is responsible for projecting it back to original dimensions. Parameters of adapter is much less than that of transformer. Adapter reorganizes and extracts information of the original language model on specific task. Then it is added with original information to next layer. The difference to [5] is that adapter used in our model has no a skip-connection for the output of feed forward. Instead we extract this step as a separate route. Skip-connection will be repetitive if the outputs of multi-adapter are added, which is unnecessary. In adapter-tuning, the top-layer and the adapter weights are co-trained, but the parameters of the original network are frozen.

3.2   Transformer with Adapters

We proposed a simple and effective method to use a trained adapter to do transfer learning. Figure 1 shows the transformer layer with adapter. Each feedforward layer in transformer followed by one or multi adapter. The model adds adapter layer to transformer for per task. Adapter module itself has a skip-connection internally. In this way, the adapter will not affect the transformer structure, but only as part of an insertion. As shown in Fig. 1, only parameters from layers in blue—adapter are trained, and all the rest parameters are frozen in training stage. Layer normalization parameters are fixed in our model when adapt pre-trained model for new tasks. Keeping the layer normalization parameter fixed can completely achieve independence of each adapter, which enables the layer normalization to be shared by many tasks and avoids catastrophic forgetting in finetune or transfer learning. If an adapter trained without updating the weights of layer normalization, the performance will not be worse or even better in our experiment, see Sect. 4.3.

3.3 Transfer Learning Without Forgetting

The most common method for transfer learning between tasks based on a pre-trained language model, is to train $task_1$ first, and then train $task_2$ on the same model. But it always suffers catastrophic forgetting. Training a model with new information will overwrite previously learned knowledge. For this, we use a completely different method, as shown in Fig. 1. Transformer layer with two adapter layer inside. Suppose $adapter_1$ has been trained on source task— $task_1$, and $adapter_2$ is newly defined for the target task—$task_2$. The outputs of $adapter_1$ and $adapter_2$ are added to the next layer.

$$In = output(feedforwardLayer) \tag{1}$$

$$A_i = Adapter_i(In) \tag{2}$$

$$LayerOutput = In + A_1 + A_2 \tag{3}$$

where In is the output of feedforward layer and input of adapter. A_i stands for $adapter_i$. During the training process for target $task_2$, parameters of $adapter_1$ remain unchanged, and only weights of $adapter_2$ are trained. It enables model to use the existing knowledge to learn new tasks without overwriting the learned adapters.

4 Experiment

We conduct several experiments to test our method and explore different aspects of its behavior. The results prove that our method has a good performance both in target and source task after domain adaptation or transfer learning, which is better than the previous model.

Table 1. Target Task: The performance of different model. Evaluate on the test set of MRPC and dev set of RTE using accuracy. Parameters indicates how many parameters are trained in the fine-tuning or training stage in total.

	Models	MRPC	RTE	Trained parameters
Target task	finetune	83.59	67.50	100.0%
	finetune+TL	86.37	**80.50**	100.0%
	adapter	85.04	68.59	**2.1%**
	adapter+TL	**87.11**	<u>80.14</u>	**2.1%**
Source task (MNLI)	finetune+TL	60.18	73.67	100.0%
	adapter+TL	**83.69**	**83.69**	2.1%

4.1   Datasets

We conducted two groups of experiments. The first group is task-to-task transfer learning; the second group is QA domain adaptation. For task-to-task transfer learning, the source and target task are from GLUE [24]. We chose Multi-Genre Natural Language Inference Corpus (MNLI) [26] as the source data. MNLI is a crowdsourced collection of 433k sentence pairs with textual entailment annotations. In order to test the transfer learning ability of our model from task with large scale data to task with limited data, the training data sets for target data was less than 5k. They are MRPC [3], and RTE [24]. MRPC is to predict whether the sentences in the pair are semantically equivalent. RTE is to predict if the premise entails the hypothesis.

For question answering domain adaptation, We use SQUAD v1.1 [18] as the source data. SQuAD contains more than one hundred thousand question-answer pairs. To test our methods, we use 6 narrow question answering domain data sets that released by [27] as the target task, including the following domains: biomedical (MS-BM), computing (MS-CP), film (MS-FM), finance (MS-FN), law (MS-LW) and music (MS-MS). Each domain has Thousands of examples.

4.2   Experiments Setting

The implementation is based on adapter[1] and Bert[2]. For Bert, all of our analyses are done with the Bert base which has 110M parameters to make our results comparable to other work, since it has been widely used as a baseline.

The different methods listed below are models that are often compared in our experiments. These methods are based on the Bert language model. Source task is large labeled data which helps the model learn the target task. Target task is a narrow domain task or a task with limited data.

– **finetune** Vanilla finetune for specific task;

---

[1] https://github.com/google-research/adapter-bert.
[2] https://github.com/google-research/bert.

Table 2. Influence on whether to train layer norms inside Bert or not using adapter model. We evaluate on the dev set of MNLI (Acc.) and SQuAD (F1/EM), test set of MRPC (Acc.).

Task	MNLI	MRPC	SQuAD
Adapter+TL (Trained LayerNorm)	83.44	84.57	**88.43/81.07**
Adapter+TL (Fixed LayerNorm)	**83.69**	**85.04**	88.41/80.67

- **finetune+TL** Directly fine-tune the model on the stream of tasks one after another. Train source task first, then target task;
- **adapter** Train adapter on a specific task;
- **adapter+TL** First, train parameters of $adapter_1$ on source task. Second, add the model with $adapter_2$ for target task, and fix the parameters of $adapter_1$ and train the weights of $adapter_2$ only.

We set epoch to 5 for both adapter and Bert. In our transfer learning experiment, adapter size is 64 as default. The adapter size is the parameter that we tune for adapter. In the domain adaptation process, we set adapter size to 32 or 64, and select a better model based on the dev set. The learning rate is always $3e^{-4}$ for adapter and $2e^{-5}$ for Bert.

4.3   Task-to-Task Transfer Learning

To get an understanding of the performance of our method, We conduct two different transfer learning methods in this experiment, including adapter+TL and finetune+TL. Besides, we also tried two other methods— using an adapter model to learn target task and finetune—directly finetune target task on the pre-trained Bert base model. We use MNLI as the source task, and MRPC and RTE as the target tasks. The experimental results are shown in Table 1.

In terms of target task performance (The top half of Table 1), we can see that, adapter+TL performs much better than adapter, especially on RTE. It shows that our transfer learning method is very effective. Compared to the method of finetune+TL, adapter+TL also shows better performance and is more efficient. Transfer learning based on adapter has only a few trainable parameters. Fine-tuning requires the total number of Bert parameters. In contrast, adapters require only 2.1% parameters (adapters of size 64).

The bottom half of Table 1 shows the model performance on source data— MNLI after training each of the target task. Regardless of the target task, the accuracy of the model on the data set MNLI has not decreased. Table 1 tells us that, our transfer learning setup using adapter can prevent the existing knowledge from being overwritten, as the parameter of source adapter is fixed in the transfer learning process. The previous learned knowledge of model can be retained permanently and reused repeatedly.

Table 3. The upper part of the table is the result of testing the SQuAD after the domain adaption. The bottom half of the table is the test results of each QA domain. In the left half of the table, we get the data of finetune, +ewc, +newc, +cd, +l2, +all and gem from [27].

Domain	finetune+TL	+ewc	+newc	+cd	+l2	+all	gem	Adapter+TL	Increase
Target task									
MS-BM	68.30	68.20	68.00	68.04	68.24	67.87	68.02	**70.53**	+2.23
MS-CP	70.57	71.21	71.41	69.33	69.57	69.49	70.4	**72.20**	+0.79
MS-FM	74.73	74.75	74.36	73.73	74.85	75.78	74.63	**78.06**	+2.28
MS-FN	69.13	70.42	70.60	69.07	70.05	69.15	69.54	**73.14**	+2.54
MS-LW	69.99	70.73	71.59	70.57	70.91	68.59	68.87	**71.89**	+0.30
MS-MS	73.56	73.19	73.07	72.97	73.43	72.5	72.73	**76.29**	+2.73
Avg.	71.04	71.41	71.50	70.57	71.17	70.56	70.70	**73.68**	+2.18
Source task (SQuAD)									
MS-BM	72.55	74.24	76.51	72.36	74.14	77.32	74.14	**88.09**	+10.77
MS-CP	68.41	69.63	75.65	76.92	75.98	77.86	73.37		+10.23
MS-FM	73.82	75.17	79.75	75.28	74.71	81.42	76.89		+6.67
MS-FN	72.59	74.27	75.52	73.22	74.84	78.18	76.16		+9.91
MS-LW	71.93	81.11	81.05	78.77	77.97	83.11	75.90		+4.18
MS-MS	72.59	78.06	83.56	75.67	74.29	83.54	76.99		+4.53
Avg.	71.98	75.32	78.67	75.36	75.31	80.24	75.57		+7.85

Influence on Training LayerNorm or Not. Weights of layer normalization being fixed or not is the key to whether the model can perform continuous learning. Keeping the weight of layer normalization fixed make each adapter achieve completely independent of each other. Table 2 shows model performance with or without training the weights of layer normalization.

In Table 2, we can see that after fixing the parameters of layer normalization, the accuracy of model is improved on MNLI and MRPC, and the F1 score on the SQuAD has only decreased by 0.02%. It implies that our method can accumulate knowledge by training more adapters for different tasks, and avoid catastrophic forgetting.

4.4 Domain Adaptation Without Forgeting

To test our model's ability to overcome catastrophic forgetting during domain adaptation and keep the performance of target task optimal, we measure both source data and target domain in this experiment. And we assume have no access to data from the source domain.

We use SQuAD as source domain task, and 6 narrow domain data sets as the target domain task. In this domain adaptation experiment, source domain and target domain tasks share one output layer. Parameters of output layer only trained on source task. The evaluation metric is standard macro-averaged F1, and reported performance on the development set of SQuAD and test sets of 6

Table 4. Performance on QA target domain. Parameters represents how many parameters using in fine-tuning or training stagein total.

	Trained parameters	MS-BM	MS-CP	MS-FM	MS-FN	MS-LW	MS-MS	Avg.
Train examples	–	22,134	3,021	3,522	6,790	3,105	2,517	–
finetune	100.0%	68.69	66.69	74.05	69.03	67.50	69.61	69.26
finetune+TL	100.0%	70.18	70.66	**78.21**	71.93	70.41	75.62	72.83
adapter	2.1%	69.39	67.92	74.77	69.45	69.04	69.45	70.00
adapter+TL	2.1%	**70.53**	**72.20**	78.06	**73.14**	**71.89**	**76.29**	**73.68**

narrow domain target tasks as [27]. In addition to the method finetune+TL, We also compare the following models in our experiments:

- **ewc** Elastic weight consolidation [7] slows down the learning on certain weights based on how important they are to previously seen tasks;
- **newc, l2, cd, and multi-penal** These methods are all proposed in [27]. newc is an improved model of ewc. l2 and cd are two different penalties. Multi-penal means combine different distance metrics altogether;
- **gem** Gradient episodic memory, introduced by [11], using an episodic memory to store a subset of the observed examples and allows beneficial transfer of knowledge from previous tasks.

Our experimental results are shown in Table 3. The bottom half of the Table 3 is the test results for each QA domain. It can be seen that our model has the highest F1 score on all target domain. Except that the accuracy of MS-CP and MS-LW is improved by less than 1%, the rest are improved by at least 2%. The highest is an increase of 2.73% points on MS-MS. The upper part of the Table 3 shows the result of testing the SQuAD after the domain adaption. It can be seen that adapter+TL has a higher accuracy than the results of all models on the left. The highest increase is 10.77% points, and the minimum is 4.18% points. During the domain adaptation training process, since the parameters of $adapter_{SQuAD}$ and output layers trained for the SQuAD corpus are fixed, the knowledge about the SQuAD in the model will always be retained.

Table 4 shows the performance of methods with or without transfer learning. MS-BM has the most training data. The performance of adapter+TL on MS-BM is 1.14 % higher than that of adapter. The training data sets of other target domains are relatively small. The smaller the training data of the target domain, the worse the performance of the adapter method. However, the performance of the adapter+TL is very stable. For example, the training data set of MS MS is the smallest, and F1 score of adapter+TL is 6.84 % higher than the adapter. As can be seen from the table, compared with finetune+TL, adapter+TL requires much less training parameters, and its domain adaptability is strong.

Influence of Epoch. To study the model performance in different training stages, we select two target tasks with less training data as our target tasks in transfer learning and domain adaptation. The source tasks are MNLI and

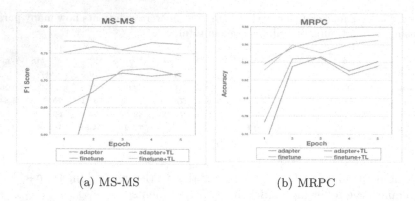

(a) MS-MS   (b) MRPC

Fig. 2. The performance of the model with the different training epochs. X-axis represents different epochs. Y-axis corresponds to the accuracy on MRPC and F1 score on MS-MS.

SQuAD respectively. Figure 2 records the model performance on two tasks. Overall, transfer learning performs better on these low-resource tasks. We can see that adapter+TL has the highest accuracy on MRPC where epoch is 1 and it shows steady growth on both MRPC and MS-MS. But the performance of finetune+TL has some fluctuation on both task. There are too many parameters to be trained for finetune method. If the data of task is relatively small, it is not enough for the pre-trained model to learn the task well. In this case, the model is prone to two problems: catastrophic forgetting and overfitting. With the increase of epoch, the performance of our method increases steadily and rarely fluctuates. It may be because the parameters of $adapter_{source}$ remain fixed in training process, that is, this part of the knowledge will not be forgotten. At the epoch 1, the performance of adapter is the lowest compared with to the other three methods. When training an adapter, the weights are initialized at random. When epoch was small, the parameters are not well learned.

Influence of Adapter Size. To further investigate the robustness of our method to the adapter size, We compare the performance of model with different adapter size. Figure 3 shows the results. Adaptor-based transfer learning is significantly better than training an adapter for a task alone. When the adapter size is 1, the performance of the adapter+TL on both two target tasks is even higher than the highest performance of adapter. And compared to finetune+TL, which requires 100% training parameters, our method has closed performance, which requires less than 0.1% parameters of Bert.

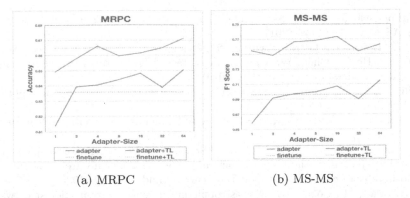

(a) MRPC   (b) MS-MS

Fig. 3. Model performance for different adapter size. We compare adapters of different sizes with fine-tuning all the parameters. X-axis represents the adapter size. Y-axis corresponds to the accuracy on MRPC and fi score on MS-MS. The parameters of adapter of size 64 is less than 2.1% of Bert. Adapter+TL can achieve the comparable results as finetune+TL, but the parameter of adapter+TL is only 2.1% of finetune+TL.

5   Conclusion

We have presented a task-to-task transfer learning method with parameter-efficient adapter based on the language model. It can be used to learn a narrow data task with its learned task while fully preserving the existing representation. Our experiments demonstrate that our proposed method is parameter-efficient and can overcome catastrophic forgetting in transfer learning and domain adaptation.

Acknowledgement. This work is funded by the Humanity and Social Science Youth foundation of Ministry of Education (19YJCZH230) and the Fundamental Research Funds for the Central Universities in BLCU (No. 17PT05).

References

1. d'Autume, C.D.M., Ruder, S., Kong, L., Yogatama, D.: Episodic memory in lifelong language learning. arXiv preprint arXiv:1906.01076 (2019)
2. Devlin, J., Chang, M.W., Lee, K., Toutanova, K.: BERT: pre-training of deep bidirectional transformers for language understanding. arXiv:1810.04805 (2018)
3. Dolan, W.B., Brockett, C.: Automatically constructing a corpus of sentential paraphrases. In: Proceedings of the Third International Workshop on Paraphrasing (IWP2005) (2005). https://www.aclweb.org/anthology/I05-5002
4. French, M.R.: Catastrophic forgetting in connectionist networks. Trends Cogn. Sci. **3**(4), 128–135 (1999)
5. Houlsby, N., et al.: Parameter-efficient transfer learning for NLP. In: ICML. PMLR (2019)
6. Howard, J., Ruder, S.: Universal language model fine-tuning for text classification. In: ACL (2018). https://www.aclweb.org/anthology/P18-1031

7. Kirkpatrick, J., et al.: Overcoming catastrophic forgetting in neural networks. PNAS **114**, 3521–3526 (2017)
8. Li, Z., Hoiem, D.: Learning without forgetting. ECCV (2016)
9. Liu, X., He, P., Chen, W., Gao, J.: Multi-task deep neural networks for natural language understanding. In: ACL (2019)
10. Liu, Y., et al.: Roberta: a robustly optimized BERT pretraining approach. arXiv:1907.11692 (2019)
11. Lopez-Paz, D., Ranzato, M.: Gradient episodic memory for continual learning. In: NIPS (2017)
12. McClelland, J.L., McNaughton, B.L., O'Reilly, R.C.: Why there are complementary learning systems in the hippocampus and neocortex: insights from the successes and failures of connectionist models of learning and memory (1995)
13. McCloskey, M., Cohen, N.J.: Catastrophic interference in connectionist networks: the sequential learning problem. In: Psychology of Learning and Motivation. Elsevier (1989)
14. Pan, S.J., Yang, Q.: A survey on transfer learning (2009)
15. Parisi, G.I., Kemker, R., Part, J.L., Kanan, C., Wermter, S.: Continual lifelong learning with neural networks: a review. Neural Netw. **113**, 54–71 (2019)
16. Peters, M.E., et al.: Deep contextualized word representations. In: Proceedings of NAACL (2018)
17. Radford, A., Narasimhan, K., Salimans, T., Sutskever, I.: Improving language understanding by generative pre-training (2018)
18. Rajpurkar, P., Zhang, J., Lopyrev, K., Liang, P.: SQuAD: 100,000+ questions for machine comprehension of text. In: ACL (2016)
19. Rebuffi, S.A., Bilen, H., Vedaldi, A.: Efficient parametrization of multi-domain deep neural networks (2018)
20. Ruder, S.: Neural transfer learning for natural language processing. Ph.D. thesis, National University of Ireland, Galway (2019)
21. Rusu, A.A., et al.: Progressive neural networks. arXiv preprint arXiv:1606.04671 (2016)
22. Sun, F.K., Ho, C.H., Lee, H.Y.: LAMAL: language modeling is all you need for lifelong language learning. arXiv:1909.03329 (2019)
23. Talmor, A., Berant, J.: MultiQA: an empirical investigation of generalization and transfer in reading comprehension. arXiv preprint arXiv:1905.13453 (2019)
24. Wang, A., Singh, A., Michael, J., Hill, F., Levy, O., Bowman, S.R.: GLUE: a multi-task benchmark and analysis platform for natural language understanding (2018). arXiv:1804.07461
25. Wiese, G., Weissenborn, D., Neves, M.: Neural domain adaptation for biomedical question answering. In: Proceedings of the 21st Conference on Computational Natural Language Learning (CoNLL 2017) (2017)
26. Williams, A., Nangia, N., Bowman, S.: A broad-coverage challenge corpus for sentence understanding through inference. In: ACL (2018)
27. Xu, Y., Zhong, X., Yepes, A.J.J., Lau, J.H.: Forget me not: reducing catastrophic forgetting for domain adaptation in reading comprehension. Computing Research Repository (2019)
28. Yang, Z., Dai, Z., Yang, Y., Carbonell, J., Salakhutdinov, R., Le, Q.V.: XLNet: generalized autoregressive pretraining for language understanding. arXiv:1906.08237
29. Zhang, Y., Yang, Q.: A survey on multi-task learning. arXiv:1707.08114 (2017)

Key-Elements Graph Constructed with Evidence Sentence Extraction for Gaokao Chinese

Xiaoyue Wang[1], Yu Ji[1], and Ru Li[1,2(✉)]

[1] School of Computer and Information Technology, Shanxi University,
Taiyuan, China
`wangxy0808@163.com`, `jiyu0515@163.com`, `liru@sxu.edu.cn`
[2] Key Laboratory of Computational Intelligence and Chinese Information Processing
of Ministry of Education, Shanxi University, Taiyuan, China

Abstract. Multiple choice questions from university admission exams (Gaokao in Chinese) is a challenging AI task since it requires effective representation to capture complicated semantic relations between sentences in the article and strong ability to handle long text. Face the above challenges, we propose a key-elements graph to enhance context semantic representation and a comprehensive evidence extraction method inspired by existing methods. Our model first extracts evidence sentences from a passage according to the corresponding question and options to reduce the impact of noise. Then combines syntactic analysis techniques with graph neural network to construct the key-elements graph bases on the extracted sentences. Finally, fusing the learned graph nodes representation into context representation to enhancing syntactic information. Experiments on Gaokao Chinese multiple-choice dataset demonstrate the proposed model obtains substantial performance gains over various neural model baselines in terms of accuracy.

Keywords: Multiple-choice reading comprehension · Evidence sentence extraction · Graph neural network

1 Introduction

Multiple-choice machine reading comprehension (MRC) task [1–3] is especially tricky which aims to select the correct option from the given candidates associated with this question, the majority of answer options cannot be directly extracted from the given texts thus to answer the questions usually need high reasoning and comprehension ability.

Supported by the National Key Research and Development Program of China (No. 2018YFB1005103) and the National Natural Science Foundation of China (No. 61772324) and the Postgraduate Education Innovation Project of Shanxi Province (No. 2020SY019).

© Springer Nature Switzerland AG 2020
X. Zhu et al. (Eds.): NLPCC 2020, LNAI 12431, pp. 403–414, 2020.
https://doi.org/10.1007/978-3-030-60457-8_33

This work focuses on multiple-choice questions in Gaokao Chinese. A highly challenging multiple-choice MRC task is from the Chinese University Admission Examination (Gaokao in Chinese), which called GCRC as follows. The question format in GCRC[1], as shown in Fig. 1. Unlike its counterparts which rely on numerical reasoning and specialized field knowledge, GCRC focuses on testing language comprehension. All of the questions in this dataset are answerable without any other knowledge.

Previous work on multiple-choice datasets [4–6] usually using the entire passage as input, analyzing the relationship between the passage and option, then selecting the most appropriate option. However, this makes interpreting their predictions extremely difficult and could introduce some noise because not every sentence in the article contains relevance information with question/option [7]. Especially in the dataset with a relatively long article such as GCRC (average 1,134.15 words per passage).

Some researchers noticed this problem and proposed some solutions, e.g., [8] viewed this problem as a textual entailment task then determine the relevance between the article sentence and answer option. These methods overlook the relevance between extracted evidence sentences, which may have the possibility of information redundancy. [9] proposed ROCC to fix this problem. However, most of the options in multiple-choice questions are not complete sentences that will affect the model result judgment, and they need to combine with its corresponding questions.

For the shortcomings of the above methods, we propose a comprehensive method about evidence sentence extraction. We treat evidence sentence extraction as textual entailment task. Then we supplement missing information in options, manual annotation evidence sentences of some questions to construct evidence sentences corpus and fine-tune pre-trained model on it. After getting prediction results, we use ROCC to filter duplicated information.

For information encoding, with the emergence of sizeable pre-trained models [10,11], more and more researchers directly using these pre-trained models as encoder layer [6,12], these models treat context as a sequence and process it without considering inherent hierarchical structure which is crucial for semantic understanding. As shown in Fig. 1, the options are highly similar to the article content, but the semantics is different as the difference in the syntactic structure. If do not grasp the syntactic structure in the sentences, the model is likely to be confused by the appearance then get the wrong conclusion.

Face the above problem. We consider infusing syntactic information into the context representation to enhance its semantic representation. Besides, dependency tree has graph-like structures bringing to play the recent class of neural networks, namely, graph convolutional networks(GCN) which have been widely used in open domain MRC tasks [13,14] to solve multi-hop problems [15–17]. It can learn representations and get the association between nodes. Furthermore, we also notice that not all components of one sentence are useful for question answering that use all of the components to construct the graph will

---

[1] Datasets and codes are available on https://github.com/jfzy-lab/GCRC.

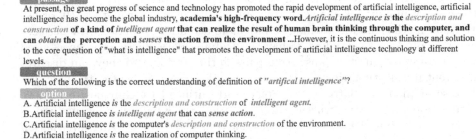

passage
At present, the great progress of science and technology has promoted the rapid development of artificial intelligence, artificial intelligence has become the global industry, **academia's high-frequency word.**_Artificial intelligence is_ **the** _description and construction_ **of a kind of** _intelligent agent_ **that can realize the result of human brain thinking through the computer, and can** _obtain_ **the perception and** _senses_ **the action from the environment** ...However, it is the continuous thinking and solution to the core question of "what is intelligence" that promotes the development of artificial intelligence technology at different levels.

question
Which of the following is the correct understanding of definition of _"artifical intelligence"_?

option
A. Artificial intelligence _is_ the _description and construction_ of _intelligent agent._
B. Artificial intelligence _is_ _intelligent agent_ that can _sense action._
C. Artificial intelligence _is_ the computer's _description and construction_ of the environment.
D. Artificial intelligence _is_ the realization of computer thinking.

answer   A

Fig. 1. A sample Gaokao-Chinese QA problem that require syntactic analysis.

introduce noise. These observations motivate us to develop a neural network that could efficiently extract evidence sentence and propose a Key-elements Graph NetworkKGN) for GCRC, which reduces the impact of noise information and understand semantics further by capturing syntactic association between crucial elements.

We experiment on GCRC, which questions collected from 2005–2019 Chinese Gaokao examinations to evaluate model performance. Experimental results show that we can achieve better performance than the same model that considers the full context and not fusion with syntactic information. Moreover, the comparison between ground truth evidence sentences and automatically selected sentences indicates that there is still room for improvement.

Our primary contributions are as follows:

- To the best of our knowledge, this is the first work to fusion syntactic information in multiple-choice MRC task;
- We improve the performance of evidence sentence extraction on multiple-choice MRC.
- We also conduct a detailed error analysis of the experimental results and summarize the directions that need to be explored in depth. We hope our attempts and observations can encourage the research community to develop more explainable MRC models and study models that have a deeper understanding of semantics.

2   Related Work

2.1   Evidence Sentence Extraction for Reading Comprehension Task

Evidence sentence extraction method in reading comprehension tasks can be divided into two categories from whether training data is needed.

In the first category, previous work (e.g., [7]) have used entailment resources or annotated some question manually to train components for extracting evidence sentences for MRC.

In the second category for those not provided ground-truth evidence sentences to train model, some works rely on reinforcement learning [18,19] or use attention mechanism for learning to pay more attention to better evidence sentences [4–6]. As a supplement to have no training data, these approaches need large amounts of question/answering pairs during training so they can discover the latent justification. However, because there is no clear indicator, the precision of these methods is relatively low. Some works utilize IR techniques to retrieve justification from both structure and unstructured KBs [20]. Our method is inspired by it, but these methods have not considered the missing information of the option, which is crucial for exploring the relation between option and sentence in the passage.

2.2 Application of Graph Neural Network in Question Answering

Most applications of graph neural network for question answering exist in multi-hop QA [13,14], which requires a model to integrate scattered pieces of evidence across multiple documents to predict the right answer. For example, MHQA-GRN [21], Coref-GRN [22] and CogQA [17] construct an entity graph based on co-reference resolution or sliding windows. Entity-GCN [23] considers different types of edges and entities in the graph. CogQA employs an MRC model to predict answer spans and possible next-hop spans and then organizes them into a cognitive graph.

Nevertheless, these methods did not consider the inherent hierarchical structure of natural language. They usually treat text as a sequence. When two key elements are far away, the sequence characteristics determine that they cannot capture the relationship between the two elements. But the hierarchical structure will shorten the distance between the elements in space.

3 Method

3.1 Evidence Sentences Extractor

We propose a new evidence sentences extraction model, as shown in Fig. 2, with three components: (i) an option rephrasing module, which combines and rewrite option into a complete sentence without grammatical errors; (ii) a sentence relevance module, which learns to focus on the relevance sentences; (iii) a filter module, which from the three aspects of coverage, relevance and redundancy further select the evidence sentences extracted in the previous step.

Option Rephrasing Module: That not all of the answer options is a complete sentence. For example, as shown in Fig. 2 *option A* lacks subject information. If directly use the option to explore its relationship with passage sentence, the missing information will affect subsequent judgment. Alternatively, directly concatenating questions with answer options; the result of this method usually is a grammatically wrong sentence.

Toward these, we use the regular expression to get the rephrase option R ensure the integrity of information.

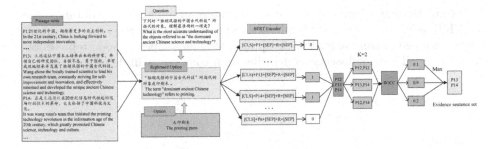

Fig. 2. The procedure of evidence sentence extraction.

Sentence Relevance Module: The goal of this module is to extract the article sentence, which contains the critical information required for judging the correctness of rephrased option R. We can use a pre-trained entailment model to obtain this:

$$\alpha_i = f_e(P_i, R) \tag{1}$$

$$P_{label} = argmax(softmax(W^T\alpha_i + b)) \tag{2}$$

$f(.)$ is the entailment function, $\alpha_i \in R^d$ is the importance of the sentence P_i, which is one sentence in passage $P = \{P_1, P_2, \ldots, P_n\}$, to the rephrased option R. $W^T \in R^{2 \times d}$ is a learnable parameter matrix.

Filter Module: After using the entailment model to get a coarse sentences set. We use ROCC [9] to further filter redundant evidence sentences. First we create candidate evidence sets by generating $\binom{n}{k}$ groups of sentence from the coarse sentences set, using multiple values of k, n is the number of sentences in the coarse sentence set.

For every evidence set, we calculate the ROCC score, which evaluates the probability that this group of evidence sentences could judge the correctness of the corresponding answer option. We then rank the evidence sets in descending order of ROCC score in descending order of ROCC score and choose the top set as the group of evidence sentences E that is the output of ROCC for the given rephrased option R.

Due to space constraints, we do not introduce the ROCC method in detail. We combine the evidence sets of all the answer options of a question, and perform the deduplication operation to get a context $C = \{c_1, c_2, \ldots, c_m\}$ which can be seen as the short version of the article, c_i is one evidence sentence.

3.2   Key Elements Graph Network

As illustrated in Fig. 3, the proposed Key-elements Graph Network (KGN) consists of three main components: (*i*) Graph Construction Module; (*ii*) Context

Encoding Module, where initial representations of graph nodes are obtained via a BERT-based encoder; (*iii*) Graph Reasoning Module, where graph-attention-based message passing algorithm is applied to jointly update node representations. The following sub-sections describe each component in detail.

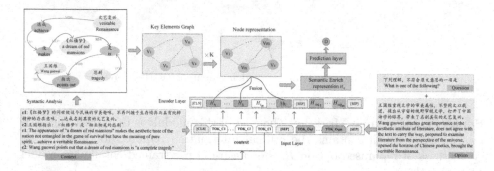

Fig. 3. Model architecture of the proposed Key-Elements Graph Network.

Graph Construction: Each sentence in context C contains multiple entities. We tried to use named entity recognition technology to extract entities, but due to datasets covered domain are various, it is hard to find a common type entity that plays an important role in all of the categories. So we just use part-of-speech tagging technology to label nouns in C to construct entity set $N = \{n_1, n_2, \ldots, n_j\}$, j is the total number of entities in the context.

In order to highlight the details mentioned above which are easy to overlooked, we use syntactic analysis technology to extract the elements that have a direct syntactic connection to n_i that in entity set N. Repeat the same step for each sentence in the context C, after that the extracted elements are combined with the entity set to form a key elements graph nodes set $V = \{v_1, v_2, v_3, \ldots, v_n\}$, n denote the number of key elements node in a graph. In experiments, we set $n = 40$ (padded where necessary), each node $v_i = \{t_j\}_{j=b}^{e}$ is a text span in C, where b/e is the starting/ending position of the text span.

After constructing the nodes of the key-elements graph, we define the edge between nodes as follows: 1. for every pair of entities appear in the same sentence in context (within-sentences-level links); 2. for key elements with entities that have a syntactic association in the same sentence (within-sentence-level links). 3. for every pair of entities with the same mention text in context (across-sentence-level links). 4. the last entities in the previous sentence and first entity in the current sentence in context (across-sentence-level links). Notice the across-sentence-level links ensure that entities across multiple sentences are connected in a certain way.

Encoding Query and Context: We treat the answer option and the question as a whole, denoted as new option O_q, and use "[SEP]" to separate it from the context. The node representations are initialized by feeding the concatenated sequence of context and the new option to pre-trained BERT model. We denoted the encoded context representation as $H_C = \{h_{t_1}, h_{t_2}, \ldots, h_{t_l}\} \in R^{l \times d}$, and the encoded of new option as $H_{O_q} = \{h_{o_1}, h_{o_2}, \ldots, h_{o_m}\} \in R^{m \times d}$, where the l, m are the length of the context and the new option, respectively and d is the size of hidden states.

For key-elements nodes, which are a span in the context, each of them the representation is calculated from (i) concatenate the hidden state of the encoded context H_C from the start position to end position. (ii) then use an avg-pooling layer to obtain its final representation. To this end, we obtain the initial representations of all graph nodes $H_V \in R^{n \times d}$, where n is the number of nodes.

Graph Reasoning: After context encoding and obtain initial representations of graph nodes, KGN performs reasoning over the graph, where the contextualized representations of all the graph nodes are transformed into higher-level features via a graph network.

For graph propagation, we use Graph Attention Network(GAT) [24] to perform message passing over the graph and capture syntactic relation between two nodes. Specifically, GAT takes all the nodes as input, and updates node feature h_i through its neighbors N_i in the graph. Formally,

$$h'_i = \sigma\left(\sum_{j \in N_i} \alpha_{ij} W h_j\right) \tag{3}$$

where $W \in R^{d \times d}$ is a weight matrix to be learned, $\sigma(.)$ denotes an activate function, and α_{ij} is the attention coefficients, which can be calculated by:

$$\alpha_{ij} = \frac{\exp(\sigma(W_2[h_i; h_j]))}{\sum_{k \in N_i} \exp(\sigma(W_2[h_i; h_k]))} \tag{4}$$

where $W_2 \in R^{d \times 2d}$ is a weight matrix and $[;]$ is the concatenation operation. After graph reasoning, we obtain the updated key-elements graph representations $H_G = \{h_{g_1}, h_{g_2}, \ldots, h_{g_n}\} \in R^{n \times d}$.

Integration: In this module, the graph representations H_G are fused into context H_C to obtain the semantic enriched context representations.

For each node v_i in graph, we add the representation h_{g_i} with context token representation according to its start and end position in context. For the other tokens in context which not belong to nodes, we add each token representation h_{t_i} with a special vector close to $\overrightarrow{0}$. After that, we obtain the semantic enrich representation and then concatenate it with the new option, to get the output of KGN which denotes as H_S.

3.3 Prediction

For answer prediction, we feed the output into two feed forward layers to get the final representation $O'_i \in R^d$, which is the representation for each context-question-option triplet.

$$O_i = FFN_1(H_{S_i}) \tag{5}$$

$$O'_i = FFN_2(O_i) \tag{6}$$

where $FFN(.)$ is a feed forward layer, if O_k is the correct option for a question, then the objective function can be computed as follows:

$$L(O_K|C,Q,O_i) = -\log \frac{\exp(W_3^T O'_K)}{\sum\limits_{j=1}^{m} \exp(W_3^T O'_j)} \tag{7}$$

where $W_3 \in R^d$ is a learnable parameter matrix, and m is the number of answer options in a question.

4 Experiments

In this section, we describe our experiments on GCRC, comparing KGN with several state-of-art approaches in multiple-choice MRC task and providing detailed analysis.

4.1 Datasets

GCRC: We collected the raw data from real and simulated Chinese University examinations across 15 years, as shown in Fig. 1 each question in GCRC contains a passage, related question and, four answer options. Table 1 provides statics on GCRC. Note each article could have one or multiple associated questions.

Table 1. Statistic of GCRC

Question number	7,886	Article number	3,179
Article max length (#tokens)	3,050	Article max length (#sentences)	107
Article min length (#tokens)	152	Article min length (#sentences)	4
Article avg length (#tokens)	1,134.15	Particle avg length (#sentences)	24.77

Evidence Sentences Corpus: Due to there is no Chinese corpus related to evidence sentences of multiple-choice reading comprehension. We randomly select 500 questions from the dataset and manually annotating corresponding evidence sentences for each answer option. After a series of cross-validation and re-labeling work, we get the evidence sentence set which contains 45,311 sentence pairs. The training, evaluation and test set include 36,254, 4,528 and 4,529 sentence pairs, respectively.

4.2   Experiment Settings

Baselines: Regarding to answer prediction, we compare our model against with several strong baselines on machine reading comprehension.

- **BERT** [10]: contains multiple bidirectional Transformer [25] layers and was pre-trained on large scale datasets. BERT has achieved very good performance for most current reading comprehension datasets. As such, we have employed the BERT-base model on Chinese documents in our experiments to assess its capabilities on our new dataset.
- **ALBERT** [26]: is an improved version of BERT, which proposes two parameter reduction techniques to lower memory consumption and increase training speed of BERT. This model performs very well on a few benchmark datasets, like RACE, SNLI.
- **DCMN** [5]: uses BERT as backbone and models passage-question, question-option and passage-option relationships bidirectionally. It exploits a gate mechanism to effectively combine information from two directions, achieving competitive performance on RACE.

Evidence Sentence Extraction: we are first taking BERT as the backbone and fine-tune the model with the manual labeled evidence sentence dataset. After that, we use ROCC to decrease the redundancy of extracted sentences and the filter K is set to 3.

Key-Elements Graph: to construct the key-elements graph, we use Stanford-CoreNLP to analyze the syntactic dependency and use BERT as the backbone of model, the input max length is set to 512, the train batch size is set to 32 and the gradient accumulation step is set to 8. Adam optimizer is used with learning rate = 1e-5. For the graph encoder, the number of layers is set to 2.

4.3   Evaluation

Effectiveness of KGN. As shown in Table 2, the use of KGN with evidence sentence extraction method improves the accuracy over the plain BERT model by 7.56 points on dev set. We suffer up to a 2.02 points drop in accuracy on dev set with KGN when removing the elements that have syntactic relation with entities in the context. This indicates that infusing of syntactic information is helpful.

Table 2. Performance comparison with baselines and the ablation study. The best performance is in bold. "+ evi" means use evidence sentence extraction method.

Model	BERT	BERT + evi	ALBERT	ALBERT + evi	DCMN	DCMN + evi	KGN	KGN-syn
dev acc	32.61%	36.29%	29.06%	32.11%	30.83%	32.64%	**40.17%**	38.15%
test acc	30.33%	31.34%	28.05%	29.57%	30.24%	32.12%	**36.13%**	34.27%

Effectiveness of Evidence Sentences Selection. The proposed KGN relies on effective evidence selection to find the critical information required for answering the question correctly.

Table 3. Ablation study of evidence sentence extraction method.

Model	Precision	Recall	F1
BERT-wwm	73.78%	63.84%	68.45%
BERT-wwm + option rephrased	77.29%	**65.34%**	70.81%
BERT-wwm + option rephrased + ROCC	**78.55%**	64.84%	**71.04%**

As illustrated in Table 3, that rephrase the option improves the F1 score over the plain entailment model by 2.36 points. This indicates that rephrase option making the information more complete. By using ROCC to further filter irrelevant sentences, the precision gets an additional improvement of 1.26 points. The above results show the effectiveness of our proposed method.

4.4   Error Analysis

To analyze the lack of capabilities of the model, we choose a representative example from mistake predictions, as shown in Fig. 4. To answer the question, the model needs to know the *"little spring insect"* in options refers to *"fossil"* in the passage. About 87% of errors (the remaining errors are difficult to be summarized as a certain category) are related to this situation. The result turns out that the model cannot tackle these problems. To tackle this problem, model need to have the ability to solve the cross-sentence co-reference problem.

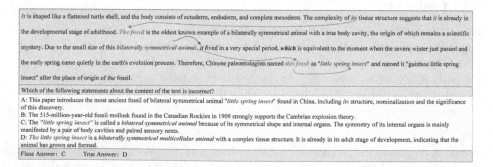

Fig. 4. The procedure of evidence sentence extraction.

5 Conclusion

This paper faces with the characteristics of questions from Gaokao Chinese examinations presents a model named KGN which infused syntactic information and improves the performance of the evidence sentence extraction model. Our experimental results show that the adopted KGN, together with other neural models, could make the model accuracy get a big improvement. Meanwhile, we notice that even if most of the evidence sentences have been extraction, the impact of noise information is significantly reduced and KGN enhances the semantic information. The improvement is still limited, which may cause us to think - does the model understand semantics?

In the future, we will study the co-reference problem involved in reading comprehension tasks and explore how to improve the comprehension ability of reading comprehension model.

References

1. Mihaylov, T., Clark, P., Khot, T., Sabharwal, A.: Can a suit of armor conduct electricity? A new dataset for open book question answering. In: Proceedings of the 2018 Conference on Empirical Methods in Natural Language Processing, Brussels, Belgium, October–November 2018, pp. 2381–2391. Association for Computational Linguistics (2018)
2. Dua, D., Wang, Y., Dasigi, P., Stanovsky, G., Singh, S., Gardner, M.: DROP: a reading comprehension benchmark requiring discrete reasoning over paragraphs. In: Proceedings of the 2019 Conference of the North American Chapter of the Association for Computational Linguistics: Human Language Technologies, Minneapolis, Minnesota, June 2019, Volume 1 (Long and Short Papers), pp. 2368–2378. Association for Computational Linguistics (2019)
3. Khashabi, D., Chaturvedi, S., Roth, M., Upadhyay, S., Roth, D.: Looking beyond the surface: a challenge set for reading comprehension over multiple sentences. In: Proceedings of the 2018 Conference of the North American Chapter of the Association for Computational Linguistics: Human Language Technologies, New Orleans, Louisiana, June 2018, Volume 1 (Long Papers), pp. 252–262. Association for Computational Linguistics (2018)
4. Wang, S., Yu, M., Chang, S., Jiang, J.: A co-matching model for multi-choice reading comprehension (2018)
5. Zhang, S., Zhao, H., Wu, Y., Zhang, Z., Zhou, X., Zhou, X.: Dual co-matching network for multi-choice reading comprehension. CoRR, abs/1901.09381 (2019)
6. Ran, Q., Li, P., Hu, W., Zhou, J.: Option comparison network for multiple-choice reading comprehension (2019)
7. Wang, H., Yu, D., Sun, K., Chen, J., Roth, D.: Evidence sentence extraction for machine reading comprehension. In: Proceedings of the 23rd Conference on Computational Natural Language Learning (CoNLL) (2019)
8. Trivedi, H., Kwon, H., Khot, T., Sabharwal, A., Balasubramanian, N.: Repurposing entailment for multi-hop question answering tasks (2019)

9. Yadav, V., Bethard, S., Surdeanu, M.: Quick and (not so) dirty: unsupervised selection of justification sentences for multi-hop question answering. In: Proceedings of the 2019 Conference on Empirical Methods in Natural Language Processing and the 9th International Joint Conference on Natural Language Processing (EMNLP-IJCNLP) (2019)

10. Devlin, J., Chang, M.-W., Lee, K., Toutanova, K.: BERT: pre-training of deep bidirectional transformers for language understanding (2018)

11. Yang, Z., Dai, Z., Yang, Y., Carbonell, J., Salakhutdinov, R., Le, Q.V.: XLNet: generalized autoregressive pretraining for language understanding (2019)

12. Trivedi, H., Kwon, H., Khot, T., Sabharwal, A., Balasubramanian, N.: Repurposing entailment for multi-hop question answering tasks. CoRR, abs/1904.09380 (2019)

13. Welbl, J., Stenetorp, P., Riedel, S.: Constructing datasets for multi-hop reading comprehension across documents (2017)

14. Yang, Z., et al.: HotpotQA: a dataset for diverse, explainable multi-hop question answering (2018)

15. Feldman, Y., El-Yaniv, R.: Multi-hop paragraph retrieval for open-domain question answering. CoRR, abs/1906.06606 (2019)

16. De Cao, N., Aziz, W., Titov, I.: Question answering by reasoning across documents with graph convolutional networks. CoRR, abs/1808.09920 (2018)

17. Ding, M., Zhou, C., Chen, Q., Yang, H., Tang, J.: Cognitive graph for multi-hop reading comprehension at scale (2019)

18. Choi, E., Hewlett, D., Uszkoreit, J., Polosukhin, I., Berant, J.: Coarse-to-fine question answering for long documents. In: Proceedings of the 55th Annual Meeting of the Association for Computational Linguistics (Volume 1: Long Papers) (2017)

19. Geva, M., Berant, J.: Learning to search in long documents using document structure (2018)

20. Yadav, V., Bethard, S., Surdeanu, M.: Alignment over heterogeneous embeddings for question answering. In: Conference of the North (2019)

21. Song, L., Wang, Z., Yu, M., Zhang, Y., Florian, R., Gildea, D.: Exploring graph-structured passage representation for multi-hop reading comprehension with graph neural networks (2018)

22. Dhingra, B., Jin, Q., Yang, Z., Cohen, W.W., Salakhutdinov, R.: Neural models for reasoning over multiple mentions using coreference (2018)

23. De Cao, N., Aziz, W., Titov, I.: Question answering by reasoning across documents with graph convolutional networks (2018)

24. Veličkovié, P., Cucurull, G., Casanova, A., Romero, A., Liò, P., Bengio, Y.: Graph attention networks (2017)

25. Vaswani, A., et al.: Attention is all you need (2017)

26. Lan, Z.-Z., Chen, M., Goodman, S., Gimpel, K., Sharma, P., Soricut, R.: Albert: a lite BERT for self-supervised learning of language representations. arXiv, abs/1909.11942 (2019)

Knowledge Inference Model of OCR Conversion Error Rules Based on Chinese Character Construction Attributes Knowledge Graph

Xiaowen Zhang, Hairong Wang$^{(\boxtimes)}$, and Wenjie Gu

School of Computer Science and Engineering, North Minzu University, Yinchuan 750021, China
bmdwhr@163.com

Abstract. OCR is a character conversion method based on image recognition. The complexity of the character and the image quality plays a key role in the conversion accuracy. The OCR conversion process has the characteristics of irregular conversion errors and the combination between incorrect conversion words and context of original location in certain text scenarios is established in semantic. In this paper, we propose an OCR conversion error rules inference model based on Chinese character construction attribute knowledge graph to analyze and inference the structure and complexity of Chinese characters. The model integrates a variety of coding methods, extracts features of entities and relationships of different data types with different encoder in the knowledge graph, uses convolutional neural networks to learn and inference the unknown error rules in the OCR conversion. In addition, in order to enable the triple feature matrix to fully contain the construction attribute information of the Chinese characters, a feature crossover algorithm for feature diffusion of the triple feature matrix is introduced. In this algorithm, the relation matrix and the entities matrix are crossed to generate the new feature matrix which can better represent the triple of knowledge graph. The experimental results show that, compared with the current mainstream knowledge inference model, the OCR conversion error rules inference model incorporating the feature cross algorithm has achieved important improvements in MRR, Hits@1, Hits@2 and other evaluation indicators on public data sets and task-related data sets.

Keywords: Knowledge inference · Knowledge graph · OCR · Convolutional neural network · Text error correction

1 Introduction

With the rapid development of computer technology, in the popular research application fields such as question answering system and intelligent recommendation, to have complete and powerful functions, a large amount of high-quality, high-precision text data is required. A real problem is that not all texts have regular text documents that can be processed directly, including public papers in databases, electronic versions of historical documents, etc., all exist in the form of PDFs or images. These documents need to be converted. Natural language processing operations can only be performed in the form

© Springer Nature Switzerland AG 2020
X. Zhu et al. (Eds.): NLPCC 2020, LNAI 12431, pp. 415–425, 2020.
https://doi.org/10.1007/978-3-030-60457-8_34

of text for use in question answering systems, open retrieval and other fields [1]. The current PDF or image conversion to text is mainly based on optical character recognition (Optical Character Recognition, OCR) technology [2]. The mainstream OCR technology can correctly recognize most of the text content, but there are still a lot of recognition errors caused by similar text. OCR recognition errors are different from common text errors, such as input errors and garbled transmission, and have their own characteristics. Therefore, text error correction for OCR recognition errors is of great significance to the current development of the field of artificial intelligence and semantics, and it is also a problem to be solved urgently.

Benefiting from the rapid development of the application of knowledge graph and the maturity of deep learning technology, knowledge inference, as one of the main methods of using knowledge graph, has received a lot of research. Knowledge graph is a kind of knowledge base with knowledge triples as the basic structure, which has more flexible knowledge representation ability than traditional data structure. Knowledge inference based on the knowledge graph is to characterize the knowledge graph, using machine learning algorithms, deep learning models, etc. to perform inference and calculations to obtain unknow knowledge. Bordes A et al. [3] proposed TransE, a inference prediction model that uses triple vector equations to automatically supplement missing triple information in a low-dimensional space; Wang Z et al. [4] proposed TransH based on the TransE model., Using negative triples to solve the problem of poor inference models in one-to-many, many-to-one and many-to-many complex scenarios; in order to solve the problem of mutual coverage of entity relationship feature spaces, Lin Y et al. [5] proposed The TransR model is used to perform the backward feedback of the weights of the connected entities when training the feature vector; because TransR splits the feature space, it brings about the problems of unobvious features in the interval and feature explosion. Ji G, Liu K, etc. [6] proposed Improved model TransSparse to solve this problem; Zhang W et al. [7] designed a model TransH for feature tiling projections in different vector spaces to fuse the vectors obtained from entity relations training in different feature spaces; TransH passed Constructing an instance of negative triples to improve the effect of entity relationship feature training, but the data skew problem of the data set itself has not been solved. Kanojia V et al. [8] modified the rules for generating negative triples to effectively improve this problem. In order to cope with the semantic understanding and knowledge representation challenges brought by multi-modal data, Pezeshkpour P et al. [9] proposed a MKBE model for knowledge inference based on multi-modal data. The model uses TextGan, ImageGan and other models for feature learning on multimodal data, and uses Distmult and ConvE models to implement feature inference and calculation. Compared with TransE, TransSparse, TransH and other models, it has been greatly improved. In the feature extraction of text data, the model ignores the sequence of the text itself, and loses part of the semantic information contained in the text content.

This paper proposes an OCR conversion error rule inference model based on the Chinese character construction attributes knowledge graph. With the Chinese character construction attributes knowledge graph as the background knowledge, the specific feature extraction of different data types in the knowledge graph is carried out by using the volume The product neural network performs knowledge inference, and automatic generation of OCR conversion error rules between Chinese characters missing in knowledge graph; this paper also designs a feature crossover algorithm for the triple feature matrix, based on the Hadamard multiplication on the triple entity matrix and The relation matrix is feature-enhanced to improve the inference ability of the knowledge inference model.

2 Biao-Xing Code and Knowledge Graph of Chinese Character Construction Attribute

Biao-Xing code is a kind of shape code designed by experts and scholars based on the similarity between Chinese character radicals and English letters, which is led by the national key Torch Program project. There is a certain similarity between the Chinese character and the English letter in the shape after the decomposition of the Chinese character. The corresponding English letter is designed for each Chinese character radical by the Biao-Xing code. The writing order of the Chinese character is taken and the corresponding English letter of the sub radical is used to code. The 3-4-digit code corresponding to the overall construction property of the Chinese character is obtained. Because the Biao-Xing code in the split of Chinese characters in line with the intuitive, and has the theoretical support of Chinese characters. Therefore, the use of Biao-Xing codes to supplement the knowledge graph of Chinese characters not only has reasonable interpretability, but also can make full use of the similarity between OCR conversion error Chinese characters. Table 1 shows the Biao-Xing code and OCR conversion errors intuitively by taking several errors in the OCR conversion process as examples.

Table 1 shows the two wrong Chinese characters (徇and 锌) that are identified in the OCR conversion process, as well as the Biao-Xing codes and strokes of the corresponding two wrong characters. It can be found that the coding distance between the correct character and the wrong character is only 1 bit, and the number of strokes is very close. Starting from the form code and strokes of Chinese characters, this paper

Table 1. Example of OCR conversion error.

Chinese characters	Biao-Xing code	Strokes
徇	VHO	7
拘	FHO	8
句	HOI	5
锌	ZIKX	12
粹	GMIX	14

(continued)

Table 1. (*continued*)

Chinese characters	Biao-Xing code	Strokes
梓	MIKX	11

constructs a knowledge graph of Chinese character construction attributes, including Chinese characters themselves, corresponding shape codes of Chinese characters, strokes of Chinese characters, and error rules between Chinese characters. The knowledge graph contains five kinds of relations and more than 20000 entities, including Chinese character shape code, Chinese character stroke, shape code stroke, and Chinese character Chinese character error rules. At the same time, it also includes more than 900 OCR conversion error rules in practical application scenarios.

3   Multi Encoder Knowledge Inference Model

This section introduces a knowledge inference model based on different data formats. The knowledge graph of Chinese character construction attributes contains many types of data such as numbers, words and text sequences. The traditional knowledge inference model is rough in the process of data vectorization, and uses a single feature extraction method for different data types. This method is not ideal in multimodal data, it can not effectively distinguish the features between different data, and there is the possibility of excessive feature extraction for single small sample data. Therefore, this paper uses multiple coding models to encode the three tuples of different data types in the knowledge graph, uses MLP model to vectorize digital type data, and uses GRU model to extract features of text type data, and carries out matrix splicing for the three tuple feature matrix of different data types after feature extraction. A new feature matrix of the three tuple is obtained by using the feature cross algorithm to spread the feature. The convolution model of ConvE graph is used to infer the feature matrix. The model framework is shown in Fig. 1:

In the graph, Es, R and Eo represent the feature matrices of the head entity, relation entity and tail entity of the triplet after being vectorized by multiple encoders. Es and R are respectively obtained from the head entity Chinese character id of the triple contained in the knowledge graph and all the relationships contained in the knowledge graph through full connection layer initialization, while Eo is obtained from all tail entities of the triple contained in the knowledge graph through the differential vectorization method according to their different data types. The tail entity in the error rule triple is the Chinese character id, which shares the same with the Chinese character id of its head entity A feature matrix after initialization of full connection layer. The tail entity strokes of the stroke triplet of Chinese characters are digital entities, which are vectorized and encoded by MLP multi-layer perceptron. The tail entity of the Biao-Xing code is the one-to-one correspondence of each Chinese character. It is treated as a text sequence in the model. Firstly, the word vector is initialized by using the open-source word vector for word representation Glove [10], and then the sequence vector is learend and trained

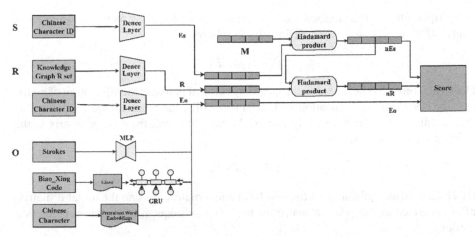

Fig. 1. Multi encoder knowledge inference model.

by GRU model to generate the feature matrix that can represent the Biao-Xing code. Chinese characters are initialized by using the open source Chinese vectors for word representation [11] pre trained by Tencent AI Lab as the feature matrix of Chinese characters. After the first level multi encoder vectorization, the corresponding head entity feature matrix Es, relational feature matrix R and tail entity feature matrix Eo are obtained. Then, the feature cross algorithm is used to cross the head entity feature matrix Es and relationship feature matrix R to generate more representative feature matrix nEs, nR and Eo as the input of convolution prediction model. The convolution prediction of the input three tuple feature matrix by the fractional function realizes the prediction of the error rule relationship between different Chinese character id. The knowledge graph can be represented by a set of triples $G = \{(s, r, o)\} \in \varepsilon \times R \times \varepsilon$. The task of relational prediction is to learn a scoring function $\varphi : \varepsilon \times R \times \varepsilon \to R^1$. Give a triple $x = (s, r, o)$. It's score $\varphi(x) \in R^1$ proportional and x is a real possibility. ConvE the scoring model is shown below:

$$\varphi_r(e_s, e_o) = f(vec(f([\overline{e_s}; \overline{r_r}] * \omega))W)e_o \tag{1}$$

The loss function of the model is as follows:

$$L(p, t) = -\frac{1}{N} \sum_i (t_i \cdot \log(p_i) + (1 - t_i) \cdot \log(1 - p_i)) \tag{2}$$

4 Feature Crossover Algorithm

After getting the triple matrix composed of Es, R and Eo, in order to strengthen the features of entities and relations of triples, the head entities and relation matrices of triples can fully learn the knowledge contained in the knowledge graph. We introduces a feature crossover algorithm. Firstly, in the process of model training, we define one for each triple relation $1 \times$ Embed Size's feature cross vector, construct the feature cross matrix $M \in n_r \times$ *Embed Size*, define nEs as follows"

$$nEs = M_r^\circ Es \tag{3}$$

Here, the $^\circ$ refers to Hadamard multiplication, a kind of pairwise multiplication of matrices. By Hadamard multiplication with each row of Es, the relation features defined as size are diffused to the head entity matrix. At the same time, the relation matrix in the training triple is fed back by feature.

$$nR = nEs^\circ R \tag{4}$$

By Hadamard multiplication of the new head entity matrix nEs and the initial R matrix, nR is obtained as the relation matrix of the input subsequent convolution prediction model.

Algorithm 1. Feature crossover algorithm

Input:
 R (Relation matrix, $n_r \times embed\_dim$), Es (Head entity matrix, $n_s \times embed\_dim$).
 M (Feature cross matrix, $n_r \times embed\_dim$).
Output:
 nR (Relation matrix after feature crossing), nEs (head entity matrix after feature intersection).
1:    for t in n_r:
2:    t represents the sequence of the current training triple correspondence in the relational dictionary
3:    $t_1' = t \times M$
4:      for i in n_s:
         $nE_s = Hadamard(one - hot(i) \times E_s, t_1')$
5:      end for
6:      for j in n_s:
7:        j represents the sequence of the head entity of the current training triplet
8:        $nR = Hadamard(j \times nE_s, R)$
9:      end for
10:   end for

Because the feature crossover algorithm dynamically adjusts the feature matrix of the triple head entity and the relation feature matrix, the original score function of the ConvE can not effectively evaluate the feature matrix after the feature crossing. The optimization of the score function of the ConvE model is as follows:

$$f(s, r, o) = \sigma(\tanh(M_r \times Es + nEs \times R + b)nEo^T) \tag{5}$$

As well as:

$$f(s, r, o) = \sigma(\tanh(M_r \times Es) + M_r \times Es \times R + b)nEo^T \tag{6}$$

The model is optimized by minimizing the cross entropy of each output of the full connection layer. The loss function is defined by:

$$\sum_{(s,r)} \sum_o t_o^{s,r} \log(p_o^{s,r}) + (1 - t_o^{s,r}) \log(1 - p_o^{s,r}) + \lambda \sum \|\theta\|_2^2 \tag{7}$$

λ controls the L2 regularization terms of Es, R, Eo and bias of the model, so that the model can be trained iteratively based on gradient.

5   Experiment and Result Analysis

In this paper, an knowledge inference model of OCR conversion error rules based on the Chinese character construction attributes knowledge graph is proposed, and the feature crossover algorithm for the triple feature matrix is integrated. This section will carry out experimental design, validation and result analysis.

5.1   Experimental Design

This paper focuses on knowledge inference on multi data type data sets. The public dataset Movielens, which also contains a variety of data types, contains various background information of users and movies, as well as users' ratings of different movies. The background knowledge of users and movies in the data set, and the rating information of users on films are constructed as a knowledge graph of film rating. The multi encoder knowledge inference model is used for feature extraction and inference calculation of film rating knowledge graph to complete the missing rating information in the knowledge graph. In this paper, 901 error rules are obtained by statistics and manual revision in the actual application scenario of OCR transformation. The multi encoder knowledge inference model is used for feature extraction and inference calculation of Chinese character construction attributes knowledge graph, and the unknown OCR conversion error rules between Chinese characters are predicted. The specifications of the two datasets are shown in Table 2.

Table 2.   Dataset statistics.

	MovieLens	Error rules
Link type	13	5
Entities	2625	20,881
Link triples	100,000	63,544

From Table 2, we can find that there are great differences in the number of relations and entities between the two datasets, which is a challenge to the model.In order to fully test the performance of the model and the rationality of the dataset, three models, namely TransE, MKBE (Dismult), MKBE (ConvE) are selected as the comparison models of the proposed models in this paper, and they are carried out on the open dataset Movielens and the error rule dataset The experimental results of several models were compared. The Multi Encoder Knowledge Inference model proposed in this paper is named MEKI, and the experimental results of MEKI model on the knowledge graph constructed by error rule data set and Chinese characters are tested. At the same time, in order to verify the promotion effect of the feature crossing algorithm proposed in this paper, the MEKI model is marked as MEKI-Fc (Feature Cross). The two models are tested on Movielens data set, error rule data set and Chinese character construction attributes knowledge graph to verify the effectiveness of the model and algorithm.

5.2 Results and Analysis

In this paper, MEKI, MEKI-Fc and MKBE-D (Dismult), MKBE-C (ConvE) and TransE are tested on Movielens data set and error rule data set respectively. MRR and Hits @ are selected to evaluate the effect of the model. The final evaluation results are shown in Table 3 and Table 4:

Table 3. Results on Movielens dataset.

Model	MRR	Hits@1	Hits@2	Hits@3	Model
TransE	0.496	0.224	0.365	0.531	TransE
MKBE-D	0.650	0.424	0.73	0.791	MKBE-D
MKBE-C	0.726	0.512	0.83	0.882	MKBE-C
MEKI	0.738	0.536	0.872	0.9035	MEKI

Table 4. Results on error rules dataset.

Model	MRR	Hits@1
TransE	0.7735	0.547
MKBE-C	0.7917	0.5923
MEKI	0.8653	0.731
MEKI-Fc	0.8933	0.7873

Compared with Table 3 and Table 4, we can see that the proposed multi encoder knowledge inference model MEKI in this paper can evaluate MRR, MRR, and MRR without fusion feature cross algorithm Hits@1, Hits@2, Hits@3 Compared with the best MKBE-C model, the experimental results on Movielens dataset increased by 1.2%, 2.4%, 3.8% and 2.15%, respectively. Compared with MKBE-C, MEKKI-Fc, a multi encoder knowledge inference model, achieved the best results in all indicators. Compared with MKBE-C, MEKI-Fc increased by 2%, 4.69%, 6.1% and 3.3% respectively, and MEKI-Fc increased by 0.8%, 2.29%, 2.3% and 1.15% respectively compared with MKBE-C.

Similarly, MEKI-Fc and MEKI achieved the first and second best results on the error rule dataset, and the indicators of the two models were significantly higher than that of MKBE-C, which performed best in the comparison model. MEKI-Fc achieved the best results in all indicators, compared with the MRR, MRR and MRR of MKBE-C, which performed best in comparison model Hits@1. The index is improved by 10.2% and 19.5% in turn. Compared with the multi encoder knowledge inference model without feature crossing algorithm, MEKI is increased by 7.36% and 13.87% respectively.

Experiments show that MEKI-Fc achieves the best results on both evaluation datasets. The Movielens dataset contains 13 relationships and 2625 entities, and the error rule dataset contains 5 relationships and 20881 entities. Compared with the error rule data set, Movielens dataset has more relations and fewer nodes. The results show that MEKI has better prediction ability than MEKI FC on the data sets with complex relationships and fewer nodes. It shows that the targeted processing based on multi coding can obtain more representative feature matrix and ultimately affect the prediction ability of the model. Compared with MEKI-Fc, the index of MEKI and MEKI-Fc is increased by 19.5% on the data set with relatively simple entity relationship and a large number of nodes, which indicates that the feature matrix of nodes and relationships has been fully learned and differentiated, which verifies the effectiveness of multi coding targeted processing for feature learning of different data.

At the same time, the MEKI-Fc model integrated with feature crossing algorithm is compared with the MRR, MRR and MRR of MEKI model on Movielens Hits@1, Hits@2 and Hits@3 8%, 2.29%, 19% and 1.15% respectively. In the error correction data set, it is improved by 2.8% and 5.63%, which shows the effectiveness of the feature crossing algorithm. The feature crossover algorithm calculates the Hadamard product between the initial three tuple eigenmatrixes after multi coding processing, and iteratively accumulates the distance between the three tuple eigenmatrices in the training process. The more irrelevant the triples are, the larger the accumulated distance is in the training iteration process. Until fully trained, the characteristic interval distribution of triples conforms to the correlation between triples. In the convolution prediction layer, the inference ability of the model is strengthened from the perspective of feature matrix reinforcement learning.

The knowledge graph of Chinese characters construction attributes includes word, code, stroke and OCR conversion error rules between Chinese characters. In order to explore the role of Chinese character construction attributes in error rule inference, the knowledge graph of Chinese character construction attributes was segmented and the performance of MEKI and MEKI-Fc models on different Chinese character construction attributes knowledge graph was tested. The experimental results are shown in Table 5.

Table 5. Results based on different knowledge subgraph.

Model	Dataset	MRR	Hits@1
MEKI	W + S	0.8072	0.614
	W + C	0.845	0.69
	W + S + C	0.8653	0.731
MEKI-Fc	W + S	0.8135	0.627
	W + C	0.8632	0.7265
	W + S + C	0.8933	0.7873

It can be seen from Table 5 that MEKI model and MEKI-Fc model achieve their best results when the knowledge graph of Chinese character construction attributes includes Chinese character (W), Biao-Xing code (c) and stroke (s). Moreover, the MEKI-Fc model integrated with feature crossing algorithm is better than MEKI model in each parallel index, which proves that the feature crossing algorithm can improve the inference ability of the model Efficacy. The application of MEKI model in the complete knowledge graph of Chinese character construction attributes Hits@1 Compared with Chinese character + stroke subgraph and Chinese character + shape code knowledge subgraph, the index increased by 11.7% and 6.62% respectively. The application of MEKI-Fc model in complete Chinese character construction attributes knowledge graph Hits@1 Compared with Chinese character + stroke subgraph and Chinese character + shape code subgraph, the index increased by 16.03% and 6.08% respectively.

6 Conclusion

This paper focuses on the inference and prediction of OCR conversion error rules based on Chinese character construction attributes. A modified knowledge inference model of OCR conversion error rules is proposed. The semantic richness of feature matrix is ensured by feature extraction for multimodal data. The experiment shows that it has good effect on prediction of OCR conversion error rules. This paper proposes a feature crossover algorithm for the triple knowledge structure, which effectively improves the effect of knowledge inference based on triple feature matrix. Experiments based on different knowledge subgraph show that Chinese character construction attributes have a good indication in the prediction and correction of OCR conversion errors. Experiments show that the accuracy rate of the proposed method in OCR conversion error rule inference reaches 87%, and the coverage rate reaches 89%. It can comprehensively cover most of the errors that may be encountered in the process of text extraction based on OCR transformation. It has guiding significance for assisting the text error correction after OCR recognition.

Acknowledgment. This work has been support by the North Minzu university key research project (No. 2019KJ26), the Ningxia first-class discipline and scientific research projects (electronic science and technology) (NO. NXYLXK2017A07) and the Natural science foundation of Ningxia Province (NO. 2020AAC03218).

References

1. Fink, F., Schulz, K.U., Springmann, U.: Profiling of OCR'ed historical texts revisited. In: Proceedings of the 2nd International Conference on Digital Access to Textual Cultural Heritage, Gottingen, pp. 61–66. Association for Computing Machinery (2017)
2. Bast, H., Claudius, K.: A benchmark and evaluation for text extraction from pdf. In: Proceedings of the 17th ACM/IEEE Joint Conference on Digital Libraries, Toronto, pp. 99–108. IEEE Press (2017)
3. Bordes, A., Usunier, N., Garcia-Duran, A., Weston, J., Yakhnenko, O.: Translating embeddings for modeling multi-relational data. In: Proceedings of the 26th International Conference on Neural Information Processing Systems, Lake Tahoe, vol. 2, pp. 2787–2795. Curran Associates Inc. (2013)
4. Wang, Z., Zhang, J., Feng, J., Chen, Z.: Knowledge graph embedding by translating on hyperplanes. In: Proceedings of the Twenty-Eighth AAAI Conference on Artificial Intelligence, Quebec, pp. 1112–1119. AAAI Press (2014)

5. Lin, Y., Liu, Z., Sun, M., Liu, Y., Zhu, X.: Learning entity and relation embeddings for knowledge graph completion. In: Proceedings of the Twenty-Ninth AAAI Conference on Artificial Intelligence, Austin, pp. 2181–2187. AAAI Press (2015)
6. Ji, G., Liu, K., He, S., Zhao, J.: Knowledge graph completion with adaptive sparse transfer matrix. In: Proceedings of the Thirtieth AAAI Conference on Artificial Intelligence, Phoenix, pp. 985–991. AAAI Press (2016)
7. Wen, Z.: Knowledge graph embedding with diversity of structures. In: Proceedings of the 26th International Conference on World Wide Web Companion, Perth, pp. 747–753. International World Wide Web Conferences Steering Committee (2017)
8. Pouya, P., Liyan, C., Sameer, S.: Embedding multimodal relational data for knowledge base completion. ArXiv, abs/1809.01341 (2018)
9. Kanojia, V., Maeda, H., Togashi, R., Fujita, S.: Enhancing knowledge graph embedding with probabilistic negative sampling. In: Proceedings of the 26th International Conference on World Wide Web Companion, Perth, pp. 801–802. International World Wide Web Conferences Steering Committee (2017)
10. Pennington, J., Socher, R., Manning, C.: Glove: global vectors for word representation. In: Proceedings of the 2014 Conference on Empirical Methods in Natural Language Processing, Doha, vol. 14, pp. 1532–1543. Association for Computational Linguistics (2014)
11. Yan, S., Shuming, S., Jing, L., Haisong, Z.: Directional skip-gram: explicitly distinguishing left and right context for word embeddings. In: Proceedings of the 2018 Conference of the North American Chapter of the Association for Computational Linguistics: Human Language Technologies, New Orleans, vol. 2, pp. 175–180. Association for Computational Linguistics (2018)

Explainable AI Workshop

Interpretable Machine Learning Based on Integration of NLP and Psychology in Peer-to-Peer Lending Risk Evaluation

Lei Li[1(✉)], Tianyuan Zhao[1(✉)], Yang Xie[1], and Yanjie Feng[2]

[1] Beijing University of Posts and Telecommunications, Beijing 100876, China
leili@bupt.edu.cn, zhaotianyuan13@163.com
[2] Shanghai University of International Business and Economics, Shanghai 201620, China

Abstract. With the rapid development of Peer-to-Peer (P2P) lending in the financial field, abundant data of lending agencies have appeared. P2P agencies also have problems such as absconded with ill-gotten gains and out of business. Therefore, it is urgent to use the interpretable AI in Fintech to evaluate the lending risk effectively. In this paper we use the machine learning and deep learning method to model and analyze the unstructured natural language text of P2P agencies, and we propose an interpretable machine learning method to evaluate the fraud risk of P2P agencies, which enhances the credibility of the AI model. First, this paper explains model behavior based on the psychological interpersonal fraud theory in the field of social science. At the same time, the NLP and influence function in the field of natural science are used to verify that the machine learning model really learns the information of part-of-speech details in the fraud theory, which provides the psychological interpretable support for the model of P2P risk evaluation. In addition, we propose "style vectors" to describe the overall differences between text styles of P2P agencies and understand model behavior. Experiments show that using style vectors and influence functions to describe text style differences is the same as human intuitive perception. This proves that the machine learning model indeed learn the text style difference and use it for risk evaluation, which further shows that the model has a certain machine learning interpretability.

Keywords: Interpretable machine learning · Natural Language Processing (NLP) · Fraud theory in psychology · AI in Fintech · Peer-to-Peer (P2P) lending risk evaluation

1 Introduction

P2P lending is a kind of private lending model that gathers small amounts of money to lend to people in need of funds. The main process is to use the Internet credit company as an intermediary platform to provide information release and transactions through the Internet. China's P2P lending company have developed rapidly due to its advantages of convenience, high interest rate. However, there are also many problems, such as absconded with ill-gotten gains and difficult withdrawing. At present, the risk assessment

© Springer Nature Switzerland AG 2020
X. Zhu et al. (Eds.): NLPCC 2020, LNAI 12431, pp. 429–441, 2020.
https://doi.org/10.1007/978-3-030-60457-8_35

of P2P lending agencies is still very scarce. In particular, P2P network lending has generated a lot of data, especially unstructured natural language text, which contain more plentiful information than structured one. These data can be used to effectively evaluate the risk fraud in the lending process, and then analyze its interpretability according to the effect of different machine learning models, which is significant to verify whether the behavior of the model conforms to human cognition, and can enhance the user's understanding and trust of the system. These are significant to reduce the risk of online lending, strengthen market supervision, assist in making policies and decisions, and establish a good financial investment environment.

In the current information age, data processing and analysis is very important. Admittedly, machine learning and deep learning can automatically process and analyze a large number of data, but the interpretability of their models does not have sufficient theoretical support. Only interpretable models can be applied to the market more safely, which is necessary in financial industry that requires a high degree of accuracy and stability. The current research of machine learning interpretability is mostly based on the methods in the field of natural science, which explain the model behavior through the analysis of model structure and data, but rarely analyze whether the model conforms to human cognitive behavior in the field of social science.

In summary, this paper uses machine learning method to model and analyze unstructured natural language text information in P2P lending companies, and to evaluate the potential fraud risks of various companies from the perspective of machine learning interpretability. For the first time, this paper proposes a psychological fraud theory based on social sciences to explain the results of P2P lending model risk assessment. At the same time, we use the influence function and computational linguistics technology in the field of natural sciences to verify that the machine learning model really learns the important information in the fraud theory, which provides the interpretable support for the machine learning model of risk fraud. The main contributions include two points:

(1) For the explicit details features such as part-of-speech distribution, we combine psychology and computational linguistics to propose and verify an interpretable machine learning in P2P lending risk evaluation.
(2) For the implicit abstract features such as doc2vec, we propose a machine learning interpretability research based on text style. First, we define a style vector, and then combine the influence function and least square method to describe the overall difference of P2P company text, and use it in risk evaluation.

2 Related Work

The existing P2P risk assessment is mainly based on the theory of economics and personal credit risk, using the method of combining theoretical research with case analysis. For example, the credit risk assessment of P2P lending investment decision based on examples [1] and the enhancement of P2P lending investment decision [2]. However, there is still less work to identify the operational risk of P2P lending from the perspective of fraud theory. In previous work, we proposed a data-driven risk assessment framework [3] for 4554 unstructured natural language text data of P2P companies, and NLP technologies such as keywords [4], LDA [5], word2vec [6] and doc2vec [7] were used to extract the features of the text for each P2P company, and then meta-learning method were used to integrate multiple machine learning and deep learning models. Experiments showed that the precision of risk identification using text-based features such as company profile and executive profile was higher than that of numerical features (volume, yield, etc.). Textual features include not only explicit features such as part-of-speech distributions, but also implicit features such as doc2vec. In this paper, in order to further analyze the interpretability of the evaluation results, we build on that work and propose an interpretable machine learning method based on the combination of psychology and computational linguistics for the explicit features, and propose text style-based machine learning interpretability research for implicit features.

Although researchers are eager to explore the interpretable truth from the performance of machine learning model, there is little consensus on the specific definition and evaluation method of machine learning interpretability [8], and even less research on the interpretable machine learning of P2P lending risk fraud. At present, there are three kinds of interpretable evaluation methods in general. The first type is ante-hoc interpretability: the model itself is interpretable due to its simple structure and easy to understand, such as decision tree [9], generalized linear model [10], etc. The second type is post-hoc interpretability: for the trained model, the relationship between the input and output of the sample is analyzed by using the interpretable method to explain the working mechanism and operation principle of the model, such as the influence function [11] and LIME [12]. The third type is based on the multi-disciplinary point of view: through philosophy, psychology and other theories to explain the model of human cognition. What makes psychology stand out is that many theories of psychology have been proved and verified in a large number of psychological experiments (such as cognitive psychology [13] and experimental psychology [14]).

Koh PW et al. [11] use the influence function to track the prediction results of the model and trace them to the training samples through the learning algorithm, so as to obtain the training points with the greatest influence on the prediction results. Compared with influence function, other interpretable algorithms (such as decision tree) simply analyze the relationship between model input and output from the perspective of feature itself or the principle of easily interpretable model, while influence function is strictly defined and proved by reasoning in the paradigm of machine learning. The whole process is very consistent with the research process of machine learning. This is why the influence function is chosen as the focus of this paper to study the interpretability of machine learning.

In psychology, Criteria-Based Content Analysis (CBCA) [15] is usually used to identify cases and adult lies. The CBCA theory is able to distinguish between lies and the truth because the person who is actually experiencing the event gives a more detailed description, and therefore meets more CBCA criteria. Interpersonal Deception Theory (IDT) is also used to explain, predict and identify lying behaviors in interpersonal situations. According to the theory, liars use the following strategies to control the information in a conversation in order to avoid getting caught: (a) Quality Manipulations: liars will deviate completely or partially from the facts and will use fewer adjectives and adverbs to make the meaning of the sentence ambiguous; (b) Quantity Manipulations: liars use fewer words and sentences and cannot provide rich details.

In summary, the previous researches mainly focused on the analysis of numerical and textual information, involving a variety of machine learning and deep learning models. However, the current research rarely analyzes the risk fraud evaluation results of P2P companies from the perspective of machine learning interpretability. Also, the research on interpretability is only the analysis of the model mechanism in natural science, and rarely can be given from the psychological theory of social science. There is also rare research of the efficacy of implicit features used in machine learning models from a textual perspective. These have caused great obstacles to the application of artificial intelligence in the financial field.

3 Model

3.1 Machine Learning Based on Integration of Psychology and NLP

(1) Text Details of CBCA and IDT in Psychology.

CBCA theory points out that fraud can be identified by identifying "general description" and "detailed description". The CBCA theory states that people who actually experience the event will make a more detailed description and therefore will meet more CBCA standards. The IDT theorizes that at least four types of cues are involved in lie detection as shown in Table 1: the number of words, the use of pronouns, the emotional vocabulary, and the cognitive complexity of the presenter.

Table 1. CBCA&IDT detailed description.

Detailed feature	Content
Number of words	Distribution of part-of-speech
Number of details	Specific place, time, person, etc.
Unusual details	Unusual but meaningful details of people, objects and events
Redundant details	Peripheral information with no actual contribution to the statement

(2) Extract Part-of-speech Details Based on NLP.

According to Table 1, for company profile text, we can get part-of-speech sequence and frequency of each part-of-speech at the same time after tagging. The 42 part-of-speech include: adjectives, adverbs, nouns, adjective morphemes, distinguishing words, conjunctions, adverbs, interjections, prefixes, orientation words, idioms, abbreviations, suffixes, idioms, numerals, noun, nominal morpheme, person name, place name, organization, other proper names, onomatopoeia, preposition, quantifier, pronoun, personal pronoun, demonstrative pronoun, place word, time word, time word morpheme, auxiliary word, auxiliary morpheme, auxiliary word, idioms, verbs, adverbs, nominal verbs, intransitive verbs, verbal morphemes, mood words, state words, state morphemes.

(3) Use Influence Functions to Verify the Importance of each Part-of-speech.

The influence function algorithm [11] can observe the change of model parameters by increasing the weight of training samples or disturbing the training samples. The prediction results of the model can be traced back to the training samples, so as to obtain the training data with the greatest influence on the prediction results, and then further analyze the influence degree of each feature on the final results of the model. The influence function (I) of a single training sample (z) on all model parameters (θ) is as follows:

$$I_{up,\ params}(z) \overset{\text{def}}{=} \frac{d\hat{\theta}_{\epsilon,z}}{dx}\Big|_{\epsilon=0} = -\mathrm{H}_{\hat{\theta}}^{-1}\nabla_\theta L\left(z, \hat{\theta}\right) \tag{1}$$

$$H_\theta \overset{\text{def}}{=} \frac{1}{n}\sum\nolimits_{i=1}^n \nabla_\theta^2 L\left(z_i, \hat{\theta}\right) \tag{2}$$

Where ϵ is the weight of sample z relative to other training samples, H_θ is the Hessian second-order partial derivative matrix, including the influence of all N training samples on the model parameter θ. The gradient $\nabla_\theta L\left(z, \hat{\theta}\right)$ includes the influence of a single training sample z on model parameter θ, where L is loss of training samples.

In the experiment, we use part-of-speech features to train a variety of machine learning models, obtain the importance of each part-of-speech feature through the influence function, verify whether the detailed information extracted by the machine learning model is the same as the detailed information believed by psychological theory, and explain the behavior of the machine learning model from a psychological perspective.

3.2   Interpretable Machine Learning Based on Text Style

For executive profile texts, there are large differences in text styles between normal and abnormal companies. We believe that it is the machine learning model that captures such differences in text styles that has a high accuracy rate. Therefore, this paper proposes to study the interpretability of machine learning based on text styles.

(1) Detailed Description.

There are obvious differences in the text style between the normal and abnormal executive profile texts in the two categories. Table 2 lists the detailed analysis. It can be seen that the distribution of language structural units provides an important basis for the analysis of text style. Through the statistics of language structure features in different texts, we can get the consistency or difference features of text style. The distribution data of language structure, such as part-of-speech, becomes a kind of measurement feature reflecting different types of language style. After the NLP method is used to extract 42 part-of-speech features, we also use the 200 dimensional doc2vec for feature representation. Because the part-of-speech distribution features are not comprehensive. Some important text style information, such as context semantic relation, will be implicitly reflected in the doc2vec in some way. Therefore, it is necessary to analyze the interpretability of doc2vec carefully.

Table 2. Text style of executive profile.

Business status	Text style of executive profile
Normal	With a bright resume and detailed introduction, they graduated from a well-known university, mostly with a master's degree or above. The career experience is complete, and the work content of each stage has a relatively specific description, and also has important positions in well-known companies
Abnormal	Short length, low education, working in a small or unknown company, work content is not detailed

(2) The interpretability of text style based on style vector and influence function.

Most of the previous studies use doc2vec as a feature representation method directly. Although the precision of text classification using doc2vec is high, and the semantic, grammatical and emotional information of context can be well combined with words, it still ignores the important role of the rich part of speech details of text. Therefore, this paper proposes "style vector" to describe style differences.

For the positive and negative executive profiles, we use doc2vec method to get their 200 dimensional doc2vec features. First, we make a difference between the values of each dimension and take the absolute value. For the 42 dimensional part-of-speech features of the two categories, the average value of each dimension is calculated, and the new 42-dimensional part-of-speech features are concatenated behind the new vector to obtain a new 242-dimensional style vector. Secondly, we use the influence function to get the influence coefficient of each dimension feature. Thus, 242 points are obtained (x_i, y_i) $(i = 1, 2,\ldots 242)$, where x is the influence coefficient and Y is the value of the style vector. Then the least square method is used to fit the line equation of 242 points. Finally, the slope of the line equation is used to describe the style difference, so as to enhance the interpretability of the model. The principle of the straight line fitting based on the least square method is as follows: if the regression straight line equation is, its slope and intercept can be obtained according to formula (3) and formula (4).

$$\hat{b} = \frac{\sum_{i=1}^{n} x_i y_i - n\bar{x}\bar{y}}{\sum_{i=1}^{n} x_i^2 - n\bar{x}^2} \tag{3}$$

$$\hat{a} = \bar{y} - \hat{b}\bar{x} \tag{4}$$

4   Experiments and Analysis

4.1   Data Source

We have collected data about 4,554 P2P companies from a third-party platform of network lending, the Home of Network Loan (https://www.wdzj.com). There are four categories graded from 0 to 3, and different categories represent different business status.

Table 3. The status and numbers of the four categories.

Label	Business status	Number
0	Normal	1849
1	Out of business	1263
2	Difficult withdrawing	595
3	Absconded with ill-gotten gains	847

The companies with label 1–3 are all abnormal companies. The significance of all kinds of data is shown in Table 3.

The company profile mainly includes business content, scope of business, operation philosophy, social responsibility, etc. That information can fully describe a company, and the description information of different types of companies varies greatly, which plays a significant role in the subsequent risk category assessment.

4.2 Interpretable Machine Learning Based on Integration of Psychology and NLP

(1) Detailed description.

By counting the frequency of part-of-speech, the company profile text has the following rules: the quantitative relationship of each part-of-speech is noun > adjective > pronoun > adverb > preposition, and the number of these part- of-speech is much higher than other unimportant part-of-speech. And the number of the representative part-of-speech of the company from normal state to Absconded with ill-gotten gains is decreasing, the specific data is shown in the Table 4. By analyzing the text of the company profile, it is found that the company profile that operates normally contains a larger number of representative part-of-speech such as nouns, adjectives, as well as places, organizations, etc., which are rich details in CBCA and IDT theory. Unusual details: some companies operating abnormally include a large number of words such as exposure, rights protection and resolution. Redundant details: the company profile of abnormal company has too much space to publicize the corporate culture.

Table 4. Frequency of representative part-of-speech in some companies.

Company	Label	Noun	Adjective	Preposition	Adverb	Pronoun	Place
Xin**	0	405	62	46	28	25	7
Ren**	0	90	11	13	11	4	2
Qian**	1	33	3	5	1	0	2
Hua*	1	17	1	1	2	0	1
Shuo*	2	14	0	1	0	0	1
Jun***	2	19	0	2	5	3	2
Tai***	3	10	1	1	0	1	1
Shi**	3	6	0	0	1	0	1

In this case, this paper analyzes the representative part-of-speech of each company to verify that these abnormal companies do exist fraud. It not only conforms to the behavior of fraud in psychological fraud theory, but also provides psychological explanation and support for many machine learning and deep learning models.

(2) Importance of Part-of-speech Features.

For normal and abnormal companies, it is still relatively simple to quantify the part-of-speech distribution only from a statistical perspective. Therefore, it is necessary to combine the influence function to analyze the specific importance of each part-of-speech feature. We call the importance of each part-of-speech feature based on the influence function as the "influence coefficient". The larger the influence coefficient, the more important the feature is.

We used multiple models such as Logistic Regression, SVM [16], CNN [17], LSTM [18]. Among them, the results of the Logistic Regression model are the best. At the same time, the decision tree and the LIME model are used as the comparative experiments of the influence function, and the specific results are shown in Table 5.

Table 5. Importance of part-of-speech features.

Part-of-speech	Influence coefficient	Decision tree	LIME
Suffix	1.21	0.33	0.43
All nouns	0.65	0.24	0.21
Conjunction	0.6	0.09	0.11
All adjectives	0.51	0.11	0.14
Idioms	0.48	0.04	0.06
All pronouns	0.38	0.09	0.08
Quantifier	0.27	0.05	0.09
Idioms and allusions	0.13	0.03	0.06
Preposition	0.11	0.03	0.02
Interjection	0.09	0.05	0.04
Abbreviations	0.09	0.01	0.01
Adverb	0.07	0.03	0.02
Numeral	0.06	0.01	0.01
Prefix	0.06	0.05	0.03

Through the experiment of part-of-speech features based on the influence function, it is found that: nouns, adjectives, pronouns are of high importance, and suffixes, conjunctions, idioms, quantifiers, prepositions and other part-of-speech are of high importance, which fully coincides with the part-of-speech details in CBCA and IDT theories. Companies with good credit usually contain more important details, while companies with fraudulent intent have less quantity and quality of details. The location words and organization groups are also important, which also correspond to the location and organization details in the fraud theory. At the same time, the importance degree of the part-of-speech features based on the influence function is more obvious in the numerical difference, and the importance degree of each part-of-speech is very clear, which shows that the influence function algorithm has a high interpretability.

To sum up, for the three interpretable algorithms of influence function, decision tree and LIME, the influence function is better than the other two algorithms in both the ability to interpret the model and the applicable scope. Meanwhile, influence function also verifies that it is more appropriate to interpret fraud theory in psychology.

(3) Experimental Results.

Psychological fraud theory believes that texts rich in details have stronger authenticity, and reflected in natural language processing are more abundant in terms of nouns and adjectives. In this experiment, the importance of each part-of-speech feature is obtained through influence function, decision tree and LIME. Also, it is proved that part-of-speech features, such as nouns, adjectives and pronouns, which represent details are indeed very important. Moreover, the precision of classifier based on part-of-speech features can reach 80%. It shows that the details extracted by NLP that can be considered important by machine learning exactly coincide with details that are considered important in psychology, and it is proved by influence function that these important details make the precision of machine learning model higher.

Therefore, this section explains the model behavior based on the psychological fraud theory in the field of social science, and verifies that the machine learning model really learns the important information in the fraud theory by using the NLP technology in the field of natural science, thus providing the interpretable support for the machine learning model of risk fraud.

4.3   The Interpretability of Text Style Based on Style Vector and Influence Function

According to the previous experimental results, the normal company's executive profiles are usually very detailed, complete and convincing, while the abnormal company's executive profiles are usually not detailed. According to the theories of CBCA and IDT related to psychological fraud theory, we believe that companies with low quality executive profiles are more likely to have fraud intentions, and this intuitive difference in text style also provides with a new method of interpretable research.

(1) Interpretable Research Based on Doc2vec.

Most of the previous studies use doc2vec as a feature representation method directly. Although the accuracy of using doc2vec for text classification is high, there is a problem that the specific meaning of each dimension of dec2vec and the relationship between each dimension can not be explained. Therefore, this experiment focuses on the analysis of the interpretability of doc2vec.

For normal and abnormal executive profile texts, firstly, 200 dimension doc2vec are used to represent the features of all positive and negative executive profiles, and then average all positive and negative executive profiles to form a new 200 dimension doc2vec (for example, the blue curve in the Fig. 1 is a normal company). Similarly, all negative executive profiles also obtain a new 200 dimension doc2vec (for example, the orange curve in the Fig. 1 Abnormal company). Then, the influence function is used to analyze the doc2vec itself, and two rules are found, which can understand and explain the behavior of the model: (1) there are positive and negative opposites between the values of different categories in the same dimension of doc2vec. (2) The absolute value of the difference in the same dimension of doc2vec is positively related to the importance of dimension. The larger the absolute value is, the larger the influence coefficient is, which means the more important the features of the dimension are.

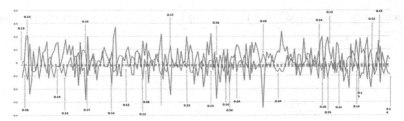

Fig. 1. Doc2vec-200 dimensions (Color figure online)

(2) Research on the Interpretability of Text Style Based on Style Vector and Influence Function.

From the typical content of the executive profile (Table 6), it is found that the executives of class a text graduated from famous universities with complete professional experience and have held important positions in well-known companies; while the executives of class B and C text have poor educational background and the companies they have held are not well-known, and they have not held important positions at the same time. From the perspective of human intuitive feelings, there is a big difference in the style of class A, B and C texts, and a small difference in the style of class B and C texts. At the same time, it also gives people the feeling that the operating risk of A-class companies may be lower than that of B-class and C-class companies, and the probability of A-class companies constituting fraud to users may also be lower.

Table 6. Typical contents of executive profile.

Text	Executive profile	State
A	***, Bachelor of science, Peking University. He has successively held CEO, CTO, vice president and other senior positions in Founder group of Peking University, China interactive media group, with profound technical management, team management ability and rich experience in industries	Normal
B	***Graduated from the school of management, Qingdao University of science and technology. I worked as an administrative assistant in Qingdao priority Export Co., Ltd in 2004–2006. I worked as an administrative manager in Ningbo Aksu Nobel Chemical Co., Ltd in 2007–2013	Abnormal
C	***, worked in 2005, engaged in real estate projects since 2008 in small loan business. Rich experience in business management	Abnormal

For the data in Table 6, we use the style vector in Sect. 3.2 to construct feature. Through the method of Sect. 3.2, the scatter diagram in Fig. 2 is obtained by combining style vector formed by the text of class A and class B with influence function, and the scatter diagram in Fig. 3 is obtained by combining style vector formed by class B and class C text with influence function. It is found from the figure that the slope of straight line fitted by each point in Fig. 2 is larger than that in Fig. 3. It shows that the larger the difference of text style is, the larger the slope of line based on style vector and influence coefficient is.

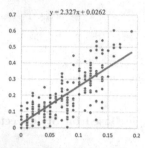
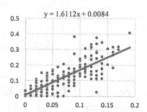

Fig. 2. Class A and B   **Fig. 3.** Class B and C

Then we use the text with a large style difference between class A and class B to retrain the machine learning model. At this time, the accuracy of risk identification reaches 100%; while using the text with a small style difference between class B and class C to retrain the machine learning model, the accuracy is only 74.03%. It can be seen that in the actual task of risk identification of text classification, due to the existence of noise data, using all the data to train the model often can not achieve the highest accuracy. The training data can be effectively filtered by using style vector to analyze the interpretability of text style, so as to improve the accuracy of machine learning model.

In this case, where the text style of executive profiles varies widely, through the above experiments, it is found that using style vector to describe the differences of text style is the same as human's intuitive feeling, which shows that style vector can describe the differences between text styles. Moreover, the larger the slope of the line based on the style vector and the influence coefficient is, the greater the style difference of the text is, and the higher of accuracy in risk identification is. It shows that the machine learning model really learns the text style difference in human cognition and uses it in risk judgment, which further shows that the model has certain machine learning interpretability.

5 Conclusions

To sum up, in view of the evaluation and analysis of the fraud risk of P2P Internet loan companies, this paper proposes to explain the model behavior based on the psychological interpersonal fraud theory in the field of social science, and uses NLP and influence function in the field of natural science to verify that the machine learning model does learn the details of the fraud theory, which also provides the heart for the machine learning model of P2P risk evaluation The support of the interpretability of Neo Confucianism. On the other hand, machine learning interpretability research based on text style not only improves the accuracy of the model, but also provides interpretability of text style for P2P risk assessment model from the perspective of text style. In the future, we will do further research on the risk assessment of P2P companies, especially the analysis of more model interpretability, extraction of better semantic features and optimization of classification model.

Acknowledgements. This work was supported by Beijing Municipal Commission of Science and Technology [grant number Z181100001018035]; National Social Science Foundation of China [grant number 16ZDA055]; National Natural Science Foundation of China [grant numbers 91546121, 71231002]; Engineering Research Center of Information Networks, Ministry of Education; Beijing BUPT Information Networks Industry Institute Company Limited; the project of Beijing Institute of Science and Technology Information.

References

1. Guo, Y., Zhou, W., Luo, C., et al.: Instance-based credit risk assessment for investment decisions in P2P lending. Eur. J. Oper. Res. **249**(2), 417–426 (2016)
2. Luo, C., Xiong, H., Zhou, W., et al.: Enhancing investment decisions in P2P lending: an investor composition perspective. In: ACM SIGKDD International Conference on Knowledge Discovery and Data Mining, San Diego, CA, USA, August. DBLP, pp. 292–300 (2011)
3. Zhao, T., Li, L., Xie, Y., et al.: Data-driven risk assessment for peer-to-peer network lending agencies. In: 2018 5th IEEE International Conference on Cloud Computing and Intelligence Systems (CCIS). IEEE (2018)
4. Hendricks, D., Roberts, S.J.: Optimal client recommendation for market makers in illiquid financial products. In: Altun, Y., et al. (eds.) ECML PKDD 2017. LNCS (LNAI), vol. 10536, pp. 166–178. Springer, Cham (2017). https://doi.org/10.1007/978-3-319-71273-4_14
5. Jin-Qun, H.E., Liu, P.J.: The documents classification algorithm based on LDA. J. Tianjin Univ. Technol. **4**, 28–31 (2014)
6. Mikolov, T., Chen, K., Corrado, G., et al.: Efficient estimation of word representations in vector space. Computer Science (2013)
7. Le, Q.V., Mikolov, T.: Distributed representations of sentences and documents. Eprint Arxiv, vol. 4, pp. 1188–1196 (2014)
8. Doshi-Velez, F., Kim, B.: Towards a rigorous science of interpretable machine learning. arXiv: 1702.08608v2 (2017)
9. Wang, X., He, X., Feng, F., et al.: TEM: tree-enhanced embedding model for explainable recommendation. In: The 2018 World Wide Web Conference (2018)
10. Mclis, D.A., Jaakkola, T.: Towards robust interpretability with self-explaining neural networks. In: Proceedings of the 32nd International Conference on Neural Information Processing Systems, pp. 7775–7784. Curran Associates Inc., Red Hook (2018)
11. Koh, P.W., Liang, P.: Understanding black-box predictions via influence functions. In: Proceedings of the 34th International Conference on Machine Learning, vol. 70, pp. 1885–1894 (2017). JMLR.org
12. Ribeiro, M.T., Singh, S., Guestrin, C.: "Why should I trust you?": explaining the predictions of any classifier. In: Proceedings of the 2016 Conference of the North American Chapter of the Association for Computational Linguistics: Demonstrations. ACM (2016)
13. Lombrozo, T.: Causal–explanatory pluralism: how intentions, functions, and mechanisms influence causal ascriptions. Cogn. Psychol. **61**(4), 303–332 (2010)
14. Byrne, R.M.J., Mceleney, A.: Counterfactual thinking about actions and failures to act. J, Exp. Psychol. Learn. Mem. Cogn. **26**(5), 1318–1331 (2000)
15. Wu, S., Jin, S.H., Cai, W.: Detecting deception by verbal content cues. Progress Psychol. Sci. **20**(3), 457–466 (2012)
16. Das, S.P., Padhy, S.: A novel hybrid model using teaching–learning-based optimization and a support vector machine for commodity futures index forecasting. Int. J. Mach. Learn. Cybernet. **9**(1), 97–111 (2018)
17. Kim, Y.: Convolutional neural networks for sentence classification. Eprint Arxiv (2014)
18. Minami, S.: Predicting equity price with corporate action events using LSTM-RNN. J. Math. Financ. **08**(1), 58–63 (2018)

Algorithm Bias Detection and Mitigation in Lenovo Face Recognition Engine

Sheng Shi[1], Shanshan Wei[1], Zhongchao Shi[1], Yangzhou Du[1(✉)], Wei Fan[1], Jianping Fan[1], Yolanda Conyers[2], and Feiyu Xu[3]

[1] AI Lab, Lenovo Research, Beijing, China
{shisheng2,weiss3,shizc2,duyz1,fanwei2,jfan1}@lenovo.com
[2] Lenovo Group, Morrisville, USA
yolanda2@lenovo.com
[3] SAP Cloud, Walldorf, Germany
fei.yu.xu@sap.com

Abstract. With the advancement of Artificial Intelligence (AI), algorithms brings more fairness challenges in ethical, legal, psychological and social levels. People should start to face these challenges seriously in dealing with AI products and AI solutions. More and more companies start to recognize the importance of Diversity and Inclusion (D&I) due to AI algorithms and take corresponding actions. This paper introduces Lenovo AI's Vision on D&I, specially, the efforts of mitigating algorithm bias in human face processing technology. Latest evaluation shows that Lenovo face recognition engine achieves better performance of racial fairness over competitors in terms of multiple metrics. In addition, it also presents post-processing strategy of improving fairness according to different considerations and criteria.

Keywords: Explainable Artificial Intelligence · Diversity and inclusion · Algorithm fairness · Bias detection and mitigation

1 Introduction

Artificial Intelligence (AI) [1,2] has had get a tremendous advancement in recent decades. Remarkable surges in AI capabilities have led to a number of innovations which impact nearly all aspects of our society. However, the development and use of these AI technologies have to deal with tech and non-tech challenges simultaneously. AI must be developed in a trustworthy manner to ensure reliability, safety and accuracy.

Companies which use and develop AI technology must be aware of Diversity and Inclusion (D&I) challenges [3]. Workplace diversity is understanding, accepting, and valuing differences between people of different races, ethnicities, genders, religion and so on. Inclusion is an organisational effort and practices in which different groups or individuals from different backgrounds are culturally and socially accepted and welcomed, and equally treated [4,5]. For example,

X. Zhu et al. (Eds.): NLPCC 2020, LNAI 12431, pp. 442–453, 2020.
https://doi.org/10.1007/978-3-030-60457-8_36

face recognition should not bring uneven accuracy in terms of light or dark skin color. Recommendation algorithms should not introduce gender bias in job recommendations or auto-suggest bias words in search engine. Machine translation should cover both male and female cases when translating from sex-insensitive language such as Turkish. Speech recognition should take care of persons with impaired speech, such as by a stroke or ALS. With the advancement of AI technology, algorithms bring more fairness challenges in ethical, legal, psychological and social levels. People should start to face these challenges seriously in dealing with AI products and AI solutions. More and more companies are starting to recognize the importance of D&I and take corresponding actions.

Lenovo has paid a great attention to D&I and started to make efforts on algorithm fairness in building technology and solutions. The vision of Lenovo 3S strategy is 'Smarter Technology for All', where the key driver of 'Smarter Technology' is our diversity. The most innovative AI solutions require an ever-increasing diversity of inputs. To ensure 'Technology for All', we must be inclusive. We take actions to leverage the diversity of inputs from our global customers and build the best technology for the world. As a first step, we evaluated and consolidated the diversity performance of our in-house face recognition engine. In the future, we will evaluate other AI algorithms in terms of D&I, identify key issues, build standards for AI products, improve core algorithms, carry out the D&I awareness from design, manufacturing, verification, marketing and custom cares. We might be able to create a community or an association for AI around D&I and collaborate with the industry to improve D&I of AI solutions in the global society.

2 Related Work

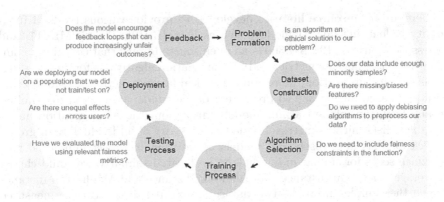

Fig. 1. Fairness in the lifecycle of an AI application (Image courtesy of K. Browne and J. Draper [9])

There has been a recent surge of discussion on algorithm fairness and bias in the machine learning field. As fairness is a complex and multi-faceted concept that depends on context and culture, there are many different mathematical definitions [6]. Researchers have shown that it is impossible to satisfy all definitions of fairness at the same time [7]. In addition, bias can make its way into the AI system at any point in the development lifecycle, from the problem framing, dataset collection, to algorithm selection and objective function, as shown in Fig. 1. As the different bias handling algorithms address different parts of the model lifecycle, it is a big challenge to understand how, when and why to use each algorithm. Fairness research keeps as an active field, because of the variety of bias metrics and the effectiveness of mitigation strategies [8].

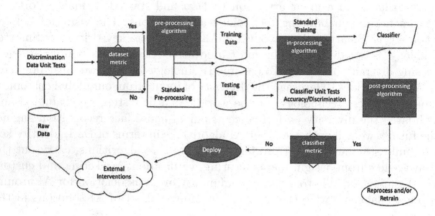

Fig. 2. Bias processing in the machine learning pipeline. (Image courtesy of IBM Research, AIF360 Toolkit [15])

There are open-source libraries developed to provide various levels of functionality in learning fair AI models such as FairML [10], Themis-ML [11] and Fairness Comparison [12]. AIF360 is an open source library that contains a comprehensive set of fairness metrics and bias mitigation algorithms for datasets and models [13]. In this Section, we introduce typical fairness metrics and mitigation techniques based on AIF360 to promote a deeper understanding of discrimination and bias in machine learning models throughout the AI application lifecycle. Table 1 lists fairness metrics divided by category of 'individual' and 'group' to check for bias in datasets and models. If we want to detect individual fairness which seeks for similar individuals to be treated similarly, we could choose the average Euclidean distance, Mahalanobis distance and Manhattan distance between the samples from the two datasets. Group Fairness can be measured either on the training data or on the learned model. If bias detection on training data is required, Dirichlet-smoothed base rates could be used. Where fairness on models is concerned, a large collection of fairness metrics based on confusion matrix, such as average odds difference, false discovery rate ratio could be used. In addition, where both individual and group fairness are concerned, then the generalized entropy index and Theil index [14] etc. could be used. When a single metric does not fit all contexts, we would have to use multiple metrics simultaneously to detect bias.

Table 1. Fairness metrics

Fairness	Metric	
Individual fairness	Euclidean distance	
	Mahalanobis distance	
	Manhattan distance	
Group fairness	Data	Dirichlet-smoothed base rates
		Smoothed empiricial differential fairness
		Statistical parity difference of base rate
		Disparate impact on base rate
		Average odds difference
	Model	Average abs odds difference
		Statistical parity difference
		Disparate impact
		Equal opportunity difference
		Differential fairness bias amplification
		Select rate
		Error rate difference
		True positive rate difference
		False omission rate ratio
		False discovery rate ratio
Both	Generalized entropy index	
	Theil index	
	Coefficient of variation	

Bias can make its way into a machine learning pipeline at different stages. According to the location where bias mitigation algorithms can intervene in a complete machine learning pipeline, these algorithms can be categorized as pre-processing, in-processing and post-processing [16]. As shown in Fig. 2, the choice among algorithm categories can partially be made based on the user's personal opinion to intervene at different parts of a machine learning pipeline. Pre-processing can be used if it is allowed to modify the training data. As reweighing [17] only changes weights applied to training samples, it is an ideal option in the event that the application does not allow to edit the sample. Other algorithms like optimized pre-processing [18] and disparate impact remover [19] edit features values or labels by different criteria. If the user is allowed to change the learning procedure for a machine learning model, then in-processing bias mitigation can be used. Adversarial debiasing [20] adopts the idea of adversarial network to maximize the classifier prediction accuracy and simultaneously reduce discrimination. Prejudice remover [21] adds a discrimination-aware regularization term to learning objective function. In addition, post-processing can be only used if we treat the learned model as a black box without any ability to modify the training data and learning algorithm. Post-processing algorithms [22–24] reduce discrimination by changing output labels with different criteria.

3   Bias Evaluation

This Section mainly introduces our Lenovo face recognition engine (LeFace) in terms of bias mitigation strategy and bias evaluation with competitors. The quality of machine learning models heavily depends on the quality of training data. If the training data is discriminatory, no matter which classifier inducer is applied, it will result in biased models. Therefore, we used the following strategy to train the face recognition and improve diversity performance. Firstly, we designed and developed a semi-automatic data collecting, cleaning and labeling system. The collected training data contains great diversity in race, age, gender, pose, light-environment, etc. This data system cleans and labels face data with the algorithm scripts and manual work cycle to clean and label face data through a coarse-to-fine process. Then, data augmentation is applied to generate a balanced training dataset. In addition, LeFace adopts an attention mechanism to feed the network with as balanced as possible data during training period. LeFace adopts multi-stage training and online data augmentation strategies. A base model is trained with the source-balanced data to get balanced performance on different races. Afterwards we introduce online data augmentation to generate hard samples for fine-tuning the model. The hard level increases as the fine-tune times grow. After rounds of fine-tune, LeFace gets high performance model with great balance in different races.

Racial Faces in-the-Wild (RFW) database [25] can be used to fairly evaluate and compare the recognition ability of the algorithm against different races. It contains four testing subsets, namely African, Asian, Caucasian and Indian. Each subset contains about 3000 individuals with 6000 image pairs for face verification. Based on RFW, we compare LeFace with the Face++ recognition API [26]. Table 2 lists the face verification accuracies of the two recognition APIs. Comparing to Face++, we can see LeFace provides the best verification accuracy. Moreover, by comparing ROC curves shown in Fig. 3, we preliminarily judge that LeFace is less discriminatory on different races.

Table 2. Face verification accuracy on RFW database

Model	RFW			
	Caucasian	Indian	Asian	African
LeFace	0.9730	0.9518	0.9518	0.9523
Face++	0.9392	0.8855	0.9250	0.8742

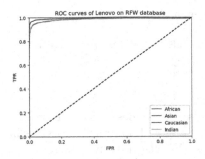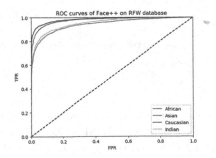

Fig. 3. The ROC surves of LeFace (left) and Face++ (right) on RFW database

As described in Sect. 2, there are many dedicated metrics used to measure the fairness on different models. We use Statistical Parity Difference (SPD), Equal Opportunity Difference (EOD), Average Odds Difference (AOD) and Theil Index (TI) to measure the model's discrimination in different angles. As the database is divided into four groups according to the protected attribute of race, we extended the fairness metrics by using standard deviation versions.

$$std(\mathbf{x}) = \sqrt{\sum_{i=1}^{n} (x_i - \bar{x})^2 / (n-1)} \tag{1}$$
$$\bar{x} = \sum_{i=1}^{n} x_i / n$$

Statistical Parity Standard Deviation (SPSD) is the standard deviation of the rate of favorable outcomes received by different groups. SPSD measures bias by analyzing disparity of acceptance rates of all groups.

$$SPSD = std(Pr\{\hat{y} = 1 | R = Caucasian\}, ..., Pr\{\hat{y} = 1 | R = African\}) \tag{2}$$

Equal Opportunity Standard Deviation (EOSD) is the standard deviation of true positive rates (TPR) among different groups.

$$EOSD = std(TPR\{R = Caucasian\}, ..., TPR\{R = African\}) \tag{3}$$

Average Odds Standard Deviation (AOSD) is the average standard deviation of false positive rate (FPR) and true positive rate (TPR) among different groups.

$$AOSD = 0.5 * std(TPR\{R = Caucasian\}, ..., TPR\{R = African\}) \tag{4}$$
$$+ 0.5 * std(FPR\{R - Cuucasian\}, ..., FPR\{R = African\})$$

Theil Index [14] is to use existing inequality indices from economics to measure how unequally the outcomes of an algorithm benefit different individuals or groups in a population. Firstly, we designed a benefit mapping function to map predictions to benefits. Since all outcomes of a classifier can be decomposed into true positives (TP), true negatives (TN), false positives (FP) and false negatives (FN), the benefit function needs to assign a benefit score to each of

Table 3. Benefit mapping function

	True positives	True negatives	False negatives	False positives
Benefit	1	1	0.25	0

these prediction types. As we consider accurate outcomes as more desirable than inaccurate ones, we would choose a benefit mapping function that assigns higher value to true positives and true negatives. As false positives might be worse than false negatives for face recognition, we assigns the lowest value to false negatives. The benefit mapping function is shown in Table 3. After designing a benefit mapping function predictions to benefits, we measure the fairness by calculating Theil index.

$$TI = \frac{1}{n} \sum\nolimits_{i=1}^{n} \frac{b_i}{\bar{b}} log \frac{b_i}{\bar{b}} \tag{5}$$
$$\bar{b} = \sum\nolimits_{i=1}^{n} b_i/n$$

Table 4 lists the bias metric results on different recognition APIs. These metrics measure model's discrimination in different angles. Simulation experiment results show that when variance of four probability values is smaller than 0.02, the model can be considered discrimination-free. By comparing EOSD, AOSD and Theil Index, it shows Face++ API have potential discrimination for different races. Leface is more fair than Face++ API on different races.

Table 4. Fairness metrics on different recognition APIs

Model	RFW			
	SPSD	EOSD	AOSD	Theil index
LeFace	0.0012	0.0109	0.0141	0.0226
Face++	0.0001	0.0318	0.0417	0.0650

4 Comprehensive Fairness by Post-processing

Given the different distributions of LeFace predicted similarity shown in Fig. 4 for each group, we can study the optimal face verification model under different constraints on allowed predictors, as follows.

Race Blind: Race blind has no constraint with race. It will search for a single threshold at which the verification accuracy is highest overall.

Max Accuracy: Max accuracy has no fairness constraints. It will pick the threshold that maximizes accuracy for each group.

Demographic Parity: Demographic parity picks a threshold for each group such that the fraction of group members that be verified positive is the same.

Equal Opportunity: Equal opportunity searches for a threshold for each group such that the true positive rates across different groups are consistent.

Equal Odds: Equal odds that are proposed in [22] requires both the true positive rates and false positive rates to be consistent. In order to achieve the purpose of equal odds, we pick two thresholds for each group. If LeFace predicts similarity above both thresholds, the predicted result will be positive. If similarity lies between these two thresholds, the predicted result will be changed selectively.

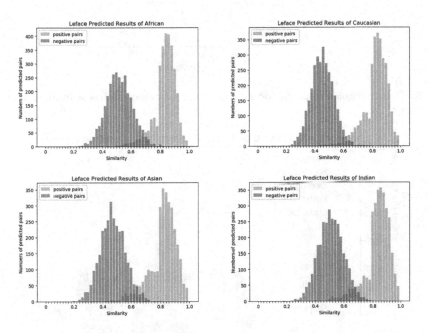

Fig. 4. Distribution of LeFace predicted similarity of 6000 pairs in test sets of (a) African, (b) Caucasian, (c) Asian, (d) Indian

Figure 5 shows different thresholds of different post-processing methods previously explained. The True Positive Rate (TPR) of post-processing strategy to achieve fairness in different perspectives is shown in Fig. 6. Under max-accuracy and demographic parity, we find that positive pairs in Caucasian group would have a higher probability to be verified positive. Under race-blind, the positive pairs in Asian and African group would have a lower probability to be verified positive. In addition, equal opportunity and equal odds are two notions of nondiscrimination. The difference between equal odds and equal opportunity is that under equal opportunity, the classifier can make use of its better accuracy among Caucasian, while an equal odds classifier must classify every pairs as poorly as

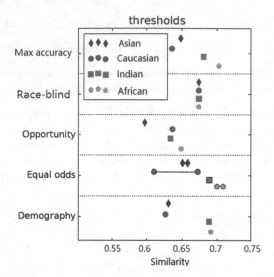

Fig. 5. The thresholds of post-processing strategy to achieve fairness in different perspectives

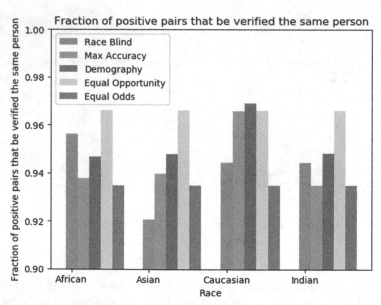

Fig. 6. The True Positive Rate (TPR) of post-processing strategy to achieve fairness in different perspectives

the hardest group. Table 5 lists the accuracy achieved by each method. We find that a max accuracy threshold gets 0.9583, while equal opportunity registers 0.9426 and equalized odds registers 0.9532. Eliminating the discrimination of algorithms will certainly reduce the accuracy slightly.

Table 5. The accuracy of post-processing strategy to achieve fairness in different perspectives

Method	Max-accuracy	Race-blind	Demographic	Equal opportunity	Equal odds
Accuracy	0.9583	0.9537	0.9561	0.9426	0.9532

5   Conclusion and Future Work

Lenovo has paid a great attention to D&I and have made initial efforts on algorithm fairness in building technology and solutions. We have evaluated and consolidated the diversity performance of Lenovo Face Recognition Engine. In the future, we will evaluate other AI algorithms in terms of D&I, identify key issues, build standard for AI products, improve cores algorithm, carry out the D&I awareness from design, manufacturing, verification, marketing and custom cares. Specifically, there should be the following strategy.

The Evaluation of AI Technology with Respect to D&I: Testing AI technology in terms of D&I issues, for example, (a) diversity issues in face recognition; (b) inclusive performance in speech recognition with respect to gender or dialects or age; (c) gender and ethnicity bias problems in recommendation engine, machine translation, and conversational agents.

Creation of D&I Standard for AI Technology: Building up corporate-level standard or industry-level AI D&I standard that products need to follow, issuing a license or certificate, as done by https://www.licenses.ai/.

Improvement of AI Technology with Respect to D&I: When the D&I performance of our AI technologies are known through tests and evaluations, we need to consider to improve core algorithms, by (a) balancing the distribution of training data, (b) refining machine learning model, (c) post-processing with rules or black-list; (d) human verification in case of lower confidence of algorithm output.

Building of Applications with AI Technology for D&I: When core algorithms are good enough in terms of D&I performance, we can use them to build new applications and solutions or empower existing solutions and products.

Development of AI Empowered Universal Product Design: The design and practices need to be iterated: discovering issues → refining standards → improving algorithms → upgrading applications → evaluating and testing again.

In the future, we might be able to create a community or an association for AI around D&I and collaborate with the industry to improve D&I of AI solutions in the global society.

References

1. Goodfellow, I., Bengio, Y., Courville, A.: Deep Learning. MIT Press (2016). http://www.deeplearningbook.org

2. Hastie, T., Tibshirani, R., Friedman, J.: The Elements of Statistical Learning. SSS. Springer, New York (2009). https://doi.org/10.1007/978-0-387-84858-7_910.1007/978-0-387-84858-7_9

3. Muheidat, F., Tawalbeh, L.: Team based learning: the role of equity, diversity, and inclusion in team formation. In: 2018 Research on Equity and Sustained Participation in Engineering, Computing, and Technology (RESPECT), pp. 1–2 (2018)

4. Hespanhol, L., Davis, H., Fredericks, J., Caldwell, G.A., Hoggenmueller, M.: Digital outreach: designing technologies for diversity, participation and social inclusion, pp. 648–650, November 2017

5. Siau, K.: How can AI help to enhance diversity and inclusion? In: 25th Americas Conference on Information Systems, AMCIS, August 2019

6. Narayanan, A.: Translation tutorial: 21 fairness definitions and their politics. In: Conference on Fairness, Accountability, and Transparency (2018)

7. Kleinberg, J.M., Mullainathan, S., Raghavan, M.: Inherent trade-offs in the fair determination of risk scores. CoRR, abs/1609.05807 (2016)

8. Friedler, S.A., Scheidegger, C., Venkatasubramanian, S., Choudhary, S., Hamilton, E.P., Roth, D.: A comparative study of fairness-enhancing interventions in machine learning. In: Proceedings of the Conference on Fairness, Accountability, and Transparency (2019)

9. Browne, K., Draper, J.: https://www.slideshare.net/KrishnaramKenthapadi/fairness-and-privacy-in-aiml-systems-187923831/

10. Adebayo, J.A.: FairML: toolbox for diagnosing bias in predictive modeling. Master thesis, Massachusetts Institute of Technology (2016). https://github.com/adebayoj/fairml

11. Bantilan, N.: Themis-ml: a fairness-aware machine learning interface for end-to-end discrimination discovery and mitigation. CoRR, abs/1710.06921 (2017)

12. Zehlike, M., Castillo, C., Bonchi, F., Hajian, S., Megahed, M.: Fairness measures: datasets and software for detecting algorithmic discrimination. http://fairness-measures.org/

13. Zehlike, M., Castillo, C., Bonchi, F., Hajian, S., Megahed, M.: Fairness measures: datasets and software for detecting algorithmic discrimination. http://fairness-measures.org/

14. Speicher, T., et al.: A unified approach to quantifying algorithmic unfairness: measuring individual & group unfairness via inequality indices. CoRR, abs/1807.00787 (2018)

15. https://community.ibm.com/HigherLogic/System/DownloadDocumentFile.ashx?DocumentFileKey=618c7917-8d2b-ca78-5ecc-2286486b9c69&forceDialog=0

16. Alessandro, B., ONeil, C., Laatta, T.: Conscientious classification: a data scientists guide to discrimination-aware classification. Big Data **5**, 120–134 (2017)

17. Kamiran, F., Calders, T.: Data preprocessing techniques for classification without discrimination. Knowl. Inf. Syst. **33**(1), 1–33 (2011)

18. Calmon, F., Wei, D., Vinzamuri, B., Ramamurthy, K.N., Varshney, K.R.: Optimized pre-processing for discrimination prevention. In: Guyon, I., et al. (eds.) Advances in Neural Information Processing Systems, vol. 30, pp. 3992–4001. Curran Associates Inc. (2017)

19. Feldman, M., Friedler, S.A., Moeller, J., Scheidegger, C., Venkatasubramanian, S.: Certifying and removing disparate impact. In: Proceedings of the 21th ACM SIGKDD International Conference on Knowledge Discovery and Data Mining. Association for Computing Machinery, New York (2015)

20. Zhang, B.H., Lemoine, B., Mitchell, M.: Mitigating unwanted biases with adversarial learning. CoRR, abs/1801.07593 (2018)

21. Kamishima, T., Akaho, S., Asoh, H., Sakuma, J.: Fairness-aware classifier with prejudice remover regularizer. In: Flach, P.A., De Bie, T., Cristianini, N. (eds.) ECML PKDD 2012. LNCS (LNAI), vol. 7524, pp. 35–50. Springer, Heidelberg (2012). https://doi.org/10.1007/978-3-642-33486-3_3
22. Hardt, M., Price, E., Srebro, N.: Equality of opportunity in supervised learning. CoRR, abs/1610.02413 (2016)
23. Pleiss, G., Raghavan, M., Wu, F., Kleinberg, J., Weinberger, K.Q.: On fairness and calibration. In: Guyon, I., et al. (eds.) Advances in Neural Information Processing Systems, vol. 30, pp. 5680–5689. Curran Associates Inc. (2017)
24. Kamiran, F., Karim, A., Zhang, X.: Decision theory for discrimination-aware classification. In: 2012 IEEE 12th International Conference on Data Mining, pp. 924–929 (2012)
25. Wang, M., Deng, W., Hu, J., Tao, X., Huang, Y.: Racial faces in the wild: Reducing racial bias by information maximization adaptation network. In: 2019 IEEE/CVF International Conference on Computer Vision (ICCV), pp. 692–702 (2019)
26. Face++ research toolkit. www.faceplusplus.com

Path-Based Visual Explanation

Mohsen Pourvali(✉), Yucheng Jin, Chen Sheng, Yao Meng, Lei Wang,
Masha Gorkovenko, and Changjian Hu

Lenovo, Beijing, China
{mpourvali,jinyc2,shengchen1,mengyao1,wanglei63,mgorkovenko,
hucj1}@lenovo.com

Abstract. The ability to explain the behavior of a Machine Learning
(ML) model as a black box to people is becoming essential due to wide
usage of ML applications in critical areas ranging from medicine to commerce. Case-Based Reasoning (CBR) received a special interest among
other methods of providing explanations for model decisions due to the
fact that it can easily be paired with a black box and then can propose a
post-hoc explanation framework. In this paper, we propose a CBR-Based
method to not only explain a model decision but also provide recommendations to the user in an easily understandable visual interface. Our evaluation of the method in a user study shows interesting results.

Keywords: Explainable artificial intelligence · Case-based reasoning ·
Classification

1 Introduction

The ability to explain the behavior of a ML model to people is becoming essential
due to wide usage of ML applications in critical areas ranging from medicine to
commerce.

Most of the current explanation methods assign scores to *input* features, by
which features that have highest influence on the model's decisions are identified.
Explaining the underlying reasons for an image classification model's decision to
a human is easier than explaining the decision of a text classification model.

In an image, we can represent segments of the image as concepts [3], and
a model's decision can be understood by a human if we explain it using these
concepts. For example, in an image of a girl, her hair is a concept, and it is
easily understandable for an AI novice if we explain to her that this part of the
image was the main reason that model thinks this is a picture of a girl. The
understandable concepts in text could be a sentence or paragraph, like saying
which sentence is the main reason for a model decision. But, in tabular data, it
is hard to explain the reasons for a model's decision through concepts. We define
this difficulty as **Feature Inability** and **Feature Ambiguity** problems.

© Springer Nature Switzerland AG 2020
X. Zhu et al. (Eds.): NLPCC 2020, LNAI 12431, pp. 454–466, 2020.
https://doi.org/10.1007/978-3-030-60457-8_37

Feature Inability: The first problem is that each feature in tabular data individually (like a single pixel in an image) is not able to explain the reason behind the model's decision, and also unlike what a collection of pixels in images as segments/super-pixel of image can do for understandability of an explanation, a collection of features in tabular data is not quite understandable by a human since finding the relations between the features is difficult.

Feature Ambiguity: Another problem is that the meaning of a feature solely in tabular data might be ambiguous to a human, like a single pixel in an image is. But, unlike images, in which a collection of coherent pixels makes it understandable for a human, in tabular data even a collection of features still doesn't change the ambiguity of the features. For instance, in an image of a dog, a single pixel is not meaningful, but it is possible to select a segment of pixels (e.g., the dog's leg) which is understandable for a human. In tabular data, features are like scattered pixels in that even a collection of them are possibly not understandable to a human.

A collection of coherent pixels as a segment of an image shows relations between the features/pixels in that segment which are understandable and meaningful to human eyes. But in tabular data, even if there is a relation between two features, it might be unclear to a human. And this is because of the nature of images: images come from a real world object, so all features already are defined and are put together, and there is an order that makes it easy to separate features in meaningful segments. Also, in text data, we can see this meaningful order and segmentation (e.g., sentence, paragraph) but not exactly like what exists in images. In tabular data, there is no meaningful order and segmentation in features. The two above mentioned issues also indicate the importance of a visualization of the explanation that enables user to interpret the underlying reasons for a model decision. A good explanation for a model's prediction of an instance may not be a complete explanation of all the reasons for the prediction, but it could be a contrastive explanation comparing how the prediction is different from the prediction for another instance [11]. Another factor for a good explanation could be providing a few recommendations to the user. For example, if you apply for a loan and your application is rejected, you might want to not only know the reasons but also to understand the agent's reasoning in a bid to strengthen your next application [9].

We propose a Hybrid method to address these issues for any probability-based classification model. We first establish an explanation algorithm by taking advantage of *Facts* and *Foils* concepts. Regarding explanations, people are not only interested in why event P happened, they also want to know why not event Q happened instead of event P. The event that did happen P is referred to as Fact, and the contrasting event that did not happen Q is referred to as Foil [8]. A Foil could be any sample to be compared with a Fact. We consider the better samples and the best sample in a Path-Based fashion to compare with a Fact. This explanation exposes more hidden knowledge of the samples, model, and data to users. Indeed, we try to answer three questions which may also be asked by the user, which are: why did a *better* event not happen; why did the *best* event not happen; and an important question, which is how to touch these events. We then present our Path-Based explanation with a visual interface which is easily understandable for a user.

2 Related Works

CBR enables us to present a post-hoc mechanism to not only predict the model result of a query case, but also explain the model's decision by using examples which are similar to the case with respect to the model. Indeed, CBR as a more interpretable system can be paired with a black box in a way that provides explanatory samples based on model prediction, to generate a *twin-system* [5]. Authors in [5] survey similar approaches that use CBR in a post-hoc fashion as one particular solution to the eXplainable Artificial Intelligence (XAI) problem. For example, [1] uses a learned model as distance metric to find explanatory cases for an Artificial Neural Network (ANN) in the medical domain. Authors use Euclidean distance to measure similarity between latent features (i.e., hidden units activation vector of ANN model) of the case to be explained and all the training dataset, and then they present cases with small Euclidean distance to the query case as the similar cases to the query case to then explain the ANN reasoning for the query case. In [12], authors select explanatory cases based on their similarity in their local important features to the query case to be explained. [2] evaluate the usefulness of CBR in terms of retrieving explanatory cases to explain a prediction, and show that it is more convincing than an explanation based on rules. Visualization of CBR-paired systems can even enhance transparency and understandability of the proposed explanation. [10] show that knowledge-intensive tasks require a better explanation than just a set of retried cases. Local information of a query case that enables the user to easily identify similarity of the cases must be visible to the user. [7] proposes a CBR system able to classify a query case using an automatic algorithm, but also through visual reasoning. Authors in [7] select similar cases from the feature/input space of the model.

This work is inspired by [7], our approach in this context is a post-hoc approach that explains the underlying reasons for a model decision, in which similar points are selected in the model result/output space. In our approach the samples sit next to each other for a specific goal, which is to build a path from the query case to the best case in each class. These samples are selected from the candidate cases that their model results are close to, and a direct line in the model output space is drawn between the query case result and the best case. We only use three colors in the visual interface, which makes it easier for the user to identify the dominant color. It also can be modified for colorblind people by using different shapes for each color. Providing a path from the model output of a query case to the best result of the model can depict an **evolution** process, and in turn can help the user to understand how (s)he can get a better result from the model. Furthermore, it can provide **recommendations** for this aim.

3   Our Proposed Method

Providing a path from a model's result of a sample case to the best result of the model can depict an evolutionary process, and in turn can help the user to understand how (s)he can get a better result from the model. Furthermore, a path on which there are several cases from other classes implies a form of analogical reasoning: Case-Based Reasoning (CBR) in which the solution for a new case is determined using a database of previous known cases with their solutions. Cases similar to the new case are retrieved from the database, and then their solutions are adapted to the case. This situation provides an Interpretable Classification, in which a user can classify the new case according to his own knowledge and the knowledge retrieved from CBR. In this paper we do not use CBR to classify new cases; we select similar/explanatory cases from the *output* of a ML model to visually explain the model's result for a query case. The proposed visual interface aims at identifying what is the dominant color? However, this explanation can either be a supporting or nonsupporting proof for the model decision.

A path from a query case to the best case of each class in the model result space provides a better understanding of the model due to evaluation of the similar cases that appear on the path. A visual interactive explanation with an embedded path that constructs CBR in ML results space provides a transparent insight of the ML, which can be used also to evaluate different ML models. Each specific model has its own best case, path, and explanatory cases on the path.

Assuming a classification model with N classes $\mathbb{C} = \{C_1, C_2, .., C_N\}$ trained on a training dataset and testing dataset, for a single case E as input to be explained and its probability E' as result of the model for that case, our explanation algorithm works as follows: It selects two classes as default, the class of the query case result and the class with the highest probability (the selection can also be based on the user desire), and then it generates two paths, each one from E' to a point M_i which is the best result (i.e., highest probability) obtained for a case in class C_i. A path is generated by connecting a collection of points in the probability space that are very close to the direct line connecting E' to M_i in 3-Dimension space.

In general, the workflow of the approach has two steps. In the first step, a 3-Dim model results space is generated and two paths with similar cases in each are indicated. In the second step, a visual explanation for input/query case is presented.

First Step: Given a vector $E = [e_0, e_1, e_2, ..., e_{N-1}]$ with N dimensions as a distribution over N classes for a classification model with an input case p_i, (a) two classes C_1 and C_2 based on user desire or default classes are selected, and the rest of the classes' probabilities are reduced to one dimension e'_3 to generate a new vector $E' = <e_1, e_2, e'_3>$. We use Multidimensional Scaling (MDS) for dimension reduction to preserve distances involving the query case, (b) from each class, the best sample is selected which is a result of the model for a sample

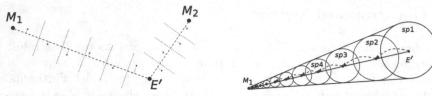

(a) Two paths to the best cases in class C_1 and class C_2

(b) Various distributions of Explanatory Samples over the path

Fig. 1. 2-dim visual illustration of paths and explanatory samples space.

that has highest probability in corresponding dimension of its distribution. (c) two paths from E' to C_1 and C_2 are conducted by identifying the nearest cases to the path as Explanatory Cases (EC), shown in Fig. 1a. In order to depict the evolution process for the sample case E', each path is divided into several areas, and from each area an EC is selected. Indeed, these ECs build the paths through which we can see how features of a sample case are changed to reach the best result in each class. Each EC is a case from the corresponding class for which the result of the model is close to the direct line/path between E' and the best result in that class. Indeed, the path is a direct line in 3-Dim between the model result of the query case and the best case, and ECs are the closest point in model result space to this line. The Explanatory Cases are selected from the testing data, which is a small portion of ground truth cases. This reduces the computational/memory allocation cost (specially MDS cost), and it is able to provide a comparable environment by using different and new testing data that introduces new best cases, various paths and recommendations, which in turn provides comparison metrics to evaluate different ML models. We select ECs from inside different step areas separated with dotted lines perpendicular to the paths shown in Fig. 1b. These areas are not necessarily equal areas, since the distribution of ECs over an specific path is not normal, thus, the more dense the distribution, the more ECs are selected. For example, assume that the distribution of points close to the query case is dense(bigger cycles in Fig. 1b) and density is being reduced by getting away from the query case. In this case, more ECs are selected from the area around the query case. To implement this, we first map all of the candidate ECs (i.e., close to the path) to a one-dim array, and then by using a constant distance of index in the array we select one EC from each area.

The distance between a point (model result) and direct line (path) is calculated using the following formula:

$$d_i = \frac{\left| \overline{p_i E'} \times \overline{s} \right|}{|\overline{s}|} \tag{1}$$

Algorithm 1. Algorithm for recording the recommendations

---

    function SuggRecord(E, EC_i)

        for all not equal f in Features(E, EC_i) **do**

          $Combs = Coalitions(f, coalition\_length)$

        for c in $Combs$ **do**

          Swap(E, EC_i, c)

          $dis_1 = 1$ - OneDimDistance(E', p_i)

          $dis_3 = 1$ - Euclidean(E', p_i)

          $min = 1$ - ($\alpha \times dis_1 + (1 - \alpha) \times dis_3$)

          Record f with lowest min

---

where $p_i = [p_{i0}, p_{i1}, p_{i2}]$ is the probability vector of a candidate explanatory case EC_i, E' is the query case, and $s = [(e'_0 - p_{i0}), (e'_1 - p_{i1}), (e'_2 - p_{i2})]$ is the directing vector of the line.

We use a weighted linear combination of Euclidean and one-dimensional distance to record the recommendations for each pair of the query case and explanatory case, shown in Algorithm 1. The goal is to minimize the distance between the model result of the query case and a specific explanatory sample on the path. Indeed, similar to Shapley Values [14], we try to find a feature's value that has the highest contribution to increase probability of the query case in a class. But here, there is only one sample, i.e., the sample in the step that we want to get there, and coalitions of features are limited to those which are not equal in value, comparing features of E and EC_i[1].

Second Step: In the second step, we generate a Visual Explanation as shown in Fig. 2, which is inspired by Rainbow Boxes [6]. As it is shown in Fig. 2, the corresponding model's input case query for vector E' is in the middle of the explanation, and the best case for each class is located at each corner. The two classes at corners of the explanation are based on user desire or are default classes. Characteristics of the visual interface are explained in Sect. 4.

Our proposed explanation for a single case in tabular data can address the two problems mentioned before. Regarding Feature Inability, using CBR with cases which are considered to be better than the query case provides an understandable explanation for the user, by allowing comparison of a collection of connected features that have the same path in common. Regarding Feature Ambiguity, a path that explains the evolutionary process of changing a feature's value to enhance the probability of being selected as a better member of a class (in model point of view), and building a coalition of cases with similar or different feature's value all aims at one goal: helping to disambiguate the features and their relations.

---

[1] In our experiments we use coalitions with only a single member.

4   Visual Interface

Figure 2 shows the visual interface designed for an ML classification model that predicts *legal* cases, and that its three target classes are *No*, i.e., the case is not legal, *Low*, i.e., the case is legal with low level, and *Hight*, i.e., the case is legal with high level. Two user-desired classes are *High* and *No* corresponding to C_1, C_2, respectively, and important local features identified by LIME are shown on the left side. The characteristics of the Visual Explanation are as follows:

- The ECs on each path are identified by different colors corresponding to different classes, e.g., Red for class High and Blue for class No, shown in Fig. 2.
- The value inside each box is the feature value; thus, the user is able to explore the feature's change through each path to the best result of the model.
- As it can be seen in Fig. 2, the length of each box is different, and it is proportional to the importance of the corresponding feature for that box. For example, the feature placed in the first row is the most important one. To rank importance, we use LIME [13] with the aim of finding a local feature importance for query case.
- Looking at the dominant color in Fig. 2, the user can recognize at a glance that class *High* is a better choice to classify the query case, and *High* is indeed the model target result for the query case.
- Furthermore, we can see more information in Fig. 2, like a suggestion which represents how we can get a better result from the model. For example, if we walk in the path to class *No*, we will get a better result for the query case if we only replace value of feature $RprTp_-$ by 0 instead of 5. In other words, if we want to have a better result of the model, and we can only go one step toward the best result of the model in class *No*, and also are allowed to only change one feature's value, then, feature $RprTp_-$ would be one of the best features and for which value 0 is one the best value to choose. We identify this information by replacing a feature's values of the query with the feature's values of the specific sample on the path, shown in Algorithm 1.
- At top right of the interface in Fig. 2, by applying natural language, the result of LIME is presented in understandable way for the user. We also use this result to examine visual-based and text-based explanations.
- Right below the LIME result there is a recommendation panel in 2, this part shows the first possible recommendation directing to the best sample in a target class. The first and second recommendations for each step in each direction are shown with thick and dotted outline borders for the corresponding feature box, respectively.
- Another piece of information that we can see in Fig. 2 is the priority of a feature's value. On the path to the best sample in class *No* it is shown that from sample 1 to sample 6 the feature whose value is best replaced with query case is $RprTp_-$; but for the last sample, which is the best sample also, the best feature becomes $f\_RetCount$. Indeed, for sample 6 and the best sample, all of the important features have the same values, and it is expected that

still the value of feature *RprTp_* will be the best choice to be replaced with 5. But as it is shown, *f_RetCount* is the first recommendation, since the value for *f_RetCount* in all the samples except the last one is less than 2. Considering the two last samples, which are the same in most important features, it shows that value 305 for feature *f_RetCount* has a higher impact in class *No* compared to the value *0* for feature *RprTp_*.

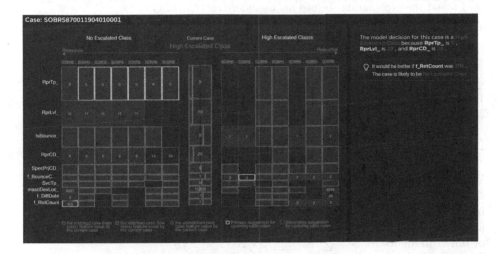

Fig. 2. A snapshot of the visual interface

The core of the visual interface is written in the Python language. The application backend service uses the Java language to unify processes, and the frontend is uniformly built using VUE. Due to the large latency of python core processing data, an asynchronous interaction is established through Kafka as a message middleware.

5 Experimental Setup

To evaluate our designed visualization, we measure the user-perceived quality of the visualization by using the System Causability Scale [4], which is a simple and rapid evaluation tool to measure the quality of an explanation interface or an explanation process itself.

5.1 Dataset

We used an imbalanced dataset consisting of about 1 million real cases logged in a repair center for mobile devices. This data is used to train a classification model with 30 input features to classify escalation of a case into 3 classes *No*, *Low*, and *High*. The visualization shows how a queried case is likely to match two selected classes based on the case-based reasoning algorithm.

Table 1. Ten question items of System Causability Scale

Statements
1. I found that the data included all relevant known causal factors with sufficient precision and granularity.
2. I understood the explanations within the context of my work.
3. I could change the level of detail on demand.
4. I did not need support to understand the explanations.
5. I found the explanations helped me to understand causality.
6. I was able to use the explanations with my knowledge base.
7. I did not find inconsistencies between explanations.
8. I think that most people would learn to understand the explanations very quickly.
9. I did not need more references in the explanations: e.g., medical guidelines, regulations.
10. I received the explanations in a timely and efficient manner.

5.2   Evaluation Measures

We compose a questionnaire based on the System Causability Scale which consists of ten statements (Table 1). Participants are asked to rate each statement by using a five-point likert scale that ranges from strongly agree to strongly disagree. In the end, the quality of visualization is indicated by the average rating of ten statements $SCS = \sum_i rating_i/5 * 10$.

In addition, we also asked three additional questions to collect the subjective feedback for the visualization.

1. How do you think the visualization can help you make a decision?
2. Is it more likely that you trust the prediction result when the visualization is presented? Why?
3. Which one (visual explanation versus textual explanation) is more effective for increasing the transparency of reasoning algorithm?

5.3   Study Procedure

We asked participants to follow the following procedure to perform a task by using the presented visualization.

Task: Based on the visualization in Fig. 2, please reduce the risk of escalation for the queried case by adjusting its feature values. i.e. convert a case of high escalation to a case of no escalation. To better judge if participants understand the visualization, the task includes a restriction that the value of feature $RprTp_-$ is not allowed to change.

1. The participants were asked to attend a training to get familiar with the experimental task and the main functions of visualization.

2. After finishing the training, the participants write down how to adjust the feature value of queried case with the purpose of *no escalation*.
3. Finally, the participants filled out the questionnaire and answered three open questions.

5.4 Participants

We recruited 5 participants from a high-tech company to test the visualization based on a given task. The demographics of the participants are shown in Table 2.

Table 2. Participants' demographics.

ID	Age	Sex	Occupation	Working experience (years)	Education
1	42	Male	Visual designer	20	Bachelor
2	35	Female	Interaction designer	10	Master
3	28	Male	Software developer	6	Bachelor
4	28	Female	Visual designer	6	Bachelor
5	27	Female	Visual designer	5	Bachelor

6 Results and Discussions

6.1 Objective Results

We measure the actual quality of visualization by the effectiveness of the actions (Table 3) the participants took to reduce the escalation risk for the queried case. The result shows that three of the five participants took actions that were exactly the same as the ones that the system suggested. Although P1 did not take the optimal action, P1's actions are still reasonable for the task goal. P4's action seems to be not logical since the value of feature RprLvL is not 1 for all presented cases.

Table 3. Actions taken by the participants.

ID	Actions
1	RprLvL: 19→11, RprCD : 25→6
2	mascDevLoc: 15205→8227, f_RetCount: 1→305
3	RprLvL: 19→1
4	RprLvL: 19→11, f_RetCount: 1→305, RprCD_: 25→6
5	f_RetCount: 1→305, RprCD_: 25→6

6.2   Questionnaire Results

Figure 3 shows the results of participants responses on the System Causability Scale (SCS). The average score of SCS is 0.588 and standard deviation is 0.143. Although the score does not indicate a good quality of explanation according to the reference value 0.680, the visualization still is rated high for some aspects such as 5. Understanding causality, 7. No inconsistencies, and 10. Efficient.

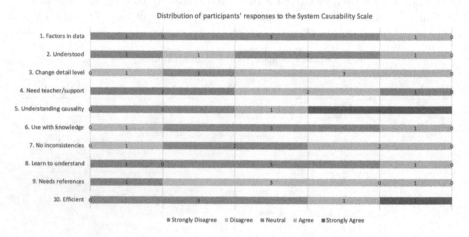

Fig. 3. Distribution of participants' responses to the System Causability Scale

In addition, all participants think that the visualization can help them make a decision if they have been trained for using this visualization. As we assumed, all participants state that they tend to trust the prediction result more if the visualization is presented. However, regarding a preferred method of explaining the case-based reasoning, not all participants prefer the visualization because they can simply know how to achieve their goal just by following the textual suggestion, and the complexity may also hinder them from using the visualization properly. E.g., they were struggling with understanding the way that the weight of features was presented and the relevance of the case in each escalation class. The participants who are in favor of visualization thought it allows them to freely explore the system and deeply understand the logic of reasoning.

6.3   Discussion

Overall, despite the high complexity, most of the participants value the visualization in terms of **understanding causality, efficiency, support in decision making, and user trust**. After a simple training, four out of five participants can take an optimal action to decrease the escalation class without violating the restriction of adjusting feature, which implies that participants are able to trade off among multiple features that can be adjusted.

The overall score of SCS is lower than the suggested score for good quality of explanation. Arguably, this visualization is designed for users with professional knowledge in a specific application domain. However, all participants do not have knowledge on repairing service of mobile phones needed in the user scenario. Therefore, most participants reported that they need substantial support and training before using the visualization.

7 Conclusion

We proposed a visual explanation based on an evolutionary path through CBR. We discussed the difficulty of explaining model decisions in tabular data, and inability and ambiguity of single features in this data. We then presented a coherent visual explanation by which a user can see the relation between samples and features through a set of connected samples, which are placed side by side each other with one step improvement in quality between them. Our experiments showed that, by answering the three questions implied by the Fact and Foil concept (why not a little better event, why not the best event, and how to achieve the event) a user can better understand a the decision of a model that uses tabular data.

In the future we intend to extend this work to other data types. We want to expand this method in text data by exploiting a knowledge graph to also visualize semantic relations of samples and features through an evolutionary path explanation.

References

1. Caruana, R., Kangarloo, H., Dionisio, J., Sinha, U., Johnson, D.: Case-based explanation of non-case-based learning methods. In: Proceedings of the AMIA Symposium, p. 212. American Medical Informatics Association (1999)
2. Cunningham, P., Doyle, D., Loughrey, J.: An evaluation of the usefulness of case-based explanation. In: Ashley, K.D., Bridge, D.G. (eds.) ICCBR 2003. LNCS (LNAI), vol. 2689, pp. 122–130. Springer, Heidelberg (2003). https://doi.org/10.1007/3-540-45006-8_12
3. Ghorbani, A., Wexler, J., Zou, J.Y., Kim, B.: Towards automatic concept-based explanations. In: Advances in Neural Information Processing Systems, pp. 9277–9286 (2019)
4. Holzinger, A., Carrington, A., Müller, H.: Measuring the quality of explanations: the system causability scale (SCS). KI-Künstliche Intelligenz 34, 1–6 (2020)
5. Keane, M.T., Kenny, E.M.: How case-based reasoning explains neural networks: a theoretical analysis of XAI using post-hoc explanation-by-example from a survey of ANN-CBR twin-systems. In: Bach, K., Marling, C. (eds.) ICCBR 2019. LNCS (LNAI), vol. 11680, pp. 155–171. Springer, Cham (2019). https://doi.org/10.1007/978-3-030-29249-2_11
6. Lamy, J.-B., Berthelot, H., Capron, C., Favre, M.: Rainbow boxes: a new technique for overlapping set visualization and two applications in the biomedical domain. J. Vis. Lang. Comput. 43, 71–82 (2017)

7. Lamy, J.-B., Sekar, B., Guezennec, G., Bouaud, J., Séroussi, B.: Explainable artificial intelligence for breast cancer: a visual case-based reasoning approach. Artif. Intell. Med. **94**, 42–53 (2019)
8. Lipton, P.: Inference to the Best Explanation. Taylor & Francis, New York (2004)
9. Lipton, Z.C.: The mythos of model interpretability. Queue **16**(3), 31–57 (2018)
10. Massie, S., Craw, S., Wiratunga, N.: Visualisation of case-base reasoning for explanation. In: Proceedings of the ECCBR, pp. 135–144 (2004)
11. Molnar, C.: Interpretable Machine Learning. Lulu.com (2020)
12. Nugent, C., Cunningham, P.: A case-based explanation system for black-box systems. Artif. Intell. Rev. **24**(2), 163–178 (2005)
13. Ribeiro, M.T., Singh, S., Guestrin, C.: "Why should i trust you?" explaining the predictions of any classifier. In: Proceedings of the 22nd ACM SIGKDD International Conference on Knowledge Discovery and Data Mining, pp. 1135–1144 (2016)
14. Shapley, L.S.: A value for n-person games. Contrib. Theory Games **2**(28), 307–317 (1953)

Feature Store for Enhanced Explainability in Support Ticket Classification

Vishal Mour, Sreya Dey$^{(\boxtimes)}$, Shipra Jain, and Rahul Lodhe

SAP, Bengaluru, India
{vishal.mour,sreya.dey01,shipra.jain01,rahul.lodhe}@sap.com

Abstract. In order to maximize trust between human and ML agents in an ML application scenario, humans need to be able to easily understand the reasoning behind predictions made by the black box models commonly used today. The field of explainable AI aims to maximize this trust. To achieve this, model interpretations need to be informative yet understandable. But often, explanations provided by a model are not easy to understand due to complex feature transformations. Our work proposes the use of a feature store to address this issue. We extend the general idea of a feature store. In addition to using a feature store for reading pre-processed features, we also use it to interpret model explanations in a more user-friendly and business-relevant format. This enables both the end user as well as the data scientist personae to glean more information from the interpretations in a shorter time. We demonstrate our idea using a service ticket classification scenario. However, the general concept can be extended to other data types and applications as well to gain more insightful explanations.

Keywords: Explainable AI · Feature store · Text classification

1 Introduction

In today's world, almost all significant aspects of a person's life are affected by decisions taken by a machine learning model. Ranging from our shopping experience to medical diagnosis, from online matchmaking to home loan applications, the impact of ML is hard to measure and impossible to ignore.

With the advent of technology, the ML models that provide these decisions are becoming increasingly hard to interpret. When a model takes a decision, it is often very hard to determine why it did so. This might not be a major concern in some scenarios, but given the life altering capabilities of some decisions where ML is involved today, it is very important for a prediction given by a model to be interpretable and explainable. For example, an user might not be as impacted by a product recommendation on an online apparel store as by the decision to reject their home loan application by an ML model.

Like any other field of interaction, the interaction between AI models and human agents, both as end users and data scientists, is majorly based on trust. To

© Springer Nature Switzerland AG 2020
X. Zhu et al. (Eds.): NLPCC 2020, LNAI 12431, pp. 467–478, 2020.
https://doi.org/10.1007/978-3-030-60457-8_38

cement this trust and consequently, improve the system, ML model predictions need to be explained. This accountability of an ML system, combined with its performance, is the acceptance criteria for an ML model to be used by the human agent. Also, from the perspective of a data scientist, it is very important to be able to trust the system they are working on. Explainable ML systems, that look inside the black box working of a model, and gives insight into predictions taken, can help a data scientist understand the model better. It also helps them to correct for any bias, that the model interpretations throw light upon.

1.1 Evolution of Explainable AI

Explainable AI (XAI) refers to methods and techniques in the application of artificial intelligence such that the results of the solution can be understood by humans. The underlying concept behind XAI is not new. Early reasoning systems dating back to the 70s, such as MYCIN [1], GUIDON [2], SOPHIE [3], and PROTOS [4,5], explored the idea of explaining their underlying reasoning for diagnostic, instructional, or machine-learning purposes. Later, truth maintenance systems were developed which generated explanations by tracing reasoning from conclusions to assumptions through logical inferences. By the 90s, work started on tools to explain inherently opaque neural network models [6].

In recent times, concerns about bias, specially concerning race and gender, in AI models being used for criminal sentencing, recruiting and assessing creditworthiness, have emerged in various forums and publications [7]. This has led to a greater focus on Explainable AI and development of several methods and tools for explaining AI models and their decisions. Several regulations such as the GDPR and research forums such as the International Joint Conference on Artificial Intelligence: Workshop on Explainable Artificial Intelligence (XAI), strongly focus on the practice and development of XAI methods.

1.2 Our Proposal

For any Explainable AI method, human interpretability of the explanations themselves and the speed of explanations are two very significant criteria for acceptance. Firstly, the explanations generated by an explanation tool need to cater to all user personae using the system. For an ML model, this includes, but is not limited to, data scientists, data engineers, product owners, business analysts, domain experts, business users and application users. Explanations need to be customized such that it is useful for all personae. Here, an "one-size-fits-all" approach would not work. An explanation plot that seems very useful to a data scientist might seem cumbersome and useless to the end user of the model. For example, consider a neural network model designed for detecting pneumonia from lung images. Highlighting the activated nodes in the intermediate layers of the model might convey relevant information to a data scientist in this case, but for the end user, let's say a doctor who uses this model to support their diagnosis decision, an explanation such as the most contributing regions of the original lung image might be more useful. Secondly, if the time taken to produce explanations for a model prediction is much longer than the time taken for the prediction itself, it is often not useful. To summarize, interpretable explanations need to be provided and they need to be provided fast.

Many methods have been developed for this. We will discuss some of them in the next section. However, in many applications, the results generated by these methods need to be processed in order to address the interpretability and usability criteria mentioned above. Instead of delivering off the shelf explanations produced by explanation libraries, we need to process the explanations to a format understandable and useful to the business user, application user or end user. This addresses one of the two requirements we mentioned above. However, for these processed explanations to be useful, they also have to be produced quickly. The processing of the explanations should not add a lot of processing overhead.

To address both these issues, we propose the use of feature store concept in the model explanation stage of the ML life cycle. This avoids redundant feature computations and facilitates quick processing of global as well as local explanations, especially in systems where there are several deployed models which are using the same features.

We demonstrate the use of feature store for explanation processing using a service ticket classification scenario. We use open sources libraries such as LIME [8] and Contextual AI [10]. We implement a feature store for storing raw data, processed features and mappings between raw and derived features. This store is then used for two purposes: a) reading required features during model training, and b) processing explanations for these models. We generate global and local explanations from LIME, and process them using appropriate feature store mappings to produce more readable explanations. We also conduct error analysis using Contextual AI, and process these results using feature store mappings to get error analysis in terms of raw, interpretable features. We also apply this concept to two other datasets, and explain how a Feature Store can help in processing explanations in each case.

2   Related Work

In this section, we'll briefly introduce the tools and concepts that we use in the paper.

2.1   Local Interpretable Model-Agnostic Explanations

Local Interpretable Model-agnostic Explanations (LIME) [8], as the name suggests, is a model-agnostic method for generating interpretable explanations by approximating a model in the locality of a data point.

Although LIME is based on locally faithful explanations, LIME also provides Submodular pick (SP) algorithm to provide global explanations for a model.

From a set of data point instances, it generates a small set of representative, non-redundant explanations.

We used the Python implementation of LIME [9], to get both local and global explanations on our ticket classification model.

2.2 Contextual AI

Contextual AI [10] is an open source library for generating machine learning explanations at different stages of the machine learning pipeline - data, training, and inference. Its offerings include feature data analysis, global model explanations and feature importances, local explanations and error analysis. Internally, the library uses features from LIME and SHAP [11].

We have used Contextual AI for error analysis of our ticket classification model. Contextual AI selects top features for data points wrongly classified by the model.

2.3 Feature Store

Feature Store is a concept of having a data management layer that allows people across an organization to curate, share, and use a common set of features for their machine learning problems. This ensures that the data used across models for training and validation is consistent. It also saves redundant work done in curating the same features by multiple teams for their modelling requirements. By data reuse and cutting down the time spent in feature engineering, there is a significant reduction in overall modeling time. Many organizations use either their internal feature store implementation or external feature store solutions for managing data for training and validating models across teams.

3 Our Work

In this section, we demonstrate our proposal by implementing a feature store and extending it to enrich model explanations with additional information to improve human interpretability. For the purpose of demonstrating the concept, we use a service ticket classification problem. However, this idea can be used in any scenario where explanations need to be processed to make them more usable. We shall discuss this later in detail.

3.1 Data and Problem Statement

The dataset [12] used in this paper is an anonymized collection of support tickets with different target labels. Each row has the following fields: **title**, **body**, **ticket_type**, **category**, **sub_category1**, **sub_category2**, **business_service**, **urgency** and **impact**. The first 2 fields, **title** and **body**, are text fields and the rest are categorical features.

Our aim is to create two separate models: one for predicting the **ticket_type** of a ticket and the other for predicting the **category** of the ticket. As both models will be trained on the same dataset, we want both these models to read features for training and inference from a central feature store.

We divide the dataset into training and test data and add it to the feature store. At this stage the feature store contains only the original features corresponding to each row. Then, we process the raw data and create additional features as shown in Algorithm 1.

Algorithm 1: Text Processing in Feature Store

Input: *title,body*
Output: *text_stop_words_removed, text_stemmed,*
$\qquad\qquad$ *text_stemmed_reverse_map*
1 Concatenate *title* and *body* to get *text*.
2 Remove stop words from *text* to get *text_stop_words_removed*
3 Run stemming on *text_stop_words_removed* to get *text_stemmed*
4 Store reverse map dictionary from stemmed word to original word(s) in
$\quad$ *text_stemmed_reverse_map*

Each row in the feature store has the following fields after processing: **title, body, ticket_type, category, sub_category1, sub_category2, business_ service, urgency, impact, text_stop_words_removed, text_stemmed** and **text_stemmed_reverse_map**.

Now, any model that uses this data for training, can access the feature store directly. This saves redundant time spent in doing the same preprocessing steps by multiple modelers. Also, the raw data and all its processed versions are present in the same location. This ensures that if a feature is used in various ML models in an organization, it is consistent across the models. Also, the feature store serves as a one-stop location for the raw, intermediate and final features and their mapping to one another. This leads to easier and more scalable data management. Often we data scientists observe that it requires a lot of manual effort to maintain data sources for multiple models deployed over time. With the feature store in place, this problem is mitigated.

3.2 Experiments and Results

We build two models on the dataset to demonstrate the concept of using feature store for feature retrieval and explanation processing. The first model classifies the support ticket text into one of two **ticket_type**(s). The second classifies the ticket into one of 13 **category**(s). The fields **ticket_type** and **category** are independent of each other.

Predicting Ticket Type

In this section, we build a Naive Bayes Classifier model for predicting the binary target variable **ticket_type** from the ticket text. For the train and test data, the columns **text_stemmed**, **ticket_type** and **text_stemmed_reverse_map** are read from the feature store for each data point.

Local Explanation Using LIME

We use LIME Text Explainer for explaining the model prediction for the sample in Table 1.

Table 1. Sample data for local explanation

Title	New purchase po
body	Purchase po dear purchased has please log allocation please log retrieve old device after receive item please take consideration mandatory receipts section order make receipt item ordered how video link kind regards administrator
text_stemmed	New purchase po purchase po purchased log allocation log retrieve old device receive item take consideration mandatory receipts section order make receipt item ordered video link administrator

As the model is trained on the **text_stemmed** field, local explanations from LIME on the sample in Table 1 looks like Fig. 1.

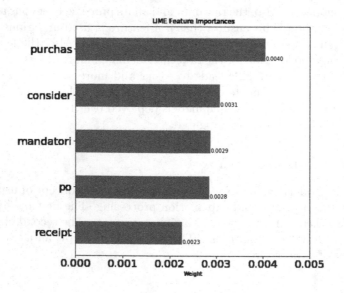

Fig. 1. LIME local explanations

Top feature names shown in the local explanation are stemmed versions of words. For the end user, these do not convey useful information. In order to process the explanations, we use the Feature Store built earlier, to extract the reverse mapping from stemmed words to their original forms. Note that, since multiple words in the same document can map to the same stemmed word form, the reverse map is an 1:n mapping. For this sample, the reverse mapping extracted from the feature store is shown in Table 2.

Table 2. Reverse mapping for stemmed words

text_stemmed_reverse_map	'new': {'new'}, 'purchas': {'purchase', 'purchased'}, 'po': {'po'}, 'log': {'log'}, 'alloc': {'allocation'}, 'retriev': {'retrieve'}, 'old': {'old'}, 'devic': {'device'}, 'receiv': {'receive'}, 'item': {'item'}, 'take': {'take'}, 'consider': {'consideration'}, 'mandatori': {'mandatory'}, 'receipt': {'receipt', 'receipts'}, 'section': {'section'}, 'order': {'order', 'ordered'}, 'make': {'make'}, 'video': {'video'}, 'link': {'link'}, 'administr': {'administrator'}

Using the reverse mapping extracted above from the feature store, we process the local explanation for the above instance. The resultant processed explanation is shown in Fig. 2.

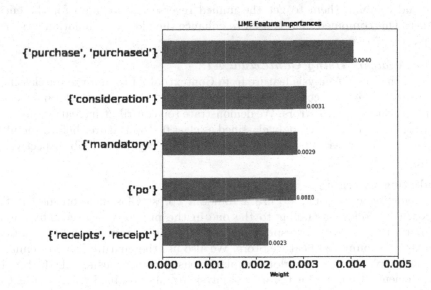

Fig. 2. LIME local explanations enhanced using reverse mapping from feature store

Global Explanation Using LIME Submodular Pick

We use LIME Submodular Pick for explaining the model trained. The output from LIME is shown in Fig. 3.

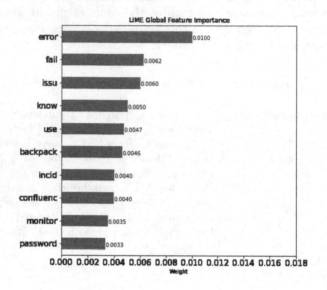

Fig. 3. LIME global explanations

We use reverse mapping from Feature Store for each document in the training data and combine them to get the unified reverse feature map for the entire dataset. This combined map is used to enhance the global explanation as shown in Fig. 4.

Error Analysis Using Contextual AI

We used the Error Analysis feature from Contextual AI to analyze misclassification errors and get top contributing features for each group (correct_target_class, predicted_class) of such errors. We demonstrate top contributing features for documents of class 1 being wrongly classified as class 0. Top features before and after processing using reverse feature map are shown in Fig. 5a and 5b respectively.

Predicting Category

For predicting **category**, we use a Random Forest Classification model. The approach we follow is similar to the one in the previous section. This model also reads the features corresponding to the required training and test dataset from the pre-computed Feature Store. We also use the Feature Store to enhance the local explanations and global explanations generated using LIME. Similar enhancements are done for the error analysis results obtained using Contextual AI. We are showing the enhanced explanations for this problem in Figs. 6 and 7 respectively.

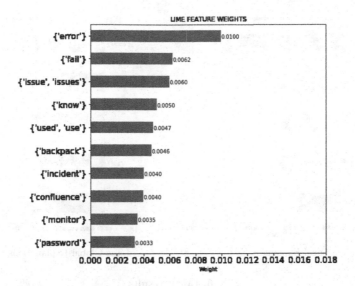

Fig. 4. LIME global explanations enhanced using reverse mapping from feature store

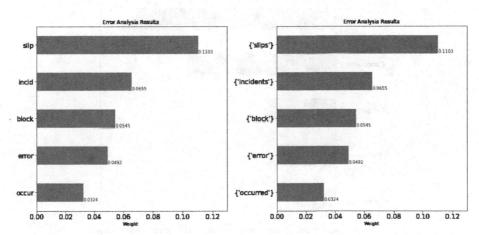

Error Analysis Results obtained from Con-   Error Analysis Results above processed us-
textual AI   ing reverse mapping

Fig. 5. Error analysis results when Class 1 tickets are misclassified as Class 0

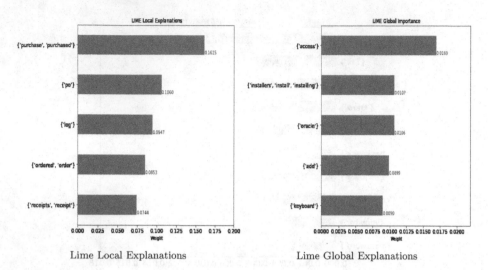

Lime Local Explanations   Lime Global Explanations

Fig. 6. LIME results

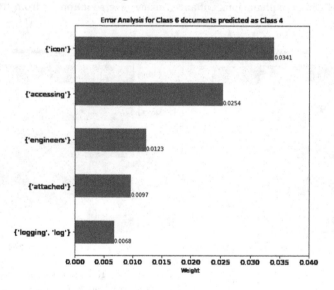

Fig. 7. Error analysis results

3.3   Applications on Other Datasets

The concept of using a feature store for enhancing explanations can be extended to other types of datasets (like tabular data) and applications too. In general, if a function f is used to map raw data to processed features, recording the inverse map of f in the feature store can help us decode the explanations, with considerable savings in redundant processing across models using the same data. We discuss two such scenarios below.

Predicting Item Production Times

Problem: Predict the time taken for a material to be produced by a machine, using historical data and current production plan.

Raw Features: Historical time taken for this machine to produce this material is one of the raw features present in the data, along with the production plan details.

Computed Feature Stored in Feature Store: Root Mean Squared value of time taken for the machine to produce the particular material in the last 5 instances. Lets call this feature $rms\_prod\_time\_5$. We also store the mapping of each value of $rms\_prod\_time\_5$ to the original 5 data values it is calculated from.

Enhanced Explanations: When the local explanation shows $rms\_prod\_time\_5$ as a contributing factor, we use the feature store to access the actual data for the last 5 days, and show these values to the user, which is more interpretable for them.

Predicting Customer Churn

Problem: For a telecommunication company offering multiple services, predict whether a customer will churn, using their account, billing and demographic information.

Raw Features: Information of accounts held by customers along with other features like billing history and personal details.

Computed Feature Stored in Feature Store: We compute the number of services offered by the company which a user is subscribed to. Lets call this feature $number\_of\_subs$. This is one of the features the churn prediction model is trained on. The feature store also stores the list of the account numbers for each service held by each consumer.

Enhanced Explanations: If the local explanation shows $number\_of\_subs$ as a contributing factor for the churn prediction for a user, we use the feature store to access the list of the accounts for each service held by the consumer, and show these values to the analyst running the explainer, which can be used to target offers to the service account.

4   Conclusion and Future Directions

In this paper, we present the idea of using feature store for enhancing explanations from standard libraries to make them more usable and interpretable for the end user. The idea, demonstrated here using a text classification scenario, can be applied to other problems and data types. We plan to take this work further and work on integration of this solution with other commonly used explanation libraries like SHAP and InterpretML.

References

1. Fagan, L.M., Shortliffe, E.H., Buchanan, B.G.: Computer-based medical decision making: from MYCIN to VM. Automedica **3**(2), 97–108 (1980)
2. Clancey, W.: Knowledge-Based Tutoring: The GUIDON Program. The MIT Press, Cambridge (1987)
3. Brown, J.S., Burton, R.R., De Kleer, J.: Pedagogical, Natural Language, and Knowledge Engineering Techniques in SOPHIE I, II, and III. Intelligent Tutoring Systems. Academic Press (1982). ISBN 0-12-648680-8
4. Bareiss, R., Porter, B., Weir, C., Holte, R.: Protos: an exemplar-based learning apprentice. In: Machine Learning, vol. 3. Morgan Kaufmann Publishers Inc. pp. 112–139 (1990). ISBN 1-55860-119-8
5. Bareiss, R.: Exemplar-Based Knowledge Acquisition: A Unified Approach to Concept Representation, Classification, and Learning. Perspectives in Artificial Intelligence (2014)
6. Tickle, A.B., Andrews, R., Golea, M., Diederich, J.: The truth will come to light: directions and challenges in extracting the knowledge embedded within trained artificial neural networks. IEEE Trans. Neural Networks **9**, 1057–1068 (1998)
7. O'Neil, C.: Weapons of Math Destruction: How Big Data Increases Inequality and Threatens Democracy. Crown Books, New York (2016)
8. Ribeiro, M.T., Singh, S., Guestrin, C.: "Why should I trust you?": explaining the predictions of any classifier. In: Knowledge Discovery and Data Mining (KDD) (2016)
9. Ribeiro, M.T., et al.: LIME: explaining the predictions of any machine learning classifier. https://github.com/marcotcr/lime. Accessed 14 July 2020
10. Wang, J., Saito, S., Chai, W.T., Patil, A.: Contextual AI. https://contextual-ai.readthedocs.io/en/latest/. Accessed 4 July 2020
11. Lundberg, S., Lee, S.: A Unified Approach to Interpreting Model Predictions, Advances in Neural Information Processing Systems, vol. 30 (2017)
12. Żak, K.: Support Ticket Classification Dataset. https://github.com/karolzak/support-tickets-classification. Accessed 14 July 2020

Student Workshop

Incorporating Lexicon for Named Entity Recognition of Traditional Chinese Medicine Books

Bingyan Song[1], Zhenshan Bao[1], YueZhang Wang[1], Wenbo Zhang[1(✉)], and Chao Sun[2]

[1] College of Computer Science, Beijing University of Technology, Beijing 100124, China
sonby97@emails.bjut.en, {baozheshan,zhangwenbo}@bjut.edu.cn,
yzwang18@163.com
[2] College of Chinese Medicine, Capital Medical University, Beijing 100069, China
sunchaotcm@ccmu.edu.cn

Abstract. Little research has been done on the Named Entity Recognition (NER) of Traditional Chinese Medicine (TCM) books and most of them use statistical models such as Conditional Random Fields (CRFs). However, in these methods, lexicon information and large-scale of unlabeled corpus data are not fully exploited. In order to improve the performance of NER for TCM books, we propose a method which is based on biLSTM-CRF model and can incorporate lexicon information into representation layer to enrich its semantic information. We compared our approach with several previous character-based and word-based methods. Experiments on "Shanghan Lun" dataset show that our method outperforms previous models. In addition, we collected 376 TCM books to construct a large-scale of corpus to obtain the pre-trained vectors since there is no large available corpus in this field before. We have released the corpus and pre-trained vectors to the public.

Keywords: Named entity recognition · Enhanced embedding · BiLSTM-CRF · TCM books · Information extraction

1 Introduction

As a distinct medical system with diagnosis and treatment, Traditional Chinese Medicine (TCM) has always played a significant role in Chinese society for thousands of years and has attracted more and more attention worldwide [1]. The TCM books contain detailed and valuable information of the whole medical procedure such as the experience of syndrome differentiation and clinical diagnosis. It is a practical task to systematically study the mechanism to obtain understandable and applicable empirical knowledge to assist doctors during their treatment. Named entity recognition (NER) in TCM books is the first step of the above task.

NER of TCM books have the following difficulties: 1) At present, TCM books have not been fully digitized and it is difficult to obtain large-scale of available corpus. 2) Most of the TCM books are written in ancient Chinese, which is quite different from

© Springer Nature Switzerland AG 2020
X. Zhu et al. (Eds.): NLPCC 2020, LNAI 12431, pp. 481–489, 2020.
https://doi.org/10.1007/978-3-030-60457-8_39

modern Chinese. Thus, the general Chinese word segmentation tools like Jieba may produce many errors which will negatively impact the final performance.

As a result, little research has been done on NER of TCM books. Meng et al. [2] used Conditional Random Field (CRF) model to automatically recognize the terms in "Shanghan Lun" (伤寒论). They used part-of-speech and word boundaries as features, but did not make full use of information from large-scale of unlabeled corpus. Ye et al. [3] used CRF to extract symptomatic drug information from "Jingui Yaolue" (金匮要略) and added the feature of TCM diagnosis key-value pairs [4]. This method put some prior knowledge of TCM into the model yet it also greatly increased the complexity and time cost of manual labeling. Li et al. [5] recognized the symptom terminologies of the "Traditional Chinese Medical Cases" based on LSTM-CRF. However, due to the limitation of available corpus and accuracy of word segmentation, they only used this one book as corpus and utilized purely character-based method for recognition. Word information, which has been proved to be useful [6], was not exploited.

Therefore, inspired by Ma et al. [7], we incorporate lexicon information into the character representation so that we can utilize word information and reduce the negative impact of inaccurate word segmentation at the same time. Previous work has been done on combing word-level information like Lu et al. [8] and Wang et al. [9] yet they haven't considered all the possible matched words for a character in one sentence.

To summarize, our main contributions of this work are as follows: 1) In order to get more accurate pre-trained vectors, we firstly collect 376 TCM books to construct a large-scale of unlabeled corpus to make up for the deficiencies of corpus in TCM books. Then, we combine the open source tool Jiayan[1] to complete the word segmentation of TCM books to solve the problem that the Chinese general word segmentation tools are basically invalid for ancient Chinese. To our best knowledge, this is the first publicly available large corpus and pre-trained vectors[2] for TCM books. 2) We propose to encode the matched words, obtained from the lexicon, into the representation layer to enrich the semantic information of character embeddings. 3) Experimental results on annotated data of "Shanghan Lun" show that our method outperforms previous models for NER of TCM books.

2   TCM Corpus and Pre-trained Word Vectors

2.1   TCM Corpus

At present, large-scale of accurate and easily accessible corpus in TCM field are hard to obtain yet the corpus is indispensable in the process of mining TCM knowledge. Therefore, we collect 376 TCM books from the Han Dynasty to the Qing Dynasty, including the basic theories, medical diagnosis, herbal medicine, and many other categories. The specific content can be found in our open source project.

---

[1] https://github.com/jiaeyan/Jiayan.
[2] https://github.com/Sporot/TCM_word2vec.

2.2 Pre-trained Vectors

Learning word vector representations from unlabeled data can help optimize a variety of NLP learning tasks and make them have better performance [10]. The word vector is a distributional representation feature obtained by training a neural network language model [11]. Compared with the one-hot encoding method that represents each word as a sparse vector with only one bit being 1, and the others being 0, the word vector method retains the rich language regularity of words [12].

Word Segmentation. The accuracy of word segmentation is crucial for the quality of the word vectors. However, the corpus of TCM books is quite different from common Chinese corpus. Many characters in ancient Chinese often have rich semantics and usually have been treated as one word. For example, each character in "后思水者 (those who think about water later)" has its own independent meaning, while most commonly used word segmentation tools are not applicable of dealing with this. Therefore, we combine Jiayan, a segmentation tool specialized for ancient Chinese, to tackle this problem. To test the performance of each segmentation tool, we select 537 sentences from "Jingui Yaolue" and manually annotate with word segmentation results. According to the results in Table 1, Jiayan is far better than other general word segmentation tools for TCM books.

Table 1. The performance of word segmentation tools for TCM books

Tools	Precision (%)	Recall (%)	F1 score (%)
Jieba	56.70	43.63	49.32
pkuseg	57.07	46.26	51.12
thulac	56.72	46.89	51.34
Jiayan	**86.95**	**81.34**	**84.05**

Pre-trained Vectors. Based on the above word segmentation, we use Word2Vec[3] [13] to obtain word vectors from the corpus introduced in Sect. 2.1. In order to verify the necessity of the domain corpus, we also use the common corpus Chinese Wikipedia for comparison. There are two main methods for evaluating the quality of word vectors [14]: First one is the intrinsic way such as semantic relevance, which evaluates the accuracy of its semantic representation by calculating the similarity between word vectors. We select one sample word "呕吐 (vomit)" which is a common symptom term both in TCM and Chinese Wiki and another word "恶寒 (aversion to cold)" which is common in TCM but rare in Chinese Wiki. The top 2 similar words of each sample are shown in Table 2. From Table 2, it can be seen that similar words obtained from TCM corpus are more precise. And the words unique to TCM books, such as "厥逆 (cold limbs)", may not be found in the general corpus. The second is the extrinsic method that measuring the effect of word vectors on NER tasks which will be described in Sect. 4.1.

---

[3] https://radimrehurek.com/gensim/models/word2vec.html.

Table 2. Semantic evaluation of word vectors

Example words	Vector dimension	Corpus	Top 2 similar words/Similarity value
呕吐 (Vomit)	50	TCM	呕恶(Nausea)/0.936，吐食(Vomit)/0.915
		Chinese Wiki	腹痛(Bellyache)/0.976，咳嗽(Cough)/0.974
	200	TCM	**呕哕(Vomit)/0.809，呕恶(Nausea)/0.783**
		Chinese Wiki	头晕(Dizziness)/0.921，耳鸣(Tinnitus)/0.911
	300	TCM	呕逆(Queasiness) /0.765，呕哕(Vomit)/0.759
		Chinese Wiki	腹泻(Diarrhea)/0.940，腹痛(Bellyache)/0.921
恶寒 (Aversion to cold)	50	TCM	恶风(Aversion to wind)/0.884，发热(Pyrexia)/0.879
		Chinese Wiki	泄泻(Diarrhea)/0.965，腹胀(Ventosity)/0.964
	200	TCM	**恶风(Aversion to wind)/0.841，怯寒(Chilly)/0.801**
		Chinese Wiki	瘰疬(Scrofula)/0.910，泄泻(Diarrhea)/0.904
	300	TCM	恶风(Aversion to wind/0.592, 憎寒(hate cold)/0.552
		Chinese Wiki	泄泻(Diarrhea)/0.891，瘰疬(Scrofula)/0.883

3   Neural Architecture for NER of TCM Books

Same as the generic character-based neural NER model, our proposed method for TCM books contains three stacked layers as shown in Fig. 1. We describe the details of these layers as below.

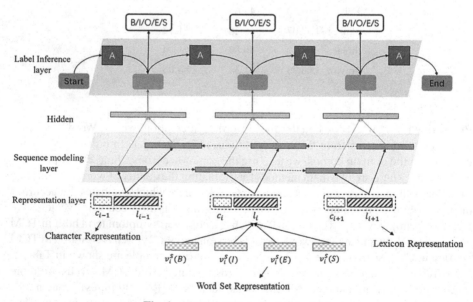

Fig. 1. Main architecture of our model

3.1 Representation Layer Incorporating Lexicon Information

Due to the inaccuracy of Chinese word segmentation, lots of researchers choose to use character-based models. For a character-based Chinese NER model, the smallest unit of a sentence is a character c_i and the sentence is seen as a character sequence $s = \{c_1, \ldots, c_n\}, c_i \in V_c$, where V_c is the character vocabulary. Each character c_i is represented by a dense vector x_i^c.

To utilized lexicon information, we make each character c corresponds to four word sets marked by the four segmentation labels "BIES", motivated by Ma et al. [7]. The word set $B(c)$ consists of all lexicon matched words on s that begin with c. Similarly, $I(c)$ consists of all lexicon matched words on s that begin with c occurs, $E(c)$ consists of all lexicon matched words that end with c, and $S(c)$ is the single-character word comprised of c. And if a word set is empty, a special word *"None"* is used to indicate this situation. We have explained it with an example shown in Fig. 2.

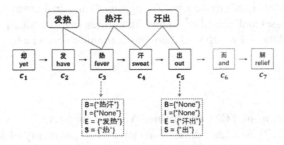

Fig. 2. An example of getting word information

In order to retain information as much as possible and reduce the negative impact of imperfect word segmentation, we concatenate the representations of the four word sets to represent them as a whole and use it to augment the character representation:

$$x_i^l = e^s(B, I, E, S) = \left[v^s(B) \oplus v^s(I) \oplus v^s(E) \oplus v^s(S)\right], \tag{1}$$

$$x_i^e \leftarrow \left[x_i^c; x_i^l\right]. \tag{2}$$

Here, v^s denotes the function that maps a single word set to a dense vector. According to the basic idea that the more times a character sequence occurs in the data, the more likely it is a word, we get the weighted representation of the word set T by:

$$v^s(T) = \frac{1}{Z} \sum_{w \in T} z(w) e^w(w), \tag{3}$$

Specifically, $Z = \sum_{w \in B \cup I \cup E \cup S}$ is the normalized term and $z(w)$ denote the frequency of w occurring in our TCM corpus. e^w denotes the word embedding look up table which can be obtained from the same TCM corpus. In this way, we introduce the pre-trained word embeddings into the character representation to utilize lexicon information for NER of TCM books.

3.2 Sequence Modeling and Label Inference Layer

For NER of TCM books, we use the popular architecture of the bidirectional long-short term memory network (BiLSTM) for sequence modeling [15]. BiLSTM contains two LSTM [16] cells that model the sequence in the left-to-right (forward) and right-to-left (backward) directions with two distinct sets of parameters. The concatenated hidden states at the ith step of the forward and backward LSTMs $h_i = [\overrightarrow{h_i} \odot \overleftarrow{h_i}]$ forms the context-dependent representations of c_i. On top of the biLSTM layer, a sequential CRF [17] layer is used to perform label inference. The Viterbi Algorithm [18] is used to find the path achieves the maximum probability.

4 Experiments

4.1 Dataset

We chose "Shanghan Lun" written by Zhongjing Zhang in Eastern Han Dynasty as the annotation dataset and tagged the symptom entities in this book. There were 17081 pieces of labeled data and we divided them into a training set and a test set according to 7:3.

4.2 Results

Different Dimensions of TCM Pre-trained Vector. In Sect. 2.2, we have already found that different TCM vector dimensions have different ability of semantic expression. Therefore, we test four dimensions of their recognition effectiveness on our dataset. From Table 3, we can see that with the increase of the dimension, the recognition performance will be improved. However, it will not continue to improve and it may even decline when reaches a certain value. In this work, 200 dimension gains the best recognition performance which is 74.38%.

Table 3. Recognition results using different vector dimensions

Vector dimensions	Precision (%)	Recall (%)	F1 score (%)
50	76.54	67.82	71.92
100	76.09	71.45	73.70
200	**76.80**	**72.11**	**74.38**
300	76.12	72.60	74.32

Different Corpus of Pre-trained Vector. In order to further verify the necessity of the domain corpus, we choose the same dimension of pre-train vector from TCM corpus and Chinese Wiki corpus introduced in Sect. 2.2. From Table 4, it can be seen that, with the same vector dimension, results of using TCM corpus is far better than using Chinese Wiki which proves the importance of constructing domain corpus.

Table 4. The recognition results from different corpus of pre-trained vector

Corpus	Vector dimension	Precision (%)	Recall (%)	F1 score (%)
Chinese Wiki	50	70.49	61.88	65.91
TCM	**50**	**76.54**	**67.82**	**71.92**

Different Models. We compare several previous models with our proposed methods. Table 5 shows the results on the same dataset introduced in Sect. 4.1.

HMM. The HMM model we used here can be found on Github[4].

CRF. The CRF toolkit we used here is CRF++[5]. Except the entity labels, we didn't add any self-defined features.

BiLSTM-CRF. This model's architecture is the same as the one we introduced in Sect. 3.2, while its representation layer is composed by either character or word embeddings.

Table 5. The recognition results from different models

Input	Method	Precision (%)	Recall (%)	F1 score (%)
Char	HMM	55.95	55.86	55.91
	BiLSTM-CRF	66.24	59.12	62.48
	CRF	**76.68**	**63.53**	**69.07**
Word	HMM	57.74	53.81	55.70
	BiLSTM-CRF	61.59	56.40	58.88
	CRF	61.61	57.21	59.33
Proposed	Char+TCM-Lexicon	**76.80**	**72.11**	**74.38**
	TCM-Lexicon	64.86	59.08	61.83

The methods of the "Char" group are character-based. The methods of the "Word" group are word-based that build on the word segmentation results generated by Jiayan. From the table, we can obtain several informative observations. First, by replacing the input from character to word, the F1-score of all the methods decreased. This shows the problem of directly using the imperfect word segmentation. Second, the char-based BiLSTM-CRF achieved a relatively low performance and was 6.58% worse than char-based CRF. This may indicate that the former model is more dependent on large-scale of annotated data. Finally, our proposed method that incorporates lexicon information in the representation layer, obtained a large improvement over the other models. This verifies its effectiveness on this dataset.

---

[4] https://github.com/luopeixiang/named_entity_recognition.

[5] https://code.google.com/archive/p/crfpp.

5 Conclusion and Future Work

In this work, in order to achieve a high-performing NER system of TCM books, we propose a method based on BiLSTM-CRF which can exploit the useful information from lexicon and large-scale of unlabeled data. Concretely, we collect 376 TCM books to construct a large-scale of corpus first and then add lexicon information into the character representation to enrich its semantic information. Experimental study on "Shanghan Lun" dataset shows that our method can obtain better performance than the comparative methods. In the future work, we plan to combine the TCM domain knowledge to further improve the performance.

References

1. Tang, J., Bao, Y.: Traditional Chinese medicine. Lancet. **372**(9654), 1938-1940 (2008)
2. Meng, H., Xie, Q.: Automatic identification of TCM terminology in Shanghan Lun based on Conditional Random Field. J. Beijing Univ. Tradit. Chin. **38**(9), 587–590 (2015)
3. Ye, H., Ji, D.: Research on symptom and medicine information abstraction of TCM book Jin Gui Yao Lue based on conditional random field. Chin. J. Libr. Inf. Sci. Tradit. Chin. Med. **040**(005), 14–17 (2016)
4. Wang, G., Du, J.: POS tagging and feature recombination for ancient prose of TCM diagnosis. Comput. Eng. Design **3**, 835–840 (2015)
5. Li, M., Liu, Z.: LSTM-CRF based symptom term recognition on traditional Chinese medical case. J. Comput. Appl. **38**(3), 835–840 (2018)
6. Zhang, Y., Jie, Y.: Chinese NER using lattice LSTM. In: Proceedings of the 56th Annual Meeting of the Association for Computational Linguistics, ACL, Melbourne, pp. 1554–1564 (2018)
7. Ma, R., Peng, M., Zhang, Q., et al.: Simplify the usage of lexicon in Chinese NER. In: Proceedings of the 58th Annual Meeting of the Association for Computational Linguistics, pp. 5951–5960 (2020)
8. Wang, Q., Zhou, Y., Ruan, T., et al.: Incorporating dictionaries into deep neural networks for the Chinese clinical named entity recognition. J. Biomed. Inform. **92**, 103133 (2019)
9. Lu, N., Zheng, J., Wu, W., et al.: Chinese clinical named entity recognition with word-level information incorporating dictionaries. In: Proceedings of the 2019 International Joint Conference on Neural Networks (IJCNN), pp. 1–8. IEEE (2019)
10. Guo, J., Che, W., Wang, H., Liu, T.: Revisiting embedding features for simple semi-supervised learning. In: Proceedings of the 2014 Conference on Empirical Methods in Natural Language Processing (EMNLP), ACL, Stroudsburg, pp. 110–120 (2014)
11. Mnih, A., Hinton, G.E.: A scalable hierarchical distributed language model. In: Advances in Neural Information Processing Systems, pp. 1081–1088 (2009)
12. Collobert, R., Weston, J.: A unified architecture for natural language processing: Deep neural networks with multitask learning. In: Proceedings of the 25th international conference on Machine learning, pp. 160–167 (2008)
13. Mikolov, T., Sutskever, I., Chen, K., Corrado, G.S., Dean, J.: Distributed representations of words and phrases and their compositionality. In: Advances in Neural Information Processing Systems, pp. 3111–3119 (2013)
14. Siwei, L., Kang, L., Shizhu, H.: How to generate a good word embedding. IEEE Intell. Syst. **31**(6), 5–14 (2016)

15. Greenberg, N., Bansal, T., Verga, P., McCallum, A.: Marginal likelihood training of BiLSTM-CRF for biomedical named entity recognition from disjoint label sets. In: Proceedings of the 2018 Conference on Empirical Methods in Natural Language Processing, pp. 2824–2829 (2018)
16. Hochreiter, S., Schmidhuber, J.: Long short-term memory. Neural Comput. 9(8), 1735–1780 (1997)
17. Lafferty, J.D., Mccallum, A., Pereira F.: Conditional random fields: probabilistic models for segmenting and labeling sequence data. In: Eighteenth International Conference on Machine Learning, pp. 282–289. Morgan Kaufmann Publishers Inc. (2001)
18. Forney, G.D.: The viterbi algorithm. Proc. IEEE 61(3), 268–278 (1973)

Anaphora Resolution in Chinese for Analysis of Medical Q&A Platforms

Alena Tsvetkova[1,2]([✉])

[1] HSE University, 20 Myasnitskaya, Moscow 101000, Russia
adtsvetkova@edu.hse.ru
[2] Semantic Hub, 4 Ilyinka, Moscow 109012, Russia

Abstract. In medical Q&A platforms, patients share information about their diagnosis, give advice and consult with doctors, this creates a large amount of data that contains valuable knowledge on the side effects of drugs, patients' actions and symptoms. This information is widely considered to be the most important in the field of computer-aided medical analysis. Nevertheless, messages on the Internet are difficult to analyze because of their unstructured form. Thus, the purpose of this study is to develop a program for anaphora resolution in Chinese and to implement it for analysis of user-generated content in the medical Q&A platform. The experiments are conducted on three models: BERT, NeuralCoref and BERT-Chinese+SpanBERT. BERT-Chinese+SpanBERT achieves the highest accuracy—68.5% on the OntoNotes 5.0 corpus. Testing the model that showed the highest result was carried out on messages from the medical Q&A platform haodf.com. The results of the study might contribute to improving the diagnosis of hereditary diseases.

Keywords: Anaphora resolution · Chinese Natural Language Processing (NLP) · User-generated content · BERT

1 Introduction

Anaphora is a linguistic phenomenon in which the interpretation of one expression (anaphor) depends on another expression in the context (antecedent). Anaphora resolution is a fundamental stage for many NLP tasks, such as machine translation, automatic text summarizing. Anaphora resolution in Chinese is more challenging comparing with English [5]. This is due to the several features of the Chinese language such as no gaps between words, zero anaphora and others. The user-generated content in Chinese is characterized by the use of idiomatic expressions (chengyu) and omission of punctuation marks which affect the accuracy of automatic analysis.

Nowadays, the Internet offers numerous opportunities to research different spheres of our life even healthcare and medicine. A lot of medical platforms allow people not only to receive detailed information about diseases but also to discuss their symptoms with other patients or doctors. Messages published in a medical Q&A platform present the unique source of information. Nevertheless, it is difficult to analyze this data because

© Springer Nature Switzerland AG 2020
X. Zhu et al. (Eds.): NLPCC 2020, LNAI 12431, pp. 490–497, 2020.
https://doi.org/10.1007/978-3-030-60457-8_40

user-generated content suffers from bias and noise. Consequently, there is a need for special instruments that allow to extract and process big data. Thus, the purpose of this research is to develop a computer program for resolving anaphora in Chinese and to implement it for analysis of user-generated content in medical Q&A platforms.

2 Related Work

The first attempts to resolve anaphora was rule-based [1, 17]. There are three kinds of major technical approaches to anaphora resolution: rule-based models [8], machine learning [13] and hybrid approach [19]. Some works are devoted to zero anaphora resolution in Chinese [19, 21]. In medical domain conducted studies about anaphora resolution mainly focus on the analysis of the health records [16] and scientific papers [10].

Peng et al. [15] propose a multi strategic model for anaphora resolution in texts extracted from a Chinese micro-blog. The model combing SVM and the set of linguistic characteristics for classification. Zhu et al. [23] describe that determining whether the noun phrases in a sentence are animate or inanimate improves the results of anaphora resolution. Authors develop the model using the bidirectional LSTM layer and the CRF structure. Converse [5] in a dissertation uses a rule-based approach based on the Hobbs algorithm and machine learning implemented by the maximum entropy method. Lin et al. analyze coreference and ellipsis resolution for creating a virtual patient dialogue system by rule-based methods [11] and BERT [12]. As a training data researches consider recorded conversations in the Hualien Tzu Chi Hospital.

Nevertheless, there is a lack of research examining the user-generated content in Chinese medical Q&A platforms. Our study seeks to contribute to filling this gap by implementing an anaphora resolution model to automatic analysis of user-generated content. The proposed approach could be applied in order to provide an early diagnosis to patients with hereditary diseases.

3 Methodology

In this work, machine learning methods are chosen to develop anaphora resolution models, therefore, the NeuralCoref scripts and pretrained BERT models are used as a basis. The NeuralCoref scripts have a multilayer perceptron architecture, while BERT is a pretrained neural network with Transformer architecture.

Pre-trained models made a breakthrough in NLP because these models such as BERT can be implemented for a broad range of tasks. In this study, experiments were conducted in BERT, Chinese-BERT-wwm, ALBERT, RoBERTa, SpanBERT. In comparison with ALBERT and RoBERTa, BERT shows the highest result. In the first experiment anaphora resolution is considered a classification task, therefore, we use BertTokenizer and BertForTokenClassification as an additional layer.

For the third experiment we use more a complicated architecture combining Chinese BERT-wwm and SpanBERT as an additional layer. SpanBERT extends BERT by masking contiguous random spans rather than random tokens [9]. Chinese BERT-wwm [6] was released by researchers from Harbin University of Technology. During its pretraining, the [MASK] tag closes not one token, as in the official model, but a whole word, which provides a better result.

BERT supposes character-based tokenizer for Chinese. This approach has drawbacks: the relative position of the symbol should be taken into account. However, this method is simple and quick to implement, since additional pre-processing are not needed. However, when using BERT, it is not possible to use a different tokenizer, because indexes (symbol numbers) and tensors will not be matched.

As a second experiment, the anaphora resolution model is configurated based on the NeuralCoref 4.0 scripts [18]. NeuralCoref is a pipeline extension for spaCy. The NeuralCoref model belongs to ranking models and is implemented based on the algorithm proposed by K. Clark and C. D. Manning [4]. The NeuralCoref model was created for English, therefore, in this study, a number of changes are made to apply it to Chinese. Training has three stages, at each different types of data pass through a multilayer perceptron. At the first stage *All pairs*, all possible pairs of mentions and their antecedents are generated. At the *Top pairs* stage, the most probable coreferential pairs or chains are formed based on the variables. Then the final stage is *Ranking*, at which the probability of coreference of each pair is estimated.

For tokenization, we choose Chinese text segmentation Jieba. Comparing with BERT, Jieba is a word-based tokenizer. It was found that the Jieba tokenizer works well with colloquial words, but it makes mistakes when dividing drug names into words, which can affect the quality of analysis of medical texts.

4   Datasets

In the case of anaphora resolution, the training data is the annotated corpus. There are a number of corpora with annotated coreference links such as OntoNotes, Chinese ACE 2004 and Chinese ACE 2005, Penn Chinese Treebank.

OntoNotes 5.0 [14] is the largest corpora with annotated coreference links. Moreover, the corpus includes various genres of texts, including those close to user-generated content. It should be noted that this corpus includes not only anaphora, but also coreference. For the NeuralCoref model the training corpus is created from OntoNotes 5.0 based on CoNLL 2012 scripts. The BERT model is also trained on the OntoNotes 5.0, but for this model we use JSON-files, not a conll-files as for the NeuralCoref model. Each line contains a sample for a token from UTF-8.

For training, we also use CLUEWSC2020 dataset [2]. It differs from an annotated corpus, it contains only antecedent, anaphor and sentences. This dataset allows conduct quick testing because of the small amount of data and a structure that is specially designed for anaphora resolution. Moreover, this dataset is considered to be up-to-date source as it was released in March 2020 for the NLPCC Shared Task. We convert the dataset into a convenient form. For this purpose, we use IO-markup (Inside Out). O is an outside tag, S1 is an antecedent, S2 is an anaphor.

5 Experimental Results

During the experiments, three models were developed: the BERT model trained on CLUEWSC2020, the NeuralCoref and BERT-Chinese-wwm + SpanBERT trained on the Chinese portion of OntoNotes 5.0.

5.1 BERT Model Trained on CLUEWSC2020

For fine tuning we choose the default parameters proposed by Devlin et al. [7] because they show high scores for the task of Named Entity Recognition in Chinese texts [20, 22]. The size of the batch is selected 64, the number of training epoch - 10. The main parameters of the model: 12 layers, 768 – size of hidden layer, 12 attention heads.

Through the test of the model, the final evaluation result is as follows (Table 1):

Table 1. Evaluation of the BERT model on CLUEWSC2020.

	Precision	Recall	F1-score
Anaphor	77%	90%	83%
Antecedent	38%	5%	9%

The model trained to determine the anaphor in the antecedent-anaphor pair, but it does not cope with the determination of antecedent. The quality of the model can be improved only by increasing the training sample so the OntoNotes 5.0 corpus [14] is used in the following experiments.

5.2 Multilayer Perceptron (NeuralCoref) Trained on OntoNotes 5.0

When visualizing the training of the model, it can be seen that the training process is conditionally divided into three parts: All pairs, Top pairs, Ranking. At each stage, a leap in quality occurs (Fig. 1).

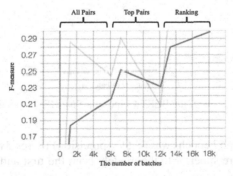

Fig. 1. The training process of the NeuralCoref model on OntoNotes 5.0.

The accuracy of the model is within 62–42% for the task of resolving coreference. In general, the model has trained to resolve coreference, but the quality could be improved (Table 2).

Table 2. Evaluation of the NeuralCoref model on OntoNotes 5.0.

MUC			B^3			CEAF			Avg. F1
P	R	F	P	R	F	P	R	F	
62%	30%	41%	54%	20%	30%	42%	18%	26%	32%

To improve the results, the Chinese model for SpaCy [3] could be retrained in order to create a vector representation of all tokens. It can be assumed that a change in hyperparameters and an increase in the number of epochs will also improve the quality.

5.3 BERT-Chinese + SpanBERT Model Trained on OntoNotes 5.0

For the third experiment we use more complicated architecture. The model type is defined as e2e-coref model. The basis of the model is BERT-wwm [6]. Other layers for a particular task are SpanBERT. SpanBERT, developed by Joshi et al. [9], showed the highest result in resolving coreference on OntoNotes for English [2]. However, this model has not been used previously for the Chinese language.

For BERT-Chinese + SpanBERT model training the values of hyperparameters are selected empirically. The main parameters are epoch number – 20, size of batch – 2800. The learning process is visualized by the F-measure (Fig. 2).

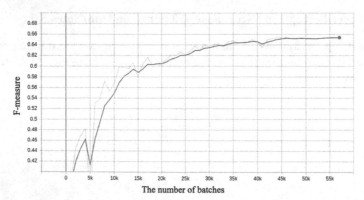

Fig. 2. The training process of the BERT-Chinese + SpanBERT model on OntoNotes 5.0.

The best result after 57 epochs was 68.5% (precision) for resolving coreference. The results of this model are superior to the models from the first and second experiments (Table 3).

Table 3. Evaluation of BERT-Chinese + SpanBERT model for Chinese on OntoNotes 5.0.

	Precision	Recall	Avg. F1
SpanBERT	68.5%	65.4%	65.4%

This model, as the NeuralCoref model, solves a broader task than was determined. Since the task of resolving coreference is more complicated, it can be assumed that the model will demonstrate a higher result if the filter of anaphoric pronouns is applied.

5.4 Main Results

The results of the models are presented in Table 4. The quality of the first model is not added to the general table, since it was trained and tested on another dataset.

Table 4. Comparison of the results of the created models: BERT-Chinese + SpanBERT and NeuralCoref on OntoNotes 5.0.

	Precision	Recall	Avg. F1
SpanBERT	**68.5%**	65.4%	65.4%
NeuralCoref	62.5%	30.6%	32.2%

In general, as the BERT-Chinese + SpanBERT achieves 68.5% on the OntoNotes 5.0 corpus, the results is quite high. Comparing with the results of the SpanBERT model for English, which shows an F-score of 79.6%, it is worth noting that the pretrained models for English perform better than for other languages. It can be assumed that experiments with hyperparameters and enlarged batch size will lead to a higher result.

6 Implementation for Analysis of User-Generated Content in a Medical Q&A Platform

Testing the BERT-Chinese + SpanBERT model, which showed the best result, is carried out on manually selected patient messages from the haodf.com medical platform. For testing, a program has been created that receives a number of sentences in the form of an array, feed the model, and gives a prediction in the form of clusters: pairs or chains. The genre of text could be chosen from those presented in OntoNotes. Working with user-generated content, the text type is configured as "wb" (web data).

It was found that animated anaphoric pronouns in user messages in medical services are used when mentioning the fact of kinship in several cases:

1) the user, describing his situation, writes that relatives have similar symptoms;
2) the user describes the medical history of his relative.

Inanimate anaphoric pronouns often refer to the name of the medicine, body parts, or physical manifestations.

Analyzing the results of the model, a problem was noticed: the model does not recognize words with English letters. It does not resolve an anaphor chain, where the antecedent is indicated by such words as X 光 检查 X 'x-ray' or ct 'computed tomography'. In addition to that, the model is sensitive to punctuation marks.

For full-scale testing of the, it is necessary to create an annotated corpus from user-generated content. Thus, the anaphora resolution model can be used to analyze the user content of medical platforms to extract the fact of kinship from the text in the diagnosis of hereditary diseases, to extract entities related to symptoms or medication.

7   Conclusion

This study may contribute to the body of knowledge on the automatic analysis of the Chinese language. Using the methods of NLP, three models for resolving the pro-noun anaphora in Chinese texts were developed in this study. Particularly, BERT, SpanBERT and NeuralCoref are used as a basis of models. OntoNotes 5.0 and CLUEWSC2020 dataset are selected for training. Among the models, BERT-Chinese + SpanBERT shows the highest accuracy – 68.5% on the OntoNotes 5.0 corpus. The model copes with a broader task: it solves not only anaphora, but also coreference. Moreover, the best performing model was tested in the messages from medical Q&A platfrom haodf.com. The features of user-generated content were highlighted.

The findings of this study are two-fold. Firstly, the research may advance the methods that can be implemented to the Chinese language considering its unique semantic, lexical and grammatical features. Secondly, the findings of this research may provide practical benefits for automatically analyzing clinical texts in Chinese in order to improve the healthcare services.

References

1. Bobrow, D.G.: A question-answering system for high school algebra word problems. In: Proceedings of AFIPS '64 (Fall, Part I), New York, pp. 591–614. Association for Computing Machinery (1964)
2. Chinese Language Understanding Evaluation Benchmark: datasets, baselines, pre-trained models, corpus and leaderboard. https://github.com/CLUEbenchmark/CLUE. Accessed 05 June 2020
3. Chinese models for SpaCy. https://github.com/howl-anderson/Chinese_models_for_SpaCy. Accessed 05 June 2020
4. Clark, K., Manning, C.D.: Deep reinforcement learning for mention-ranking coreference models. In: Proceedings of the 2016 Conference on Empirical Methods in Natural Language Processing, Austin, Texas, pp. 2256–2262. ACL (2016)
5. Converse, S.: Pronominal anaphora resolution in Chinese. Doctoral dissertation (2006)
6. Cui, Y., et al.: Revisiting pre-trained models for chinese natural language processing. arXiv preprint arXiv:2004.13922 (2020)
7. Devlin, J., Chang, M.-W., Lee, K., Toutanova, K.: BERT: pre-training of deep bidirectional transformers for language understanding (2018)

8. Dong, G., Zhu, Y., Cheng. X.: Research on personal pronoun anaphora resolution in Chinese. In: Application Research of Computers, pp. 1774–1779. China Academic Journal Electronic Publishing House (2011)
9. Joshi, M., et al.: SpanBERT: improving pre-training by representing and predicting spans. In: Transactions of the Association for Computational Linguistics, pp. 64–77. MIT Press (2020)
10. Kilicoglu, H., Demner-Fushman, D.: Coreference resolution for structured drug product labels. In: Proceedings of BioNLP 2014, Baltimore, pp. 45–53. Association for Computational Linguistics (2014)
11. Lin, C.-J, Pao, C.-W., Chen, Y.-H., Liu, C.-T. Ellipsis and coreference resolution in a computerized virtual patient dialogue systemJ. Med. Syst. **40**(9), 206 (2016). https://doi.org/10.1007/s10916-016-0562-x
12. Lin, C.-J., Huang, C.-H., Wu, C.-H.: Using BERT to process Chinese ellipsis and coreference in clinic dialogues. In: 2019 IEEE 20th International Conference on Information Reuse and Integration for Data Science (IRI), Los Angeles, CA, USA, pp. 414–418. IEEE (2019)
13. Ng, V.: Supervised noun phrase coreference research: the first fifteen years. In: Proceedings of the 48th Annual Meeting of the Association for Computational Linguistics, Association for Computational Linguistics, pp. 1396–1411 (2010)
14. OntoNotes Release 5.0. Linguistic Data Consortium. https://catalog.ldc.upenn.edu/LDC2013T19. Accessed 05 June 2020
15. Peng, Y., Zhang, Y., Huang, S., Chen, R., You, J.: Resolution of personal pronoun anaphora in Chinese micro-blog. In: Hong, J.-F., Su, Q., Wu, J.-S. (eds.) CLSW 2018. LNCS (LNAI), vol. 11173, pp. 592–605. Springer, Cham (2018). https://doi.org/10.1007/978-3-030-04015-4_51
16. Son, R.Y., Taira, R.K., Kangarloo, H.: Inter-document coreference resolution of abnormal findings in radiology documents. In: Proceedings of the 11th World Congress on Medical Informatics (MEDINFO). IOS Press, Amsterdam (2004)
17. Winograd, T.: Understanding Natural Language. Academic Press, New York (1972)
18. Wolf, T.: State-of-the-art neural coreference resolution for chatbots. https://medium.com/huggingface/state-of-the-art-neural-coreference-resolution-for-chatbots-3302365dcf30#7f43. Accessed 05 June 2020
19. Wu, D.S., Liang, T.: Zero anaphora resolution by case-based reasoning and pattern conceptualization. Expert Syst. Appl. **36**(4), 7544–7551 (2009)
20. Xue, K., et al.: Fine-tuning BERT for joint entity and relation extraction in Chinese medical text. In: 2019 International Conference on Bioinformatics and Biomedicine (BIBM), pp. 892–897. IEEE (2019)
21. Yin, Q., Zhang, W., Zhang, Y., Liu, T.: Chinese zero pronoun resolution: a collaborative filtering-based approach. ACM Trans. Asian Low Resour. Lang. **19**(1), 1–20 (2020)
22. Zhang, K., Liu, C., Duan, X., Zhou, L., Zhao, Y., Zan, H.: BERT with enhanced layer for assistant diagnosis based on Chinese obstetric EMRs. In: 2019 International Conference on Asian Language Processing (IALP), Shanghai, Singapore, pp. 384–389. IEEE (2019)
23. Zhu, Y., Song, W., Liu, X., Liu, L., Zhao, X.: Improving anaphora resolution by animacy identification, Dalian, pp. 48–51. IEEE (2019)

Evaluation Workshop

Weighted Pre-trained Language Models for Multi-Aspect-Based Multi-Sentiment Analysis

Fengqing Zhou, Jinhui Zhang, Tao Peng, Liang Yang$^{(\boxtimes)}$, and Hongfei Lin

School of Computer Science and Technology, Dalian University of Technology,
Dalian 116024, Liaoning Province, China
{zhoufengqing,wszjh,taop}@mail.dlut.edu.cn
{liang,hflin}@dlut.edu.cn

Abstract. In recent years, aspect-based sentiment analysis has attracted the attention of many researchers with its wide range of application scenarios. Existing methods for fine-grained sentiment analysis usually explicitly model the relations between aspects and contexts. In this paper, we tackle the task as sentence pair classification. We build our model based on pre-trained language models (LM) due to their strong ability in modeling semantic information. Besides, in order to further enhance the performance, we apply weighted voting strategy to combine the multiple results of different models in a heuristic way. We participated in NLPCC-2020 shared task on Multi-Aspect-based Multi-Sentiment Analysis (MAMS) and won the first place in terms of two sub-tasks, indicating the effectiveness of the approaches adopted.

Keywords: Aspect-based sentence analysis · Multi-Aspect-based Multi-Sentiment Analysis · Pre-trained language model

1 Introduction

Sentiment analysis is a typical task in natural language processing. Aspect-based sentiment analysis (ABSA), as a fine-grained sentiment analysis, has drawn many researchers' attention. The target of ABSA is to identify the sentiment polarity of the specific aspect with the context, which has widely applications, such as analyzing product reviews [1], detecting public opinion on social media [2] and so on. Here is an example, "The food is pretty good but the service is horrific.". The sentiment polarity of two aspect terms "food" and "service" are positive and negative respectively.

Existing methods to address the task of ABSA are usually explicitly model the relations between aspect and context using deep learning models [3–5]. Besides, some works focus on constructing multi-task framework to jointly tackle

---

F. Zhou and L. Yang—Both authors contributed equally to this paper.

X. Zhu et al. (Eds.): NLPCC 2020, LNAI 12431, pp. 501–511, 2020.
https://doi.org/10.1007/978-3-030-60457-8_41

the aspect extraction and polarity classification [6,7]. With the rapid development of pre-trained LMs (BERT [8], ERNIE [9], XLnet [10] etc.), which are obtained from large scale of unlabelled data, researchers can apply fine-tuning on these models to satisfy the different targets with various tasks. Pre-trained LMs also show promising performance on the task of ABSA [11–13], hence, we introduce pre-trained LMs into our system.

There are several public accessible datasets for ABSA, including SemEval-2014 Restaurant Review dataset, Laptop Review dataset [1] and Twitter dataset [2]. The above three datasets have become the benchmark datesets for ABSA recently, but the sentences of which usually contain only one aspect term or multiply aspect terms with the same sentiment polarity. In 2019, Jiang et al. [14] build a more challenging dataset named MAMS (Multi-Aspect-based Multi-Sentiment Analysis), where each sentence contains at least two aspects with different sentiment polarities. In details, MAMS consists of two sub-tasks: aspect-term sentiment analysis (ATSA) and aspect-category sentiment analysis (ACSA).

Our system tackle the MAMS (a challenging dataset for ABSA) as a sentence pair classification, using pre-trained language models as our feature extractor. Moreover, Bidirectional GRU (Bi-GRU) is connected to the last hidden layer of pre-trained LMs to enhance the representation of aspects and contexts. Finally, we apply weighted voting strategy to integrate outputs of models with different architectures and training steps, which can further improve the accuracy for the classification. Therefore, our contributions are summarized as follows:

- Based on pre-trained LMs, we optimize the model architecture to be suitable for the task of MAMS.
- We adopt a heuristic weighted voting strategy to combine the results of multiple models to further improve the performance on the MAMS task.
- The official evaluation results show that our system achieves the best performance (1/17) in terms of "ATSA" and "ACSA" sub-tasks, which indicates the effectiveness of our method[1].

2   Related Work

Since end-to-end framework can extract hidden features automatically, Neural network based models are becoming the mainstream approach to study the task of ABSA. Tang et al. [3] design two elaborate models, Target-Dependent LSTM and Target-Connection LSTM model, to obtain better sentence representation for specific aspect. Ma et al. [4] propose Interactive Attention Network (IAN) to interactively learn the attention weights between aspects and contexts, then generate better representations. Xue et al. [5] use convolutional neural networks and gating mechanisms to extract aspect related sentiment features.

Neural network based model are the dominant approach on the task of ABSA until BERT is proposed. BERT, as a typical pre-trained LM, has obtained state-of-the-art results on eleven NLP tasks. Pre-trained LM based models have show

---

[1] Code: https://github.com/BaiDing213/NLPCC2020-MAMS.

the promising performance in many NLP tasks, so as the ABSA. Li et al. [11] apply BERT to generate contextualized embedding and feed them into the end-to-end neural model, achieving competitive results. Sun et al. [12] regard the aspect term as an auxiliary sentence, forming sentence pair together with the context, then put the sentence pair into BERT to train a classification model. Xu et al. [13] adopt post-training on BERT to enhance both domain and task knowledge and prove that the approach of post-training before fine-tuning is effective. Wang et al. [15] define a unified aspect-oriented dependency tree structure and use relational graph attention network (R-GAT) to better encode the syntax information of new tree structure for sentiment prediction. Tang et al. [16] propose a dependency graph enhanced dual-transformer network which contains flat representations and graph-based representations learnt from Transformer and the corresponding dependency graph respectively. The two modules are interactively integrated and the model obtains SOTA results on five public datasets.

With the development of computing power and the large-scale available corpora, in addition to BERT, more and more variants of pre-trained LMs are proposed, constantly improving the performance on many NLP tasks. For example, XLnet [10] is a type of permutation language model, which solves the problem of auto-regressive model that can not model bidirectional information. Roberta [17] takes dynamic masking and removes the task of next sentence prediction. ERNIE [9] adopts knowledge masking strategies and continual pre-training to imitate the learning process of humans. Albert [18] introduces sentence order prediction to optimize training process and factorizes embedding parameterization to reduce the scale of the model.

3 Proposed System

The architecture of our system is shown in Fig. 1. Firstly, we regard the aspect term or category as an auxiliary sentence by following the work of Sun et al. [12]. Then, the constructed sentence pairs are fed into the pre-trained LM based model. Finally, predicting results are generated by the weighted voting strategy. Details will be described as follow.

3.1 Problem Definition

Given a sentence $s = \{w_1, w_2, \cdots, w_n\}$, and an aspect term $a_{ij}^k = \{w_i, w_{i+1}, \cdots, w_j\}$, we aim to predict the sentiment polarity of a_{ij}^k depending on the context. a_{ij}^k is a sub-sequence of s or pre-defined aspect category, and k is higher than 2, which indicates that a sentence contains at least two aspect terms or categories. The sentiment polarity of aspect term or category is among positive, negative and neutral. Obviously, it's a task of classification of three categories.

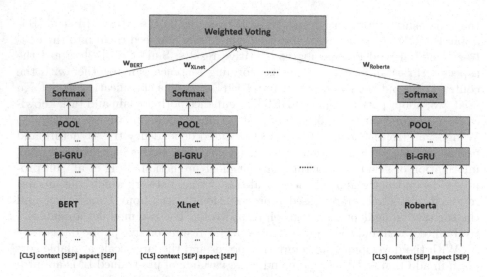

Fig. 1. Overall architecture of our system

3.2   Pre-trained LM Based Model

After defining the problem, we regard ABSA as a task of sentence pair classification. Our work is mainly based on the popular pre-trained LMs. Here, we
take BERT for example. We concatenate context and aspect as $\{[CLS]\ s\ [SEP]\ a_{ij}^k\}$, where $[CLS]$ is a token for classification and $[SEP]$ is another token for
separating different sentences.

BERT can directly follow by a dense layer on the $[CLS]$ token to fine-tune
the sentence pair classification. But in here, we feed the output of the last hidden
layer of BERT into Bi-GRU, aiming to get a higher level representation of context
and aspect pair.

$$H^k = BERT(s, a^k) \tag{1}$$

$$S^k = Bi\text{-}GRU(H^k) \tag{2}$$

The dimension of H^k and S^K are $(batch\_size, seq\_len, hidden\_dim_{BERT})$ and
$(batch\_size, seq\_len, 2 \times hidden\_dim_{Bi-GRU})$. We use max-pooling strategy and
average-pooling strategy to capture distinct and overall features respectively.

$$\begin{aligned} h_{max}^k &= MaxPool(S^k) \\ h_{avg}^k &= AvgPool(S^k) \end{aligned} \tag{3}$$

The dimension of h_{max}^k and h_{avg}^k are $(batch\_size, 2 \times hidden\_dim_{Bi-GRU})$.
Then h_{max}^k and h_{avg}^k are concatenated together and fed into a dense layer followed
by a softmax layer to perform final predictions.

$$prob^k = Softmax(Dense([h_{max}^k : h_{avg}^k])) \tag{4}$$

Finally, the training loss of classification is obtained by the cross entropy between predicted probability $prob^k$ and ground truth label $label^k$.

$$Loss = -\sum label^k log(prob^k) \tag{5}$$

3.3   Voting Strategy

We use weighted voting strategy to combine the outputs of different models. The weight of specific model depends on the performance on the validation set or is given heuristically. The maximum of the weighted sum indicates the final predicted label.

4   Experiments and Details

4.1   Dataset

Experiments are conducted on a challenging dataset named MAMS [14], which contains two sub-tasks: aspect term sentiment analysis (ATSA) and aspect category sentiment analysis (ACSA). Aspect terms usually appear in the context, and we aim to predict the reviewer's sentiment polarities towards them. Aspect categories is predefined by the MAMS task, and the categories includes "food", "service", "staff", "price" etc. Meanwhile, sometimes aspect categories may not directly appear in the context, which make the task of ACSA more challenging. The detailed statistics of dataset can be found in Table 1.

Table 1. Statistics of MAMS dataset

	Train	Validation	Test
ATSA	11186	3668	3608
ACSA	7090	1789	3713

4.2   Implement Details

We try two neural network based models (LSTM + attention and TD-LSTM [3]) and five different types of pre-trained LMs, including Bert, ALBert, RoBERTa, Xlnet and ERNIE. We construct pretrained LM based models following the description in part 3.2. The models related to ERNIE are constructed by the deep learning framework of paddlepaddle[2], while other models are based on the lib of transformers presented by huggingface[3]. The batch size is set to 4. We use Adam optimizer [19] to train our models. The learning rate is 1e−5. The hidden

---

[2] https://www.paddlepaddle.org.cn.
[3] https://github.com/huggingface/transformers.

Table 2. The macro-f1 score of different models on validation set

Model	ATSA	ACSA
lstm+attention	64.19	68.28
td-lstm	64.95	65.06
ernie-base	83.67	82.80
ernie-large	84.06	**83.21**
bert-base	83.15	80.45
bert-large	83.26	81.53
albert-base	83.02	78.73
xlent-large	83.67	81.11
roberta-large	**84.18**	82.01

dimension of Bi-GRU is 256. We tune the hyper-parameters for all baselines on the validation set.

Besides, We choose different architecture of pre-trained models due to their performance on the validation set (albert-base, bert-base, bert-large, roberta-large, xlnet-large, ernie-base, ernie-large). Each model is fine-tuned on the train set separately, then we save the middle state of each model which gains the best result on the validation set. Specially, ERNIE-related models generally outperform other models, so we save the best two middle states. That is to say, we save an extra middle state for ERNIE-related models.

In the voting stage, the weights of ERNIE-unrelated models are set to 1 and the weights of ERNIE-related models are given heuristically depending on the performance on the validation set.

4.3   Results and Analysis

Table 2 shows the results of different models on the validation set. From the table, we can see that the performance of the models based on neural network is much lower than that of pre-trained LM based model in both tasks, so our system does not adopt the method based on neural network. Besides, the performance of ERNIE-related models are better than other pre-trained language models on both ATSA and ACSA. Especially on the task of ACSA, the f1-score of ernie-large model is at least 1% higher than other ERNIE-unrelated models. The reason can be attributed that word-awared tasks are important parts in the pre-training stage of ERNIE, which helps to capture semantic relationships more accurately. Besides, ERNIE-related models also obtain competitive results in the task of ATSA, indicating that ERNIE can better model the relationships between aspect terms or categories and contexts.

In the voting stage, we integrate the outputs of different models with various strategies and results are shown in Table 3.

Due to more knowledge obtained from various corpora, it's obvious to find that the performance of integrated models are better than single models. We save

Table 3. Results of different voting strategies on validation set

voting strategy	model	ernie-avg	ernie-wtd	other-avg	mixed
weight	bert-base	–	–	1	1
	bert-large	–	–	1	1
	albert-base	–	–	1	1
	xlnet-bert	–	–	1	1
	roberta-large	–	–	1	1
	ernie-base-1	1	1.01	–	1.01
	ernie-base-2	1	1.02	–	1.02
	ernie-large-1	1	1.11	–	1.11
	ernie-large-2	1	2.13	–	2.13
voting results	ATSA	84.81	84.92	85.41	**85.61**
	ACSA	83.93	84.01	82.72	**84.59**

best two middle state of ERNIE-related models for their better performance in single model evaluation. As presented in Table 3, we integrate ERNIE-related models with same weight (ernie-avg) and different weights (ernie-wtd). Higher weight means that the model obtains better result on the validation set or the scale of model is larger. The performance of different weights is better than that of same weight as expected. Combined with the results of ERNIE-unrelated models, the overall performance is further improved on both ATSA and ACST tasks.

In the test stage, we merge train set and validation set to a larger dateset, aiming to train a more generalized ERNIE-related model. Based on this larger dateset, we only fine-tune the ERNIE-related model due to their better performance in both single model and integrated model. Obviously, we have no access to "validation set" to evaluate the best middle states of the model. Hence, we save the middle states at the same step where the ERNIE-related model obtain the best performance on the original validation set. Likewise, we save the best two middle states for each ERNIE-related model and follow the previous voting strategy.

Table 4. Weights for different models on test set

Model & weight	bert base/large	albert-base	xlnet-base	roberta-large
	1	1	1	1
	ernie-base-1	ernie-base-2	ernie-large-1	ernie-large-2
	1.01	1.02	1.11	2.13
	-base- merge-1	-base- merge-2	-large- merge-1	-large- merge-2
	1.06	1.07	1.16	2.18
Result	ATSA: 84.38 ACSA: 80.47			

As shown in Table 4, according to the analysis mentioned above, we conduct weighted voting strategy to combine all the outputs of different models. The weights of ERNIE-unrelated models are all set to 1, and weights of ERNIE-related are higher, which is given in a heuristic way. The official evaluation results show that we achieve the macro-f1 score of 84.38% and 80.47% on ATSA and ACSA respectively. The average macro-f1 score is 82.42%, and we won the first place among all the participants of NLPCC 2020 Shared Task 2 (Multi-Aspect-based Multi-Sentiment Analysis).

The decline of macro-f1 score in ACSA (84.59% → 80.47%) on test set is more obviously than that of ATSA (85.61% → 84.38%) compared to the results on validation set. The reasons may be as follows:

① Some aspect categories do not directly appear in the contexts, which indicates that models need to implicitly build the connections between entities and aspect categories;

② The scale of train set for ACSA is relatively small compared with ATSA, while the number of test examples is quite close as shown in Table 1;

③ The assumption that larger dataset makes the model more generalized might not be applicable to ACSA, and the step with saving the middle states for larger dataset might not be optimal for ACSA.

4.4 Case Study

To explore the advantages and disadvantages of our proposed model, some cases from validation set are listed for analyzing the reasons why the macro-f1 score drop sharply on the task of ACSA, and corresponding prediction results with different voting strategies as shown in Table 5.

Case 1: Applying ernie-avg strategy leads to a wrong prediction, while using ernie-wtd strategy, where strong model has higher weight, then the voting result is correct.

Case 2: It's a relative simple example, where the sentiment word "bad" is unrelated to the waiter, and thus most strategies are correct.

Case 3: The sentence contains a misspelling, where the word "aweful" should be "awful", which leads all models to make a wrong prediction. Maybe careful pre-processing will solve this kind of bad case to a large degree.

Case 4: All strategies make wrong predictions in this case. Only focusing the word "refused" will lead to a negative polarity towards the staff (chef), while the overall sentence are expressing the carefulness of the chef.

Case 5 & 6: These two cases share the same context but with different aspect categories. All strategies predict positive polarities. While the ground truth labels are neutral and positive for "staff" and "service" respectively. The latter is reasonable for the context explicitly contains the positive phrase "great service", while the former is kind of ambiguous in a way. When the service is great, reviewer will be satisfied with the staff who provide service. In the task of ACSA, the boundaries between some aspect categories are not so clear, which makes it a more challenging task.

Table 5. Some examples and outputs of different strategies. "P", "N" and "M" denote sentiment polarities of "positive", "negative" and "neutral" respectively. Green letters indicate that the strategy make correct predictions and red letters indicate wrong predictions.

#	context sentence	aspect	-avg	-wtd	other -avg	mixed	label
1	It's not going to win any awards for its decor, but the food is good, the portions are big, and the prices are low	prices	N	P	P	P	P
2	I told the waiter that my drink tasted very bad and asked if he could swap it out for a Petron Margarita	waiter	M	M	N	M	M
3	I went there for a late dinner last night with a friend and the service was aweful	service	P	P	P	P	N
4	It's a joy to watch the chef work, who refused to take my order but seeing him open my live scallop made me understand why	staff	N	N	N	N	P
5	Also, when i was waiting to be seated the bartender gave great service and mixed a mean cocktail for me	staff	P	P	P	P	M
6	Also, when i was waiting to be seated the bartender gave great service and mixed a mean cocktail for me	service	P	P	P	P	P

5   Conclusion

In this paper, based on the pre-trained LMs, we build our system for the task of MAMS, and weighted voting strategy is adopted to merge the outputs of different models together. Official evaluation results of NLPCC 2020 shared task 2 shows that our system yields the best performance in 17 participants, which proves the effectiveness of our work.

From the analysis in case study, we can infer that MAMS, as a fine-grained sentiment analysis, needs more semantic knowledge, or syntactic structure information to better capture the accurate relationships between aspects and contexts. Therefore, in the future, knowledge base and graph neural network combined with syntactic dependency analysis will be explore on this task.

Acknowledgements. This work is supported by a grant from the National Key Research and Development Program of China (No. 2018YFC0832101), the Natural

Science Foundation of China (No. 61702080, 61632011, 61806038, 61976036), the Fundamental Research Funds for the Central Universities (No. DUT19RC(4)016), and Postdoctoral Science Foundation of China (2018M631788).

References

1. Pontiki, M., et al.: SemEval-2016 task 5: aspect based sentiment analysis. In: 10th International Workshop on Semantic Evaluation (SemEval 2016) (2016)
2. Dong, L., Wei, F., Tan, C., Tang, D., Zhou, M., Xu, K.: Adaptive recursive neural network for target-dependent Twitter sentiment classification. In: Proceedings of the 52nd Annual Meeting of the Association for Computational Linguistics (Volume 2: Short Papers), pp. 49–54 (2014)
3. Tang, D., Qin, B., Feng, X., Liu, T.: Effective LSTMs for target-dependent sentiment classification. In: Proceedings of the 26th International Conference on Computational Linguistics: Technical Papers, pp. 3298–3307 (2016)
4. Ma, D., Li, S., Zhang, X., Wang, H.: Interactive attention networks for aspect-level sentiment classification. In: Proceedings of the 26th International Joint Conference on Artificial Intelligence, pp. 4068–4074 (2017)
5. Xue, W., Li, T.: Aspect based sentiment analysis with gated convolutional networks. In: Proceedings of the 56th Annual Meeting of the Association for Computational Linguistics (Volume 1: Long Papers), pp. 2514–2523 (2018)
6. Xue, W., Zhou, W., Li, T., Wang, Q.: MTNA: a neural multi-task model for aspect category classification and aspect term extraction on restaurant reviews. In: Proceedings of the Eighth International Joint Conference on Natural Language Processing (Volume 2: Short Papers), pp. 151–156 (2017)
7. He, R., Lee, W.S., Ng, H.T., Dahlmeier, D.: An interactive multi-task learning network for end-to-end aspect-based sentiment analysis. In: Proceedings of the 57th Annual Meeting of the Association for Computational Linguistics, pp. 504–515 (2019)
8. Devlin, J., Chang, M., Lee, K., Toutanova, K.: BERT: pre-training of deep bidirectional transformers for language understanding. In: Proceedings of the 2019 Conference of the North American Chapter of the Association for Computational Linguistics: Human Language Technologies, pp. 4171–4186 (2019)
9. Sun, Y., et al.: Ernie 2.0: a continual pre-training framework for language understanding. arXiv preprint arXiv:1907.12412 (2019)
10. Yang, Z., Dai, Z., Yang, Y., Carbonell, J.G., Salakhutdinov, R., Le, Q.V.: XLNet: generalized autoregressive pretraining for language understanding. In: Advances in Neural Information Processing Systems 32: Annual Conference on Neural Information Processing Systems 2019, pp. 5754–5764 (2019)
11. Li, X., Bing, L., Zhang, W., Lam, W.: Exploiting BERT for end-to-end aspect-based sentiment analysis. arXiv preprint arXiv:1910.00883 (2019)
12. Sun, C., Huang, L., Qiu, X.: Utilizing BERT for aspect-based sentiment analysis via constructing auxiliary sentence. In: Proceedings of the 2019 Conference of the North American Chapter of the Association for Computational Linguistics: Human Language Technologies, pp. 380–385 (2019)
13. Xu, H., Liu, B., Shu, L., Yu, P.S.: Bert post-training for review reading comprehension and aspect-based sentiment analysis. arXiv preprint arXiv:1904.02232 (2019)
14. Jiang, Q., Chen, L., Xu, R., Ao, X., Yang, M.: A challenge dataset and effective models for aspect-based sentiment analysis. In: EMNLP-IJCNLP, pp. 6281–6286 (2019)

15. Wang, K., Shen, W., Yang, Y., Quan, X., Wang, R.: Relational graph attention network for aspect-based sentiment analysis. arXiv preprint arXiv:2004.12362 (2020)
16. Tang, H., Ji, D., Li, C., Zhou, Q.: Dependency graph enhanced dual-transformer structure for aspect-based sentiment classification. In: Proceedings of the 58th Annual Meeting of the Association for Computational Linguistics, pp. 6578–6588 (2020)
17. Liu, Y., et al.: Roberta: a robustly optimized BERT pretraining approach. arXiv preprint arXiv:1907.11692 (2019)
18. Lan, Z., Chen, M., Goodman, S., Gimpel, K., Sharma, P., Soricut, R.: Albert: a lite BERT for self-supervised learning of language representations. arXiv preprint arXiv:1909.11942 (2019)
19. Kingma, D.P., Ba, J.: Adam: a method for stochastic optimization. arXiv preprint arXiv:1412.6980 (2014)

Iterative Strategy for Named Entity Recognition with Imperfect Annotations

Huimin Xu, Yunian Chen, Jian Sun, Xuezhi Cao, and Rui Xie[✉]

Meituan-Dianping Group, Shanghai, China
{xuhuimin04,chenyunian,sunjian20,caoxuezhi,rui.xie}@meituan.com

Abstract. Named entity recognition (NER) systems have been widely researched and applied for decades. Most NER systems rely on high quality annotations, but in some specific domains, annotated data is usually imperfect, typically including incomplete annotations and non-annotations. Although related studies have achieved good results on specific types of annotations, to build a more robust NER system, it is necessary to consider complex scenarios that simultaneously contain complete annotations, incomplete annotations, non-annotations, etc. In this paper, we propose a novel NER system, which could use different strategies to process different types of annotations, rather than simply adopts the same strategy. Specifically, we perform multiple iterations. In each iteration, we first train the model based on incomplete annotations, and then use the model to re-annotate imperfect annotations and update their weights, which could generate and filter out high quality annotations. In addition, we fine-tune models through high quality annotations and its augmentations, and finally integrate multiple models to generate reliable prediction results. Comprehensive experiments are conducted to demonstrate the effectiveness of our system. Moreover, the system is ranked first and second respectively in two leaderboards of NLPCC 2020 Shared Task: Auto Information Extraction (https://github.com/ZhuiyiTechnology/AutoIE).

Keywords: NER · Imperfect annotations · Iterative strategy

1 Introduction

NER is one of the most important tasks in natural language processing (NLP). NER systems can identify named entities like person, TV, location, organization, etc. in texts, which can be applied to other NLP tasks, including information extraction, question answering, information retrieval, etc. Most NER algorithms focus on supervised learning approaches, which rely on high quality annotated corpus. However, high quality annotated data with ground-truth is usually difficult to obtain for some specific domains due to their complexities, such as word sense disambiguation, grammatical, professional word, or even typos.

In a real business scenario, There may be complete annotations and incomplete annotations, and non-annotations in a corpus. We refer to the latter two

© Springer Nature Switzerland AG 2020
X. Zhu et al. (Eds.): NLPCC 2020, LNAI 12431, pp. 512–523, 2020.
https://doi.org/10.1007/978-3-030-60457-8_42

types of annotations as imperfect annotations in this paper. **Complete annotations** represent the sequences that are verified and labeled completely correct. **Incomplete annotations** represent that sequences are labeled, but there may be missing or error caused by manual annotation or supervision. **Non-annotations** are sequences without any labels, which may be newly generated and not annotated yet, or really have no entities. Figure 1 shows an example sequence with three annotations.

	雪	山	飞	狐	金	庸	武	侠	剧
Complete annotations	B-TV	I-TV	I-TV	E-TV	B-PER	E-PER	O	O	O
Incomplete annotations	O	O	O	O	B-PER	E-PER	O	O	O
Non-annotations	O	O	O	O	O	O	O	O	O

Fig. 1. Examples of different annotations.

There is a lot of literature studying these annotations. For complete annotations, previous works focus on feature-engineered supervised systems and feature-inferring neural network systems [29]. The former systems focus on extracting features that have a good ability to distinguish entities [17,20,21], while the latter systems can automatically infer useful features for entity classification by using deep learning models [3,12,18]. For incomplete annotations, some works focus on modifying the model structure to learn from inexpensive partially annotated sequences [7,19], while the other work focuses on using iterative training strategy to relabel entities and update their weights, to improve weights of the high quality labeled entities and reduce weights of the unlabeled or mislabeled entities in a sequence [13]. For non-annotations, previous work focus on rule-based systems and unsupervised systems [16]. The former systems rely on lexicon resources and domain-specific knowledge [9,14], while the latter systems use lexical resources, lexical patterns, and statistics computed on a large corpus to infer mentions of named entities [4,31]. Although these works have achieved satisfactory results for a specific type of annotations, to our best knowledge, few papers have taken into account the differences between different types of annotations.

Different annotations cannot be simply processed by the same strategy. Using complete annotations can help NER algorithms quickly learn a high available model, while identifying and using incomplete annotations and non-annotations could help NER algorithms improve fault tolerance and cover more entity types, thereby improving the generalization of the algorithm. In order to work better in a real business environment, it is necessary to be able to process various annotations flexibly in a NER task. Thus, how to build a flexible and high accurate NER system based on various and complex annotations is the focus of this paper.

In this paper, we use iterative strategy to build robust models and propose flexible and efficient strategies to deal with different types of annotations.

We first use complete and incomplete annotations to train a base model. During the training process of each iteration, the base model will be used to relabel incomplete annotations and non-annotations, and then we could generate and filter out high confidence annotations for the next iteration. In addition, we use high quality annotations and its augmentations to fine-tune the base model to achieve higher performance. Finally, with ensembles of different models, we could build a more reliable system.

Comprehensive experiments are conducted to demonstrate the effectiveness of our system. We evaluate and verify the system on a complex corpus released by NLPCC 2020 Shared Task: Auto Information Extraction. The experimental results show that our system can effectively deal with different types of annotations and won first and second place respectively in two leaderboards of the NLPCC 2020 competition.

The rest of this paper is organized as follows: Sect. 2 introduces the related work. We describe our algorithm in Sect. 3. Sect. 4 shows the experimental results and analysis. Finally, we conclude this paper in Sect. 5.

2   Related Work

For NER task, HMM [23], MEMN [2] and CRF [15] are some traditional methods. Recently, neural network based embedding layers and conditional random fields (CRF) are often used in end-to-end model. Embedding layer can extract features of sentences. For example, word2vec [22], ELMo [26], BERT [6], Bidirectional LSTM (BiLSTM) and convolutional neural network (CNN) based models are used to obtain character-level or word-level representations. CRF often in the last layer of a model, can learn label constraints, such as tag "E" appears after tag "B" in "BIOE" annotation system.

Many researchers study the NER task with fully annotated data, however, obtaining a fully annotated dataset is expensive. Most of data is incomplete. The entity is not correctly labeled, but wrongly labeled as "O" which will disturb the training process. Some previous works [1,7] try to make assumptions on the data with "O" labels. However, there also are partly annotated entities or words with "O" labels in their assumptions which is unrealistic. Thus, Jie etc. [13] propose to regard the missing labels as latent variables and using classifier stacking technique to model them. Latent-variable CRF is also utilized in Chinese NER which is explored by Yang etc. [30] and in a biomedical NER task by Greenberg etc. [8].

Distant supervision is also a popular method in an incomplete annotation scenario, which can generate amounts of labeled data for new entities automatically. It assumes that if a string appears in a predefined entity dictionary, the string is likely to be an entity. Yang etc. [30] propose a distantly supervised approach to address both incomplete annotation problem and noisy annotation problem. Peng etc. [25] formulate the NER task with only unlabeled data and named entity dictionaries as a positive-unlabeled (PU) learning problem. Their model is also distantly supervised.

Other models like large margin learning framework [1], a modified structured perceptron framework [7,19] and CrossWeight [28] try to solve incomplete annotation problem from model structure aspect or data cleaning aspect. Some works [24,27] also study weakly supervised methods, but these methods usually perform worse on specific language or it's difficult to implement in a real-world scenario.

In addition, to combining multiple advantages in these works, we also consider some other aspects which can make our model perform better. Firstly, we design a more robust base model and propose an effective iterative strategy on an extremely incomplete dataset (only 30% entity labels appear in training data); secondly, we propose a data augmentation method to automatically generate more samples; Finally, we obtain more reliable prediction by integrating multiple model results.

3   Approach

We propose a novel and scalable system to deal with different types of annotations flexibly according to the characteristics of data. The system consists of three main modules, i.e., base model, iterative strategy and data augmentation, as shown in Fig. 2. Base model is a classic NER framework, including word representation layer, contextual embedding layer and output layer. Then, we propose an iterative strategy to reconstruct imperfect annotations. Finally, a specific data augmentation method is used to expand high quality annotated corpus. Next, we give a detailed description.

3.1   Base Model

Word Representation Layer. Given a word sequence $x = \{x_1, x_2, \cdots, x_t\}$ whose label sequence is $y = \{y_1, y_2, \cdots, y_t\}$, $y_i \in [B, I, E, O]$. First, we map each word in the sequence to a high-dimensional vector space. Because the pre-trained language model (e.g., Bidirectional Encoder Representations from Transformers, BERT [6]) has shown marvelous improvements across various NLP tasks, we adopt Chinese BERT to encode word sequences to word embeddings.

In addition, word segmentation and part-of-speech (POS) tagging are useful for Chinese NER. Therefore, we utilize HanLP [10] to divide the sequence into words and tag the POS of each character. For each character, word embeddings generated by Chinese BERT [5] and POS embeddings are concatenated as final word embeddings $w = \{w_1, w_2, \cdots, w_t\}$.

Contextual Embedding Layer. Long-Short Term Memory (LSTM) Neural Network [11] addresses the vanishing gradient problems and is capable of modeling long-term contextual information along the sequence. BiLSTM captures the context from both past and future time steps jointly while vanilla LSTM only considers the contextual information from the past. So, we use BiLSTM to get hidden states as contextual representation of word sequences $H = \{h_1, h_2, \cdots, h_t\}$.

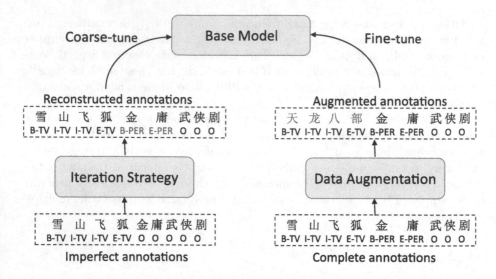

Fig. 2. Architecture of the base model.

Output Layer. The goal of base model is to predict a label sequence that marks the positions of entities. CRF is often used in the sequence tagging model because it captures dependency between the output tags in a neighborhood. During this training, the loss function is formalized as below.

$$\jmath = \sum_{i=1}^{n} l(CRF(H^{(i)}), y^{(i)})$$

where $l(CRF(H^{(i)}), y^{(i)})$ is the negative log-likelihood of the model's prediction $CRF(H^{(i)})$ compared to label sequence $y^{(i)}$.

3.2 Training Process

High quality annotated corpus is very valuable and difficult to obtain, especially in some specific fields, such as finance, mother-infant, healthcare, etc. Most of imperfect annotations suffer from low accuracy, and the performance of the model will be affected when using them directly. Therefore, we propose an iterative strategy and data augmentation method to improve the diversity of data and enrich the entities information.

Iterative Strategy. Since there are lots of unlabeled entities in imperfect annotations that seriously damage the performance, we propose an iterative strategy to reconstruct them to contain more entity information.

Algorithm 1 shows the iterative strategy of reconstructing imperfect annotations. Firstly, considering the imbalanced credibility of labels, we assign different weights W to each character of each sample. Specifically, the weight of each label of the complete annotations is 1, the weight of the "O" labels in imperfect annotations are 0.6, and the rest are 0.95.

Then, we use incomplete annotations to train the model, and the number of epochs increases with the number of iterations. This is because we find that the precision of the first few epochs of the model is relatively high, the recall is slightly low, so we can obtain reconstructed annotations with high confidence.

Finally, the trained model is used to predict imperfect annotations. According to the prediction results, imperfect annotations are relabeled and the weights of labels are reset to the predicted confidences. In order to ensure the accuracy of relabeling, we only relabel the positions which meet the following requirements:

- The original label is "O";
- The predicted labels are complete entity;
- The confidence of the predicted labels is greater than 0.7.

In addition, in order to avoid the error accumulation of relabeling, reset the model's parameters before each iteration. After K iterations, we obtain the reconstructed annotations.

Algorithm 1. Iterative Strategy.

Input: K: number of Iterations; W: weights of samples; M: base model; D_{ic}: incomplete annotations; D_{non}: non-annotations.
Output: D_{re}: reconstructed annotations.
1: Save initial parameters of model M as M_{init};
2: Set weights W to each sample;
3: **for** $k = 1 \rightarrow K$ **do**
4:     Reset the parameters of the model M to M_{init};
5:     Train model M with D_{ic} for k epochs, get model M_k;
6:     Use model M_k to predict the D_{ic} and D_{non};
7:     Update the weights W and relabel D_{ic} and D_{non} according to the prediction results, get reconstructed annotations D_{re}.
8:     Reclassify D_{re} to get D_{ic} and D_{non} according to whether the sequences contain any labels.
9: **end for**

Data Augmentation. Since the number of high quality annotated corpus is so limited, we adopt a specific data augmentation method to expand complete annotations.

Firstly, we get an entity dictionary from complete annotations whose entities are absolutely right. In detail, for a randomly selected (with a probability of 5%) sequence from complete annotations, we replace the entity in the sequence with the other from the entity dictionary then generating a new sample. There are three kinds of entity types, i.e., TV, person and serial. These three types of entities are unevenly distributed, thus we take different replacement-probability (i.e., 10%, 20%, 100%) for three types. All new samples form the augmented annotations. During the training phase, we use data augmentation technique in each epoch.

Training. Since noises are inevitably introduced by iterative strategy, and augmented annotations are relatively correct. Therefore, the reconstructed annotations are first used to train the model, and then the augmented annotations are used to fine-tune. The weighted cross entropy loss function is used in the training. Algorithm 2 shows the training process.

Algorithm 2. Pipeline of training.

Input: M: base model; D_{re}: reconstructed annotations; D_{cp}: complete annotations;
Output: Trained model.
1: Train model M with D_{re} for K epochs;
2: **for** $l = 1 \rightarrow L$ **do**
3:     Get augmented annotations D_{aug} from D_{cp};
4:     Train model M with D_{aug} for one epoch.
5: **end for**

Ensemble. In order to improve the robustness of the model, we run S times with different random seeds and get S models. Then we propose two ensemble processes: (E1) S models vote for each character in each sequence and choose the label with the highest number of votes; (E2) For each character in each sequence, choose the label with the highest confidence in S models.

4   Experiments

4.1   Setting

Data and Metrics. The corpus is from the caption texts of YouKu video. Three types of entities (TV, person and serial) are considered in this task. This dataset is split into three subsets, 10,000 samples for training, 1,000 samples for developing and 2,000 samples for testing. In the training set, 5,670 samples are not labeled, and 4,330 samples are incompletely annotated. For training data, entities are labeled by matching a given entity list. The entity list is made up of specific categories, which may cover around 30% of entities appearing in the full corpus. For developing and testing data, samples are fully annotated. Just like the other works, we adopt precision, recall and F-Score as metrics.

Experimental Details. The experimental details are introduced below, including settings of hyper-parameters and model details.

1) We use HanLP [10] to get the POS embedding for each sentence. The pretrained BERT model is "chinese_wwm_ext"[1] released by Cui [5]. During the whole training process, parameters of BERT module are fixed.

---

[1] https://github.com/ymcui/Chinese-BERT-wwm.

2) We set learning rate as 0.001, batch size as 256 and we use the RMSProp optimizer for the whole training process. We set $K = 10$ for coarse-tuning stage and $L = 20$ for fine-tuning stage.

4.2   Results

Our experimental results include four parts: (1) comparing with baselines, (2) fine-tune, (3) model ensemble strategies, (4) results on NLPCC2020 shared task: Auto Information Extraction. All metrics are computed on testing data. The following is a detailed introduction for each part.

Comparing with Baselines. Firstly, we make comparisons among our coarse-tuning models and baseline models. The BERT+CRF model is released by the organizer and it is adapted from HardLatentCRF [13]. In our work, we use BERT/POS+BiLSTM+CRF as base model. The iterative model is the base model trained with iterative strategy. As shown in the first two rows of Table 1, the two baseline models and our base model perform poorly when trained directly on the imperfect 10,000 training data. However, our base model outperforms two baseline models. When using our well-designed iterative strategy, we make a comparison between our base model and the iterative model. We can see that the iterative model gets a growth of 10.85% compared with our base model.

Table 1. Performance comparison between different baseline models and our models with different strategies.

	Model	Precision	Recall	F-Score
Baselines (w/o Dev)	HardLatentCRF [13]	65.69	36.30	46.76
	BERT+CRF [13]	63.51	64.45	63.98
Coarse-tune (w/o Dev)	Base model	68.24	65.31	66.74
	Iterative model	81.28	74.21	77.59
Fine-tune (with Dev)	Base model	86.62	80.55	83.47
	Iterative model	85.83	**83.93**	84.87
	Iterative model (data augmentation)	87.20	83.02	85.06
Ensemble	Ensemble model (E1)	**87.36**	82.47	84.85
	Ensemble model (E2)	87.27	83.06	**85.11**

As described in Sect. 3, we propose an iterative strategy to reconstruct imperfect annotations. To explore the further capabilities of iterative strategy, we draw the performance curve on the test data during the training process of the model. As shown in the sub-figure (a) of Fig. 3, the first ten epochs are in the coarse-tuning stage, and the rest twenty epochs are in the fine-tuning stage. The blue and red curves correspond to the fifth and sixth rows in Table 1, respectively. Without the iterative strategy, the training process is more unstable in the coarse-tuning stage. In the sub-figure (b), we can see that the number of valid entities increases with the number of iterations until the training converges.

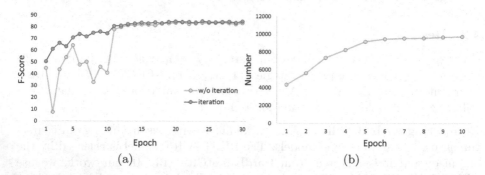

Fig. 3. Sub-figure (a) is the model training curves. Sub-figure (b) represents the number of valid entity increases when training with relabeling the unlabeled sentences.

Fine-tune. The results trained on the imperfect $10,000$ training data are not satisfactory, thus we propose to fine-tune on the developing data. In the third part of Table 1, models are firstly trained on the $10,000$ training data and then fine-tuning on the developing data. On the metric of F-Score, the iterative model performs better than the base model by 1.40%. Compared with the iterative model without fine-tuning in the four row, our fine-tuned iterative model gets growth of 7.28%.

In order to get more fully annotated data when fine-tuning the iterative model on developing data, we use the data augmentation technique in our iterative model. We firstly obtain an entity dictionary from developing data, then we randomly replace some entities to generate new samples. As shown in the seven row of Table 1, our iterative model (with data augmentation) gets the best results on the metric of precision and F-Score.

In the coarse-tuning stage, we get a comparable iterative model, and we get a huge improvement in the fine-tuning stage. We can conclude that our iterative strategy and the idea of fine-tuning on developing data is effective.

Ensemble. During the full training process, we find the models in different training stages have different performance. Some models have better performance on the metric of recall, and others may have better precision. Thus, we try to integrate multiple models in different stages. There are two ensemble strategies as described in Sect. 3. The experimental results are shown in the last two rows of Table 1. By comparing the two strategies E1 and E2, we can see that The E2 strategy is more effective. Compared with the models without ensemble, our ensemble model (E2) has both higher precision and F-Score.

Results on NLPCC2020 Shared Task: Auto Information Extraction. There are two leaderboards in the final contest. The metric of F-Score is computed on testing data. The competition results are shown in Table 2 and Table 3.

We show the top 3 ranked models and the baseline model in each leaderboard. The baseline model is released by the organizer. Table 2 is a ranking of model performance without external data and developing data. Our model performs best among the ranked models, especially outperforming the second place by 5.46% on the F-Score metric. The other leaderboard is the ranking of performance when using developing data, augmented data and integrating models from different training stages. As shown in Table 3, with all the data and ensemble considered, our overall performance is competitive and outperforms the baseline model by 4.00%.

Table 2. Leaderboard1.

Model	F-Score
Rank1 (ours)	77.32
Rank2	71.96
Rank3	71.86
Baseline	63.98

Table 3. Leaderboard2.

Model	F-Score
Rank1	85.00
Rank2 (ours)	84.87
Rank3	84.75
Baseline	80.87

5   Conclusion

In this paper, we considered a complex corpus that contains complete annotations, incomplete annotations, and non-annotations. Unlike most NER systems, only a single strategy is used to process an annotated corpus. We use specific strategies for processing different types of annotations and integrate these strategies to obtain reliable prediction results. To further improve the performance of base models, we use high quality corpus to fine-tune models. In addition, considering the robustness of the system, we also support data augmentation to enhance the diversity of the corpus. These strategies make the system more applicable to real business scenarios. We verify the effectiveness of our approach through comprehensive experiments, and won first and second place respectively in two scenarios provided by NLPCC 2020 Shared Task: Auto Information Extraction. Although our work is evaluated in NER tasks, we believe that the idea of this paper can be well applied to other fields with imperfect labeled sequences.

References

1. Carlson, A., Gaffney, S., Vasile, F.: Learning a named entity tagger from gazetteers with the partial perceptron. In: Learning by Reading and Learning to Read, Papers from the 2009 AAAI Spring Symposium, Technical Report SS-09-07, Stanford, California, USA, 23–25 March 2009, pp. 7–13. AAAI (2009)

2. Chieu, H.L., Ng, H.T.: Named entity recognition: a maximum entropy approach using global information. In: Proceedings of the 19th International Conference on Computational Linguistics-Volume 1, pp. 1–7. Association for Computational Linguistics (2002)
3. Chiu, J.P.C., Nichols, E.: Named entity recognition with bidirectional LSTM-CNNs. Trans. Assoc. Comput. Linguist. **4**, 357–370 (2016)
4. Collins, M., Singer, Y.: Unsupervised models for named entity classification. In: Fung, P., Zhou, J. (eds.) Joint SIGDAT Conference on Empirical Methods in Natural Language Processing and Very Large Corpora, EMNLP 1999, College Park, MD, USA, 21–22 June 1999. Association for Computational Linguistics (1999)
5. Cui, Y., et al.: Pre-training with whole word masking for Chinese BERT. arXiv preprint arXiv:1906.08101 (2019)
6. Devlin, J., Chang, M., Lee, K., Toutanova, K.: BERT: pre-training of deep bidirectional transformers for language understanding. In: Burstein, J., Doran, C., Solorio, T. (eds.) Proceedings of the 2019 Conference of the North American Chapter of the Association for Computational Linguistics: Human Language Technologies, NAACL-HLT 2019, Minneapolis, MN, USA, 2–7 June 2019, Volume 1 (Long and Short Papers), pp. 4171–4186. Association for Computational Linguistics (2019)
7. Fernandes, E.R., Brefeld, U.: Learning from partially annotated sequences. In: Gunopulos, D., Hofmann, T., Malerba, D., Vazirgiannis, M. (eds.) ECML PKDD 2011. LNCS (LNAI), vol. 6911, pp. 407–422. Springer, Heidelberg (2011). https://doi.org/10.1007/978-3-642-23780-5_36
8. Greenberg, N., Bansal, T., Verga, P., McCallum, A.: Marginal likelihood training of BiLSTM-CRF for biomedical named entity recognition from disjoint label sets. In: Proceedings of the 2018 Conference on Empirical Methods in Natural Language Processing, pp. 2824–2829 (2018)
9. Hanisch, D., Fundel, K., Mevissen, H., Zimmer, R., Fluck, J.: ProMiner: rule-based protein and gene entity recognition. BMC Bioinform. **6**(S-1) (2005)
10. He, H.: HanLP: Han Language Processing (2020). https://github.com/hankcs/HanLP
11. Hochreiter, S., Schmidhuber, J.: Long short-term memory. Neural Comput. **9**(8), 1735–1780 (1997)
12. Jiang, Y., Hu, C., Xiao, T., Zhang, C., Zhu, J.: Improved differentiable architecture search for language modeling and named entity recognition. In: Inui, K., Jiang, J., Ng, V., Wan, X. (eds.) Proceedings of the 2019 Conference on Empirical Methods in Natural Language Processing and the 9th International Joint Conference on Natural Language Processing, EMNLP-IJCNLP 2019, Hong Kong, China, 3–7 November 2019, pp. 3583–3588. Association for Computational Linguistics (2019)
13. Jie, Z., Xie, P., Lu, W., Ding, R., Li, L.: Better modeling of incomplete annotations for named entity recognition. In: Burstein, J., Doran, C., Solorio, T. (eds.) Proceedings of the 2019 Conference of the North American Chapter of the Association for Computational Linguistics: Human Language Technologies, NAACL-HLT 2019, Minneapolis, MN, USA, 2–7 June 2019, Volume 1 (Long and Short Papers), pp. 729–734. Association for Computational Linguistics (2019)
14. Kim, J., Woodland, P.C.: A rule-based named entity recognition system for speech input. In: Sixth International Conference on Spoken Language Processing, ICSLP 2000/INTERSPEECH 2000, Beijing, China, 16–20 October 2000, pp. 528–531. ISCA (2000)
15. Lafferty, J., McCallum, A., Pereira, F.C.: Conditional random fields: Probabilistic models for segmenting and labeling sequence data (2001)

16. Li, J., Sun, A., Han, J., Li, C.: A survey on deep learning for named entity recognition. IEEE Trans. Knowl. Data Eng., 1 (2020)
17. Liu, S., Tang, B., Chen, Q., Wang, X.: Effects of semantic features on machine learning-based drug name recognition systems: word embeddings vs. manually constructed dictionaries. Information **6**(4), 848–865 (2015)
18. Liu, Y., Meng, F., Zhang, J., Xu, J., Chen, Y., Zhou, J.: GCDT: a global context enhanced deep transition architecture for sequence labeling. In: Korhonen, A., Traum, D.R., Màrquez, L. (eds.) Proceedings of the 57th Conference of the Association for Computational Linguistics, ACL 2019, Florence, Italy, 28 July–2 August 2019, Volume 1: Long Papers, pp. 2431–2441. Association for Computational Linguistics (2019)
19. Lou, X., Hamprecht, F.: Structured learning from partial annotations. arXiv preprint arXiv:1206.6421 (2012)
20. McCallum, A., Li, W.: Early results for named entity recognition with conditional random fields, feature induction and web-enhanced lexicons. In: Daelemans, W., Osborne, M. (eds.) Proceedings of the Seventh Conference on Natural Language Learning, CoNLL 2003, Held in cooperation with HLT-NAACL 2003, Edmonton, Canada, 31 May – 1 June 2003, pp. 188–191. ACL (2003)
21. McNamee, P., Mayfield, J.: Entity extraction without language-specific resources. In: Roth, D., van den Bosch, A. (eds.) Proceedings of the 6th Conference on Natural Language Learning, CoNLL 2002, Held in cooperation with COLING 2002, Taipei, Taiwan, 2002. ACL (2002)
22. Mikolov, T., Chen, K., Corrado, G., Dean, J.: Efficient estimation of word representations in vector space. arXiv preprint arXiv:1301.3781 (2013)
23. Morwal, S., Jahan, N., Chopra, D.: Named entity recognition using hidden Markov model (HMM). Int. J. Nat. Lang. Comput. (IJNLC) **1**(4), 15–23 (2012)
24. Nadeau, D., Turney, P.D., Matwin, S.: Unsupervised named-entity recognition: generating gazetteers and resolving ambiguity. In: Lamontagne, L., Marchand, M. (eds.) AI 2006. LNCS (LNAI), vol. 4013, pp. 266–277. Springer, Heidelberg (2006). https://doi.org/10.1007/11766247_23
25. Peng, M., Xing, X., Zhang, Q., Fu, J., Huang, X.: Distantly supervised named entity recognition using positive-unlabeled learning. arXiv preprint arXiv:1906.01378 (2019)
26. Peters, M.E., et al.: Deep contextualized word representations. arXiv preprgreenberg2018marginalint arXiv:1802.05365 (2018)
27. Riloff, E., Jones, R., et al.: Learning dictionaries for information extraction by multi-level bootstrapping. In: AAAI/IAAI, pp. 474–479 (1999)
28. Wang, Z., Shang, J., Liu, L., Lu, L., Liu, J., Han, J.: CrossWeigh: training named entity tagger from imperfect annotations. arXiv preprint arXiv:1909.01441 (2019)
29. Yadav, V., Bethard, S.: A survey on recent advances in named entity recognition from deep learning models. In: Bender, E.M., Derczynski, L., Isabelle, P. (eds.) Proceedings of the 27th International Conference on Computational Linguistics, COLING 2018, Santa Fe, New Mexico, USA, 20–26 August 2018, pp. 2145–2158. Association for Computational Linguistics (2018)
30. Yang, Y., Chen, W., Li, Z., He, Z., Zhang, M.: Distantly supervised NER with partial annotation learning and reinforcement learning. In: Proceedings of the 27th International Conference on Computational Linguistics, pp. 2159–2169 (2018)
31. Zhang, S., Elhadad, N.: Unsupervised biomedical named entity recognition: experiments with clinical and biological texts. J. Biomed. Inform. **46**(6), 1088–1098 (2013)

The Solution of Huawei Cloud & Noah's Ark Lab to the NLPCC-2020 Challenge: Light Pre-Training Chinese Language Model for NLP Task

Yuyang Zhang[1,2]($\boxtimes$), Jintao Yu[1,2], Kai Wang[1,2], Yichun Yin[1,2], Cheng Chen[1,2], and Qun Liu[1,2]

[1] Huawei Noah's Ark Lab, Beijing, China
Zhangyuyang4@huawei.com
[2] Huawei Cloud and AI, Shenzhen, China

Abstract. Pre-trained language models have achieved great success in natural language processing. However, they are difficult to be deployed on resource-restricted devices because of the expensive computation. This paper introduces our solution to the Natural Language Processing and Chinese Computing (NLPCC) challenge of Light Pre-Training Chinese Language Model for the Natural Language Processing (http://tcci.ccf.org.cn/conference/2020/) (https://www.cluebenchmarks.com/NLPCC.html). The proposed solution uses a state-of-the-art method of BERT knowledge distillation (TinyBERT) with an advanced Chinese pre-trained language model (NEZHA) as the teacher model, which is dubbed as TinyNEZHA. In addition, we introduce some effective techniques in the fine-tuning stage to boost the performances of TinyNEZHA. In the official evaluation of NLPCC-2020 challenge, TinyNEZHA achieves a score of 77.71, ranking 1st place among all the participating teams. Compared with the BERT-base, TinyNEZHA obtains almost the same results while being 9× smaller and 8× faster on inference.

Keywords: Pre-trained language model · Knowledge distillation · TinyNEZHA

1 Introduction

Pre-trained language models (PLMs), such as BERT [4], have shown promising results in natural language processing. Many efforts have been paid to improve the PLMs with more parameters, larger corpus and more advanced pre-training tasks. However, PLMs often have a considerable amount of parameters and need long inference time, which are difficult to be deployed on resource-restricted devices or some NLP application scenarios that pursue high concurrency. Therefore, compressing these PLMs into smaller and faster models is an imperative topic.

Nowadays, there are many compression methods for pre-trained language models, such as distillation, pruning, and quantization. To build a platform that can comprehensively evaluate these compression methods in Chinese PLMs, the NLPCC-2020

© Springer Nature Switzerland AG 2020
X. Zhu et al. (Eds.): NLPCC 2020, LNAI 12431, pp. 524–533, 2020.
https://doi.org/10.1007/978-3-030-60457-8_43

challenge provides four different kinds of tasks, including co-reference resolution, key-word extraction, entity recognition and machine reading. This challenge requires partic-ipants to build a light model which uses less than 1/9 model size and 1/8 inference time compared with BERT-base.

For this challenge, we developed a competitive system called TinyNEZHA, which combines the techniques of Chinese PLM (NEZHA) and model distillation (TinyBERT). We trained our models on the Huawei Modelarts platform (https://www.huaweicloud. com/product/modelarts.html). In the final evaluation, TinyNEZHA ranks first place and outperforms the runner-up system by 2.4 points.

2   Related Work

With the emergence and development of pre-trained language models, the contradiction between the increasing number of model parameters and limited hardware condition have also emerged. People began to attach importance to the study of model compression methods. Google released smaller models such as BERT-small and BERT-tiny, which provided a baseline for latecomers [4]. Hugging Face introduced DistillBert in 2019, a knowledge distillation method for pre-trained language models, which uses three losses to let student models learn the knowledge of teacher models [5]. Google's Albert uses parameter sharing to significantly reduce the model's parameters while retaining the similar performance of the large model [6]. Stanford University changed the original pre-trained language model tasks by the idea of confrontation. They propose a new self-supervised task by replacing some tokens in the original text, and then train another model to find the tokens where the original text is replaced [7]. Their small Electra model also achieved outstanding results on many NLP tasks [8]. Google's MobileBERT redesigns the standard Transformer model and uses distillation to make the small student model perform excellent [9].

3   Light Pre-Training Chinese Language Model for NLP Task Tasks

Light Pre-Training Chinese Language Model for NLP Task contains four sub-tasks, CLUEWSC2020, CSL, CLUENER, and CMRC2018. The split of data sets for each task is shown in Table 1.

Table 1. The split of four task datasets

Tasks	Train	Dev	Test
CLUEWSC2020	1,244	304	290
CSL	20,000	3,000	3,000
CLUENER	10,748	1,343	1,345
CMRC2018	10,420	1,002	3,219

3.1 CLUEWSC2020 Task

CLUEWSC2020 is a task of Chinese conference resolution. It requires the model to infer whether the pronoun in a sentence refers to the given noun. The inference accuracy is the score of this task. A typical example of this dataset is as follows (Table 2):

Table 2. An example of the CLUEWSC2020 dataset

Index1	Index2	value
target	span2_index	27
	span1_index	3
	span1_text	伤口
	span2_text	它们
label		false
text		裂开的伤口涂满尘土，里面有碎石子和木头刺，我小心翼翼把它们剔除出去。

3.2 CSL Task

Table 3. An example of the CSL dataset

index	value
id	2963
abst	通过对黑旺铁矿地貌、水文地质条件、地理位置以及矿坑水的水量水质、供水路线、供水规模等分析可知,利用黑旺矿坑水向淄博市中心城区供水具有水量、水质保障和较强的可操作性,并对此提出相关建议.
keyword	"矿坑水", "淄博市","生活供水","黑旺铁矿"
label	0

CSL is a paper keyword extraction task. It requires the model to determine whether a set of keywords given in the data set are all paper's keywords. If there is a wrong keyword in the given keywords, the label is 0, otherwise the label is 1. The inference accuracy is used as the score for task evaluation. The dataset example is as follows (Table 3):

3.3 CLUENER Task

CLUENER task is a task for Chinese entity recognition. The model needs to identify which token in the sentence is an entity and which of the ten types of entity it is. This task uses the mean F1 value of all the entities as the task score (Table 4).

Table 4. An example of the CLUENER dataset

Index	neType	value	position
text		彭小军认为，国内银行现在走的是台湾的发卡模式，先通过跑马圈地再在圈的地里面选择客户	
label	address	台湾	15,16
	name	彭小军	0,2

3.4 CMRC2018 Task

The CMRC2018 task is a reading comprehension task. This task provides a paragraph of text and several questions. The answers can be found in the paragraph. The model needs to infer the span of each question's answer in the paragraph. If the prediction of the model hits one of the answer given by the task, it is considered correct. The task uses the EM value as an evaluation score (Table 5).

Table 5. An example of the CMRC2018 dataset

Index1	Index2	Index3	value
data	context_text		所谓的"傻钱"策略，其实就是买入并持有美国股票这样的普通组合。这个策略要比对冲基金和其它专业投资者使用的更为复杂的投资方法效果好得多。
	qas	query_text	什么是傻钱策略？
	qas	answers	["所谓的"傻钱"策略，其实就是买入并持有美国股票这样的普通组合", "其实就是买入并持有美国股票这样的普通组合", "买入并持有美国股票这样的普通组合"]

4   Methodology

In the NLPCC-2020 Challenge, our team adopted the distillation method to miniaturize the pertained language model, let a small student model learn the knowledge of a large teacher model. The student and teacher models use the NEZHA pre-trained language model structure because of its excellent performance on Chinese tasks [10]. Based on the organizer's data and training scripts, we have made little optimizations and modifications to achieve better results. The following is divided into three parts to detail the application of TinyNEZHA in the task.

4.1 NEZHA

Most pre-trained language models are based on a multi-layer transformer structure. The famous BERT, GPT, and XLNET are all like this, NEZHA is no exception. NEZHA adopts a multi-layer transformer structure, but on this basis, it uses functional relative position embedding instead of previous parametric absolute position embedding. We choose the fixed sinusoidal functions mainly because it may allow the model to extrapolate to sequence lengths longer than the ones encountered during training.

At the same time, NEZHA adopts the whole word masking technology (WWM). During model pre-training, you not only randomly mask a single token but mask the whole Chinese word piece, which is segmented by a word segmentation tool called JIEBA in advance [11]. In the WWM pre-training dataset, each sample contains several masked Chinese words, and the total number of masked Chinese characters is roughly 12% of its length, and 1.5% randomly replaced characters. Besides, NEZHA also uses mixed-precision training and LAMB optimizer to make pre-training more rapidly [12]

[13]. More data can be used for pre-training within the same period to achieve better results.

4.2 TinyBERT

TinyBERT Transformer distillation technology uses two-step distillation to miniaturize the large pre-trained model. Firstly it's essential to choose a good teacher model. It represents the upper limit of the student model. Here we chose the NEZHA-base model as a teacher. Secondly, we need to determine the parameters of the student model structure. In a general sense, in the same structure, more parameters mean stronger and better, and so do the pre-trained language model. However, considering the limited parameter number of the model and the constraints of running time, we chose a 4-layer, 312 Hidden size model, a 6-layer, 300 Hidden size model, and an 8-layer, 256 Hidden size model as student models. The model also used the NEZHA structure (Fig. 1).

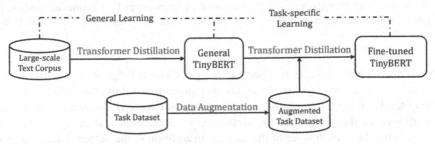

Fig. 1. The illustration of TinyBERT learning

We used a two-step distillation in our solution. The first step of distillation allows the student model to learn the teacher's knowledge on an extensive unlabeled data set. The second step of distillation is to let the student model learn on the downstream task data to make the student model more focused on specific tasks. However, the training data for the four downstream tasks are not sufficient for task distillation. For example, the training set of CLUEWSC2020 only has about 1200 data. The small amount of data dramatically limits the effectiveness of the second distillation step. To improve efficiency, we used data augmentation technology to generalize similar data to supplement data for tasks. We use the data augmentation method to predict and replace some tokens in the original text through a pre-trained language model. When predicting the masked tokens, the pre-trained language model predicts multiple results based on probability, which allows us to control the amount of data generalization. Data augmentation helps us get a much better student model, and there are about two points of improvement on CLUE classification tasks (Fig. 2).

In the distillation process, students need to learn the knowledge of the teacher model. Here we used the vector representation of each Transformer layer and the distribution of self-attention between tokens as the information that students learn from the teacher model [14]. But the number of the student model's Transformer layer is less than that of the teacher model. We calculate the ratio of the teacher and student model layers,

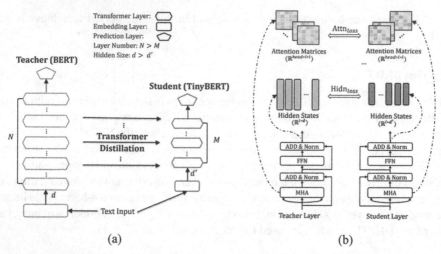

Fig. 2. An overview of Transformer distillation: (a) the framework of Transformer distillation, (b) the details of Transformer-layer distillation consisting of attention based distillation and hidden states based distillation

and then, the student model learns the teacher model's knowledge according to the rate. For example, the second layer of the eight-layer student model fits the third layer of the 12-layer teacher model; the fourth layer of the student fits the sixth layer of the teacher, the sixth layer of the student fits the ninth layer of the teacher and the eighth layer of the student fits the twelfth layer of the teacher. In addition to the output hidden states of the Transformer layer and the distribution of attention, the student model also learn the hidden states of the teacher model's Word Embedding layer. After the second step of distillation, the student model's logit outputs through the task layer fit the logits outputs by the teacher model [15]. At last, we fine-tuned the student models on the task datasets. Of course, you can also skip fine-tuning the models because fitting the teacher model's logits is equal to fine-tuning on a soft label. But to get better verification results, our models are still fine-tuned on the task datasets.

According to experience, the deeper the neural network, the stronger its expressive ability. But for the miniaturized model, due to the limitations of model parameters and running time, a deeper layer means a smaller Hidden size. It's difficult to decide how many layers and hidden size is the best. To achieve better results in the competition and explore the impact of the model structure on the task results, we submitted the six-layer and eight-layer models' results. The results show that thin and tall models can improve task results significantly. However, due to the limited number of experiments, the best model structure under the same parameters cannot be obtained.

To get a good general TinyBERT model, Chinese Wiki and News data is used for the first step of distillation. We distilled the model with 128 max_sequence_length for 1,000,000+ steps with a batch size of 256. After that we continued to distill the 512 max_sequence_length model for 200,000 steps. On the second step of distillation, we augmented the task data by 20 times first and trained for 10 epochs on the augmented data. The learning rate was set to 1e−4 during two distillation steps.

4.3 Fine-Tuning

The CLUE organizer provided the participants with task data and fine-tuning scripts. We have made some modifications on this basis to achieve better results on the task. First of all, we used adversarial training during fine-tuning [16]. It added noise to the model input and made the model more robust. Secondly, for the CLUEWSC2020 data set, we generated more data by data augmentation, to solve the problem of the lack of data. Finally, we verified the model every 100 or 200 steps and selected the model that performs best on the verification dataset for testing and submission. Different hyperparameters affect the result. We had tried 3 to 8 different hyperparameters on every task and chose the best result to submit.

5 Evaluation

In the distillation process, to get a small model with a good result on the task, first of all, you must find a teacher model with excellent results, to increase the upper limit of the student model. Therefore, we first fine-tuned the NEZHA teacher model on the tasks. Our teacher model's results are much better than the baseline of BERT-base.

Our distillation process has two steps. In the first step, the student model learns the teacher model's knowledge on the unlabeled dataset. To compare with our final results, we fine-tuned it on the downstream tasks directly. It can be found that the results of the general student model are not satisfactory. Then we performed task distillation and used data-augmented task data. After task distillation, the four-layer student model performed much better on all four tasks (Table 6).

Table 6. Results of our models on dev dataset.

Model	CLUEWSC2020	CSL	CLUENER	CMRC2018
NEZHA-base	87.5	83.27	81.38	71.08
TinyNEZHA-4L(GD)	63.45	75.06	73.42	54.24
TinyNEZHA-4L(GD+TD)	69.07	79.5	77	62.07
TinyNEZHA-6L	73.03	80.53	78.68	66.39
TinyNEZHA-8L	75.32	83.07	79.29	67.66

GD means General Distillation, the first step of Transformer distillation. TD means Task Distillation, the second step of Transformer distillation.

As can be seen from the evaluation results. Firstly, doing two-step distillation will greatly improve the results of the student model on the four tasks, it achieved an average increase of five points; Secondly, the results of the deeper and thinner model are closer to the teacher model, but pay attention to controlling the amount of model parameters and running time.

To improve our result, we tried the six-layer and eight-layer models. Due to the limitation of model size and time, we adopted 6-layer, 300 Hidden size, and 8-layer,

252 Hidden size configurations. Their performance on the task test dataset is as follows
(Table 7):

Table 7. Test results of TinyNEZHA models with different layers

Model	CLUEWSC2020	CSL	CLUENER	CMRC2018
NEZHA-4-312	66.2	79.767	75.583	69.1
NEZHA-6-300	74.138	81.2	76.459	72
NEZHA-8-252	71.379	82.933	78.058	74.250

Consistent with evaluation results, deeper and thinner models achieved better results
on the test set. However, we found that some tasks on the test set are different from the
results of the evaluation set. This may be due to uneven data distribution or the amount
of data is too small. But the overall performance on the four tasks can be the advantage
of the deeper and thinner model (Table 8).

Table 8. Scores of top three teams

Team	Score
Huawei Cloud & Noah's Ark Lab	77.71
Tencent Oteam	76.89
Xiaomi AI Lab	75.85

After scoring the task scores, running time, and model parameters, we got the first
place with a score of 77.71.

6 Conclusion and Future Work

This paper introduces the technology and performance of TinyNEZHA on the NLPCC-
2020 Challenge: Light Pre-Training Chinese Language Model for NLP Task. Firstly
the student model learns the output representation and attention distribution of each
Transformer layer of NEZHA-base on the large unlabeled corpus. Secondly, we augment
the data of downstream tasks by predicting and replacing some tokens in origin data
through the pre-trained language model. Thirdly the general-distilled student model
learns from the fine-tuned teacher model on the augmented data. Finally, we fine-tuned
the student model on the downstream task data.

TinyNEZHA technology has performed well in this competition, but it still has a lot
of room for improvement. First of all, we found that it is not the best way for the student
model to learn the teacher model according to the hierarchical ratio during the distillation
process. Choosing different layers' output of the student model fits different layers'

output of the teacher model, leading to different results. Some of these patterns allow the student model to achieve considerable improvements in various tasks. Secondly, the compression method of distillation is only one way to achieve miniaturization of the model. We are also studying miniaturization methods such as quantization and pruning. The integration of multiple miniaturization methods in the future is also an important research direction.

References

1. NLPCC2020. http://tcci.ccf.org.cn/conference/2020/index.php. Accessed 10 Mar 2020
2. Cui, Y., et al.: Pre-training with whole word masking for Chinese Bert. arXiv preprint arXiv: 1906.08101 (2019)
3. Wu, X., Lv, S., Zang, L., Han, J., Hu, S.: Conditional BERT contextual augmentation. In: Rodrigues, J.M.F., et al. (eds.) ICCS 2019. LNCS, vol. 11539, pp. 84–95. Springer, Cham (2019). https://doi.org/10.1007/978-3-030-22747-0_7
4. Devlin, J., et al.: BERT: pre-training of deep bidirectional transformers for language understanding. arXiv preprint arXiv:1810.04805 (2018)
5. Sanh, V., et al.: DistilBERT, a distilled version of BERT: smaller, faster, cheaper and lighter. arXiv preprint arXiv:1910.01108 (2019)
6. Lan, Z., et al.: Albert: a lite BERT for self-supervised learning of language representations. arXiv preprint arXiv:1909.11942 (2019)
7. Bose, A.J., Ling, H., Cao, Y.: Adversarial contrastive estimation. arXiv preprint arXiv:1805. 03642 (2018)
8. Clark, K., et al.: ELECTRA: pre-training text encoders as discriminators rather than generators. arXiv preprint arXiv:2003.10555 (2020)
9. Sun, Z., et al.: MobileBERT: a compact task-agnostic bert for resource-limited devices. arXiv preprint arXiv:2004.02984 (2020)
10. Wei, J., et al.: NEZHA: neural contextualized representation for chinese language understanding. arXiv preprint arXiv:1909.00204 (2019)
11. Sun, J.: Jieba Chinese word segmentation tool, 21 January 2018–25 June 2018. https://github. com/fxsjy/jieba (2012)
12. Micikevicius, P., et al.: Mixed precision training. arXiv preprint arXiv:1710.03740 (2017)
13. You, Y., et al.: Reducing BERT pre-training time from 3 days to 76 minutes. arXiv preprint arXiv:1904.00962 (2019)
14. Clark, K., et al.: What does BERT look at? An analysis of BERT's attention. arXiv preprint arXiv:1906.04341 (2019)
15. Hinton, G., Vinyals, O., Dean, J.: Distilling the knowledge in a neural network. arXiv preprint arXiv:1503.02531 (2015)
16. Madry, A., et al.: Towards deep learning models resistant to adversarial attacks. arXiv preprint arXiv:1706.06083 (2017)

DuEE: A Large-Scale Dataset for Chinese Event Extraction in Real-World Scenarios

Xinyu Li, Fayuan Li, Lu Pan, Yuguang Chen, Weihua Peng⁽✉⁾, Quan Wang, Yajuan Lyu, and Yong Zhu

Baidu Inc., Beijing, China
{lixinyu13,lifayuan,panlu01,chenyuguang,pengweihua, wangquan05,lvyajuan,zhuyong}@baidu.com

Abstract. This paper introduces DuEE, a new dataset for Chinese event extraction (EE) in real-world scenarios. DuEE has several advantages over previous EE datasets. (1) **Scale:** DuEE consists of 19,640 events categorized into 65 event types, along with 41,520 event arguments mapped to 121 argument roles, which, to our knowledge, is the largest Chinese EE dataset so far. (2) **Quality:** All the data is human annotated with crowdsourced review, ensuring that the annotation accuracy is higher than 95%. (3) **Reality:** The schema covers trending topics from Baidu Search and the data is collected from news on Baijiahao. The task is also close to real-world scenarios, e.g., a single instance is allowed to contain multiple events, different event arguments are allowed to share the same argument role, and an argument is allowed to play different roles. To advance the research on Chinese EE, we release DuEE as well as a baseline system to the community. We also organize a shared competition on the basis of DuEE, which has attracted 1,206 participants. We analyze the results of top performing systems and hope to shed light on further improvements.

Keywords: Event extraction · Dataset · Performance evaluation

1 Introduction

Event extraction (EE) is an important yet challenging task in natural language understanding. Given an event mention, an event extraction system ought to identify event triggers with specific event types, as well as their corresponding arguments with specific argument roles [1]. Table 1 presents an example of the EE task.

Though important, there are only a few EE datasets that are publicly available to the community. ACE 2005[1] is the most influential benchmark for EE,

---

[1] https://www.ldc.upenn.edu/sites/www.ldc.upenn.edu/files/english-events-guidelines-v5.4.3.pdf.

© Springer Nature Switzerland AG 2020
X. Zhu et al. (Eds.): NLPCC 2020, LNAI 12431, pp. 534–545, 2020.
https://doi.org/10.1007/978-3-030-60457-8_44

Table 1. A sample instance from DuEE.

Instance	Annotated results	

余文乐与王棠云结婚诞下余初见后，便像很多人那样，成了孩子奴喜欢晒娃。
 	
After Wenle Yu married to Tangyun Wang and gave birth to Chujian Yu, like many others, he became a child slave and liked to post photos of the child.
	[
	{
	"EventType": "人生.结婚",
	"Trigger": "结婚",
	"EventArguments": [
	{"text": "余文乐",
	"role": "结婚双方"},
	{"text": "王棠云",
	"role": "结婚双方"}]
	},
	{
	"EventType": "人生.生子/女",
	"Trigger": "诞下",
	"EventArguments": [
	{"text": "王棠云",
	"role": "产子者"},
	{"text": "余初见",
	"role": "出生者"}]
	}
	]
		[
		{
		"EventType": "Life.Marrige",
		"Trigger": "married to",
		"EventArguments": [
		{"text": "Wenle Yu",
		"role": "Married Person"},
		{"text": "Tangyun Wang",
		"role": "Married Person"}]
		},
		{
		"EventType": "Life.Delivery",
		"Trigger": "gave birth to",
		"EventArguments": [
		{"text": "Tangyun Wang",
		"role": "Puerpera"},
		{"text": "Chujian Yu",
		"role": "Newborn"}]
		}
		]

where most researchers carry their experiments on [2–9]. It is a multilingual corpus contains English, Arabic, and Chinese data. The 2016 and 2017 TAC KBP Event Track[2] also provide a multilingual benchmark for EE, consisting of English, Spanish, and Chinese data. Both datasets, however, are rather small in scale and have little influence for Chinese EE. Chinese Emergency Corpus (CEC) [10] is specifically designed for Chinese EE. It is also a small dataset covering merely five event types about different emergencies. The lack of large-scale datasets greatly hinders the development of EE technology.

This paper presents DuEE[3], a large-scale dataset specifically designed for Chinese EE in real-world scenarios. DuEE has the following advantages.

Scale: DuEE consists of 19,640 events categorized into 65 event types, along with 41,520 event arguments mapped to 121 argument roles, which, to our knowledge, is the largest Chinese EE dataset so far. Table 2 highlights the advantage of DuEE over previous datasets in terms of scale.

Quality: DuEE provides rich annotations including triggers, event types, event arguments, and their respective argument roles. They are all human annotated with crowdsourced review, ensuring the annotation accuracy is higher than 95%.

Reality: The schema covers trending topics from Baidu Search and the data is collected from news on Baijiahao. The settings are also close to real-world scenarios, in the sense that:

---

[2] https://tac.nist.gov/2016/KBP/guidelines/summary_rich_ere_v4.2.pdf.
[3] http://ai.baidu.com/broad/download.

Table 2. Advantage of DuEE over existing EE datasets in terms of scale.

Dataset	Language	#Documents	#Events	#Event types
ACE 2005	Arabic	403	2,267	33
	Chinese	633	2,521	33
	English	599	4,090	33
TAC KBP event track	Chinese	167	2,542	18
	English	167	2,542	18
	Spanish	167	2,542	18
CEC	Chinese	332	5,954	5
DuEE(this paper)	**Chinese**	**11,224**	**19,640**	**65**

1. A single instance is allowed to contain multiple events, e.g., the instance in Table 1 mentions two events, one of the type "人生.结婚 (Life.Marrige)" and the other of the type "人生.生子/女 (Life.Delivery)".
2. Different event arguments are allowed to share the same argument role, e.g., "余文乐 (Wenle Yu)" and "王棠云 (Tangyun Wang)" share the same role of "结婚双方 (Married Person)" in the first event.
3. An argument is allowed to play different roles, e.g., "王棠云 (Tangyun Wang)" plays the role of "结婚双方 (Married Person)" in the first event and that of "产子者 (Puerpera)" in the second event.

These settings make EE an even more challenging task on DuEE.

We release DuEE as well as a baseline system[4] to the community so as to advance the research on Chinese EE. We also organize a shared competition[5] on the basis of DuEE, which has attracted 1,206 participants from all over the world. We analyze the results of top performing systems and hope to shed light on further improvements.

The rest of this paper is organized as follows. Section 2 describes the construction process of DuEE and Sect. 3 gives its statistics. After that, Sect. 4 introduces the shared competition and analyzes the results of top performing systems. The concluding remarks are finally presented in Sect. 5.

2   Dataset Construction

Compared with the EE task, the corpus construction procedure for such task is also a challenging work. As illustrated in Fig. 1, we conducted the process in a few steps. Event schema construction aims to collect the most common event types and argument roles for each event type in real world. Data collection and filtering generate large-scaled dataset to be annotated. In annotation procedure, we would conduct an annotation-review loop until the correctness meets predefined standard.

---

[4] https://github.com/PaddlePaddle/Research/tree/master/KG/DuEE_baseline.
[5] http://lic2020.cipsc.org.cn/.

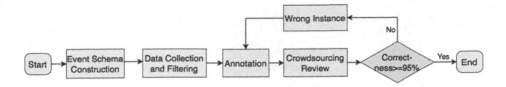

Fig. 1. Overall construction process of DuEE.

Table 3. Schema examples in DuEE dataset.

Event type	Argument roles
人生.结婚 Life. Marriage	时间，结婚双方 Time, Married Person
人生.产子/女 Life. Delivery	时间，产子者，出生者 Time, Puerpera, Newborn
灾害/意外.地震 Disaster/Accident. Earthquake	时间，震中，震级，震源深度，死亡人数，受伤人数 Time, Epicenter, Magnitude, Focal Depth, Number of Death, Number of Injured
产品行为.发布 Product. Release	时间，发布产品，发布方 Time, New Product, Publisher

2.1 Event Schema Construction

For EE task, all information would be extracted according to predefined schema. Therefore, schema construction is critical to the quality of the event extraction corpus. Event schema could be explained as a set of templates, each of which should contain exactly one event type and several corresponding argument roles under this event type:

$$Schema = \{(EventType, ArgumentRole_1, ArgumentRole_2, ...)\}$$

In order to collect the most common event types in real world, we firstly collected 3,600 trending topics from Baidu Search. After that, we analyzed the event type for each topic and selected 9 most frequently appeared event types finally, which include 65 sub-types in detail.

For each event type, related argument roles would be then defined. Argument roles are mainly entities such as organization and numbers such as price. Besides, seldom appeared roles would be excluded. Finally, we collected 121 different kinds of argument roles for all event types. For each event type, there would be 3.2 argument roles in average. Table 3 illustrated some examples of event type together with their argument roles.

2.2 Data Collection and Filtering

In this paper, we use news from Baijiahao , an authoring platform provided by Baidu, as our original document source. We sampled news published from May

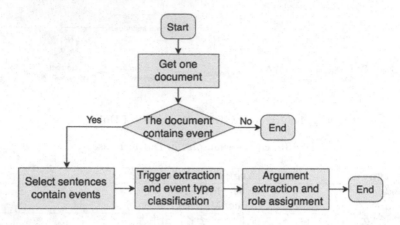

Fig. 2. The procedure of annotation.

1st, 2019 to Oct. 30th, 2019 in the database as the initial candidate news, and obtained more than 800,000 news finally. After that, a two-level filtering process was conducted to further select news more worth annotation.

A rule-based filtering was conducted in the first place. In general, we deduplicated news with the same title to decrease the duplication. But there are still quite a lot of news without any events mentioned. Thus, a classification-based filtering was conducted to identify potential news containing events. We used our pretrained classification model to identify if a news containing any event. To prevent from missing valuable news, we only filtered out news with high probability as a none-event news. After the two-level filtering process, we obtained 200,000 news in total as documents would be then annotated.

2.3   Data Annotation

In order to achieve high quality for the corpus, document annotation and crowd-sourcing review were both adopted to annotate all selected documents.

Document Annotation. The annotation was conducted on an event annotation platform, and the annotation procedure actually contains several steps as illustrated in Fig. 2. Annotators should firstly recognize if the document contains any event could be classified as one of the predefined event types. Only documents containing corresponding events would be carried on with latter annotation procedure. For one document, sentences containing at least one particular event should be firstly selected as an instance. After that, the annotators would be asked to extract triggers, typically verbs or norminalizations, that most directly describe the occurrence of events from the instance. For each trigger, the event type it indicated should also be clarified at the same time. As long as the event type was settled down for an event trigger, all argument roles to be annotated would be confirmed automatically. Therefore, annotators would

Fig. 3. An example of the review instance.

be asked to extract event arguments and assign specific argument roles to each extracted argument in a similar way.

Besides, there could be multiple event triggers within one instance, one event trigger could be assigned to different event types as it might indicate the occurrence of multiple events with different types. Ordinarily, not all predefined argument roles could always be found in one event and sometimes, there might not exist any required event argument. Thus, we do not place restrictions on the number of roles in an event. One argument could play different roles in an instance and multiple event arguments could also be assigned to the same argument role. An example could be observed in Table 1. Additionally, we further annotated possible aliases for each argument in the test dataset in case some aliases would indicate the target argument in the same way.

Crowdsourced Review. Another group of annotators were asked to review whether each annotated argument was correct on a crowdsourcing platform. In order to decrease the difficulty for review and increase the efficiency at the same time, we constructed judgement questions according to the results of formal document annotation. Judgement questions were grouped by event, which means there would be multiple problems to review for an event if several arguments were extracted. Figure 3 gives an example of the review instance. For questions judged as wrong ones, we would then re-annotate corresponding instances until the correctness reaches 95%.

Table 4. Statistics of DuEE training, dev and test sets.

Dataset	Training set	Dev set	Test set
#Instances	11,958	1,498	3,500
#Events	13,478	1,790	4,372
#Arguments	29,052	3,696	8,772

3   Dataset Statistics

According to the construction procedure introduced above, we build the largest
Chinese event extraction dataset, DuEE, which contains 19,640 events categorized to 65 different predefined event types, and 41,520 event arguments mapped
to 121 unique predefined argument roles. Different from existing datasets, we
provide our dataset in sentence level. There're 16,956 instances in total, each
instance might contain several sentences as sometimes it costs a few sentences
to describe an event.

As shown in Table 4, DuEE dataset is split into three parts, a training set,
a development set and a test set, there is no overlap among these three sets.
Currently, the training set and development set are available to download.

We further analyzed the data distribution over event types and argument
roles separately, and corresponding results are shown in Fig. 4 and Fig. 5. We
could see that the distribution of argument roles is closely related to that of
event types. While event type "Competition.Result" accounts for 15% of all
events, we could see that related argument roles also take up a great part of all
arguments, like "Winner" and "Loser". Argument roles like "Time" and "Location" generally appear in most events and thus have high frequency.

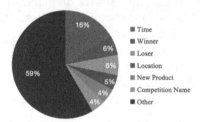

Fig. 4. Event type distribution.   **Fig. 5.** Argument role distribution.

4   Evaluation on DuEE

4.1   Shared Competition

We hosted an EE task based on DuEE dataset in 2020 Language and Intelligence Challenge. Given predefined schema and instances composed of sentences,

Table 5. Evaluation results of top performing systems.

System No.	Precision	Recall	F1	System No.	Precision	Recall	F1
S1	87.58%	84.29%	85.90%	S6	85.39%	84.04%	84.71%
S2	87.33%	83.52%	85.38%	S7	86.80%	82.66%	84.68%
S3	86.04%	84.68%	85.35%	S8	84.62%	84.70%	84.66%
S4	87.39%	83.39%	85.34%	S9	84.12%	84.48%	84.30%
S5	86.80%	82.76%	84.73%	S10	85.86%	82.66%	84.23%

this task aims to identify possible predefined event types for each instance, and extract event arguments playing certain roles. This competition match outputs of participants' systems with the manually annotated results, and score according to the matching F1.

For each predicted argument, we calculate its matching score with annotated results in token level, and the matching procedure is case insensitive. If an argument has multiple annotated mentions, the mention with the highest matching score will be used. We assume the matching score for each argument as $m_i (0 \leq m_i \leq 1)$, and m_i could be calculated as follows:

$$P_i = \frac{N_i^c}{L_i^p}, \quad R_i = \frac{N_i^c}{L_i^a}, \quad F1_i = \frac{2 \times P_i \times R_i}{P_i + R_i} \tag{1}$$

$$m_i = M_{et} \times M_{ar} \times F1_i \tag{2}$$

N_i^c stands for the number of common characters between the ith predicted argument and the chosen annotated result. L_i^p and L_i^a are the length of the predicted argument and the annotated one separately. While M_{et} and M_{ar} indicate the correctness of related event type and argument role separately, both of which would be either 0 or 1. Given m_i, the final F1 score would be calculated as follows:

$$P = \frac{1}{N_P} \times \sum_{i=1}^{N_P} m_i, \quad R = \frac{1}{N_A} \times \sum_{i=1}^{N_P} m_i, \quad F1 = \frac{2 \times P \times R}{P + R} \tag{3}$$

where N_P stands for the number of all predicted arguments and N_A indicates the number of all annotated ones. The final result is ranked according to the F1 score.

4.2 Results and Analysis

The overall competition results are published in the competition website. Table 5 lists the performance of top participant systems, and the results are ordered by their F1 scores. For further understanding of our dataset and related EE technologies, we would like to provide a detailed analysis on the outputs of top performing systems.

Table 6. Error types in predicted results of top performing systems.

Error Type	Error Description	Example	Ratio
Event type error	The predicted event type is wrong.	一年曝婚变? 阿娇老公被传出轨嫩模网红爆料者发文公开道歉解释 **Prediction**: {"Event type": "人生. 出轨", "EventArguments": [{"role": "出轨方", "text": "阿娇老公"}]} **Annotation**: {"Event type": "交往. 道歉", "EventArguments": [{"role": "道歉方", "text": "爆料者"}]}	17.4%
Non-existing role error	The event type is matched, but the sentence doesn't contain any argument of the predicted role.	王者荣耀: 四冠教练 Gemini 宣布卸任, 这名边路英雄彻底火了! **Prediction**: {"EventType": "组织关系. 辞/离职", "EventArguments": [{"role": "原所属组织", "text": "王者荣耀"}, {"role": "离职者", "text": "四冠教练 Gemini"}]} **Annotation**: {"EventType": "组织关系. 辞/离职", "EventArguments": [{"role": "离职者", "text": "四冠教练 Gemini"}]}	37.0%
Completely mismatched argument error	Predicted event type and role are correct, but the argument completely mismatches with golden result.	保时捷女司机首发声: 想死的心都有了所长丈夫已被暂时停职 **Prediction**: {"EventType": "组织关系. 停职", "EventArguments": [{"role": "停职人员", "text": "保时捷女司机"}]} **Annotation**: {"EventType": "组织关系. 停职", "EventArguments": [{"role": "停职人员", "text": "所长丈夫"}]}	23.2%
Argument boundary error	Predicted event type and role are correct, and the argument is partially matched with the golden result.	悲剧! 绍兴世茂一名 35 岁女子坠楼身亡! **Prediction**: {"EventType": "人生. 死亡", "EventArguments": [{"role": "死者", "text": "名 35 岁女子"}]} **Annotation**: {"EventType": "人生. 死亡", "EventArguments": [{"role": "死者", "text": "一名 35 岁女子"}]}	22.4%

Error Types for Predicted Results. We collected the predicted results of 10 top performing systems and analyzed error types for wrong predicted arguments, Table 6 shows the final result. "Event type error" could easily appear when there exist common characters between the name of wrong predicted event type and the text. It reveals that the EE system actually needs fine understanding of the context. The most common error type stands on "Non-existing role error", in detail, the extracted phrase could actually be not an entity sometimes and in other scenario, the extracted entity does not act in the corresponding event. This happens due to there being 121 roles in total, which promotes the difficulty for

Table 7. Recalls on single-valued problems and multi-valued ones.

Type	Recall	Type	Recall
Single-event instances	87.8%	Single-argument roles	85.9%
Multi-events instances	73.4%	Multi-arguments roles	72.8%

Table 8. Two types of unrecalled multi-arguments roles.

Type	Instance example	Recall
Multiple arguments are adjacent	今年5月27日，A股上的**海润光伏、福建众和股份、成都华泽钴镍材料**3家公司复盘，直接一字跌停，躺在地板上无法动弹。 Event type: 财经/交易.跌停 Argument role: 跌停股票 Multi-arguments: 海润光伏, 福建众和股份, 成都华泽钴镍材料	56.5%
Multiple arguments are not adjacent	北京时间6月4日，中国男足在广州正式进行训练，最新消息显示，**恒大国脚黄博文**因伤退出，这已经是第二位退出本次集训的恒大国脚，之前**徐新**就因伤退出。在两人退出后，恒大的国脚人数只剩下5人，远远少于国安的8人。 Event type: 组织关系.退出 Argument role: 退出方 Multi-arguments: 恒大国脚黄博文, 徐新	73.5%

argument extraction. When an extracted argument completely mismatch with any annotated results of clarified role, we call it as a "Completely mismatched argument error". And the wrongly extracted argument usually share the same entity type with annotated ones. This indicates that EE systems should be good at analyzing semantic roles in the text. For "argument boundary error", in most cases, the length of predicted arguments are shorter than the annotated ones. This indicates the difficulty to capture the complete description over arguments in DuEE, and sometimes, incomplete predicted results could not actually indicate target arguments.

Single-Valued v.s. Multi-valued Problems. As illustrated in Table 5, we could know that top performing systems tend to have lower recall scores compared to their precision scores, thus we carried out detailed analysis for that. Firstly, we found that the recall performance for instances with multiple events would be 14.4% lower than single-events instances as shown in Table 7, and instances with multiple events account for 19.5% in the test dataset. Events in one instance are usually related to each other and could share the same arguments, an example could be found in Table 1. After that, we also found that when there're multiple arguments to predict for one particular role, the recall would be 13.1% lower as illustrated in Table 7. We further sampled instances with multi-arguments roles, and found that we could categorize such samples into two types according to whether multiple arguments are adjacent to each other. We also took two arguments as adjacent if they are connected by a simple separator. Example instances and corresponding recalls for both types are shown in Table 8. We could know that it would be a great challenge to achieve high recall performance for multi-arguments extraction problems, especially when arguments are adjacent to each other.

5   Conclusion

This paper presents DuEE dataset, the largest high-quality Chinese event extraction dataset constructed from real world hot topics and news, whose construction procedure is also described in detail. We introduced a technical evaluation based on DuEE and analyzed the outputs of top performing systems. The results not only show that DuEE is helpful for further research in Chinese EE techniques but also provide solid baseline for proposed corpus. Finally, the analysis reveals that further research is needed for multi-valued event extraction problems, which could include multi-events detection and multi-arguments extraction in detail. At the same time, more research should also concentrate on event extraction systems that could perform well at much more event types with limited sample sizes, which would be a great work for realistic problems.

References

1. Ji, H., Grishman, R.: Refining event extraction through cross-document inference. In: Proceedings of ACL 2008: Hlt, pp. 254–262 (2008)
2. Chen, Y., Xu, L., Liu, K., Zeng, D., Zhao, J.: Event extraction via dynamic multi-pooling convolutional neural networks. In: Proceedings of the 53rd Annual Meeting of the Association for Computational Linguistics and the 7th International Joint Conference on Natural Language Processing (Volume 1: Long Papers), pp. 167–176 (2015)
3. Chen, Y., Liu, S., He, S., Liu, K., Zhao, J.: Event extraction via bidirectional long short-term memory tensor neural networks. In: Sun M., Huang X., Lin H., Liu Z., Liu Y. (eds.) Chinese Computational Linguistics and Natural Language Processing Based on Naturally Annotated Big Data, NLP-NABD 2016, CCL 2016. Lecture Notes in Computer Science, vol. 10035, pp. 190–203. Springer, Cham (2016). https://doi.org/10.1007/978-3-319-47674-2_17
4. Nguyen, T.H., Cho, K., Grishman, R.: Joint event extraction via recurrent neural networks. In: Proceedings of the 2016 Conference of the North American Chapter of the Association for Computational Linguistics: Human Language Technologies, pp. 300–309 (2016)
5. Liu, X., Luo, Z., Huang, H.Y.: Jointly multiple events extraction via attention-based graph information aggregation. In: Proceedings of the 2018 Conference on Empirical Methods in Natural Language Processing, pp. 1247–1256 (2018)
6. Nguyen, T.H., Grishman, R.: Graph convolutional networks with argument-aware pooling for event detection. In: Thirty-Second AAAI Conference on Artificial Intelligence (2018)
7. Sha, L., Qian, F., Chang, B., Sui, Z.: Jointly extracting event triggers and arguments by dependency-bridge rnn and tensor-based argument interaction. In: Thirty-Second AAAI Conference on Artificial Intelligence (2018)

8. Yang, S., Feng, D., Qiao, L., Kan, Z., Li, D.: Exploring pre-trained language models for event extraction and generation. In: Proceedings of the 57th Annual Meeting of the Association for Computational Linguistics, pp. 5284–5294 (2019)

9. Wadden, D., Wennberg, U., Luan, Y., Hajishirzi, H.: Entity, relation, and event extraction with contextualized span representations. In: Proceedings of the 2019 Conference on Empirical Methods in Natural Language Processing and the 9th International Joint Conference on Natural Language Processing (EMNLP-IJCNLP), pp. 5788–5793 (2019)

10. Zhu, F., Liu, Z., Yang, J., Zhu, P.: Chinese event place phrase recognition of emergency event using maximum entropy. In: 2011 IEEE International Conference on Cloud Computing and Intelligence Systems, pp. 614–618. IEEE (2011)

Transformer-Based Multi-aspect Modeling for Multi-aspect Multi-sentiment Analysis

Zhen Wu, Chengcan Ying, Xinyu Dai$^{(\boxtimes)}$ ⓘ, Shujian Huang, and Jiajun Chen

National Key Laboratory for Novel Software Technology, Nanjing University,
Nanjing 210023, China
{wuz,yingcc}@smail.nju.edu.cn, {daixinyu,huangsj,chenjj}@nju.edu.cn

Abstract. Aspect-based sentiment analysis (ABSA) aims at analyzing the sentiment of a given aspect in a sentence. Recently, neural network-based methods have achieved promising results in existing ABSA datasets. However, these datasets tend to degenerate to sentence-level sentiment analysis because most sentences contain only one aspect or multiple aspects with the same sentiment polarity. To facilitate the research of ABSA, NLPCC 2020 Shared Task 2 releases a new large-scale Multi-Aspect Multi-Sentiment (MAMS) dataset. In the MAMS dataset, each sentence contains at least two different aspects with different sentiment polarities, which makes ABSA more complex and challenging. To address the challenging dataset, we re-formalize ABSA as a problem of multi-aspect sentiment analysis, and propose a novel Transformer-based Multi-aspect Modeling scheme (TMM), which can capture potential relations between multiple aspects and simultaneously detect the sentiment of all aspects in a sentence. Experiment results on the MAMS dataset show that our method achieves noticeable improvements compared with strong baselines such as BERT and RoBERTa, and finally ranks the 2nd in NLPCC 2020 Shared Task 2 Evaluation.

Keywords: ABSA · MAMS · Neural network · Transformer · Multi-aspect Modeling

1 Introduction

Aspect-based sentiment analysis (ABSA) is a fine-grained sentiment analysis task, which aims to detect the sentiment polarity towards one given aspect in a sentence [14,17,20]. The given aspect usually refers to the aspect term or the aspect category. An aspect term is a word or phrase explicitly mentioned in the sentence representing the feature or entity of products or services. Aspect categories are pre-defined coarse-grained aspect descriptions, such as *food*, *service*,

---

Z. Wu and C. Ying—Authors contributed equally.

X. Zhu et al. (Eds.): NLPCC 2020, LNAI 12431, pp. 546–557, 2020.
https://doi.org/10.1007/978-3-030-60457-8_45

and *staff* in restaurant review domain. Therefore, ABSA contains two subtasks, namely Aspect Term Sentiment Analysis (ATSA) and Aspect Category Sentiment Analysis (ACSA). Figure 1 shows an example for ATSA and ACSA. Given the sentence "*The salmon is tasty while the waiter is very rude*", the sentiments toward the two aspect terms "*salmon*" and "*waiter*" are respectively positive and negative. ACSA is to detect the sentiment polarity towards the given pre-defined aspect category, which is explicitly or implicitly expressed in the sentence. There are two aspect categories in the sentence of Fig. 1, i.e., *food* and *waiter*, and their sentiments are respectively positive and negative. Note that the annotations for ATSA and ACSA can be separated.

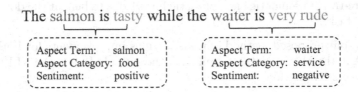

The salmon is tasty while the waiter is very rude

Aspect Term:	salmon	Aspect Term:	waiter
Aspect Category:	food	Aspect Category:	service
Sentiment:	positive	Sentiment:	negative

Fig. 1. An example of the ATSA and ACSA subtasks. The terms in red are two given aspect terms. Note that the annotations for ATSA and ACSA can be separated. (Color figure online)

To study ABSA, several public datasets are constructed, including multiple SemEval Challenges datasets [18–20] and Twitter dataset [5]. However, in these datasets, most sentences consist of only one aspect or multiple aspects with the same sentiment polarity, which makes ABSA degenerate to sentence-level sentiment analysis [9]. For example, there are only 0.09% instances in Twitter dataset belonging to the case of multi-aspects with different sentiment polarities. To promote the research of ABSA, NLPCC 2020 Shared Task 2 releases a Multi-Aspect Multi-Sentiment (MAMS) dataset. In the MAMS dataset, each sentence consists of at least two aspects with different sentiment polarities. Obviously, the property of multi-aspect multi-sentiment makes the proposed dataset more challenging compared with existing ABSA datasets.

To deal with ABSA, recent works employ neural networks and achieve promising results in previous datasets, such as attention networks [6,16,25], memory networks [2,22], and BERT [9]. These works separate multiple aspects of a sentence into several instances and process one aspect each time. As a result, they only consider local sentiment information for the given aspect while neglecting the sentiments of other aspects in the same sentence as well as the relations between multiple aspects. This setting is unsuitable, especially for the new MAMS dataset, as multiple aspects of a sentence usually have different sentiment polarities in the MAMS dataset, and knowing sentiment of a certain aspect can help infer sentiments of other aspects. To address the issue, we re-formalize ABSA as a task of multi-aspect sentiment analysis, and propose a **T**ransformer-based **M**ulti-aspect **M**odeling method (TMM) to simultaneously detect the sentiment polarities of all aspects in a sentence. Specifically, we adopt the pre-trained RoBERTa [15] as backbone network and build a multi-aspect scheme for MAMS based on transformer [23] architecture, then employ multi-head attention to learn the sentiment and relations of multi-aspects. Compared with existing works, our method has three advantages:

1. It can capture sentiments of all aspects synchronously in a sentence and relations between them, thereby avoid focusing on sentiment information belonging to other aspects mistakenly.
2. Modeling multi-aspect simultaneously can improve computation efficiency largely without additional running resources.
3. Our method applies the strategy of transfer learning, which exploits large-scale pre-trained semantic and syntactic knowledge to benefit the downstream MAMS task.

Finally, our proposed method obtains obvious improvements for both ATSA and ACSA in the MAMS dataset, and rank the second place in the NLPCC 2020 Shared Task 2 Evaluation.

2   Proposed Method

In this section, we first re-formalize the ABSA task, then present our proposed Transformer-based Multi-aspect Modeling scheme for ATSA and ACSA. The final part introduces the fine-tuning and training objective.

2.1   Task Formalization

Prior studies separate multiple aspects and formalize ABSA as a problem of sentiment classification toward one given aspect a in the sentence $s = \{w_1, w_2, \cdots, w_n\}$. In ATSA, the aspect term a is a span of the sentence s representing the feature or entity of products or services. For ACSA, the aspect category $a \in A$ and A is the pre-defined aspect set, i.e., {*food, service, staff, price, ambience, menu, place, miscellaneous*} for the new MAMS dataset. The goal of ABSA is to assign a sentiment label $y \in C$ to the aspect a of the sentence s, where C is the set of sentiment polarities (i.e., positive, neural and negative).

In this work, we re-formalize ABSA as a task of multi-aspect sentiment classification. Given a sentence $s = \{w_1, w_2, \cdots, w_n\}$ and m aspects $\{a_1, a_2, \cdots, a_m\}$ mentioned in s, the objective of MAMS is to simultaneously detect the sentiment polarities $\{y_1, y_2, \cdots, y_m\}$ of all aspects $\{a_1, a_2, \cdots, a_m\}$, where y_i corresponds to the sentiment label of the aspect a_i.

2.2   Transformer-Based Multi-aspect Modeling for ATSA

Recently, Bidirectional Encoder Representations from Transformers (BERT) [4] achieves great success by pre-training a language representation model on large-scale corpora then fine-tuning on downstream tasks. When fine-tuning on classification tasks, BERT uses the specific token [CLS] to obtain task-specific representation, then applies one additional output layer for classification. For ABSA,

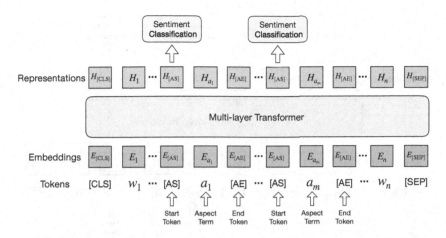

Fig. 2. Transformer-based Multi-Aspect Modeling for ATSA. In the above example, the aspect a_i may contain multiple words, and each word of the sentence might be split into several subwords. For simplicity, here we do not represent them with subword tokens.

previous work concatenates the given single aspect and the original sentence as the input of BERT encoder, then leverages the representation of [CLS] for sentiment classification [9].

Inspired by BERT, we design a novel Transformer-based Multi-Aspect Modeling scheme (TMM) to address MAMS task with simultaneously detecting the sentiments of all aspects in a sentence. Here we take ATSA subtask as example to elaborate on it. Specifically, given a sentence $\{w_1, \cdots, a_1, \cdots, a_m, \cdots, w_n\}$, where the aspect terms are denoted in the original sentence for the ease of following description, we propose two specific tokens [AS] and [AE] to respectively represent the start position and end position of aspect in the sentence. With the two tokens, the original sentence $\{w_1, \cdots, a_1, \cdots, a_m, \cdots, w_n\}$ can be transformed into the sequence $\{w_1, \cdots, [AS], a_1, [AE], \cdots, [AS], a_m, [AE], \cdots, w_n\}$. Based on this new input sequence, we then employ multi-layer transformer to automatically learn the sentiments and relations between multiple aspects.

As shown in Fig. 2, we finally fetch the representation $\mathbf{H}_{[AS]}$ of the start token [AS] of each aspect as feature vector to classify the sentiment of aspect.

2.3 Transformer-Based Multi-aspect Modeling for ACSA

Since aspect categories are pre-defined and may be not mentioned explicitly in the sentence, the above TMM scheme needs some modifications for ACSA. Given the sentence $s = \{w_1, w_2, \cdots, w_n\}$ and aspect categories $\{a_1, a_2, \cdots, a_m\}$ in s, we concatenate the sentence and aspect categories, and only use the token [AS] to separate multiple aspects because each aspect category is a single word, finally forming the input sequence $\{w_1, w_2, \cdots, w_n, [AS], a_1, [AS], a_2, \cdots, [AS], a_m\}$. As Fig. 3 shows, after multi-layer transformer, we use the representation $\mathbf{H}_{[AS]}$ the indication token [AS] of each aspect category for sentiment classifcation.

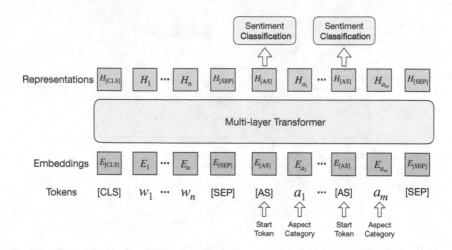

Fig. 3. Transformer-based Multi-Aspect Modeling for ACSA.

2.4   Fine-Tuning and Training Objective

As aforementioned, we adopt the pre-trained RoBERTa as backbone network, then fine-tune it on the MAMS dataset with the proposed TMM scheme. RoBERTa is a robustly optimized BERT approach and pre-trained with the larger corpora and batch size.

When in the fine-tuning stage, we employ a softmax classifier to map the representation $\mathbf{H}^i_{[AS]}$ of aspect a_i into the sentiment distribution $\hat{\mathbf{y}}_i$ as follow:

$$\hat{\mathbf{y}}_i = \mathrm{softmax}(\mathbf{W}_o\mathbf{H}^i_{[AS]} + \mathbf{b}_o), \tag{1}$$

where $\mathbf{W}_o$ and $\mathbf{b}_o$ respectively denote weight matrix and bias.

Finally, we use cross-entropy loss between predicted sentiment label and the golden sentiment label as training loss, which is defined as follows:

$$Loss = -\sum_{s\in D}\sum_{i=1}^{m}\sum_{j\in C}\mathbb{I}(y_i = j)\log \hat{y}_{i,j}, \tag{2}$$

where s and D respectively denote a sentence and training dataset, m represents the number of aspects in the sentence s, C is the sentiment label set, y_i denotes the ground truth sentiment of aspect a_i in s, and $\hat{y}_{i,j}$ is the predicted probability of the j-th sentiment towards the aspect a_i in the input sentence.

3   Experiment

3.1   Dataset and Metrics

Similar to SemEval 2014 Restaurant Review dataset [20], the original sentences in NLPCC 2020 Shared Task 2 are from the Citysearch New York dataset [7].

Each sentence is annotated with three experienced researchers working on natural language processing. In the released MAMS dataset, the annotations for ATSA and ACSA are separated. For ACSA, they pre-defined eight coarse-grained aspect categories, i.e., *food, service, staff, price, ambience, menu, place,* and *miscellaneous.* The sentences consisting of only one aspect or multiple aspects with the same sentiment polarities are deleted, thus each sentence at least contains two aspects with different sentiments. This property makes the MAMS dataset more challenging. The statistics of the MAMS dataset are shown in Tabel 1.

Table 1. Statistics of the MAMS dataset. Sen. and Asp. respectively denotes the numbers of sentences and given aspects in the dataset. Ave. represents the average number of aspects in each sentence. Pos., Neu. and Neg. respectively indicate the numbers of positive, neutral and negative sentiment.

Datasets		Sen.	Asp.	Ave.	Pos.	Neu.	Neg.
ATSA	Train	4297	11186	2.60	3380	5042	2764
	Dev	1000	2668	2.67	803	1211	654
	Test	1025	2676	2.61	1046	1085	545
ACSA	Train	3149	7090	2.25	1929	3077	2084
	Dev	800	1789	2.24	486	781	522
	Test	684	1522	2.23	562	612	348

NLPCC 2020 Shared Task 2 uses Macro-F1 to evaluate the performance of different systems, which is calculated as follows:

$$Precision(P) = TP/(TP + FP), \qquad (3)$$

$$Recall(R) = TP/(TP + FN), \qquad (4)$$

$$F1 = 2 * P * R/(P + R), \qquad (5)$$

where TP represents true positives, FP represents false positives, TN represents true negatives, and FN represents false negatives. Macro-F1 value is the average of F1 value of each category. The final evaluation result is the average result of Macro-F1 values on the two subtasks (i.e., ATSA and ACSA). In this work, we also use standard Accuracy as the metric to evaluate different methods.

3.2 Experiment Settings

We use pre-trained RoBERTa as backbone network, then fine-tune it on downstream ATSA or ACSA subtask with our proposed Transformer-based Multi-aspect Modeling scheme. The RoBERTa has 24 layers of transformer blocks, and each block has 16 self-attention heads. The dimension of hidden size is 1024. When fine-tuning on ATSA or ACSA, we apply Adam optimizer [10] to update model parameters. The initial learning rate is set to 1e-5, and the mini-batch size is 32. We use the official validation set for hyperparameters tuning. Finally, we run each model 3 times and report the average results on the test set.

3.3   Compared Methods

To evaluate the performance of different methods, we compare our RoBERTa-TMM method with the following baselines on ATSA and ACSA.

- **LSTM**: We use the vanilla LSTM to encode sentence and apply the average of all hidden states for sentiment classification.
- **TD-LSTM**: TD-LSTM [21] employs two LSTM networks respectively to encode the left context and right context of the aspect term, then concatenates them for sentiment classification.
- **AT-LSTM**: AT-LSTM [25] uses the aspect representation as query, and employs the attention mechanism to capture aspect-specific sentiment information. For ATSA, the aspect term representation is the average of word vectors in the aspect term. For ACSA, the aspect category representation is randomly initialized and learned in the training stage.
- **ATAE-LSTM**: ATAE-LSTM [25] is an extension of AT-LSTM. It concatenates the aspect representation and word embedding as the input of LSTM.
- **BiLSTM-Att**: BiLSTM-Att is our implemented model similar to AT-LSTM, which uses bidirectional LSTM to encode the sentence and applies aspect attention to capture the aspect-dependent sentiment.
- **IAN**: IAN [16] applies two LSTM to respectively encode the sentence and aspect term, then proposes the interactive attention to learn representations of the sentence and aspect term interactively. Finally, the two representations are concatenated for sentiment prediction.
- **RAM**: RAM [2] employs BiLSTM to build memory and then applies GRU-based multi-hops attention to generate the aspect-dependent sentence representation for predicting the sentiment of the given aspect.
- **MGAN**: MGAN [6] proposes fine-grained attention mechanism to capture the word-level interaction between aspect term and context, then combines it with coarse-grained attention for ATSA.

In addition, we also compare strong transformer-based models including BERT$_{BASE}$ and RoBERTa. They adopt the conventional ABSA scheme and deal with one aspect each time.

- **BERT$_{BASE}$**: BERT$_{BASE}$ [4] has 12 layers transformer blocks, and each block has 12 self-attention heads. When fine-tuning for ABSA, it concatenates the aspect and the sentence to form segment pair, then use the representation of the [CLS] token after multi-layer transformers for sentiment classification.
- **RoBERTa**: RoBERTa [15] is a robustly optimized BERT approach. It replaces the static masking in BERT with dynamic masking, removes the next sentence prediction, and pre-trains with larger batches and corpora.

3.4   Main Results and Analysis

Table 2 gives the results of different methods on two subtasks of ABSA.

Table 2. Main experiment results on ATSA and ASCA (%). The results with the marker * are from official evaluation and they do not provide accuracy performance.

Model	ATSA		ACSA	
	Acc.	F1	Acc.	F1
LSTM	48.45	47.45	45.86	45.04
BiLSTM-Att	71.91	71.04	69.84	69.28
TD-LSTM	75.01	73.80	–	–
AT-LSTM	67.95	66.87	68.39	67.98
ATAE-LSTM	65.26	64.48	66.41	66.15
IAN	70.02	68.88	–	–
RAM	75.58	74.46	–	–
MGAN	75.37	74.40	–	–
BERT$_{BASE}$	82.12	81.29	72.88	72.91
RoBERTa	83.71	83.17	77.44	77.29
RoBERTa-TMM	85.64	85.08	78.03	77.79
RoBERTa-TMM$_{ensemble}$	–	85.24*	–	79.41*

The first part shows the performance of non-transformer-based baselines. We can observe that the vanilla LSTM performs very pool in this new MAMS dataset, because it does not consider any aspect information and is a sentence-level sentiment classification model. In fact, LSTM can obtain pretty good results on previous ABSA datasets, which reveals the challenge of the MAMS dataset. Compared with other attention-based models, RAM and MGAN achieve better performance on ATSA, which validates the effectiveness of multi-hops attention and multi-grained attention for detecting the sentiment of aspect. It is surprising that the TD-LSTM obtains competitive results among non-transformer-based baselines. This result indicates that modeling position information of aspect term may be crucial for the MAMS dataset.

The second part gives two strong baselines, i.e., BERT$_{BASE}$ and RoBERTa. They follow the conventional ABSA scheme and deal with one aspect each time. It is observed that they outperform the non-transformer-based models significantly, which shows the power of pre-trained language models. Benefiting from the larger datasets, batch size and the more parameters, RoBERTa obtains better performance than BERT$_{BASE}$ on ATSA and ACSA.

Compared with the strongest baseline RoBERTa, our proposed Transformer-based Multi-aspect Modeling method RoBERTa-TMM still achieves obvious improvements in the challenging MAMS dataset. Specifically, it outperforms RoBERTa by 1.93% and 1.91% respectively in accuracy and F1-score for ATSA. In terms of ACSA, the improvement of RoBERTa-TMM against RoBERTa is relatively limited. This may be attributed to that the predefined aspect categories are abstract and it is challenging to find their corresponding sentiment spans from the sentence even in the multi-aspect scheme. Nevertheless, the improvement in ACSA is still substantial because the data size of the MAMS dataset is sufficient and even large-scale for ABSA research. Finally, our RoBERTa-TMM-based ensemble system achieves 85.24% and 79.41% respectively for ATSA and ACSA in F1-score, and ranks the 2nd in NLPCC 2020 Shared Task 2 Evaluation.

3.5 Case Study

Sentence: Food was OK – fish was cooked well.		RoBERTa-TMM	RoBERTa
Aspect term: Food	Sentiment: neutral	Food: neutral ✓	Food: positive ✗
Aspect term: fish	Sentiment: positive	fish: positive ✓	

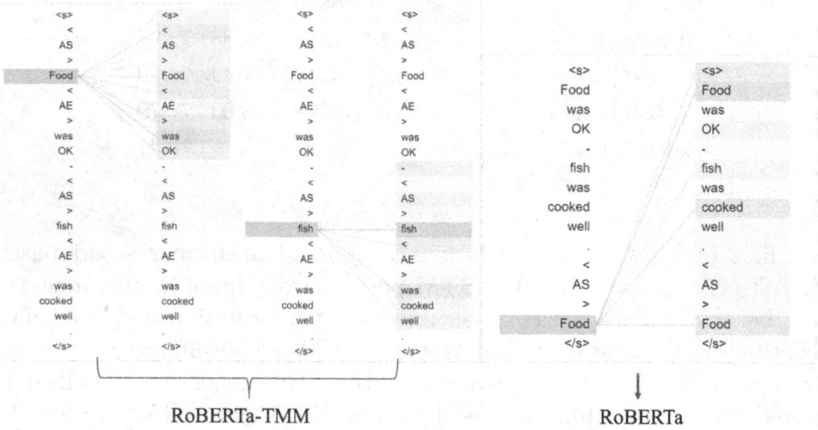

Fig. 4. Attention visualization of RoBERTa-TMM and RoBERTa in ATSA. The words in red are two given aspect terms. The darker blue denotes the bigger attention weight. (Color figure online)

To further validate the effectiveness of the proposed TMM scheme, we take a sentence from ATSA as example, and average the attention weight of different heads in RoBERTa-TMM and RoBERTa models, finally visualize them in Fig. 4.

From the results of attention visualization, we can see that the two aspect terms in the RoBERTa-TMM model capture the corresponding sentiment spans correctly through multi-aspect modeling. In contrast, given the aspect term "*Food*", RoBERTa mistakenly focuses on the sentiment spans of the other aspect term "*fish*" due to lacking other aspects information, thus making wrong sentiment prediction. The attention visualization indicates that the RoBERTa-TMM can detect the corresponding sentiment spans of different aspects and avoid wrong attention as much as possible by simultaneously modeling multi-aspect and considering the potential relations between multiple aspects.

4   Related Work

4.1   Aspect-Based Sentiment Analysis

Aspect-based sentiment analysis (ABSA) has been studied in the last decade. Early works devote to designing effective hand-crafted features, such as n-gram features [8,11] and sentiment lexicons [24]. Motivated by the success of deep learning in many tasks [1,3,12], recent works adopt neural network-based methods to automatically learn low-dimension and continuous features for ABSA. [21] separates the sentence into the left context and right context according to the aspect term, then employs two LSTM networks respectively to encode them from the two sides of sentence to the aspect term. To capture aspect-specific context, [25] proposes the aspect attention mechanism to aggregate important sentiment information from the sentence toward the given aspect. Following the idea, [16] introduces the interactive attention networks (IAN) to learn attentions in context and aspect term interactively, and generates the representations for aspect and context words separately. Besides, some works employ memory network to detect more powerful sentiment information with multi-hops attention and achieve promising results [2,22]. Instead of the recurrent network, [26] proposes the aspect information as the gating mechanism based on convolutional neural network, and dynamically selects aspect-specific information for aspect sentiment detection. Subsequently, BERT based method achieves state-of-the-art performance for the ABSA task [9].

However, the above methods perform ABSA with the conventional scheme that separates multiple aspects in the same sentence and analyzes one aspect each time. They only consider local sentiment information for the given aspect and possibly focus on sentiment information belonging to other aspects mistakenly. In contrast, our proposed Transformer-based Multi-aspect Modeling scheme (TMM) aims to learn sentiment information and relations between multiple aspects for better prediction.

4.2   Pre-trained Language Model

Recently, substantial works have shown that pre-trained language models can learn universal language representations, which are beneficial for downstream NLP tasks and can avoid training a new model from scratch [4,13,15,27]. These pre-trained models, e.g., GPT, BERT, XLNet, RoBERTa, use the strategy of first pre-training then fine-tuning and achieve the great success in many NLP tasks. To be specific, they first pre-train some self-supervised objectives, such as the masked language model (MLM), next sentence prediction (NSP), or sentence order prediction (SOP) [13] on the large corpora, to learn complex semantic and syntactic pattern from raw text. When fine-tuning on downstream tasks, they generally employ one additional output layer to learn task-specific knowledge.

Following the successful learning paradigm, in this work, we employ RoBERTa as the backbone network, then fine-tune it with the TMM scheme on the MAMS dataset to perform ATSA and ACSA.

5   Conclusion

Facing the challenging MAMS dataset, we re-formalize ABSA as a task of multi-aspect sentiment analysis in this work and propose a novel Transformer-based Multi-aspect Modeling scheme (TMM) for MAMS, which can determine the sentiments of all aspects in a sentence simultaneously. Specifically, TMM transforms the original sentence and constructs a new multi-aspect sequence scheme, then apply multi-layer transformers to automatically learn to sentiments clues and potential relations of multiple aspects in a sentence. Compared with previous works that analyze one aspect each time, our TMM scheme not only helps improve computation efficiency but also achieves substantial improvements in the MAMS dataset. Finally, our method achieves the second place in NLPCC 2020 Shared Task 2 Evaluation. Experiment results and analysis also validate the effectiveness of the proposed method.

Acknowledgements. This work was supported by the NSFC (No. 61976114, 61936012) and National Key R&D Program of China (No. 2018YFB1005102).

References

1. Bengio, Y., Ducharme, R., Vincent, P.: A neural probabilistic language model. In: NeurIPS 2000, Denver, CO, USA, pp. 932–938 (2000)
2. Chen, P., Sun, Z., Bing, L., Yang, W.: Recurrent attention network on memory for aspect sentiment analysis. In: EMNLP 2017, Copenhagen, Denmark, 9–11 September 2017, pp. 452–461 (2017)
3. Dahl, G.E., Yu, D., Deng, L., Acero, A.: Context-dependent pre-trained deep neural networks for large-vocabulary speech recognition. IEEE Trans. Speech Audio Process. **20**(1), 30–42 (2012)
4. Devlin, J., Chang, M., Lee, K., Toutanova, K.: BERT: pre-training of deep bidirectional transformers for language understanding. In: NAACL-HLT 2019, Minneapolis, MN, USA, 2–7 June 2019, Volume 1 (Long and Short Papers), pp. 4171–4186 (2019)
5. Dong, L., Wei, F., Tan, C., Tang, D., Zhou, M., Xu, K.: Adaptive recursive neural network for target-dependent twitter sentiment classification. In: ACL 2014, 22–27 June 2014, Baltimore, MD, USA, Volume 2: Short Papers, pp. 49–54 (2014)
6. Fan, F., Feng, Y., Zhao, D.: Multi-grained attention network for aspect-level sentiment classification. In: EMNLP 2018, Brussels, Belgium, 31 October–4 November 2018, pp. 3433–3442 (2018)
7. Ganu, G., Elhadad, N., Marian, A.: Beyond the stars: improving rating predictions using review text content. In: WebDB 2009, Providence, Rhode Island, USA, 28 June 2009 (2009)
8. Jiang, L., Yu, M., Zhou, M., Liu, X., Zhao, T.: Target-dependent twitter sentiment classification. In: ACL 2011, 19–24 June 2011, Portland, Oregon, USA, pp. 151–160 (2011)
9. Jiang, Q., Chen, L., Xu, R., Ao, X., Yang, M.: A challenge dataset and effective models for aspect-based sentiment analysis. In: EMNLP-IJCNLP 2019, Hong Kong, China, 3–7 November 2019, pp. 6279–6284 (2019)

10. Kingma, D.P., Ba, J.: Adam: a method for stochastic optimization. In: ICLR 2015, San Diego, CA, USA, 7–9 May 2015, Conference Track Proceedings (2015)
11. Kiritchenko, S., Zhu, X., Cherry, C., Mohammad, S.: NRC-Canada-2014: detecting aspects and sentiment in customer reviews. In: SemEval@COLING 2014, Dublin, Ireland, 23–24 August 2014, pp. 437–442 (2014)
12. Krizhevsky, A., Sutskever, I., Hinton, G.E.: ImageNet classification with deep convolutional neural networks. In: NeurIPS 2012, 3–6 December 2012, Lake Tahoe, Nevada, United States, pp. 1106–1114 (2012)
13. Lan, Z., Chen, M., Goodman, S., Gimpel, K., Sharma, P., Soricut, R.: ALBERT: a lite BERT for self-supervised learning of language representations. In: ICLR 2020, Addis Ababa, Ethiopia, 26–30 April 2020 (2020)
14. Liu, B.: Sentiment analysis and opinion mining. Synth. Lect. Hum. Lang. Technol. **5**, 1–67 (2012)
15. Liu, Y., et al.: RoBERTa: a robustly optimized BERT pretraining approach. CoRR (2019)
16. Ma, D., Li, S., Zhang, X., Wang, H.: Interactive attention networks for aspect-level sentiment classification. In: IJCAI 2017, Melbourne, Australia, 19–25 August 2017, pp. 4068–4074 (2017)
17. Pang, B., Lee, L.: Opinion mining and sentiment analysis. Found. Trends Inf. Retr. **2**(1–2), 1–135 (2007)
18. Pontiki, M., et al.: SemEval-2016 task 5: aspect based sentiment analysis. In: SemEval@NAACL-HLT 2016, San Diego, CA, USA, 16–17 June 2016, pp. 19–30 (2016)
19. Pontiki, M., Galanis, D., Papageorgiou, H., Manandhar, S., Androutsopoulos, I.: SemEval-2015 task 12: aspect based sentiment analysis. In: SemEval@NAACL-HLT 2015, Denver, Colorado, USA, 4–5 June 2015, pp. 486–495 (2015)
20. Pontiki, M., et al.: SemEval-2014 task 4: aspect based sentiment analysis. In: SemEval@COLING 2014, Dublin, Ireland, 23–24 August 2014, pp. 27–35 (2014)
21. Tang, D., Qin, B., Feng, X., Liu, T.: Effective LSTMs for target-dependent sentiment classification. In: COLING 2016, 11–16 December 2016, Osaka, Japan, pp. 3298–3307 (2016)
22. Tang, D., Qin, B., Liu, T.: Aspect level sentiment classification with deep memory network. In: EMNLP 2016, Austin, Texas, USA, 1–4 November 2016, pp. 214–224 (2016)
23. Vaswani, A., et al.: Attention is all you need. In: NeurIPS 2017, 4–9 December 2017, Long Beach, CA, USA, pp. 5998–6008 (2017)
24. Vo, D., Zhang, Y.: Target-dependent twitter sentiment classification with rich automatic features. In: IJCAI 2015, Buenos Aires, Argentina, 25–31 July 2015, pp. 1347–1353 (2015)
25. Wang, Y., Huang, M., Zhu, X., Zhao, L.: Attention-based LSTM for aspect-level sentiment classification. In: EMNLP 2016, Austin, Texas, USA, 1–4 November 2016, pp. 606–615 (2016)
26. Xue, W., Li, T.: Aspect based sentiment analysis with gated convolutional networks. In: ACL 2018, Melbourne, Australia, 15–20 July 2018, Volume 1: Long Papers, pp. 2514–2523 (2018)
27. Yang, Z., Dai, Z., Yang, Y., Carbonell, J.G., Salakhutdinov, R., Le, Q.V.: XLNet: generalized autoregressive pretraining for language understanding. In: NeurIPS 2019, 8–14 December 2019, Vancouver, BC, Canada, pp. 5754–5764 (2019)

Overview of the NLPCC 2020 Shared Task: AutoIE

Xuefeng Yang[1(✉)], Benhong Wu[1], Zhanming Jie[2], and Yunfeng Liu[1]

[1] ZhuiYi Technology, ShenZhen, China
{ryan,wubenhong,glen}@wezhuiyi.com
[2] Singapore University of Technology and Design, Singapore, Singapore
zhanming_jie@mymail.sutd.edu.sg

Abstract. This is an overview paper of the NLPCC 2020 shared task on AutoIE, which aims to evaluate the information extraction solutions under low data resource. Given an unlabeled corpus, entity lists covering 30% entities in the corpus and some labeled validation samples, participants are required to build a named entity recognition system. There are 44 registered teams and 16 of them submitted results, the top system achieve 0.041 and 0.133 F1 score improvement upon the baseline system with or without labeled validation data respectively. The evaluation result indicates that it is possible to use less human annotation for information extraction system. All information about this task may be found at https://github.com/ZhuiyiTechnology/AutoIE.

Keywords: Named entity recognition · Low resource natural language processing

1 Introduction

Information extraction (IE) [2] aims to build intelligent system which may extract entities, attributes and relations from unstructured text. The extracted structure knowledge may be used as an individual application or supporting downstream applications like dialogue system [1] and information retrieval [6]. The important role IE played in language intelligence makes it a hot topic, and many IE systems have been developed in the last decades. The openIE [4] system does not assume the categories of information while ontology based IE systems [11] use predefined categories. In recent years, data driven machine learning models dominates the novel solutions developed for ontology based IE, and many progress have been obtained [5,13].

Large amount of data is necessary for data driven approaches, and it is very expensive to annotate a full labeled dataset. This limitation reveal the significant problem in practical IE application, especially for application specific information. Focusing on specific problem, the participants challenge to build NER system with no direct human annotation in this evaluation task. Given an unlabeled corpus and a list of entities (gazetteers), the proposed solutions need to

X. Zhu et al. (Eds.): NLPCC 2020, LNAI 12431, pp. 558–566, 2020.
https://doi.org/10.1007/978-3-030-60457-8_46

Train Sample

Unlabeled Corpus	Entity List
爸爸回来了140522标清	笑傲江湖
笑傲江湖25精彩片段高清	于谦
德云社郭德纲相声专长重庆站	郭德纲

Valid Sample

1	4	0	9	1	5	华	晨	宇	天	天	向	上	录	制	无	剧	透	小	花	絮
O	O	O	O	O	O	B-PER	I-PER	E-PER	B-TV	I-TV	I-TV	E-TV	O	O	O	O	O	O	O	O

Fig. 1. Sample of train and valid data. Train samples do not contain linked labels while samples for validation are fully annotated. The entity list only include around 30% entities occurring in unlabeled corpus.

learn labels and models simultaneously. This setting is very common in practical application scenario because unlabeled corpus and the entities list are not expensive for the interesting information. What costs most in the developing process is annotating the links between entities and unlabeled text.

The task provides a dataset with 13000 samples, including 10000 train, 1000 valid and 2000 test samples. The 10000 train samples are not annotated, and 1851 entities in three categories are provided as lists to support the auto labeling process for train samples. Both valid and test samples are fully annotated. The sample is shown in Fig. 1.

There are totally 44 teams that sign in this shared task, and 16 of them submitted their solutions before the deadline. The good news is that most submitted systems defeat the baseline and top ranked systems improve the performance significantly. Without labeled validation samples, top system achieves 0.133 F1 score improvement, and 0.041 F1 score increase is obtained when there are 1000 labeled samples.

This overview is organized as follows. Section 2 will review some important works in related directions, and details of this evaluation task is provided in Sect. 3. After introducing the task setting, some important factors and the proposed solutions are analyzed in Sect. 4. Finally, the conclusion is given in Sect. 5.

2   Related Work

Firstly, we will review some widely used named entity recognition datasets for Chinese. Weibo dataset is initially provided in [15]. There are 4 categories entities and 1890 samples in total, the source corpus is from social media and full of oral presentations. Resume NER dataset [19] is from 1027 resume summaries in Sina Finance. There are 16565 entity annotations in 8 types, and the job title type nearly covers half of the labels. The clue ner dataset [17] is available recently, which contains 10 types of entities and 12091 samples.

Dealing with noise label in NER has draw some attention. Relabel is an effective method to solve this problem [10]. The proposed solution trains multi models simultaneously with subset of the whole dataset, these subsets has no intersection with each other. The label for each subset is estimated by other models and new models are trained with these updated labels. Bnpu [14] proposed that unbiased risk can be calculated by entity rate and the risk of both positive and unlabeled examples. The entity rate is initialized by a exist labeled data set and estimate by the predict result of bnpu. Then model will be trained with the estimated unbiased risk. To address false negative problem, AutoNER [16] employs fuzzy CRF which may predict multiple labels for entity candidate and the candidate entities are mined by auto phrase toolkit. The proposed LSTM-CRF-PA [18] can learn from incompletely labeled data directly, and select the distantly supervised instances with reinforcement learning.

From the perspective of machine learning, the challenge in this task is very close to the noise label problem which receives much attention recently. Clean-Net [12] is a strong baseline used in this field. CleanNet builds an reference set embedding and query embedding by attention mechanism, simple threshold based on the similarity between the reference set and the query image leads to good results. Co-teaching in [7] train two networks simultaneously, and the data for next mini-batch is filtered by the other network. An two stage strategy is employed in [8], the labels are corrected after regular training phrase. O2U-Net is proposed in [9], it addresses the problem by adjusting the hyper-parameters of the deep network to make its status transfer from overfitting to underfitting cyclically, which is very simple but effective.

3   Evaluation Task

The AutoIE evaluation task aims to decrease the cost of building IE system, especially for the NER problem with domain specific entity type. This evaluation task is strongly related to two research problems, which are learning from knowledge and data efficiency. Generally, these problems are very important for data driven machine learning applications.

3.1   Setting

For the NER application, there are two facts; first, the most common knowledge about entity recognition is a entity list which describing many entities belonging to the same category. Entity lists are not expensive because there are many existing lists and it is easy to create one by human if the coverage requirement is not high. Secondly, although full labeled dataset for training may cost a lot, annotating a small dataset for validation and testing is acceptable. AutoIE task is designed based on these two facts. To be specific, participants are required to build IE system with entity list and unlabeled corpus, and there is also a small size labeled data for validation.

3.2 Dataset

The dataset used in this task is originally from [10] and extended for supporting this evaluation. The contextual sentences are from the Youku video descriptions. Three types of entities are interested in this evaluation, including TV name, Person and TV number.

The whole dataset are divided as train, valid and test. In the training dataset, the corpus contains 10000 samples without annotations. Besides the corpus, three lists of interested entity types are provided. These entities may cover around 30% entities occurring in the unlabeled corpus. Validation dataset contains 1000 full labeled samples, and there is no restriction about how to use these validation data. Finally, 2000 full labeled samples are reserved for testing the submissions. The statistic of dataset may be found in Table 1.

Table 1. Statistic of dataset

Part	Size	Avg length	Entity num			List size		
			TV	PER	NUM	TV	PER	NUM
Train	10000	16.49	8957	4028	1036	1215	614	22
Valid	1000	15.81	843	420	94	Null	Null	Null
Test	2000	16.56	1722	863	185	Null	Null	Null
All	13000	16.45	11522	5311	1315	Null	Null	Null

There are restrictions for the usage of external resources. Larger entities lists in any form are not allowed and other corpus of video descriptions sentences are forbidden.

3.3 Baseline

The system in [10] achieves state of art result for incomplete label problem in NER application, and it is employed as the baseline system for our evaluation.

Figure 2 shows the pipeline of automatically labeling procedure used in this baseline. Initially, the labels are obtained by string matching with the entities

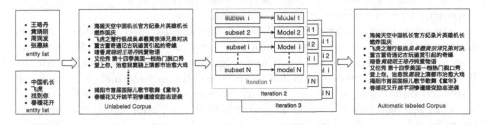

Fig. 2. Illustration of baseline system

list. After achieving these noise labels, models are trained with subset of the corpus. The labels in the next iteration are updated by the models learned in the previous iteration. Finally, a automatically labeled corpus is employed to learn the final model.

4   Task Analysis

Firstly, empirical studies about the influence of the entity list size, pretrained models and labeled data size are conducted to explore this AutoIE evaluation task. After the factors analysis, submitted systems are reviewed and evaluation result are provided.

4.1   Factor Analysis

In order to understand the effect of different factors, the performances of baseline system with different setting are studied. Three different factors that may affect the performance are included which are pretrained model, size of labeled data and entity coverage of given list.

Effect of Pretrained Models. Pretrained model are widely used in NLP tasks. The performance effect of different pretrained model on this AutoIE task is empirically studied, including Bert, RoBERTa and RBTL3.

As show in Table 2, RoBERTa achieves the best result in 3 pretrained models, but the improvement over Bert is just 1%.

Table 2. Pretrained models

Pretrained model	Precision	Recall	F1 score
Bert	79.01	82.82	80.87
RoBERTa	80.02	82.45	81.22
RBTL3	72.96	75.62	74.27

Size of Labeled Data. In this section, the effect of labeled data size on baseline system is analyzed. For comparison, 300, 500 and 700 samples are randomly selected from all 1000 valid samples. Besides the sample size, all other hyper parameters are the same for the experiments.

The performance with different labeled data size is listed in Table 3. Apparently, as the increase of labeled data size, precision, recall and f1 score are also improved, but recall increased more significantly than precision. With the labeled data size increased from 300 to 1000, recall improved 6.8% but precision improved only 2.5%, which means recall is more sensitive to labeled data size. Another interesting and reasonable result is that the performance improvement decrease when the data size increase linearly and there is almost no difference between 700 and 1000.

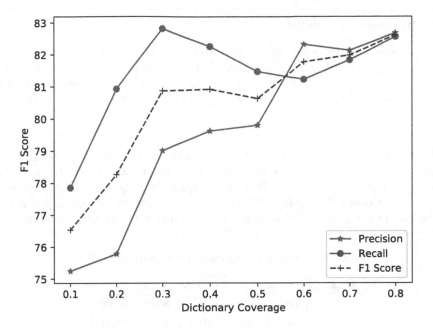

Fig. 3. F1 score with different coverage from 0.1 to 0.8

Table 3. Labeled data size

Labeled data size	Precision	Recall	F1 score
300	76.49	76.02	0.7645
500	77.87	78.04	0.7796
700	78.98	81.98	0.8045
1000	79.01	82.82	0.8087

Entity Coverage. Experiments with different entity coverage from 0.1 to 0.8 is conducted, entity coverage refers to the proportion of entities in the given list to all entities in the training set. For example, 0.5 coverage means 0.5 recall may be obtained using string match between the entity list and the unlabeled corpus. And the precision of all those dict match training set are around 82% to 85%.

Figure 3 shows the change of precision, recall and f1 score as we increase the entity coverage. As show in the figure, with the entity coverage increases, the performance of baseline system rise significantly when dictionary coverage no more than 0.3. But with the dictionary coverage exceeding 0.4, f1 score is less sensitive to the entity coverage rate. This indicates 0.3 coverage is a good choice for this baseline system with the consideration of lower cost is better.

4.2 Submission Analysis

9 of 16 teams propose better solutions than the baseline system when 1000 valid samples are employed, and all 7 submissions achieve better performance under the circumstance that no valid full label data is available. This promising result indicates that algorithm development plays an important role for NER problem under low resource.

Evaluation Results. The evaluation result of top3 submissions are given in Table 4 and 5. Apparently, all three systems significantly increase the performance with or without 1000 validation samples, and the best solution make a improvement over 0.04 and 0.13 F1 score. Another interesting conclusion is that the solutions are more effective when the full label data are not available.

Table 4. Evaluation leaderboard with validation data

Rank	System name	Precision	Recall	F1 score
1	Sophie	84.02	85.99	85.00
2	Hair loss knight	87.80	82.13	84.87
3	Hermers	85.96	83.57	84.75
4	Baseline	79.01	82.82	80.87

System Review. Top 3 ranking system are reviewed in this shared task. The sophie team divides training dataset into 2 parts by string matching between entity lists and corpus. For the incomplete annotation part, two-fold cross iterative training is applied. Self iterative training is used for the samples without any matched entities. The Hair loss knight team proposes a novel iteration strategy, and the annotation types is analyzed. They design the training procedure and set the training epoch increase with iteration. In addition, data augment and label confidence filter method are employed with the iteration strategy. The Hermers team studied the problem from three perspectives including contextual semantic representation, word merging layer and prediction majority voting. Different existing pretrained models are compared for this task, and the conclusion is that

Table 5. Evaluation leaderboard without validation data

Rank	System name	Precision	Recall	F1 score
1	Hair loss knight	80.99	73.79	77.32
2	yunke_ws	67.68	76.82	71.96
3	Hermers	76.03	68.12	71.86
4	Baseline	63.51	64.45	63.98

Chinese BERT-wwm-ext [3] may provide best features. For the word merging layer, word representation based on jieba word segmentation is concatenated to the character representation.

5   Conclusion

This paper briefly presents an overview of the AutoIE evaluation task in NLPCC 2020. The evaluation result of the first AutoIE is very exciting and promising, and this has given us strong confidence on the future. Despite all the top solutions increase the performance significantly, evaluation results on more datasets are expected. We believe these proposed solutions may help in practical information extraction applications.

References

1. Chen, H., Liu, X., Yin, D., Tang, J.: A survey on dialogue systems: recent advances and new frontiers. SIGKDD Explor. Newsl. **19**(2), 25 35 (2017). https://doi.org/10.1145/3166054.3166058
2. Cowie, J., Lehnert, W.: Information extraction. Commun. ACM **39**(1), 80–91 (1996). https://doi.org/10.1145/234173.234209
3. Cui, Y., et al.: Pre-training with whole word masking for Chinese BERT. arXiv preprint arXiv:1906.08101 (2019)
4. Etzioni, O., Banko, M., Soderland, S., Weld, D.S.: Open information extraction from the web. Commun. ACM **51**(12), 68–74 (2008). https://doi.org/10.1145/1409360.1409378
5. Gogar, T., Hubacek, O., Sedivy, J.: Deep neural networks for web page information extraction. In: Iliadis, L., Maglogiannis, I. (eds.) AIAI 2016. IAICT, vol. 475, pp. 154–163. Springer, Cham (2016). https://doi.org/10.1007/978-3-319-44944-9_14
6. Greengrass, E.: Information retrieval: a survey (2000)
7. Han, B., et al.: Co-teaching: robust training of deep neural networks with extremely noisy labels. In: Bengio, S., Wallach, H., Larochelle, H., Grauman, K., Cesa-Bianchi, N., Garnett, R. (eds.) Advances in Neural Information Processing Systems, vol. 31, pp. 8527–8537. Curran Associates, Inc. (2018). http://papers.nips.cc/paper/8072-co-teaching-robust-training-of-deep-neural-networks-with-extremely-noisy-labels.pdf
8. Han, J., Luo, P., Wang, X.: Deep self-learning from noisy labels. In: The IEEE International Conference on Computer Vision (ICCV), October 2019
9. Huang, J., Qu, L., Jia, R., Zhao, B.: O2U-Net: a simple noisy label detection approach for deep neural networks. In: 2019 IEEE/CVF International Conference on Computer Vision (ICCV), pp. 3325–3333 (2019)
10. Jie, Z., Xie, P., Lu, W., Ding, R., Li, L.: Better modeling of incomplete annotations for named entity recognition. In: Proceedings of the 2019 Conference of the North American Chapter of the Association for Computational Linguistics: Human Language Technologies, Volume 1 (Long and Short Papers), pp. 729–734. Association for Computational Linguistics, Minneapolis, Minnesota, June 2019. https://doi.org/10.18653/v1/N19-1079, https://www.aclweb.org/anthology/N19-1079

11. Karkaletsis, V., Fragkou, P., Petasis, G., Iosif, E.: Ontology based information extraction from text. In: Paliouras, G., Spyropoulos, C.D., Tsatsaronis, G. (eds.) Knowledge-Driven Multimedia Information Extraction and Ontology Evolution. LNCS (LNAI), vol. 6050, pp. 89–109. Springer, Heidelberg (2011). https://doi.org/10.1007/978-3-642-20795-2_4

12. Lee, K.H., He, X., Zhang, L., Yang, L.: CleanNet: transfer learning for scalable image classifier training with label noise. In: The IEEE Conference on Computer Vision and Pattern Recognition (CVPR), June 2018

13. Lin, Y., Ji, H., Huang, F., Wu, L.: A joint neural model for information extraction with global features. In: Proceedings of the 58th Annual Meeting of the Association for Computational Linguistics, pp. 7999–8009 (2020)

14. Peng, M., Xing, X., Zhang, Q., Fu, J., Huang, X.: Distantly supervised named entity recognition using positive-unlabeled learning. In: Proceedings of the 57th Annual Meeting of the Association for Computational Linguistics, pp. 2409–2419. Association for Computational Linguistics, Florence, July 2019. https://doi.org/10.18653/v1/P19-1231, https://www.aclweb.org/anthology/P19-1231

15. Peng, N., Dredze, M.: Named entity recognition for Chinese social media with jointly trained embeddings. In: Proceedings of the 2015 Conference on Empirical Methods in Natural Language Processing, pp. 548–554. Association for Computational Linguistics, Lisbon, September 2015. https://doi.org/10.18653/v1/D15-1064, https://www.aclweb.org/anthology/D15-1064

16. Shang, J., Liu, L., Gu, X., Ren, X., Ren, T., Han, J.: Learning named entity tagger using domain-specific dictionary. In: Proceedings of the 2018 Conference on Empirical Methods in Natural Language Processing, pp. 2054–2064. Association for Computational Linguistics, Brussels, October–November 2018. https://doi.org/10.18653/v1/D18-1230, https://www.aclweb.org/anthology/D18-1230

17. Xu, L., et al.: ClUENER 2020: fine-grained name entity recognition for Chinese. arXiv preprint arXiv:2001.04351 (2020)

18. Yang, Y., Chen, W., Li, Z., He, Z., Zhang, M.: Distantly supervised NER with partial annotation learning and reinforcement learning. In: Proceedings of the 27th International Conference on Computational Linguistics, pp. 2159–2169. Association for Computational Linguistics, Santa Fe, August 2018. https://www.aclweb.org/anthology/C18-1183

19. Zhang, Y., Yang, J.: Chinese NER using lattice LSTM. In: Proceedings of the 56th Annual Meeting of the Association for Computational Linguistics (Volume 1: Long Papers), pp. 1554–1564. Association for Computational Linguistics, Melbourne, July 2018. https://doi.org/10.18653/v1/P18-1144, https://www.aclweb.org/anthology/P18-1144

Light Pre-Trained Chinese Language Model for NLP Tasks

Junyi Li[1]([✉]), Hai Hu[1,2], Xuanwei Zhang[1,4], Minglei Li[1,5], Lu Li[1,3],
and Liang Xu[1]

[1] CLUE Team, Shenzhen, China
ljyduke@gmail.com
[2] Indiana University, Bloomington, USA
[3] Central China Normal University, Wuhan, China
[4] iQIYI Inc., Beijing, China
[5] Speech and Language Innovation Lab, Huawei Cloud and AI, Shenzhen, China
https://www.cluebenchmarks.com/

Abstract. We present the results of shared-task 1 held in the 2020 Conference on Natural Language Processing and Chinese Computing (NLPCC): Light Pre-Trained Chinese Language Model for NLP tasks. This shared-task examines the performance of light language models on four common NLP tasks: Text Classification, Named Entity Recognition, Anaphora Resolution and Machine Reading Comprehension. To make sure that the models are light-weight, we put restrictions and requirements on the number of parameters and inference speed of the participating models. In total, 30 teams registered our tasks. Each submission was evaluated through our online benchmark system (https://www.cluebenchmarks.com/nlpcc2020.html), with the average score over the four tasks as the final score. Various ideas and frameworks were explored by the participants, including data enhancement, knowledge distillation and quantization. The best model achieved an average score of 75.949, which was very close to BERT-base (76.460). We believe this shared-task highlights the potential of light-weight models and calls for further research on the development and exploration of light-weight models.

Keywords: Chinese language processing · Pre-trained language
models · Model lighting

1 Introduction

Pre-trained language models have become a very important component in recent Natural Language Processing (NLP) research and applications. They have been applied to many NLP tasks and have achieved great successes. Part of the progress of this trend was promoted by different datasets, competitions and leader-boards. Among these pre-trained models, BERT shows great advantages and achieve substantial performance improvements [3]. In industry, BERT and its various updated versions such as RoBERTa and ALBERT have been used

© Springer Nature Switzerland AG 2020
X. Zhu et al. (Eds.): NLPCC 2020, LNAI 12431, pp. 567–578, 2020.
https://doi.org/10.1007/978-3-030-60457-8_47

for many NLP problems, e.g., text classification, sequence labelling and machine reading comprehension [3,7,9,19].

However, very few datasets, competitions and leader-boards have been created in Chinese to evaluate the performance of models over Chinese NLP tasks. Furthermore, the sheer size of the transformers prevent them from being used in resource-lean scenarios, or cases where inference speed is a priority.

There have been attempts to remedy these issues. With regard to Chinese NLP datasets, Meituan-Dianping has recently released a sentiment classification task in AI-Challenger[1]. CLUE [18] has published a large-scale and comprehensive benchmark for Chinese Natural Language Understanding (NLU), with a total of nine NLU tasks, a small diagnostic dataset and a large pre-training corpus. Additionally, Tianchi[2], Kesci[3], Baidu AI[4] and some language conference like NLPCC[5] are also holding NLP challenges in Chinese to facilitate research in this area. Meanwhile, people began to pay attention to the Chinese language model Tencent [20], Baidu [11] and Huawei [15] also trained Chinese model on Chinese corpus. In terms of modelling, researchers have realized the importance of small models in industry, and proposed multiple methods to trim down large models like BERT, e.g., knowledge distillation [5,6,10,14], model pruning and quantification [4]. For task-agnostic knowledge distillation, MSRA proposed a way to do compression of pre-trained Transformers [14]. Researchers from CMU and Google released MobileBERT for compressing and accelerating the BERT model [12]. Huawei presented TinyBERT to transfer knowledge from huge models to light and task-specific models [6].

However, to the best of our knowledge, there is no shared-task in Chinese NLP that focuses exclusively on small and light models where model size and inference speed are taken into consideration in evaluation.

In this work, we introduce shared task 1 on NLPCC 2020: Light Pre-Trained Chinese Language Model for NLP Tasks. This task evaluates pre-trained models with limited model size and inference speed over four different tasks.

Six teams have submitted their results on our evaluation system and some of them are continuing to work on the tasks after the deadline of this task[6]. The top submission, which took advantage of NEZHA with TinyBERT distillation technology, achieved an average score of 75.949, which was close to 76.460 from BERT-base. Other submissions explored knowledge distillation, data augmentation and optimization scheme. In the following sections, we present our datasets, a review of the official baselines and submissions to our shared-task. Finally, a conclusion about this task is given in the last section.

---

[1] http://ai.chuangxin.com/.
[2] https://tianchi.aliyun.com/competition/gameList/activeList.
[3] https://www.kesci.com/.
[4] https://ai.baidu.com/.
[5] http://tcci.ccf.org.cn/conference/2020/cfpt.php.
[6] See most recent results at https://www.cluebenchmarks.com/nlpcc2020.html.

2 Task Description

2.1 Task Overview

The main purpose of this task is to train a light language model and evaluate it over four different NLP tasks. We comprehensively consider the number of model parameters, model accuracy, and model inference time, which will be used together as the model evaluation criteria. Here is our introduction to the data set. Along with this task, a huge Chinese corpus is released[7].

This task contains four different datasets, which are given in Table 1. Two of them are classification datasets, one of them is Name Entity Recognition dataset and the last one is Machine Reading Comprehension dataset. All the dataset used in this task are Chinese and the details about them will be described in Sect. 3.

The participants should train a pre-trained model and fine-tune it over training/evaluation dataset. After that, the predicted results using the fine-tuned model should be submitted to our evaluation system[8].

2.2 Evaluation Criteria

The results are evaluated using accuracy for each task. The final score is calculated by taking the average of scores over all four tasks. Besides, we will take into account the model parameters and inference time. The preliminary rounds including two factors:

- Model size: $< 12M$ $(1/9 * 110M)$.
- Inference time: $1/8 *$ (time of BERT-base) on the same task

We offer an equation here to calculate the scores among all participants.

We do not require the inference time of the contestants to be reproduced exactly on our local machine but required their live broadcast or recorded broadcast of inference time for model eligibility. Finally, we take speed and model size measured by ourselves locally as the basis for calculating the score.

The score is computed according to the formula below:

$$final\_score = P/100 * 0.8 + 0.1 * (1 - S_{Lite}/(0.9 * S_{BERT})) + 0.1 * (1 \ \ T_{Lite}/T_{BERT})$$

where

- P: scores on average
- S: Size of model
- T: Average time for inference given all the test data
- BERT: BERT base
- Lite: light model

---

[7] https://github.com/CLUEbenchmark/LightLM.
[8] https://www.cluebenchmarks.com/nlpcc2020.html.

Table 1. Dataset description.

Task name	Training data	Evaluation data	Test data
CSL	20k	3k	3k
CLUEWSC2020	1,244	304	290
CLUENER	10,748	1,343	1,345
CMRC 2018	10k	3.4k	4.9k

3   Dataset Description

There are four different datasets in this shared task. Overview of them is in Table 1.

3.1   CSL

Chinese Winograd Schema Challenge (CSL) is a variant of the Turing test, first introduced in [18]. The main purpose of it is to determine the common sense reasoning ability of AI systems. The computer program participating in the challenge needs to answer a special but simple common-sense question: the pronoun disambiguation problem, which is to judge whether the given nouns and pronouns refer to the same reference. Among them, the label, true means that the reference is consistent, false means that the reference is inconsistent (Table 2).

3.2   CMRC 2018

CMRC 2018 [2] is a span-extraction based dataset for Chinese machine reading comprehension. This dataset contains about 19,071 human-annotated questions from Wikipedia paragraphs. In CMRC 2018, all samples are composed of contexts, questions, and related answers. Furthermore, the answers are the text spans in contexts (Table 3).

3.3   CLUENER2020

This dataset was created by CLUE in 2020 [16]. It is a fine-grained dataset for named entity recognition in Chinese, containing 10 categories: person names, organization names, positions, company names, addresses, game names, governmental bodies, scenes, book names and movie names (Table 4).

3.4   CLUEWSC2020

The Chinese Winograd Schema Challenge dataset is an anaphora resolution task where the model is asked to decide whether a pronoun and a noun (phrase) in a sentence co-refer (binary classification), following similar datasets in English (e.g., [8,13]). Sentences in the dataset are manually-picked from 36 contemporary

Table 2. An example from CSL

item_index	item_value	item_value(en)
id	1	1
abst	" 为解决传统均匀 FFT 波束形成算法引起的 3 维声呐成像分辨率降低的问题, 该文提出分区域 FFT 波束形成算法. 远场条件下, 以保证成像分辨率为约束条件, 以划分数量最少为目标, 采用遗传算法作为优化手段将成像区域划分为多个区域. 在每个区域内选取一个波束方向, 获得每一个接收阵元收到该方向回波时的解调输出, 以此为原始数据在该区域内进行传统均匀 FFT 波束形成. 对 FFT 计算过程进行优化, 降低新算法的计算量, 使其满足 3 维成像声呐实时性的要求. 仿真与实验结果表明, 采用分区域 FFT 波束形成算法的成像分辨率较传统均匀 FFT 波束形成算法有显著提高, 且满足实时性要求."	"in order to solve the traditional FFT beamforming algorithm of 3 d sonar imaging resolution to reduce the problems, this paper points FFT beamforming algorithm is put forward. The far field condition, to ensure the imaging resolution as constraint conditions, to partition number at least as the goal, USES the genetic algorithm as a means of optimizing the imaging area is divided into multiple regions. Select a beam direction in each area, obtain each receiving array yuan received the demodulation output when the direction of the echo, as uniform raw data in the area of traditional FFT beamforming. Optimize the FFT calculation process, reduce the amount of calculation of the new algorithm, make it meet the requirements of 3D imaging sonar about instantaneity, and experimental results show that the image resolution of FFT beamforming algorithm is better than that of conventional FFT beamforming algorithm.
keyword	[" 水声学", "FFT", " 波束形成", "3 维成像声呐"]	["Underwater acoustics ", "FFT", " Beamforming ", "3D imaging sonar"]
label	1	1

literary works in Chinese. Their anaphora relations are then manually-annotated by linguists, amounting to 1,838 questions in total. Example questions are shown in Table 5. Specifically, the annotators were asked to find sentences that satisfy the two criteria: 1) it has one pronoun (*he, she, it,* etc.), 2) there are more than one potential antecedents before the pronoun. If a sentence has three potential antecedents (for instance the sentence in Table 5), then three questions should be made out of this sentence, where at least one of them will have a "yes" label. They were also requested to keep the balance between different pronouns, and a balance between the binary choices. A complete list of literary works used to create the CLUEWSC dataset can be found in Appendix A.1.

After 1,838 questions were collected, we used the sentences from three authors as the development set (Lu Yao, A Lai and Chen Ran), another three authors

Table 3. An example from CMRC2018

passage	passage (en)
工商协进会报告，12 月消费者信心上升到 78.1，明显高于 11 月的 72。另据《华尔街日报》报道，2013 年是 1995 年以来美国股市表现最好的一年。这一年里，投资美国股市的明智做法是追着 "傻钱" 跑。所谓的 "傻钱" 策略，其实就是买入并持有美国股票这样的普通组合。这个策略要比对冲基金和其它专业投资者使用的更为复杂的投资方法效果好得多。	The CONFEDERATION of Commerce and Industry reported that consumer confidence rose to 78.1 in December, up from 72 in November. According to *the Wall Street Journal*, 2013 was the best year for U.S. stocks since 1995. This year, the smart way to invest in THE U.S. stock market was to go after dumb money. The 'dumb money' strategy is simply a common mix of buying and holding U.S. stocks. This strategy works much better than the more complex investment methods used by hedge funds and other professional investors.
Quesiton 什么是傻钱策略	Question (en) What is a stupid money strategy?
Answer1 "所谓的 "傻钱" 策略，其实就是买入并持有美国股票这样的普通组合"	Answer1 (en) "The 'dumb money' strategy is a common mix of buying and holding U.S. stocks."
Answer2 "其实就是买入并持有美国股票这样的普通组合"	Answer2 (en) "It's just a common mix of buying and holding U.S. stocks."
Answer3 "买入并持有美国股票这样的普通组合"	Answer3 (en) "It's a common mix of buying and holding U.S. stocks."

Table 4. The distribution of the training/evaluation set in CLUENER2020 dataset is as follows (Note: All entities appearing in a piece of sample are marked. If two address entities appear in a piece of sample, they will be treated as two entities) [16]

Training dataset	Evaluation dataset
address: 2829	address: 364
book: 1131	book: 152
company: 2897	company: 366
game: 2325	game: 287
government: 1797	government: 244
movie: 1109	movie: 150
name: 3661	name: 451
organization: 3075	organization: 344
position: 3052	position: 425
scene: 1462	scene: 199

as the test set (Wang Shuo, Liu Zhenyun and Wang Meng), all the rest as the training set. We did not randomly choose the dev and test sets from all 18k questions because this may add biases to the dataset. For example, if sentences from the same novel are in train, dev and test sets at the same time, the model might learn from the training data that the pronouns may be more likely to refer to the main character in the novel. This can be avoided if the sentences in the dev and test sets are not from the same sources as the training data.

Table 5. An example from CLUEWSC2020, from Wang Shuo's (王朔) novel *Little Red Flowers* (《看上去很美》). These three questions are based on the same text and same pronoun, but have different anaphora candidates.

qustion	text	pronoun	candidate	answer
1	李阿姨下意识地开始数孩子人头儿，正要恍然大悟，老院长进来分散了她的注意力。		李阿姨 Aunt Li	yes
2	Eng: Aunt Li started to count the number of kids.	她 she/her	孩子 kids	no
3	While about to realize (what had happened), the old (kindergarten) principal came in and distracted *her* attention.		老院长 old principal	no

4 Baselines

We offer baselines for all four tasks. Code for these baselines can be found here[9]. Baselines we provided are based on RoBERTa-tiny-clue published by CLUE in [17], whose number of parameters is only 7.5M. Some results are predicted by our baselines with carefully training, achieving more than 67[10].

The way to deal with these four tasks is not complicated and it is the same as the description for four tasks in the original paper.

For CSL, NER and CMRC, the data processors are the same as its type of task. WSC is a little different from the other three. We take it as a single sentence classification problem and just join the samples with an underscore. This could be a point to improve this baseline.

5 Submissions

This shard task lasted for about 2 months from April to May. All submissions were evaluated over our systems. In total, we received submissions from six different teams for the final evaluation. Three teams submitted their description papers. We will describe each of them briefly below.

From the submissions, data augmentation is an important part of their results. Some results submitted from participants are using the baseline we offered.

---

[9] https://github.com/CLUEbenchmark/LightLM/tree/master/baselines.
[10] Recently, 69.289 is the best score of our baseline.

Tencent Oteam. The submission from Tencent Oteam used RoBERTa-tiny-clue. [17] as backbone model. They perform knowledge distillation with RoBERTa-large-WWm as the teacher model and backbone model as the student model. Apart from model compression, they also draw external data for training to improve performance. They conduct data selection for CLUENER task. A BERT-tiny model is trained as domain classifier to select relevant corpus for CLUENER task [1]. Then they use the relevant external corpus for distillation. To be concrete, they generate pesudo labels on relevant external corpus through teacher model, and then train student model with those pesudo labels. Finally, they get the second place among all the submitted result.

Xiaomi AI Lab. The submission from Xiaomi AI Lab proposes a method of training a pre-trained language model from scratch. This scheme can still produce a comparable result compared with other task-related distillations. Moreover, data augmentation is a big contributor to their performance. In the end, they get the third place.

Huawei Cloud & Noah's Ark Lab. The submission from Huawei Cloud & Noah's Ark lab proposes a new knowledge distillation solution named TinyNEZHA, which combines the tricks of TinyBERT [6] and a model named NEZHA [15] together. Besides, they also use the data augmentation to generalize more training data for training. Ultimately, The result they submitted is generated by a six-layer model with 300 dimensions and get the first place among all the submitted result.

6   Results

Table 7 lists the top 25 of the submitted results. The teams are ranked by the score over four tasks. As seen in Table 7, the best-performing model[11], submitted by Huawei Cloud & Noah's Ark lab, achieves an F1 score of 75.949, which is very close to the result of BERT-base[12].

We evaluate all the submitted source files in terms of the formula described above and it shows in Table 6.

Table 7 shows the average score of selected submissions for the four tasks. Table 6 calculates the final score using the formula mentioned above for the top 3. The inference time is obtained by running the submitted models and the BERT-base model respectively with the scripts provided by participants over the NER task.

---

[11] Huawei Cloud & Noah's Ark lab submitted Rank 3 instead of the best one.
[12] Thanks to Xiaomi AI Lab. They submitted this BERT-base model, which is though not totally fine-tuned.

Table 6. Results of this task

Name	Parameters	Inference Time	Average_score	Final_score
Huawei Cloud & Noah's Ark lab	10780384	5.108310103	75.949	0.777126778
Tencent Oteam	7547592	8.723785877	73.507	0.768969257
Xiaomi AI Lab	12111968	8.785942492	72.77	0.758543871

Table 7. Top 25 of the submitted results

Rank	Name	Score	CLUEWSC2020	CSL	CLUENER	CMRC2018
1	Huawei Cloud & Noah's Ark lab	76.655	71.379	82.933	78.058	74.25
2	**BERT-base**	**76.047**	**74.828**	**81.267**	**77.441**	**70.65**
3	Huawei Cloud & Noah's Ark lab	75.949	74.138	81.2	76.459	72
4	Tencent Oteam	73.507	73.448	74.167	75.613	70.8
5	Xiaomi AI Lab	72.77	67.931	78.567	75.483	69.1
6	Huawei Cloud & Noah's Ark lab	72.514	66.207	79.767	75.583	68.5
7	mi-ailab-nlp-app	72.045	67.931	79.033	75.166	66.05
8	Tencent TEG	69.704	63.448	76.767	74.851	63.75
9	mi-ailab-nlp-app	68.577	62.414	76.733	73.262	61.9
10	Huawei-ICS-NLP	67.885	63.793	75.5	72.996	59.25
11	mi-ailab-nlp-app	67.421	62.414	72.733	72.287	62.25
12	mi-ailab-nlp-app	67.237	62.759	72.433	71.507	62.25
13	test-baseline1	66.58	60.69	72.033	71.745	61.85
14	dlnu-5.20	63.423	62.414	66	66.429	58.85
15	dlnu-5.19	63.337	62.069	66	66.429	58.85
16	dlnu-xiaomi	62.043	62.414	66	60.908	58.85
17	民大 F4	62.043	62.414	66	60.908	58.85
18	中国平安财产险科技中心	61.191	60.69	68.567	60.805	54.7
19	中国平安财产险科技中心	60.777	60.69	68.067	59.65	54.7
20	xiaomi	60.76	62.414	65.967	60.908	53.75
21	dlnu-5.14	60.376	62.414	64.433	60.908	53.75
22	dlnu-5.15	60.29	62.069	64.433	60.908	53.75
23	dlnu-5.13	58.91	62.414	58.567	60.908	53.75
24	nlp-test-light	57.772	63.793	75.5	32.543	59.25
25	Huawei-ICS-NLP	49.714	55.862	67.2	60.894	14.9

The best result is submitted by Huawei Cloud & Noah's Ark lab, and the final score is 0.7771, which is 0.0082 and 0.0186 points ahead of the second and third team respectively.

From the results submitted, the first two use the method of knowledge distillation, which shows that it can indeed bring better results than simply training a small model from scratch. At the same time, it can be seen from the paper submitted by everyone that the thin and deep model is indeed easier to achieve better results than the wide and shallow model.

7 Conclusion

We describe the results of NLPCC shared task 1, which focuses on the performance of the model with limited parameters and inference speed.

Firstly, data augmentation is undoubtedly a very important step for a great result. The means of data augmentation and the part of data processing will have a great impact on the results, which are shown in the three papers submitted and the results in Table 7.

Secondly, the three teams have made different choices and combination in the selection of the distillation method, teacher model and student model. How to choose a proper method of distillation in different situations and how to make a great combination of teacher and student model are both great problems to be solved. There are not enough experiments in these results, so we can't make a firm conclusion from this result, but this could be future work.

Finally, we also think the way to understand and preprocess data will have an impact on the final performance, but this is a very task-specific method.

From the competition, the number of NLP developers doing Chinese language model lighting is indeed limited, but participants are of high quality. This phenomenon shows that in the industry, there is a real focus on the practical business deployment of models. Through this contest, it is also hoped to promote the development of Chinese language model lighting, Chinese language processing and some language-agnostic techniques.

Acknowledge. Many thanks to NLPCC for giving us this opportunity to organize this task and people who take part in this task.

A Appendix

A.1 List of Literary Works Selected in CLUEWSC2020

Annotator	Work	Author	n_questions
1	一地鸡毛	刘震云	51
2	一句顶一万句	刘震云	46
	看上去很美	王朔	48
	青春万岁	王蒙	44
3	人兽鬼	钱钟书	50
	内心之死	余华	44
	围城	钱钟书	96
	流浪地球	刘慈欣	58
	球状闪电	刘慈欣	53
	第七天	余华	46
	这边风景	王蒙	52
4	宝刀	阿来	50
	尘埃落定	阿来	55
	平凡的世界	路遥	47
	无处告别	陈染	50
	玩的就是心跳	王朔	49
	私人生活	陈染	50
	黄叶在秋风中飘落	路遥	52
5	四牌楼	刘心武	48
	红顶商人胡雪岩	高阳	49
	遍地枭雄	王安忆	51
	金瓯缺	徐兴业	53
	钟鼓楼	刘心武	48
	长恨歌	王安忆	51
6	刘子超专栏	刘子超	49
	前山夏牧场	李娟	50
	北方大道	李静睿	49
	枕边书	李静睿	44
	深山夏牧场	李娟	51
	穿越印度的火车之旅	刘子超	56
7	你别无选择	刘索拉	47
	兄弟	余华	52
	哺乳期的女人	毕飞宇	47
	在细雨中呼喊	余华	49
	推拿	毕飞宇	50
	混沌加哩格楞	刘索拉	53

References

1. Chen, B., Huang, F.: Semi-supervised convolutional networks for translation adaptation with tiny amount of in-domain data. In: Proceedings of The 20th SIGNLL Conference on Computational Natural Language Learning, pp. 314–323 (2016)
2. Cui, Y., et al.: A span-extraction dataset for Chinese machine reading comprehension. arXiv preprint arXiv:1810.07366 (2018)
3. Devlin, J., Chang, M.W., Lee, K., Toutanova, K.: BERT: pre-training of deep bidirectional transformers for language understanding. arXiv preprint arXiv:1810.04805 (2018)
4. Gordon, M.A., Duh, K., Andrews, N.: Compressing BERT: studying the effects of weight pruning on transfer learning. arXiv preprint arXiv:2002.08307 (2020)
5. Hinton, G., Vinyals, O., Dean, J.: Distilling the knowledge in a neural network. arXiv preprint arXiv:1503.02531 (2015)
6. Jiao, X., et al.: TinyBERT: Distilling BERT for natural language understanding. arXiv preprint arXiv:1909.10351 (2019)
7. Lan, Z., Chen, M., Goodman, S., Gimpel, K., Sharma, P., Soricut, R.: ALBERT: a lite BERT for self-supervised learning of language representations. arXiv preprint arXiv:1909.11942 (2019)
8. Levesque, H., Davis, E., Morgenstern, L.: The winograd schema challenge. In: Thirteenth International Conference on the Principles of Knowledge Representation and Reasoning (2012)
9. Liu, Y., et al.: RoBERTa: a robustly optimized BERT pretraining approach. arXiv preprint arXiv:1907.11692 (2019)
10. Sanh, V., Debut, L., Chaumond, J., Wolf, T.: DistilBERT, a distilled version of BERT: smaller, faster, cheaper and lighter. arXiv preprint arXiv:1910.01108 (2019)
11. Sun, Y., et al.: Ernie: Enhanced representation through knowledge integration. arXiv preprint arXiv:1904.09223 (2019)
12. Sun, Z., Yu, H., Song, X., Liu, R., Yang, Y., Zhou, D.: MobileBERT: a compact task-agnostic BERT for resource-limited devices. arXiv preprint arXiv:2004.02984 (2020)
13. Wang, A., et al.: SuperGLUE: a stickier benchmark for general-purpose language understanding systems. arXiv e-prints (2019)
14. Wang, W., Wei, F., Dong, L., Bao, H., Yang, N., Zhou, M.: MiniLM: deep self-attention distillation for task-agnostic compression of pre-trained transformers. arXiv preprint arXiv:2002.10957 (2020)
15. Wei, J., et al.: NEZHA: neural contextualized representation for Chinese language understanding. arXiv preprint arXiv:1909.00204 (2019)
16. Xu, L., et al.: CLUENER 2020: fine-grained named entity recognition dataset and benchmark for Chinese. arXiv preprint arXiv-2001 (2020)
17. Xu, L., Zhang, X., Dong, Q.: CLUECorpus 2020: a large-scale Chinese corpus for pre-traininglanguage model. arXiv preprint arXiv:2003.01355 (2020)
18. Xu, L., Zhang, X., Li, L., Hu, H., Cao, C., Liu, W., Li, J., Li, Y., Sun, K., Xu, Y., et al.: Clue: A chinese language understanding evaluation benchmark. arXiv preprint arXiv:2004.05986 (2020)
19. Yang, Z., Dai, Z., Yang, Y., Carbonell, J., Salakhutdinov, R.R., Le, Q.V.: XLNet: generalized autoregressive pretraining for language understanding. In: Advances in Neural Information Processing Systems, pp. 5753–5763 (2019)
20. Zhao, Z., et al.: UER: an open-source toolkit for pre-training models. arXiv preprint arXiv:1909.05658 (2019)

Overview of the NLPCC 2020 Shared Task: Multi-Aspect-Based Multi-Sentiment Analysis (MAMS)

Lei Chen[1], Ruifeng Xu[2], and Min Yang[1]([⊠])

[1] Shenzhen Institutes of Advanced Technology, Chinese Academy of Sciences, Shenzhen, China
{lei.chen,min.yang}@siat.ac.cn
[2] Harbin Institute of Technology (Shenzhen), Shenzhen, China
xuruifeng@hitsz.edu.cn

Abstract. In this paper, we present an overview of the NLPCC 2020 shared task on Multi-Aspect-based Multi-Sentiment Analysis (MAMS). The evaluation consists of two sub-tasks: (1) aspect term sentiment analysis (ATSA) and (2) aspect category sentiment analysis (ACSA). We manually annotated a large-scale restaurant reviews corpus for MAMS, in which each sentence contains at least two different aspects with different sentiment polarities. Thus, the provided MAMS dataset is more challenging than the existing aspect-based sentiment analysis (ABSA) datasets. MAMS attracted a total of 50 teams to participate in the evaluation task. We believe that MAMS will push forward the research in the field of aspect-based sentiment analysis.

Keywords: Multi-Aspect-based Multi-Sentiment Analysis · Aspect term sentiment analysis · Aspect category sentiment analysis

1 Introduction

Aspect-based sentiment analysis has attracted increasing attention recently due to its broad applications. It aims at identifying the sentiment polarity towards a specific aspect in a sentence. A target aspect refers to a word or a phrase describing an aspect of an entity. For example, in the sentence "The salmon is tasty while the waiter is very rude", there are two aspect terms "salmon" and "waiter", and they are associated with "positive" and "negative" sentiment, respectively.

Recently, neural network methods have dominated the study of ABSA since these methods can learn important features automatically from the input sequences and be trained in an end-to-end manner. [1] proposed to model the preceding and following contexts for the target via two separate long-short term memory (LSTM) networks. [2] proposed to learn an embedding vector for each aspect, and these aspect embeddings were used to calculate the attention weights

© Springer Nature Switzerland AG 2020
X. Zhu et al. (Eds.): NLPCC 2020, LNAI 12431, pp. 579–585, 2020.
https://doi.org/10.1007/978-3-030-60457-8_48

to capture important information for aspect-level sentiment analysis. [3] developed the deep memory network to compute the importance degree and text representation of each context word with multiple attention layers. [4] introduced the interactive attention networks (IAN) to interactively learn attention vectors for the context and target, and generated the representations for the target and context words separately. [5] extracted sentiment features with convolutional neural networks and selectively output aspect-related features for sentiment classification with gating mechanisms. Subsequently, Transformer [6] and BERT-based methods [7] have achieved noticeable success on ABSA task. [8] combined the capsule network with BERT to improve the performance of ABSA. There are also several studies attempting to simulate the process of human reading cognition to further improve the performance of ABSA [9,10].

So far, several ABSA datasets have been constructed, including SemEval-2014 Restaurant and Laptop review datasets [11], and Twitter dataset [12]. Although these three datasets have since become the benchmark datasets for the ABSA task, most sentences in these datasets consist of only one aspect or multiple aspects with the same sentiment polarity, which makes the ABSA task degenerate to the sentence-level sentiment analysis. Based on our empirical observation, the sentence-level sentiment classifiers (TextCNN and LSTM) without considering aspects can still achieve competitive results with more advanced ABSA methods (e.g., GCAE [5]). On the other hand, even advanced ABSA methods (e.g., AEN [13]) trained on these datasets can hardly distinguish the sentiment polarities towards different aspects in the sentences that contain multiple aspects and multiple sentiments.

In NLPCC 2020, we manually annotated a large-scale restaurant reviews corpus for MAMS, in which each sentence contains at least two different aspects with different sentiment polarities, making the provided MAMS dataset more challenging compared with existing ABSA datasets [8]. Considering merely the sentence-level sentiment of the samples would fail to achieve good performance on MAMS dataset.

This NLPCC 2020 shared task on MAMS has attracted a total of 50 teams to register, and 17 teams submitted the final results. We provide training and development sets to participating teams to build their models in the first stage and evaluate the final results on the test set in the second stage. The final ranking list is based on the average Macro-F1 scores of the two sub-tasks (i.e., ATSA and ACSA).

2   Task Description

Conventional sentiment classification aims to identify the sentiment polarity of a whole document or sentence. However, in practice, a sentence may contain multiple target aspects in a single sentence or document. For example, the sentence "the salmon is tasty while the waiter is very rude" expresses negative sentiment towards the "service" aspect, but contains positive sentiment concerning the "food" aspect. Considering merely the document- or sentence-level sentiment cannot learn the fine-grained aspect-specific sentiment.

Aspect-based sentiment analysis [11], which aims to automatically predict the sentiment polarity of the specific aspect in its context, has gained increasing popularity in recent years due to many useful applications, such as online customer review analysis and conversations monitoring. Similar to SemEval-2014 Task 4, NLPCC-2020 MAMS task also includes two subtasks: (1) aspect term sentiment analysis (ATSA) and (2) aspect category sentiment analysis (ACSA). Next, we will describe the two subtasks in detail.

2.1 Aspect Term Sentiment Analysis (ATSA)

The ATSA task aims to identify the sentiment polarity (i.e., positive, negative or neutral) towards the given aspect terms which are entities presented in the sentence. For example, as shown in the Fig. 1, the sentence "the salmon is tasty while the waiter is very rude" contains two aspect terms "salmon" and "waiter", the sentiment polarities towards the two aspect terms are positive and negative, respectively. Different from the ATSA task in SemEval-2014 Task 4, each sentence in MAMS contains at least two different aspect terms with different sentiment polarities, making the our ATSA task more challenging.

2.2 Aspect Category Sentiment Analysis (ACSA)

The ACSA task aims to identify the sentiment polarity (i.e., positive, negative or neutral) towards the given aspect categories that are pre-defined and may not presented in the sentence. We pre-defined eight aspect categories: food, service, staff, price, ambience, menu, and miscellaneous. For example, the sentence "the salmon is tasty while the waiter is very rude" contains two aspect categories "food" and "service", the sentiment polarities towards the two aspect categories are positive and negative, respectively. For our NLPCC-2020 ACSA task, each sentence contains at least two different aspect categories with different sentiment polarities.

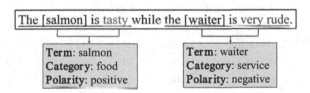

Fig. 1. An example for the ATSA and ACSA tasks.

3   Dataset Construction

Similar to SemEval-2014 Restaurant Review dataset [11], we annotate sentences from the Citysearch New York dataset collected by [14]. We split each document in the corpus into a few sentences, and remove the sentences consisting more than 70 words. The original MAMS dataset was presented in [8]. In NLPCC-2020 shared task, we relabel the MAMS dataset by providing more high-quality validation and test data.

For the ATSA subtask, we invited three experienced researchers who work on natural language processing (NLP) to extract aspect terms in the sentences and assign the sentiment polarities with respect to the aspect terms. The sentences that consist of only one aspect term or multiple aspects with the same sentiment polarities are deleted. We also provide the start and end positions for each aspect term in the sentence.

For the ACSA subtask, we pre-defined eight coarse aspect categories: food, service, staff, price, ambience, menu, place and miscellaneous. Five aspect categories (i.e., food, service, price, ambience, anecdotes/miscellaneous) are adopted in SemEval-2014 Restaurant Review Dataset. We add three more aspect categories (i.e., staff, menu, place) to deal with some confusing situations. Three experienced NLP researchers were asked to identify the aspect categories described in the given sentences and determine the sentiment polarities towards these aspect categories. We only keep the sentences that consist of at least two unique aspect categories with different sentiment polarities.

The detailed statistics of the datasets for ATSA and ACSA subtasks are reported in Table 1. The released datasets are stored in XML format, as shown in the Fig. 2. Each sample contains the given sentence, aspect terms with their sentiment polarities, and aspect categories with their sentiment polarities. In total, the ATSA dataset consists of 11,186 training samples, 2,668 development samples, and 2,676 test samples. The ACSA dataset consists of 7,090 training samples, 1,789 development samples, and 1,522 test samples.

Table 1. Statistics of MAMS dataset.

Dataset		Positive	Negative	Neutral	Total
ATSA	Training	3,380	2,764	5,042	11,186
	Development	803	654	1,211	2,668
	Test	1,046	545	1,085	2,676
ACSA	Training	1,929	2,084	3,077	7,090
	Development	486	522	781	1,789
	Test	562	348	612	1,522

4   Evaluation Metrics

Both ATSA and ACSA tasks are evaluated using Macro-F1 value that is calculated as follows:

$$Precision(P) = \frac{TP}{TP + FP} \tag{1}$$

```
<sentence id="2846">
  <text>
    Not only was the food outstanding, but the little 'perks' were great.
  <\text>
  <aspectTerms>
    <aspectTerm term="food" polarity="positive" from="17" to="21" />
    <aspectTerm term="perks" polarity="positive" from="51" to="56" />
  </aspectTerms>
  <aspectCategories>
    <aspectCategory category="food" polarity="positive" />
    <aspectCategory category="service" polarity="positive" />
  </aspectCategories>
</sentence>
```

Fig. 2. Dataset format of MAMS task.

$$Recall(R) = \frac{TP}{TP + FN} \tag{2}$$

$$F1 = 2 * \frac{P * R}{P + R} \tag{3}$$

where TP represents true positives, FP represents false positives, TN represents true negatives, and FN represents false negatives. We average the F1 value of each category to get Macro-F1 score. The final result for the MAMS task is the averaged Macro-F1 scores on the two sub-tasks (i.e., ATSA and ACSA).

5   Evaluation Results

In total, there are 50 teams registered for the NLPCC-2020 MAMS task, and 17 teams submitted their final results for evaluation. Table 2 shows the Macro-F1 scores and ranks of these 17 teams. The Macro-F1 results confirmed our expectations. It is noteworthy that we have checked the technique reports of the top three teams and reproduced their codes. Next, we briefly introduce the implementation strategies of the top-3 teams.

The best average Macro-F1 score (82.4230%) was achieved by the *Baiding* team. They tackle the MAMS task as a sentence pair classification problem and employed pre-trained language models as the feature extractor. In addition, the bidirectional gated recurrent unit (Bi-GRU) is connected to the last hidden layer of pre-trained language models, which can further enhance the representation of aspects and contexts. More importantly, a weighted voting strategy is applied to produce an ensemble model that combines the results of several models with different network architectures, pre-trained language models, and training steps.

The *Just a test* team won the 2nd place in the MAMS shared task. They achieved a Macro-F1 score of 85.2435% on the ATSA task and 79.4187% on the ACSA task. The averaged Macro-F1 score was 82.33%, which was slightly worse than that of the *Baiding* team. The RoBERTa-large is used as the pre-trained language model. The *Just a test* team added a word sentiment polarity prediction task as an auxiliary task and simultaneously predicted the sentiment polarity of all aspects in a sentence to enhance the model performance. In addition, a data augmentation via EDA (Easy data augmentation) [15] is adopted to further improve the performance, which doubled the training data.

The *CUSAPA* team won the third place, which achieved a Macro-F1 score of 84.1585% on the ATSA task and 79.7468% on the ACSA task. The averaged Macro-F1 score was 81.9526%. The *CUSAPA* team employs a joint learning framework to train these two sub-tasks in a unified framework, which improves the performance of both tasks simultaneously. Furthermore, three BERT-based models are adopted to capture different aspects of semantic information of the context. The best performance is achieved by combing these models with a stacking strategy.

Table 2. Macro-F1 scores (%) on the MAMS dataset.

Team	ATSA	ACSA	Average	Rank
Baiding	84.3770	**80.4689**	**82.4230**	**1**
Just a test	**85.2435**	79.4187	82.3311	**2**
CUSAPA	84.1585	79.7468	81.9526	**3**
PingAnPai	84.5463	79.1408	81.8436	4
DUTSurfer	84.1994	78.5792	81.3893	5
wesure01	83.3898	78.3331	80.8615	6
Xiao Niu Dui	83.9645	76.5508	80.2576	7
To be number one	82.4616	76.8539	79.6577	8
AG4MAMS	82.1669	77.0149	79.5909	9
rain2017	80.1005	78.6458	79.3732	10
NLPWUST	81.2856	75.7212	78.5034	11
CABSA	81.6573	72.4605	77.0589	12
MXH42	80.9779	72.1240	76.5510	13
FuXi-NLP	77.9562	73.5253	75.7407	14
YQMAMS	84.0473	47.1836	65.6154	15
W and Triple L	61.3888	63.4616	62.4252	16
HONER	55.9910	49.3538	52.6724	17

6 Conclusion

In this paper, we briefly introduced the overview of the NLPCC-2020 shared task on Multi-Aspect-based Multi-Sentiment Analysis (MAMS). We manually annotated a large-scale restaurant reviews corpus for MAMS, in which each sentence contained at least two different aspects with different sentiment polarities, making the provided MAMS dataset more challenging compared with existing

ABSA datasets. The MAMS task has attracted 50 teams to participate in the competition and 17 teams to submit the final results for evaluation. Different approaches were proposed by the 17 teams, which achieved promising results. In the future, we would like to create a new MAMS dataset with samples from different domains, and add a new cross-domain aspect-based sentiment analysis task.

References

1. Tang, D., Qin, B., Feng, X., et al.: Effective LSTMs for target-dependent sentiment classification. In: Proceedings of COLING, 3298–3307 (2016)
2. Wang, Y., Huang, M., Zhu, X., et al.: Attention-based LSTM for aspect-level sentiment classification. In: Proceedings of the 2016 Conference on Empirical Methods in Natural Language Processing, pp. 606–615 (2016)
3. Tang, D., Qin, B., Liu, T.: Aspect level sentiment classification with deep memory network. arXiv preprint arXiv:1605.08900 (2016)
4. Ma, D., Li, S., Zhang, X., et al.: Interactive attention networks for aspect-level sentiment classification. arXiv preprint arXiv:1709.00893 (2017)
5. Xue, W., Li, T.: Aspect based sentiment analysis with gated convolutional networks. In: Meeting of the Association for Computational Linguistics, vol. 1, pp. 2514–2523 (2018)
6. Vaswani, A., Shazeer, N., Parmar, N., et al.: Attention is all you need. In: Advances in Neural Information Processing Systems, pp. 5998–6008 (2017)
7. Devlin, J., Chang, M.W., Lee, K., et al.: BERT: pre-training of deep bidirectional transformers for language understanding. arXiv preprint arXiv:1810.04805 (2018)
8. Jiang, Q., Chen, L., Xu, R., et al.: A challenge dataset and effective models for aspect-based sentiment analysis. In: Proceedings of the 2019 Conference on Empirical Methods in Natural Language Processing and the 9th International Joint Conference on Natural Language Processing (EMNLP-IJCNLP), pp. 6281–6286 (2019)
9. Lei, Z., Yang, Y., Yang, M., et al.: A human-like semantic cognition network for aspect-level sentiment classification. In: Proceedings of the AAAI Conference on Artificial Intelligence, vol. 33, pp. 6650–6657 (2019)
10. Yang, M., Jiang, Q., Shen, Y., et al.: Hierarchical human-like strategy for aspect-level sentiment classification with sentiment linguistic knowledge and reinforcement learning. Neural Netw. **117**, 240–248 (2019)
11. Pontiki, M., Galanis, D., Pavlopoulos, J., Papageorgiou, H., Androutsopoulos, I., Manandhar, S.: SemEval-2014 task 4: aspect based sentiment analysis. In: Proceedings of the 8th International Workshop on Semantic Evaluation (SemEval), pp. 27–35 (2014)
12. Dong, L., Wei, F., Tan, C., Tang, D., Zhou, M., Xu, K.: Adaptive recursive neural network for target-dependent twitter sentiment classification. In: Proceedings of the 52nd Annual Meeting of the Association for Computational Linguistics (Volume 2: Short papers), vol. 2, pp. 49–54 (2014)
13. Song, Y., Wang, J., Jiang, T., Liu, Z., Rao, Y.: Attentional encoder network for targeted sentiment classification. arXiv preprint arXiv:1902.09314 (2019)
14. Ganu, G., Elhadad, N., Marian, A.: Beyond the stars: improving rating predictions using review text content. In: WebDB (2009)
15. Wei, J., Zou, K.: EDA: easy data augmentation techniques for boosting performance on text classification tasks. arXiv preprint arXiv:1901.11196 (2019)

Author Index